FIFTH EDITION

EDUCATIONAL LEADERSHIP

A Bridge to Improved Practice

PAULA A. CORDEIRO
University of San Diego

WILLIAM G. CUNNINGHAM
Old Dominion University

PEARSON

Boston Columbus Indianapolis New York San Francisco Upper Saddle River
Amsterdam Cape Town Dubai London Madrid Milan Munich Paris Montreal Toronto
Delhi Mexico City São Paulo Sydney Hong Kong Seoul Singapore Taipei Tokyo

Vice President and Editorial Director: Jeffery W. Johnston
Senior Acquisitions Editor: Meredith D. Fossel
Associate Editor: Anne Whittaker
Editorial Assistant: Andrea Hall
Vice President, Director of Marketing: Margaret Waples
Senior Marketing Manager: Christopher Barry
Senior Managing Editor: Pamela D. Bennett
Project Manager: Kerry Rubadue
Senior Operations Supervisor: Matthew Ottenweller
Senior Art Director: Diane Lorenzo

Text Designer: S4Carlisle Publishing Services
Cover Designer: Jayne Conte
Permissions Administrator: Rebecca Savage
Cover Image: Fotolia
Media Project Manager: Rebecca Norsic
Full-Service Project Management: Lynn Steines, S4Carlisle Publishing Services
Composition: S4Carlisle Publishing Services
Printer/Binder: Courier Companies, Inc.
Cover Printer: Courier Companies, Inc.
Text Font: Palatino LT Std

Credits and acknowledgments borrowed from other sources and reproduced, with permission, in this textbook appear on appropriate page within text.

Every effort has been made to provide accurate and current Internet information in this book. However, the Internet and information posted on it are constantly changing, so it is inevitable that some of the Internet addresses listed in this textbook will change.

Copyright © 2013, 2009, 2006, 2003, 2001 by Pearson Education, Inc. All rights reserved. Printed in the United States of America. This publication is protected by Copyright and permission should be obtained from the publisher prior to any prohibited reproduction, storage in a retrieval system, or transmission in any form or by any means, electronic, mechanical, photocopying, recording, or likewise. To obtain permission(s) to use material from this work, please submit a written request to Pearson Education, Inc., Permissions Department, One Lake Street, Upper Saddle River, New Jersey 07458 or you may fax your request to 201-236-3290.

Library of Congress Cataloging-in-Publication Data

Cunningham, William G.
  Educational leadership : a bridge to improved practice / William G. Cunningham, Paula A. Cordeiro. — 5th ed.
    p. cm.
  ISBN-13: 978-0-13-267812-4—ISBN-10: 0-13-267812-8   1. School management and organization—Study and teaching (Higher)—United States.   2. Problem-based learning—United States.   3. School administrators—Training of—United States.   I. Cordeiro, Paula A.   II. Title.
  LB1738.5.C86 2013
  371.200973—dc23

                                                                                        2012000384

10 9 8 7 6 5 4 3 V092 15

ISBN 10:   0-13-267812-8
ISBN 13: 978-0-13-267812-4

PREFACE

Educational Leadership: A Bridge to Improved Practice, Fifth Edition provides a comprehensive discussion of the field of educational administration. This book describes how successful and effective schools and administrators operate in an increasingly challenging, fast-paced, demanding, and perhaps revolutionary environment. Readers are offered an integrated view of the knowledge base, research, and practice of administration within a context of multiple perspectives and a wide range of thinking.

NEW TO THIS EDITION

- The text has been divided into three sections, each followed by a PBL project. The first five chapters fall within what we term *The Foundations of Educational Leadership*. These chapters focus on the context, standards, and practice of the discipline of education within the field of leadership studies. A variety of leadership assessment instruments are included and provide the reader with an understanding of his/her leadership style and beliefs. The second section is entitled *Instructional Leadership and Student Learning*. This section includes Chapters 6 through 9, which are the heart of the text because they emphasize how leadership can help to improve teacher and student learning. The final section, *Operational Support for Effective Teaching and Learning*, shifts to operational responsibilities and legal and regulatory issues. This section explores major leadership responsibilities related to student support services, legal and compliance issues, and finance and stewardship. A brief overview of problem-based learning (PBL), two expert essays explaining how best to use PBL, and one additional PBL project are included in the appendices.

- We have added a new chapter entitled *Technology and Learning*. Since the previous edition, there has been exponential growth in the use of technology at all levels of schooling. School leaders need to be well versed in the technologies available to teachers and students and how they can be integrated into the curriculum. As school leaders struggle through trial and error to forge new approaches to learning that work, knowing where to find evidence on the effective use of technology and how best to apply research findings is crucial.

- Three new expert opinions have been added. Award-winning Connecticut Superintendent Kathleen Binkowski talks about the superintendent and leadership team's role in improving student achievement. Professor and technology researcher Chris Devers discusses the importance of school leaders creating environments that cultivate the use of empirically validated strategies for improving learning through the use of technology. Discussing a topic that is rarely mentioned in a textbook written to help prepare school leaders,

Ian Martin, a school counseling professor, explores how principals can empower counselors to become leaders and contributors to school improvement.

■ A chapter on human resource management has been deleted. Earlier editions placed too much emphasis on work that is usually done by central office staff rather than at the school level. Topics such as teacher recruitment and selection, collective bargaining, and staff development have been updated and placed in related areas in other chapters.

■ Each chapter has been updated to include the most widely recognized research and best administrative practices to focus attention on the latest challenges facing the discipline. All demographic information has been updated with the most recently available data, as well as new research findings and policy implications. Additionally, the suggested readings section at the conclusion of each chapter lists some of the most recent books available on the chapter's topics.

■ MyEdLeadershipLab˚ is integrated in the student text, enhancing the teaching and learning experiences.

HOW TO USE THIS BOOK

The book's format allows the reader to choose among areas of concentration and those of review. Some chapters are important to a reader because of his or her present professional status, whereas others may be simply informative. Although the topics flow logically from one chapter to the next, selected chapters and even portions of chapters can be studied separately, or in a different sequence depending on the needs of the reader or instructor.

Earlier chapters can be skipped without losing touch with the essence of later chapters, or vice versa, although we recommend that they be scanned to obtain a sense of content. Each topic is introduced and placed in a practical perspective as part of an integral system of leadership that is developed throughout a person's professional life. The text provides a comprehensive reference of key information useful in improving educational practice.

Each chapter follows the same basic format and begins with a vignette that reflects the life of a school administrator. Questions and comments are located throughout each chapter to make overall theory–practice connections to encourage readers to enrich their understanding of problems in practice and to suggest how leadership might be applied in a variety of settings. Illustrations, expert opinions, quotes, Web sites, and examples are often used to highlight key points, trends, and issues.

All chapters conclude with suggested activities through which readers can begin to build their educational leadership platforms. Artifacts can be collected to demonstrate a reader's ability to connect knowledge to his or her responsibilities. The portfolio artifacts and reflective writings can be collected for each chapter to create a cumulative portfolio documenting the reader's growth and understanding of administrative practice.

A number of nationally noted scholars and practitioners from a variety of fields have provided original, expert reflections on critical topics within each chapter. These contributions provide insights into many key areas of educational administration from those who have been involved in the most promising activities within the field. These insights help model and encourage readers in the development of well-thought-out and supported analysis of key issues. They also allow the reader to relate his or her reflective thinking to that of noted experts in the field. Each contribution encourages the reader to think through, discuss, and debate key issues surrounding educational administration.

The book is divided into three sections with each section followed by a PBL project. The PBL projects can be used in a variety of ways. Although a project might connect with all major topics in the book, the projects following each section are specifically tied to the content in the preceding chapters. One approach to using a project is to schedule it before reading the text. The text can serve as a resource when readers select only chapters that are necessary to address issues adequately and appropriately. Another way to incorporate the projects is for readers to complete a project approximately midway through the book. This approach permits readers to become comfortable with the content, begin the development of an administrative platform, and begin developing a portfolio. Alternatively, a PBL project could be used as a culminating activity. The appendix contains an additional project covering most content areas of the text. No solutions are provided to projects. The PBL projects are designed to stimulate inquiry, to create deep reflection, to foster group dynamics, and to challenge perspectives regarding key issues, values, and needs.

We encourage you to be introspective and reflective as you apply the collective wisdom within the field to current issues in the context of today's education. Through dozens of vignettes, problem-based projects, concrete examples, original expert opinions, assessment instruments, collected artifacts, and reflective writings, the book focuses attention on the successful application of the expansive knowledge contained within. Finally, we very much hope this book will serve as a valuable resource as you work in a school leadership position.

MyEdLeadershipLab™

MyEdLeadershipLab™ connects your course content to video- and case-based real-world scenarios, and provides:

- *Building Ed Leadership Skills* exercises that offer opportunities for candidates to develop and practice skills critical to their success as school leaders. Hints and feedback provide scaffolding and reinforce key concepts.
- *Assignments & Activities* assess candidates' understanding of key concepts and skill development. Suggested responses are available to instructors, making grading easy.
- *Multiple-Choice Quizzes* help candidates gauge their understanding of important topics and prepare for success on licensure examinations.

Access to MyEdLeadershipLab˜ can be packaged with this textbook or purchased as a standalone. To find out how to package student access to this website and gain access as an Instructor, go to www.MyEdLeadershipLab.com, email us at edleadership@pearson.com, or contact your Pearson sales representative.

ACKNOWLEDGMENTS

The authors appreciate the wise counsel of their editor Meredith Fossel and Associate Editor Anne Whittaker. Much of the content of this book is drawn from the life work of researchers, scholars, and practitioners who have dedicated their professional lives to an improved understanding of education and administration. We appreciate their dedication and critically important insights. We are also indebted to reviewers for various editions who provided invaluable feedback, insights, and resources: Bruce Barnett, University of Texas at San Antonio; Martin Burlingame, Oklahoma State University; John C. Daresh, University of Texas–El Paso; Lynn H. Doyle, Old Dominion University; Lorenzo Flores, Governors State University; Athanase Gahungu, Chicago State University; Tom Glass, University of Memphis; Maria-Luisa Gonzalez, New Mexico State University; Larry W. Hughes, University of Houston; Richard A. King, University of Northern Colorado; Otis Lovette, University of Louisiana at Monroe; Rosita L. Mercano, Northern Illinois University; Mark D. Myers, Indiana University–Purdue University Fort Wayne; Ulrich C. Reitzug, University of North Carolina, Greensboro; Floria Trimble, National University, Los Angeles; and Eileen Yantz, Gaston College. Special thanks go to each of the experts who contributed original pieces reflecting on the contents of the chapters and who have made such significant contributions to our field. Particular thanks go to Kate Sheridan, who helped procure the permissions and checked references helping to make this book a reality. We deeply appreciate the careful editing of each chapter by David J. O'Brien. His insights and support are greatly valued.

We would also like to thank our parents, Jerry and Margaret Cunningham and Manuel Cordeiro; sister, Gail Penn; spouse, Sandra L. Cunningham; children Kerri and her husband Chuck Joyner; grandchildren Katie and Cody; Michael and his wife Dottie; and grandchildren, Cierra, Merrick, Keenan, Shealyn, Braidyn, and Alayna for their continuing encouragement and support and the happiness and love we enjoy. We hope you find this book worthy of the greatness of the people who have had such profound influences on our lives. Part of each is in this work.

Many friends and colleagues who teach and practice educational administration provided counsel, inspiration, and direction as they have given of their time and interest. Last, but certainly not least, are the thousands of educational leadership students who first breathe such exciting life into this subject and then into our schools. We wish them Godspeed on their noble journeys. To them all, we offer appreciation and great thanks.

Paula A. Cordeiro
William G. Cunningham

CONTENTS

CHAPTER 5
Leadership Theory and Practice   137

PBL Project 1: Marveling at the Results: Power, Roles, Relationships, and School Reform   183

PART II INSTRUCTIONAL LEADERSHIP AND STUDENT LEARNING   191

CHAPTER 6
Leading Learning in Schools   192

LEADERSHIP MATTERS   192

ADULT LEARNING   195

EFFECTIVE SCHOOL LEADERSHIP PRACTICES   197

ACCELERATING STUDENT AND ADULT LEARNING   198

DEVELOPING AND SUPPORTING TEACHER LEADERSHIP   198
> ■ Leadership and the Change Process *Michael Fullan, University of Toronto*   200

STRUCTURES AND PROCESSES THAT PROVIDE OPPORTUNITIES FOR TEACHER COLLABORATION   202
> Study Groups   202   /   Instructional Walk-Throughs   203   /   Teacher Conferences   203   /
> School Visitations   204   /   District and/or School Instructional
> Conferences   204   /   Action Research (AR)   205   /   Learning
> Communities   205   /   Networks for School Personnel   206

SUPPORTING THE CHANGE PROCESS   206
> ■ Principals as Instructional Leaders: Modeling and Supporting Teaching and Learning
> *Paul V. Bredeson, University of Wisconsin–Madison*   207

RECRUITMENT, SELECTION, INDUCTION, SUPPORT, AND EVALUATION   209
> Staff Planning   209

RECRUITMENT   209

THE TEACHER SELECTION PROCESS   212
> The Interview   212   /   Interview Questions   214

PEER MENTORING AND COACHING   215

PERFORMANCE APPRAISAL AND EVALUATION   216
> Planning the Evaluation   216   /   Collecting Performance Data   217

USING INFORMATION   218

CHAPTER 7

Technology and Learning   225

CHAPTER 8

Diversity and Language Learning   251

CHAPTER 11
Law and Policy   359

THE FOUNDATIONS OF EDUCATIONAL LEADERSHIP

CHAPTER 1

LEADERSHIP STANDARDS, VALUES, AND PRACTICE

MyEdLeadershipLab™

Visit the MyEdLeadershipLab™ site for *Educational Leadership: A Bridge to Improved Practice*, Fifth Edition to enhance your understanding of chapter concepts. You'll have the opportunity to practice your skills through video- and case-based Assignments and Activities as well as Building Leadership Skills units, and to prepare for your certification exam with Practice for Certification quizzes.

EDUCATIONAL LEADERSHIP

The 20-year period beginning the 21st century provides one of the great opportunities to obtain educational administration positions. According to the U.S. Department of Labor, over 52% of the nation's 92,330 principals and 20% of vice and assistant principals will retire over the next 12 years. For example, 48% of elementary school principals are age 50 or older. Moreover, an additional 1.5 million elementary and middle school students are expected in public schools by 2015. In some regions of the nation, this translates into a shortage of qualified applicants for at least the next 10 years. However, some researchers note that the problem is not in the *quantity* of candidates, but in the *quality*. Additionally, many candidates avoid certain schools and districts, such as those with low salaries or high-poverty and/or high-minority populations making the school leadership "shortage" more acute in certain regions. Thus, as some scholars note, the perceived shortage problem is one of distribution and poor leadership preparation, rather than inadequate supply. According to the Department of Labor's *Occupational Outlook Handbook 2010–11*, job opportunities in most regions of the nation should be excellent because of a large number of expected retirements and fewer qualified applications for some positions.

Fink and Brayman (2006) found that turnover and shortages of principals resulted "from the aging of the baby boom generation, principals' mobility, and the pressures of the standardization agenda which have created additional difficulties . . . and undermine the capacity of incoming and outgoing principals to lead their schools" (p. 83).

At the same time, the number of qualified candidates willing to assume positions of school leadership is growing smaller (Young, Petersen, & Short, 2002). According to the National Association of Secondary School Principals (NASSP), half of all surveyed districts, including 45% of those classified as suburban, reported shortages of qualified candidates for principalships at all levels. School districts across the country are studying ways to increase the number of candidates for administrative positions, including the superintendency.

School districts are identifying future leaders who can think thoroughly and quickly about complex issues, collaborate with diverse groups, show good judgment, stay on the cutting edge of school improvement, and lead needed school reforms. These leaders will be risk takers and coalition builders who can obtain broad support.

In all states, educational leaders will have to meet established educational administrative licensure requirements. Over 40 states now require a master's degree with some administrative courses for an administrative and supervision license. These state requirements were developed to ensure the quality of the preparation of our future practicing school leaders. They exist to protect the health, safety, and welfare of the public and to ensure knowledge and skills important for competent practice. In addition, many states and local districts now offer leadership academies to complement the training received in universities and to provide in-service development for practicing administrators.

A growing number of states, particularly southern states, have established cutoff scores on various forms of assessment as a prerequisite to receiving licensure. A licensure test is designed to determine if individuals possess occupation-relevant knowledge and skills at the time of entry into their profession. The belief is that school administrators should be held accountable to the same high standards as teachers. The Interstate School Leaders Licensure Consortium (ISLLC) standards (see Box 1.1) guide and shape the 6-hour Educational Testing Service (ETS) School Leadership Licensure Assessment (SLLA) and the scoring of the exercises. Currently more than 40 states have adopted the ISLLC standards into their administrative certification program requirements.

At least 13 states now use the SLLA as part of the administrative licensure process. A number of states have developed other formal assessments, for example, the Connecticut Administrative Test (CAT). The CAT assesses the candidate's ability in the areas of instructional supervision, school improvement, data-driven decision making, and student learning. Other states have developed two- and three-tier licensing systems, to encourage continuous development of educational leaders. The idea is to support involvement of local educational agencies (LEA) in the training of administrators and to formalize the mentoring for new administrators over a certain period of time. State-funded principal leadership academies in

BOX 1.1

ISLLC STANDARDS FOR SCHOOL LEADERS

STANDARD 1

A school administrator is an educational leader who promotes the success of all students by facilitating the development, articulation, implementation, and stewardship of a vision of learning that is shared and supported by the school community.

STANDARD 2

A school administrator is an educational leader who promotes the success of all students by advocating, nurturing, and sustaining a school culture and an instructional program conducive to student learning and staff professional growth.

STANDARD 3

A school administrator is an educational leader who promotes the success of all students by ensuring management of the organization, operations, and resources for a safe, efficient, and effective learning environment.

STANDARD 4

A school administrator is an educational leader who promotes the success of all students by collaborating with families and community members, responding to diverse community interests and needs, and mobilizing resources.

STANDARD 5

A school administrator is an educational leader who promotes the success of all students by acting with integrity, with fairness, and in an ethical manner.

STANDARD 6

A school administrator is an educational leader who promotes the success of all students by understanding, responding to, and influencing the larger political, social, economic, legal, and cultural context.

The Interstate School Leaders Licensure Consortium (ISLLC) Standards were developed by the Council of Chief State School Officers (CCSSO) and member states. Copies may be downloaded from the council's website at www.ccsso.org.

Council of Chief State School Officers. (1996). *Interstate School Leaders Licensure Consortium (ISLLC) standards for school leaders.* Washington, DC: Author.

some states offer professional development programs, as well. These states establish and continuously fund such statewide academic programs to ensure a stable source of learning opportunities for principals and other school leaders. North Carolina has had a leadership academy located at UNC-Chapel Hill for more than 20 years.

Practitioner-oriented professional associations also provide input on the identification, preparation, and practice of educational leaders. They have local, state, and national meetings; academies; and conferences for the purpose of providing professional development while shaping the latest thinking in educational leadership. They publish newsletters, journals, and books that help administrative students and practitioners to keep current in their field. They have a long-standing commitment to the improvement of education and have championed the cause for innovation and experimentation.

Those preparing to be administrators as well as practicing administrators should associate with a professional association that best meets their needs. Some of the older and most well-known professional associations include the following:

PROFESSIONAL ASSOCIATION	EXAMPLE OF A MAJOR PRACTITIONER AUDIENCE
Council of Chief State School Officers (CCSSO)	State superintendents
National School Boards Association (NSBA)	School board members
American Association of School Administrators (AASA)	Superintendents
Association for Supervision and Curriculum Development (ASCD)	Central office personnel and supervisors
National Association of Secondary School Principals (NASSP)	High school principals
Middle School Principal Association (MSPA)	Middle school principals
National Association of Elementary School Principals (NAESP)	Elementary school principals
National Education Association (NEA)	Teachers
American Federation of Teachers (AFT)	Teachers
Phi Delta Kappa (PDK)	Educators in general

One example of the profound influence that professional associations might have on the preparation of future school administrators can be found in the work of the CCSSO, which, in conjunction with the National Policy Board for Educational Administration (NPBEA)—a joint board representing a number of educational professional associations—created ISLLC to develop standards for the preparation and assessment of school leaders. These six standards have been adopted by a majority of the states and have influenced state administrative licensure requirements, the design of the ETS Administrative Assessment, and the development of educational administrative programs across the United States (for more information see npbea.org).

Many educational leadership programs have met the Council for the Accreditation of Educator Preparation (CAEP, formerly called NCATE) standards. CAEP has authorized the Educational Leadership Constituent Council (ELCC), an affiliation of four administration groups, to review preparation programs for educational leaders and provide recognition for those programs that meet the standards.

Schools, school divisions, state departments of education, the U.S. Office of Education, professional associations, and universities form a rich network of organizations focused on improving the teaching/learning process as well as other aspects of education by enhancing organizational and individual effectiveness. Administrators benefit from a knowledge base, skills, ethical principles, and contextual understanding that provide the intellectual grounding needed for effective leadership. They build on a core of knowledge and skills in which theory and practice are integrated to improve performance.

Effective administrators are prepared to respond to the larger political, social, economic, legal, and cultural context of schools. Administrators are expected to apply a variety of policies, laws, regulations, and procedures in creative ways. They are expected to operate and maintain safe and clean buildings, equipment, and grounds while keeping attention focused on instruction. When you assume the role of an educational administrator, you will influence the direction of schooling so that each student leaves school having the capacity to engage in self-governance and self-development and to contribute to the economic benefits of our society.

Thomas Jefferson noted that schooling is necessary for democracy to survive. Each administrator is expected to be a catalyst in the process by which multiple voices, conflicting values, and diverse expectations are molded into a vision for education. The vision must meet the tests of justice, fairness, and equity. Thus, schooling is a profoundly human enterprise, an institution that nourishes liberty and democracy and provides access to economic benefits. It is also a technological enterprise that integrates the latest advances into the curriculum and instructional process.

Communicating, facilitating, team building, coaching, managing conflict, involving others in decision making, and acting politically are a few of the major skills to be developed in the context of technological advancement, assessment and accountability, diversity, new knowledge, and limited resources, among many other elements. Effective administration requires cooperation among departments, government agencies, staff members, professional groups, political office holders, school board members, media, universities, publishers, and many others.

Research, Theory, and Practice

Although there is no sense of total agreement on what educational administrators need to know and be able to do, conceptually there is widely accepted consensus that there are some foundational factors central to the practice of educational administration. Certainly the mission includes commitment to effective operation and continuous improvement of our schools, but it is far more than that. The desirable aspects of effective leadership are influenced by beliefs related to caring, pedagogy, moral stewardship, renewal, accountability, passion, charisma, civility, economic utility, reform, democratic character, social justice, and competence. The need is to provide a comprehensive account of educational leadership without oversimplifying its complex, dynamic, and interactive nature.

Educational leadership preparation programs throughout the United States are under intense scrutiny and criticism. Certainly there has been no greater scathing nor controversial attack than that by Arthur Levine (2005) who stated, "Some observers have expressed serious reservations about whether these institutions are capable of re-engineering their leadership preparation programs to effectively educate aspiring principals and superintendents to lead high performing schools. . . . The typical course of study for the principalship has little to do with the job of being a principal" (p. 27). Joseph Murphy (1990) talks about "the bankruptcy of the traditional ways of doing things" (p. 2). I am reminded of the quip, "If your horse dies, it is best to get off." Others have called these programs "bridges to nowhere." This criticism is not new and has been debated since the mid-1980s with the critical attack by the National Commission of Excellence in Educational Administration. In 2003, the Broad Foundation and Fordham Institute called for an opening up and deregulating of the field. This is occurring in a number of states where administration and supervision licensure is being opened up to "career switchers" and "alternative providers," such as the Broad Academy, Southern Regional Education Board (SREB) Modules, and district-run programs. Elmore (2006) has raised questions regarding principal preparation related to "how it is being taught, what is being taught, and the connections of theory with practice." He feared that existing programs were "disassociated from current practice" (p. 3).

There are a number of efforts under way to reform educational administration preparation programs, including collaborative partnerships, experiential learning, reflective practice, structured dialogue, technological models, problem-based learning, and engagement in authentic practice. A majority of universities have revamped their programs and are continuing to do so, with support from the Council for the Accreditation of Educator Preparation (CAEP, formerly called NCATE) and/or their state departments of education. Unfortunately, these reform agendas and innovations seem to have gone largely unnoticed by the critics, a point made quite strongly by Creighton and Young in "Taking Back our Profession: Revisited" (2005), a response to Arthur Levine's scathing attack on school leadership preparation. Fenwick English (2006), a UCEA president, has expressed concern that the assault on educational leadership programs, and education in general, is part of a well-organized extreme radical right conspiracy to implement their agenda for reform, including the corporatizing and privatizing of educational leadership preparation and public schools in the United States.

HUMAN CAPITAL AND THE ACCUMULATED KNOWLEDGE BASE

There exists a diverse variety of sometimes conflicting perspectives on how one might better understand educational administration. These views tend to rise and fall in importance in relation to the social and political events of the times. However, Willower and Forsyth (1999) find a number of unifying elements in the scholarship in educational administration from which are derived a variety of frameworks for addressing educational problems. The decision as to what will best serve the practitioner will most likely come down to its utility when it is being employed and the benefits of its results.

Certainly, educational administration practice is a blending of knowledge, practice, politics, ethics, traditions, and new visions. No one perspective or approach will provide a complete and universal explanation for practitioners; however, having an understanding of these diverse perspectives provides great benefit. The challenge then becomes finding ways to integrate the different perspectives, values, and approaches to improve the outcomes of education and the functioning of educational organizations (Donmoyer, 1999a).

Current Conditions and Expectations

From 2008–2009 through 2020–2021, public elementary and secondary school enrollment is projected to increase from 49.3 to 52.7 million students, but with differences across states. The number of students enrolled in public charter schools more than tripled from 340,000 students in 1999–2000 to 1.6 million in 2010–2011 with slightly more than 5% of all public schools being charter schools. Public charters have spread nationwide since the first one started in Minnesota in 1992. Today, there are more than 5,000 charter schools. There are wide variations in regions of the country with regard to the number of charter schools. California is home to 912 charters, more than any other state. Also, by 2010 some 10% of all elementary and secondary school students were enrolled in private schools. Between 1989 and 2009, the percentage of public school students who were White decreased from 68% to 55%, and the percentage of those who were Hispanic doubled from 11% to 22%. In 2009, some 21% of children ages 5–17 (or 11.2 million) spoke a language other than English at home, and 5% (or 2.7 million) spoke English with difficulty. Seventy-three percent of those who spoke English with difficulty spoke Spanish as a first language. The number of children and youth ages 3–21 receiving special education services was 6.5 million in 2008–2009, corresponding to about 13% of all public school enrollment. In 2009, some 19% of 5–17-year-old children were in families living in poverty (see Chapter 8 for more details), compared with 15% in 2000 and 17% in 1990 (NCES, 2010).

By 2010, federal, state, and local spending on public education exceeded $900 billion. Yet, only about 75% of U.S. students graduate from high school, which ranks the United States 16th among the 30 member countries of the Organization for Economic Cooperation and Development (OECD). These dropout problems are far more severe in urban districts, where by age 9 students are on average three grade levels behind in reading and math. Sousa (2005) reports that although decoding problems are only seen in 10% to 15% of students in middle schools, comprehension problems are seen in 85% of the cases. These comprehension skills are higher-level thinking skills needed for educational success in middle schools.

Today, a major concern is U.S. students' performance on international tests. In 2004, U.S. 15-year-old children performed well below the mean for the 30 OECD countries. They ranked 21st in math and 23rd in problem solving. The United States is also losing ground to European nations in the percentage of citizens with college degrees. Marc Tucker (1990), vice-chairman of the New Commission on the Skills of the American Workforce concluded, "The fact that other nations are outperforming the United States in education is both a threat and an opportunity. The threat is the real possibility of a significant decline in our standard of living. The opportunity is the chance to learn from them by studying the world's most effective educational systems, gleaning the lessons we need to exceed their performance." As a result, communities are placing increasing demands on administrators and teachers to provide more effective schools. This has placed greater emphasis on the importance of administrators, whose abilities are seen as absolutely crucial to the effectiveness of the nation's schools. The "principal's abilities are central to the task of building schools that promote powerful teaching and learning for all students" (Davis, Johnson-Reid, Saunders, Williams, & Williams, 2005, p. 8).

The job, however, has evolved into an almost overwhelming set of responsibilities. Anne Grosso De León (2006) states:

> Alas, the critical role of instructional leader is only one of a dizzying array of roles the school principal is required to play in today's educational environment. According to a recent study on school leadership published by the Stanford Educational Leadership Institute with support from the Wallace Foundation, . . . [t]he role of principal has swelled to include a staggering array of professional tasks and competencies. Principals are expected to be educational visionaries, instructional and curriculum leaders, assessment experts, disciplinarians, community builders, public relations and communications experts, budget analysts, facility managers, special programs administrators, as well as guardians of various legal, contractual, and policy mandates and initiatives. In addition, principals are expected to serve the often conflicting needs and interests of many stakeholders, including students, parents, teachers, district office officials, unions, and state and federal agencies. (p. 2)

See also the School Leadership Study (srnleads.org/resources/publications .html).

The expectations for both our schools and our administrators have dramatically increased. The responsibilities of both have expanded to include instructional leadership and student achievement. The traditional focus on management (organization, staffing, and resources) and a safe, clean, well-managed, disciplined school today is only half the story; the demand now is for a new kind of leader focused on instructional leadership, school improvement, and student achievement with an emphasis on high academic standards and expectations. Research has shown that the most pervasive challenges and issues that educational administrators face are related to the expanding expectations of their role as instructional leaders (DiPaulo & Tschannen-Moran, 2003). Cantano and Stronge (2006) state, "The stress today is on instructional leadership and student performance. Principals are being asked to incorporate practices that are responsive to the most crucial needs of their schools with regard to raising student achievement—the most essential instructional leadership task" (p. 223).

Principals have to varying degrees always been responsible for instructional leadership; however, that role has reached a new level of demand and complexity. It is only recently that researchers have been able to identify specific instructional leadership behaviors that are related to student achievement (Blase & Blase, 1998; Leithwood, Day, Sammons, Hopkins, & Harris, 2006; Fuller, Young, Barnett, Hirsch, & Byrd, 2007). Research has provided evidence that school leaders strongly influence student learning (Henderson et al., 2005; Leithwood, Seashore-Louis, Anderson, & Wahlstrom, 2004; Marks & Printy, 2003; O'Donnell & White, 2005; Waters, Marzano, & McNulty, 2003). See Chapter 6 to learn more about these positive links to student achievement. Leithwood and Jantzi (2006) found that school leader behavior (setting directions, developing people, redesigning the organization, managing instructional programs) and school conditions made the largest contributions to standardized total effects on student achievement. Certainly this increasing pressure for instructional leadership comes from the principals' obligation to ensure that their schools meet state academic standards monitored through high-stakes testing systems—the standards and accountability movement. "The political pressure of high-stakes accountability requires principals to improve instruction and student achievement while balancing the need to maintain facilities, supervise student conduct, and manage budgets. The concern regarding expanding roles is that it will result in a significant amount of conflict and overload and affect principal effectiveness" (Cantano & Stronge, 2006, p. 231). Add to this daunting list the glaring, seemingly intractable issue of "equity" and any administrator will have his or her hands full. Certainly educational leaders must be well prepared to handle this complex set of expectations.

An important set of knowledge, skills, and dispositions is needed to effectively lead schools and improve student achievement in an increasingly complex and diverse context. Today's principals need to have a wide repertoire of leadership and management skills; a deep understanding of curriculum, instruction, assessment, and adaptations to unique contexts; and knowledge of the various components and operational systems that are required to support effective schools. An example of some of the practices required for successful school leadership includes facilitating student learning, building professional learning communities, fostering teacher professional development, providing instructional feedback, improving teacher practices, resolving challenges using data to monitor progress, identifying problems, and working with staff in proposing and implementing improvements. Even though leaders are expected to devote the bulk of their efforts to instructional leadership, they also have responsibility for the routine management and operational tasks of running a school (LaPointe & Davis, 2006; Goldstein, Halverson, & Murphy, 2007).

Leithwood and Jantzi (2006) showed that critical leadership practices include setting direction, helping individual teachers, fostering collaboration, and providing management and support. These expectations require administrators to have a coherent and clear set of values focused on supporting student achievement. All of this places a huge responsibility on those who wish to take on administrative responsibility in education and become highly qualified administrators, committed to the improvement of student achievement. Future educational leaders must be well equipped to meet the ever-increasing demands placed on their leadership and the schools they lead. There is a great deal to be learned and it is the responsibility of each person who aspires to become a future leader to develop the essential knowledge, skills, and dispositions. In recent years, research has converged on the importance of three aspects of the principal's job:

1. Developing a deep understanding of how to support teachers
2. Managing the curriculum in ways that promote student learning
3. Developing the ability to transform schools into more effective organizations that foster powerful teaching and learning for all students (Davis, Darling-Hammond, LaPointe, & Myerson, 2005)

There is a set of shared values, beliefs, knowledge, skills, and dispositions about effective administrative practice that is widely accepted and provides a foundation and scaffolding on which to build effective practice.

Administrative Succession

Leadership succession has often been described as a career ladder that narrows at the top. The educational administrative career path starts with being a new teacher. Usually the path begins after finishing college and becoming certified as a teacher. According to the Department of Labor, kindergarten, elementary school, middle school, and secondary school teachers held about 3.5 million jobs in 2008. Of the teachers in those jobs, about 180,000 were kindergarten teachers, 1.5 million were elementary school teachers, 660,500 were middle school teachers, and 1.1 million were secondary school teachers (Occupational Outlook Handbook, 2010–2011 Edition). According to Orfield and Lee (2006) the number of teachers grows along with an accelerating growth of nonwhite public school students and the racial diversity of the teaching force remains low. Teachers of color are a much smaller percentage of the teaching force than students of color are in comparison to the entire student enrollment. Researchers report that new teachers are more diverse than their veteran colleagues; however, the entire teaching force still remains overwhelmingly white (Shen, Cooley, & Wengenke, 2004; Kirby, Berends, & Naftel, 1999).

Analysis of teacher data from 1994–2000 (Guarino, Sanlibarney, & Daley, 2006) suggest that hires in education were 73% female and 39% minority. The teaching force is 1.2% Asian American, 4.7% Hispanic, 9.6% African American, 80% Caucasian, and 5.5% other. Among new teachers, 96% felt the job involved work they loved to do and 97% felt that it contributed to society. Qualifications and attributes sought in hiring teachers are prior successful teaching experience, class management skills, good character, and ability to work with diverse learners, interpersonal skills, and a variety of teaching strategies. Public school teachers in high-poverty schools were more likely than their counterparts to leave teaching (10% versus 9%) but less likely to change schools (13% versus 19%). However, some studies have suggested that fewer than 40% of teachers remained in the profession over 5 years (Lankford, Loeb, & Wyckoff, 2002). Teachers who experienced induction and mentoring support in their first year of teaching were less likely to leave. Of teachers who left, 22% believed that they had not received adequate support or resources to perform their jobs. Teachers were concerned about safety (89%), being underpaid (78%), working conditions (76%), scapegoat status (76%), limited opportunities for advancement (69%), and teacher autonomy and discretion (42%).

As the administrative candidate becomes more comfortable and effective, he or she should take on some extracurricular activities, such as tutoring, club sponsor (e.g., debate, sports, drama), PTA, testing, and so on. It is also advisable to make one's intention known to the department head, assistant principal, and principal. Moreover, the candidate should solicit or volunteer for opportunities to gain experience in school operations, academic instruction, assessment and evaluation, special education, safety, fund raising, community services, school improvement, summer school administration, and other services that exemplify talents, skills, motivation, and intentions. This is also a good time to become more active in professional associations and staff development. The candidate should dress the part, to walk and talk the part, and gain needed political support.

The candidate might also apply for a department chair/head position or to serve as a grade-level team leader if that position exists in the elementary school. These positions challenge problem-solving and people skills, curriculum and instructional knowledge, leadership, communication (oral and written), and creative talents. Candidates, when observed, should show leadership abilities and the potential for upward mobility. Motivation, knowledge, experience, and performance will determine the number of years it will take to obtain an administrative position; a fast-track approach can accomplish this in 3 to 5 years.

Some school districts have such administrative positions as dean of students, peer coaches, and cluster leaders. Time at the school, evaluations, professional behavior, instructional proficiency, ethics, school involvement, relationships (student to teacher, teacher to teacher, teacher to parent, and teacher to administrator), and positive interactions are factors considered for applicants for administrative positions. The following provides an example of the requirements needed by applicants for assistant principal or principal positions.

1. Hold the postgraduate professional license with an elementary, middle, high school principalship endorsement or administration/supervision pre-K–12 endorsement
2. Have 3 years or more of successful experience as a teacher, administrator, or supervisor, with preferably 2 years at the level applied for
3. Have demonstrated leadership and personal characteristics necessary for working with students, teachers, and parents

At each education level—whether elementary, middle, or high school—the candidate will need experience at that particular level due to differences in the population, curriculum, and agenda. Some states also require satisfactory performance on a leadership test like the Administrative PRAXIS or the ETS School Leadership Licensure Assessment (SLLA). Almost all principals have advanced degrees and engage in professional development programs. Almost half have presented at a workshop, meeting, or training activity. Nearly all individuals who were promoted had participated in workshops or conferences during the previous year and had attended association meetings and visited other schools. According to the U.S. Department of Education (USDOE) National Center for Education Statistics (NCES), the average principal had served 14 years as a teacher and 9 years as a principal (nces.ed.gov).

Most educational leaders begin their administrative careers as assistant principals. This position immediately presents a dilemma for those who aspire to the principalship—meet the job expectations that usually focus on a series of narrow technical tasks or develop the broader leadership skills that are expected of principals—in other words, be a managerial specialist or an instructional leader (Daresh, 2002). The principal will gradually release greater authority and control to those whom they are grooming to become educational leaders. They will take on the role of mentors and coaches as these people take on greater responsibility. After 3 to 7 years, many motivated assistant principals are promoted to principal positions.

Hart (1993) describes a period of "organizational socialization" of the new principal into existing school culture. She introduced the idea of four stages in leadership transition—looking ahead, enchantment, disenchantment, and equilibrium. While going through the process of enculturation into a school, principals are typically left on their own to fend for themselves (Fink & Brayman, 2006). Over time, new experiences and new challenges help develop the needed understanding of the significant responsibility placed on the principal, as principals refine their view of what the job requires. Some districts have recognized the need to better support principals in this process and have developed leadership academies or other such programs to better introduce principals to the realities of the job. During this period, individuals tend to acquire a new mindset, different from that of being an assistant principal or teacher, which some describe as "reality shock" or "street smarts." Perhaps the best and most immediate help can be gained from a mentor who can give advice and perspective. Also, a principal who continues to hone his or her skills and achieve greater success might look toward promotion to a position that has an opportunity for even greater impact—an influence over the entire school district.

Those seeking promotion to a director, coordinator, or assistant/associate superintendent position would have had successful terms as principals and assistant principals in middle schools or high schools. They must have accomplishments that will set them apart from the rest—for example, holding an important office in a distinguished professional organization. Their schools would have passed all state required standards or made notable progress toward meeting that goal. Their schools or personnel might have created or contributed to implementing new learning strategies or instructional programs. Most states require a master's degree and certification in pre-K–12 administration and supervision; however, a doctorate is often preferable.

Many superintendents are hired from other states and are interviewed by the local school boards. Superintendents need to have impeccable records and have served at various levels in the education system. They will have a long list of programs and innovations that have contributed to education, technology, student achievement, the community, and the school district as a whole. They often will have written articles or reviews on specific educational topics. Examples of some qualities school boards will be looking for include:

- Leadership experience as a superintendent or assistant superintendent of a school system, as well as successful experience as a teacher and principal
- High standards of ethical and moral conduct; a role model who holds high expectations for students and for personnel
- Outstanding experience, understanding, and abilities relating to budgets and to the budgeting process
- Educational leadership, with special knowledge and expertise in curriculum and instruction and a proven record in improving student achievement
- Commitment to fostering cooperative relationships with personnel, the school board, and the community
- Excellent communications and interpersonal skills, and successful work experience in a multicultural community

CORE EDUCATIONAL LEADERSHIP VALUES

Educational leaders should reflect on the values that have been put forth as important (for example, see the ISLLC standards in Box 1.1). The educational leader should determine how these values are or are not being practiced within schools. These value statements can help individuals to experience and reflect on the moral aspects of leadership in a more systemic way. Hopefully, this process will sensitize administrators to the moral and ethical issues that will confront them as leaders.

Appendix 1.A at the end of this chapter provides a list of some of the generally held dispositions or beliefs that typically guide the work of educators (based on ISLLC and the SLLA). This is not a comprehensive list; however, it does bring out some of the core beliefs about education. These values will assist you to know what to do and how to assess your work regarding successful outcomes. It is recommended that you check your own assumptions against this list and the assumptions that seem to exist within your educational site. Which do you disagree with? Which do you feel would disagree with what exists at your site? Discuss disagreements with your instructor, classmates, and administrative mentor.

Give some thought to how what you agree or disagree with might influence your behavior as an educational leader. You might want to discuss this with your instructor, administrator, and/or fellow students. You might have others complete this instrument and then provide feedback to one another.

The greater the agreement between your assumptions and those of the profession and organization, the greater the probability of success as an educational leader. You might ask value-oriented questions regarding:

1. What leadership strategy will you use and how will you know if it is successful?
2. How will you incorporate your knowledge of research and best practice in what you do?

GROUNDING MORAL EDUCATIONAL LEADERSHIP IN THE INTRINSICALLY MORAL ENTERPRISE OF LEARNING

ROBERT J. STARRATT
Boston College

The moral demands of educational leadership go well beyond considerations of specific acts of moral choice (when to tell or withhold the truth about what one knows about a student; whether to compromise with pressure groups who want to impose a point of view in certain areas of the curriculum or lose one's job over the issue; whether to retain a mediocre teacher with political connections, and so on). The much more essential work of moral educational leadership is to create a schoolwide learning environment that promotes the moral integrity of learning as the pursuit of the truth about oneself and one's world, however complex and difficult that task may be.

Schooling implicates learners in the enterprise of appropriating the way by which their society interprets and understands itself and the world. This knowledge helps or hinders learners to identify who they are (as citizens, as workers, as gendered and racial beings, or simply as human beings), what they are worth, what they are responsible for, how they exist in nature and society, and how they might conduct themselves in their personal and public lives. Since this knowledge is received or presented as heuristic as well as an expressive cultural production of that society (McCarthy, 1997a), schools ought to assist the learner in exploring how this knowledge was generated and on what assumptions that generation rests.

Learning involves an encounter with an aspect of reality, albeit an interpreted and culturally grounded reality. The learner cannot intentionally deny its existence or arbitrarily make it into its opposite without disfiguring the integrity of that reality and violating the intrinsic moral obligation to acknowledge on its own terms the reality one encounters. Learning requires a coming to terms with what a person is learning, whether it is a scientific fact such as "ice floats on water," a historical assertion that "Lincoln freed the slaves," or a depiction of a moneylender like Shylock in *The Merchant of Venice*. That learning conveys a multitude of meanings, some of which should be honored (slavery is immoral), some of which should be questioned (since most of the mass of an iceberg is below water, how can it be said to float on water? Where does money come from and how is it accumulated?), and some of which should be repudiated or denounced (Hitler's assertion of the superiority of the Aryan race).

The obligation to come to terms with what one knows, to explore its use and its misuse, to avoid its distortion or manipulation is both a moral and an intellectual obligation (if for scholars, why not for younger learners as well?). Learning is a moral search as well as an intellectual search for truth—truth about ourselves, about our community, about our history, about our cultural and physical world. The truth, of course, will never be final or complete; rather, it will be tentative, incomplete, fallible, partial, and generative. But the truth will ultimately involve human beings with choices about themselves and about the kinds of communities they want to create.

This is what schools are supposed to be about. Hence, those who would lead schools toward this approach to teaching and learning are inescapably involved in a moral enterprise. This understanding of moral educational leadership implies a different conversation between educational leaders and other teachers and parents about curriculum, about assessment of student performances, and about teacher assessment. It also implies a different kind of academic preparation of administrators, one in which the moral dimensions of their own learning are continuously explored and the ongoing creation and reconstruction of their own self-identity is pursued.

3. How will you confront conflicts that develop and how will you know if that approach is successful?
4. What are your beliefs concerning bringing about needed change?
5. How will you establish relationships and communicate to other professionals and clerical helpers on the staff?
6. How do you want to be seen by others? Is that a realistic expectation?
7. How do you want to be perceived as an administrator?

ETHICAL MODELS

Starratt created a model (1994) that is depicted as a triangle with each side labeled with one of three ethics: the ethic of care, the ethic of justice, and the ethic of critique. Each of these overlapping ethics raised different questions that school leaders need to consider.

The Ethic of Caring

The notion of an ethic of caring has been promoted by Carol Gilligan (1982) and Nel Noddings (1992). According to Noddings (1992), "Caring is a way of being in relation, not a set of specific behaviors" (p. 17). Caring includes modeling, dialogue, practice, and confirmation. Modeling for educators means demonstrating that we care, rather than simply saying it. Dialogue must be in the sense that Paolo Freire (1973) espouses: open ended and sincere. This dialogue allows teachers and administrators to show they care by listening fully. Noddings's fourth component of caring—confirmation—involves affirming and encouraging the best in others. Noddings believes that "when we confirm someone, we spot a better self and encourage its development" (p. 25). An important question to ask about a school environment from the perspective of an ethic of care is—What do our relationships ask of us?

The Ethic of Justice

Justice involves equity and fairness in relation to individual and community choice. How a school is governed is a crucial part of the ethic of justice, which demands that administrators serve as advocates for students, including advocating for optimal learning conditions. Justice addresses issues of educational equity, opportunity of resources, emotional and physical security, and health and social environment. An example of a question to ask from the perspective of an ethic of justice is—How shall we govern ourselves?

Justice involves individuals acting impartially and a community that governs its actions fairly. As Starratt (1996) maintains, "To promote a just social order in the school, the school community must carry out an ongoing critique of those structural features of the school that work against human beings" (p. 194). One habit of the heart that schools must embrace is the habit of questioning and self-criticism. If the questions raised come from the ethics of caring and justice, they are closely related to the ethic of critique.

The Ethic of Critique

The ethic of critique is based on critical theory. According to Foster (1986), critical theory "questions the framework of the way we organize our lives or the way our lives are organized for us" (p. 72). Foster argues that the school administrator must be a critical theoretician. Through dialogue, she or he must ask and help others to ask questions that challenge the status quo. The ethic of critique promotes questions such as: Who benefits from this? Who holds power? Whose voice has not been heard? Who is privileged?

The ethic of critique facilitates conversation and dialogue between people in organizations. The ethic of critique obliges the moral agent to question unjust and uncaring social arrangements and work to change such injustice. The recent focus on "social justice" is rooted in this ethic of critique. There is a rejection of oppression in any form and a call for new frameworks of action. It is crucial to the ethic of critique to address conflict with civility.

FOUNDATIONS OF ETHICAL BEHAVIOR: STANDARDS FOR GOOD PRACTICE

Beck (1994), Starratt (1996), English (2008), Shapiro and Stefkovich (2010), and others writing on the topic of ethics have identified standards of good practice that can serve school administrators as a foundation for ethical behavior. Standards of good practice include being conscious (aware and informed), encouraging dialogue, modeling, and being reflective. In recent years, researchers have described various approaches that can help educational administrators develop skills to function as ethical school leaders (Craig, 1999; Duke & Grogan, 1997; Mertz, 1997a; Shapiro & Stefkovich, 2010), including the following:

- Examining situations from a variety of perspectives, including feminism, postmodernism, liberation theology, and critical theory (see Chapter 6)
- Writing personal essays, or educational platforms, describing ethical principles or values that students subscribe to
- Examining dilemmas from consequentialist and nonconsequentialist points of view
- Utilizing data from values instruments such as the Personal Values Inventory and the Hall-Tonna Inventory that supply information on several areas of human growth

- Comparing and contrasting ethical codes of conduct from a variety of organizations
- Learning and using group dynamics training
- Reading ethical dilemmas rooted in particular contextual variables because "leadership does not exist apart from context" (Duke & Grogan, 1997, p. 145)

Craig (1994) believes that "virtue can be developed through arduous practice" and that "treating others justly and respectfully over a long period of time may result in a virtuous person" (p. 134).

Codes of Ethics

According to Shapiro and Stefkovich (1997), a legal perspective focuses on the interpretation of state and federal codes of ethics. These codes are rule bound.

Standards also exist for many professional associations. Go to the Web site for your professional organization and find their "statement of ethics." These standards can be viewed as a beginning step for a school administrator when developing a personal educational platform that includes the principles he or she advocates. The codes of ethics stress the common values of honesty, integrity, due process, civil and human rights, and above all, the students' well-being. Ethics assist with individual ethical quandaries. Leaders must be aware of the beliefs they have and the dispositions that they display because they have a profound influence on their behavior. In addition to the professional association code of ethics, many state statutes have also codified codes of ethics for public employees. Such codes can be important in ascertaining what might be considered "immorality," "moral turpitude," "incompetency," and "conduct unbecoming of a professional," which may be used as grounds for dismissal. In this way, the power of ethical codes is quite high, demanding that school personnel perform at the highest level in all facets of their responsibilities. As Dantley (2005) suggests, "Leadership of this nature is not only transformative but it is also principled and purposive. . . . Principled leadership emanates from a sense of the need to ground the work of education in a context of morality and meaning. . . . " (p. 15). Codes of ethics contain some principles that educational administrators might want to include when developing a personal platform.

AASA'S STATEMENT OF ETHICS FOR EDUCATIONAL LEADERS

An educational leader's professional conduct must conform to an ethical code of behavior, and the code must set high standards for all educational leaders. The educational leader provides professional leadership across the district and also across the community. This responsibility requires the leader to maintain standards of exemplary professional conduct while recognizing that his or her actions will be viewed and appraised by the community, professional associates, and students.

The educational leader acknowledges that he or she serves the schools and community by providing equal educational opportunities to each and every child. The work of the leader must emphasize accountability and results, increased student achievement, and high expectations for each and every student.

To these ends, the educational leader subscribes to the following statements of standards.

The educational leader:

1. Makes the education and well-being of students the fundamental value of all decision making.
2. Fulfills all professional duties with honesty and integrity and always acts in a trustworthy and responsible manner.
3. Supports the principle of due process and protects the civil and human rights of all individuals.
4. Implements local, state, and national laws.
5. Advises the school board and implements the board's policies and administrative rules and regulations.
6. Pursues appropriate measures to correct those laws, policies, and regulations that are not consistent with sound educational goals or that are not in the best interest of children.
7. Avoids using his/her position for personal gain through political, social, religious, economic, or other influences.
8. Accepts academic degrees or professional certification only from accredited institutions.
9. Maintains the standards and seeks to improve the effectiveness of the profession through research and continuing professional development.
10. Honors all contracts until fulfillment, release, or dissolution mutually agreed upon by all parties.
11. Accepts responsibility and accountability for one's own actions and behaviors.
12. Commits to serving others above self.

Source: AASA, Printed with permission.

EDUCATIONAL LEADERSHIP PLATFORMS

Senge and colleagues (2000) state: "Reflection and inquiry are not practiced much: People everywhere are impeded from working together effectively by the conflicting views of the world. But the discovery of oneself, the ability to see something in your own behavior that was invisible to you before, and appreciation of what's productive and what's painful in your attitudes—awareness of these capabilities seems pretty intrinsic to the human condition. . . . There is something integral in the core idea that manifests at all different levels and can be seen from all different angles" (pp. 560–561). Thus, it is important that administrators and those whom

they influence have a clear understanding of the foundational principles, concep-
tualizations, philosophy, and values on which they base their judgments.

Empathy, integrity, fairness, respect, honesty, optimism, self-esteem, self-
confidence, determination, and self-awareness are essential to good leadership.
In addition to administrative knowledge and skills, beliefs, opinions, values, and
attitudes provide the foundation for the actions of leaders. They are seen by the
school community as the educational values and beliefs of the leader and often
become the mood of the school. These relatively intangible qualities of the principalship spur leaders, their staff, and the entire school to superior performance.

People need to connect emotionally as well as intellectually in order to succeed. There is some wisdom in establishing the right level of passion and emotion
when communicating with others. Too much or too little can easily turn others off
to what you are saying. Simple things like eye contact can be very important along
with effective listening and oral communication skills. Sensing where to focus attention is certainly another of those intangible and hard-to-describe skills. These
can all be embodied in the platform on which one stands. Sergiovanni and Starratt
(2001) refer to one's personal philosophy as a *platform*. An individual's platform
"is made up of those basic assumptions, beliefs, attitudes and values that are un-
derpinnings of an educator's behavior" (Sergiovanni & Starratt, 2001, p. 84).

An educational leadership platform is a document that provides a description of one's values, beliefs, and philosophies about educational leadership. It is a
self-reflective document providing a framework for administrative action. It helps
administrators determine if their actions are aligned with their espoused beliefs.
Barnett (1991) stresses the importance of platform development in helping administrators "to identify the moral dilemmas they will face as administrators and to
articulate the standards of practice they will use in judging situations" (p. 135).
The platform is a statement that systematically and accurately states the principles, ethics, and values that underlie a person's actions. It is crucial that administrators reflect on the basis of the choices they will ultimately make.

Educators carry on their work, make decisions, and plan instruction on the
basis of their platforms; thus, these platforms should be clearly articulated and espoused. This concept is based on the political model in which parties are expected
to develop platforms to aid supporters and voters to make the clearest, best, most
informed choices for themselves. Knowing the platform and being aware of any
inconsistencies with practice or other platforms is immensely helpful. Argyris and
Schön (1978) refer to these inconsistencies as differences between espoused theory
and theory-in-use. Espoused theories detail philosophies, beliefs, values, assumptions, theories, and paradigms underlying behavior; theory-in-use represents the
way people actually implement them. Argyris and Schön (1978) state:

> When someone is asked how he would behave under certain circumstances, the an-
> swer he usually gives is his espoused theory of action for the situation. This is the
> theory of action to which he gives allegiance and which, upon request, he communi-
> cates to others. However, the theory that actually governs his actions is his theory-in-
> use, which may or may not be compatible with his espoused theory; furthermore, the
> individual may or may not be aware of the incompatibility of the two theories. (p. 11)

Argyris and Schön (1978), Cunningham (1982), Blake and McCanse (1991), and Sagor and Barnett (1994) suggest that the best first step in improving organizational functioning is for practitioners to discover and make explicit any differences between espoused theory and theory in use. An administrator needs to clearly state her or his espoused theory—that is, her or his administrative platform. The administrator then compares this platform to her or his behavior within the organization. When platform and behavior are incompatible, the administrator decides which to alter. It is best for all concerned when actual behavior is compatible with espoused values and theories. When it is not, trust breaks down and the organization becomes ineffective. Thus, the development of an educational and administrative platform is essential for all administrative action.

Individual platforms should be in general agreement with the philosophy, mission, goals, and direction of the school system. When they are not, administrators should endeavor to explain why such differences exist.

Platforms often include a statement of the person's philosophy of leadership, preferred leadership style, and the process by which he or she works with teachers, other school community members, and other foundational areas related to leadership practices. Ovando (2004) found platform development to be a powerful learning experience—enhancing self-awareness and value clarification. Platforms provide an opportunity for reflection while they serve "as a foundation for school leadership practice" (Ovando, 2004, p. 37). The platform serves as a guide for school leadership performance as it is consulted as a point of reference. Sharing one's platform with peers is enlightening, enhances understanding, and is useful in bringing out areas of agreement and disagreement.

Sergiovanni and Starratt (1998) describe how to get started:

> Once we have written down the elements of our platform, we can with further reflection begin to group them in clusters and place them in some order of importance. . . .
>
> [Some] will find the writing exercise too tedious and will seek out a colleague to discuss this whole question. The free flow of shared ideas frequently stimulates the process of clarification. . . . Still others may go to a formal statement of goals that the school or system has in print to begin the process. (p. 244)

Sergiovanni and Starratt (1998) refer to this as a work in progress that should be periodically revisited and updated. Colleagues, students, and professors should challenge the leader to prove that his or her platform is more than espoused theory. The leader's theory in use must be observable in his or her actions. They go on to suggest that regardless of how individual platforms are developed, administrators should compare them with those of other colleagues to provide an opportunity to reflect on "areas of agreement or disagreement." Sometimes this comparison leads to modification and sometimes to acceptance of greater diversity in perspectives. It usually helps to build collegiality, understanding, alignment, and—when the platform is compatible with behavior—trust, integrity, cooperation, and continuous improvement, which creates organizational effectiveness (Cunningham & Gresso, 1993). Chapter 6 provides a number of instruments that can be used for "guided reflection" related to values, beliefs, experiences, and, ultimately, practices.

THE KNOWLEDGE BASE IN EDUCATIONAL ADMINISTRATION

There is considerable debate and little agreement regarding a specific knowledge base for educational administration (Hoy & Miskel, 2008). Obviously, no "cookbook" tells practitioners what paradigms, values, methods, or models to use; what issues and operational areas to address; or how to apply specific skills in various different contexts. Administrative knowledge is a complex array of theories, ideologies, skills, ethical principles, paradigms, and practices that are applied to a diverse set of issues.

The synthesis of knowledge in educational administration can be conceptualized as comprising seven factors: functions, skills, ethics, structure, operational areas, context, and issues. Table 1.1 presents a comprehensive model of the complexity of educational administration. Even though in practice factors cannot be separated, it is probably best to focus on and integrate one factor at a time. Each leads to some truth, but none by itself affords an adequate understanding. Together they provide a more complete understanding of educational leadership.

THE KNOWLEDGE BASE IN EDUCATIONAL ADMINISTRATION: A PRACTICAL REASONING

ROBERT DONMOYER
The University of San Diego

The search for a scientific knowledge base for the educational administration field has taken various forms during the past 100 years. Initially, scholars in the emerging field took their cue from efficiency experts in business. For instance, Elwood P. Cubberly, who often has been called the father of the educational administration field, wrote in 1909: "Our schools are, in a sense, factories in which the raw products (children) are to be shaped and fashioned into the products to meet the various demands of life" (p. 383). Cubberly, like many other 20th-century scholars (e.g., Good, Biddle, and Brophy, 1975; Thorndike, 1910), assumed that educational researchers could, through experimentation, create a knowledge base that would lead to standardizing the teaching and learning process. This belief turned out to be wrong.

Later, educational administration scholars, motivated at least in part by the failure of Cubberly and his contemporaries to produce a definitive knowledge base that could be used to "choreograph" educational practice, focused their work on creating social science theory. They assumed that the theories scholars generated (not the findings of particular studies, per se) could direct educational practice. The lack of success of this so-called theory movement can be seen in PRIMIS, a computerized set of documents developed by the University Council of Educational Administration (Hoy, 1994) that ostensibly organizes the knowledge base for the field. Rather than providing a coherent and relatively consistent vision of educational administration practice, the document base presents a plethora of different—and at times conflicting—theoretical perspectives. These perspectives can be useful

(continued)

TABLE 1.1 Key Factors in Effective Administration

ADMINISTRATIVE FUNCTIONS*	SKILLS	ETHICAL STANDARDS	STRUCTURE AND ORGANIZATION	OPERATIONAL AREAS	CONTEXT	ISSUES
■ Plan	■ Leadership	■ Honesty	■ President	■ Finance	■ Community	■ Safe schools
■ Organize	■ Problem analysis	■ Integrity	■ U.S. Department of Education	■ Curriculum and instruction	■ Taxpayers	■ Multiculturalism
■ Actuate/direct	■ Decision making	■ Loyalty/fidelity	■ Secretary of Education	■ Human resource development	■ Special-interest groups	■ Inclusion
■ Coordinate	■ Delegation	■ Promise keeping	■ Governors	■ Research and development	■ Teachers/ parents/kids	■ Technology
■ Control/evaluate	■ Supervising and motivating	■ Fairness	■ State school boards	■ Business and logistics	■ Chamber of commerce	■ Synchronous and asynchronous learning
	■ Interpersonal sensitivity	■ Concern for others	■ State superintendents	■ Physical plant	■ College professors/ researchers	■ Standardized testing (high-stakes testing)
	■ Oral communication	■ Respect for others	■ State departments of education	■ Pupil personnel	■ Media/TV	■ Assessment
	■ Written communication	■ Law-abiding/ civic duty	■ Local school boards		■ City council	■ Vouchers
	■ Assessment	■ Pursuit of excellence	■ Superintendents		■ Religious organizations	■ Charter schools
	■ Legal, policy, and political applications	■ Personal accountability	■ Central administrators		■ Private business	■ School choice
	■ Public relations		■ Principals		■ Professional associations	■ Achievement gap
	■ Technology		■ Teachers		■ Textbook manufacturers	■ Global education
	■ Social		■ PTA		■ Industry	■ Environmentalism
					■ Government	■ Alternative certification
					■ International groups	■ Best practices
					■ Technologists	■ Comprehensive school reform
						■ Preschool education
						■ Childhood obesity
						■ Differentiated instruction

*Henri Fayole (1949).

to school administrators as they think about what actions to take and which policies to implement; a theoretical knowledge base containing many different, often conflicting theories, however, does not provide the sort of direction to administrators and policymakers that theory movement advocates envisioned. (For a more detailed discussion of the issue, see Donmoyer, 1999a.)

As is often the case, there are echoes of the past in the present (see, for example, National Research Council, 2002b; Whitehurst, 2003). It is a virtual certainty, however, that current efforts to develop a definitive knowledge base for the field will be no more successful than efforts in the past have been because of two problems that have not—and will not—go away.

One problem is that of *idiosyncrasy.* Anthropologists allude to this problem when they note that normally there is as much variation within a culture or group as there is between cultures and groups. Observant teachers certainly understand what anthropologists are talking about. They know (either from experience or from reading research), for example, that 4th-grade African-American males tend to respond positively to certain strategies and negatively to others; however, they also know that not all African-American 4th-grade students fit the general pattern. Skilled teachers understand that they must always see children as unique individuals rather than merely as types; by contrast, researchers intent on producing a general knowledge base for the field can only speak in terms of general categories (i.e., ideal types). Consequently, the knowledge researchers produce, though not useless, cannot be translated into formulas or recipes that policymakers and administrators can mandate with any certainty about the results that will be produced. Indeed, the problem of idiosyncrasy suggests that deviation from a "scientifically validated" standardized program will be required for certain students to succeed.

The second problem, which can be labeled *the problem of values,* can best be explained by using an example: Assume that a team of researchers has been hired to determine whether a kindergarten program created from the developmental theories of Piaget produces more learning than a kindergarten program that is rooted in Skinnerian behaviorism. Before the team can begin to study the programs and their effects, the team must answer a question that, ultimately, is a value question: How should learning be defined in the study? If the research team's values are consistent with the way Piaget conceptualizes learning, they almost certainly will select a definition—and outcome measures consistent with the definition—that reflects Piaget's view of learning. The same can be said of researchers who prefer Skinner's way of thinking. Whatever definition is selected will have a significant impact on which program is judged more successful; the definition—and the values implicit in it—will determine what data count and, in fact, what data get counted. That is why educational research in the past—and any educational research that will be done in the future—will inevitably support differing, and at times even contradictory, courses of action.

So, do the two problems discussed earlier mean that educational administration cannot develop a knowledge base? And, because a knowledge base is generally thought to be a prerequisite for classifying a field as a profession, does that mean that educational administrators cannot be considered professionals? Not necessarily.

There is at least one very prestigious profession, the profession of law, in which what counts most is not a knowledge of facts and theories but, rather, a knowledge of how to think and reason (Donmoyer, 2007). To be sure, lawyers do understand legal principles (which also, at times, conflict) and know about particular legal cases (the raw material employed in the legal reasoning process). This knowledge is

(continued)

secondary, however, to knowledge about how to employ legal principles and case knowledge in the process of legal reasoning about a particular case. Given the problems outlined earlier, one could argue that knowing how to reason in a way that applies general principles to particular contexts (and also enriches understanding of the general principles in the process) may be as important in the educational administration field as it is in the field of law. Consequently, although the knowledge base question in educational administration has not generally been conceptualized in this practical reasoning way in the past, the legal reasoning analogy may be helpful when thinking both about how school administrators should be educated, how they should approach their work, and how to make educational administration a profession.

CONCLUSION

Our frames of reference, our paradigms, and our mental models are invisible elements that influence the way we think and our ability to envision the future. We can operate "without thinking" if we never reflect on frames of reference or develop platforms that make our belief systems explicit. New frames can accentuate previously unnoticed possibilities; new relationships, previously unseen, can become viable. For these reasons, administrators should continually revisit and reflect on their platforms.

We must understand the current conditions in education and the positions to which we aspire. What do leaders need to know? What is important? These are essential questions in taking on the responsibilities of leadership in our schools. Our practice is held captive by our theory, our knowledge base, and our experiences. We must ensure that the ideas, positions, and theories that enjoy privileged positions of unquestioned supremacy and thus are viewed as the "truth" are themselves questioned when new ways of seeing things evolve. The challenge is in how we pursue knowledge and how knowledge is expanded.

MyEdLeadershipLab™

Go to Topic 1: *Vision and Mission* in the MyEdLeadershipLab™ site (www.MyEdLeadershipLab .com) for *Educational Leadership: A Bridge to Improved Practice,* Fifth Edition, where you can:

- Find learning outcomes for *Vision and Mission* along with the national standards that connect to these outcomes.
- Complete Assignments and Activities that can help you more deeply understand the chapter content.
- Apply and practice your understanding of the core skills identified in the chapter with the Building Leadership Skills unit.
- Prepare yourself for professional certification with a Practice for Certification quiz.

PORTFOLIO ARTIFACTS

- Define the values or ethics that guide your behavior as an educational leader.

- Describe how your leadership behavior models personal and professional ethics, integrity, justice, and fairness.

- Reflect on your teaching philosophy, beliefs, and leadership platform, recognizing their impact and influence on the performance of others.

- Develop a comprehensive leadership platform (include philosophies of education and leadership).

- Examine what accreditations (state and national) your local colleges/schools of education hold. Discuss with your fellow students what implications statement #8 in the NAESP Code of ethics might have.

- Examine past agendas of school board meetings or attend a school board meeting and relate the work of the school board to your philosophy and values.

- Review administrative job descriptions and the policy manual within a school district.

- Discuss with a principal what it will take to be promoted to an administrative position.

- Attend a conference or a superintendent's administrative meeting and report back on the content and what you learned.

KEY TERMS

- Ethics
- Human capital
- Instructional leadership
- ISLLC Standards
- Knowledge base

- Leadership
- Leadership platform
- Management
- Organizational socialization

- Paradigms
- Theory in use
- SLLA

SUGGESTED READINGS

English, F. (2011). *The SAGE handbook of educational leadership: Advances in theory, research, and practice* (2nd ed.). Thousand Oaks, CA: Sage.

Fullan, M. (2003). *The moral imperative of school leadership*. Thousand Oaks, CA: Corwin.

Glickman, C. (2003). *Holding sacred ground: Essays on leadership, courage, and endurance in our schools*. San Francisco, CA: Jossey-Bass.

Houston, P. (2006). *The spiritual dimensions of leadership*. Thousand Oaks, CA: Sage/Corwin Press.

Shapiro, J. P., & Stefkovich, J. A. (2010). *Ethical leadership and decision making in education: Applying theoretical perspectives to complex dilemmas.* New York, NY: Routledge.

Starratt, R. (2004). *Ethical leadership*. San Francisco, CA: Jossey-Bass.

APPENDIX 1A

Ethical Statements Underlying Current Thinking and Practice

Please indicate your agreement or disagreement with the following statements:

Standard 1: Development, articulation, implementation, and stewardship of a vision

Agree   *Disagree*

_____   _____   All students can and will learn.

_____   _____   Everything that occurs in the school should be focused on student learning.

_____   _____   It is important to work with all groups including those whose opinions may conflict.

_____   _____   Students should be actively involved in the learning process.

_____   _____   The overarching concern is to ensure that students have the knowledge, skills, and values needed to become successful adults.

_____   _____   A key responsibility is to promote success by facilitating the development and implementation of a vision of learning.

_____   _____   It is highly unlikely that success will occur unless those involved buy into and share the vision.

Standard 2: Advocating, nurturing, and sustaining a school culture and instructional program

Agree   *Disagree*

_____   _____   Decisions should be based on research and best practice considerations.

_____   _____   It is essential that students and staff feel valued and important.

_____   _____   Curriculum and instructional decisions should be based on the understanding that there are a variety of ways in which students can learn.

_____   _____   Professional development is an important part of school improvement.

_____   _____   It is important that the leader has knowledge of learning theory and principles of effective instruction.

_____   _____   A variety of supervisory models should be employed.

_____   _____   The primary focus is on the design, implementation, evaluation, and refinement of curriculum and instruction.

_____   _____   It is important for students to demonstrate successful application of knowledge and skills they have acquired.

_____   _____   All barriers to student learning should be identified, clarified, and addressed.

Standard 3: A safe, efficient, and effective learning environment

Agree   *Disagree*

_____   _____   It is important to appraise effectiveness and manage decisions to enhance learning and teaching.

_____   _____   It is important to establish good and respectful relationships with colleagues, students, parents, and community.

_____   _____   An effective leader must trust people and their judgments.

_____   _____   An important focus of leadership effort is the effective resolution of conflict.

_____   _____   It is important to align resources to the goals of the school.

_____   _____   It is as important that the school plant operates safely and efficiently as it is that the curriculum and instruction is in place.

_____   _____   It is important to set high expectations.

_____   _____   Leaders need knowledge of measurement, evaluation, and assessment strategies and use multiple sources of assessment data.

_____   _____   Schools should be places where children feel safe and protected from harmful activity.

Standard 4: Collaborating with families and community members and responding to diverse interests

Agree   *Disagree*

_____   _____   Diverse stakeholders should be treated equitably.

_____   _____   It is essential to involve families and other stakeholders in school decision-making processes.

_____   _____   It is important to give credence to and incorporate individuals whose values and opinions may conflict.

_____   _____   The school operates as an integral part of a larger community.

_____   _____   Families are partners in the education of their children.

_____   _____   Resources of the family and community need to be brought to bear on the education of students.

_____   _____   It is very important that the public be informed about what is occurring within their schools.

Standard 5: Acting with integrity, fairness, and in an ethical manner

Agree   *Disagree*

_____   _____   Schools should be freely open to public scrutiny.

_____   _____   It is important that you clearly examine and understand your personal and professional values.

_____   _____   The right of every student to a free, quality education should be a primary value of all educators.

_____   _____   All decisions should be based on the inherent worth and dignity of all.

_____   _____   It is important to apply policy, procedures, and laws fairly, wisely, and consistently.

_____   _____   A leader should accept the consequences for upholding one's principles and actions and not try to blame others.

_____   _____   The leader should use all the power of his or her office to constructively and productively service all students and their families.

_____   _____   The leader cannot favor either instruction or operations when planning his or her work efforts.

Standard 6: Understanding, responding to, and influencing the larger context

Agree   *Disagree*

_____   _____   Programs and activities should recognize a variety of ideas, values, and cultures.

_____   _____   It is important to address emerging trends that support school goals.

_____   _____   A very important role of leadership is to actively participate in the political and policymaking context in the service of education.

_____   _____   You must work within a framework of laws to protect student rights and improve student opportunities.

CHAPTER 2

CONTEXT AND PERSPECTIVE FOR EDUCATIONAL LEADERS

MyEdLeadershipLab™

Visit the MyEdLeadershipLab™ site for *Educational Leadership: A Bridge to Improved Practice*, Fifth Edition to enhance your understanding of chapter concepts. You'll have the opportunity to practice your skills through video- and case-based Assignments and Activities as well as Building Leadership Skills units, and to prepare for your certification exam with Practice for Certification quizzes.

PALA MIDDLE SCHOOL

Understanding the Context

You are the new principal of Pala Middle School. The principal whom you replaced is quite bitter that he was not appreciated for maintaining a fine school in the face of confusion, conflict, and criticism. He stated, "They did not understand the many problems I faced from hiring teachers—to maintaining accountability." The teachers seem to be fed up with the lack of respect they receive and concerned about the inability of leadership to envision the kind of school the community and state are demanding. Because salaries of community members had significantly outpaced those of educators, the teachers in a professional association survey ranked "salary" as their number one concern. Safety and discipline were also high on their list. Family life within the community had

deteriorated and tension within the school was on the increase.

In discussing the principal's position with you, Superintendent Dunigan said, "The previous principal was unable to properly interpret the federal, state, and local demands and school board and district expectations for the school and thus generated resistance, divisiveness, and mistrust, which ultimately ended in ideological battlegrounds and no school improvement." You are concerned that the curriculum, instruction, and support services have not kept pace with current demands.

The federal government is placing a strong emphasis on an education preparing students to be successful in various sectors of the

U.S. economy. The theme of this movement is creating a high school diploma that counts. The proposal now being debated within the state is the creation of opportunity grants (vouchers) to allow students to select the school they want to attend if the school they are attending receives low marks. They are encouraged to attend schools that will enhance their skills in the workforce and prepare them for success in college and/or in the workplace.

If a school does not meet high academic standards regarding the "must have" competencies, the students are encouraged to use opportunity grants to go to better schools. This competition in public education is believed by policymakers to improve public education.

Another major theme for school reform that is gaining support and enthusiasm is small schools with less bureaucracy and more personal environments. A number of schools in your district have applied for and received grants from foundations over the past few years to develop these small, personalized charter schools that use best practices. In addition, there are also a number of excellent small private schools within the district. Both small charter and private schools have achieved success on the state standardized tests and are fully accredited. Other schools within the district have not been doing as well and a number of schools have performance levels that are not considered acceptable. Pala Middle School is considered a low-performing school.

There is much controversy regarding these new initiatives. A number of parents within your school attendance zone see the recent focus on standards and tests as creating a factory approach to education. There is also a strong movement within the state to suggest that much of this reform is to discredit public schools and provide a new emphasis for privatization. They use the concept of school choice and the creation of opportunity grants as examples of how this transition might take place. You have been drawn into the middle of this debate because your district has a grant from the state to test the concept of opportunity grants.

Pala Middle School has received accreditation from the Southern Association of Colleges and Schools (SACS), but needs improvement. You are considered a "challenged school" that is not meeting its challenges. You have the highest number of students eligible for free/reduced price lunches in the district. Your school did not receive full accreditation because several of the standards were found to be inadequate, the staff has been somewhat humiliated, and morale is very low. Parents have now been granted a green light to abandon Pala Middle School and 160, 13% of students, have opted to use their opportunity grants to transfer to other public and private schools next year. The parents of those leaving sometimes mention their concern about public school ideology and finding schools that are more relevant to their belief systems. With drops in enrollment at Pala and a few other schools, the loss of students within the public schools, the overcrowding of students in high-performing and charter schools, and everyone involved feeling great pressure and tension, the superintendent and board have become very concerned.

You have been instructed to reflect on the experimental opportunity grant program and to make suggestions on what should be done next. You are to focus on potential allies to make the public schools better able to serve all children, to work on any campaign needed to improve the present situation, to shift resources, and to take the best next steps for the school and district given its present context.

✳ **How will you begin to gain control of Pala Middle School given the present context?**

CONTEXTUAL KNOWLEDGE

Most experts today recognize and accept the importance of context to the practice of educational administration. They might not agree on how best to characterize context, but few question its importance. Duke (1998) states: "One clear message from the preceding review of recent scholarship is that leadership is situated. It cannot be understood, in other words, apart from context. The context of leadership, however, may be characterized in various ways" (p. 182). Leaders today cannot be successful without having a broad understanding of the social, political, and economic dynamics that influence and shape U.S. education.

To a great extent, the quality of education depends on the effectiveness of school leaders to be able to respond to diverse groups and pressures as they continuously work to improve schools (Edmonds, 1979; Lezotte, 1988b; Leithwood, & Riehl, 2005). The call is for leaders with political savvy and a moral compass to understand the social, economic, and human demands, the governmental and community agendas, as well as the professional expectations and responsibilities of the work. Schools are part of a much larger global system, linked to society through both formal and informal structures of governance and influence that shape almost all educational decisions (for more information see ed.gov).

⁕ How will the existing contextual factors shape what you will do as the principal of Pala Middle School? What contextual factors will have the most significant impact in the near future?

BROAD, COMPLEX CONTEXT

Schooling is a federal interest, a state responsibility, and a local operation. The United States has 50 systems of public education that are being strongly influenced by world, national, state, and local pressures and expectations (see Chapter 4 for greater detail). Add to this the significant number of interest groups—the *Encyclopedia of Associations* lists 1,221 national and international education associations—and you begin to understand the diversity of thinking local school leaders must be prepared to contend with, even before they face students and their parents.

There are about 49.3 million students enrolled in public schools, of which 1.5 million are enrolled in public charter schools. Additionally, there are 5.9 million students enrolled in private schools, meaning that approximately 10% of the nation's K–12th-grade students attend private schools. In the fall of 2009, there were 132,656 elementary and secondary public schools, while there were 33,740 elementary and secondary private schools. Most private schools are independent, nonsectarian schools while others are faith based, with the largest group being Catholic schools. There are a total of 7,510 Catholic schools in the nation.

Citizens across the nation are becoming increasingly interested in what is taught, read, viewed, and discussed in our public schools. People use pressure, legislation, mandates, and other forms of political action to ensure that decisions conform to their interests. The educational leader is responsible for seeing that the final decisions are representative of the whole and are in the best interests of the children (Deluca, 1999).

Educational leaders are caught among conflicting desires of elected and governmental officials, business leaders, diverse communities, teachers and staff, boards of education, interest groups, students and families, educational experts, and others, all of whom have their own agendas. The related pressures seem to be increasing along with the ever-growing number of social problems and issues that find their ways into the schools. As educators become enmeshed in the web of issues being debated by various constituencies, they can find themselves at the center of the controversies, particularly if they do not understand the history and objectives of the groups with which they are dealing.

The following statement suggested by Razik and Swanson (1995) is even truer today than it was over 15 years ago:

> For better or for worse, this is, indeed a dynamic and exciting period in human history. Because of the fluidity of the situation, it is a period of unparalleled opportunity and potential danger. To capitalize on the opportunities and to minimize the dangers demands extraordinarily wise leadership in all sectors and in all enterprises including education. . . .
>
> The context of educational leadership today is different from any other time in history. It is essential that contemporary issues and processes be understood if leadership is to result in relevant action. (pp. 70–71)

The challenge of leaders is to identify the "turning-points" and be prepared to exert necessary leadership.

✳ **Which individuals or groups should you, as principal at Pala Middle School, meet on a regular basis?**

FEDERAL TURNING POINTS

The involvement of the federal government in education has shifted directions during the past 250 years and is sometimes categorized by eras of influence. This is not a precise categorization because some of the impact from an era continues to influence education during later eras. What follows is one way of looking at the historical involvement of the federal government in U.S. education.

Education Origins

Education was not mentioned in the U.S. Constitution. As a result of the 10th Amendment, ratified in 1791, it became a responsibility of each state. As states adopted constitutions, they consolidated powers over education that had been exercised by local communities. The states established minimum standards and guidelines, leaving a large amount of the power for operating the school systems to local communities. The U.S. school system was built on a concept of universal opportunity for education to all of its citizens. Thousands of acts and laws passed in each of the states placed schools in the public domain, granting compulsory taxing power, setting schools up as quasimunicipal corporations, establishing legal rights, setting up standards, providing for governance, and so forth.

Educators such as Horace Mann, Henry Barnard, William H. McGuffey, Johann Herbart, and later John Dewey were powerful forces in shaping American education. School enrollments increased by geometric proportions, and public education became one of the great enterprises in the nation. At the same time, social and economic concerns in a changing world were making new demands on schooling.

Because the constitution is silent about support for public education, the federal government must use implied powers for which it does have responsibility to support involvement in education. These implied powers come from the general welfare clause, parts of the First Amendment, and both the due process and equal protection clauses of the 14th Amendment. To date, as shown in Table 2.1, five major federal responsibilities have been used to justify federal involvement in education: (1) land grant, (2) public relief and welfare, (3) national defense, (4) equal opportunity, and (5) economic competitiveness and school safety. This table is not inclusive but provides a sampling of legislation related to education. In addition, a number of pieces of legislation, although not directed specifically at education, certainly have a significant impact—such as the Fair Labor Standards Act and the Equal Employment Opportunity Act.

TABLE 2.1   Key Examples of Federal Involvement in Education

LAW		PURPOSE
LAND GRANT, AGRICULTURE, AND VOCATION		
Land Ordinance	1785	Provided for orderly distribution of public land by surveying the land
Northwest Ordinance	1787	Encouraged use of public monies for the maintenance of public schools in the newly created townships
Ohio Statehood Enabling	1802	First of the enabling acts, which provided land grants for public schools in newly created states
Smith–Hughes Act	1917	Provided matching funds to help states develop high school vocational programs
Relief "New Deal"	1930s	Encouraged education as part of the Public Works Administration, Civilian Conservation Corps, National Youth Administration, Works Progress Administration, and others

LAW		PURPOSE
Lanham Act	1941	Provided funds to construct and operate schools where federal activity created burdens on local governments; expanded in 1980 by Impact Laws 815 and 874, which provided money for school construction and district operating costs, respectively
National School Lunch Program	1946	Provided funds for school lunch programs in public and nonpublic school; expanded in 1954 to include a school milk program
NATIONAL DEFENSE		
National Defense Education Act	1958	Provided graduate fellowships in education—particularly in the sciences, mathematics, and foreign languages; extended in 1964 (supported student loans, local/state/national partnership, encouraged curriculum reform)
Peace Corps Act	1961	Established a program to supply teachers and technicians for underdeveloped nations for 2-year time periods
Manpower Development and Training Act	1962	Established up-to-date training programs for youth whose lack of education prevented them from obtaining employment
EQUAL EDUCATIONAL OPPORTUNITY		
Vocational Education Act	1963	Extended 1950 impact laws and NDEA and provided funds for construction of vocational schools and development of expanded vocational education offerings
Civil Rights Act	1964	Intended to discourage racial discrimination throughout society with particular emphasis on hastening desegregation in the nation's schools
Elementary and Secondary Education Act (ESEA)	1965	Provided large sums of money for a broad range of educational concerns; improved state department of education, compensatory education, and innovative programs
Bilingual Education Act	1968	Provided funds for instruction of children with limited English proficiency

(continued)

TABLE 2.1   **Key Examples of Federal Involvement in Education (Continued)**

LAW		PURPOSE
Emergency School Aid Act	1972	Provided federal support for voluntary desegregation of local schools
Family Educational Rights and Privacy Act	1974	Established a student's right to privacy
Education for All Handicapped Children	1975	Forbade exclusion of or discrimination against persons solely because of their handicapping condition (provided Act PL 94-142 some funds for children in poverty)
WORLD CLASS ECONOMIC COMPETITIVENESS AND SAFETY		
National Assessment of Educational Progress	1983	Created a national testing program for the assessment of educational results
Americans with Disabilities Act	1990	Protected the rights of individuals with disabilities through high standards, accommodations, and employment practices and services
Job Training Partnership	1991	Designed program to help at-risk youth be successful in schools and jobs
Family and Medical Leave Act	1993	Allowed employees to take 12 weeks a year of unpaid leave for circumstances such as childbirth, adoption, or illness of family member
Goals 2000: Educate America Act	1994	Established eight national goals for public education (two new goals concerning teacher education and parental participation); provided funds for standards-based reforms
Improving American Schools Act	1994	(Reauthorization of the ESEA Act) Strongly encouraged state and LEA's involvement in education, especially in setting high standards; moved ESEA toward school-based reform; promoted innovative programs
Safe and Drug-Free Schools and Communities Act	1994	(Reauthorization of title IV) Supported school and community efforts in the war against drugs
Telecommunications Act	1996	Mandated FCC to make telecommunications services affordable for all schools and libraries

LAW		PURPOSE
Amendments to the Individuals with Disabilities Education Act	1997	Attempted to overcome barriers that have prevented children with disabilities from being educated effectively
Children's Internet Protection Act	2000	Schools and libraries are required to block access to sexually explicit material for children
Alternative Routes to Teacher Certification Act	2001	Provided for the establishment of a commission to review and make recommendations to Congress and the states on alternative and nontraditional routes to teacher certification
No Child Left Behind Act	2002	Developed school accountability for results, provided freedom to states and communities, encouraged proven educational methods, and provided more choices for parents
Education Sciences Reform Act	2002	Overhauled the Office of Educational Research and Improvement (OERI); eliminated OERI and replaced it with a new Academy of Education Science that could oversee educational research, statistics gathering, program evaluation, and dissemination of information
Teacher Recruitment and Retention Act	2003	Provided for loan forgiveness for math, science, and special education teachers and for those in the poorest schools and some rural schools
Deleting Online Predators Act	2004	Schools and libraries are required to block access to commercial Web sites that allow for the creation of Web pages, discussion boards, chat rooms, or e-mail service
IDEA Reauthorization	2004	Aligned IDEA with the accountability measures under NCLB
American Recovery and Reinvestment Act	2009	Funds Race to the Top (R2T, RTTT or RTT) designed to spur reforms in K–12 education
Elementary and Secondary Education Act		Scheduled to be reauthorized 2012

National Defense

In 1939, the U.S. Office of Education was transferred to the Federal Security Agency. The first act passed under the national security and defense emphasis was the National Science Foundation Act in 1950. This act provided funds for study and research in scientific fields and was administered by the National Science Board, composed of 24 members and a director. The Hoover task force, Commission on Government Organization, created in 1955, concluded that the U.S. Office of Education had "meager influence and no control." In addition, of the 3 billion federal dollars being spent on education at the time, only 1% went through the U.S. Office of Education. The rest went through a number of blue-ribbon boards and commissions and over 20 other federal agencies. The commission recommended a number of changes in the executive branch of government. In 1953, the Department of Health, Education, and Welfare was created, placing greater responsibility for the administration and control of educational matters within this office.

The Soviet Union's launching of Sputnik in October 1957 opened the floodgates of seething criticism of the American educational system. It was a rude awakening to Americans who had been taught that most Soviets did not have access to electricity or running water; unfairly or not, the schools were blamed for the Soviets' technical success over America. From all sides came demands for changes in the way Americans were schooled. National security and defense were increasingly used as a justification for greater federal involvement in education. The result was the passage of the largest federal education legislation to date: the National Defense Education Act (NDEA) of 1958. This act was to address changes in curriculum, methods, and requirements, including higher standards, more training in science and mathematics, better provision for bright students, and harder study for all students. The act was particularly designed to strengthen science, mathematics, and foreign languages. This legislation introduced the era of excellence with its emphasis on enrichment, ability grouping, gifted education, and accelerated and enrichment programs. It also established more local/state/ national partnerships to improve American education. This was the first piece of legislation aimed specifically at improving instruction in academic or nonvocational subjects and in broadening the involvement of those influencing curriculum and instruction.

Equal Educational Opportunity

Before the 1950s, poor inner-city communities, particularly African-American communities, saw education as their only hope for improved quality of life. The education system had shown some signs of meeting their needs through the approaches that grew out of progressive child-centered education. Progressive educators in the 1950s and 1960s argued that teachers had the responsibility of making education relevant to the needs and background of the child. John Dewey, identified as the leader of this movement, believed that society should be interpreted to children through their daily living in the classroom, in a framework that is genuine and meaningful to them as students. During this time, education began to become accessible to all, enabling students to progress at their own speed. However, the reforms that grew out of the NDEA act and related thinking reversed the progressive child-centered focus and reverted to a subject-centered focus on basics, achieving excellence, with major focus on math, science, and foreign language skills. The curriculum was expanded to include much more learning within each grade level. Those who could not keep up often failed and later dropped out of school.

At the same time, the U.S. Supreme Court and legislative activity were placing greater attention on equal opportunity without discrimination. Although we have reserved the discussion of the influence of the courts to Chapter 11, a few cases having a profound impact on U.S. education will be mentioned here. Certainly *Brown v. Board of Education* in 1954 and *Swann v. Charlotte-Mecklenburg Board of Education* in 1971 were such groundbreaking Supreme Court cases. Both grew out of a long, protracted struggle for civil rights and the end of segregation. The two decades between these decisions marked an effort to counteract the racial discrimination—in housing, education, jobs, transportation, and restaurants and other public places—that existed in the United States. Some of the U.S. Supreme Court decisions at this time included the invalidation of school prayer, equality of voting rights and representation, a number of antidiscrimination decisions, and reaffirmation of the freedom of religion, speech, press, and association.

Amid the sense of volatility regarding fundamental civil liberties, especially within urban communities, legislators and others were providing a powerful political push to address growing concerns. Crime, especially among juveniles and young adults, had increased significantly. The signs of problems were easily seen in New York, Cleveland, and other cities in early 1964 through boycotts of city school systems. Redevelopment, education, and jobs were the major themes. A 2-year period of rioting and looting began in the summer of 1964 in the Harlem and Bedford-Stuyvesant sections of New York. Other cities repeating this tragic pattern were Los Angeles (Watts), Chicago, Atlanta, San Francisco, Cleveland, Pittsburgh, Baltimore, St. Louis, Omaha, and Milwaukee, as well as Rochester, NY; Springfield, MA; Pompano Beach, FL; and Birmingham and Tuscaloosa, AL. Demonstrations and marches were also occurring throughout the nation.

The Kerner Commission was created in 1967 to investigate the riots. The report (Kerner Commission, 1968) concluded that the typical rioter was an underemployed school dropout whose hopes were raised by earlier progressive, student-centered improvements, only to be later crushed by experiences with NDEA-supported subject-centered, back-to-basics types of school changes. These experiences helped create a climate that resulted in violence. The typical citizen within the community who tried to stop the riots—the counterrioter—was a high school graduate with a job. Education and income were the only factors that distinguished the counterrioters from the rioters. General practices of racism were also high on the Kerner list of causes.

This introduced greater federal involvement in education for the purpose of encouraging equality of educational opportunity. The most significant piece of legislation under the equality movement is the Elementary and Secondary Education

Act (ESEA) of 1965, a broad program of support for children from low-income families. The first six titles of this bill supported compensatory education, instructional materials, supplementary services, innovative programs, strengthening state departments, and libraries. Literature such as Charles E. Silberman's *Crisis in the Classroom*, describing school as a "grim, joyless place" where spirit is repressed and the joy of learning and creating is lost, added support for student-centered innovations. The programs created under the ESEA legislation were now complemented by progress in Head Start programs, desegregation, student-centered education, and open classrooms.

In the 1970s, the busing of children to schools outside their neighborhoods to improve racial balances overshadowed all other education issues. The significant *Swann v. Charlotte-Mecklenburg Board of Education* decision established that there was "no basis for holding that the local school authorities may not be required to employ bus transportation as a tool of school desegregation. Desegregation plans cannot be limited to the walk-in school." This decision launched busing as a legal approach to achieving school desegregation when housing patterns blocked them from occurring naturally. This was another very turbulent period in American education.

Certainly an additional factor in forming national opinion was the increased interest by media, particularly television, in gaining an understanding of what was occurring in the United States and the world. The vast resources of the media are able to solidify support, intentionally or unintentionally, for issues and reforms that they view as important and/or necessary. Television, for the first time, offered a glimpse into the difference between affluence and poverty, helping to fuel the frustration and rage of those living in poverty.

The 1970s ended with a concern that a significant number of American youth did not perform satisfactorily on standardized tests of reading, writing, and arithmetic—the three Rs. The first major international comparison of achievement in mathematics revealed that U.S. student scores fell below those of Japan and Britain. At the same time, significant cutbacks were made in funding for public schools, and the equalization of state educational funding formulas were challenged (*Rodriguez v. San Antonio Independent School District*, 1973). A separate cabinet-level U.S. Department of Education came into existence on September 24, 1979. This new cabinet position was to fulfill a promise to the National Education Association (NEA) and to improve relations with U.S. teachers, who had been engaging in a string of teacher strikes over issues such as salary increases, cost-of-living clauses, lesson-preparation time, class size, and extra-duty pay.

World Class Economic Competitiveness and Support—the 1980s

The 1980s began with teachers openly expressing dissatisfaction with their jobs—41% in an NEA teacher poll responded that they would not become teachers if they had to do it over again. Educators argued that the tax revolt of the 1970s had reduced state and local funds to education, and federal cuts only contributed to the difficulties within local districts.

A blitz of national reports criticized U.S. education, including one by the U.S. Secretary of Education's appointed National Commission on Excellence in Education (1983). The report, titled *A Nation at Risk*, purposefully alarmist in tone, began:

> Our nation is at risk. Our once unchallenged preeminence in commerce, industry, science and technological innovation is being overtaken by competitors, throughout the world. The educational foundations of our society are presently being eroded by a rising tide of mediocrity that threatens our very future as a nation and a people. . . . If an unfriendly foreign power had attempted to impose on America the mediocre educational performance that exists today, we might well have viewed it as an act of war. (p. 5)

American students compared unfavorably to foreign students in inferential skills, science and math achievement had declined, and illiteracy was a huge national problem. The recommendations were to launch a core curriculum, raise academic standards, lengthen the school day and year, improve teacher quality, and attract capable teachers. National attention turned to the need for higher academic standards, tougher subjects, rigorous testing, and stiffer high school graduation requirements. Also important were high-level cognitive skills, critical thinking skills, active and authentic learning, technology application, logic and reasoning skills, functional and operational literacy, interpersonal skills, work ethic, multicultural respect, problem solving and reasoning, and analytical skills. Educators found that the collective American mood had swung once again—excellence was more important than equality of opportunity and equity. President Ronald Reagan was urging prayer in public schools, legislation for tuition tax credits, vouchers, choice in public and private schools, and a smaller federal role in education. Amid all the criticism of the schools there was a bright spot: 80% of the nation's school-age population now graduated from high school, far more than in most other countries.

Education had entered the political arena full swing, and regardless of causes, politicians felt compelled to make their mark on education. There is no sign that they will retreat from this position anytime in the near future. The National Governors' Association 1986 report, *Time for Results*, states early on that, "better schools mean better jobs" (p. 2). Governor Lamar Alexander's (Tennessee) summary of the report (1986, p. 7) reaffirmed the governors' readiness to provide "the leadership needed to get results on the hard issues that confront the better school movement . . . (and) to lead the second wave of reform in American education policy." The governors shared the belief "that real excellence can't be imposed from a distance. Governors don't create excellent schools; communities—local school leaders, teachers, parents, and citizens—do." The states would work on recommendations, standards, assessment, and accountability. In a report titled *Results in Education: 1987*, the members of the National Governors' Association noted that "states will have to assume larger responsibilities for setting educational goals and defining outcome standards, while, at the same time, stimulating local inventiveness" (p. 3).

At the same time, the country was developing a very wealthy class of people whose income was significantly higher than that of the middle class, creating the largest economic gap in U.S. history. In the 1980s the United States, the wealthiest 1% of the population held 36% of the country's wealth—a higher proportion than any other country in the world (Ginsberg, Lowi, & Weir, 1995). Sixty-four percent of the increase in earnings in the 1980s went to this top 1%. Over 50% of total U.S. income was paid to the wealthiest 20% of the population. At the same time, the taxes on this extraordinarily wealthy group of Americans were being cut, placing the burden of government on the middle class. During the Reagan administration, the top personal tax bracket dropped from 70% to 28% and corporate taxes were cut in half. The Tax Reform Act of 1986 effected a 53% tax decrease for the wealthy and an 18% increase in federal taxes for middle- to upper-middle-class taxpayers (Bartlett & Steele, 1994). The government also began a period of scaling back services to its citizens, particularly those of middle and lower socioeconomic status.

✳ **Select contextual elements that are having and/or will have the most pronounced influence on Pala Middle School.**

THE 1990S

In 1991–1992, a total of 30 superintendents of urban school districts—Los Angeles, Atlanta, Boston, Cleveland, Columbus, Charlotte-Mecklenburg, Charleston, St. Louis, Kansas City, and Washington, DC, to name a few—lost their jobs. Carter and Cunningham (1997) suggest that the cost of turnover has weighed heavily on local school districts and the staff who are trying to hold them together. Paul Houston, executive director of the American Association of School Administrators (AASA), suggests:

> The current role is indeed a troubled one. The condition of children in this country has deteriorated, while the challenges facing them have escalated. And the critics are in full force. Superintendents find themselves defending the system they lead, demanding accountability so they can keep the doors open and morale up, while at the same time they must search for ways to transform the system to meet an uncertain future . . . . Much of the solution to this problem rests in the ability of school leaders to build conditions of support for schools from among those most interested in seeing schools succeed. (Carter & Cunningham, 1997, pp. ii–iv)

The 1990s were also a period of great concern regarding the large increase in juvenile violent crimes. More and more of our young were lost to crime and violence. In this setting, President George H. W. Bush and the nation's governors came together at the historic first Educational Summit in Charlottesville, Virginia.

The second educational summit was held in March 1996, with 49 corporate leaders, 41 governors, and 30 educators, staff advisors, and policy experts (observers) attending. Louis V. Gerstner, CEO of IBM and cochair of the summit, stressed that "we set standards and learn how to measure against them." The attendees endorsed the idea of each state developing "internationally competitive academic standards" and rigorous new tests to measure whether students meet the standards. The third national education summit occurred in the fall of 1999 when government and business leaders stressed the importance of standards, accountability, and high-quality teachers.

❋ **How might you and the staff begin to respond to the contextual demands being placed on Pala Middle School?**

THE FIRST DECADE OF THE 21ST CENTURY

On January 8, 2002, President Bush signed the No Child Left Behind Act of 2001 (NCLB), creating a seismic shock throughout public education. This reauthorization of the Elementary and Secondary Education Act of 1965 encourages evidence-based schooling by looking at adequate yearly progress (AYP) on accountability goals for all students as well as breakdowns for the following subgroups:

- Economically disadvantaged
- Children with disabilities
- Children of different race and ethnicity
- Children with limited English proficiency

NCLB required that schools produce annual report cards for parents, teachers, and state officials regarding school progress in core subjects.

By 2011, thirty-nine states had standards in place in math, science, and reading/language arts, which were to be assessed at three different points during the students' progression through grades (see ed.gov/nclb/landing.jhtml). States are also asked to select and set goals for an "additional indicator" that reflects specific values and priorities. Most states have chosen attendance rates.

A minimum 95% student participation rate is required. No more than 1% of the students at tested grade levels can be provided alternative/lowered standards (for example, at the IEP determined level); all the rest must pass the standardized tests at the grade level. Students in the 5th grade who are working at the 3rd-grade level take the assessment at the 5th-grade level. Each school system is responsible to collect and disaggregate data, determine AYP goals to ensure school accountability for students on achievement tests, identify schools needing improvement and corrective action, take corrective actions, provide supplemental educational services, and report results to the state Department of Education. Schools that fail to achieve adequate progress might require corrective actions such as academic reviews, school improvement plans, adding new curriculum, increasing lengths of school year/day, appointing outside experts as advisors, restructuring or reconstituting school organization, replacing relevant staff, governance changes, and/or providing parental choice options.

Low-performing schools make AYP if they increase the number of students at the "proficient" level by 10% from the previous year, even if the performance level is below state goals. Schools identified as "in need of improvement" must offer families the option to transfer their children to high-performing schools within the district. Students in schools identified as "in need of improvement" for 2 or more years must offer students access to supplemental academic assistance—in after-school or weekend programs to improve academic performance. Schools that have been identified for "corrective action" for 6 years and fail to make adequate progress are identified for "restructuring" (see ed.gov/nclb/landing.jhtml).

This legislation has heated up the battle over vouchers (see Chapter 12). In *Zelman v. Simmon Harris*, the Supreme Court ruled that the First Amendment's establishment clause (see Chapter 11) did not prohibit voucher programs—including using public funds to pay tuition for private schools. *Zelman* moved the issue to state legislatures and courts. In Florida, it was proposed that a student in a school found to be "failing" for 2 out of 4 years can receive an "opportunity scholarship" to attend a qualifying private school. In *Bush v. Holmes*, the Florida Supreme Court ruled that the "opportunity scholarship" program violated Article IX, Section 1(A) of the Florida Constitution which in part states, "Adequate provision shall be made by law for a uniform, efficient, safe, secure, and high quality system of free public schools that allows students to obtain a high quality education and for the establishment, maintenance, and operation of institutions of higher learning and other public education programs that the needs of the people may require."

Despite widespread debate and controversy over this highly visible piece of legislation, NCLB celebrated its tenth anniversary on January 2012. Inadequacies, difficulties, and impossibilities of this legislation have been topics of discussion since its enactment in 2002; however, the lofty goal of having 100% of U.S. children reach grade-level standards by 2014 is still the light at the end of the tunnel for many school systems. According to an article from the State News Service (2007), "As of 2006, all 50 states and the District of Columbia have accountability plans in place as well as reading/language arts and mathematics assessments for grades 3–8, plus one high assessment in high school."

Many educators truly embrace this piece of legislation as being the ticket to the improvement of education for all children. However, those on the other side of the fence have still raised concerns, especially in 2007 when NCLB was scheduled for reauthorization. Wendy Puriefoy, president of the Public Education Network (publiceducation.org/nclb) who publishes "Everything You Wanted to Know about NCLB: The One-Stop Resource for Community and Parent Leaders" stated, "NCLB presents an opportunity and a challenge. The opportunity to close the achievement gap for the low performing students and schools. The challenge to be personally accountable for assuming that no one child is left behind" (p. 2). As is historically the case, school systems and persons responsible for educating U.S. children have risen to the challenge and are paving the way for no child to be left behind.

There is also an expectation that there will be a highly qualified teacher in all classrooms. These are teachers demonstrating "subject knowledge" and "teaching skills" in reading, writing, mathematics and other basic subject areas that must be in place in every classroom. This requirement is also tied in with Title II of the Higher Education Act of 1998. The focus in this area is on professional development in mathematics and science, reforming certification/licensing requirements, alternative routes (Troops to Teachers, Teach for America, etc.) to certification, recruitment and retention initiatives, reforming tenure, teacher testing, and merit pay.

The Education Trust (2006) has examined state assessment results from 2003 to 2005 and found inconsistent progress across grade levels and states (edtrust.org). The data are helping educators take steps toward closing the achievement gap, bringing students to proficiency in reading and math, and in providing information about student performance. The data shows that schools can improve and meet state goals and can identify schools that far exceed them. Although the data help greatly to identify student, teacher, and school needs, it is highly unlikely that schools will meet the policy expectations of this act. The Education Trust suggests that there is no chance that schools will get all students to grade level by 2014 at the rate of progress that is now occurring. Looking at the results from 37 states, 23,812 schools were identified in 2002–03 as not making adequate progress.

In a comparative study (Education Trust, 2006) of results from state assessment and the National Assessment of Educational Progress (NAEP) it was concluded that a number of states had set the bar too low (see nces.ed.gov/ nationsreportcard/nde). According to NAEP, just 29% of the nation's 8th-grade students demonstrate proficiency in reading and math, which is a much lower rate than exists on state assessments. For example, NAEP found that 29% of the nation's 8th-grade students do not read at even the most basic level—49% African American, 45% Latino, and 43% low-income (nces.ed.gov/nationsreportcard/ reading). These findings suggest that state assessments have been set at a much lower standard than national expectations would dictate. Sixty-two percent of teachers and 27% of superintendents think that too many students pass through the system without learning at even a minimal level.

Principals are beginning to recognize that to improve student performance on these high-stakes tests, they must focus on standards (Thomas, 2004). All stakeholders, but especially teachers, need to understand the need to teach to, assess, and monitor student progress based on state content standards. Principals play a vital role in making sure the NCLB data is appropriately analyzed and reported, and that teachers are clear about the knowledge and skills embedded in the standards. There is some concern, however, that such a focus on standards can be overdone.

Some of the most significant findings regarding achievement problems were at the middle and high school level where there is a need to dramatically increase efforts to improve secondary schools, especially for low-income students and students of color. In response to this data and concerns regarding the economy, the nation's governors committed to efforts to transform high schools into institutions that prepare all students for the demands of college, the 21st-century workforce, and society (National Governors Association, 2005). Suggestions regarding what schools have to do include providing opportunities for all students to complete a challenging academic core of courses (core curriculum aligned with college-admission standards), creating early warning systems (benchmarks) to identify students needing additional help, increasing attention to reading and literacy, recruiting of high-quality teachers for our struggling schools, assigning the most effective teachers to the most vulnerable, struggling students, supporting and mentoring new teachers with laser-like focus on improving instruction and curriculum, and eliminating the funding gap (see cges.org).

In the Phi Delta Kappa 2006 Summit on Public Education, Sandy Kress, one of the architects of the NCLB legislation, stated that the sanctions in NCLB are not terribly onerous. He also doubted that writing a plan, replacing some staff members, reorganizing the school, bringing in a team, hiring outside advisors, or transferring students had much to do with actually raising student achievement. He argued, "I just defy anybody to actually find any research that would suggest that those are successful strategies." Bill Sanders, a senior research fellow at the University of North Carolina, suggested NCLB sanctions emphasize "teaching to the bubble kids," referring to the students closest to achieving higher proficiency levels, while ignoring children who are truly far behind and those who have performed quite well on previous tests. This has created a problem where higher-performing students are regressing toward the mean and very low performers fall further behind because less attention and resources are focused on these groups of students. Such critics wanted to see the law changed so it encourages academic progress for all students—moving each student up the ramp. The standards would be tailored to each student individually and would extend up to the top of the ramp.

Other criticism reflects concerns about narrowing the instructional focus, resulting in an impoverished definition of reading, writing, or mathematics; ignoring content domains not tested; questioning the realistically obtainable goals for all children ("Goldilock standards"); stressing less desirable instructional practices to achieve goals; taking away from instructional time for testing; misaligning instructional materials with tests; putting too much pressure on educators; treating all children the same; and branding children, schools, and communities—to name but a few of the more prevalent themes. Some states have begun to seek federal waivers from some parts of the NCLB act (Foster, 2004).

Probably the greatest concern is the cost of this program to the states. The National Association of State Boards of Education estimated the cost of developing, scoring, and reporting results of reading and math tests at somewhere between $2.7 billion and a frightening $7 billion over the life of the new law. Science tests would cost extra. The Education Council reported a figure at between $300 and $400 million each year, which works out to be approximately $4 billion.

The bottom line, however, is that the average 2003 scores of students in both reading and math increased over the scores from 1990. The percentage of students ranked at or above basic, proficient, and advanced levels were also higher in 2003. For example, the number of 4th-grade students rated as proficient rose from 13% in 1990 to 32% in 2003. During this same time period, children in grades 1 through 5 attending a parent-chosen public school (other than their assigned school) increased from 12% to 17%. The percentage of classes taught by a highly qualified teacher has risen to 91%. Moreover, more reading progress was made by 9-year-old children in the 5 years ending in 2004 than in the previous 24 years combined, and reading and math scores for 9-year-old children and 4th-grade students have reached all-time highs. Between 2003 and 2005, an additional 235,000 4th-grade students learned fundamental math skills.

THE SECOND DECADE OF THE 21ST CENTURY

As we enter the second decade of the 21st century, the Obama administration has released a blueprint for the reauthorization of ESEA and the act is expected to be passed by Congress in 2012 (see 2.ed.gov/nclb/landing.jhtml). The blueprint includes key topics being discussed nationally such as college and career readiness standards, the rewarding of excellence and promotion of innovation, school choice, turning around low-performing schools and science, technology, and engineering and mathematics (STEM) education, among others.

Common Core Standards

By mid-2011, 42 states had adopted the Common Core State Standards, which are in mathematics and language arts. These standards define the knowledge and skills students should have within their K–12 education careers so that they will graduate high school able to succeed in entry-level, credit-bearing academic college courses and in workforce training programs. The Common Core State Standards Initiative is coordinated by the National Governors Association Center for Best Practices (NGA Center) and the Council of Chief State School Officers (CCSSO). According to CCSSO, the standards, developed in collaboration with teachers, school administrators, and experts, build upon strengths and lessons of current state standards, are evidence based, and are aligned with college and work expectations.

There is considerable national debate and discussion about whether having common standards will improve academic achievement. Some politicians, practitioners, and scholars maintain that the standards were developed and adopted by states too quickly. They argue that the standards do not pay sufficient attention to the need for an interdisciplinary curriculum and that they disregard the role that schools play in preparing students for citizenship.

According to Porter, McMaken, Hwang, & Yang (2011) the Common Core Standards emphasize cognitive skills, and devote less time to memorization and performing procedures and more time to demonstrating understanding and analyzing written material. Momentum for the Common Core Standards continues to grow, and supporters maintain that the standards will be beneficial because currently there is too much variation from state to state and all children need to have access to a similar education. In addition, advocates assert that common standards not only bring coherence, but are more rigorous than most states' current standards.

The Achievement Gap

The achievement gap in the United States is large and persistent. NAEP consistently reports that the average 8th-grade minority student's scores are about the same as the average white 4th-grade student. Females scored higher than males in both grades. Nearly two out of three African-American and Hispanic students are reading below grade level by 4th grade and by the end of high school, African-American and Hispanic students perform about the same on assessments as white 8th-grade students.

Many, if not most, of these children live in high-poverty urban school districts where conditions mirror inequalities in those aspects of schooling, early life, and home circumstances that research has linked to school achievement. For example, at the 4th-grade level, 71% of Hispanic students, 70% of African-American students, and 23% of white students are eligible for the free or reduced-price lunch program. These students tend to be concentrated in low-income schools where the achievement gap is the greatest. The number of poor children will continue to grow (see edtrust.org) because middle-income families are declining as both the number of wealthy and poor households grow.

In March 2004, Association for Supervision and Curriculum Development (ASCD) identified the achievement gap as a priority issue and stressed the grave consequences of persistent gaps in student achievement. Certainly, NCLB legislation and AYP are identifying schools with huge achievement gaps and pinpointing schools in serious need of attention. This legislation states "all students will reach high standards, at a minimum attaining proficiency or better in reading, language arts, and mathematics by 2013–2014." AYP in particular is motivating schools to do something about achievement gaps. Schools will not have sanctions placed on them if they can reduce the percentage of students at the below proficient level by 10%. Suggestions for administrators include taking responsibility, using data to reshape curriculum and instruction, finding ways to provide extra instruction, and assigning the strongest teachers to those who need them the most.

Gerry House (2005) in his AASA article, "Reclaiming Children Left Behind" states, "Institutions with a long history of failure will not become havens of success by continuing to do what they have always done or making a few minor adjustments. Bold systemic change that revolutionizes every aspect of school is required" (p. 10). Many argue that this problem will also require governments, communities, neighborhoods, and families to create conditions that remove barriers and support cognitive development. Helping minority and underachieving students to become part of the American dream continues to be a challenge. We have yet to develop a clear understanding of our nonlearners and how they can be helped to achieve. However, there are many notable efforts under way to address these concerns. Various types of schools, often with foundation support, take approaches such as innovative citizenship, academic pressure and tough love, uniforms and separate classes for boys and girls, communitarian ethics and thematic group projects, self-designed projects and internships, and project-based courses keyed to careers in technology (gatesfoundation.org). The Annenberg

Institute (annenberginstitute.org) is dedicated to improving the conditions and outcomes of schooling, especially in urban communities and in schools serving disadvantaged children. An approach being tried in a number of low-achieving schools is mastery learning. Mastery learning (Bloom, 1971; Guskey, 2005) stipulates that instructors provide students with opportunities (or time) to practice and actively engage in the most important higher-level skills. This concept also stresses the importance of special feedback with directions on how to correct any learning errors. Research has shown that mastery learning closes gaps in achievement of different groups of students.

Guskey (2005) states that:

> The impediments to learning in students' environments outside of school should never become a basis for lowering expectations about what can be done to help them learn well in school. The feedback, correctives, enrichment process, and instructional alignment elements of mastery learning represent powerful tools that teachers can use to capitalize on the influence they have . . . . They offer the tools needed to help students of different racial, ethnic, and socioeconomic backgrounds learn excellently, succeed in school, and gain the many positive benefits of that success. (p. 87)

Others are arguing for quality preschool programs (the first 5 years of life are the most important learning years) in these low-socioeconomic status schools.

Ruby Payne (1995) is credited with providing great insights regarding the nonfinancial challenges that poverty presents to students and teachers. Her premise is based on children's deficiencies and deprivations (emotional, mental, role models, knowledge, and so on), which prevent them from succeeding in school and cause them to act out in antisocial or self-injurious ways (Grogan-Kaylor, 2004). For example, Payne advises that children from generational poverty will "argue loudly with the teacher," make "angry responses" and/or "inappropriate or vulgar comments," be "disrespectful to the teacher," "physically fight," "cheat or steal," "harm other students verbally or physically," and "have their hands always on someone else" (Payne, 1995, pp. 103–104). Children might actually laugh when disciplined, which is a "way to save face in matriarchal poverty" (Payne, 1995, p. 103). Children in poverty often do not value learning and are unfamiliar with goals and rules. The foundational causes of these behaviors must be channeled in more acceptable ways so that these children can interact more successfully and be welcomed in the school and ultimately in the work environment. Children from poverty have very limited planning, scheduling, and prioritizing skills, which must be addressed if schools are to be successful.

To turn much of this around, Payne suggests that these students need support systems, role models, confidence, social skills, protection, structure, and nutrition, all of which are often taken for granted within schools. Payne stresses the importance of providing low-income students with emotional resources so that they are better able to deal with school dynamics and so they can develop the needed stamina and persistence to succeed. The idea is to break old poverty habits and adopt new habits, with mainstream mores that are more compatible with teaching and learning. There are some, however, who are concerned that such deficit theories may actually stereotype "children of poverty" and cause teachers and others to see all these children in the same way and for the same reasons (Davis, Johnson-Reid, Saunders, Williams, & Williams, 2005). This standardized perspective might inhibit diagnosis and prescription and cause educators not to suspect and/or report symptoms of emotional or learning disabilities, abuse, trauma, abandonment, and neglect. It may also cause educators to generalize deficits as an excuse for why these children cannot learn.

However, this is not what Payne had in mind. She states, "The key to achievement for students from poverty is in creating relationships with them" (1995, p. 32). She goes on to identify relationships as the most significant motivator for students. Williams (2003), in her book *Closing the Achievement Gap: A Vision for Changing Beliefs and Practices*, further emphasizes the critical importance of relationships in closing the achievement gap. Williams's research suggests that "turnaround" schools that are closing the achievement gap employ the strategies of:

1. Focusing on relationships between teachers and students
2. Attending to needs of the "whole child," including a sense of belonging and respect
3. Employing school-based mentoring
4. Adopting a career exploration/school program to increase career focus
5. Establishing family/school/community partnerships

Research additionally suggests that mentoring relationships increase educational achievement through prompting better attendance, improving students' chances of going on to postsecondary education, and promoting better attitudes toward school (see mentoring.org).

The Education Trust (2006) found that elementary schools had made the most progress in raising achievement and closing the achievement gap. Middle and high schools have improved achievement slightly, especially in mathematics, but have had no impact on the achievement gap. Perhaps one of the more promising efforts occurred under the direction of Dr. Mel G. Riddle, named 2006 Met Life/NASSP National High School Principal of the Year, at J. E. B. Stuart High School in Falls Church, Virginia. He noticed that low socioeconomic status kids didn't come to school often enough and could not read—74% of his high school students were reading more than 3 years below grade level. He held a literacy summit to study high school reading assessment data, a rarity, and established literacy coaches with the outcome that all teachers in the school are "teachers of reading." Today the school is a national model for serving disadvantaged students, named a "breakthrough high school" by the Gates Foundation and NASSP.

Research on the achievement gap clearly challenges the universally accepted assumption that literacy is mastered by the middle school grades (Knickerbocker & Rycik, 2006). Wise (2005) found that two thirds of 8th-grade students read below grade level. In 1999, the International Reading Association cited a neglect of adolescent literacy by schools and called for the continued development of adolescent reading and writing (Ivey, 2002). Only 54% of all American students read in the "at or above basic" range. In a middle school in Virginia, it was discovered that 95% of students who read at grade level pass the Standards of Learning (SOL) tests; however, only 64% of the students who read below grade level pass the SOL tests. The data are fairly convincing that reading intervention is needed at all grade levels, but perhaps most drastically at the middle school level.

Segregation, Poverty, and Low-Performing Schools

There is a growing concern that as a result of continued white flight to suburban and rural neighborhoods and a string of court rulings to limit the use of desegregation strategies our schools are becoming re-segregated. Freeman (2010) recognized that segregation and poverty is no longer an inner-city problem only and that there are a growing number of large pockets of poverty and segregated communities within the suburbs as the above middle class move into walled communities, exclusive areas, and rural areas leaving old suburban neighborhoods that are on the decline. These changes are now continuing the segregated housing patterns with few if any options for educators to continue the progress made through the 1954 *Brown v. Board of Education* decision.

There are very different beliefs regarding how this growing concern might be addressed. Tatem (2010) suggests that better facilities, better equipment and supplies, more curricular options, and often (although not always) more highly trained teachers in segregated schools—and all schools for that matter—is the best solution to these challenges. Tatem (2010) states:

> Because of segregated housing patterns, neighborhood schools are most often segregated schools. Not much can be done about that without housing policy that encourages the development of racially integrated neighborhoods. But that does not mean that schools serving children of color cannot be the beacons of educational opportunity for which previous generations struggled. The presence of white children should not be required to ensure students have adequate facilities, a challenging curriculum, well-qualified teachers, and a learning atmosphere conducive to success. (p. 30)

Another view is that the best solution is to continue to implement the strategies suggested by the landmark Brown decision. These individuals are convinced that poor inner-city children will receive a better education in integrated classrooms and that separate schools will always be inherently unequal. Kozol (2010) suggests:

> People who devote their lives to tinkering with clever ways to close the achievement gap by "demanding more" of children and their principals and teachers within segregated settings are, knowingly or not, upholding the same failed and tainted promises given to people in the United States more than a century ago by *Plessy v. Ferguson*. They are ripping to shreds the legacy of the Brown decision and Dr. Martin Luther King. Only those oblivious to history would dare deceive us in this shameful manner. (p. 29)

He further suggests that charter schools, favored by the Obama administration, are more profoundly segregated than most other public schools. Kozol maintains that magnet schools have generally failed to achieve much, if any, diversity. The debate continues to revolve around the issue whether success can be achieved through high expectations conveyed by teachers and administrators working in partnership with engaged parents in poor urban communities, regardless of the educational setting, or that it is only through integrated schools that the children of the poor will have the same full opportunity as the above-middle-class children in their desegregated schools. Desegregation approaches typically integrate the solving of local community problems into the core of their educational solutions. Regardless of approach, the benefits of expenditures to improve the education of the below-middle-class, poor, and segregated are to reduce spending on special education, grade retention, high school dropouts, juvenile and criminal justice, and welfare payments. They can be justified based on significant cost–benefit ratios (Freeman, 2010).

The Obama administration has come down on the side of improving schools as they now exist and providing more options within the school districts. Because we already know a lot about creating effective schools and obtaining high-quality teaching and learning, educators should use what they know to focus on improving existing schools. Educators are in a position to have the opportunity to customize schooling in ways that simply were not possible a decade ago. Certainly technology-rich environments and charter schools are two examples of ways that such changes are being made possible. This can be done in more ways than could possibly be reviewed in this text and will be discussed more in Chapter 7.

Hess and Meeks (2010) suggest two possible types of restructuring:

> The first is *structural unbundling*, in which we loosen our grip on traditional ideas about "teacher," "school," or "school system" and explore how to deliver schooling in new and effective ways. The second dimension is *content unbundling*, or unbundling the "stuff" of learning. In this dimension, we revisit assumptions about the scope and sequence of what students are expected to learn and explore new, more varied approaches to curriculum and coursework. This distinction may not be immediately clear, so consider a couple of examples. A virtual classroom in which a distinguished math instructor in Boston is teaching students in Birmingham online represents a clear change in the structure and delivery of schooling. But there is no reason to expect that the math lessons he or she delivers will be sequenced or organized any differently than a traditional classroom setting. Conversely, adapting curriculum content and schedules to better suit individual student and teacher needs in real time is an example of content unbundling. (p. 42)

In a compelling article about high performance in high-poverty schools, Reeves (2003) discusses the common characteristics of 90/90/90 schools. He coined this term in 1995 and it refers to 90% or more of the students being eligible for free and reduced lunch, 90% or more of the students are members of an ethnic minority group, and 90% or more of the students meet or exceed district or state academic standards in reading and another area. Common characteristics of these schools include: a focus on academic achievement; clear curriculum choices;

frequent assessment and multiple opportunities for improvement; an emphasis on nonfiction writing; and collaborative scoring of student work.

High-poverty schools are often the low-performing schools, as well. These schools struggle the most to pass state assessment tests and are often placed on probation. As a result, U.S. Secretary of Education Arne Duncan set a national priority to turn around the country's 5,000 lowest-performing schools. He called for rapid, large-scale reform in individual schools—not just incremental school improvement. Based on research from 2004 to 2008, Salmonowicz (2009) and his colleagues from the University of Virginia reviewed the literature on low-performing schools and interviewed dozens of turnaround specialists from 18 districts in four states. They also visited numerous schools in the midst of turnaround initiatives, and surveyed turnaround specialists and their faculties. From his year as a turnaround teacher and experience as a researcher, Salmonowicz developed the following suggestions for those in schools and districts who are considering the possibility of school turnaround or who already are engaged in the process. Having both conducted research on and worked in low-performing schools facing a large-scale reform to turn them around, he offers seven recommendations for educators in schools that are facing such reforms:

1. Ensure that more than enough resources are available
2. Ensure that the principal understands what "turnaround" means
3. Determine key priorities that you must get right the first time—and get them right
4. Show teachers that success in challenging schools is possible
5. Make literacy the centerpiece of your turnaround plan
6. Provide frequent, targeted, professional development
7. Don't scale up until you have a model that works (Salmonowicz, 2009)

The most prevalent way that school districts are using to turn around low-performing urban schools are through charter schools. The *U.S. News and World Report* has labeled a charter high school near Fenway Park in Boston as one of the nation's best high schools. The school has an open-admissions policy and three quarters of its students live in poverty, yet nearly 100% of its graduates win places at 4-year colleges. This occurs as a result of a lot of intensive instructional support, which is quite expensive. In addition, slightly less than half of the entering freshmen transfer back to Boston's traditional public schools, and half of those who stay take 5 years to graduate. Also, this highly successful school costs $35,000/per student/ per year. Thomas Toch (2009) believes that because the success in this school was based on very labor-intensive practices, requiring large amounts of personal interaction between students and teachers, technology is not likely to be a significant factor in transforming urban education or ultimately reducing the cost of urban education. According to Toch (2009), "It's expensive work, but there really doesn't seem to be a viable alternative" (p. 41).

Charter schools have received a great deal of support in recent years. The 2010 Gallup Poll suggests that charter schools are popular even though they are often misunderstood. Arne Duncan, Secretary of Education, believes there are three things needed to have good, successful charter schools:

> First, you have to have a very high bar for entry. This is not "let a thousand flowers bloom." I would argue that there are far too many low-performing charters. We had a lot of charters in Chicago, but I closed three charter schools because they weren't performing. The chance to educate our kids is like a sacred obligation. You really need to have a very clear vetting process so you're only allowing the best of the best to do that. Once you've done that, two other things have to happen. You have to give these schools real autonomy. These are by definition educational entrepreneurs who have a different vision of education. You have to free them from the bureaucracy and give them the chance to innovate and create. Third, you have to tie that autonomy to real accountability. We had 5-year performance contracts. If they're not performing, you need to close them down. When those three things happen, you can have remarkable, remarkable results for children. It's a piece of the answer. It's by no means the whole answer. (Richardson, 2009, p. 26)

The jury is still out on the success of charter schools; however, many educators in traditional schools are asking that traditional school systems have the autonomy that charter schools enjoy today (Toch, 2010). This is a response that the New York City system is taking to try to improve their lowest performing urban schools. Also, Secretary of Education Arne Duncan has pressed states during the evolution of the federal Race to the Top school reform competition to lift caps on the number of new charter schools they permit. However, a problem is that in addition to the high cost to be successful in charter schools, it also is difficult to attract the talented teachers and principals willing to work the long hours needed to launch new schools in difficult environments. Toch (2010) stated, "It's been hard to expand charter schooling outside major urban centers where entrepreneurial young educators want to live and where foundation funding is concentrated. The Charter School Research Project reports that 41% of California's charters are in Los Angeles and 90% of Illinois' charters are in Chicago" (p. 71). Certainly, charter schools and addressing the needs of our struggling youth is an effort still in development. However, regardless of its shortcomings, it is an effort that seems to have the political support to ultimately succeed. Time and future projects and research will help educators to determine the viability and success of this approach.

Another approach to the problems of the poor and the achievement gap is early childhood education. This is based on a number of research studies that have shown that 30% of low-income children have no familiarity with print, 60% do not know the alphabet, and only 6% understand numerical sequence. These programs have become more important with the recognition that about half the gap in school achievement is present at the time of school entry. Many are beginning to question whether "race to the top" can succeed when so many of our children are not even at the starting line.

Freeman (2010) suggests that high-quality care and education for 3- to 5-year-old children can make a significant contribution in closing achievement gaps and promoting social mobility:

> There is no one-shot inoculation for neutralizing the consequences of disadvantage and enhancing social mobility. Rather, a meaningful approach requires a concerted and sustained effort that starts before birth and continues through childhood and adolescence . . . When the realities of working families means that it is often necessary for both parents to work outside the home, increased funding for early care and education can ease the burden of young families who otherwise would not be in a position to afford it. (p. 676)

Research has shown that early childhood education does have a very positive impact and that those in these programs showed considerable improvement in literacy, language, and math skills when entering kindergarten, much of this continued through the 2nd grade, and these students were less likely to have to repeat a grade (Doggett & Wat, 2010). Doggett and Wat conclude:

> Gaps in learning and development among low- and middle-income children appear well before kindergarten. Without a robust early education strategy to promote greater access, higher quality, and stronger Pre-K through 3rd-grade alignment—and without investments to support these activities—we will never close the achievement gap. There is some good news. As educators and policy makers review the research and accumulate more experience, they are learning that high-quality Pre-K for all children is an indispensable part of an effective school reform strategy. They are also realizing that when teaching and learning practices are coordinated between Pre-K programs and elementary grades, they can maximize the gains children reap in the early years. (p. 9)

Over 40 states are now looking into offering some type of pre-kindergarten program and eight states are looking into a pre-kindergarten program for all children.

ACHIEVEMENT GAP AND EARLY CHILDHOOD EDUCATION

Poverty in the United States, as discussed earlier, is no longer a problem that is found mainly in our urban core; the problem has slowly migrated into the suburbs. Census data from the 2005 American Community Survey reveal new patterns of income inequality, residential mobility, and spatial segregation that make the suburbs more like its urban counterpart. For the first time, a larger number of America's poor are living in the suburbs than in the cities. This is placing greater challenges on suburban school systems that are now facing similar challenges as the more urban systems (Freeman, 2010). This decentralizing of the poor has placed increased burden on the suburbs, which do not have as extensive of a social support system as does the central cities. All of this has increased the concern about the achievement gap and how educators can address this problem, which has confronted American Education for the past 50 years. Closing this achievement gap continues to be a very complex and challenging problem.

In 2007, only 60% of Georgia's Latino students and 63% of economically disadvantaged students graduated from high school. A large percentage of students in American schools who fall behind end up dropping out of school. Research (Ramirez & Carpenter, 2009) suggests, however, that living in two-parent homes and spending more time on homework decreases the likelihood of dropping out. This is because a large percentage of students who fall behind end up dropping out of school.

Low income is associated with a variety of factors that directly affect students' educational prospects such as limited access to prenatal care, lower quality nutrition, exposure to lead, less access to books and computers, and so on (Cummins, 2009).

Freeman (2010) states:

> The years between birth and age 5 are critical to brain development and later success, and children who receive quality early care and education exhibit improved cognition, language, motor skills, adaptive skills, and socio-emotional functioning that collectively translate into better academic performance. Given today's tight fiscal environment, well-focused investments in early education development programs yield higher public and private economic benefits than do investments later in life such as on-the-job training. Cost–benefit analyses of early child development programs are encouraging in that they point to positive socialization effects and measurable long-term economic benefits such as decreased rates of criminal conduct and higher adult earnings. Economists from the Federal Reserve Bank of Minneapolis calculated a 12% rate of return for dollars invested in early childhood education because of reduced spending on special education, grade retention, high-school dropouts, juvenile and criminal justice, and welfare payments. . . . Because about half the gap in school achievement is present at the time of school entry, an integrated system of high-quality care and education for 3- to 5-year-old children can make a significant contribution in closing achievement gaps and promoting social mobility. (p. 676)

It continues to be widely accepted that academic achievement opens doors—it is a proven, universal currency of privilege.

Ragan and Reid (2009) suggest:

> The federal government supports states as they develop pre-kindergarten and other early education efforts. For the next 3 years, the federal government should provide states 25 cents on each additional dollar the states invest to launch or expand their current enrollments in Pre-K, with first priority accorded to children from low-income families, children for whom English is not the home language, or those at high risk of school failure. Eligibility for these funds should be contingent on states having a long-term plan to provide universal preschool for 3- and 4-year-old children. (p. 577)

Murphy (2009) discusses certain caveats that educators need to keep in mind when devising achievement gap interventions. He argues that there is no silver bullet to solving the achievement gap and that race is an important factor, but a more critical issue is socioeconomic status. Murphy also insists that a coherent design needs to include both out-of-school factors (e.g., academically oriented summer programs in elementary school) and in-school variables (e.g., more rigorous curriculum). Additionally, he reminds educators that there are no short-term solutions.

The frameworks for helping eliminate school achievement gaps should spotlight increasing achievement among low-skilled children more than reducing gaps between groups. Efforts to mitigate the achievement gaps should be less concerned with the different factors between white and minority students or any other group, and more concerned with what is holding students back in a school district or community. The need for early childhood education and reduction of the achievement gap is compelling and the potential for future investment is promising. Research has suggested that much of a child's brain development occurs in the first few years of their life. This development occurs as a result of the experiences the child receives during these early years. One challenge for educators who are interested in reducing the achievement gap is to expand access to quality early education.

NEW TECHNOLOGICAL DEMANDS

Another pressing issue having a major impact on student learning is technology. The International Society for Technology in Education (ISTE) released a set of computer proficiency standards titled the "National Technology Standards for Students" (NET-S). They also published a guidebook, *National Education Technology Standards for Students: Connecting Curriculum and Technology,* for school leaders, showing how to integrate the standards and technology throughout the curriculum (ISTE, 2000). The goal of school systems is to "produce technology-capable kids," meaning "kids who are able to use technology effectively by applying their technical skills" (for more information see iste.org and Chapter 7).

In 2001, the Collaborative for Technology Standards for School Administrators (TSSA) approved a set of standards that described what educational administrators should know about technology. For example, administrators must (a) demonstrate the ability to use technology to collect and analyze data and other information to improve decision making; (b) understand current technologies that can be integrated into all aspects of the teaching and learning process; (c) understand the elements and characteristics of long-range planning for the use of current and emerging technology; and (d) attain technology skills for instructional planning, budgeting, technical support, personnel, and safety.

The National Education Technology Standards for Administrators (NETS-A) states that administrators should "advocate, on the state and national levels, for policies, programs, and funding opportunities that support implementation of the district technology plan." Recent issues revolve around how students and staff should use this new educational technology. This has introduced issues related to legal matters, purchasing/updating computer hardware and software, training needs, applications software, and programming for instruction and administration, as well as policy and procedural initiatives. Technology opens up access to massive amounts of current information and communication networks with people around the world as communication and computer technologies converge (see Chapter 7).

This has become far more pressing because federal and state funding has resulted in educational technology rapidly spreading into K–12 schools across the nation (Nance, 2003). There have been great strides in the area of implementing technology in education. The access students have to computers since the 1990s has increased significantly. In 1998 and 2003, the student-to-computer ratio went from 12 to 1 to 4.4 to 1 (NCES, 2003). Today, public schools average one computer for every 3.8 students. In 1994, only 3% of classrooms had Internet access compared to 93% in 2003 (Parsad & Jones, 2005). (See Chapter 7 for a more in-depth discussion.)

✳ **What additional issues will most likely develop over the next 5 years that you will need to consider in providing leadership at Pala Middle School? What factors will be important? Explain your answer.**

GOVERNANCE AND PRIVATIZATION

Efforts are now under way to find ways to allow schools to experiment and innovate beyond the "shackles" of policy and tradition. More than 40 states have authorized charter schools, and many have been looking at various forms of school choice programs, school vouchers, year-round learning, and magnet schools. Although parents have expressed a high level of satisfaction with charter schools (Gill, Timpane, Rose, & Brewer, 2001), they have made no innovations in curricular and instructional practice (Lubienski, 2003). The focus of charter school improvements has been on organizational and governance structures. According to Fashola and Slavin (1998), the key reforms now needed are in curriculum and instruction, programs for at-risk students, and family support.

By 2003, school choice had greatly expanded. Seventeen states have interdistrict open enrollment programs; public voucher programs—which are more controversial—exist in three states; and numerous private voucher programs are operating mostly in urban areas. Parents may use education vouchers (public funds) to enroll their children in private schools, including religious schools.

This new direction opens up the opportunity for businesspeople to operate schools for profit and, if school vouchers are created, possibility that for-profit schools might replace public schools. Supporters argue that such approaches offer opportunities for improved student achievement. As a result, there are an increasing number of private organizations that provide support for education and who hope to both manage and operate schools.

Levine (2000) suggests, "The private sector has two entrance points to the public school marketplace. They can directly enter by creating for-profit schools or managing existing schools in the manner of Christopher Whittle's Edison Schools which started in the early 1990s. Or one can enter the field by providing support services, and learning materials as Sylvan does" (p. 8). He believes the "companies that provide support and noninstructional services for elementary and secondary schools will be more lucrative than those that create or manage schools" (p. 9). The greatest concern expressed in for-profit schools is that the profit will take precedence over the children and that it will separate the diversity that exists in schools in this country by providing a different level of educational service, based largely on parents' wealth and the amount they can afford to pay for their children's education. There is also a concern that a fragmented educational system will be a threat to U.S. society, national unity, and democratic socialization, creating balkanization, growing segregation, and increased civil unrest.

If the present conditions in education do not change, we can expect to see a further push toward increased privatization through charters, vouchers, public funding for private and parochial schools, and various forms of school takeovers. In 2002, New York Mayor Michael Bloomberg reached an agreement with state legislative leaders that removed power from the local boards and gave him control over the schools. Another takeover occurred in Philadelphia in 2001, when the school board was disbanded and the state took control of the schools. Vouchers received strong support in the Supreme Court's June 2003 decision in the Cleveland voucher case, *Zelman v. Simmon Harris*. By a 5–4 margin, the Supreme Court upheld a program in which school district voucher receipts were being used for religious schools on the grounds that it was a "true private choice" and thus not unconstitutional. The theme was that the programs were neutral in respect to religion and were a genuine expression of parent choice. In this way, the district/state may pay the tuition of students who wish to attend private schools, even religious schools. This ruling may not have a significant impact because 37 states have amendments that prohibit using public money to support religious schools; however, the voucher battle is expected to heat up in state legislatures. Typically, referendums on vouchers and tuition tax credits have failed, especially when they take money away from public schools; however, the present political/legal climate is no longer clear on this issue (for more information see mcrel.org).

EQUITY AND SOCIAL JUSTICE

According to Darling-Hammond (1997), schools in the 90th percentile of income spent nearly ten times more than schools in the 10th percentile. Such conditions do not provide equitable treatment for economically disadvantaged students. In the past, this inequity, some might argue injustice, has had a particularly harsh effect on African-American, Latino, and Native American children. Darling-Hammond (1997) suggests, "Perhaps the single greatest source of inequity in education is this disparity in the availability and distribution of well-qualified teachers" (p. 273) (see leadershipforsocialjustice.org).

Equity or social justice can be discussed from a number of different perspectives—political, economic, opportunity, and results. The equity movement has resulted in the improved access of minority children, women, and the handicapped to various school programs and activities. This issue is receiving greater attention as a result of the growing achievement gaps and the extraordinary economic gaps among people. Pounder, Reitzug, and Young (2002) talk about "inequitable outcomes" that are characterized by "patterned polarization" of school achievement and economic opportunity and welfare (p. 270).

The focus on multicultural issues related to curriculum, instruction, textbooks, literature, and cultural studies also show an increasing interest in social justice. Pounder et al. (2002) clearly illustrate the recent direction of the social justice discourse:

> Literally millions of students, every year, are not served well by our schools. Schools across our nation in districts large and small with different resources and different student populations are failing to educate, failing to nurture, failing to develop, failing to protect, and failing to include all students . . . the students who are affected most are typically from marginalized groups (e.g., students of color, students with disabilities, low-income students, girls, and gay/lesbian students). (p. 271)

These topics were a major theme of the 2006 and 2007 UCEA conferences.

Social justice helps define part of the ethical, moral, and democratic dimension of leadership. Leaders will need to continuously stress the values of equity and excellence and ensure that it becomes part of their organization's vision. In discussing this type of leader, Schewick and Skrla (2003) found that such a leader:

> Understands that it is our responsibility, even our sacred or spiritual responsibility— to create such schools. This leader understands that this responsibility is central to our country's long history of dedication to equity for all people—for working people, the poor, women, people of color, people with disabilities, for any people who have been excluded. (p. 100)

This will not always be an easy position to take and leaders will want to be well connected to allies who can provide moral support. Most transformations will require strong, outstanding leaders and issues related to equity and social justice are no exception.

Grogan (2002) claims that social justice leaders must continue to challenge the status quo, which favors one group over others. The primary goal is the improvement of "life chances" of children who have in the past been minimized by the system. Recently, the issues have been expanded to environmental pollution and domination over nature. This focus is on understanding the relationships between ecological and cultural systems and not jeopardizing the environment for future generations (Furman & Gruenewald, 2004).

No country has taken the concerns of equality and social justice more seriously than the United States. This goal has necessitated "creating policies that favor children most at risk—policies that, by definition, are partial, biased and unequal. Given an unlevel playing field, only redistributive policies offer the possibilities of equalizing educational opportunities" (Cooper, Fusarelli, & Randall, 2004, p. 51).

According to a number of reports, many parents and communities are not attending to their children. Marian Wright Edelman, founder and president of the Children's Defense Fund, calls them "back seat" children. Two-parent income earners, single-parent homes, mobility, divorce, poverty, and/or very busy lifestyles have changed the experiences children have within the family. They are often confronted by social issues such as crime, neglect, poverty, abuse, disease, addiction, and violence. An example legislation that attempts to address equity is included in the NCLB Act of 2002, which states that, "Assessment results and state progress objectives must be broken out by poverty, race, ethnicity, disability, and limited English proficiency to ensure that no group is left behind."

STATE ROLES AND RESPONSES

Education is mentioned in every state constitution. The legislatures in every state other than Hawaii, which has a state school system, continue to follow the original pattern of local control of public education (see Chapter 4 for greater detail). State boards of education date back to 1784, and the first state superintendent of public instruction emerged in 1854. State superintendents have been successful in marshaling public opinion, lobbying state legislatures, providing professional leadership, establishing direction, and setting minimum standards. Although the state legislature is charged with the primary responsibility of maintaining a system of public education, the governor's desires are not lightly ignored. Governors influence education through their platform positions, educational appointments, and veto of bills. The state board of education is often appointed by the governor and determines policies and appoints the chief state school officer. The state department of education is responsible for implementing these policies.

State education departments did not really come of age until after the passage of the Elementary and Secondary Education Act in 1965. Title V of this act provided money to significantly increase the number of state department officials as well as providing training, equipment, and encouragement for research and development efforts. Within 3 years after the passage of this act, many state departments of education doubled in size, with much of the support coming from federal funds.

The major areas of focus at the state level are academic standards, instructional programs, textbook selection, certification of personnel, facilities standards, financial support, data collection and distribution, testing, inspecting and ensuring appropriate compliance, and regulation of nonpublic schools.

The major theme across America at the turn of the 21st century was "get the scores up." Reform in 2001 was often a matter of conforming instruction to fit final tests. Students were exposed to sets of practice tests and drill-and-skill teaching and packaged programs, as they hustled through units and chapters to complete a year's worth of standards. This has created an era of "test-centered" curriculum.

Tests are becoming a major determiner of what the curriculum should and should not include, thus transferring control of the curriculum and teaching and learning to groups that control the exams. In expressing some concerns regarding the standards movement, and particularly the related sanctions, Darling-Hammond and Falk (1997) maintain that:

> Ultimately, raising standards for students so that they learn what they need to know requires raising standards for the system, so that it provides the kinds of teaching and school settings students need in order to learn. . . . Genuine accountability requires both higher standards and greater supports for student, teacher, and school learning. (p. 198)

There is at least some evidence that state standardized testing is having a positive impact. Detert, Kopel, Mauriel, and Jenni (2000) state:

> Our data suggest that while educators may not agree with state-wide testing, the tests are serving as an impetus for continuous improvement efforts, including goal setting, baseline data, and benchmarks. Most sites with highly publicized state tests are using them successfully as a rallying point for improvement efforts and as a concrete reason to analyze and study their data and the processes relating to these tests. (pp. 179–180)

An American Association of School Administrators poll concluded that tests can provide useful feedback to improve instruction, but they should not be the *only* benchmarks, *competencies*, *performance standards*, or any other current term in the accountability movement. Thus, tests are only a sample of what students need to know and may end up narrowing teacher focus.

✳ **What role would your state most likely play in Pala's renewal efforts?**

CHANGING POPULATIONS IN THE 21ST CENTURY

The world in which we live is shrinking, and we need a better understanding of other countries and cultures. Futurists suggest that the next two decades will produce more change than has occurred in the last century. The half-life of knowledge is approximately 8 years—that is, half of what you learn will be obsolete in 8 years. The world store of knowledge is growing at an exponentially increasing rate. However, our children may not be prepared for this knowledge explosion.

In *Beyond Rhetoric*, the National Commission on Children (1991) said of American children:

> [A]mong all races and income groups, and in communities nationwide, many children are in jeopardy. They grow up in families whose lives are in turmoil. Their parents are too stressed and too drained to provide nurturing, structure and security that protect children and prepare them for adulthood. Some others are unsafe at home and in their neighborhoods. (p. 5)

Some of the quality-of-life factors that are worsening include child abuse, the number of children in poverty, obesity, drug abuse, lack of health insurance coverage, out-of-pocket health costs, urban poverty, and crime. Other significant trends that affect education are national and global interdependence, increasing institutional change in both pace and complexity, the obsolescence of knowledge, terrorism, and a worsening ecology. Children today are exposed to a constant barrage of violence on television and in movies and computer games. They are even sometimes permitted to buy semiautomatic and automatic weapons when they "come of age."

Twenty-four percent of children in the United States live with one parent and 4% live with neither parent. Eight percent have attempted suicide. Forty-five percent of high school students reported sexual intercourse. Thirty-four percent of children have seen some form of violence and are scared during some part of their day. Eighty-one percent of youth report that they use alcohol by 12th grade. Approximately 50% of 12th-grade students reported moderate to heavy drinking. Thirty percent have ridden with a driver who had been drinking. Sixteen percent of all white children and 37% of all African-American and Hispanic children live in poverty (NCC, 1991).

A central factor in the quality-of-life decline is that the real buying power of American families is decreasing except among the wealthiest income brackets. There is a significant increase in the poorest and richest families with a resulting decline in the middle class. Wealth in this country is being controlled by an ever-decreasing number of American citizens. At the same time, taxes have been increased for the middle and working classes and decreased for the wealthy. As a result, income and economic power are being concentrated in fewer and fewer hands.

Another factor affecting education is that the Hispanic populations will continue to increase faster than the overall population. The non-Hispanic white population will drop from 65% in 2003 to 56% by 2020. By 2010, the number of African-American students will decline by more than 6%. By 2025, nearly one in four school-aged children will be Hispanic.

In July 2011, there were more than 315 million people in the United States, 8 million more than the forecast. This increase was caused by immigration— primarily by Latinos, now comprising more than 16% of the population and growing by nearly 10% every 2 years. The number of Asian and Pacific Islander children is projected to rise by 14% (see nces.ed.gov). As more Americans marry across racial lines, however, such categories will perhaps be less meaningful.

The need for multicultural education has increased as the face of classrooms has changed dramatically. Bemak, Chung, and Siroskey-Sabdo (2005) state, "21st century urban schools face unique challenges in being culturally responsive and providing quality education to culturally diverse and low-income students" (p. 381). Administrators must be sensitive to the diversity that exists within their schools. Partnerships with communities and parents become imperative due to the need to understand family structures and to accommodate learning differences. Thus, teachers must implement multicultural education in the classrooms in addition to meeting standards. Bemak et al. (2005) warn, "As schools become increasingly diverse in the 21st century, the ability to understand and respond appropriately to students' cultural, racial, economic, social, and learning differences will become increasingly important prerequisites to effective school leadership" (p. 385).

The number of older Americans—the graying population—is increasing within our society. Overall, the elderly are the fastest growing segment of the population. Today only one household in four has a school-age child. As fewer adults have contact with children in their daily lives, there will probably be less political support for children in the future. Labor-intensive work is being outsourced to other nations, forcing American labor to compete with low-income workers in developing nations.

The estimated U.S. federal budget deficit, approaching $14 trillion over the next few years, may slow economic growth and further reduce federal support to cash-strapped state and local education budgets. Some calculations maintain that every family of four now owes over $90,000 just to pay off the national debt. We are now spending more on interest on the national debt than we are on national defense. There is real concern about running out of fossil fuels, which are now essential to American life and the economy, early in the next century. Many are quite concerned with the potentially devastating effects of global warming.

> ✳ **What structure and process will best allow schools like Pala to be both proactive and responsive to contextual issues at the federal, state, and local levels?**

SEGREGATION, DESEGREGATION, AND INTEGRATION

The U.S. educational system has responded to issues of desegregation and integration in a variety of ways. Programmatic options include magnet programs, programs for at-risk children, bilingual programs, and Afrocentric programs or schools, to name but a few. Since *Brown v. Board of Education* (1954), school desegregation has become one of the most hotly debated education issues nationwide. Some argue that prior to *Brown*, school segregation was legal and that it is still present in the form of single-sex schools, single race and ethnic schools (i.e., Afrocentric schools), some bilingual programs, and alternative schools or programs that separate special education students.

It is evident that an educational leader must not only understand the programmatic possibilities and their context, but also the social and cultural factors that influence program development decisions. Clearly, the needs of the community that Tanner discusses in Chapter 8 are one of the key issues at the heart of a school's curriculum.

Magnet Schools

Magnet schools can be found at all grade levels in both private and public schools. Magnet programs are differentiated by their curriculum, special focus area, and instructional approach (e.g., Montessori, Paideia, math and science, project-based learning). The formats of magnet schools vary. Some programs are schoolwide, or whole-school magnets, in which all students would be involved in the "magnet" area (e.g., in a schoolwide global education magnet, all students would in some ways be involved in the global education curriculum). Another type is often called a "school-within-a-school program" (SWAS) or "program within a school" (PWS). Only some students in a particular school are involved in the magnet program. Another format might be a grade-level magnet in which only certain grade levels are offered a particular curricular focus.

Recent years have seen a decline in magnet schools. This may particularly be due to the growth of charter schools that have unique themes, but also according to Hossell (2005) there are no school districts in the United States that have had an extensive system of magnet schools that have not closed a few because of budget cuts. She maintains that magnets are victims of their own success because during the last 15 years most local schools have computer technology and science labs, which once made magnet schools unique (see educationnext.org/magnetschools/).

Today, nearly all large school districts have magnet schools. In the 2001–2002 school year, there were 3,000 magnet schools nationwide. There are numerous reasons for the growth of magnet schools. They include: families wanting more choice; the appeal of schools that have unique offerings; the notion that magnets, like some charter schools, are supposed to help students with particular career choices; and the fact that they are a voluntary approach to school desegregation, among others.

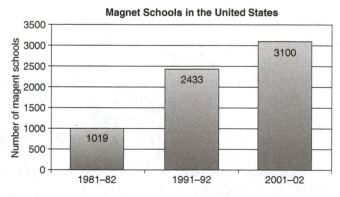

FIGURE 2.1   Enduring Attraction

Source: National Center for Education Statistics (NCES) and estimated from Source Book of the Magnet Schools Association of America.

CONCLUSION

Federal and state involvement in U.S. education centers around the recurring themes of educational excellence and educational opportunity. Educational excellence seeks to set higher standards; strengthen the curriculum, particularly in math and the sciences; set higher standards for coursework and graduation; and develop more rigorous grading, testing, homework, and discipline. Educational opportunity prompts efforts to improve school attendance, provide needed services, ensure that all learners achieve minimum standards, and provide for multiculturalism, inclusiveness, and diversity. The school choice movement began in the last quarter of the 20th century and continues to gain momentum. The last 30 years have witnessed the growth of homeschooling, charters, magnets, and more recently virtual schools. The bottom line is to create schools that are constantly improving themselves and meeting the ever-changing demands of society.

Local school leaders are often challenged by conflicting desires, expressed at the federal, state, and local levels as part of the great national debate on education. While local control and grassroots democracy remain a cherished tradition, the political power of localities has eroded. Despite the crush of competing agendas and distractions, educational leaders must help to bring everyone's attention and efforts to bear on important educational goals for the future. All who have a stake in successful schools must be involved in the efforts to improve them. Cetron and Cetron (2004) offer the following:

> [W]e are cautiously optimistic about the future of education. In any poll, U.S. voters—the people who must pay for our schools—consistently cite education as the highest priority. . . . If technology brings new challenges for our schools, it also provides a means to make schools more effective. The challenge in the twenty-first century will be to spell out and develop successful schools. (p. 29)

MyEdLeadershipLab™

Go to Topic 1: *Vision and Mission* in the MyEdLeadershipLab™ site (www .MyEdLeadershipLab.com) for *Educational Leadership: A Bridge to Improved Practice*, Fifth Edition, where you can:

- Find learning outcomes for *Vision and Mission* along with the national standards that connect to these outcomes.
- Complete Assignments and Activities that can help you more deeply understand the chapter content.
- Apply and practice your understanding of the core skills identified in the chapter with the Building Leadership Skills unit.
- Prepare yourself for professional certification with a Practice for Certification quiz.

PORTFOLIO ARTIFACTS

- Examine your school or district's vision or mission. Compare and contrast it with another school district.

- Share information with colleagues regarding new ideas and directions acquired from the state or federal department of education or professional meetings.

- Demonstrate an understanding and articulation of the context that is operating within your school district.

- Examine the accountability systems to produce reports of local, state, and federal compliance by a school system.

- Interview a key central office administrator responsible for curriculum related issues. Investigate what state, national, and professional organization standards are built into the curriculum.

- Join a professional education association (see Chapter 1, page 5 for examples). Become involved in an advocacy issue the organization is working on.

- Attend a "Day on the Hill" event sponsored by a professional association. This might be in Washington, DC or at your state capitol.

- Attend a Senate, House of Representatives, city council, chamber of commerce, or civic organization meeting.

KEY TERMS

- Achievement gap
- Adequate yearly progress (AYP)
- Accountability
- *Brown* decision
- Charter school
- Common core standards
- Desegregation
- Elementary and Secondary Education Act (ESEA)

- Equal educational opportunity
- Equity and social justice
- High-stakes testing
- No Child Left Behind (NCLB)
- Magnet schools
- Millennials
- School choice

- *Swann v. Charlotte-Mecklenburg Board of Education*
- Virtual school
- Vouchers

SUGGESTED READINGS

Burris, T. (2006). *The impact of politics in local education.* Blue Ridge Summit, PA: Rowman E. Littlefield Education.

Leithwood, K. (2006). *Making schools smarter.* Thousand Oaks, CA: Corwin Press.

Mitchell, D. E., Crowson, R. L., & Shipps, D. (Eds.). (2011). *Shaping education policy: Power and process.* London, England: Routledge.

Noguera, P., & Yonemura-Uisrey, J. (Eds.). (2007). *Unfinished business: Closing the racial achievement gap in our schools.* San Francisco, CA: Jossey-Bass.

Tyack, D. (2003). *Seeking common ground: Public schools in diverse society.* Cambridge, MA: Harvard University Press.

CHAPTER 3

SCHOOL REFORM
AND INNOVATION

MyEdLeadershipLab™

Visit the MyEdLeadershipLab™ site for *Educational Leadership: A Bridge to Improved Practice*, Fifth Edition to enhance your understanding of chapter concepts. You'll have the opportunity to practice your skills through video- and case-based Assignments and Activities as well as Building Leadership Skills units, and to prepare for your certification exam with Practice for Certification quizzes.

MILTON MIDDLE SCHOOL

Reform at Milton

You are the principal at Milton Middle School. Your math, social studies, science, and English departments all seem to be ready to focus effort on improving student achievement in the areas of reading, writing, mathematics, and science. The school board and Superintendent Melville have suggested that you select one of the evidence-based models (see pages 79–83) for improving instruction, collect information about the model, develop a proposal on why the model best fits Milton, and on approval join the network of nationwide educators involved in developing and implementing the model. It is quite important to the board and Superintendent Melville that the model selected is compatible with the integration of technology into each of the core subject areas. The combined reform model and integrated technology plan will be used at a later time at Milton to develop a comprehensive school improvement plan. You are now doing some of the initial groundwork regarding possible content for the plan; the process for school improvement planning and the budget will be devised at a later date.

The school district does not have a policy regarding curriculum implementation and instructional reform to ensure consistent and high-quality decision making. A policy is needed regarding agreed-on criteria for evaluating and approving reforms for the school. In fact, a number of the teachers are familiar with national reform efforts under way by prominent individuals and groups nationwide that they believe hold considerable promise for Milton Middle School. Each of the models will need to be evaluated in regard to its educational merit and the technology integration initiative in order to select the one that is most compatible with the school's need to realign its core curriculum. Some members of the community and a number of teachers who are loyal to the existing curriculum have already begun to express concern that you and some of the teachers are chasing after the latest fads and not supporting existing programs. The school student council made an appeal, however, that the principal and teachers come up with a plan to remedy "the shortcomings" at the school, so all students will be prepared to meet the challenges they will face as adults and to take on meaningful roles in society. To convince parents, teachers, and students, information will need to be available on successful comprehensive school reform (CSR) efforts that are under way in other school divisions. Final decisions regarding reform will be based on which CSR initiatives are most compatible with the goals set for Milton Middle School as well as on their potential impact on student achievement.

※ **Develop some general guidelines regarding the content of curricular and instructional reforms and the criteria that will be used to evaluate the comprehensive school reform models.**

THE CONTEXT FOR SCHOOL REFORM

The demand for school reform has required educational administrators to become agents of change. At the same time, they are feeling the pressures of the standards movement, new forms of assessment, new curricular and instructional demands, and overall changing job expectations—instructional leadership more than management. The central goal of educators' work today is to improve student achievement. When teachers perceive instructional leadership behaviors to be appropriate, supportive, and responsive with regard to raising student achievement, they grow in commitment, professional involvement, and willingness to innovate. Marks and Printy (2003) state, "When the principal elicits high levels of commitment and professionalism from teachers and works interactively with teachers in a shared instructional leadership capacity, schools have the benefit of integrated leadership, they are organizations that learn and perform at high levels" (p. 393).

Most discussions of the role of educational administrators today stress the responsibility for keeping up with new ideas and facilitating innovation. As one principal stated, "We should always be growing and trying something new and experimenting" (Biddle & Saha, 2006, p. 73), the No Child Left Behind (NCLB) legislation has placed a demand on low-performing schools to improve their students' academic achievement annually. Schools are now expected to use the result of "student assessments" to look into different innovative strategies and instructional practices to determine which seem to encourage the highest student achievement. There is an effort to create a continual improvement cycle within curriculum, instruction, and assessment.

This focus on pedagogy tends to strengthen collaborative teamwork within the schools. Principals in high-performing schools were able to point to programs, interventions, and professional development opportunities that contributed to success. When schools are transformed, it is often, according to Christman (2005) related to "changes in the school's instructional practices and programs" (p. 20). Christman further states, "Schools and districts can bring about student achievement and sustain achievement if they are willing to examine their practices and embrace change" (p. 20). In almost all cases of school improvement, schools made a transition from one mode of operation to another.

✳ **What will be needed for reform to be successful at Milton Middle School?**

Finding New Directions

The improvements that are now called for address "what and how" subjects are taught, as well as how progress is measured and evaluated. They get at the technical core of the teaching and learning process. Students' performance, experiences, preparation, and outcomes become the driving force for the new reforms.

Certainly no educational improvements will occur if an organization has not built the capacity to change. To succeed, members must use a great deal of care to create a culture and approach that motivates and supports participants. According to Brown and Anfara (2003), the capacity to support continuous improvement requires the administrator's knowledge and skill in the following areas:

1. Understand the nature, needs, strengths, and limitations of staff members
2. Understand the relevance of the reform in terms of need, practicality, and complexity
3. Assess the readiness of staff to become involved
4. Ensure that the necessary resources and support are available, including the time to accomplish the task
5. Work collaboratively with a critical mass of diverse constituents (teachers, community members, parents, etc.)
6. Understand that change is difficult and will be met with resistance
7. Acknowledge that teachers must "own" the intended reform
8. Ensure that excessive authority is not imposed from above
9. Provide the professional development and education necessary to properly implement the intended reform
10. Remember that structural changes will not ensure fundamental changes in the purposes, priorities, and functioning of a school by themselves
11. Acknowledge that reform is a developmental process (p. 30)

Improvements will not occur unless educators are encouraged to think about the significant opportunities that exist for their schools. Without a strong vision of what great 21st century schools look like, it is highly unlikely that capacity-building efforts will have much impact on classrooms, schools, or students. Capacity and vision must proceed hand in hand if we are to achieve any level of success.

The basic research on planning and innovation has focused on decision making and the implementation process (Allison, 1971; Cohen & March, 1974; Etzioni, 1986; Hughes & Achilles, 1971; Janis & Mann, 1977; Lindblom, 1980; March & Simon, 1959; Mintzberg, 1989). Other authors see innovation as a series of choices that organizations and thus individuals are constantly confronting in order to decide what is better than the previous idea (Hall & Hord, 1987; Rogers, 1995). Probably the most important factor related to the speed of adoption and its ultimate success is the relative advantage as perceived by those who influence the decision and its ultimate success.

Innovations typically begin with the recognition of a need or problem. This recognition can occur through the political process, the rise of social problems, or a sense of present difficulties and future needs. Everett Rogers (1995) states:

> Many, but not all, technical innovations come out of research. The purpose of research is to advance knowledge, practice and/or to solve practical problems. Rogers defines development as "the process of putting a new idea into a form that is expected to meet the needs of an audience of potential adopters. . . . This represents an arena in which researchers come together with change agents. How are innovations evaluated? One way is through clinical trials, scientific experiments that are designed to determine prospectively the effects of an innovation in terms of efficacy, safety and the like. (p. 160)

It takes the genius of creative ideas, a vision of the future, and knowledge of where we need to be to spark individuals to improve schools. The capacity is essential, but so are the ideas. Those participating in the improvement of schools will need to orient their common efforts toward a shared vision of improvement as they develop creative insights, invent new schools, and prepare all students for life in a knowledge society (Carter & Cunningham, 1997). Eventually, when innovations are successful and are an improvement on what currently exists, leaders who serve as the innovative catalysts in their disciplines spread them.

The creation of effective new schools ultimately depends on the ability of educators to visualize how improved schools look. Vision converts ideas, knowledge, experience, and futurist thinking into a reality that is clearly understood and achievable by practitioners. Vision provides the bridge between innovative ideas and purposeful, coordinated action. Therefore, it is critically important that educators be aware of the latest thinking, of what holds the greatest promise for improving education (Sparks, 1997). The vision of an ideal school helps them to rework and reshape existing curriculum content, instructional methods, and delivery systems (americaspromise.org).

Reeves recognizes four steps to ensuring lasting change. First, the leader must define what will not change. He warns that the average person is resistant to change; therefore, the leader must be aware of specific traditions and values within the school that will be preserved. This method "places change within the context of stability" (Reeves, 2007) in order not to send the message that everything prior to the change was bad or wrong, insulting colleagues and creating unnecessary battles. "Effective change leaders identify and build on traditions rather than compete with them" (Reeves, 2007, p. 18). Second, the leader must remember that actions speak louder than words. A leader who talks about a collaborative environment but continues to lecture, dictate, and demand will not receive the desired results. "The greatest impediment to meaningful cultural change is the gap between what leaders say they value and what they actually do" (Reeves, 2007, p. 18). Third, leaders must use the right tools for change. Leaders must understand what works for his or her group. Various tools for change are rituals, traditions, threats, coercion, training, procedures, role modeling, and vision. Lastly, leaders must be willing to get "down and dirty" along with everyone else. "If the leader believes that every job has value and there is no such thing as unimportant work in schools, then the leader must demonstrate that belief in actions" (Reeves, 2007, p. 19).

Common Themes in a Changing World

Some policymakers are suggesting that the United States is facing "the perfect storm" and education is in the center of it. Major themes include globalization and higher demand for skilled and educated workers, and thus higher demand for an education system that can produce them. Kirsh was the research director of a 2006 study entitled "America's Perfect Storm: Those Forces Changing Our Nation's Future" (see ets.org/stormreport). The report studies the convergence of three powerful sociological and economic forces that are influencing our nation's future:

- A shifting labor market increasingly rewarding education and skills
- Changing demographics including a rapidly growing Hispanic population
- A growing achievement gap, particularly for minority and low socioeconomic status children

These researchers express concern over the decreasing number of jobs that are able to support a family and the resulting dangerous implications for many American workers. The report suggests that we must enhance learning levels, reading and math skills, attention to and resources for early childhood education, conditions that positively affect young children, programs that keep kids from dropping out of school, and continuing and adult education. Major focus must be placed on narrowing the existing achievement gaps in American education.

Schools must prepare all students for either promising careers or postsecondary education, emphasizing the crucial role of technology. As a result, there is an increased focus (Rivero, 2006) on:

- Mastery of core subject areas
- Learning skills such as critical thinking and problem solving, as well as interpersonal and self-directional skills
- Using 21st-century tools such as communication and information technologies to develop learning skills
- Learning global awareness as well as business and civic literacy

"We have a framework that lays out the skill set that we believe high-school graduates need to have in the global economy," says Ken Kay, past president of the Partnership for Twenty-First Century Skills. "The difference in the twenty-first century, in our view, is that these skills need to be integrated into the student's understanding of his or her core subjects."

This begins with preschool education, which some believe will provide lifetime dividends (Bracey, 2003). Research suggests that those who attend preschool have higher school completion rates, higher test scores, earn more money, have reduced crime rates, and fewer special education placements. As in many such programs, it is the cost–benefit analysis of the investment that is receiving attention.

There continues to be a national concern for how to improve high schools. In a 2006 NSBA survey of readers of their journal asking their views of the most important need, they found that:

- 38% focused on improving the quality of teaching and teachers
- 23% concentrated on technology and curriculum reform
- 20% emphasized the creation of smaller, more personal schools
- 19% chose other reforms

The traditional emphasis on acquiring knowledge and skills is giving way to a greater emphasis on learning how to think intelligently and the application of knowledge as needed within a specific context. The thinking is based on Bloom's (1956) higher order of learning: analysis, synthesis, and evaluation. School boards stress actively applying learning, moral reasoning, writing and speaking effectively, researching information, using new technologies, and listening to and understanding others. The potential to better customize learning to each student's needs can be supported by technological advances. Will education remain teacher and institutionally controlled or will it become more learner controlled?

Suggested changes from the new Commission of Skills of the American Workforce (2006) include:

- Universal preschool would be available for all 3- and 4-year-old children.
- High school students would take state exit exams in the 10th grade. Those who passed would go on to community college or other job training or would attend high school for another 2 years to prepare for college entrance.
- Teachers would be recruited from the top third of high school graduates. There would be considerable pay increases for teachers "willing to work the same hours per year as the other professionals typically do." Teachers who work in poor-achieving urban schools, in remote areas, or in fields where there are shortages would be paid more as well.
- Money to fund the schools would come from the state.

New schools are expected to provide many more learning options for students who have different learning styles and brain functioning. They must incorporate what we have learned from brain research, including that on infant and toddler development and learning (Gardner, 1993). Teachers need to help students develop understanding, inferential skills, and strategic knowledge and to advance their thinking skills. The most powerful models in instruction are interactive and generative—engaging and encouraging the learner to construct and produce knowledge in meaningful ways.

More than ever before, technology is at the forefront of a rapidly changing world. Information technology is driving change at an accelerated rate. Like their forebears, children must become pioneers as they move into a future of change and great adventure, where technology allows them to access information from anywhere in the world in a matter of seconds.

According to the National Commission on Teaching and America's Future (NCTAF), a child's education should be authentically grounded; subjects should be integrated (NCTAF, 1996). It is clear that we need citizens who can think strategically to create visions, learn in a constantly changing environment, build knowledge from a wide range of sources, understand systems in diverse contexts, and collaborate both locally and globally using technology.

The President's Committee of Advisors on Science and Technology's Report to the President (1997) stated that the private sector demands workers with the skills needed to compete in the "information society." There is a potential for radically different methods of teaching and learning using the range of technological possibilities—changing what is learned, how it is learned, how it is measured, and what the teacher does in the classroom.

The types of reforms required are major in scope, discontinuous with the past, and transformational. Box 3.1 summarizes some of these major new demands

BOX 3.1

NEW DEMANDS TO CHANGE PEDAGOGICAL MODELS

From	To
Teacher–curriculum centered	Learner centered
Acquisition of knowledge and skills	Intelligent thinking and knowledge application
Individual tasks	Collaborative work (speaking and listening skills)
Passive learning (listener)	Active learning (collaborator)
Printed media	Technological tools
Grade focus	Achievement focus
National perspective	Global perspective
Independent efforts	Combined efforts
Abstract learning (facts)	Authentic learning (relationships, inquiry, invention, understanding)
Rote learning (drill and practice)	Problem solving (communication, creativity, access, expression)
Paper-and-pencil tests (norm referenced)	Demonstrations and performances (criterion referenced)
Discipline based	Integrative/interdisciplinary/PBL approaches

LEADING INNOVATIVE SCHOOLS

STEPHANIE PACE MARSHALL, PHD
Illinois Mathematics and Science Academy, Aurora, Illinois

What does it take to lead an innovative school (and by that I mean a transformative and generative learning community) for the 21st century? What are the conditions that leaders-in-learning must create to prepare students to be pioneers in an unknown land? In the past, we behaved as if we believed that by understanding the parts we would discern the behavior of the whole and that analysis would inevitably lead to synthesis. By design, we constructed and operated our schools as we understood our world, and this produced learning disabled institutions that have suppressed reflective thought, creativity, and the innate and inexhaustible capacity for lifelong learning.

We designed a linear system built on predictive models of change and a belief that learning was incremental, when in fact human systems are not predictable; change is non-linear and learning is dynamic and patterned. Human beings do not follow the logic of cause and effect. We crave connectedness and meaning, we seek lasting and deep relationships, we grow by sharing and not by keeping secrets, and we need to trust and be trusted to feel safe enough to dare.

As a result, leaders of innovative learning communities need to create learning and teaching environments that enable learners to direct their own learning toward greater rigor, coherence, and complexity; to increase their intellectual, social, and emotional engagement with others; and to foster collaborative and dynamic approaches to learning that enable learners to develop thoughtful and integrative ways of knowing.

We must create a learning culture that provides a forum for risk, novelty, experimentation, and challenge and that redirects and personalizes learning. We must create learning communities for learners of all ages that can give power, time, and voice to their inquiry and their creativity. Such a community is governed by the principles of learning, not school, and is:

- *Personalized, flexible, and coherent.* Questions that are significant to the human condition drive the curriculum, and knowledge is not separated in distinct and unconnected disciplines.
- *Internally and externally connected.* It is not bounded by physical, geographic, or temporal space (because learning happens everywhere, student learning must transcend classroom and school boundaries).
- *Rich in information and flexible and diverse learning experiences.* It has pathways for all learners (students are actively engaged in meaningful research and inquiry; they study "big and important" concepts in the context of interdisciplinary problems that matter and that are relevant to the real world; students are engaged in meaningful research and serious inquiry).
- *Intergenerational in the configuration of learning experiences.* Margaret Mead has said that the healthiest learning environment occurs when three generations are learning together.
- *Grounded in collaborative inquiry.* Students engage with adults and peers and draw on the experiences of the entire group; learners are honored as capable of creating and generating knowledge, not just acquiring information.
- *Focused on complex cognition, problem finding, and problem resolution.* Students are engaged in authentic and meaningful dialogue with members of the internal and external community; they are taught skills that enable them to deal with complexity and with ambiguity and paradox.

(continued)

Creating these conditions for generative learning is the work of innovative leaders, and it is fundamental to the creation of an environment that enables exceptional learning for all students.

Parker Palmer (1998), in his simple yet profound book *The Courage to Teach,* offers the following essential insight about leaders and leading within a learning setting:

> If we are to have communities of discourse about teaching and learning—communities that are intentional about the topics to be pursued and the ground rules to be practiced—we need leaders who can call people toward that vision.
>
> Good talk about good teaching is unlikely to happen if presidents and principals, deans and department chairs . . . do not expect it and invite it into being. . . . This kind of leadership . . . involves offering people excuses and permission to do things that they want to do but cannot initiate themselves. . . . . (p. 156)

Palmer (1998) continues:

> Becoming a leader of that sort—one who opens, rather than occupies, space—requires [an] "inner journey" . . . beyond fear into authentic self-hood, a journey toward respecting otherness and understanding how committed and resourceful we all are.
>
> As those inner qualities deepen, the leader becomes better able to open spaces in which people feel invited to create communities of mutual support. . . . [L]eaders call us back to the heart of teaching and learning, to the work we share and to the shared passion behind that work. (p. 161)

Lee Bolman and Terry Deal (1995) in *Leading with Soul* confirm Palmer's assertion, "Leadership is a relation rooted in community" (p. 56) whose essence is "not giving things or even providing visions, it is offering one's self and one's spirit" (p. 102).

As leaders, we have been trying to fix the parts. We now realize we must first change the way we think and relate with one another. We must create a new way of seeing and being in the world and this will cause us to change what we do. We must take our metaphor for leading, not from a machine but from the biology of living systems in the natural world.

As leaders, we must seek to gain insight from the paradoxes that continuously confront our systems. We must:

- Create comfort with ambiguity.
- Create opportunities to allow energy, information, and the human spirit to flow within and throughout the system by facilitating authentic dialogue about teaching and learning.
- Promote diversity of all kinds.
- Establish communal relationships of meaning by inviting the hearts and souls of people into the learning environment.
- Look for patterns and relationships and explicitly identify and name them in order to promote the organization's sense of self and integrity.
- Celebrate the power of community and the human spirit.
- Create common language to build common meaning.
- Create trusting, responsible, and lovable learning communities.

For leaders in innovative schools, our role is not to control but to facilitate authentic learning by creating conversations that matter—conversations of community that invite the entire organization into shaping its future and into answering questions:

1. What is possible now?
2. What do we want to be in the world?
3. How can the world be different because of us?

Until recently, threats to organizational survival were largely external in nature and driven by precipitous events that leaders could strategically defend against. Now our threats are mostly internal, and their dynamic and systematic complexity requires leaders who can think and act in integrated, systematic, and spiritful ways.

The vision of educational leadership for innovative schools has changed from knowing what to do in order to control and manage to knowing how to live in order to unleash the synergy of the system. This is both our greatest challenge and our greatest opportunity.

We need courageous leaders who can think and act in integrative, systematic, and soulful ways and who are not afraid to create transformational learning communities that learn their way into the future by inviting and engaging in development of the fullness of human capacity.

on education. New reforms must prove themselves in the classroom, and when successful they must be woven into the basic fabric of the school and school district (Cunningham & Gresso, 1993; Elmore, Peterson, & McCarthy, 1996; Goerty, Floden, & Oday, 1996; Murphy, 1991; Murphy & Hallinger, 1993) (for more information see nctaf.org).

INNOVATIVE PROGRAMS

One approach, called *comprehensive school reform (CSR)*, seeks to improve student performance by addressing and aligning all aspects of the school's operations using the guiding philosophy, vision, and practices of a specific model. These models typically bring a clear blueprint for how the school should be operated in regard to standards, curriculum, and instructional practices. Interest in this approach grew in 1998 when Congress appropriated $150 million for the CSR demonstration program presently called the CSR Program (CSRP), now under Title I of the NCLB Act. NCLB/CSRP encourages schools to adopt an established, scientifically based reform model.

According to Borman, Hewes, Overman, and Brown (2003), "Schools that implement CSR models for 5 years or more showed particularly strong effects, and the benefits were consistent across schools of varying poverty levels" (p. 125). These programs have now been implemented in thousands of schools serving millions of students and can be transported to schools throughout the United States. In many cases, the developer provides professional development, technical support, curricular materials, performance assessment, pedagogical practices, and so on to help educators successfully implement the philosophy and/or programs.

The U.S. Department of Education (2003) defines CSR on the basis of the following eleven components:

1. Employs proven methods for student learning, teaching, and school management that are founded on scientifically based research and effective practices and have been replicated successfully in schools

2. Integrates instruction, assessment, classroom management, professional development, parental involvement, and school management
3. Provides high-quality and continuous teacher and staff professional development and training
4. Includes measurable goals for student academic achievement and establishes benchmarks for meeting those goals
5. Is supported by teachers, principals, administrators, and other staff throughout the school
6. Provides support for teachers, principals, administrators, and other school staff by creating shared leadership and a broad base of responsibility for reform efforts
7. Provides for the meaningful involvement of parents and the local community in planning, implementing, and evaluating school improvement activities
8. Uses high-quality external technical support and assistance from an entity that has experience and expertise in schoolwide reform and improvement, which may include an institution of higher education
9. Includes a plan for the annual evaluation of the implementation of the school reforms and the student results achieved
10. Identifies the available federal, state, local, and private financial and other resources that schools can use to coordinate services that support and sustain the school reform effort
11. Meets one of the following requirements: Either the program has been found, through scientifically based research, to significantly improve the academic achievement of participating students, or strong evidence has shown that the program will significantly improve the academic achievement of participating children.

Borman and colleagues (2003) completed a meta-analysis of 29 CSR models examining the costs of the programs and their effectiveness. They found the strongest evidence for: Direct Instruction, the School Development Program, and Success for All. Showing promising evidence were: the Accelerated School Project, America's Choice School Design, Atlas Communities, the Expeditionary Learning Outward Bound, and Roots and Wings. Showing some possible evidence were: Montessori, Paideia, and Talent Development High Schools. The remaining seventeen programs showed little evidence and the authors called for more research to be conducted on those models before they are adopted by other schools. Some of the conclusions that they drew from their analysis are the following:

- Effects of CSR appear greater than effects of other interventions.
- Models meeting the highest standard are the only CSR models to succeed across varying contexts and study designs and to be expected to improve test scores.

- The strong effect after the fifth year of implementation can be explained by cumulative impact or self-selection artifacts.

These researchers concluded:

> We challenge the developers and the educational research community to make a long-term commitment to research-proven educational reform and to establish a marketplace of scientifically based models capable of bringing comprehensive reform to the nation's schools. (pp. 169–170)

EVIDENCE-BASED EDUCATIONAL REFORM

Identifying and selecting a comprehensive school reform model can be a challenging undertaking. A good place to begin is by reviewing the research at these two websites:

Institute for Education Sciences's What Works Clearinghouse (ies.ed.gov/ncee/wwc/).

> The What Works Clearinghouse (WWC) quick reviews provide education practitioners and policymakers with timely and objective assessments of the quality of the research evidence from recently released research papers and reports. These reviews focus on studies of the effectiveness of education or school-based interventions serving students in grades Pk-12, as well as those in a post-secondary setting.

Data-Driven Reform in Education (CDDRE)

The Best Evidence Encyclopedia is a free Web site created by the Johns Hopkins University School of Education's Center for Data-Driven Reform in Education (CDDRE) under funding from the Institute of Education Sciences, U.S. Department of Education. It is intended to give educators and researchers fair and practical information about the strength of the evidence supporting a variety of programs available for students in grades K–12. The Best Evidence Encyclopedia provides summaries of scientific reviews produced by many authors and organizations, as well as links to the full texts of each review (bestevidence.org/).

There are many prominent efforts to improve classroom and schoolwide instruction. Some of the leading initiatives and programs include:

Accelerated Schools Project (K–8), H. Levin.   A schoolwide reform model, the Accelerated Schools Project (ASP) is based on the notion that students in at-risk situations can learn at an accelerated pace by offering enriched curricula and instruction similar to that used for gifted education. ASP was designed as an inquiry-based professional development model with a clearly articulated philosophical base, which encourages active and reflective experimentation and evaluation. Training and training materials provided (acceleratedschools .net).

Association for Direct Instruction (K–6).   The Association for Direct Instruction emphasizes carefully planned lessons that are designed around a highly specific knowledge base and a well-defined set of skills (adihome.org).

Coalition of Essential Schools (K–12), T. Sizer.   The Coalition of Essential Schools (CES) features a set of "common principles," interdisciplinary instruction, authentic projects, and mastery that are intended to be used by schools to shape their own reform efforts (essentialschools.org).

Core Knowledge (K–8), E. Hirsch.   Core Knowledge is based on the premise that to function well in society, people need a common base of knowledge. Schools are responsible for providing this knowledge to students. Curriculum guidelines are provided (coreknowledge.org).

Development Studies Center (K–6).   The Development Studies Center (DSC) promotes children's academic, ethical, and social development by helping schools and after-school programs become caring, inclusive communities and stimulating, supportive places in which to learn. DSC has developed evidence-based programs for in-school and out-of-school use. Professional development is provided (devstu.org).

Edison Schools (K–12).   Edison establishes partnership schools with the school district or charter schools and provides an educational program, technology plan, Success for All, and management system. Curriculum materials are provided (edisonlearning.com).

Expeditionary Learning (K–12).   Expeditionary Learning is based on two central ideas: Students learn better by doing, not listening, and developing character, high expectations, authentic projects, and a sense of community is as important as academic skills (elschools.org).

Foxfire Fund (K–12).   The Foxfire Funds' "Core Practices" guide instructional methods, materials, and strategies and encourage active, learner-centered, community-focused education (foxfire.org).

High Schools That Work (9–12), SREB.   High Schools That Work is designed to raise the academic achievement of career-bound high school students by upgrading the academic core and combining content of college prep studies with vocational studies (sreb.org/page/1078/high_schools_that_work.html).

High Scope (K–3).   High Scope works to improve children's problem-solving and independent-thinking skills. It is based on the belief that children should be active participants in their own learning. It features manipulatives, learning centers, portfolio assessment, and so on (highscope.org).

International Baccalaureate (Ages 3–19).   International Baccalaureate (IB) programs can be found in 140 countries and include: Primary Years Program (PYP), Middle Years Program (MYP) and IB Diploma Program.

IB curricula help develop the intellectual, personal, emotional, and social skills to live, learn, and work in a rapidly globalizing world (ibo.org/).

Literacy Collaborative, Ohio State University.   A schoolwide restructuring model that focuses on classroom-based instruction, depending on Reading Recovery as a "safety net" for those students still not succeeding. Developed by the Reading Recovery program at Ohio State, the Literacy Collaborative (LC) provides support for students who are not receiving RR. LC involves the whole school—especially teachers and families—in a comprehensive and reflective approach to literacy instruction, which is appropriate for all children (lcosu.org).

Linked Learning (Secondary).   Linked learning connects strong academic with real-world experience in a wide range of fields, such as engineering, media and the arts, and biomedical and health sciences—helping students gain an advantage in high school, college, and career. This integrated approach helps students build a strong foundation of success for college, career, and in life (connectedcalifornia.org).

MicroSociety (K–8).   MicroSociety provides its network schools, after-school community centers, summer programs, and multi-site initiatives with a comprehensive range of services and support programs. Students collaborate with parents, teachers, and community members to create a community of commerce and governance; children create and manage business ventures that produce goods and services (microsociety.org).

Montessori (Primarily Early Childhood).   Montessori incorporates the understanding of children's natural tendencies as they unfold in specific multiage group environments. The curriculum is interdisciplinary and active (montessori .edu).

National Institute for Direct Instruction (K–6).   Direct Instruction provides reading, language arts, and math curricula along with highly scripted lesson strategies, extensive writing, highly interactive lessons, flexible grouping, and frequent assessments so that by 5th grade, students are at least a year and a half beyond grade level (nifdi.org).

Paideia (K–12), M. Adler.   The Paideia Model changes classroom practice through three "columns" of instruction: didactic teaching, coaching, and Socratic seminars (paideia.org).

Reading Recovery, Ohio State University.   Reading Recovery (RR) is a pullout, one-on-one reading intervention for the lowest achieving students in 1st grade (i.e., the lowest 20%). RR is designed to bring those students up to grade level. The intervention helps children make the difficult transition from decoding to comprehension (readingrecovery.org).

Reggio Emilia (Primarily Early Childhood).   Reggio Emilia is an educational philosophy focused on preschool and primary education. The model is built on the principles of respect, responsibility, and community through exploration and discovery in a supportive and enriching environment based on the interests of the children through a self-guided curriculum (reggioalliance.org/).

Roots and Wings (Pre-K–8), R. Slavin.   Used in conjunction with the Success for All reading program, Roots and Wings seeks to improve academic achievement in elementary schools, using prescribed curriculum, integrated science and social studies, cooperative learning, and support teams. Materials are provided (successforall.net).

School Development Program (K–8).   Based on the theory that children learn better when they form strong relationships with adults, this program aspires to develop personal, social, and moral strengths in students. Training, manuals, and teaching materials are provided (schooldevelopmentprogram.org).

School of One (Middle/Intermediate Schools).   Currently part of the New York City Department of Education, the School of One identifies the specific academic needs of every student and then accesses a large bank of carefully reviewed educational resources, and uses sophisticated technology to find the best matches among students, teachers, and resources. Currently, the model is only used in mathematics (schoolofone.org/).

Success for All (Pre-K–8), R. Slavin.   The Success for All (SFA) Pre-K–8 program strives to ensure students' success in reading through nine components, such as a prescribed curriculum, cooperative learning, family support, and one-on-one tutoring. It involves a comprehensive school-restructuring process designed for schools with large populations at risk for learning failure. SFA balances a skills-oriented instructional approach with a heavy emphasis on collaboration and teamwork among educators (successforall.net).

Talent Development High School (9–12).   Talent Development High School aims to reorganize students and teachers in a school and to focus instruction on students' academic needs and career interests by dividing large urban high schools into smaller units (mdrc.org/publications/408/execsum.html).

Additionally, many of these programs offer after-school activities for all children to further supplement regular classroom work (Slavin, Madden, Dolan, & Waskik, 1996). Another possible theme is the creation of an inviting, engaging school climate that begins with teachers earning the trust and respect of their students' families and welcoming and supporting students in the classroom (Comer, Joyner, & Haynes, 1996). Schools are improved by increasing parental presence and through the use of child-centered concepts and beliefs for all students. Other factors include applying action research; increasing instructional time and student engagement; aligning curriculum, instruction, and assessments; and using a developmental approach.

Generalizing, finding new examples, carrying out applications, working through understanding, performances, and other activities press learners to think well beyond what they already know (Gardner, 1993). Learning is often structured around consequences, impacts, dramatizations, connectability, relationships, insights, and responsibilities, which help to induce understanding.

Rubrics and portfolios provide examples of ongoing assessment throughout the learning process to support reflective activities. The emphasis is on students' active engagement with teachers in the assessment of their own and classmates' work. Thus, use of generative topics, an understanding of goals and performances, and ongoing assessment are the core elements of all teaching for understanding (Gardner & Boix-Mansilla, 1994; Perkins & Blythe, 1994; Simmons, 1994).

Other Innovative Models and Their Benefits

This brief overview of prominent national programs and initiatives provides limited information on a few of the major reform efforts existing in the United States today. There are numerous other efforts under way, including John Goodlad's School Renewal Project, Phillip Schlechty's Center for Transforming America's Schools, Dorothy Rich's Mega Skills, Lawrence Lezotte's Effective Schools, and William Spady's Transformational Approach to Outcome-Based Education, among others.

In evaluating some of these schoolwide reform models, Fashola and Slavin (1998) conclude that:

> It is apparent from the discussion of the currently available schoolwide reform models that much more research is needed to make available a substantial "shelf" of proven models. Yet what we do know now is that schools need not start from scratch in designing effective schoolwide plans. A wide array of promising programs are available, backed up by national networks of trainers, fellow users, materials, assessment and other resources. . . . Once a school has chosen to affiliate with a national program, it can then work out how to implement the national

model with integrity, intelligence, and sensitivity to local needs and circumstances. (p. 378)

Before adopting any new model or initiative, it is essential to ensure it has a strong evidence/research base. Once the reform is selected and implemented, the key issue regarding any reform is whether it lasts over time and becomes institutionalized or embedded into the structure and norms of the organization. Shifting district and state policies and priorities often cause the abandonment of reforms. Less structured reforms that place fewer demands on the system and its resources seem to fare better in regard to sustainability. But this begs the question of whether smaller focused initiatives result in greater student learning. Datnow (2005) found that "if a school is not planning on sticking with a reform for long, it is perhaps best not to start at all. Teachers become frustrated with the endless cycle of reforms that progress through schools and, over time, become increasingly skeptical of them" (p. 148).

> ✳ **Using the criteria developed earlier, select a comprehensive school reform model and provide a rationale for why this model was chosen.**

USING EVIDENCE-BASED STRATEGIES TO BUILD A MODEL OF TEACHING AND LEARNING

The previous section described Comprehensive Reform Models. Embedded in those models are many teaching and learning strategies that are key to the success of those models. This section describes those strategies that the research evidence has found to be of significant importance in improving academic achievement.

The Evidence-Based Teaching and Learning Strategies

A key question for a school leader to ask is—what teaching and learning instructional strategies should I be promoting in my school? And, where do I find the evidence that these strategies will result in greater student achievement? There are several good references, however, Hattie's book *Visible Learning: A Synthesis of Over 800 Meta-analyses Relating to Achievement* (2009) is the most comprehensive reference to date. This excellent book describes the evidence of the contributions to learning from: the child, home, school, curricula, teacher, and approaches to teaching. For example, Hattie's analysis of the research findings points out that a *whole language* approach to reading instruction "has negligible effects on learning to read" (p. 139), while Hattie's analysis supports the conclusions of the National Reading Panel's report (2000) that phonics instruction is a powerful approach to teaching children to read.

A FRAMEWORK FOR SCHOOL IMPROVEMENT

CARL GLICKMAN, LEW ALLEN, AND JAMES WEISS
The University of Georgia

School leaders need to ensure that the focus, structure, and process of their work with faculty and staff is always focused on teaching and learning. In more than a decade of successful collaborations with more than 100 K–12 public schools (The League of Professional Schools), we have found that a commitment to the beliefs and practices of democracy in learning and in governance is essential. This is accomplished through a three-part framework.

The framework consists of a covenant of teaching and learning, a shared governance process, and an action research process. The goal of implementing this three-part framework is to create a school that is a self-renewing learning community that is focused on students. All three parts of the framework are of equal importance; neglect of any one will greatly compromise a school's efforts.

COVENANT OF TEACHING AND LEARNING

A covenant captures the beliefs that people in a school and its immediate community hold about exemplary teaching and learning. A school's goals, objectives, activities, curriculum, and instructional practices are filtered through the question: Are they within the letter and spirit of our covenant?

A covenant of teaching and learning allows a school to embrace certain instructional practices that are consistent with the beliefs of the school community, as well as to discern practices that are not. Without a covenant to help define and clarify a school's beliefs and practices, the collective energy of the individuals in the school is often fragmented or focused on the immediate issues of the day rather than on what all would agree, in their more reflective moments, should be done to achieve the long-term goals of the school community.

It is important that a covenant of teaching and learning reflect the voices of everyone in the school. The collegial discussions and deep reflections about teaching and learning that go into creating a covenant are crucial. A covenant written in isolation deprives those not involved of the experience of participating in a collegial dialogue about their deeply held, and often unexamined, beliefs about teaching and learning. A covenant that does not reflect all voices in the school will not likely serve as a guide to people's work.

SHARED GOVERNANCE

Shared governance is the process through which people democratically decide how to bring the covenant to life in the school. The shared governance process includes agreements as to how decisions are made and which roles will be assumed by administrators, teachers, staff, students, parents, and community members. Defining the structure and composition of decision-making bodies and the process by which decisions are made are crucial components. Time and energy must be taken to ensure that everyone understands the rules so that all can benefit from them. Rules of governance must be democratically established before decisions are made, not as decisions are being made.

A clearly written shared governance model that lays out how decisions are to be made ensures that all in the school know the rules, and the processes and procedures will not change on the whims of a few or for expediency. Schools trying to implement a new decision-making process sometimes find themselves with two decision-making processes functioning at once: the old process and the new process. Creating a specific shared governance model can help a school pick its way through this difficult transition.

(*continued*)

ACTION RESEARCH

Action research can first help a school identify, clarify, plan, and evaluate actions that will bring the beliefs articulated in its covenant to life. A school's ability to bring about school-wide renewal that benefits students is closely tied to its capacity to study and reflect on how its practices are affecting students.

Staying focused on student goals is remarkably difficult. It is easier to document whether programs, new initiatives, or new structures have been put in place than it is to study what is happening to students. For example, it is much easier to study whether teachers are using more cooperative learning techniques in their classrooms than it is to gather data on the effects that cooperative learning is having on students. An action research process that is focused on students can help keep a school on track while informing the decision-making process as to what is working and what needs further attention.

SUMMARY

A school renewal framework will provide a school with a structure that allows it to define for itself where it wants to go (covenant), how it wants to get there (shared governance), and how it will know if it is making progress (action research). Everyone in the school is systematically and collegially learning about and getting better at creating experiences for students that support this concept. Teachers are part of a community of learners working together to bring about a common vision of what their school is all about.

Charter Schools

Forty states have authorized the creation of charter schools, which provide a publicly funded alternative to traditional schools. In 2011, there were more than 5,200 charter schools operating in more than 40 states serving more than 1 million students (National Alliance for Public Charter Schools, 2011). Charters allow these schools some degree of exemption from normal regulations and encourage innovation and experimentation with curriculum and instructors. This movement has generated heated debate as to whether it will actually improve student achievement. Advocates argue that freeing schools from the bureaucratic stranglehold of policies, procedures, and standard operating practices (SOP) will give administrators and teachers the flexibility to improve schools through innovation. Opponents are concerned that funds will be siphoned off to these schools in an effort to increase privatization of American education and ultimately benefit the wealthy and harm the middle class and poor. Only about 10% of the charter schools nationally are managed by private companies, but most charter proponents are excited about opening education to competition in the marketplace. The NCLB legislation only allows children in failing schools to attend publicly funded charter schools.

Public charter schools often operate in partnership with nonprofit, for-profit, and public organizations that provide resources to help the schools improve. There have been a number of success stories regarding these charter schools, although the jury is still out on the overall success of charter schools (Ferrero, 2006; Lubienski, 2003). The National Assessment Governing Board (2004) found that on average, charter school students scored lower on NAEP assessments than did students in traditional public schools, particularly students eligible for free and reduced-priced lunches. Lubienski (2003) calls into question the expectations that charter schools will actually result in innovations in classroom instruction. Regardless of the initial findings, there is still strong national support for charter schools.

One of the more recent developments is the virtual school. Although there are numerous definitions of virtual schools, we define a virtual school as an educational organization that offers K–12 courses using Internet or web-based methods. Virtual schools began at the secondary level but are now operating at K–12 levels, often supplementing instruction in rural and small schools.

In 2001, 14 states allowed statewide virtual charter schools (Clark, 2001). By 2008, that number increased to 25 states having virtual schools (Christensen, Johnson, & Horn, 2008). Virtual schools can typically enroll students statewide and can become a choice option for students attending failing schools. In 2000, there were fewer than a dozen virtual schools; by 2006, this figure grew to about 200. The National Center for Education Statistics estimates that 36% of all school districts offer some kind of virtual learning activities (Revenaugh, 2006). West Ed estimated that 40,000 to 50,000 students were enrolled in online courses in 2001–2002. Christensen, Johnson, & Horn in their bestselling book, *Disrupting Class,* noted that by 2008 more than 1 million students were enrolled in blended or fully online courses. They predict, ". . . that by 2019 about 50 percent of high school courses will be delivered online" (p. 98).

Virtual schools use computer-based learning to deliver personal education programs through synchronous and asynchronous learning systems that are provided through the Internet. Students can work independently at times and at other times interact directly with the teachers, ask questions, and talk with other students. The system is designed to serve "highly motivated independent learners." The schools have proved to be highly controversial and the disputes regarding them are largely unresolved (Huerta & Gonzalez, 2006).

Using the Web in Pre-K–12 Education

According to the National Center for Education Statistics (NCES, 2003), 99% of public schools in 2001 had access to the Internet (big6.com; ala.org). All students, however, do not have the same level of access to technology. According to 2002 statistics from NCES, this digital divide means that while 66% of Caucasian and Asian children have easy access to technology, just 45% of African-American children and 37% of Hispanic youth have this same access. A major challenge for administrators will be to expand the use of technology in instruction and to narrow the digital divide. Quite often, searching on the Web is incorporated into classroom projects; however, a major problem is the selection of good sites. Agosto (2002) found that students are not apt to work at getting high-quality information but to quickly choose the first information that they find related to their topics. Kuiper, Volman, and Terwell (2005) state "the literature therefore argues strongly for using the Web in the context of inquiry activities. In this way the Web serves a function in the curriculum, and children learn that finding information on the Web is not an objective in itself. Specific attention must be paid to learning to assess the relevance and reliability of information" (p. 326).

Students also have access to external resources such as museums, subject-matter experts, out-of-state peers, the Library of Congress, and other resources to improve the quality of learning within the school (see blogger.com; edublogs.org; schoolblogs.com; seedwiki.com; kidsclick.org; turnitin.com; noodletools.com). Success is related to how well students translate a query into keywords and combine keywords, how well they can make quick decisions about locating quality in the vast information that they find, and how well they can use the information to answer specific questions. Jones (2002) believes that students need opportunities to access preselected sites as well as to freely search the Web. In all cases, support from the teacher is absolutely essential.

Librarians may have an expanded role as they grow in their understanding of specific student needs and become familiar with related online resources—subject-specific search engines, databases, references, catalogs, links, and so on. They will be responsible for creating virtual libraries with easy access. Pathfinders can be used to lay out pathways—keywords, concepts, questions, sites, media, blogs, wikis—to help students find information for particular assignments (see ipl.org/div/pf/).

* **Would a charter school be an appropriate option for reforming Milton Middle School? Why or why not?**

REFORM AND INNOVATION IN THE NEXT DECADE

A sea change is taking place in both Pre-K–12 and higher education. Many factors are coalescing and are having an enormous impact on the traditional public school as it existed 25 or 30 years ago. At that time, there were basically two options for families to choose from for their children—public and private schools. Today, there are numerous options within public and private schools including virtual, charter, magnet schools, and home schools. With schools having access to the Internet, students and teachers are engaging with the world in a multitude of different ways: from a class in the USA using Skype and a camera to see and talk with a class in Australia, to students synchronously and asynchronously talking with experts in any number of fields about any topic they are investigating. As the costs of public education increase and pressure from numerous stakeholders expressing discontent due to the lack of achievement of too many children grows, more and more options will be made available to children and families.

Educators today have inherited a model that rose in the early part of the 20th century and does not fit a 21st-century world requiring high-quality, customized learning opportunites. The next few years will see the rapid expansion of personalized learning. Personalized learning tailors the curriculum, learning environment, and pedagogy in order to meet the needs of individual learners, often with the extensive use of technology. In order to provide this type of learning to all children, an array of providers and options will dramatically reconfigure Pre-K–12 schooling.

THE LEADERSHIP CHALLENGE

As previously noted, a key issue regarding any reform is whether it lasts over time and becomes institutionalized or embedded into the structure and norms of the organization. And, in fact, many reforms will require significant changes to the structure, pedagogy, and curriculum of schools. Institutionalization can be structural (becomes a concrete part of the standard operating procedures) and/ or cultural (becomes embraced by members of the organization). Does the reform become a part of the fabric of the school or district? Certainly, the timing and conditions—incentives, resources, factions, legacies of prior projects, change process, and so on—must support a reform regardless of the strength or excellence of the reform. Conditions that seem to sustain reform include continuity of leadership, level of stakeholder commitment, degree to which it becomes part of the culture, lack of criticism and/or misunderstanding, principal sponsorship, workability of the reform, early success, policy support, efficacious attitudes toward the reform, central office personnel support, and perhaps most important, its usefulness in meeting students' needs (Datnow, 2005). Datnow (2005) found:

> Educators need to work hard toward the institutionalization of a reform. As the findings of this study make clear, reform sustainability does not come easily; it takes extensive time and effort. If the principal and faculty believe that a reform is working well, they would be well advised to keep district administrators informed about their successes along the way. This can help buffer the school in the face of policy and leadership changes. Finally, it would be wise to choose a reform that can help the school improve on state and district measures of accountability. (p. 148)

Innovations must have constituencies who support them and believe in them if they are to be successful. The chance of these innovations surviving is also increased if the constituency is broad based, including groups like parents, educators, policymakers, and business management. Communication is essential if support is to be developed and sustained. This includes stakeholders meetings, information sharing, ongoing updates, surveys, open forums, and other forms of networking.

One of the major tasks of educational leadership is to build both capacity and creativity within existing organizations. We now know that existing institutions must develop the capacity to envision a desired state of affairs that induces commitment to continuous improvement. As Drucker (1993) points out, "We have learned to innovate because we cannot expect that the accumulated competence, skill, knowledge, product, services and structure of the present will be adequate for very long" (p. 339). In today's world, "staying even" usually results in falling behind and, in many cases, disappearing. In fact, getting ahead often results in "staying even" so organizations must constantly reinvent themselves through innovation and responsiveness. Although the process of innovation is relatively uncomplicated, that does not mean it is easy. It is hard, systematic work.

Fullan (2003) talks about the need to understand "the process of change" while knowing that it is not always either completely understandable or predictable. There are, however, a number of enabling structures that tend to facilitate innovation, entrepreneurship, and continuous improvement. Many researchers have attempted to identify what must be done to facilitate and support the implementation of innovation, what might be called "transformative change."

According to Fullan (2003):

> What this means is that we have to work directly with schools as organizations, and use school districts as local system organizers to create new contexts that do better at student learning precisely because they provide better environments for teacher leaders and school leaders to develop in those organizations. All the way up and down the line we are talking about increasing system capacity. (pp. 105–106)

Improvement and transformation is a process made by individuals first and then by institutions. It is highly personalized as an experience and entails developmental growth in knowledge, feelings, abilities, and skills. It relates to people and capacity first and innovation and implementation second. T. E. Lawrence (1922) states, "All men dream but not equally, those who dream by night, wake in day to find it was wanting, but those who dream by day, dream with their eyes open, so to make it possible" (p. 3). As educators, we must be able to translate our innovation and creativity into improvements in teaching and learning. We must take the sparks of creativity and develop the capacity needed to support actions directed at improving our schools.

Progress occurs when we increase the number of people who conceptualize, believe in, advocate, and practice new transformational approaches. Transformation needs individuals to create innovations and champion their cause. Margaret Mead states, "Never doubt that a small group of thoughtful, committed citizens can change the world. Indeed, it's the only thing that ever has" (interculturalstudies.org/faq.html). Researchers tell us that reformers go through different stages in the innovation and implementation process and have different needs at different stages. Table 3.1 presents a continuous improvement model, which is a good starting point for approaching challenges related to improvements within an organization. The model presents a process often required to achieve success in developing shared vision, problem solving, action, and innovation.

The model brings significant parties together at key points in the planning process, helping them to become educated and make effective decisions and to become partners and develop a sense of ownership. This model focuses on

TABLE 3.1   Steps for Success in Approaching Needed Improvements

(*Note:* Gathering and dispersing information is an essential element for each of the steps discussed below)

PRESENT CONDITION	STEPS TO SUCCESSFUL INNOVATION AND PROBLEM SOLVING	TYPICAL BEHAVIOR
I. There is little recognition or understanding of needed improvement.	Awareness	Build understanding of the challenges to be faced and open up new possibilities.
II. There is a lack of knowledge about the situation and/or possible innovations.	Gather/seek information	Develop the needed knowledge base to begin the planning/renewal process. (This step has to be revisited throughout the effort.)
III. The organization is ready to begin to look at options, approaches, and innovations.	Orientation/ deliberation	Seek out information and learn more about the possible innovations and reforms.
IV. There is a need to begin pruning the options and develop a set of possible solutions.	Narrowing options/ assessment	Develop criteria, assess options and directions to be taken, and develop a universe of acceptable alternatives and approaches.
V. There is a lack of needed input on and support for possible approaches or solutions.	Political support	Assess and work within the power structure to build required support and political allies to help to ensure the success of the innovation finally selected. (This step has to be revisited throughout the effort).
VI. There is a need to make a commitment to one of the options within the possible solution set.	Decision/implementation planning	Narrow the options to the most desirable and supportable option through consensus. Initial development of an implementation plan.
VII. All needed stakeholders are not adequately aligned toward achieving the renewal effort that was selected.	Building shared values and goals	Information is provided to a wide audience so that all involved understand the innovation and realize how it will affect them. The goals, values, and mission are internalized within the organizational culture.

(*continued*)

TABLE 3.1   **Steps for Success in Approaching Needed Improvements (Continued)**

PRESENT CONDITION	STEPS TO SUCCESSFUL INNOVATION AND PROBLEM SOLVING	TYPICAL BEHAVIOR
VIII. People do not have the needed skills to successfully complete the innovation.	Development	The organizational staff members and others are readied and prepared for successful implementation of the innovation. This requires the development of staff members and others.
IX. The innovation is not part of the organization because it has not yet been implemented.	Implement and integrate	The innovation and renewal effort is implemented and obstacles and problems begin to emerge. Efforts are made to make needed modifications and to begin integrating the innovation into the organizational culture and to ensure that it works effectively.
X. The innovation has not become totally effective and is not a systemic part of the organization because it has not been fully embraced.	Refinement and coordination and expanding support	Establish a widespread pattern of use and coordinate the efforts in using the innovation and in making and sharing information regarding performance and refinements. Groups are regularly discussing the innovation as it becomes a part of routine procedure.
XI. Data has not been produced to support the effectiveness of the newly implemented innovation.	Evaluation/reflection	Collect and analyze data to make needed adjustment and to ensure and increase the effectiveness of the innovation. Share and celebrate successes and quickly respond to, learn from, and make needed adjustments regarding failures. (This behavior occurs from step IX through step XII.)
XII. There are new needs that are not being considered in the present operation of the organization.	Refocusing and renewal	Users start to become aware of new problems, new needs, and new opportunities within the very dynamic context in which they operate. The process begins anew.

Source: Based on a model for adopting educational innovation from the Research and Development Department for Teacher Education at the University of Texas at Austin.

developing and involving staff and building the needed commitment to success. It results in a great deal of development as well as a more open, comfortable, and inspiring work environment. Ultimately, it builds a consensus around a needed improvement. It is a starting point in resolving the challenges presented in the vignettes and problem-based learning activities found in this and other textbooks and, more importantly, the real-world challenges of administration.

In continuous improvement and innovation, there is a natural desire to protect the delivery system and the existing culture; the normal response is to restore the old order, rather than to risk the perils of allowing a new order of things to evolve. The evolving idea creates resistance among those who want to stick with what has worked in the past. Moving from the tried and true to a new response to changing educational expectations requires a period of confusion, learning, and inefficiency—in which the courage to move forward is incubated. Paradigm shifts involve dislocation, conflict, and uncertainty. Innovations and new paradigms are nearly always received with coolness, even mockery and hostility.

Those with vested interests will fight the changes, which is understandable. Some of the potential costs of innovation to those with a vested interest in the status quo include:

- Damage to relationships and loss of friends from confrontations
- Challenges to deeply held beliefs
- Feeling of guilt/burnout/dissidence/depression (opening Pandora's box)
- Giving up common practices and values
- Damage to personal identity
- Having to fix mistakes
- Requirement of a lot of blood, sweat, tears, and time

A large part of the innovation process requires winning over the minds and hearts of those involved, and this need exists from the very top of the organization to the very bottom.

Producing deep improvements that last and spread has continued to be a major challenge in education (Hargreaves & Fullan, 1998). Hargreaves and Goodson (2006) found that "standardization is proving to be the ultimate enemy of enduring innovation and sustainable learning communities" (p. 34). There is a difficult balance that must be achieved between sustainable achievements, which are not rigid, and transitory changes that evaporate before they are even fully understood. The complexity of educational improvement is well stated by Hargreaves and Goodson (2006):

> Focusing on and exercising leadership to secure deep learning and not just tested achievement for all students; developing clearer processes and administrative plans that will ease the problems of accelerated leadership succession; engaging with the strengths of teachers' generational missions rather than treating them with administrative disdain as only naive sources of resistance among a degenerating teaching force; finding ways to make teaching and learning more vivid and real

for the increasing number of students in cultural minorities and in poverty; not overinvesting in model schools, magnet schools, or discretionary initiatives to the cost of those around them; turning schools and districts into more activist professional learning communities; retaining standards but refraining from standardization; and, treating history and experience as strengths to be drawn on rather than obstacles to be overcome in the quest for improvement—these are the implications of the Change Over Time Study for securing truly sustainable improvements for all students, that matter, spread, and last. (p. 35)

Continually improving any organization is a very difficult and often stressful undertaking when compared to managing the status quo; however, anxiety and resistance can be decreased and overcome when the objectives, the frames of reference, and the reforms are clarified and have a sense of political support. We already know enough about what future schools need to look like. The challenge is to create an educational model that addresses current knowledge and needs and that the average teacher is capable of implementing (for more information, see techedlab.com/k12.html).

* **Develop a step-by-step implementation plan for the comprehensive school reform for Milton Middle School.**

CONCLUSION

Quantum physics suggests that order is inherent in all living systems, including education. Internal and external forces—whether negative or positive—can disturb and threaten that order or equilibrium. Under proper conditions, the system responds and evolves to a new, improved order, one that is much better suited for the new environment (Wheatley, 1992). Proper conditions suggest that (1) those within the system take advantage of the opportunities or possibilities for renewal and re-creation and (2) the entire system is allowed to adapt and improve itself. When the system recognizes that existing ideas do not seem to be working, the system can resist, retreat, tune out, tighten control, increase rigidity, and intensify traditions, or the system can regenerate, reform, renew, reconfigure, and re-create itself to better suit its new environment. Linda Darling-Hammond (1997) maintains:

> It is critical to remember that reform is never completed because everyone continually changes and everyone continually learns, experiencing fresh insights from practices, from research, and from the synergy of teachers, administrators, students, parents, and others inquiring together. Although policy supports are essential, reform can never be enforced from the top down, because people must create change in locally appropriate ways at the school and classroom levels. The importance of both context and commitment mean that local invention must be supported by policies that provide a mix of top-down support and bottom-up initiatives. (pp. 336–337)

Baseball Hall of Famer Casey Stengel once advised, "If the horse you're riding dies, it's best if you get off." Traditional education seems to be dying a slow death, and perhaps it is time to get off, or else students could be locked into the 21st century with 20th century skills and behaviors. The call is for educators to rethink education and to create new, more effective paradigms that improve the entire system. Box 3.2 presents the implications of this call for our future leaders (see also Chapters 6 and 7).

Educational leaders need to use direction and alignment to build a culture of visionaries, to encourage risk taking and experimentation, to set the pace, and to lead by example. They must discuss and translate knowledge and research for excellent schools. We must ignite the spark of individual and group genius required to really make a difference in education.

BOX 3.2

IMPLICATIONS FOR LEADERS

WE NEED TO

Have a positive impact on student learning and the classroom.
Connect district, school, and staff development plans.
Encourage bold and creative undertakings.
Provide vision and encouragement (take the long view).
Ensure adequate resources.
Rethink and re-create schools.
Keep everyone informed about research and practice.
Attract powerful constituents for support.
Make technology a driving force (an integral part of school reform).
Measure performance.
Implement improved approaches.

MyEdLeadershipLab™

Go to Topic 2: *Human Resources* in the MyEdLeadershipLab™ site (www.MyEdLeadershipLab .com) for *Educational Leadership: A Bridge to Improved Practice*, Fifth Edition, where you can:

- Find learning outcomes for *Human Resources* along with the national standards that connect to these outcomes.
- Complete Assignments and Activities that can help you more deeply understand the chapter content.
- Apply and practice your understanding of the core skills identified in the chapter with the Building Leadership Skills unit.
- Prepare yourself for professional certification with a Practice for Certification quiz.

PORTFOLIO ARTIFACTS

- Select an innovative program that you find of interest and join the network. Become an expert on that program, and begin to experiment with it in your existing setting.

- Visit the VOPOD website (http://vodpod.com/tag/education+reform) which lists dozens of the latest videos on education reform. Select one and share your review of it with a colleague.

- Videotape innovative classrooms in different school districts. Lead a group discussion to evaluate the effectiveness of the approaches appearing on the videotape.

- Integrate a current technology you have not used before into your present work setting.

- View the video case studies at http://sites.sandiego.edu/globaleducation/home/. They are of different teachers and students at various levels and types of schools. Talk with another student in your university class about one of the video cases and the role of global education in K–12 classrooms.

- Explore the Institute of Education Sciences "What Works Clearinghouse." Select one topic (e.g., dropout prevention programs) and review the summaries of the research evidence (http://ies.ed.gov/ncee/wwc/).

KEY TERMS

- Active learning
- Authentic learning
- Charter school
- Comprehensive school reform (CSR)
- Data warehousing
- Direct instruction
- Evidence based
- Home schools
- Interdisciplinary
- Magnet school
- Virtual school

SUGGESTED READINGS

Bain, A. (2007). *The self-organizing school: Next generation comprehensive school reforms*. Lanham, MD: Rowman & Littlefield Education.

Barnett, B., & the Teacher Solutions 2030 Team. (2011). *Teaching 2030: What we must do for our students and our public schools.* New York, NY: Teachers College Press.

Boix Mansilla, V., & Jackson, A. (2011). *Educating for global competence: Preparing our youth to engage the world.* New York: CCSSO & and the Asia Society.

Chen, M. (2010). *Education nation: Six leading edges of innovation in our schools.* San Francisco, CA: Jossey-Bass.

Egan, K. (2008*). The future of education: Reimagining our schools from the ground up.* New Haven, CA: Yale University Press.

Hess, F. M., & Manno, B. V. (Eds.). (2011). *Customized schooling: Beyond whole-school reform.* Cambridge, MA: Harvard Education Press.

MEDIA RECOMMENDATION

The VOPOD website (http://vodpod.com/tag/education+reform) lists dozens of the latest videos on education reform.

CHAPTER 4

SCHOOL DISTRICT ORGANIZATIONAL STRUCTURE AND LEADERSHIP

MyEdLeadershipLab™

Visit the MyEdLeadershipLab™ site for *Educational Leadership: A Bridge to Improved Practice,* Fifth Edition to enhance your understanding of chapter concepts. You'll have the opportunity to practice your skills through video- and case-based Assignments and Activities as well as Building Leadership Skills units, and to prepare for your certification exam with Practice for Certification quizzes.

SKY RANCH SCHOOL

Data Disaggregation: Building an Excellent School

You are the new principal of the 1,100-student Sky Ranch School. Sky Ranch was rezoned 5 years ago, which created a significant shift in the population attending the school. You are the third principal in this 5-year period and the school has not really recovered from the change in demographics. You have had the entire summer to meet staff, disaggregate data, meet with community members, and basically learn as much as possible about Sky Ranch School.

Listed as "Accredited with Warning," it did not make adequate yearly progress last year. In fact, state test scores have been declining for at least 5 years. The faculty insists on continuing to give the Scientific Research Associates (SRA) standardized achievement test. Last year, there were no PTA meetings scheduled due to the very low attendance in the past 2 years at similar meetings. You have studied the following tables of data concerning the school and students.

SCHOOL/STUDENT DEMOGRAPHICS	LAST YEAR	6 YEARS AGO
Number of students	1,100	999
Number of assistant principals	3	2
Number of counselors	2	2
Percent on free and reduced lunch	69%	35%
Percent eligible for special education	41%	15%
Number of office referrals	1,573	422
Number of suspensions (1–5 days)	459	38
Number of suspensions (6–10 days)	216	22
Number of suspensions (> 10 days)	55	10
Percent of white students	31	78
Percent of black students	48	22
Percent of Hispanic students	20	0
Percent of other ethnicity	1	0

STUDENT SRA TEST DATA BY PERCENTILE	PREVIOUS YEAR PERCENTAGES	6 YEARS PREVIOUS PERCENTAGES
0–10th percentile	13	0
11–20th percentile	17	4
21–30th percentile	14	4
31–40th percentile	11	6
41–50th percentile	9	9
51–60th percentile	7	14
61–70th percentile	9	20
71–80th percentile	10	17
81–90th percentile	8	18
91–100th percentile	2	8
Percent of students reading below grade level	62	

FACULTY DATA	CURRENT YEAR
Credentialed teachers	72%
Provisionally licensed teachers	28%
Average teacher age	46 years
Average experience at the school	19 years
Master's degree (or above)	10%
White teachers	87%
Minority teachers	13%
Teacher turnover	14%

Only about 15% of the teachers showed up at the reception welcoming you to the school. The teachers have had the responsibility for assigning students to classes each summer. Ability grouping persists. Lower student–teacher ratios exist in high-ability classes, and higher student–teacher ratios exist in lower ability classes. A large number of teachers rely on textbooks, do not differentiate instruction, and have only a sprinkling of hands-on activities. The teachers with master's degrees teach upper-level students.

Several newer teachers approached you during the summer and expressed hope that you will change the school. They mention that the curriculum and the teaching methods have not been revised in more than 10 years, even though the student body has very different needs. They ask for your help. During the first week of school, you learn that the assistant principal has been having difficulty locating substitutes and is especially concerned because the English department chair had a death in the family and will be out for over a week. You also have three emergency parent meetings and a serious discipline problem related to extreme violent behavior that may result in an expulsion hearing, requiring immediate attention. Besides a number of scheduling problems that need immediate action to get students assigned to appropriate classes, your bookkeeper wants to meet regarding a negative balance on the books that seems to be carried over from previous years, overlooked because the books were not audited for a couple of years. She also reminds you of the districtwide meeting of the health committee, on which you serve, later that afternoon. The senior custodian has been late to work, neglecting his duties while openly critical of the "impossible expectations that you and the teachers have for the janitorial staff" as well as being very harsh in dealing with his crew.

The previous principals were totally reactive and could never gain control of Sky Ranch or become very proactive. You are beginning to understand the problem. The superintendent is going to be much more involved with this school at the request of the school board, who want quarterly reports on school progress.

Source: Modified from a case study provided by William A. Owings, Old Dominion University, and Leslie S. Kaplan, Newport News Public Schools.

✳ **Do you as Sky Ranch principal have the needed authority from the appropriate sources to begin a reform effort? Whose assistance and support might you seek?**

RECENT FEDERAL INVOLVEMENT AND DIRECTION

The conservative right's agenda for public education tends to argue that local control and local school boards have caused many of the problems in public education. They see the need for the federal government to take greater control of the nation's schools through the establishment of national standards, expansion of national testing, elimination of teacher tenure and pensions, tying of teacher pay to teacher performance, extended school years, and the center piece, privatization of public schools. There is a growing number of citizens who believe that public education is obsolete and should be dismantled and replaced by entrepreneurship and a completely choice type system. The arguments used are that the free market system and consumer choice are the only mechanisms that will raise student achievement in this nation. In this way, good schools would thrive and bad schools would go out of business.

Ravitch (2010) argues, however, that education is a public good that government has a legal, moral, and social responsibility to provide to its citizens. She states:

> In the history of American education, crisis talk is cheap. Those who talk crisis usually have a cure that they want to promote, and they prefer to keep us focused on the dimensions of the "crisis" without looking too closely at their proposed cure. . . . The local school boards are the first line of defense for public education. Critics know this. . . . Some localities have high achievement, some have low, and the difference is economics and demography, not democracy. There is not a shred of evidence in the research literature that schools improve when democratic governance ends. . . . The business model assumes that democratic governance is a hindrance to effective education. It assumes that competition among schools and teachers produces better results than collaboration. It treats local school boards as a nuisance and an obstacle rather than as the public's representatives in shaping education policy. It assumes that schools can be closed and opened as if they were chain stores rather than vital community institutions. (p. 24)

Arne Duncan, as Secretary of Education, struggled with this exact issue. He states (2009):

> Now that I'm in Washington, I *know* that all of the good ideas don't come out of Washington. The best ideas are always going to come at the local level. So fundamentally, we want to be loose and tight. To become tight on the goals but to allow people to become much more entrepreneurial, much more creative, innovative to get there. (p. 4)

Duncan is worried about the goals because he believes they were "dummied down" at the state level and that, in many places those children who are just meeting the standard are barely able to graduate from high school and absolutely inadequately prepared to go on to a competitive 4-year university, much less graduate. As a result, Secretary Duncan and President Obama have pledged federal money to four central areas of reform that they believe will drive school improvement:

1. Adopt internationally benchmarked standards and assessments that prepare students for success in college and the workplace.
2. Recruit, develop, retain, and reward effective teachers and principals.
3. Build data systems that measure student success and inform teachers and principals how they can improve their practices.
4. Turn around the lowest-performing schools.

The federal government has approved $96.8 billion in discretionary funding provided under the American Recovery and Reinvestment Act of 2009. International research has shown that top-achieving countries have focused, coherent, and rigorous national standards (Schmidt, 2010). America has been moving toward national standards or international benchmark standards for the past quarter century and part of this funding is being used to develop standards and accompanying assessments, although we do not yet know how or by whom. The National Governors Association and the Council of Chief State School Officers have recently taken it upon themselves to develop "common core" standards in reading/writing and math for states to adopt if they like. Efforts have been made to move quickly to get most states to sign an agreement to unite around these common core standards. At this point, this means common content standards for the subject matter need to be taught at each grade level. The next question will be whether the coalition moves on to create a common test for each grade in math and reading and advances to other subject areas. At this stage, there is substantial momentum. The National Assessment Governing Board, which decides what knowledge and skills the National Assessment of Educational Progress (NAEP) should measure, is another possible candidate for the development of national standards and assessments; however, at this time it is not clear what coordinating mechanism might be used.

There is a growing concern that standardized tests are being administered to ELL children who do not speak English and thus cannot pass the tests. This has negative consequences for the child, the school, and the district. This is another issue that is being considered regarding any national standardized testing that is being developed. Illinois is one of several states to receive federal funds in 2009 to study this issue and to improve test validity for ELL students. The 23-state World-Class Instructional Design and Assessment Consortium (WIDA) is the subcontractor of Illinois' grant and is developing Spanish-language development standards for K–12 students and reliable Spanish-language proficiency-assessment systems for kindergarten students and K–2. Some educators are suggesting that the U.S. Department of Education re-establish the Office of Bilingual Education in order to focus greater attention on the growing needs of this underserved population in American schools.

A major piece of the American Recovery Act and Race to the Top is the support and involvement of the entire community in the effort to improve schools. In urban communities, this has meant the involvement of mayors in this leadership effort. Some cities like New York and Washington have placed the mayor in charge of the schools with the School Board serving in a role automatically endorsing the mayor's wishes. There is a lot of business and political input through the mayor's office and, hopefully, this will generate much broader support for education. These programs have had their share of controversies with community members and some board members expressing concern that the system is not responsive to, or even interested in, local community interests and there have been few standout successes to date. A consistent concern has been that there are no forums in which parents and other members of the public can ask questions and get timely answers. Decisions seem to be made in private within the local power structure and mayor's office. Some argue that in the absence of a school board to oversee the actions of the executive, there is no accountability. When problems develop, it is difficult to determine who is responsible and the schools usually get the lion's share of the blame even for poor policy decisions and problems in implementation. Proponents of local school boards argue that two of the three lowest-performing districts in the nation (Cleveland and Chicago), are controlled by their mayors, while the highest performing districts (Charlotte and Austin) are managed by school boards. Mayoral control, however, has impressed the Obama Administration and Secretary Duncan has strongly endorsed this idea as a means to improve achievement.

The Obama administration sees educational problems as so large, and the needs so great, that everyone in the city needs to rally around the effort. The person that has the highest probability of making that happen is the mayor. The work is so hard in large urban cities with a history of fairly dysfunctional school systems, and the challenges so intractable, that you need leaders who are in a position to mobilize the entire community and exert strong leadership if you hope to improve the quality of teaching and learning within these communities.

> Duncan (2009) suggests that improving American education is ". . . very complex, but it starts with real leadership at the top. You have to have strong, courageous leadership. . . . You have to rally the entire community behind these efforts. I've argued that if it's just the school system by itself trying to get better, you're not going to get there. You need the business community, the philanthropic community, the religious community; you need the not-for-profits, you need the parks and recreation, health and human services. This has to be citywide effort. You cannot have a world-class city without a world-class school system.
>
> You've seen a series of mayors—the mayor of New York, Mayor (Adrian) Fenty here in Washington—provide real leadership at the top to rally an entire city, not just the school district by itself. . . . I can't imagine a more important activity for a city and one that a city can rally behind than dramatically improving the quality of public education. It combines a real sense of self-interest. If you want to attract and retain jobs, you have to have an educated workforce. And the sense of altruism that our children deserve more than what we're giving them. This requires a leader at a higher level within the city; a leader at the mayor level. (p. 25)

Today, many people believe that school boards are past their prime and need elimination or major revision. Supporters say that mayoral control is needed to fill the present void and achieve greater accountability and stability. Michael Bloomberg, mayor of New York City, is a strong opponent of local school boards and local school governance. Supporters of school boards point out that test scores have not improved in cities with mayor takeovers, such as New York City, and that there has been a lack of community oversight and input. The National School Board Association is firmly opposed to mayoral control. The coming decade may well determine if school boards regain their vitality or simply slip further into irrelevance. The future of school boards is not clear but certainly the mayoral model is gaining political momentum. This places school superintendents directly responsible to the mayor or his or her designee. This is probably based on the same type of thinking that believes privately managed charter schools will be better run than public schools. The research to date shows some successes and some failures with this form of thinking. Perhaps the question at this point in time is, "What will educational governance look like?" The answer begins with "what does it look like now?"

LOCAL ORGANIZATIONAL STRUCTURE

We can easily identify the formal structure of an organization and the positions within it by organizational charts and job descriptions. "In addition to defining work roles and authority relations, formal organizations also explicitly define and codify such details as the organization's channels of communication, policies and procedures, and norms and sanctions" (Loveless & Jasin, 1998).

What makes organizations unique are the people who hold these positions, people with unique personalities and approaches to the formal roles and structures provided. As a result, an organization always has visible and invisible aspects. The invisible aspects are often unique to the organization and time, whereas the visible, formal structure is fairly consistent across all organizations and is easier to describe and understand. The formal organization defines the structure in which people work, and the informal organization addresses the less tangible human factors and groupings within an organization.

Even though the formally defined structures do not totally depict reality, being aware of them goes a long way toward helping people understand the operation of an organization. Two important aspects of formal organizational structure are norms and roles. Scott (1992) defines these two elements: "*Norms* are the generalized rules governing behavior that specify, in particular, appropriate means for pursuing goals; and *roles* are expectations for or evaluative standards employed in assessing the behavior of occupants of specific social positions" (p. 16). Scott goes on to say these are "organized so as to constitute a relatively coherent and consistent set of beliefs and prescriptions governing the behavior of participants" (p. 16). There is a constraining nature to organizational structure but also an enabling one that allows humans to accomplish more than they could through randomness and lack of structure. Each member of an organization can produce a larger outcome than he or she would be able to accomplish separately. Organization promotes this synergy effect.

THE LOCAL SCHOOL DIVISION

The primary units of structure for U.S. education are the local school divisions, which number slightly less than 14,000. Across these diverse systems, however, some general structural patterns and issues remain fairly constant. These include authority structures, political patterns, norms, roles, and assignments. Typically, in school divisions, the major layers of responsibility within the organization are school board, superintendent, central office administration, school administration, and instructional staff.

Education is usually the largest single budgetary component of local government and, in total, employs more people than state and federal governments.

The local district operates all the public schools within it and serves as the unit by which the community influences local education. The local school district is a quasi-municipal corporation that serves as an extension of state government and derives its authority from the state. It has a perpetual status, acts as an individual, survives the death of any member, and, as long as officers and employees act in good faith and fraud and collusion are absent, it has limited liabilities.

The school district is set apart from other government bodies in that it has its own board and school governance. Education is a state function, and the local board of education represents the state as well as the residents within the district. The board represents the community interests within statutory and constitutional law. A school district is either fiscally independent or it must gain approval on fiscal matters from some other governing body. Dependent boards can be appointed by the mayor (with the consent of the council) or the board of county supervisors. In many cases, board members are elected by the voting residents within the district. Independent boards must be elected. Most urban districts have dependent school boards. These dependent boards must get prior approval from elected or appointed municipal officials to determine finally and legally the size of the local levy, the tax rate, and the size of the school division budget.

The interface between the superintendent of schools and the school board is critical to the success of the educational program within the district (Carter & Cunningham, 1997). Yet only about half the states' school codes contain language defining the relationship. This lack of legislative guidance has resulted in some confusion about the status, authority, and responsibility of the school board and superintendent of schools. In general, the board is given the freedom to determine the level of trust placed in the superintendent's judgment to guide the direction of schools. School boards leave much of the decision making to the superintendent and school district staff assuming there is no evidence of community concern. It is not that board members are powerless—because they can apply sanctions of far-reaching consequences, including the hiring and firing of the superintendent.

Administrators at the central office and school level are expected to provide leadership and stewardship to ensure that policies, laws, and regulations are adhered to, that effective education occurs, and that desired goals and outcomes are achieved. Central office staff members are typically organized around specific operational areas—finance, pupil personnel, staff personnel, curriculum and instruction, business technology, and logistics—and are considered specialists (staff personnel, discussed in later chapters). Principals, like superintendents, are generalists (line personnel) and are expected to set the tone and develop the culture for the district's schools while meeting accountability requirements. As Elmore (2005) points out, "Policies do not determine whether schools are accountable. In other words, all schools operate with implicit or explicit action theories that determine to whom, for what, and how they are accountable" (p. 24). The culture of the school is established by the leadership. Coherent leadership means that the "alignment of individual values with collective expectations, reinforced by the processes of accountability, results in internal accountability" (Elmore, 2005, p. 25). Internal accountability forms the collective culture in which people will perform.

The concept of line and staff responsibilities grows out of the hierarchical structure that often exists within organizations. Authority (power) and responsibility (obligation) are delegated from the very top of the organization to the bottom. Those serving in line positions are delegated the authority and responsibility required to discharge operational functions. Communications, gradation of power, and relationships are defined by the line between superior and subordinate. Staff authority comes from the need to have experts in specific areas to provide support for line officers. The staff relationship is usually a staff-to-line managerial one that can occur at any level within the school division. The staff concept gives a horizontal dimension to the organization. The line officer typically asks for the assistance of a staff person in helping with a very specific area of responsibility.

* **What are the most pressing issues that need to be addressed? How can you, as principal of Sky Ranch School, be proactive when there are so many individuals involved in decisions that must be addressed to keep the school operating efficiently?**

THE SCHOOL BOARD

Over 95% of the nation's school board members are elected officials chosen by the voters to govern school districts. A third of the nation's districts have five-member boards. Most of the others are evenly divided between seven and nine members. Some large districts have over 20 board members. There are more than 100,000 school board members who are entrusted by the electorate to govern organizations spending many billions of tax dollars. School boards are required to adhere to state statutes and federal laws and regulations. As long as they do so, they remain in office unless turned out by the electorate at the polls. School boards who violate the dictates of public opinion for a period of time are generally removed when levels of dissatisfaction become pronounced.

Diversity is a term that appropriately applies to U.S. school boards. Over 4,000 school districts have fewer than 400 students and about 170 have more than 25,000. The greatest number of school districts still remains in rural and small-town America. However, a majority of minority children attend school in one of 25 urban districts. Board members themselves are becoming more diverse. The traditional board member has been a white male between 40 and 50 years of age, married and with a college degree. This is changing as more women and minorities seek board positions, especially in metropolitan areas (Glass, 2000).

In theory, the board of education is the policymaking body, and the superintendent and school staff execute policies. In practice, however, boards sometimes micromanage schools and educational administrators sometimes develop policy statements. The "fuzziness" of the demarcation of responsibilities often causes discontent, which can erode the effectiveness of the school division. School boards are empowered to provide strategic planning and policy for the school system, and most board members take this civic responsibility quite seriously.

Both school boards and superintendents believe that the most contentious part of their job is the relationship between each. This can cause major problems because school system effectiveness is often influenced by the quality of these relationships (Domenech, 2005). It is essential that superintendents and school board members communicate effectively in order to find the best solutions. Mountford (2004) found that board members who try to wield power in a forceful manner ("power over") can stifle open and objective discussions on critical issues. Effective communication requiring everyone to be heard in an honest and forthright exchange of viewpoints has proven to be best for children.

Research suggests that the governance training boards receive and the resulting philosophies they adopt helps to better define their roles and allows them to self-monitor their own actions. Most boards believe that their debates and discussions should be completed prior to the public meeting so that by the time a public vote is taken, they present a united front (Solomon & Preis, 2006).

The powers of local boards are: (1) those expressly granted by statute, (2) those fairly and necessarily implied in the powers expressly granted, and (3) those essential to the accomplishment of the objectives of the school district. The board has no choice but to comply with the statutes of the state. It can, however, work through established legislative channels to amend, abolish, or modify statutes that it finds are not in the best interest of the school district. The laws provide a great deal of opportunity for board members to exercise individual discretion and judgment. School boards answer to the citizens in their local communities and provide an effective mechanism through which communities can address their concerns. Public schools can, however, become the political arena in which ideological, social, economic, and religious differences are reconciled, sometimes at the expense of student needs. Serving on the board can be a stepping stone to a higher-level political position.

All boards have legal authority to determine salary and working conditions within the school division. They almost always hire and fire the superintendent of schools and approve the hiring of all other staff. They must approve the final budgets for schools and assist in obtaining needed resources. They also make decisions related to the financing of capital purchases. They resolve issues that are closely related to interpretation of community values, like family life and sex education, religious issues, acceptable moral behavior, character education, and other issues of community concern. They keep the community informed about the general condition of schools and help to build local support for school systems. They approve all policies by which the schools are governed.

School boards are involved in determining school sites, selecting architectural designs and contractors, determining attendance boundaries, entering into contracts, and bargaining with employee groups. Much of a board's time is spent interpreting rules made at other levels of government. The board provides minutes from all meetings, which serve as the official record and are open to examination by taxpayers. All board meetings must be open to the public except for special "executive sessions" in which school personnel matters are discussed. Even though meetings are open, past research suggests that fewer than 6% of Americans have ever attended a school board meeting (Glass, 2000). No state currently requires that the performance of individual board members or entire boards be subject to evaluation on a formal or regular basis.

Very active political board members' decisions are viewed, in the opinion of many superintendents, as more with an eye to what will gain the support of voters rather than what is best for the children. Tough decisions that alienate voters can result in loss of support from the board, even if the decisions are best for the school system over the long haul. Educational leaders have learned that they must have board support if they or their initiatives are to weather the heat that accompanies almost every decision (Carter & Cunningham, 1997).

Superintendents suggest that the balance has shifted to the point that political astuteness matters more than job performance. "Absolutely, politics plays a big role," said Dr. Frank Petruzielo, then superintendent of the Houston Independent School District. "Competency in many instances is not the issue, and that's what makes these jobs more difficult to perform than any other in public or private sectors" (Carter & Cunningham, 1997, p. 104). However, through research, Waters and Marzano (2006) have found five district-level leadership responsibilities (of the superintendent and the board as well as other district leaders) that correlate with student academic achievement: "Collaborative goal setting, nonnegotiable goals for achievement and instruction, board alignment with support of district goals, monitoring the goals for achievement and instruction, and the use of resources to support the goals for achievement and instruction" (p. 11). It will be wise for superintendents to give attention to these areas if they hope to survive the NCLB era.

Citizens are largely uninvolved in school governance, with only 10% to 15% voting in school board elections. Those with economic, political, and social power dominate educational policy, with little of the public dialogue, debate, and participation so important to democracy and citizenship. The results are declining participation in education and distrust of policymakers and bureaucrats (Land, 2002). Price (2001) suggests that boards and communities have become polarized, thwarting progress and frustrating parents and citizens. As a result, mayors and governors are currently, or have staged takeovers in such cities as Baltimore, Boston, Chicago, Cleveland, Oakland, New York, Philadelphia, Detroit, Newark, and Washington, DC. In the early 2000s, mayoral control over school boards increased. The political rhetoric has compared school boards to "dysfunctional families" and questioned whether they still serve a useful purpose.

Mayoral takeovers have met with qualified success in Boston, Chicago, and New York, but in most other locations have not resulted in improvement. In many cases, there has been more finger pointing than improvement. One of the chief criticisms of mayoral takeover is the loss of citizen input—particularly minority input—into the governance of the public schools.

Others argue that school boards are dynamic democratic institutions that go a long way toward making public schools public. However, this is challenged by the contention that vying for school board positions has become out of reach for potential candidates who are unable to raise needed campaign funds, secure political allies, and run a political campaign that can compete against large organized groups. Citizens argue for a need to "rebalance the governance equation in favor of lay citizens while diminishing the power of the state and of educational professionals" (Murphy, 1999).

The once-secure and cherished tradition of the U.S. school board is being challenged. The New Commission on the Skills of the American Workforce, funded by the Bill and Melinda Gates Foundation along with a number of other foundations, released a report in December 2006 entitled *Tough Choices or Tough Times*, which suggests that schools should operate under independent contractors, whether teachers or other private contractors. School boards and central office staff would write and monitor the contracts. Schools would have complete discretion on how to spend money, control staff, schedule programs, and manage the organization. Boards would be responsible for collecting data and sending it to the state. The state would ensure testing and other accountability requirements.

Anne Bryant, Executive Director of the National School Boards Association, responded to this controversial report by stating:

> We believe that a community working with its local school board and superintendent is the way to enact changes to improve the education for all children in the community. The idea of giving individual schools the autonomy to run their own building operations may sound attractive, but it is irresponsible without an adequate analysis of the time, skill, and resources that would need to be expended by building administrators. How many more administrators will each school have to hire to manage bus contracts, run the breakfast and lunch programs, or renovate and maintain their facilities? Placing the authority and control at the school level, as the report recommends, removes the school system leadership that results in efficient operation, a shared vision, and a clear accountability system on which parents and community members depend to deliver outcomes. (NSBA, 2007, p. 6)

These ideas may actually run counter to state constitutions, which often forbid giving authority over schools to entities outside the public school system.

Policy formation and overseeing schools is a very difficult job, and most school board members deserve a great deal of credit for being willing to serve the schools. They make decisions among conflicting ideologies, political pressures, and shifting economic and social conditions. They work with business, government, and community organizations to continuously improve the schools and promote student welfare. There are many opportunities for missteps in a highly public forum. In fact, many board meetings today are televised to the local community and receive full media attention. Board members are peppered with questions by critics and supporters alike and feel the same pressures that superintendents do.

✳ **What responsibilities does the school board have in supporting the administrators, teachers, and program at Sky Ranch School given its present condition? How can the school obtain the board's support, and is that feasible and/or important? Would some other governance structure improve the schools' chances of achieving school reform? Why or why not?**

THE SCHOOL SUPERINTENDENT

The superintendent is the chief executive officer for the school district, serving as the professional advisor to the board, leader of reforms, manager of resources, and communicator to the public. Thus, the superintendent has become the most visible, most vulnerable, and potentially most influential member of the organization. Educational decisions are usually made in an environment of strong pressure from various segments of the community, state, and nation. A major responsibility of the superintendency is to deal with conflicting expectations, multiple political agendas, and varying ideas without unduly creating enemies or distrust. The superintendent's success as chief executive officer is determined largely by his or her ability to deal with these pressures while running an effective and efficient school system.

The ways the superintendency has been studied show its multifaceted nature—reform and restructuring, centralization versus decentralization, acting as change agent, effectiveness, instructional impact, politics and political strategy, critical challenges, qualifications and access, leadership styles, context, and in terms of many other social and economic factors. Grogan (2000a) highlights the recent interest in ethics and leadership and the notion of the superintendency as a position with moral responsibility and an expectation to act morally and wisely. Often, the factors that are considered important in the superintendency emerge or become dormant as the social, political, and economic dramas of a community unfold.

Traditionally, the superintendency has been filled by white males, which is probably influenced by both the access to, and the administrative style of, the position. According to the American Association of School Administrators (AASA) this is slowly changing. Approximately 22% of superintendents are women, with a mean age of 54.5, of whom approximately 6% are minority; 60% have a doctoral degree. In addition, according to AASA's State of the Superintendency study, "the mean tenure for a superintendent is 5.7 years and annually the turnover rate is 17%," which is a clear improvement over past years.

Major functions of the superintendency, in descending order of time commitments devoted to the activities, are instructional leadership, finance and business management, general planning, personnel administration, school plant management, communication and public relations, and pupil services. Many superintendents have difficulty scheduling their day and often find themselves reacting to issues and crises that seem to occur on a daily basis. The majority of superintendents' interactions are with members of the school organization and board members, but there is an increasing demand from a wide variety of community groups—parents, vendors, mass media, chambers of commerce, mayors and city officials, special interest groups, civic leaders, businesspeople, clergy and church members, and police, among others. A crucial relationship to establish is with the local media, who are often in a position to set the tone for the prevailing view (Cooper, Fusarelli, & Carella, 1999; Glass, Bjork, & Brunner, 2000; Hodgkinson & Montenegro, 1999).

One of the most important challenges for the superintendent is maintaining the confidence of board members while providing needed attention to system-wide employees, the community, teachers, and ultimately student learning. Superintendents must maintain the confidence of the community for stable support in passing tax levies, restructuring educational programs, and leading schools and communities into the future (Kimball, 2005). "If public schools are to survive, fervent attention needs to be paid to the relationship between the schools and communities" (O'Callaghan & Irish, 2006). Allowing the opportunity for open discussion ultimately cultivates trust and support for the needs of the district.

Ideally, board members come from all areas and segments of the community so that all persons are represented. The more that members come from various corners of the community, the greater is the opportunity for all needs to be met. If this is not the case, the superintendent must create opportunities to meet with underrepresented groups. Later in this chapter, Paul Houston compares the superintendent to a dolphin trainer who rides on the backs of two dolphins, with a foot on each. The dolphins are the staff and the community, with the superintendent trying to maintain a stable balance.

In June 2003, the Connecticut Association of Boards of Education and the Connecticut Association of Public Schools Superintendents developed the keys to successful working relationships between the two groups. The results of their work appear in Appendix 4A at the end of this chapter (Larson & Rader, 2006, pp. 32–33). The overarching goal and focus of this governance statement is "collaboration on behalf of children." The Connecticut State Board of Education endorsed these guidelines in 2004.

To further define the superintendency as a profession, the AASA Commission on Standards for the Superintendency developed a set of professional standards (AASA, 1993). The commission stated, "All superintendents should be held accountable for the eight professional standards." The Professional Standards for the Superintendency are as follows:

- Standard 1: Leadership and District Culture
- Standard 2: Policy and Governance
- Standard 3: Communications and Community Relations
- Standard 4: Organizational Management
- Standard 5: Curriculum Planning and Development
- Standard 6: Instructional Management
- Standard 7: Human Resources Management
- Standard 8: Values and Ethics of Leadership

Superintendents are also being asked to respond to statewide standards-based reforms and assessment. This focus on what young people are learning and how well it is being learned has become a driving force in school divisions across the United States. The report Quality Counts '99 (*Education Week*, January 11, 1999) states: "The pressure is on. After years of exhorting and cajoling schools to improve, policy makers have decided to get tough. States are taking steps to reward results and punish failure in an effort to ensure that children are getting a good education and tax dollars aren't being wasted" (p. 5).

In the past, superintendents typically talked more about the budget, finance, legal considerations, and subjects of that nature. Today, the conversations are much more focused on instruction and student performance. Closing the achievement gap, without limiting the education of students at the high end, has become a pressing concern. Where needed resources will come from, given economic conditions, baby boomer retirements, widespread antitax sentiment, and federal and state priorities is still an important issue; however, it does not receive primary attention. The 2000 AASA Superintendent Survey found that the board's primary expectations for the superintendent was 40.1% as educational leader, 36.4% as managerial leader, 12.7% as political leader, 2.8% as reform leader, and 8% as other. The high-stakes environment created by NCLB legislation coupled with the chronic shortage of resources makes the superintendency a very challenging job (Peterson & Dlugosh, 2007).

Staying focused on the core business of instruction and student learning in an environment rampant with special interest groups, political distractions, conflicts, media coverage, and governance pressure is not an easy task. This environment requires lots of communication so everyone is informed and has confidence in the direction of the school district and speaks with a common voice. Mutual respect, common goals, and a concern for professionalism guide decisions. The success of the district is largely determined by the quality of the staff and the alignment of staff, board, and community toward achieving improved student performance. Recent research by the Council of Greater City Schools show that this "district-level leadership provided by school boards and superintendents is much more critical than previously imagined in improving outcomes for all children" (Carr, 2003).

According to DiPaola and Stronge (2001), there is a growing use of state and other standardized tests to evaluate school districts and superintendents. An increasing number of legislatures have decreed that compensation and contract renewal must be tied to student achievement. In response, some are suggesting that to protect the viability of the superintendency, they should be granted at least a 6-year renewable contract to provide some level of security.

> ✳ **How can the superintendent best support the administrators, teachers, and programs at Sky Ranch School? How can the school obtain the superintendent's support?**

CENTRAL OFFICE OPERATIONS

The titles of those in central office administration include deputy superintendents, assistant superintendents, directors, coordinators, and supervisors. The central office staff provides support based on organizational strategic goals and objectives, emphasizing planning, compliance, development, and accountability. Most staff in the central office provide expertise to those serving at the school level. Although central office staff personnel do not have direct control over the school, they have considerable power through their positions, knowledge, time, and resources.

The central office staff is usually broken up into various divisions or departments based on operational responsibility and school division size. Departmentalization is used to subdivide tasks among the central administrative staff. Organizational charts, available in almost all school districts, portray a rough description of this departmentalization. Most are staff positions providing support to people in line positions. Individuals in staff positions usually help in the handling of details, locating data requirements, and offering expertise in specific areas.

The line officer is typically a generalist, whereas the staff person is a specialist. The authority over operations is given to line officers, with staff officers providing advisory and consultant services. The main duties of central office staff are to:

1. Provide technical expertise.
2. Recommend courses of action.
3. Discuss plans with others in the organization to promote the exchange of information and collegial decision making.
4. Prepare written documentation to support work efforts.
5. Explain and interpret decisions made by supervisors.
6. Conduct evaluations and research, and assemble, summarize, and interpret results.
7. Provide assistance to line position personnel.
8. Inform and advise others what is occurring in the field.

One of the more recent roles is monitoring school compliance with federal and state law and local policy. The NCLB legislation has greatly expanded this role as staff members produce reports and analysis of systemwide test data and recommend needed changes.

Central administrative staff members are being called on in a number of districts to work directly with principals and teachers to improve students' test scores. The responsibility for improving test scores is being placed solidly on the principal and teachers, calling on central administration for needed financial and technical support. A key will be working together to attain high-quality professional development that is focused on improving student achievement.

Some argue (Childress, Elmore, & Grossman, 2006; Honig, 2003) that central district offices must be more involved in strategic planning focused on improving student achievement. Childress and colleagues (2006) state: "They need to develop district wide strategy for improving teaching and learning and to create an organization that is coherent with the strategy" (p. 59). In this way, central administrators are directly linked to the work of teachers and students in classrooms. They should not allow themselves to be pulled away from their focus on student achievement. They must also ensure that appropriate constituencies are aboard that support the strategies and can be counted on as allies.

The Montgomery County Maryland Public School District provides an example of developing a strategy that gave the district office a powerful lead role in improving student achievement. Central office administrators designed a curriculum for all the schools in the district. This systematic, integrated plan ensured that all schools within the district were aligned with the state tests, districtwide goals, and each grade level. They then developed systems to help teachers identify student needs and then to hold teachers and principals accountable for addressing those needs and demonstrating student progress. They created an aggressive professional development plan for teachers and principals based on these strategic plans and a districtwide information system for tracking student performance by school and classroom. They placed a major focus on literacy and investing in new technology—including Palm Pilots that quickly track students' progress. The key element of this plan was a focus on strengthening teaching and learning, clear objectives, and established accountability. The results have been a marked improvement between 2003 and 2006 on student performance data (Childress et al., 2006).

These same types of improvements have been occurring in the Chicago Public Schools where central administration developed both a systemwide strategy and an effort to get everyone together to execute the strategy. The district office overhauled the information systems and established benchmarks for student progress. School plans now contain numerical objectives for student achievement, attendance, graduation rates, gains on standardized tests, percent in advanced placements, ranking, and so on. Central offices were also asked to provide more business services to the schools in order to take over administrative tasks and free up school administrators to devote more time to strengthening instruction. Also, a number of charter schools were established to provide more educational choices. The key point is that in many districts, central administration took on an expanded role focused on systemwide strategy related to teaching, learning, and student achievement. It is essential that central office staff members are knowledgeable observers who can identify, address, and remedy predictable problems in advance (Honig, 2003). Because of the superintendent's busy schedule, he or she often has to depend on central office administrators to keep the school district running smoothly. Superintendents often have little time to supervise central office administrators directly and have to depend on their staff's ability to follow up on the vision established by the superintendent and board. It is important that the board, superintendent, and assistant superintendents focus on the strategic objectives of the school district, allowing the central office staff to support operational areas and the day-to-day operations (Glass, 1992).

Central office administration can greatly assist school staff, and their support can be key to a school's success in its continuous improvement efforts. These connected central office administrators can present ideas in palatable terms and gain the needed support and resources for local school efforts. They can also help address certain school challenges that only they have the authority to remedy. Central administrators have a much better understanding of federal and state rules and how they will support or inhibit school plans. They can help schools to interpret these rules.

THE SUPERINTENDENT AND THE LEADERSHIP TEAM'S ROLE IN IMPROVING STUDENT ACHIEVEMENT

KATHLEEN BINKOWSKI, PHD
Superintendent, Plainville Community Schools, CT

There is an increasing amount of research being conducted on the ways that school district central offices can impact student achievement. The research does not directly address organizational structures for the central office. Rather, it is focused on the characteristics of how a successful central office does the work as opposed to recommending ideal structures. A common theme emphasizes providing leadership and support to principals and teachers in contrast to monitoring school compliance.

This theme emerges when we analyze school districts described as organizational learning cultures. Staff members in these school districts are motivated by using data, such as test scores and other performance measures as indicators, to improve student learning. Further, Leithwood, Seashore-Lewis, Anderson, and Wahlstrom (2004) found some evidence suggesting that an organizational learning culture contributes to high student achievement.

In examining how districts think about and use data, Firestone and Gonzalez (2007) cite Togneri and Anderson's (2003) research that found the use of a vision statement with a focus on student achievement to be evident among school districts that have high percentages of economically disadvantaged students; these districts "beat the odds" by achieving at extraordinarily high levels. Moreover, the use of data extended beyond state assessments as they used several data sources.

In districts that stress organizational learning, the superintendent and the senior leadership team take on the role of keeping the district focus on improving instruction. The superintendent and leadership team become responsible for creating a sense of urgency around instructional improvement and

take steps to make it understood widely. The central office leadership team keeps the focus on the instructional core. As such, they play a critical role in making the "through line" explicit so that everyone understands the relationship of the vision and mission statements to the actual learning and teaching that occurs in the classroom. Another leadership role is to create an environment where staff members feel that they are part of a larger community of learners and that data collected will not be used for evaluative purposes.

Organizational learning cultures use information to identify "problems of practice" then structure administrator rounds, or walk-throughs, to collect qualitative information on instruction. The data collected during rounds complements initial data and is used to determine the "problem of practice." Administrators agree that the timely sharing of data around a "problem of practice" can assist in analyzing what students know and are able to do. Also, when teachers and department instructional leaders are part of the process, student achievement is accelerated as high-yield instructional strategies are refined and matched both to the task and student needs. In districts that are successful in improving student achievement, leaders maintain an emphasis on a limited number of areas for the long term—for example, literacy and mathematics. The superintendent and leadership team members are responsible for connecting the dots—making the "through line" explicit—so that the members of the organization are able to understand their role in improving student achievement.

An organizational learning culture is supportive of teacher and principal voice. In this culture, the superintendent creates

(continued)

opportunities for professionals to come together to learn from each other. This appears to contribute to a cultural shift where leadership becomes more distributed. As such, when professionals are able to understand their power to improve student achievement, positive energy is released throughout the district and collective efficacy takes shape. In this scenario, teachers and principals understand how they can improve student achievement and contribute to the learning community.

The top leadership of the district plays a critical role in promoting its vision. The role of the superintendent can be played out through the development of a theory of action and problem of instructional practice for the district.

Superintendent's Problem of Practice: Do we have a sense of urgency regarding raising standards and increasing rigor for our students? Is there evidence of individual and collective efficacy? Does our district theory of action have an impact on teaching, learning, and the instructional practices of administrators and teachers? Is the through line to the classroom explicit, and have we used what we learned in raising mathematics achievement to improve student achievement in other areas?

We have seen the work of instructional rounds accelerate large-scale instructional improvement at the elementary and middle school levels in mathematics and reading. Is there evidence that the power of rounds is beginning to make an impact at the high school?

Superintendent's Theory of Action. If we create a sense of urgency and participate as a professional learning community by analyzing student data to solve problems of practice in the district, then we can develop the capacity of staff members to improve student achievement. The Superintendent's Theory of Action drives the process used to build capacity for the work in the district. Districts begin to accelerate student achievement as teachers and administrators become more

proficient at analyzing student data and matching instructional strategies to the needs of students. In our district where student achievement has accelerated significantly, the district leadership team identified the following components as contributing to the improvement:

- Development and implementation of a high quality curriculum aligned to state and national frameworks clearly articulating what students should know, understand, and be able to do
- Clear vertical articulation and alignment that eliminates redundancy while spiraling concepts to increasingly higher levels
- Professional development in differentiated instruction and a commitment to challenge each student with rigorous work every day
- A focus on "high-yield" instructional strategies as defined by Marzano, Waters, & McNulty (2005) and Hattie (2009) and carefully selecting the best strategy for the task and the students
- Explicit instruction and modeling of strategies and high expectations for student use of these strategies in their work
- Constantly asking the question, "Who is doing the thinking in this lesson, activity, or task?" When students are doing the thinking around rigorous tasks that require synthesis, application, and creation of knowledge, the result is a deeper understanding of concept and true learning

School improvement efforts and changing a school's culture are very complex and rely on a combination of district responses to external prompts that create a sense of urgency. These prompts may include a strategic planning process that galvanizes the school and greater community or uses a problem-based learning scenario with district and teacher leaders developing an organizational learning culture. Additionally, a program evaluation can be designed to gather data to inform decision making in a particular content area. Each of these mechanisms can be used to create a sense of urgency by making the data public as discussions take place to respond to the strengths and challenges evident in the data.

In districts making improvements in student achievement, the board of education, superintendent, and the district leadership team are committed to working together to solve problems of practice. The board assumes the role as policymaker with the superintendent as the major architect of the district vision created through the extensive involvement of the school and greater community. Finally, of greater importance, there is a pattern of leadership stability that guides and sustains the improvement process.

That means it is very important that good relationships be developed between central administration and the school sites and that the communication flows freely in both directions. The quality of these interactions is largely determined by the level of trust that exists between central administration and the schools. Effective policy development requires an understanding of individual site needs and practices so that they can enable these practices. That means that central office administrators need time on site (Honig, 2003; Leithwood, Aitben, & Jantzi, 2001).

School administrators call frontline administrators several times a week to discuss various opportunities and challenges. Therefore, it is very important that these frontline offices have a strong understanding of systemwide knowledge and provide accurate information, avoid confusion, and support local responsiveness as well as central office understanding of site needs. Frontline administrators will not allow the majority of their time to be diverted to central office administration bureaucracy and away from working with the sites.

＊ **Define the role of the central office staff members in supporting the administrators, teachers, and programs at Sky Ranch School. How can the school obtain the central office staff members' support? How much responsibility do the central office administrators have for this school and does such responsibility create problems related to micromanagement?**

THE SCHOOL ADMINISTRATOR

Each school building is staffed by a principal and, as size warrants, any number of assistant or vice principals, teachers, and a number of others in staff and clerical positions. The principal carries out all the duties necessary to run an effective school. Principals usually serve in elementary (K–5), middle (6–8), or high schools (9–12). It is generally agreed that the high school principalship is the most demanding job, followed by the middle school, and then the elementary principalship, and this is reflected in the difference in principal pay scales.

As the educational leader of the school, the principal is responsible to the superintendent for all matters relating to the operation of the school. He or she is responsible for complementing the policies of the board and regulations of the superintendent. Some of the responsibilities of this position include:

- Supervise the school's education program and help plan, implement, and evaluate curricular and instructional programs.
- Assume responsibility for the implementation and observance of all board policies and regulations by the school's staff and students.
- Organize programs of study and schedule classes.
- Assume the implementation and evaluation of district initiatives at the building level.
- Supervise all professional, paraprofessional, administrative, and nonprofessional personnel attached to the school.
- Assist in the hiring, training, assigning, and evaluating of the school professional staff.
- Assume responsibility for the safety of the school, staff, and students and administration of the school plant.
- Provide stewardship of school resources.
- Assist in the orientation of, and ongoing professional learning opportunities for, teachers, with special responsibility for staff members' administrative procedures and instructions.
- Supervise the preparation of all school reports for the central office and make recommendations for improving the school.
- Assume responsibility for attendance, conduct, and health of students.
- Provide for extracurricular and athletic activities.
- Assist in the management and preparation of the school budget.
- Supervise the maintenance of accurate progress and attendance records for students.
- Act as liaison between the school and the community, interpreting activities and policies of the school and encouraging community participation in school life.
- Conduct staff meetings as necessary for the proper functioning of the school.

Research has shown that the principal is the single most important individual to the success of any given school (Edmonds, 1979; Lezotte, 1988a; Miller, 1995; SREB, 2010). School effectiveness research in the 1980s pointed to the importance of the principal and teachers as the main determiners of school success. Waters, Marzano, and McNulty (2003) have also confirmed through their meta-analysis a correlation of 0.25 between leadership and student achievement. They have also identified 21 areas of principal leadership responsibilities including culture, order, discipline, resources, curriculum (instruction and assessment), focus, knowledge of curriculum (instruction and assessment), visibility, contingent rewards, communication, outreach, input, affirmation, relationship, change agent optimization, ideals and beliefs, monitoring and evaluation, flexibility, situational awareness, and intellectual stimulation (Waters et al., 2003, Figure 3).

The principal is at the very heart of school improvement. In the report *America 2000: Where School Leaders Stand* (1991), AASA states: "Effective schools have at least one thing in common: sound leadership. School administrators have never had a more crucial role in American society; they must be the ones who stimulate the debate and help develop a vision of what our schools should become in communities across the nation" (p. 6). Management functions and clerical chores must not be allowed to dominate the work of the principal. In fact, the most important responsibilities focus on vision and developing and motivating staff to achieve optimum student learning outcomes.

Both the National Association of Elementary School Principals (NAESP) and the National Association of Secondary School Principals (NASSP) have established proficiencies that they believe to be critically important to principals' leadership. It is generally agreed that these proficiencies are constantly evolving to fit the context in which schools operate.

Ubben, Hughes, and Norris (2001) believe that the perception of the principal has changed from the traditional view of a manager who implements policy within the bureaucratic hierarchy.

> Instead, today's school principals have been charged with the task of shaping their schools to become outstanding beacons of productive learning. They are challenged to clarify their own values, beliefs, and positions and to engage proactively with others in the redesign and improvement of their schools. They are expected to establish conditions that foster personal empowerment and enhanced development of organizational members and to orchestrate shared power and decision making among an array of individuals both internal and external to the school setting. At the same time, they are encouraged to build a community of leaders and learners who will effectively shape the school environment to champion increased productivity among students. (p. 3)

Changing Roles

The perceptions and expectations on the school principal have changed dramatically given the changing context of education over the last 15 years. The traditional roles and responsibilities of ensuring a safe environment, managing the budget, and maintaining discipline are still in force; however, there are many new demands. As programming and associated auxiliary activity have been expanding, needed resources and support have not been forthcoming. In looking at the role of the principal as instructional leader, the National Center for School Leadership (NCSL) identified five key aspects of the role of effective principals:

1. Defining and communicating a school's educational mission
2. Coordinating curriculum
3. Supervising and supporting teachers
4. Monitoring student progress
5. Nurturing a positive learning climate

A major theme of the new changes is that principals are paying more attention to instructional leadership. This includes development and evaluations of curriculum and instruction, use of instructional time, disaggregation of data, analyzing classroom practices, faculty and staff development, student incentives, and curriculum alignment with standards. The principal also has to deal with more outside groups, thus serving as a conduit for communication and understanding (Shen & Crawford, 2003).

The conflict between management-related tasks and instructional leadership initiatives is at an all-time high, which can deplete the emotional and physical energy of the individual in this position. This condition is not helped by the layering of responsibilities placed on the schools along with major concerns related to accountability, multicultural awareness and understanding, special education/inclusion, student health and safety, and moral values. The mantra is "I must do more." Principals are more on call than ever with e-mail, cell phones, and pagers to an ever-expanding constituency. Most principals are also spending significantly more time on paperwork.

The conflicts abound and include role conflict, conflicting expectations (inclusion, diversity needs, and accountability), autonomy and mandates, and efficiency and support for needed assistance. More home–school communication is required. It is a very challenging time to be a principal, but, as always, it is an exciting time, and principals can be influential and make a difference in the lives of children and young adults.

In a study completed by Kochan, Spencer, and Matthews (2000), principals perceived the major challenges to the job as "insufficient financial resources," "control of financial matters," "being overloaded by the demands placed on them," "controlling and dealing with teacher apathy" (male principals), "building a climate of trust and enhancing morale" (female principals), "dealing with school discipline and handling conflicts," and "safety issues related to deteriorating facilities" (female principals). The most important skills indicated were organizational, interpersonal–relational, curricular and instructional, technical and administrative, and personal attributes (concern, flexibility, and personal strength).

Brown-Ferrigno (2003) asked teachers to describe their understanding of the roles and responsibilities of school principals. Different views were related to respondents' teaching experience. Differences in age and experience appeared to influence staff perceptions regarding principal responsibilities. This suggests that teachers with different levels of experience require different types of support from the principal.

In a research study describing the changing role of the principal, Goodwin (2004) states:

> The findings of this study illustrated the breadth of the interactions related to the principalship. Interactions with people in the school, in the district, in the community, the interaction of social changes with school expectations, the interaction of politics and bureaucracy with daily school life, the interaction of standards and accountability with the social and emotional needs of students, and the interaction of the expectation to be an effective instructional leader and an efficient manager are all evidence of the complexity of the position. (p. 19)

There is still a disconnect between the principal's changing role and what demands his or her daily attention. The principal needs to be an expert in so many more things—special education, standards, data-based decision making, testing, high technology, dropouts, tight budgets, lobbying, student diversity, brain research, teaching, learning, nutrition, safety, distance learning, litigation, legislation, court cases, paperwork, and the list goes on. Goodwin (2004) continues:

> The role of the principal has increased in complexity, and [so has] the principal's perceived linear conflicts between being inclusive and meeting high standards, between accountability and meeting the diverse needs of students, between being responsive to mandates and being autonomous, and between and among the roles of strategic leader, instructional leader, organizational leader, and political and community leader. (p. 19)

PRINCIPAL AS INSTRUCTIONAL LEADER

Instructional Leadership

Instructional leadership is focused on curriculum and instructional development; staff development; instructional supervision; program, teacher, and student evaluation; research and experimentation; provision of resources; and the continuous improvement of teaching and learning. NCES data shows that principals stress literacy skills, academic excellence, good work habits, personal growth, human relations, and multicultural education as important for their schools. The school manager focuses more on facilities, equipment, supplies, schedules, discipline, procedures, stewardship, critical incidents, and general compliance with efficient behavior and practice, as well as district policies, procedures, and programs. Management is associated with coordination, control, and operations of the school. Research tends to suggest that principals must first and primarily be the instructional leader, but not at the expense of effectively managing the school (Pounder & Merrill, 2001; Richards, 2000; Shen & Crawford, 2003).

Policy makers' messages today are loud and clear—academic achievement. Research (Cantano & Stronge, 2006) implies that instructional leadership is the major focus of school district policies and standards at the national and state level. Research also suggests that instructional leadership provided by the principal is a contributing factor to higher student achievement (Hallinger & Heck, 1998; Lezotte, 1994; Orr, 2006; Davis, Darling-Hammond, LaPointe, & Meyerson, 2005; Chrisman, 2005; O'Donnell & White, 2005; Marks & Printy, 2003; Owings, Kaplan, & Nunnery, 2005; Hallinger, 2005; Waters, Marzano, & McNulty, 2003).

Hoy, Tarter, and Hoy (2006) state, "The simple conclusion should encourage teachers and principals to move forward with confidence, knowing many of the significant linkages within schools that influence student learning" (p. 444). This vast body of post-1995 research on effective schools and effective principals offers new insights that will help principals to become more effective instructional leaders. Principals need to incorporate these practices that are responsive to the most crucial needs of their schools with regard to raising student achievement. Appendix 4B, at the end of this chapter, helps define what instructional leadership might look like in practice based on this extensive body of research.

Effective principals are more likely to communicate about instructional matters; to pay attention to test results; to discuss curriculum and instruction; to focus on how well learning objectives were mastered in communication to students, teachers, and parents; and to be a visible presence in and around the school. Achilles and Smith (1999) conclude:

> The stimulation of pupil academic performance is a continuing challenge for the principal. Improvement will not occur without the principal's time and attention, for "as is the principal, so is the school." The principal is the coordinator of the learning environment and must demonstrate a commitment to pupil performance. The principal, the teachers, and the pupils are a learning team. (p. 242)

Principals express their commitment to improved student performance through words, focus, and actions (see Chapter 6). They will be visible throughout the school expressing interest in instruction and learning—their presence felt and seen by everyone. They are involved in planning for instruction and know what is to be taught and make sure it is being taught. They often meet with teachers, chairpersons, lead teachers, specialists, and others collaboratively discussing various aspects of the curriculum, observed instruction, assessment, student progress, what's going well and what is not, and ultimately shaping the vision for an improved school. As an instructional leader, staff development and providing for teachers' instructional needs become a primary focus of the administrators' work so that teachers are able to do their best for children. This requires effective evaluation and monitoring of both teacher and student progress to provide the needed information for planning appropriate developmental activities (Pollard & Durodola, 2003). For an example of an educational leadership improvement protocol, see the work of Defranco and Golden (2003).

＊ **What do you see as your role as principal of Sky Ranch School? How will you marshal the needed resources to gain control of this school and ultimately improve student performance? What will be the major challenges that you will face both personally and professionally?**

SCHOOL IMPROVEMENT PLANNING

The school improvement plan (SIP) is a contract that details planned changes, sets benchmarks, and specifies the roles and responsibilities of school personnel. These plans have increased in importance since the implementation of NCLB and the state's minimum targets for academic proficiency, test participation, attendance rates, graduation rates, and dropout rates. Approximately 23,000 schools failed to make adequate yearly progress (AYP) and over 12,000 were identified for school improvement in the 2004–2005 academic year. The AYP provisions of this law serve as a signal to a school that it must plan and show improvement in order to keep from being identified as a school needing "corrective action" and external assistance or ultimately to be reconstituted. Schools must consistently show improvement and the SIP is critical in achieving this objective. Schools typically are expected to develop a 2-year school improvement plan (SIP).

The NCLB legislation stipulates that the SIP be composed of ten components:

1. Specific academic issues causing the school to miss AYP
2. Effective strategies showing exactly how the school plans to meet academic proficiencies in the future
3. Policies and practices that ensure all subgroups of students meet academic proficiency
4. Professional development opportunities related to the academic achievement problems
5. Accounting how professional development expenditures will facilitate academic goals
6. Statement of objectives for annual and measurable progress for each subgroup
7. A plan to provide written notice to all parents about its "needs improvement" status
8. Outline of state, district, and school responsibilities for improvement
9. Strategies for promoting effective parental involvement
10. Development of a teacher mentoring program

Leaders at all levels access information to evaluate and pinpoint learning needs, develop solutions, assign responsibilities, and allocate resources. Strategies might be related to such areas as curriculum alignment, classroom instruction, supplemental education services, and test preparation. The school district is responsible for providing technical assistance and support to the school. The district must also inform parents about other services offered by approved providers (Wong & Nicotera, 2007).

School administrators and staff work on school improvement plans each year. They look at the data describing student achievement in relation to state standards and decide what improvements need to be made to achieve desired outcomes. This standards-based reform requires schools to make changes in order to meet adequate yearly progress. School improvement requires district support and sponsorship but successful implementation depends on schoolwide efforts to consider problems and conceive necessary school improvement efforts. These improvement plans are best coordinated at the central administration level but developed and implemented at the school level. In this way, different improvements at each school depend on the unique conditions existing within the school, the context of the school, and staff members' own analysis of school challenges. The school improvement process provides an opportunity to develop support, to tap into individual abilities and strengths, to increase the sense of ownership, to provide people with a sense of voice, to learn to work together as a team, to let people know they are valued, to develop greater understanding, to improve communication, to create a learning organization, and to develop staff. The driving force for these efforts is improved academic performance.

POLITICS OF THE PRINCIPALSHIP

School administrators often operate in a contentious arena and vie for ways of balancing, directing, controlling, manipulating, managing, and surviving their edgy environments (Lindle & Mawhinney, 2003). Interested parties exert various forms of power over others in order to achieve their self-interests. Decisions are frequently based on who is able to apply the greatest pressure or cause the worst damage as opposed to what might be the larger good for all involved. Lashway (2006) concludes:

> In the final analysis, politics is simply the means by which people in a group make decisions when opinions differ. It serves a constructive purpose by channeling organizational conflict into solution-oriented behavior. . . . Despite this fundamentally healthy function, politics can go astray, leading participants into unproductive quibbling, dishonest communication and manipulative behavior, causing the organization to slowly bog down. . . . Blase and Blase (2003) have cited numerous examples of this abuse, ranging from unfair criticism to favoritism to sexual harassment. . . . Even a noble end does not justify every means. Principals who keep asking, "How do students benefit?" are more likely to elevate politics from game-playing to an act of leadership. (pp. 280–281)

Principals can set an example by being knowledgeable, fair, understanding, tolerant, sincere, even-handed, and compassionate in their actions and decisions. Of course, it never hurts to have good relationships with those in power.

Parents, teachers, community members, and others can become alienated when questions arise whether educational administrators are motivated by the general welfare and/or by the interests of powerful individuals and groups. This concern can create distrust and a "crisis of confidence" in the schools.

Who gets to make what kinds of decision is at the very core of politics and educational governance. This evolves into issues of who gains and who loses when the political model is used. "Whose personal beliefs and values are raised to become public beliefs and values, which all are asked or forced to accept, is what makes debate and governance so contentious" (Cooper, Fusarelli, & Randall, 2004, p. 37). Educators are responsible to ensure that the voices of diverse stakeholders are heard and carefully considered. The overarching goal is to develop decision-making processes that incorporate teachers, parents, community members, researchers, business and civic leaders, and policymakers.

Mark Gerzon, president of Mediators Foundation and codirector of the Global Leadership Network, states (2006), "Your first response is not about doing anything; it is about being aware, seeing the whole" (p. 30). Systematic political

PUTTING "Cs" INTO THE VILLAGE

PAUL C. HOUSTON, EDD
Former Executive Director, American Association of School Administrators

Many leaders are currently caught in the trap of trying to emulate the success achieved by earlier generations of "command and control" administrators. Today, you cannot command the staff or community—you can't even get them to take a number.

Rather than try to lead by command, administrators must develop and nurture relationships. I am fond of reminding my colleagues that if you stand in the middle of the road, you get hit by traffic going in both directions. However, that is also the best place from which to direct traffic. You can either get the plate number of the truck that just ran you down, or stand up and wave your arms to move the flow in a positive direction.

Educators are particularly fond of saying, "It takes a village to raise a child," but the real question for school leaders is, "What does it take to raise a village?" The villages of yesterday are gone and must be rebuilt in the new era we face. Schools are the connect points for communities. They can, and must, play the role of creating the needed network of support for children. School leaders must be the connectors, the bridge builders who bring diverse elements of the community together to support children.

School leaders must move from the "Bs" from past days of school administration (bonds, building, buses, budgets—the "stuff" of education) to the "Cs" (connections, collaborations, communication, children—the building of relationships). School system leaders must create a balance between being courageous champions for children and communities and collaborative catalysts who use their pivotal roles to bring people together to make things happen. I have called this shifting role as moving from being a superintendent of schools to being a superintendent of education. It implies reaching out beyond the traditional walls of schools and school districts to embrace a broader set of responsibilities and relationships.

School leaders will of necessity behave very differently from the way they do today. Proactive leadership that initiates contact and issues and demands both human and political sensitivities is required. Changed attitudes and new skills will be required as well as change in the organizations supporting schools such as district offices. District offices must reduce their oversight and monitoring role and replace it with the building of capacity for schools. Schools need guidance and support; they do not need control. Savvy school district leaders will make it their business to transform district offices into places of support.

School management in the 21st century is the management of relationships: the relationship of child to learning, child to child, child to adult, and school to community. There can be no barriers. It is all interconnected. Education is organic in nature and the pieces cannot be mechanically separated. The role of school leadership will be to foster and nurture the old relationships and to create new ones necessitated by the changing social conditions facing children and schools.

I have always thought that leadership comes from the ability to comfort the afflicted and afflict the comforted—helping the public understand that schools are more effective than they think and helping staff understand that they are not as effective as they think. Successful leaders find the balance between the demands and expectations of those working on the problems, and those who depend on the problems to be solved. Like a performer at a sea park who rides a pair of dolphins, you must have one foot on the back of the community and the other on the back of the staff. If you lean too far in either direction, you fall off.

(continued)

There is one final relationship that must be fostered—the relationship with the board of education. In essence, the real role of school boards is to translate the values of the community into policy for the system. It is a crucial role that, too often, is not being played appropriately. School boards are often not asked to focus on the very thing that they are there to provide—insight into what the community hopes and dreams for its children. Boards need to be helped to move away from a preoccupation with the "stuff" of education to its higher purposes. School superintendents must use their positions to help school boards play this role if any success is expected.

Successful school district leaders are moving from acting like sharks to behaving like dolphins. The role is no longer one of the lone predator, swimming menacingly through the water in search of the next meal. It is one where sophisticated communication and sonar are used, where collaboration and cooperation are stressed, and where a bit of playfulness doesn't hurt. For all those people who would hold on to the shark behavior out of fear of being swallowed up in the dangerous waters of the next century, it is good to remember that dolphins kill sharks. You do not have to be a predator to be successful. Swimming fast and not taking yourself too seriously also do not hurt.

thinking is identifying all of the elements related to the conflict and understanding the relationships among these elements. The leader must give full attention to the conflict and not allow pressure, subversion, and stress to distract from the issue—applying all mental resources to assessing and transforming the conflict. Inquiry is a way to ask questions and gather essential information to seek full understanding of complex, political situations. Leaders must not be close-minded about a political conflict nor allow this attitude to impose itself in conversation. Dialogue dissipates assumptions, misconceptions, and stereotypes. Dialogue also alleviates confusion, mistrust, and misunderstandings. Bridging is the process of closing the gaps or divisions among stakeholders. These invisible bridges are built with trust, social capital, respect, healing, empathy, understanding, courage, and collaboration.

This inclusiveness is difficult when coalitions form around specific interests, and decisions are made through bargaining, negotiation, coercion, and compromise. The quality of decisions is influenced by the political skill and acumen of the leader to channel power toward desirable outcomes. Those who have a stake in the outcome build power bases in order to influence the decision. For example, a principal may establish strong relationships with parents and community members in order to build a power base. That principal, at some risk, can then call on that power base to influence the superintendent or school board to support a schoolwide program that is not presently supported by the board and/or central administration.

One's position also provides a sense of power as long as the position holder is recognized as appropriately holding that position. The ability to have some control over another position holder's professional life also creates power. Mutual respect, high status, expertise, expressive ability, wealth, popularity, and so on can allow an individual to dominate the political process. The principal needs to know how to work through this political process in order to achieve desired outcomes.

PARENTAL INVOLVEMENT

Families are often not directly involved in their children's school activities for many reasons. In order to alter the paradigm of parent involvement, we need to begin by talking about *family* involvement. Given the changing demographics of families, schools can no longer think only about mom and dad. Simply by expanding our definition of *family*, as we think about involvement, the possible participation net is enlarged. In many families, older siblings, a grandparent, or an aunt or uncle have primary responsibilities of child care.

A second part of the paradigm needing change is the relationship between schools and families. Schools need to think of family members as *partners.* Two or more independent agents agree to work together to accomplish a common purpose that is mutually beneficial. For schools and educators, partnership means that family and school share power. Family members are given opportunities to provide ideas and advice just as educators are. Both partners are obliged to be committed and are responsible for doing their part.

Another part of the old paradigm requiring change is the way educators have traditionally viewed involvement—attendance of parents at school functions and volunteering at school. When asked how families are involved in a child's education, educators typically respond that parents are invited to a variety of school functions—open houses, parent conferences, school assemblies, sports activities—and to participate as classroom volunteers. If educators continue to think about involvement in these limited ways, little will change in the relationship between schools and families. (See Epstein's typology of parent involvement in Chapter 10.)

Research shows that when families are involved in their children's education, grades are higher, attendance is better, homework completion improves, and students are more motivated (Epstein, 2001; Epstein, Coates, Salinas, Sanders, & Simon, 2002; Henderson & Mapp, 2002; Sheldon, 2003; Van Voorhis, 2001). Epstein and Jansorn (2004) state, "Every school needs a purposeful, planned partnership program that creates a welcoming environment and engages families in activities that contribute to students' readiness for school, academic success, and positive attitudes and behaviors" (p. 10). The first step in increasing family involvement is to create a welcoming environment—positive handling of phone calls and drop-in visitors, a clean school, visible student work, a parent's space for meeting, welcoming attitudes, and so on. Next is providing needed information through a school web page, newsletter, teacher–parent conferences, and scheduled activities for parents. Parents want to get a feel for the values, beliefs, and attitudes of those who surround their children each day (partnershipschools.org).

The 6.5-million-member national Parent Teacher Association (PTA) has developed standards to encourage parent involvement in their children's education. The six factors identified by the National PTA are:

1. Regular, two-way, meaningful communication between home and school
2. Promotion and support of parenting skills
3. Active parent participation in student learning

4. Parents as welcome volunteer partners in schools
5. Parents as full partners in school decisions that affect children and families
6. Outreach to the community for resources to strengthen schools

Other organizations, such as the National Coalition for Parents' Involvement in Education (NCPIE), work to create meaningful family–school partnerships in every school. They have been further supported by the NCLB Act, which requires schools to have well-planned programs of family and community involvement to support student achievement and to communicate clearly with parents.

The principal shows that parents are valued by frequently letting teachers and students know that parents are valued at this school. Their involvement on action teams further stresses their importance. Only with the principal's ongoing support will parents, teachers, students, and others work closely together for the benefit of schools and the children they serve.

Principals need to be prepared to assist all parents. Some parents felt inadequate or unable to assist their children with school work and/or may not have had a particularly good experience at school. Horvat, Weininger, and Lareau (2003) found that middle class and above parents react collectively or at least threaten the possibility of collective involvement, which essentially trumps or neutralizes the authority of educators, thus creating a more open environment. They also seem to have closer ties to those who can provide needed information, expertise, and authority needed to effectively participate.

The working-class and poor parents tend to undertake individual response and do not receive support through broader networks. They do not have the same trappings of authority, community response, information, or expertise. They tend to be the easiest to ignore and marginalize, which can become a problem if the principal does not put in a greater effort to ensure that the staff values their participation beyond discipline and negative school experiences.

✳ **How would you involve the parents at Sky Ranch School to help turn this school around? How might you make this happen?**

ASSISTANT PRINCIPAL

Principals are in desperate need of more assistant principals if they are to meet the expanded expectations of their role. Two thirds of principals (DiPaola & Tschannen-Moran, 2003) reported that they did not have enough assistants to fulfill the expanding role of the principalship. This study also found that 65% of elementary assistant principals, 41% of middle school assistant principals, and 34% of high school assistant principals indicated they would seek a position as principal. However, 56% planned to retire in the next 10 years.

Keesor (2005) found that "the literature review indicated that the time spent by assistant principals acting as disciplinarians consumes too much time to allow other duties to be completed. As a result, being an instructional leader is problematic. . . ." (p. 65). Research (Gerke, 2004) continues to support the role of the assistant principal as primarily that of discipline; however, this is slowly changing as all leaders in education are focusing more on instruction. Assistant principals who spend time monitoring classrooms are better able to prevent problems and therefore do not have to put out fires throughout the day. Also, time spent monitoring the classrooms puts the assistant principal in the middle of daily instruction, giving a window into what is going on in the classrooms. Teachers and students become familiar with the assistant principal in the classroom setting and view him or her as more than just a disciplinarian.

Some principals assign a very limited, narrow set of responsibilities to assistant principals so that they become single-facet administrators. Assistant principals (APs) should be provided a well-rounded set of experiences to better prepare them to take on full responsibility for the school and to deepen their understanding of the school. The traditional roles of operations manager and disciplinarian in which they administer discipline, buses, attendance, schedules, student activities, and other noninstructional functions have changed with the changing role of the principal into the need to share greater power and help create an instructional leadership team.

Principals must support their assistants in working toward personal growth goals, including extending themselves more into working with teachers on instructional strategies, tutoring students, and improving the instructional climate (Bartholomew, Melendez-Delaney, Awilda, & White, 2005). Assistant principals can improve student conduct by meeting with students outside the office, meeting with students during lunch, and meeting with all newly enrolled students. This strategy allows assistant principals to stay abreast of the climate of the school, and to be aware of potential discipline problems before they occur. This additional responsibility is best supported by keeping a to-do list, planning ahead, even for the next year, and developing forms to quickly document and respond.

Pounder and Crow (2005) suggest several strategies for attracting and retaining qualified, energetic leaders. To tap into already existing talent within the school building, principals should be purposefully identifying teachers and other educators who have shown leadership talent. By steering them toward opportunities to use and develop their leadership skills and otherwise providing aspiring administrators with more practical experiences, principals can give new school leaders opportunities to practice their craft before having to actually do the job. Internships are another way of ensuring that school leaders are prepared for the challenges of the job. A method previously discussed is redefining and expanding the role of the assistant principal. Exposure to all aspects of school leadership, and not just discipline, helps equip the assistant to move to the role of principal. The strategy of shared leadership between principal and assistant can also reallocate responsibilities so as not to wear down the principal.

Thus, there is strong pressure to upgrade and expand the role of the AP. Assistant principals hold the keys to the type of instructional leadership being called for in schools today. Their responsibility for teacher evaluations could be expanded to that of a mentor or coach who actively assists teachers to improve their performance, gain skills and confidence, implement best practices, interpret feedback data, and deal with a wide range of students (Kaplan & Owings, 1999). APs could meet regularly with department heads and grade leaders to address the school's instructional concerns. Although an increase in the number of administrative assistants or deans within the school may be required along with some division of labor, in this expanded role, assistant principals will learn the same skills that make principals effective, thus preparing them to be principals. Moreover, a number of school districts have developed academies and institutes to give administrators an opportunity to develop a greater repertoire of knowledge and skill.

The assistant principalship is an excellent source of professional development for the principalship role. Principals listed the assistant principalship role as one of their most valuable experiences in preparing for the responsibilities of the principalship. This experience should allow for development in all areas with major emphasis on instructional leadership. In this way, assistant principals will be prepared to take on the changing role of the principal.

CONCLUSION

The basic operating unit of U.S. education is the local school. It is at this level that teaching and learning occur and that services are provided. The role of the school board and school district staff is to support and facilitate the development of outstanding schools. At the same time, parents and other community members are seen as partners in this process.

As the demands on education have increased, school districts are shifting the roles of all those within the district, freeing the superintendent to work more closely with the board and community power structures, sharing greater authority and responsibility with local schools, and expecting the central office staff to provide the needed support for both. The principal and teachers within the school are expected to be more entrepreneurial, having the power and authority to come up with needed school improvements and seeing them through to success. The central office administrators are to facilitate, support, and assess these efforts. The superintendent and board are to articulate core values and outcomes, obtain political support, develop alignment, provide resources, and maintain accountability for results. This entire process works best when it is open, allowing for input from parents and community members as well as public, nonprofit, and private organizations.

The principal deals briefly with the rapid events that occur and often communicates in brief encounters and unscheduled meetings. The principal also spends a good deal of time on management of school matters, instructional and curricular leadership, pupil control, teacher development, and community relations. The principal is concerned with staff issues and recognizes how necessary it is to have staff support to succeed. The biggest concern is how often urgent matters (crises, pressing problems, deadline-driven activities) have gotten in the way of what is important (instructional leadership, teacher development). Principals recognize how important it is to be a proactive instructional leader rather than a reactive manager. Fullan (1997) concludes:

> People change organizations. The starting point is not system change or change in those around us, but taking action ourselves. The challenge is to improve education in the only way it can be—through the day-to-day actions of empowered individuals. This is what's worth fighting for in the school principalship. (p. 47)

MyEdLeadershipLab™

Go to Topic 3: *Supervision* in the MyEdLeadershipLab™ site (www.MyEdLeadershipLab.com) for *Educational Leadership: A Bridge to Improved Practice*, Fifth Edition, where you can:

- Find learning outcomes for *Supervision* along with the national standards that connect to these outcomes.
- Complete Assignments and Activities that can help you more deeply understand the chapter content.
- Apply and practice your understanding of the core skills identified in the chapter with the Building Leadership Skills unit.
- Prepare yourself for professional certification with a Practice for Certification quiz.

PORTFOLIO ARTIFACTS

- Ask to serve as "principal for a day." Note the various roles, responsibilities, obligations, time commitments, and issues that occur in this single day.

- Attend a superintendent's administrative meeting.

- Attend a school board meeting in two different school districts. Compare and contrast the two meetings.

- Compare the organizational charts of two school districts of similar size. Describe the differences you see.

- Review your school system's organizational chart and the job descriptions of key leadership positions.

- Search the Web for organizations such as:

    AASA—http://www.aasa.org
    AASPA—http://www.aaspa.org
    AERA—http://www.aera.net
    ASCD—http://www.ascd.org
    CCSSO—http://www.ccsso.org
    NAESP—http://www.naesp.org
    NASSP—http://www.nassp.org

NBPTS—http://www.nbpts.org
NPBEA—http://www.npbea.org
NMSA—http://www.nmsa.org
NSBA—http://www.nsba.org
NCPEA—http://www.ncpea.net
UCEA—http://www.ucea.org

Who are their target audiences? What do they offer to members?

KEY TERMS

- Accountability
- Authority and responsibility
- Decentralization and delegation
- Dependent and independent school board
- Instructional leadership
- Leadership and management
- Line and staff
- Operational areas
- Policy and procedures
- Politics
- School improvement planning (SIP)

SUGGESTED READINGS

Fullan, M. (2008). *What's worth fighting for in the principalship?* New York, NY: Teachers College Press.

Goodman, C., & Berry, C. (2010). *Great assistant principals and the (great) principals who mentor them.* Larchmont, NY: Eye on Education.

Townsend, R. (2005). *A practical guide to effectual school board meetings.* Thousand Oaks, CA: Corwin Press.

Ubben, G., Hughes, L., & Norris, C. (2010). *The principal: Creative leadership for excellence in schools* (7th ed.). Boston, MA: Allyn and Bacon.

Woolfok, A., & Hoy, W. K. (2008). *Instructional leadership: A research based guide to learning in schools.* Boston, MA: Allyn & Bacon.

APPENDIX 4A

Roles and Responsibilities of Superintendents and School Boards

The Board's Responsibilities

- To establish and regularly review all policies, ensuring they are lawful and designed to improve the quality of the school district
- To hire, support, and conduct an annual formal evaluation of the superintendent of the schools
- To refer administrative communications, including questions, complaints, and personnel inquiries to the superintendent, as appropriate, and to follow the board-established chain of command
- To seek the superintendent's recommendation before taking action
- To adopt, advocate for, and oversee a school budget, which is responsive to district goals and meets the needs of all students
- To delegate to the superintendent responsibility for all administrative functions, except those specifically reserved to the board through board policy
- To conduct an annual self-evaluation of its own leadership, governance, and teamwork
- To ensure appropriate resources for the superintendent to carry out his or her responsibilities
- To have the board chair work with the superintendent to develop meeting agendas
- To determine and include in district policy hiring procedures that clearly define board and superintendent responsibilities
- To communicate and interpret the school district's mission to the public and to listen and incorporate appropriate community perspectives into board action
- To ensure there is a supportive, smoothly operating leadership team that advocates both for children and the community

The Superintendent's Responsibilities

- To implement policies approved by the board and recommend changes, if appropriate
- To develop, implement, and inform the board of administrative procedures necessary to implement board policy
- To serve as the school board's chief executive officer and educational leader
- To respond to communications as appropriate and ensure the adherence and appropriate response through the chain of command
- To keep board members informed about district issues in a timely manner
- To provide the board with good information for informed decision making, as appropriate
- To prepare, advocate for, and implement an annual budget that addresses district goals and meets the needs of all students and to report regularly to the board on the status of the budget and any concerns or other issues about which the board should be informed

- To oversee the organization and management of the district's day-to-day operations
- To participate, as appropriate, in the annual self-evaluation of the board
- To recommend appropriate resources to ensure all responsibilities can be accomplished
- To work closely with the board chair to develop meeting agendas
- To hire personnel for the school district as pursuant to best practice and board policy, and to ensure that each employee is properly supervised and evaluated; and to make recommendations for termination of employment
- To communicate community perspectives, research information, performance results, and educational needs to the board and to the school staff
- To serve as an effective key member of the leadership team

Joint Responsibilities

- To work together with the community to develop a vision and goals for the school district and to monitor the achievement of those goals
- To advocate for students and the school district and promote the benefits of public education
- To provide community leadership on educational issues by creating strong linkages with appropriate organizations, agencies, and other groups to provide support for healthy development and high achievement for all children
- To collectively execute their legal responsibilities
- To work collaboratively with appropriate agencies and bodies on an ongoing basis
- To collaborate with other school boards and superintendents to inform legislators of local concerns and issues relative to education
- To participate in continuing education specifically regarding their roles and responsibilities and on relevant content areas
- To support board actions and decisions
- To semiannually set aside time to discuss school board–superintendent relations
- To belong to, actively support, and participate in their professional organizations, and to each encourage the other to do so
- To institute a process for long-range and strategic planning that will position the school district for success
- To ensure that professional development opportunities, consistent with district goals, are available to all school district employees
- To serve as liaisons to the community
- To ensure adherence to federal and state laws and board policies

Copies of the entire statement, which also includes sections on hiring personnel and the relationship between the board chair and superintendent, are available at the Web sites of the Connecticut Association of Boards of Education (http://www.cabe.org) and the Connecticut Association of Public Schools Superintendents (http://www.capss.org).

Source: Larson, D., & Rader, R. (May 2006). Working together. *American School Board Journal, 196,* 5, 30–33. Reprinted with permission from *American School Board Journal,* May 2006. © 2006 National School Boards Association. All rights reserved.

APPENDIX 4B

Factors Influencing the Instructional Climate in Schools

1. *Organizational Culture (OC).* The culture of an organization identifies the beliefs and values that guide the activities and members of the school. Culture includes the processes used to delineate the vision, mission, goals, and belief/guiding principles of the organization. DuFour and Eaker (1998) assert that the most effective schools give everyone a shared sense of purpose and create shared responsibility for the purpose. The culture of the school can be seen in how the school operates, how things are done, and how decisions are made. Research suggests that cultures framed around responsibilities for, and communication about, student achievement result in superior academic progress.

   Descriptors. Focus on school-wide goals, staff input, development and communication of shared mission, values, goals, and decisions based on student achievement.

2. *Academic Emphasis (AE).* The academic emphasis of an organization defines the degree to which the school is focused on student achievement. The organization shares the accountability for all student achievement regardless of the job assignment. All involved believe in the students' ability to achieve. Leaders provide the staff time to collaborate and focus on instructional strategies and best practices as they apply to instruction. Instructional time is valued and leaders ensure noninstructional interruptions are limited or eliminated.

   Descriptors. Monitors student progress; students receive appropriate instruction; protects instructional time from interruptions; decisions are made in the best academic interest of students; data are monitored; professional development is provided; time to collaborate among staff is provided; teachers are knowledgeable and share curriculum, instructional strategy, and common assessments.

3. *Affiliation (AF).* The level of teacher support within an organization allows a sense of trust and commitment to develop among the instructional staff. Teacher support is shown through the actions and behaviors of staff within the school. Leaders take the initiative to get to know staff and encourage staff to get to know one another. Staff members achieve goals with a sense of enthusiasm and commitment.

   Descriptors. Sets a positive climate; staff members are committed to their jobs and willingly expend energy to fulfill mission; accomplishments are acknowledged; staff members actively listen to one another; time is provided to get to know one another; staff members are complimented, successes are celebrated, and teachers efforts are rewarded.

4. *Resource Support (RS).* The amount of resource support provided to the staff of an organization has an effect on the staff members' ability to meet goals. Resources such as curriculum guides, textbooks, paper, and time are critical to students' success. Teachers believe their basic instructional needs are met and resources are readily available to support goal achievement.

   Descriptors. Classroom supplies are available (pen, pencil, glue); paper is available; time is provided for planning and instruction; each student has a textbook and teacher's guides are available; each teacher has a copy of the curriculum;

science materials are available; Internet access and appropriate technology are provided; content-based manipulatives are available; sufficient materials are readily available.

5. *Learning Incentives (LI).* Learning incentives are both tangible and intangible. A systematic process for recognizing and rewarding the accomplishments of students is in place and recognitions are freely communicated to staff, parents, and students. Staff members discuss students' academic progress using the results of assessments and recognize and, when appropriate, reward student accomplishments.

   Descriptors. Monitors student progress; publicly awards achievements; stays ahead of research; encourages teacher support of students; promotes current curriculum, instruction, and assessment practices.

6. *Communication (C).* The leaders have established a systematic, two-way communication process to ensure all staff members are provided with information needed to do their job. Staff members are encouraged to share their thoughts and ideas in a nonthreatening environment. The leaders make frequent visits to classrooms to walk through and identify areas of strength and opportunities for improvement as it relates to instruction. With open communication, leaders are highly visible throughout the school and touch base with each staff member throughout the week.

   Descriptors. Classroom visits/observations; open-door policy; clear communication process; easily accessible; provides teachers opportunities to communicate with each other; positive attitude; provides parents and community with communication process; maintains high visibility; discusses school issues.

7. *Professional Development (PD).* Learning leaders promote continuous, ongoing, and job-embedded professional development for all staff members. Learning opportunities are provided for staff members based on identified needs and follow-up support is found in high-performing schools. The opportunities offered to staff members are meaningful and directly relate to jobs/positions. Staff members are provided opportunities to contribute to the choices of professional development that are offered. Learning leaders are seen participating in the professional development offerings alongside the staff.

   Descriptors. Lesson study; peer observations; examining student work; portfolios; national board certification process; self-assessment and goal setting; book study; performance observations; professional development committee; mentoring.

Source: Cunningham, W. G., & Nunnery, J. A. (2007, November 16). *Developing an effective instructional climate for all students.* Paper presented at the 2007 annual UCEA Conference in Alexandria, VA.

CHAPTER 5

LEADERSHIP THEORY AND PRACTICE

MyEdLeadershipLab™

Visit the MyEdLeadershipLab™ site for *Educational Leadership: A Bridge to Improved Practice*, Fifth Edition to enhance your understanding of chapter concepts. You'll have the opportunity to practice your skills through video- and case-based Assignments and Activities as well as Building Leadership Skills units, and to prepare for your certification exam with Practice for Certification quizzes.

ATLAS SHRUG HIGH SCHOOL

Failing Health

You are in the second year of your first principalship. Atlas Shrug High School has an enrollment of 1,600 students and 65 full-time teachers. This old school has had a number of problems, and you were brought in to take charge. The new superintendent of the district has given you considerable freedom in determining how to turn Atlas Shrug around to be more responsive to student needs and the district's new reform agenda.

Recent standardized test scores indicate that the students, most from middle-class homes, are scoring slightly below national and state averages. Only 52% are performing at or above grade level in mathematics and science, two areas of particular concern. The superintendent has noticed that a much higher percentage, over 65% of the students, receive As and Bs in their course work, and 90% earn Cs or above.

The teachers explain away these inconsistencies, such as one highly influential teacher, who states, "The tests do not measure the skills that we have traditionally believed to be important at Atlas Shrug. We have prepared students for a long while and know a lot more about these students and their parents than can be learned from any tests." In general, there are few complaints from either the teachers or the community about Atlas Shrug High School.

Few improvements have been made in the school, and teachers often express concern at how difficult and traumatic it is to try anything new. A number of innovative teachers have requested transfers. The new superintendent has charged the Office of Research to help the district gain a better understanding of the overall health of the schools within the district and their readiness for renewal efforts. The office is beginning with the Organizational Health Instrument (OHI), developed by Dr. Marvin Fairman and associates (Fairman, Holmes, Hardage, & Lucas, 1979), to look at critical dimensions of school health. The following 10 dimensions focus on the preparedness and probable success of any improvement effort within the schools:

1. *Goal focus* measures the degree to which members of the organization clearly perceive and share system goals and objectives.

2. *Communication adequacy* refers to the extent to which information flows freely and without distortion, vertically and horizontally, within the organization.

3. *Optimal power equalization* relates to the distribution of influence between subordinates and superiors within the work group.

4. *Resource utilization* measures the extent to which resources within the organization, particularly personnel, are obtained and used effectively.

5. *Cohesiveness* measures the extent to which members of the organization feel attracted to, and wish to remain with, the organization.

6. *Morale* measures the degree to which members of the work group experience feelings of well-being, satisfaction, and pleasure in being part of the organization.

7. *Innovativeness* relates the extent to which members of the work group believe the organization to be open, responsive, innovative, diverse, and supportive of creative thinking and risk taking.

8. *Autonomy* refers to the ability of the organization to deal with external pressure while maintaining its ideals and goals.

9. *Adaptation* describes the organization's ability to tolerate stress and maintain stability while coping with the demands of, and responses to, the external environment.

10. *Problem-solving adequacy* measures members' perceptions of the degree to which the organization can solve problems completely and efficiently.

The results were reported by dimension percentile score measuring in percent the degree to which each characteristic exists in a school as compared with a normal set of schools (70% and above is an acceptable score). The results for Atlas Shrug High School are as follows:

DIMENSION	PERCENTILE SCORE
Resource utilization	88
Goal focus	83
Problem-solving adequacy	80
Communication	74
Innovativeness	35
Cohesiveness	32
Autonomy	30
Morale	27
Adaptation	25
Optimal power equalization	17

"These can't be right!" responds Guy Francon, your assistant principal, who has been at the school more than 7 years. The director of research assures Francon that the data were collected very carefully and have been double checked and that these are, in fact, the perceptions of the teachers. Francon continues, "I don't mean that your figures are wrong but that the teachers are wrong. We are able to cope with external demands, the teachers do have influence, there are clear school expectations, and the morale is much higher than this shows. They say they want to be involved but they seem very passive and unwilling to put in the time. They seem satisfied with existing programs. Sometimes their recommendations are unacceptable, and we have to be accountable that good decisions have been made. After all, the administration is responsible for this school." The director of the research department explains, "The teachers' responses are not right or wrong. This is an expression of their perceptions of the school. If you don't think these perceptions are correct, it is important to find out why the teachers hold these perceptions. It is important that the profile is interpreted, along with other information regarding your school."

Other data suggest that very little change has taken place at Atlas Shrug High School over the past 10 years. Test scores are still low, grade inflation is still high, teacher evaluations and development are uninspiring, curriculum and instruction have not changed, community involvement is limited, and although there have been few complaints, morale is not good. There is no spirit or responsiveness in this school. Although no one makes waves and there are no obvious problems, the school seems to lack energy or excitement, and, worse, it seems to produce mediocre results, with little being done to improve them. You begin to ask yourself, "What is wrong in this school?"

✳ **What might explain the wide range in the percentile scores on the 10 dimensions of organizational health? Are teachers' perceptions of their organization's health, ethos, and culture important? Why or why not?**

LEADERSHIP AND MANAGEMENT

There is a saying: "I have to run very fast to get ahead of the group for I am their leader." Although this is said with tongue in cheek, there is some truth to it. Certainly, a leader must be very sensitive to the context in which the organization is embedded and the thinking, vision, and passion of those within the organization he or she is leading. Although leadership has probably been studied throughout time, there have been more intense efforts to gain greater understanding over the past 100 years. The exact nature of leadership continues to be debated; however, in much of the literature, a new sense of agreement is developing. It is important for those who plan to assume leadership positions to have some sense of the thinking regarding leadership and how that thinking has evolved. To a large extent, an administrator's leadership determines how successful his or her organization will be in delivering appropriate services and winning community support.

Administration is the broadest term related to organizational responsibility, *management* focuses on efficient use of resources, and *leadership* focuses on organizational direction and purpose. Administrators are expected to be effective leaders and efficient managers. Management focuses on the nuts and bolts of making the organization work, such as hiring, distributing resources, and enforcing policy and procedures (Hanson, 1991). Northhouse (1997) states, "Management is about seeking order and stability; leadership is about seeking adaptive and constructive change" (p. 8). Leadership is doing the right things, management is doing things right, and administration is responsible for both.

Leadership draws others into the active pursuit of the strategic goals. Scholars (Cunningham, 1982; Miles and Louis, 1990; Sergiovanni, 2001) suggest that leadership ranges from vision, mission, purpose, direction, and inspiration and management to implementing plans, arranging resources, coordinating effort, and generally seeing that things get done. You can have strong leaders who are weak managers and vice versa. Strong administrators are good at both leadership and management.

Leadership has to do with guiding improvement and infusing an organization with meaning and purpose, whereas *management* is involved with stewardship and accountability for all types of resources. Management also focuses on implementing routines in an organization and ensuring its smooth operation. Barker (1992) states, "You manage within a paradigm, you lead between paradigms" (p. 164). The line between these two concepts remains fuzzy for some, and the terms are occasionally used synonymously.

Leadership, by far the most studied aspect of administrative behavior, is especially important because we have entered a time of transformation. Reform in education is a continuous process of improvement to meet the needs of a dynamic society. Leadership in this new "era of change" requires the ability to envision an improved school and the spark to energize and lead staff to bring it about. Improvement requires perseverance, nurturing, and problem solving. Leaders must be entrepreneurial in the sense that they empower employees to meet new challenges.

Leadership has many definitions. Hoy and Miskel (2008) state, "The only assumption shared by this and most definitions is that leadership involves a social influence process in which one individual exerts intentional influence over others to structure activities and relationships in a group or organization" (p. 419). Disputes about definitions remain, however, over whether leadership is a specialized role or social influence process; over the kind, basis, and purpose of influence attempts; and over leadership versus management (Yukl, 2002). Leadership has functional, emotional, ethical, and philosophical foundations that are important in understanding and critiquing leadership approaches and styles.

The study of administration is grounded in science and philosophy, in theories and ethics. Thus, a person's epistemology—the way a person thinks and determines reality and the way that person approaches work—is critically important. The premise is that good theory provides useful knowledge to guide effective practice. The administrator's skills and abilities are improved by both theory and practice. As John Dewey suggested long ago, there is nothing as practical as a good theory. Theories provide the conceptual tools to focus the work of the administrator: They are guides to action. They provide a reasonable base for tactics and strategies that might improve the educational administrator's success. Greenfield (1995) states:

> More complete knowledge of these two realms (the nature and centrality of leadership in schools and the demand environment [context] to which it responds) will provide a basis for more powerful theories about school administration, more informed preparation curricula, and more concrete guidance regarding the specific intentions, strategies, behaviors, and process associated with effective leadership in schools. (p. 80)

Philosophical Frames and Epistemological Influences

Paradigms can provide a general overview of the development of major themes as ideas about leadership transform and evolve. Paradigms identify the main components of concepts, which embody the way something operates.

Heck and Hallinger (1999) state:

> During the past decade, the fields of education and management have both been
> in the midst of paradigm shifts. These shifts have led to the reconsideration of the
> theoretical conceptualizations as well as research methods. (p. 142)

Understanding and classifying the thinking that influences theory and knowledge
development in educational administration involves turbulent debates in regard
to types of epistemology, research orientation, and knowledge bases. Such turbulence portrays the rifts and currents alive in our field today. Before studying
leadership, it is important to gain an understanding of the many perspectives that
influence the current knowledge base.

For example, the previously dominant scientific paradigm has been eclipsed
in the postmodern age. The claim that administration is a closed scientific system
has faced severe challenges (Callahan, 1962; Greenfield, 1988; Willower, 1979).
Griffiths (1979) criticizes science and the cult of efficiency for failing to provide
ethical guidance and to theorize gender issues and for being unable to support political analysis or to adjudicate conflicts of interest. Feminist critics Carol Gilligan
(1982), Jill Blackmore (2009), and Margaret Grogan and Charol Shakeshaft (2011)
demonstrate the neglect of gender issues in administrative theory and research.
James Banks (1993) expressed concern that educational administrative research
might also be racially biased. With our dominant frames of reference for educational administration, views from other races or cultures can be relegated to the
margins in terms of legitimacy. Schewick and Young (1997) state that:

> [A]s we teach and promote epistemologies like positivism to postmodernism, we
> are at least implicitly teaching and promoting the social history of the dominant
> race at the exclusion of people of color, scholars of color and the possibility for
> research based on other race/culture epistemologies. We can, however, use our
> opposition to racism to consider the question of whether our dominant epistemolo-
> gies are racially biased and, if they are, to begin to change the situation. (p. 11)

Most criticism of logical empiricism and science has come from difficulties
with empirical adequacy as a criterion of theory choice (Evers & Lakomski, 1996;
Greenfield, 1993; Hodgkinson, 1991). Useful patterns to explain organization and
educational administration "draw on more criteria than just empirical adequacy—
such as consistency, simplicity, comprehensiveness, utility of explanation, learnabil-
ity and fecundity" (Evers & Lakomski, 1996, p. 386). Logical empiricism, traditional
science, behaviorism, critical theory, subjectivism, feminism, and postmodernism all
provide alternative and often conflicting perspectives within administrative theory.

Paradigms and the Scientific/Rational Approach

Paradigms provide frameworks of thought that rest on a belief system and some
scientific data and facts. Paradigms are the way we understand and explain our
world. They are our way of perceiving, thinking, valuing, and achieving based on

our particular explanations of complex behavior. Barker (1992) states, "A paradigm is a set of rules and regulations (written or unwritten) that does two things: (1) it establishes or defines boundaries; and (2) it tells you how to behave inside the boundaries in order to be successful" (p. 32). We see the world through our paradigms. "What may be perfectly visible, perfectly obvious to persons with one paradigm may be quite literally invisible to persons with a different paradigm" (p. 86).

In its simplest form, a paradigm is the set of rules by which something operates. When an organization's paradigm changes, the way it operates changes as well. This shift usually results in confusion, turbulence, and chaos as the changes dramatically upset the existing theoretical explanation and status quo. The changing of the rules, theory, or paradigms is the earliest sign of a significant change in our understanding of the world.

Scientists see unfounded explanations as ideologies. Under the influence of ideologies, decisions are based on personal interpretation and not on rational inquiry and analysis and scientific methods. Usually politics, not science, is used to mediate discordant ideologies, disparate value systems, and conflicting points of view. Scientists do not hold ideology in high regard because it is often based on speculation or a body of unproven doctrine. They often do not accept ideologies as truth because the concepts rest on "self-evident" or "unexamined" truths (English, 1993, p. 49). Basing decision on thought processes other than science can result in an organization's continual floundering, as it is buffeted by constantly shifting and unproven ideologies (Barker, 1992).

✳ **How do the ideas expressed about the scientific approach relate to the strategies being taken at Atlas Shrug High School?**

Political, Critical, and Constructivist Frames of Reference

Thomas Greenfield (1978, 1979, 1980, 1985, 1988) forcefully attacked many assumptions embedded in the scientific/rational approach. He believed that ends could not be separated from means, facts from underlying values, or rational thinking and action from preferences, passions, and ideologies. Each type of thinking and acting is subjective rationality—justifiable from the thinker's perspective. Greenfield recognized as important the truly irrational outbursts that influence our everyday lives and the course of history—that drive humans to do what they do. Greenfield suggested that educational administration could benefit from philosophy, history, law, political theory, sociology, and anthropology—and not solely science.

Investigation that adequately grasps administrational and organizational complexity must identify motives, emotions, attitudes, abilities, intentions, preferences, values, beliefs, relationships, and many other factors that complicate administrative practice. Understanding organizational structures, functions, and roles requires critical examination of ideology, power, force, authority, legitimization, and conflict.

The net effect of such critiques was to call into question the legitimacy and appropriateness of a single foundation of knowledge based on the scientific/rational approach and the professional status of such a knowledge base (Donmoyer, 1999a). Such challenges open up possibilities for new types of responses and free us from the rigidity of science. The result can be an educative and transformational process in which organizational aspects such as vision, goals, practices, rewards, structures, policies, and controls might be altered. Critical theorists argue that administrators are not neutral, rational, scientific bureaucrats. They operate from a value base that affects their views, decisions, and actions (Scribner, Aleman, & Maxcy, 2003).

Critical/Contextual Ideas of Gender and Race

Feminist theorists begin with a desire to offer a reconceptualization of administration based strongly on the beliefs and values of women. The present administrative knowledge base, developed under a white male perspective, is universal only to the extent that women and people of color respond like white males do. Gilligan (1982) challenges the dominant ethic of justice and proposes an ethic of care and conceptualizes moral maturity as caring for and sensitivity to the needs of others. Gilligan (1993) writes:

> As we have listened for centuries to the voices of men and the theories of development that their experience informs, so we have come more recently to notice not only the silence of women but that the different voice of women lies in the truth of an ethic of care. . . . The failure to see the different reality of women's lives and to hear the differences in their voices stems in part from the assumption that there is a single mode of social experience and interpretation. . . .
>
> While an ethic of justice proceeds from the premise of equality—that everyone should be treated the same—an ethic of care rests on the premise of nonviolence—that no one should be hurt. (pp. 173–174)

English (2008) talks about the importance of compassion, which is different from caring because it stresses both empathy and action.

Feminist critique (Noddings, 1992) stresses the importance of all people and an ethics of relationship and care. The emphasis is "on living together, on creating, on maintaining, and enhancing positive relations" (p. 21). Feminist theories encourage administrators to challenge the conflicts between self-interest and the desire to "act on behalf of others." Noddings suggests that administrative decisions are related to how we are situated, who we are, and to whom we are related. Feminist critique stresses the importance of engaging in public, moral deliberation and making and revising decisions according to the results of such debate and not solely on technical, rational, scientific, and political expertise. The emphasis is on responsibility and relationships as much as on rights and rules.

Shakeshaft (1995) focuses on differences in the way male and female administrators perceive situations. Her work is based on the belief that gender and race differences influence behavior and perspective. For example, male administrators are less likely to promote women into positions of close working proximity because they feel uncomfortable in a close working relationship and are concerned with image problems among colleagues, subordinates, and family members. Women seem to value community and relationship building more than men do. Men typically receive more feedback, and more types of feedback, than women do. Furthermore, women often receive positive feedback even when their performance is less than ideal, depriving them of an equal opportunity to improve their performance. Males fear the prospect of women's tears and often hold back negative comments. The work environment of women is also one that has elements of sexual fear and threats that can be perceived as unsafe. Shakeshaft (1995) concludes:

> The point of examining these differences is not to say one approach is right and one is wrong (the way theory and practice up to now have done), but rather to help us understand that males and females may be coming from very different places, and that unless we understand these differences, we aren't likely to work well together. (pp. 153–154)

Starratt (1991) suggests that educational administrators need to draw on both care (understanding, sensitivity, nurturing) and justice (rationality, rights, laws) to create ethical schools. (See Chapter 1.)

Concern has been expressed (Banks, 1993; Young & Brooks, 2008) that administrative epistemologies used in research and practice might be racially biased. Banks (1993) suggests, "all knowledge reflects the values and interests of its creators" (p. 4).

The bottom line is that a person's perception of truth can be blurred by his or her system of beliefs, assumptions, values, contexts, words, and decisions. These marginalized people become invisible because people in the dominant group refuse to see them.

Foster (1986) suggested that in the objective world of fact, conclusions are based on empirical evidence; in the moral world of rightness, they are based on sanctioned discourse and debates about values such as truth, justice, and equality. Foster approached administration and leadership as praxis—a practical action aimed at clarifying and resolving social conditions:

> Praxis must be thought of as practical action, informed by theory, that attempts to change various conditions. In one respect, then, change involves a raising of consciousness about possibilities by penetrating the dominating ideas or total ideologies and analyzing the possible forms of life. This orientation, while political and cultural, is also critical, because it suggests that we attempt to cut through the "natural" taken-for-granted status quo to explore new arrangements. (p. 167)

For Foster, leadership requires critical reflection and analysis by all in a process of empowerment and transformation.

Postmodernism, Poststructuralism

Postmodernists "argue that all forms of knowing have equal legitimacy, all expressions are acceptable forms of voice, and there are no hierarchies of wisdom" (Glickman, 1998, p. 40). For the practitioner who confronts the day-to-day operation of the school, utility can be the only criterion under the pressure of today's environment. West (1992) suggests, "new cultural politics of difference . . . align themselves with demoralized, demobilized, depoliticized, and disorganized people in order to empower and enable social action" (p. 65).

Postmodernism addresses the importance of creativity, imagination, and vision. In a rapidly changing environment, organizations must articulate realistic, credible, and attractive futures. Progress is the "realization of a vision" that is used to guide successful improvement. It begins as a statement of dreams that develop from inspiration and creative insights. Such thinking is more imagery than words, more perception than conception. It is the presentation of scenarios and visions that express dreams and are tempered with an understanding of what is possible— a belief in what should and can be. In discussing these frames of references, Evers and Lakomski (1996) state:

> Really massive gains over experience come from manipulating theory formulations so that they apply to matters beyond experience, enabling us to think hypothetically and act accordingly. The imagination so augmented can explore policy and decision option spaces that have not been lived through, perhaps not with precision, owing to the friability of current administrative theory and its context dependence, but with a modest prospect of beating chance. (p. 140)

Bolman and Deal (1995) suggest that leaders have lost touch with the types of understanding that give our lives passion and purpose. As they suggest, it is "about the search for something bigger. . . . Seek new sources of vigor, meaning, and hope to enrich your life and leave a better legacy for those who come after you" (pp. 11–12). These sources animate, inspire, and transform as they operate on emotional and spiritual resources and on inherent values, commitments, and aspirations. They provide a deep, noble sense of purpose and inspiration.

Postmodern thought is skeptical because most social reality and perhaps much of reality is constructed through established narratives (Foster, 2004). As John Lennon said, "Reality leaves a lot of room for the imagination." Power verifies or reinforces the truth of the narratives and supports a like-minded, well-rewarded, and self-appointed way of thinking. This has caused English (2006) to conclude:

> There are no single, unitary, undisputed views of 'reality' regarding anything, and . . . the concept of a monolithic, uncontested, internally consistent fount of universally accepted stipulations and axioms and tenets for an academic discipline is an illusion, supported only in the case of accreditation by a forced, muscular application of raw political power. (pp. 461–462)

The critics of postmodernism point out its failings but recognize that it has something to offer to our understanding. Constas (1998) states:

> We need to consider the idea that the postmodern version of educational inquiry is just another variety of discourse in education and should not be granted special

privileges . . . because I believe that an overreliance on any one disciplinary perspective is necessarily confining, it is worth exploring the way educational research may be situated, explained and enlivened. (pp. 30–31)

According to Marshall and Anderson (1995), theories provide lenses or windows that provide a particular view of social phenomena, opening up vistas not to be seen from other windows/theories. In this way, new theoretical perspectives can make visible those aspects of traditional educational phenomena made invisible by previous theoretical frames. New theories can also illuminate previously ignored phenomena, opening up new areas for critical examination (p. 169).

This has resulted in questioning of the concept of a "knowledge base" for educational leadership and substitution of a "knowledge dynamic." Because our knowledge is ever expanding, shifting, and changing, we must recognize that the foundations of our practice are, in fact, dynamic and often influenced by our current context. We must avoid a mindset that sees only one legitimate way of working or a set of one-size-fits-all standards.

✳ **Does this philosophical discussion of frames of reference have anything to do with understanding the situation and the possibilities of ultimate improvements at Atlas Shrug High School? Explain your answer.**

PARADIGMS OF LEADERSHIP: A GROWING KNOWLEDGE BASE

A person brings a personal style to any administrative position that permeates all that he or she does within the organization and serves as the screen through which he or she views organizational activity. Style is influenced by one's philosophical frames of reference and epistemology. These frames and epistemologies are reflected in the theories about leadership that have developed over the past 100 years. Frederick Taylor's (sometimes called the father of scientific management) theories are classic examples of the scientific/rational approach to administration. This scientific/rational approach views people as interchangeable parts of a machine (the bureaucracy) and studies physiological aspects and organizational structure, such as time and motion, human engineering, policy, procedure, tasks, delegation, control, and specialization (Fayol, 1949; Taylor, 1947; Urwick, 1937; Weber, 1947). These ideas are all important, but today it is widely recognized that they are by no means an adequate explanation of organizational leadership and productivity. They have been challenged by political, critical, feminine, and postmodernist frames of reference.

Mary Parker Follett (1942) was among the first to critique the mechanistic interpretation of organizations and the disregard of the human factor in the scientific approach to leadership (see Table 5.1). She was particularly concerned with the scientific belief that there is no place for debate, conflict, ambiguity, and perhaps chaos within organizations. Follett (1924) stated that these were "not necessarily a wasteful

TABLE 5.1   Benefits and Problems with Empirical Scientific Theory

CLASSICAL THEORIES	BENEFITS	PROBLEMS
Division of labor	Expertise	Boredom
Unity of command	One immediate supervisor	None
Hierarchy of authority	Disciplined coordination of power	Communication blocks
Operating procedures and regulations	Continuity and uniformity	Rigidity and lack of responsiveness
Standardization of tasks	Rationality	Lack of morale
Impersonal, objective orientation	Competition, incentive to produce	Conflict, lack of teamwork

Source: Hoy, W., & Miskel, C. (1991). *Educational administration: Theory, research, and practice.* New York, NY: McGraw-Hill. Reproduced with permission of McGraw-Hill.

outbreak of incompatibilities, but a normal process by which socially valuable differences register themselves for the enrichment of all concerned" (p. 300). Her work was later to influence the critical feminist and postmodernist theories of leadership.

Follett and other theorists spawned the human relations and organizational behavior movement. The development of this movement is usually traced back to Elton Mayo and the studies completed in the Hawthorne plant of the Western Electric Company in Chicago (Roethlisberger & Dixon, 1939). Perhaps the most important achievement of these findings was the tempering of the focus on organizational structure and the realization that the classical scientific theorists did not have all the answers.

Mayo's work directly challenged the concept that human beings could be viewed as passive cogs in a machine. One set of experiments held all other conditions constant and changed the frequency and duration of rest periods. The classic theories suggested that if people took more rests, the level of their output would go down because they would have less time to spend on the task. These experiments indicated, however, the actual productivity (output) of the employees went up when their rest pauses were increased. These puzzling findings later led to a number of other such discoveries that established the importance of studying organizational behavior. Behavioralism is concerned with psychological satisfaction, social interaction, motivation, job satisfaction, climate, ethos, group dynamics, interpersonal relations, empowerment, and organizational culture.

✳ **Which paradigms—scientific/rational and structuralist; organizational behavior, human relations, and behavioralistic theory; values, ethics, and control; political, critical, and constructivist; critical/contextual gender and race; or broad poststructural and postmodernist—best describe the perceived qualities at Atlas Shrug High School? On what basis did you draw this conclusion?**

LEADERSHIP INSTRUMENT ANALYSES

Following are some of the most popular and well-regarded theories of leadership among educational administration practitioners along with some associated self-diagnostic instruments. Complete the instruments first and analyze your results. Use them as self-reflection tools to enhance consideration of your own frames of reference and leadership style in relation to the theories presented. They can stimulate self-awareness, self-evaluation, as well as discussing, rethinking, and sometimes even changing practice, in a process referred to as "guided reflection" by Hole and McEntee (1999). Be advised, however, that people tend to record their intentions rather than their actual behavior (Argyris & Schön, 1978; Blake & McCanse, 1991). The purpose of instrument analysis is to lay the groundwork for people to initiate discussions about values, philosophies, epistimologies, perceptions, and attitudes and to stimulate reflective thinking about personal behavior. Reflections should include examples that support the responses you and colleagues provide and examples that frame behaviors first and then describe the effects of the behavior. This technique will help you see yourself while revealing how you and others view leadership.

McGregor's Theories X and Y

Douglas McGregor (1960) perceived an administrator's style as closely associated with his or her fundamental beliefs about human beings. He devised two contradictory views of human behavior, which he described as theory X and theory Y (Box 5.1). Respond to the X–Y scale presented in Box 5.1 to determine your X–Y beliefs about people (the scoring key appears in Appendix 5A at the end of this chapter). Box 5.2 presents the properties of X–Y belief patterns, which have been related to autocratic and democratic styles of leadership. The *autocratic style* is based on theory X assumptions in which leaders announce decisions, sell decisions, and invite questions about what is expected of others. In some cases, they might even test their ideas to learn how subordinates will respond in order to plan a rational strategy for forcing compliance. This approach relies heavily on the institutional authority of bureaucracy by carefully controlling the workforce, structuring the work, following standard operating procedures, emphasizing the importance of respect for positions of authority, threatening economic and professional harm to those who do not follow directives, and praising, rewarding and promoting those who do. The leader is granted the power to force followership.

The *democratic style* is based on theory Y assumptions, in which leaders delegate authority and responsibility and permit subordinates to function within defined limits. A more inclusive model, this form of leadership is collaborative; it encourages team effort to narrow possibilities and make final decisions. Leadership based on theory Y beliefs structure organizations and use leadership to facilitate and support efforts of subordinates to develop and express themselves and to act in the best interests of the organization. This style examines the values, preferences, and passions that influence a person's views, decisions, and actions. Theory Y leaders emphasize self-control and development, motivate through encouragement

BOX 5.1

THE X–Y SCALE

DIRECTIONS: As an administrator (manager, leader) you may engage in various types of behavior in relation to subordinates. Read each of the following items carefully, and then put a check mark in the appropriate column to indicate what you would do: 1 = make a great effort to do this, 2 = tend to do this, 3 = tend to avoid doing this, 4 = make a great effort to avoid this.

	1	2	3	4
1. Closely supervise my subordinates to get better work from them.				
2. Set the goals and objectives for my subordinates and sell them on the merits of my plans.				
3. Set up controls to ensure that my subordinates are getting the job done.				
4. Encourage my subordinates to set their own goals and objectives.				
5. Make sure that my subordinates' work is planned out for them.				
6. Check with my subordinates daily to see if they need any help.				
7. Step in as soon as reports indicate that the job is slipping.				
8. Push my people to meet schedules if necessary.				
9. Have frequent meetings to keep in touch with what is going on.				
10. Allow subordinates to make important decisions.				

The scoring instructions for the X–Y scale appear in Appendix 5A at the end of this chapter.

Source: McGregor, D. (1960). *The human side of enterprise.* New York, NY: McGraw-Hill. Reprinted with permission of McGraw-Hill.

and recognition of achievement, and expect quick response to and correction of any failures that occur (Tannenbaum & Schmidt, 1958). Organization members develop an understanding of themselves and prepare for and accept ownership of their work. The leader shares power, provides evaluative data, develops staff, and expects continuous improvement.

Leadership style may, in fact, influence the behavior of subordinates in such a way that the subordinates' behavior actually supports the use of the leader's preferred style, becoming a self-fulfilling prophecy. Thus, the leader's assumptions about a person and the way she or he treats that person may actually create the behavior—the Pygmalion effect—rather than vice versa. Autocratic approaches actually cause individuals to move toward immature behaviors, and democratic approaches cause people to move toward mature behaviors, whatever their initial starting points (Meyer, Kay, & French, 1965). Box 5.3 presents a continuum of immature and mature behaviors. Autocratic styles might actually trigger the

BOX 5.2

MCGREGOR'S TWO MAJOR BELIEF PATTERNS

Theory X	Theory Y
1. People dislike and will avoid work if they can.	1. People find work as natural as play and prefer it to doing nothing.
2. People will shirk responsibility, are inherently lazy, lack creativity, and are unreliable, and therefore a leader must coerce, direct, and threaten them to make them work.	2. People are capable of self-direction and self-control; are naturally creative and strive for excellence; and therefore will make personal commitments to shared organizational goals.
3. People desire security, external direction, and rigid structuring; resist change and avoid responsibility; and have little ambition.	3. People seek and accept greater self-direction and new challenges and can be trusted with both authority and responsibility.

Source: McGregor, D. (1960). *The human side of enterprise.* New York, NY: McGraw-Hill. Reprinted with permission of McGraw-Hill.

BOX 5.3

CONTINUUM OF IMMATURE AND MATURE BEHAVIORS

(Type X) Immaturity _____	Maturity (Type Y)
Passive _____	Active
Dependent _____	Independent
Limited skills _____	Diverse skills
Erratic, shallow interest _____	Well supported, strong interests
Short-term perspective _____	Long-term perspective
Unempowered, subordinate mentality _____	Empowered, equal position
Lack of awareness of potential _____	Awareness and control of self

Source: Argyris, C. (1993). *The individual and the organization: Some problems of mutual adjustment.* New York, NY: Irvington.

lazy, indifferent, and intransigent reactions that are described as type X behaviors. Democratic leadership styles might motivate the more active, responsive, and self-directed approaches described as theory Y behaviors.

✳ **Are the perceived behaviors at Atlas Shrug High School more related to theory X or theory Y beliefs? What causes you to believe this?**

NREL Behavior Matrix

There is a great deal of diversity in the personal styles that people bring to their organization. As mentioned earlier, these styles serve as screens through which the individual views people, tasks, and organizations. Sayers-Kirsch and the Northwest Regional Educational Laboratory (1985) developed an instrument to help people identify their own behavior style and to identify and understand the basic styles of others. The following abbreviated version helps individuals to better understand these differences. As you think about the four descriptors below, place yourself along the continuum near the description that best describes you (stay off the midpoint):

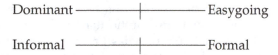

Dominant ─────────┼───────── Easygoing

Informal ─────────┼───────── Formal

The lines are next reorganized in order to develop four quadrants. Box 5.4 presents the reorganized lines in the form of a behavior matrix. Convert your marks to these axes and draw a horizontal and vertical line through your marks and determine the point where the two lines intersect. This will place you into a quadrant on the behavior matrix. After you have completed the interpretation of the matrix using Appendix 5B, hopefully you will draw the same conclusion that is supported by research, which is that successful people come from all quadrants of the matrix and an organization needs all four types of people to be successful. It is important for leaders to be reflective and to think through their strengths and weaknesses and

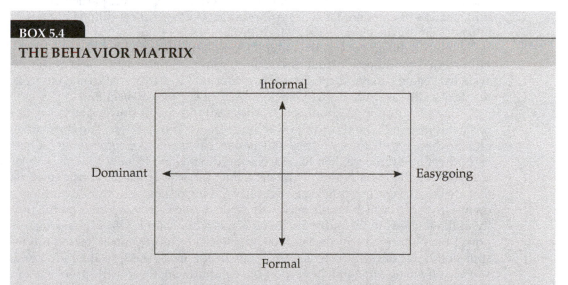

BOX 5.4

THE BEHAVIOR MATRIX

After placing yourself in one of these four quadrants, examine Appendix 5B at the end of the chapter in order to interpret the results. (Interpret and discuss the results.)

the types of people who will best complement their ability to lead and those with whom they might be most likely to be in conflict (look at Working Relationships: A Worksheet in Appendix 5B). Complete this worksheet and discuss it with others.

   * **What seems to be the dominant personal style and what impact is it having on teachers who are working at Atlas Shrug High School?**

Early Studies

Among the earliest studies from the huge body of literature on leadership were *The University of Iowa studies* (Levin, Lippet, & White, 1939), which suggested that leadership can be classified on the basis of how the leader handles several decision-making situations—authoritarian, democratic, and laissez-faire. The researchers found that subordinates preferred democratic styles, were aggressive or apathetic under authoritarian styles, and that laissez-faire produced aggressive behavior. Productivity was slightly higher under authoritarian than democratic leaders and was worse under laissez-faire leaders.

Path-goal theory (House, 1971; House & Boetz, 1990) suggests that by increasing the number and kinds of subordinate payoffs for the attainment of goals and by establishing paths to these payoffs (by clarifying the paths, reducing roadblocks and pitfalls, and increasing the opportunities for personal satisfaction along the way), the group will be able to achieve its goals. Employees work toward goals if they can see a source of satisfaction, and effective leaders make these sources contingent on subordinates' efforts. Such frameworks can be achieved through one of four distinct leadership behaviors: directive, supportive, participative, or achievement orientation. Each is appropriate under certain conditions but not in others. Subordinate characteristics include abilities, locus of control (whether the individual or others control the environment), and needs and motives. The environmental conditions include tasks, work group characteristics, and authority systems. Leader behaviors moderated by subordinate characteristics and environmental conditions result in effective performance and job satisfaction.

Compliance theory (Etzioni, 1975) creates a typology of power and how subordinates respond. The types of power are coercive, enumerative, and normative, and the three types of responses are alienation, calculation, or commitment. Coercive power uses force and fear to control subordinates and usually generates alienation among the more mature workers. Utilitarian power uses extrinsic rewards that are based on an external locus of control (giving others responsibility for one's own self-worth), which works best with a calculative response based on the utility of the rewards to the individual who is motivated in this way. The normative power uses intrinsic rewards based on an internal locus of control (taking full responsibility for oneself) in which the value of the work itself, to the individual, serves as the motivator and the response is commitment. Obviously, problems can develop when there is a mismatch of styles.

Theory Z (Ouchi, 1981) is an extension of McGregor's theory X and Y and focuses on culture. The theory Z culture exhibits trust, cooperation, collective decision making, career orientation, and teamwork. These characteristics create a sense of security, commitment, and loyalty to the organization. The employee is focused on career development and sees the organization as a community of equals who work cooperatively toward a common goal. Employees see their careers as investments over the long term that will be appreciated and rewarded.

Argyris (1993) questions the benefits of bureaucracy on the basis that it hinders employees from using their full potential. He views individuals as progressing along an immaturity to maturity continuum (see Box 5.3). As people mature, they require a greater level of independence, which bureaucracy and autocratic leadership do not support. As a result, these approaches can decrease the person's ability to reach his or her full level of development and thus make a maximum contribution to the organization. This can result in this person's becoming either aggressive or apathetic. Argyris supports a more participatory style of leadership that results in greater maturity, development, and productivity.

The Ohio State Studies

The *Ohio State studies* (Fleishman & Hunt, 1973; Hemphil & Coons, 1950; Stogdill, 1974, 1981) helped shift thinking away from a single-axis paradigm of leadership, usually with "democratic" and "autocratic" at either ends of the continuum, to a two-dimensional paradigm of leadership that includes two continuums: consideration and initiating structure. *Consideration* includes behavior indicating mutual trust, respect, and a certain warmth and rapport between the administrator and the work group. This dimension appears to emphasize a deep concern for group members and their development. It stresses such behavior as participation in decision making, encouraging communication, developing staff, supporting independent thinking, and keeping staff informed about the quality of their output.

Initiating structure includes behavior in which the supervisor organizes and defines group activities. The leader defines the role she or he expects each member to assume, assigns tasks, plans ahead, establishes work methods, pushes for improved productivity, emphasizes deadlines, encourages use of procedures, keeps staff members informed of what is expected of them, and follows up to ensure that staff members are working up to capacity. These two dimensions were found to be independent of one another; thus, a person could operate in one of four different quadrants—high on both dimensions, low on both, or high on one and low on the other.

Well over 100 studies of leadership have examined this model. The general findings suggest that consideration and initiating structure are positively related to various measures of group effectiveness, cohesiveness, and harmony. A leader who scores high on both of these dimensions would be considered more effective based on traditional values held by organizations. For example, Halpin (1956, 1966) completed a study of superintendents and found that the most effective were described as being high on both of these dimensions; Box 5.5 presents a leadership behavior instrument based on this research. (Complete the instrument before you examine the scoring instructions, which appear in Appendix 5C at the end of this chapter.) The most desirable approach to leadership, according to these researchers, is to stress both the importance of the individual and the importance of the task.

BOX 5.5

LEADERSHIP BEHAVIOR SURVEY

Instructions: Place a check mark in the column that most closely describes your behavior in group activities. Scale: 5 = always, 4 = often, 3 = occasionally, 2 = seldom, 1 = never

Behavior	1	2	3	4	5	*Behavior*	1	2	3	4	5
1. I make my attitude clear to the group.						16. I consult subordinates before taking action.					
2. I do personal favors for subordinates.						17. I emphasize the meeting of deadlines.					
3. I try out my new ideas with the group.						18. I back up subordinates in their actions.					
4. I do little things to make it pleasant to be a member of the group.						19. I encourage the use of uniform procedures.					
5. I rule with an iron hand.						20. I treat all subordinates as equals.					
6. I am easy to understand.						21. I make sure that my part of the organization is understood.					
7. I speak in a manner not to be questioned.						22. I am willing to make changes.					
8. I find time to listen to subordinates.						23. I ask that subordinates follow standard rules and regulations.					
9. I criticize poor work.						24. I am friendly and approachable.					
10. I mix with subordinates rather than keeping to myself.						25. I let subordinates know what is expected of them.					
11. I assign subordinates particular tasks.						26. I make subordinates feel at ease when talking with them.					
12. I look out for the personal welfare of individuals in my group.						27. I see to it that subordinates are working up to capacity.					
13. I schedule the work to be done.						28. I put suggestions made by my group into action.					
14. I explain my action to subordinates.						29. I see to it that the work of subordinates is coordinated.					
15. I maintain definite standards of performance.						30. I get group approval in important matters before acting.					
IS Column Total						**C Column Total**					

Source: Halpin, A. (1966). *Theory and research in administration.* Adapted by permission of Prentice Hall, Upper Saddle River, NJ.

✳ **In which of the four quadrants defined by the Ohio State studies do you believe the administration at Atlas Shrug High School would fall? Why? What benefits and what problems might this style cause?**

The New Managerial Grid

Although both were completed independently, the managerial grid (Blake & McCanse, 1991; Blake & Mouton, 1964, 1978) is a two-dimensional model that closely resembles the one in the Ohio State studies. The grid, which was the popularized version, includes various phases of training to help leaders become proficient in both dimensions of leadership. For these researchers, initiating structure was a "concern for production" and consideration was a "concern for people." Blake and McCanse (1991) identified seven different leadership styles, which they believe encompassed the most important differences among leaders, as follows (the double numbers show location on the grid).

  1. *Control and Dominate (Dictatorial).* A 9,1 person demonstrates a high concern for results and a low concern for people. The resulting style is autocratic; the person comes across like a steamroller, pushing for results without considering how his or her behavior influences others. "People" concerns—such as benefits, training, flexible work hours, and career paths—are given a low priority. Human qualities of relationships are seen as issues that slow down or impede the main focus of achieving sound results. The 9,1 does not mean to attack people, but he or she truly believes this is the only way to get the job done—and "all that other stuff is frills, anyway" that distract people from working hard.

  2. *Yield and Support (Accommodating).* The 1,9 person demonstrates a low concern for results with a high concern for others. The resulting style comes across as warm and friendly, but lacking in strength and purpose. This leader is the "nurturer" who is genuinely concerned about what people think and feel, and sees her or his role as generating enthusiasm and building morale rather than generating results. The 1,9 and 9,1 styles are diametrically opposed. Although both understand the difference in the two perspectives, they are unable to appreciate that these styles are equally harmful. Each of these orientations leads in a narrow and single-focused manner. The Achilles' heel in the 1,9 thinking is that "as long as I'm keeping people happy, results will follow." The evidence shows the opposite: Because there are never any serious consequences for poor performance, people respond by not really caring about personal or team effectiveness.

  3. *Balance and Compromise (Status Quo).* The 5,5 style is located in the middle of the grid with a medium level of concern for both results and people. Like the 9,1 and the 1,9, the 5,5 person believes there is an inherent contradiction between the two concerns. This contradiction is resolved by balancing the needs of people with results, through compromises and trade-offs rather than trying to achieve the soundest possible results. The objective is not to strive for excellence but to play it safe and work toward acceptable solutions. The 5,5 is often very informed, but his or her efforts are weakened by the objective of fitting in with popular trends.

Information gathered is not used for challenging standards and searching for creative solutions but is used to reduce or suppress controversy.

4. *Evade and Elude (Indifferent).* The 1,1 indifferent style, located in the lower left corner of the grid, represents the lowest level of concern for both results and people. This is the least visible person in a team; he or she is a "follower" who maintains a distance from active involvement whenever possible. The key word for this style is *neutral.* Such a person goes through the motions of work rituals, doing enough to get by and rarely making a deliberate effort to do more. 1,1 survival is possible in structured workplaces where the boundaries of effort are clearly defined and communication is minimal. This sort of workplace allows the 1,1 to blend in without attracting attention.

5. *Prescribe and Guide (Paternalistic).* The (1,9; 9,1), or paternalism style, results from the coming together of two individual grid styles in a way that produces a unique, joined style. Relationships with the paternalists are like parent to child where reward comes from the 1,9 influence and punishment comes from the 9,1 influence to dictate behaviors. The resulting style is a controlling and dominating person who also seeks approval and admiration. A person who complies receives rewards in the form of praise, advantage, and benefits that are more characteristic of the 1,9 style. This person is still expected to maintain the high standards of performance, but receives more support, guidance, encouragement, forgiveness, and overall "help" from the paternalist along the way. A person who does not comply receives more of a 9,1 treatment as seen in increased scrutiny, "prove to me you are worthy of my support," and "this is for your own good" attitude regarding expectations for performance.

6. *Exploit and Manipulate (Opportunistic).* The opportunist is a person who uses whatever grid style is needed to advance his or her personal goals. This person has little concern for what is best for others or the company and instead is driven by the ever-present question, "What's in it for me?" The opportunist uses whatever grid style is needed to help her or him along. The 1,9 is appealed to with 1,9 values, and the 9,1 is appealed to with 9,1 values. The opportunist succeeds by using and deceiving people in order to gain trust and support and move on. Because people learn fast, the opportunist cannot make a lasting impact without being exposed as self-serving.

7. *Contribute and Commit (Sound).* The 9,9 demonstrates a high concern for both results and people. 9,9 leadership is based on examining "what's right," not "who's right?" The 9,9 leader rises above politics and fears to constantly evaluate actual effectiveness against standards of excellence. These leaders utilize feedback and criticism to develop shared understanding of objectives, to learn from experience, and to find ways to strengthen team performance. Every member is encouraged to contribute to and challenge ideas without fear of retaliation. This attitude of openness generates strong commitment to results because members feel a personal stake in outcomes. The candor present in 9,9 teams also builds a high degree of mutual trust and respect where people are not afraid to take risks and test the limits of creativity.

(*Source: The Grid Style Summaries,* © 1998 by Scientific Methods, Inc. Reproduced by permission of the owners.)

Table 5.2 and Figure 5.1 illustrate the various approaches used in these seven leadership styles.

TABLE 5.2 Grid Styles Description Table

GRID STYLE	INTEGRATED LEVEL OF CONCERN	LEADERSHIP APPROACH	TEAM CULTURE CREATED
1. Control and dominate (Dictatorial)	Concern for results: High (9) Concern for people: Low (1)	I expect results and take control by clearly stating a course of action. I enforce results that support production and do not permit deviation.	Members are suppressed, hidden, and sullen. People become resentful and antagonistic and feel little motivation to do more than they are told. Tensions and low commitment are obvious.
2. Yield and support (Accommodating)	Concern for results: Low (1) Concern for people: High (9)	I support results that strengthen happy, warm relations. I generate enthusiasm by focusing on positive and pleasing aspects.	Members are complacent but also insecure and solicitous. People are friendly and accommodating as long as problems don't arise.
3. Balance and compromise (Status quo)	Concern for results: Medium (5) Concern for people: Medium (5)	I endorse results that are popular but caution against unnecessary risk taking. I test my opinions with others involved to ensure ongoing acceptability.	Members are accessible and outgoing but cautious and guarded when controversy arises. Creativity is inhibited by an overdependence on protocol, procedures, and bureaucracy.
4. Evade and elude (Indifferent)	Concern for results: Low (1) Concern for people: Low (1)	I distance myself from taking active responsibility for results to avoid getting entangled in problems. If forced, I take a passive or supportive position.	Members are apathetic and prefer working in isolation whenever possible. Members feel little or no personal commitment to results.
5. Prescribe and guide (Paternalistic)	Concern for results: 9 and 1 Concern for people: 1 and 9	I take control of results by defining initiatives for myself and others to take. I offer praise and appreciation for support and discourage challenges to my thinking.	Members are polarized by the favoritism in place. Favored members are not held up to the same high standards as others, which causes resentment, antagonism, and lower mutual trust and respect.
6. Exploit and manipulate (Opportunistic)	Concern for results: Inconsistent Concern for people: Inconsistent	I persuade others to support results that benefit me personally. If they also benefit others, that's even better in gaining support. I rely on whatever approach is needed to ensure collaboration.	Members operate independently with little to no mutual trust and respect. People resist sharing resources for fear of losing personal gain. Destructive competition is high.
7. Contribute and commit (Sound)	Concern for results: High Concern for people: High	I demonstrate my commitment to sound results by initiating team action. I explore all facts and alternative views to reach a shared understanding of the best solution.	Members demonstrate high levels of mutual trust and respect with each other, and creativity flourishes. Members feel high levels of commitment to results.

Source: Grid Style Description table, © 1998 by Scientific Methods, Inc. Reproduced by permission.

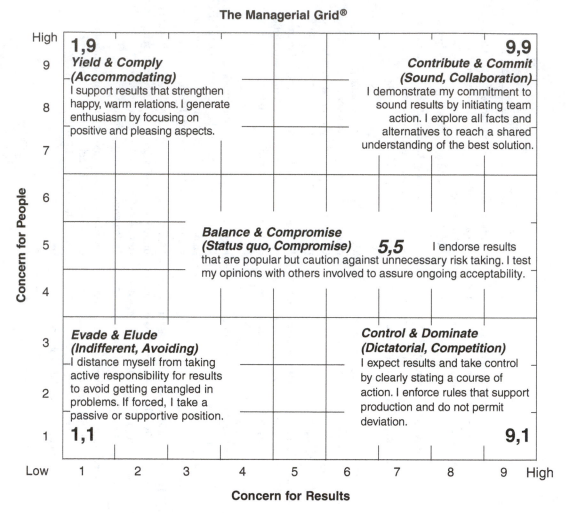

FIGURE 5.1   Summary of Preferred Management Styles

Source: Copyright 1991 Scientific Methods, Inc. Reproduced by permission.

✳ **Which of the Blake and Mouton and Blake and McCanse leadership styles should be used at Atlas Shrug High School in planning, organizing, activating, directing, and controlling? Why?**

Situational and Contingency Leadership

Fiedler (1967) found that a leader's effectiveness in a given situation depends on the fit between his or her style and the task, authority level, and nature of the group. The interactions between these various combinations yield different results in different situations. A key condition is the maturity level of the followers. Immature followers need more structure and task behavior; as maturity increases, they need less structure and more human-relations–oriented behavior. In the most favorable situation, relations between leader and followers are good when tasks are well-defined and the leader is in a position of power.

Fiedler and Cherners (1974, 1984) suggested that leadership style is a fixed personality-based trait that no amount of training will modify. They state that the relationship between leadership style and effectiveness depends on several factors in the situation. These "leader match" models became known as *contingency theories* of leadership. Leadership is, to a large extent, determined by characteristics such as relationships, structure, and power that are vested more in the position and in the leader's personal ability to establish effective relations with appropriate people within the organization. Contingency theory suggests that both high- and low-power and control positions call for task-oriented leaders. Moderate-power and control positions call for human-relationship–oriented styles (Fiedler & Garcia, 1987). These researchers expanded the study of leadership to include the qualities of the leader, the group, the task, and the situation.

Fiedler and Cherners maintain that one cannot change her or his style, but Hersey and Blanchard (1977, 1982, 1993; Hersey, Blanchard, & Johnson, 1996) suggest that leaders are expected to readily modify their styles to cope with changes in follower readiness. The situational style of leadership is influenced by the maturity and development of the work group and individual subordinates, and it varies from subordinate to subordinate. There are four appropriate styles of leadership—telling, selling, participating, and delegating—which are determined by various combinations of relationship and task behavior. Once you have identified the follower's present level of readiness, you can identify the appropriate combination of task and relationship behavior appropriate for that individual. Hersey, Blanchard, and Johnson (1996) state:

> [T]o use this model, identify a point on the readiness continuum that represents [the] follower's readiness to perform a specific task. Then construct a perpendicular line from that point to a point where it intersects with the curved line representing leader behavior. This point indicates the most appropriate amount of task behavior and relationship behavior for that specific situation.
>
> Note that the curved line never goes to either the lower left or the lower right corner. In both quadrants 1 and 4 there are combinations of both task and relationship behavior. Style 1 always has some relationship behavior and style 4 always has some task behavior. (p. 200)

Situational theories answer the question, "What is excellent leadership?" with the reply, "It depends." They believe that there is no one best way to influence others.

Contingency and Situational Leadership® theorists reject the conclusion that there is one best approach to leadership. They suggest that time available, task specificity, competence and maturity of the staff, need for involvement, authority, and dynamics of the situation determine what style should be used. Other contextual factors include group size, rewards, leader status, method of appointment, and technical background. For each level of development among the workforce, the leader should adopt a specific style of leadership; thus, leaders demonstrate a strong degree of flexibility regarding leadership style.

Vroom and Yetton (1973) developed yet another relatively complex model for determining different situations and their relationship to subordinate participation in leadership. Decision making is on a continuum that runs from unilateral at one end to a shared model in which all group members participate in the decision at the other. Factors such as quality requirements, potential conflict, acceptance, information availability, and structure are used to determine which approach should be applied in a given situation.

Vroom and Jago (1988) presented a decision tree to help leaders determine the "best" approach under different combinations of circumstances. Ubben and Hughes (1997) expanded the factors involved and stressed the importance of time available as a consideration to leadership approach.

Yukl (1989) differentiated the situational approach on the basis of whether the requirement was for a "leader" or a "manager." In the capacity of leader, a person needs an advanced repertoire of skills, and different skills are used in different situations. Participation of the workforce is important to the development of knowledge, skills, and a shared vision. Also important are gaining subordinate understanding and commitment and encouraging experimentation. In the capacity of a manager, that person is more directive, sending messages, establishing channels of command, and closely monitoring work. Followers comply with the perceived legitimacy of the leader to manage the organization. Yukl strongly argues that no single approach will suffice for all situations.

The formulas devised for matching these variables are not simple. Many critics of contingency theories argue that the nature of leadership does not vary with each situation. Critics suggest that the unpredictable aspects of shifting styles provoke suspicion, distrust, deceit, and confusion. What contingency and situational approaches ignore is the Pygmalion effect—the power that expectations and treatment have on the behavior of others. People often become what their leader expects them to become. Berlew and Hall (1988) found that what higher-level managers expected of lower-level managers determined the lower-level managers' subsequent performance and success. These findings are corroborated by the work of Edward Deming (discussed later in this chapter). Another matter of concern is that leaders can create situations that demand their preferred styles. For example, a leader can place short time constraints on decisions to justify more autocratic approaches.

University of Michigan Studies

Another series of studies originated with Likert (1967) at the University of Michigan Social Research Center. He was able to identify the following four types of leadership styles:

System 1 (Exploitative authoritative). Management does not trust subordinates, who are not free to discuss matters with supervisors and whose opinions are not sought in solving problems. Motivation comes from fears, threats, and occasional rewards. Communication comes down from higher management. Goals are ordered from on high, where all decisions are made.

System 2 (Benevolent authoritative). Management and employees exist in a master–servant relationship. There is some involvement of employees and more rewards than in system 1, with slightly better upward communications. This is a paternalistic organization, not giving much latitude to employees to "do their thing."

System 3 (Consultative). Management controls things, but employees are consulted before solutions to problems and decisions are made by management. Communication upward is better, but is still cautious. Unpleasant or unfavorable information is not offered freely. Employees feel they will perform some roles in preliminary stages of decision making and policy setting but that their contributions might not always be taken seriously.

System 4 (Participative group). Management trusts employees, regards them as working willingly toward the achievement of organizational objectives. People are motivated by rewards and are involved at all levels in discussing and deciding issues that are important to them. Communication is quite accurate and goes up, down, and across. Goals are established with the participation of the people who will have to work to achieve them.

The ideal style was identified by Likert as system 4, the participative style, which was consistently associated with more effective performance. System 3 was next best and so on, with system 1 being the least effective. (Table 5.3 provides an instrument that can be used to determine which of the four styles is most characteristic of an organization.) The University of Michigan studies complement the Ohio State studies and those completed by Blake and Mouton and Blake and McCanse.

   ✳ **Use the 10 dimensions of the Organizational Health Instrument to characterize the leadership system that now exists at Atlas Shrug High School.**

RECENT WORKS ON LEADERSHIP

It is beyond the grasp of a single volume to be exhaustive, much less definitive, when it comes to leadership theories. There is too much theoretical and empirical literature to cover in a survey of this subject; however, a number of studies and theories provide the overall recent themes in the popular literature. Much of it builds on the studies already presented in this chapter.

   To judge by the best-seller lists, there is a growing interest in the topic of leadership. The success of the 26 books of Drucker (1954, 1974, 1980, 1992, 1998,

TABLE 5.3 Leadership Style That Is Most Characteristic Within an Organization

ORGANIZATIONAL VARIABLE	1	2	3	4
How much confidence and trust does management place in subordinates?	Virtually none	Some	Substantial amount	A great deal
How free do subordinates feel to talk to superiors about the job?	Not very free	Somewhat free	Quite free	Very free
How often are subordinates' ideas sought and used constructively?	Seldom	Sometimes	Often	Very frequently
Is predominant use made of (1) fear, (2) threats, (3) punishments, (4) rewards, (5) involvement?	1, 2, 3, occasionally 4	4, some 3	4, some 3 and 5	5, 4, based on group
Where is responsibility felt for achieving organization's goals?	Mostly at top	Top and middle	At most levels	At all levels
How much cooperative teamwork exists?	Very little	Relatively little	Moderate amount	Great deal
What is the usual direction of information flow?	Downward	Mostly downward	Down and up	Down, up, and sideways
How is downward communication accepted?	With a great deal of suspicion	With some suspicion	With caution	With a receptive mind
How accurate is upward communication?	Usually inaccurate	Often inaccurate	Sometimes inaccurate	Almost never inaccurate
How well do superiors know problems faced by subordinates?	Not very well	Rather well	Quite well	Very well
Are subordinates involved in decisions related to their work?	Almost never	Occasionally consulted	Generally consulted	Fully involved
What does the decision-making process contribute to motivation?	Not very much	Relatively little	Some contribution	Substantial contribution
How are organizational goals established?	Orders are issued	Orders are issued, some comments are invited	After discussion, by orders	By group action (except in crisis)
How much covert resistance to goals is present?	Strong resistance	Moderate resistance	Some resistance at times	Little or none
Is there an informal organization resisting the formal one?	Yes	Usually	Sometimes	No—same goals as formal
What are the cost, productivity, and other control data used for?	Policing, punishment	Reward and punishment	Reward, some self-guidance	Self-guidance, problem solving

Source: Likert, R. (1967). *The human organization: Its management and values.* New York, NY: McGraw-Hill. Reproduced with permission of McGraw-Hill.

2002, 2006), a leading management and leadership philosopher, attests to the prominence of this subject. One of Drucker's works (1992) contains essays from leadership experts around the world. The books focus on the importance of core values—integrity, respect, tenacity, curiosity, learning, standards, friendliness, resilience, convictions, and courage. Leaders need to respect diversity, see the potential in all employees, and communicate persuasively. They must model a commitment to continuous education and self-growth. Effective executives believe in shared decision making.

Search for Excellence

Peters and Waterman 1992 work, *In Search of Excellence*, was the leadership and administrative book of the century based on marketplace success, with more than 5 million copies sold in 15 languages. The sequels, *A Passion for Excellence* (Peters & Austin, 1985), *Thriving on Chaos* (1987), *The Pursuit of Wow!* (1994), and *Circle of Innovation* (1997), have also done extremely well, although none has had the impact of the first book. The basic theme of this body of work is familiar—to succeed, leaders must attend to both the hard and soft components of the organization (the tasks and the people). The book develops eight attributes of leadership that are found in the most effective organizations.

Peters promotes the importance of organizations being responsive to customer needs and supporting experimentation, initiative, and risk taking to accomplish goals and satisfy highly visible customers. Slogans such as "ready, fire, aim" or "fire, fire, fire" support the try-it-now, fail, learn, shift, interact, and modify approach to leadership. Another related slogan is "fail faster, succeed sooner." "Paralysis in analysis" suggests that emphasis on long-term planning be reduced so the organization can be more spontaneous in response to quickly evolving conditions. The research stresses the importance of rich, informal communication, open forums, management by walking around (MBWA), positive reinforcement, better listening, constancy of innovation, and responsiveness to customers and employees. Mistakes are always viewed as progress, although they must be identified and corrected quickly. The bedrock of Peters's message is listening, trust, respect, innovation, and whatever else results in "turned-on" and "in-touch" people. Leaders must love change (instead of fighting it) and instill and share an inspiring vision.

✳ **Use ideas from *In Search of Excellence* to describe an effective work culture for Atlas Shrug High School.**

The 7 Habits of Highly Effective People

Covey's book *The 7 Habits of Highly Effective People* (1989) is similar to the works of Peters in its homey approach and has been phenomenally well received; it was a best seller for 14 months. There is considerable debate among academicians as to whether this book is a study of leadership or a self-help book. Covey described the 7 Habits of Highly Effective People as (Covey, Merrill, & Merrill, 1994):

> *Habit 1: Be Proactive®.*
> Take the initiative, responding and making things happen. Realize you have freedom to choose, be aware of self, develop knowledge, and practice integrity in choices.
>
> *Habit 2: Begin with the End in Mind®.*
> Start with an image or paradigm of the end in mind. Have a clear understanding of where you are going, where you are, and what it is going to take to get to the destination.
>
> *Habit 3: Put First Things First®.*
> Practice effective self-management day in and day out. All truly successful people make present decisions that help achieve desired outcomes.
>
> *Habit 4: Think Win/Win®.*
> Have a frame of mind that always seeks to have all parties feel as though they have won—the benefits to be mutually shared. Cooperation is the key.
>
> *Habit 5: Seek First to Understand, Then Be Understood®.*
> Practice empathetic listening skills so that you understand other people from their frame of reference. Listen with not only ears, but with eyes and hearts. Then, present your ideas logically, clearly, specifically, and in the context of understanding the other person.
>
> *Habit 6: Synergize®.*
> Create new alternatives. Leave your comfort zones to confront new and unknown challenges. Value differences, respect them, and use them to build on strengths. Develop unity and creativity with others. Unleash new powers, create new, exciting alternatives.
>
> *Habit 7: Sharpen the Saw®.*
> Leading people requires a tremendous amount of energy. Make a constant effort to manage health needs. Model good self-help techniques. Convince others that they are valued and should value others. Enjoy and celebrate accomplishment.
>
> (*The 7 Habits of Highly Effective People* and the 7 Habits respectively are all registered trademarks of Franklin Covey Co. Used with permission.)
>
> Vision is the fundamental force that drives everything else in our lives. It empassions us with a sense of the unique contribution that's ours to make. It empowers us to put first things first, compasses ahead of clocks, people ahead of schedules and things. (p. 116)

Many researchers have identified core values, enduring purpose, and vision as the most distinguishing characteristics of the more successful organizations. Such organizations understand the difference between what should and what should never change. In discussing vision, Collins and Porras (1994) state:

> If you do this right, you will spend only a small percentage of your time articulating the vision. The vast majority of your time will be spent bringing the organization into alignment. Yes, it's very important to stop and think about vision. But even more important, you have to align the organization to preserve the core ideology and stimulate progress toward the envisioned future, not merely write a statement. Keep in mind that there is a big difference between being an organization with a vision statement and becoming a truly visionary organization. (pp. 238–239)

Successful organizations move toward visions and practices that reinforce their core ideologies and values.

Organizations build trust and collegiality, develop people and align them toward a shared vision, and then release their creative energies to work in cooperation and harmony to achieve desired results (see the accompanying illustration).

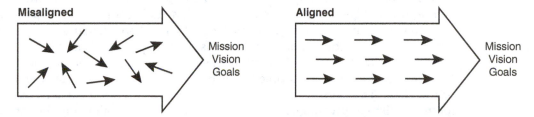

* **How might the staff at Atlas Shrug High School be aligned so that they are working toward a common shared vision for the school?**

The Learning Organization

The "learning organization" concept developed by Senge (1990a; 2008) is a generative process that enhances and extends an organization's ability to create. The concept of responsiveness is an important organizational behavior, but the real payoffs come from being generative. Clarify what is important by continually learning how to see the current reality more clearly and developing abilities to move beyond it. This new learned knowledge permeates the organization and gives coherence to diverse activities. A shared vision provides the focus and energy for learning and creates commitment (not compliance). Commitment to the vision fosters risk taking and experimentation. It is central to the daily work of those within the organization.

Vision grows out of opportunities to communicate, learn, experiment, be held accountable for results, and most of all to shape the future. Although this process can be chaotic, it most often "converges on a conclusion or course of action" (Senge, 1990a, p. 247). Senge stresses the importance of having teams develop fluency in the language of systems thinking. The system provides the unifying principles that serve to integrate the diverse activity occurring within the organization.

Successes in one classroom influence the entire system. Like Peters, Senge stresses the importance of being able to "forgive" and "forget" mistakes and knows how hard it is to provide the needed time to allow this process—understanding complexity, clarifying vision, and learning—to occur.

DePree (1989) believes that people, relationships, information, and communication—not structures—build organizational effectiveness. "Information is power but it is pointless power if hoarded" (p. 104). Effective leaders help their employees to understand the systematic forces that shape change and to see current reality. Effective leaders instill the confidence in their employees that together "we can learn whatever we need to learn in order to achieve the results we truly desire" (Senge, 1990a, p. 399).

Good to Great Schools

Another book that is a great success based on popularity and sales is Collins's *Good to Great* (2001). The author's research team completed a study to determine what distinguished "good-to-great companies" from their competitors. This is a fun book to read, rich in stimulating ideas like first who, then what; don't worry about who got credit; rigorous, not ruthless; disciplined people, thought, and action; buildup followed by breakthrough; manage the system, not the people; harness technologies; get the right people on the bus; and let the truth come out (confront brutal facts). This book challenges some conventional wisdom such as putting in too much time motivating and aligning people instead of allowing the infectious momentum to do that.

Collins sees executive leaders not as ego-driven or "larger-than-life" heroic leaders. They are ambitious, but for the organization's success; they are "plow horses" more than "show horses." Executive leaders differ from other leadership styles in that they are ambitious first and foremost for the cause, the movement, the mission, the work—not themselves—and they have the will to do "whatever it takes" to make good on the ambition. Additionally, executive leadership is not about being "soft" or "nice" or purely "inclusive" or "consensus building." The whole point is to make sure the right decisions happen—no matter how difficult or painful—for the long-term greatness of the institution and the achievement of its mission, independent of consensus or popularity.

Collins uses a bus analogy stressing the importance of getting the right people on the bus and the wrong people off the bus before deciding what must be done and who will be doing those things. The right people are those who adapt well to change, who are self-motivated, who have good character attributes (work ethic, intelligence, dedication, focus, respect, self-discipline, passion, honesty), and who freely and honestly communicate with others. Collins (2001) states:

> Those who strive to turn good into great find the process no more painful or exhausting than those who settle for just letting things wallow along in mind-numbing mediocrity. Yes, turning good into great takes energy, but the building of momentum adds more energy back into the pool than it takes out. Conversely,

perpetuating mediocrity is an inherently draining process and drains much more energy out of the pool then it puts back in. (p. 208)

✳ **List some things you might try to energize Atlas Shrug High School.**

The New Science of Leadership

Wheatley (1992; Steinberg, 1995) suggests a fundamental shift in thinking in which leaders look for order rather than control in organization. Order is inherent in living systems. It does not evolve from avoiding different or disturbing information, smoothing turbulence, defining situations, standardizing approaches, writing procedures, and telling people what to do. Discomfort is a part of greater understanding, motivation, and satisfaction, as new approaches are made successful. Order is inherent—people naturally seek to make their conditions coherent. A small change can disturb and threaten order or equilibrium and result in chaos throughout a system. But even that chaos will act within specific parameters with order and predictability; chaos has boundaries beyond which it will not go.

Disequilibrium creates growth, and under proper conditions the system will respond and evolve to a new, improved order. Successful organizations adapt and change and are free to interact with a turbulent, changing environment in such a way that it is open, free, and capable of responding and regenerating—a viable, living, adaptive, well-ordered organization. Successful organizations take advantage of the opportunities or possibilities for renewal and enhancement. Such opportunities involve longer, more thoughtful conversations, greater participation, more risk taking, more tolerance of mistakes, more openly shared information, more acceptance of chaos, more volatility of politics, and more effort toward figuring out what works and what does not work. The foundation of leadership is a welcoming of diverse and rich viewpoints, including many different people in the process of thinking together for self-renewal, and continuous improvement.

Leaders often become wary of periods of turbulence and clamp on controls, retreat, tune out information, and create rigid structure to calm the waters. Some administrators focus on holding all the pieces together and smoothing the political and ideological debate. Unfortunately, this "circle the wagons" mentality short-circuits the learning and improvement process that is needed for success and excellence by cutting off uncertainty, debate, disagreement, confusion, and conflict. Administrators who react this way stop the organization from learning, responding, and regenerating itself and force it back into equilibrium—the status quo. A principal, for example, seeing that test scores are falling, might abandon a new program and go back to simpler, more basic past standard practices to avoid the debate, concern, and confusion that result. "We'll go back to the basics in order to make sense out of all of this."

This effort to gain control cuts off learning and shuts down the natural, life-enhancing processes of responding and improving. The problem just cited might, in fact, be with the instructional strategy that worked for the old program but does not work for the new one. Organizations cannot become more fit in their present environments unless leaders are willing to risk the perils of the path through chaos, which leads to knowledge, growth, order, and regeneration. Leaders help the system to reform, renew, reconfigure, and recreate itself to better suit the new demands and environment. Rexford Brown (1983), from the Education Commission of the States, is fond of saying:

> Educational improvements will require new kinds of leadership. We need leaders to create conversations, to change the levels and kinds of discourse going on in and around schools, and to stimulate inquiry, questioning, problem solving, and a focus on learning for everyone in the system, not just students. . . . The primary conditions for this type of thoughtfulness are mystery, uncertainty, disagreement, questions, ambiguity, and curiosity. (p. 3)

✳ **Characterize what is happening at Atlas Shrug High School using Margaret Wheatley's theories regarding disequilibrium, chaos, order, and improvement. What needs to be happening?**

Total Quality Management

Advocates of total quality management (TQM) established a foothold in Japan in the 1950s and the effects of their philosophy have been growing and spreading ever since. The fundamental messages of TQM are to improve quality, serve the customer, satisfy customer requirements, encourage employee innovation, provide for the free flow of information, attack the system (not the employees), instill pride and teamwork, and create an atmosphere of innovation and continuous improvement. Mintzberg (1987) argues that successful organizations "craft strategy" as they continually learn about shifting conditions and inclusively determine "what is desired" and "what is possible." The job of a leader is to create and improve the system so that more is possible.

Deming (1986, 1991, 1993), the father of TQM, stated, "Workers are responsible for only 15 percent of the problems, the system for the other 85 percent" ([1993], p. 22). He then added that the system is the responsibility of management. The heart of Deming's approach to improving the organization is teamwork and collaboration among managers and workers. The leader provides core values, consistency of purpose, information, support, training, integration, common language, continuing feedback, improved systems, alignment, integrity, time, trust, and resources. Employees are responsible for improving themselves and the work process in such a way that the outcomes of the organization continuously improve.

TQM tenets include eliminating numerical goals, tearing down walls between work groups, and sharing information, reducing or eliminating micromanaging, and letting work teams tackle the inefficiencies and outcome problems. Matrix teams draw workers from several departments to study something in addition to their regular work; project teams pull workers for temporary work on a project; process teams look into the way work is being completed; and vertical teams take a diagonal slice through the organization to include people at different levels to create organizational vision and expand abilities. Regardless of the team, the members work together to develop one another and thus the organization.

Fear is eliminated so that people feel free to ask questions, take a stand, make suggestions, experiment, and take risks. Leaders must build the culture within the organization to support the needed transformation. The focus of everyone's work in the TQM model is excellent, quick, high-quality, and flawless service. Quality improvement is the goal of every single individual within the organization.

* **Using the TQM model, identify the causes for the problems existing at Atlas Shrug High School.**

Cultural Leadership

Schein (1985) suggests the most important thing leaders do is to help shape an effective culture in which people will complete their work. He talks about shared beliefs that define basic views of an organization and its environment. He contends that culture does the following:

> [I]nfluences the ways in which group members perceive, think, and feel about the world thereby serving to stabilize that world, give meaning to it, and thereby reduce the anxiety that would result if we did not know how to categorize and respond to the environment. (p. 312)

In fact, culture is often defined as "the way we do things around here." Hoy and Miskel (2008) describe organizational culture as "a system of shared orientations that holds the unit together and gives it distinctive identity. Culture can be examined in terms of shared assumptions, shared beliefs and values, and/or shared norms" (p. 214). Bolman and Deal (1991) believe:

> Culture is both product and process. As product, it embodies the accumulated wisdom of those who were members before we came. As process, it is continually renewed and re-created and new members are taught the old ways and eventually become teachers themselves. . . .
>
> Many of these patterns and assumptions are unconscious or taken for granted. They are reflected in myths, stories, rituals, ceremonies, and other symbolic forms. Managers who understand the power of symbols have a better chance of influencing organizations than do those who focus only on other frames. (p. 231)

They go on to say, "Beliefs, values, practices, and artifacts define for . . . members who they are and how they do things" (p. 250).

Our culture is important because it shapes the different ways we recognize and react to events, gives meaning and purpose to our work, and unites people. A useful frame for examining the many cultures of an organization is Hofstede's (1991; 2010) research of cultural practices on many levels, from the values and practices (rituals, heroes, and symbols) to the many layers of culture (national, regional, and/or ethnic/religious/linguistic; gender; generational; social class; and organizational). According to Deal and Kennedy (1982), the goal of leadership is to make something as ill-defined as culture work for leaders and for the improvement of educational performance.

Perhaps the cultural glue that holds organizations together is *trust*. In examining the effects of organizational structure and team behavior on the level of trust exhibited by educators, Henkin and Dee (2001) suggest:

> Trust benefits from the flexibility and adaptive features that distinguish organizations that operate within fluid social environments. Strong, coherent, mechanistic organizational forms, in contrast, may actually deter the development of high levels of trust. Underregulated forms of organization, we suggest, may be more effective, though less efficient, in producing and sustaining high levels of trust. . . . Collective trust can endure as long as teachers, administrators, parents, and community members work together under the assumptions that collective behaviors are rational and their collective fate and interests are coupled. (p. 59)

The process of developing improvements, interacting about needed improvements, considering alternatives, and developing plans are as important to the ability to implement improvement as is the substance of the change itself (Cunningham & Gresso, 1993; Lieberman, 1991; Sarason, 1996; Sashkin & Walberg, 1993; Schein, 1991). Bennis (1983) found that culture can give an organization transformative power to continuously improve itself. Bennis (1983) states:

> In sum, the transformative power of leadership stems less from ingeniously crafted organizational structures, carefully constructed management designs and controls, elegantly rationalized planning formats, or skillfully articulated leadership tactics. Rather, it is the ability of the leader to reach the souls of others in a fashion which raises human consciousness, builds meanings, and inspires human intent that is the source of power. Within transformative leadership, therefore, it is vision, purposes, beliefs, and other aspects of organizational culture that are of prime importance. (p. 70)

Bolman and Deal (1995) stress this theme when they identified courage, spirit, and hope as the enduring elements of leadership. This is the heart of leadership. Leaders put the organization in touch with what gives it passion, purpose, and meaning. Heart, hope, and faith are necessary for today's managers to become tomorrow's leaders, for today's sterile bureaucracies to become tomorrow's communities of meaning, and for our society to rediscover its ethical and spiritual center. Leading requires breathing spirit and passion into the life of the organization. Seek the vigor needed to enrich your life and leave a better legacy for those who come after you.

> ✳ **How would you characterize the organizational culture at Atlas Shrug High School? What cultural characteristics of the organization are having a positive impact? What characteristics are having a negative impact?**

Transformational Leadership

Burns (1978) formulated the idea of "transactional" and "transformational" leadership. "Transactional" leadership is based on defining needs, assigning clear tasks, rewarding congruent behavior, and having a command-and-control mentality. Followers are willing to trust the leader because they need to have problems solved and they believe the leader can solve them. "Transformational" leaders develop followers, help map new directions, mobilize resources, facilitate and support employees, and respond to organizational challenges. They see change as necessary and strive to cause it. In describing transformational leaders, Burns (1978) concluded:

> Leaders engage with followers but from higher levels of morality; in the enmeshing of goals and values, both leaders and followers are raised to more principled levels of judgment. . . . Much of this kind of elevating leadership asks from followers rather than merely promising them goods. (p. 455)

Bass (1998) added a third type of leadership style, which he called "laissez-faire" along with what he called "a full range leadership model." This model incorporates a number of different approaches to his three major leadership types.

Although the idea of transformational leadership was proposed by Burns (1978), Kenneth Leithwood (1992, 1999; Leithwood & Duke, 1994; Leithwood & Jantzi, 2005) and his colleagues have added greatly to our understanding of it and have examined the benefits of this approach to school reform. According to these researchers, transformational school leaders are in continuous pursuit of three fundamental goals:

1. Helping staff members develop and maintain a collaborative, professional school culture
2. Fostering teacher development
3. Helping teachers solve problems together more effectively

Transformational leaders provide the mechanisms by which solutions are transferred into subsequent practice by building the capacity of the individuals and the group.

Transformational leadership is a process to shape and elevate goals and abilities so as to achieve significant improvements through common interests and collective actions (Bennis & Nanus, 1985). School personnel are inspired to rise above self-interest goals, make commitments to continuously improve student learning, and take responsibility for instructional innovation. Bill Gates, chairman of Microsoft, states, "People like to have a sense of purpose, to feel that they're doing something unique and to actually see the impact their work is having." Effective leaders encourage experimentation and risk taking to meet the challenges posed by changing social conditions. The research on transformational leadership is limited but uniformly supportive of this approach as being effective in school leadership (Leithwood, 1992). Studies by Blase (1990) and Thurston, Clift, and Schacht (1993) support transformational leadership as an effective approach for the school principalship.

Transformational leadership lacks an explicit focus on curriculum and instruction. Marks and Printy (2003) found that when transformational and instructional leadership coexist in an integrated form of leadership, the influence on school performance as measured by the quality of its pedagogy and the achievement of its students, is substantiated. Neither of these leadership styles have a significant impact separately and the relationship only shows up when they are combined. Some of the characteristics in these two cultures include:

INSTRUCTIONAL
- Improve professional practice
- Interact around curricular and instructional reform efforts
- Coordinate curriculum
- Supervise classroom instruction
- Facilitate teacher growth
- Involve teachers in sustained dialogue and decision making about educational matters
- Include teachers as equal partners
- Acknowledge teacher professionalism
- Capitalize on teacher knowledge and skill (Darling-Hammond, 1998)
- Share instructional leadership
- Seek out ideas, insight, and expertise of teachers
- Set high expectations
- Monitor student progress
- Create communities of learners

TRANSFORMATIONAL
- Introduce innovation
- Shape cultures
- Transform school culture
- Provide intellectual direction and innovation
- Make teachers partners in decision making
- Practice problem finding/problem solving
- Stress goals of improving organizational performance
- Collaborate with stakeholders
- Increase commitment
- Articulate the larger good
- Develop followers
- Focus on mission, performance, culture (Leithwood, 1999).

Distributed Leadership

Discussions related to the concept of distributed leadership are becoming common as it has become a more popular topic. That popularity of distributed leadership has been driven by the work of Elmore (2000), Spillane, Sherer, and Caldreu (2005), and Spillane, Halverson, and Diamond (2001). Spillane's work is now part of the *distributed leadership* study in 13 Chicago public schools. Some are suggesting that "distributed leadership" is just the current label for "transformational leadership," "participative leadership," "shared leadership," and "democratic leadership," which have been previously discussed in this chapter. However, distributed leadership stresses spreading involvement including things like decision making, teamwork, and work reallocation. The model locates leadership practices within a networked web of individuals and contexts. In this form of distributed leadership, administrators parcel out responsibilities through coprincipalships, site councils, teacher leadership, and professionalism. Thus, leadership involves the practices of multiple individuals and occurs through the complex network of staff relations and interactions. Distributed leadership provides a new framework for thinking about leadership. Leadership is no longer thought of as an individual but instead as a practice in the new "flat world" of the 21st century. This might distinguish distributed leadership from shared or participative leadership in that responsibilities are shifted to others rather than shared with others. Decisions emerge from collaborative dialogues among many individuals engaged in mutually dependent activities.

Some argue that it has the potential to free up leaders from many managerial responsibilities so they can become true instructional leaders. According to Lashway (2006):

> In part, distributing leadership is an expression of the belief that, in the long run, organizational effectiveness will increase when leadership is seen as everyone's responsibility. (In the words of the aphorism, 'All of us are smarter than any of us.'). . . . Empowering others unleashes their passion, energy, and drive—all the things that create both satisfaction and success. (p. 264–265)

Distributed leadership is not an entirely new discovery. It has taken many forms, but due to changing times and the different demands placed on leadership, the methods for achieving optimum performance from administrators and staff members must change. Before, to have the power was to be the leader; then it was to delegate the power. Now it is to distribute the power. You empower staff to be more creative and innovative in order to boost morale and efficiency. The following are qualities associated with distributed leadership (DL):

1. Tries to use all knowledge and experience
2. Solves problems productively to create change by encouraging idea sharing
3. Encourages everyone to contribute knowledge to the decision-making process
4. Leads to discovering new approaches

In understanding this form of leadership, it is necessary to examine the multidirectional social influences occurring among teachers, administrators, parents, students, and other stakeholders. The quality of decisions depends on the quality of interactions—collaboration, dialogue, and communication (Scribner, Sawyer, & Watson, 2007).

Some use distributed leadership to indicate that school leadership involves multiple leaders; others argue that leadership is an organizational quality rather than an individual attribute. Still others use distributed leadership to define a way of thinking about the practice of school leadership (Gronn, 2003; Spillane et al., 2001, 2004). A common thread in research on distributed leadership is that leadership occurs through many individual actions across the organization. It acknowledges the complexity of the organization; the diversity, maturity, and interdependence of the participants within it; and America's deep cultural values of democratic governance.

Distributed leadership theory regards leadership as the aggregated (Spillane, 2006) or synchronized behavior of many individuals rather than an assigned role (Heller & Firestone, 1995). "Power is not a limited pie. It is wonderfully elastic [and] can be divided without shrinking" (Lipman-Blumen, 1996, p. 237). Power distribution might divide power and authority into multiple segments, or eliminate hierarchies altogether (Gronn, 2002). Shifting from a paradigm of command and control, the new focus is on democratic principles of participation, empowerment, dialogue, and cooperation (Furman, 2002).

Synergy and Distributed Leadership

With the locus of leadership dispersed throughout a structure of shared decision making, relationships take on greater importance than roles (Leithwood & Jantzi, 2006; Ogawa & Bossert, 1995). In distributively led organizations, leadership is a collective achievement based on the contributions of many participants. The leadership capacity of an organization is a function of the collective knowledge, skills, and dispositions of its members. Those who practice distributed leadership ethically use themselves and others as instruments for achieving goals, encouraging the assumption of responsibility at every level and discouraging passive followership. Leaders remain alert for synergistic opportunities—examining connections between people, ideas, and processes; harnessing the leadership potential of others; and nurturing potential leaders and successors along the way (Lipman-Blumen, 1996). It becomes critical to invest in, develop, and maximize participants' abilities.

A popular form of distributed leadership, teacher teams (Pounder, 1999) are a logical extension of previously discussed notions of the importance of the shared decision-making process and ownership. Studies (Scribner et al., 2007) also suggest that when teachers work in self-managing teams, students often achieve at higher levels. Social interaction, collaborative dynamics, facilitation, and conversation become an important attribute of effective leadership and the process by which teacher teams identify and solve problems. The idea is "to tap into the distributed and cumulative expertise of the school's staff" (Crow, Mathews, & McCleary, 2002). Multiple leaders emerge during the interactional process of the team and a pattern of shared team leadership evolves. As a result, purpose, autonomy, patterns of discourse, organizational conditions and structure, boundaries, access, time, exploration, commitment, and freedom all play an important role in the exercise of leadership and group functioning with the following warning Scribner et al. (2007) provide:

> However, tapping into this wellspring of leadership potential may be curtailed when organizations leave teams to their own devices without support and meaningful feedback. Similarly, teacher performance may also be constrained when collaborative activity is too tightly bound to standardized organizational expectations and monetary rewards. We have found that the line between organizational support and surveillance is quite thin. (p. 104)

Adaptive Leadership

In the last 20 years, some of the most important scholarship on leadership comes from the work of Heifetz described in his seminal work (1994) *Leadership Without Easy Answers* and developed further in *The Practice of Adaptive Leadership* by Heifetz, Linsky, and Grasgow (2009). Heifetz (1994) maintains that the four general approaches to leadership: trait, situational, contingeny, and transactional, ". . . define leadership objectively, without making value judgements (p. 18). Heifetz uses the term *adaptive leadership* and maintains that leadership is an activity that influences and mobilizes people to do 'adaptive work'." For Heifetz, adaptive work, "consists of the learning required to address conflicts in the values people hold, or to diminish the gap between the values people stand for and the reality they face" (p. 22)."

The defining characteristic of leadership is not simply the activity of gaining authority and influence, although these can be important resources, but the mobilization of people to clarify aspirations and do the adaptive work of defining and solving the problems created by the gap between those aspirations and current conditions. Monroe (2004) maintains that adaptive challenges are not like routine problems that can be solved with technical solutions. Adaptive challenges require a change in attitude, habitual ways of doing things, and even deeply held values. Exercising leadership frequently means getting people to face the internal contradictions of the situation being addressed, to examine the unconscious processes, patterns, and mental models related to effectiveness, and usually demands the orchestration of social learning among conflicting aspirations and points of view (sandiego.edu/soles/centers/leadership_institute).

Theory U

Theory U (or U Process) is a change management approach targeting leadership as a process of inner knowing and social innovation. Originally developed by Friedrich Glasl and Dirk Lemson in the 1960s, it has been a valuable tool in organizational development and social development since that time. Otto Scharmer studied the method and took the basic principles of this process and extended and enriched it into a significant theory of learning and management, which he calls *Theory U*. The intent of the principles of Theory U are to help leaders break through past unproductive patterns of behavior that prevent them from empathizing with their clients' or stakeholders' perspectives and often lock them into ineffective patterns of decision making.

Scharmer (2009) identifies seven leadership capacities that can help groups and organizations create a future that would not otherwise be possible. They include: holding the space of listening; observing; sensing; presencing; crystallizing; prototyping; and performing. Scharmer calls for collective leadership and maintains that we are often stuck inside very difficult situations and as a result we have blind spots. In the book *Presence* (Senge, Scharmer, Jaworski, &, Flowers, 2005), Scharmer first used the image of a "U" to distinguish ". . . different depths of perceiving reality and different levels of action that follow from that" (p. 87).

The leadership literature moved from looking at individual traits to examining particular situations and examining the context. Scholars have explored the types of problems leaders must address and the complexity of the process of leadership. One of the most cited scholars on leadership is Greenleaf (1977) who wrote about *servant leadership*. Greenleaf maintained that, *"Good leaders must first become good servants."* Because it is vital that school leaders show enormous respect for the people they supervise, this modeling may lead to students in turn being respected, thus creating a positive and inviting school climate.

CONCLUSION

The call to duty is a challenging one: providing better futures for students, overhauling outdated systems, breaking barriers, altering culture, broadening leadership, and developing highly effective schools. The decades ahead will offer many new challenges and opportunities and require what Fullan (1991) calls "a new ethos of innovation." Effective leadership has a long tradition of research and successfully integrated ideas. Many leadership scholars (Greenleaf, 1977; Culbertson, 1981; Griffiths, 1979; Rost, 1993; Heifetz, 1994; Hofstede, 1991; Scharmer, 2009) have made significant contributions to the practitioner's understanding of leadership in educational administration. In addition, many outstanding books are now available on the principalship and superintendency. Research and literature on leadership will always be a growing body of understanding. This body of literature is not so much a set of definite answers or a set of widely accepted beliefs as it is a lifelong struggle for understanding.

Leadership is shifting from a role of directing and controlling to one of guiding, facilitating, supporting, and coordinating efforts on behalf of schools. A wider population is now envisioned as having leadership potential, and we are flattening organizations, empowering more people, and decentralizing decision making (Hill & Ragland, 1995).

We are at a watershed in our history. Many argue that the current model of schools is outdated. How we function as a school system, how we exchange ideas, and how we learn will affect how we continuously improve our schools. Leaders will be expected to have a leadership framework (see administrative platforms in Chapter 1) expressing their primary philosophy, beliefs, and attitudes regarding leadership, learning, and teaching. Platforms will need to accommodate working together with people, focusing on issues in common, being inclusive, setting ground rules, setting attainable goals, implementing and evaluating programs, celebrating victories, and using modern technology.

In explaining his great hockey play, Wayne Gretsky stated, "You always skate to where the puck is going, not to where it's been." The call is for educators to move toward where education needs to be to improve the entire system, not to maintain the status quo of where it's been.

* **As principal of Atlas Shrug High School, describe your philosophy of leadership and state how that philosophy will inspire needed school reforms.**

MyEdLeadershipLab™

Go to Topic 4: *Instructional Leadership* in the MyEdLeadershipLab™ site (www.MyEd LeadershipLab.com) for *Educational Leadership: A Bridge to Improved Practice*, Fifth Edition, where you can:

- Find learning outcomes for *Instructional Leadership* along with the national standards that connect to these outcomes.
- Complete Assignments and Activities that can help you more deeply understand the chapter content.
- Apply and practice your understanding of the core skills identified in the chapter with the Building Leadership Skills unit.
- Prepare yourself for professional certification with a Practice for Certification quiz.

PORTFOLIO ARTIFACTS

- Revisit your leadership platform as a framework for administrative action.

- Review the scholars and theories presented in this chapter. Which one (ones) resonate with your beliefs and values. Is this evident from reading your leadership platform?

- Plan, coordinate, and lead a committee meeting (e.g., Individual Educational Plan (IEP) Self-Study Team, Student Appeals, Curriculum Revision, faculty or team meeting). Videotape the session. Reflect on your words and actions.

- Assist in the development of a relationship between the school and its business partners providing the agenda, minutes, and so forth.

- Brainstorm a list of what skills you will need as a school leader (reflect on what skills you already possess, what skills you will need to improve on, and how you will improve on skills).

- Take on a leadership role within your school division, the surrounding community, or a professional organization.

- Shadow a leader within the school division, another organization, or the community.

- Actively participate in educational, administrative, or professional leadership associations.

- Volunteer to help administer a summer school or after-school program.

KEY TERMS

- Adaptive leadership
- Bureaucracy
- Chaos theory
- Critical theorists
- Cultural leadership
- Delegation
- Distributed leadership
- Facilitation
- Leadership and management

- Leadership platform
- Learning organization
- MBWA
- Organizational health
- Participatory team management
- Postmodernism
- Presencing
- Pygmalion effect
- Servant leadership

- Situational leadership
- Synergy
- Total quality management (TQM)
- Transformational leadership
- Vision
- X–Y theory
- U theory

SUGGESTED READINGS

Collins, J. (2001). *Good to great: Why some companies make the leap . . . and others don't.* New York, NY: HarperCollins.

Cunningham, W. G., & Gresso, D. W. (1993). *Cultural leadership: The culture of excellence in education.* Boston, MA: Allyn and Bacon.

Deal, T., & Peterson, K. (2003). *Shaping school culture: The heart of leadership.* San Francisco, CA: Jossey-Bass.

Freiberg, K., & Freiberg, J. (2011). *Nanovation: How a little car can teach the world to think big and act boldly.* Nashville, TN: Thomas Nelson.

Greenleaf, R. K. (2002). *Servant leadership: A journey into the nature of legitimate power and greatness* (25th anniversary ed.). New York, NY: Paulist Press.

Grogan, M., & Shakeshaft, C. (2011). *Women and educational leadership.* San Francisco, CA: Jossey-Bass.

Heifetz, R. (1998). *Leadership without easy answers.* Cambridge, CA: Harvard University Press.

Linsky, M., & Heifetz, R. (2002). *Leadership on the line.* Cambridge, CA: Harvard Business Press.

Scharmer, O. (2009). *Theory U: Leading from the future as it emerges.* San Francisco, CA: Berrett-Koehler.

APPENDIX 5A

Directions for Scoring Box 5.1: The X–Y Scale

The column in which you placed a check mark on the X–Y scale determines whether you operated with X or Y beliefs on that particular question. Record an X or Y in the blank column at the end of the question based on the column that you checked. When you have scored all 10 questions, count the total number of Ys you have recorded (see page 150 for interpretation of results).

	1	2	3	4	X/Y
1. Closely supervise my subordinates to get better work from them.	X	X	Y	Y	
2. Set the goals and objectives for my subordinates and sell them on the merits of my plans.	X	X	Y	Y	
3. Set up controls to ensure that my subordinates are getting the job done.	X	X	Y	Y	
4. Encourage my subordinates to set their own goals and objectives.	Y	Y	X	X	
5. Make sure that my subordinates' work is planned out for them.	X	X	Y	Y	
6. Check with my subordinates daily to see if they need any help.	X	X	Y	Y	
7. Step in as soon as reports indicate that the job is slipping.	X	X	Y	Y	
8. Push my people to meet schedules if necessary.	X	X	Y	Y	
9. Have frequent meetings to keep in touch with what is going on.	Y	Y	X	X	
10. Allow subordinates to make important decisions.	Y	Y	X	X	
				Total Y =	

$10 \geq Y \geq 9$ Strong Y beliefs

$8 \geq Y \geq 7$ Y beliefs

$6 \geq Y \geq 5$ Mild X beliefs

$4 \geq Y \geq 3$ X beliefs

$2 \geq Y \geq 0$ Strong X beliefs

APPENDIX 5B

Directions for Interpreting Box 5.4: The Behavior Matrix

Below are the descriptors for each of the quadrants in the behavior matrix:

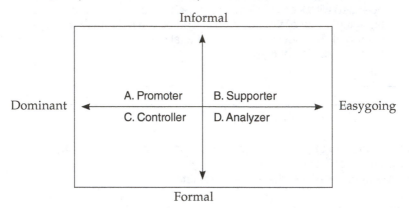

Each quadrant is associated with certain characteristics, and individuals falling in each may be described generally as follows:

Quadrant A: *The Promotional Style* (upper left). Promoters get involved with people in active, rapidly changing situations. These people are seen as socially outgoing and friendly, imaginative and vigorous. Because people react to behaviors as a result of their own value biases, some see the promotional style as dynamic and energetic whereas others perceive the same behavior as egotistical.

In a work situation, promoters can get things going but might sometimes settle for less than the best in order to get on to something else. When faced with a task, these people can generate creative ideas for work, but are less likely to follow through to get the task done. If a group or organization can accommodate this style, it will benefit from enthusiasm, but must tolerate a lack of concern for details. Promoters are frequently highly competitive and might need to learn to work with others in a collaborative manner.

Quadrant B: *The Supporting Style* (upper right). Supporters value interpersonal relations. These people try to minimize conflict and promote the happiness of everybody. Some people see the supporting style as accommodating and friendly, whereas others describe it as "wishy-washy" and "nice."

In a work situation, supporters might find it difficult to say no, therefore frequently finding themselves overcommitted. They can be counted on to do what will please others. Supporters are people oriented and nonaggressive. They will rely on others to give direction about how to get the tasks done.

Quadrant C: *The Controlling Style* (lower left). Controllers want results. They love to run things and have the job done in their own way; "I'll do it myself" is a frequent motto of the controller.

These people can manage their time to the minute. Some see them as business-like and efficient, whereas others refer to them as threatening and unfeeling.

In a work situation, controllers will make sure the job is done. They will get impatient with long discussions about "the best way" or how to please everybody. Controllers are confident in their ability, take risks, and push forward.

Quadrant D: *The Analyzing Style* (lower right). Analyzers are problem solvers. They like to get all the data before making a decision. Some say they are thorough, but others complain that they're slow. These people are frequently quiet and prefer to work alone.

In a work situation, analyzers bring valuable conceptual skills. They ask the difficult, important questions. Interpersonally, they might seem aloof and cool. Analyzers might miss deadlines, but they'll have all the reasons to support the delay.

To explore your style more in depth, join together with people of the same style and create two lists. The first list should include what you like about your selected operating style, its strengths, what it does well. The second should include what you dislike about your selected operating style, behaviors that get in the way, and its weak points. Discuss your lists with individuals who fall in the three other different quadrants. Discuss which behaviors are most important to an organization and leadership.

Complete the Working Relationships Chart, thinking of two people (preferably different behavior matrix styles) with whom you have a working relationship. Complete the questions regarding your relationship with these two individuals. Review and reflect on the implications of the information in regard to leadership.

Working Relationships: A Worksheet

My style is: _____

My strengths are: _____

	First Person	Second Person
1. Identify two people closely associated with you (i.e., superintendent, principal, spouse, etc.) and his or her style.	Name: Style:	Name: Style:
2. Identify his or her strengths.		
3. Identify what you can do to supplement or assist him or her.		
4. Identify your most likely conflict.		
5. Identify ways you can manage the conflict.		

Source: Sayers-Kirsch, S. (1985). "Understanding behavioral style." *NREL Behavioral Matrix.* Portland, OR: Northwest Regional Educational Laboratory. (Reproduced with permission of NREL.)

APPENDIX 5C

Directions for Scoring Box 5.5: Leadership Behavior Survey

The columns on the left side of the survey represent the initiating structure values. The right side columns represent consideration values. Record the column totals in the initiating structure and consideration boxes that follow. (Total the number of checks you marked in each column of Box 5.5, the Leadership Behavior Survey, and enter the totals in the following square for the appropriate column.) Multiply each of these totals by the weighted factors indicated. Add weighted factor totals for a grand total, representing the initiating structure grand total and consideration grand total. Chart both of these grand total values on the Charting Leadership Style Matrix to determine the quadrant of your selected leadership style.

Initiating Structure (left-hand column)

	IS Column Totals	Weighted Factor Totals	
Always (5)		× 4 =	
Often (4)		× 3 =	
Occasionally (3)		× 2 =	
Seldom (2)		× 1 =	
Never (1)		× 0 =	
IS Grand Total			

Consideration (right-hand column)

	C Column Totals	Weighted Factor Totals	
Always (5)		× 4 =	
Often (4)		× 3 =	
Occasionally (3)		× 2 =	
Seldom (2)		× 1 =	
Never (1)		× 0 =	
C Grand Total			

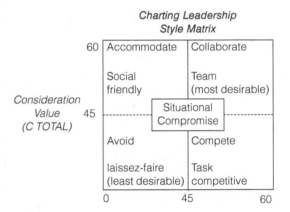

Charting Leadership Style Matrix

60	Accommodate	Collaborate
	Social friendly	Team (most desirable)
Consideration Value 45 *(C TOTAL)*	Situational Compromise	
	Avoid	Compete
	laissez-faire (least desirable)	Task competitive

0   45   60

Initiating structure Value (IS TOTAL)

Determine in which quadrant your score places you.

Source: Halpin, A. (1996). *Theory and research in administration.* Upper Saddle River, NJ: Prentice Hall. Adapted by permission of the publisher.

MARVELING AT THE RESULTS: POWER, ROLES, RELATIONSHIPS, AND SCHOOL REFORM

WILLIAM G. CUNNINGHAM
Old Dominion University

Expectations of staff members to learn from and work with one another have increased. Linda Darling-Hammond, in a background paper for the National Commission on Teaching and America's Future (1996), states: "Current efforts at school reform are likely to succeed to the extent that they are built on a strong foundation of teaching knowledge and are sustained by a commitment to structural rather than merely symbolic change" (p. 41). Dennis Sparks, former executive director for the National Staff Development Council, concurs: "Significant changes in the daily work lives of teachers must be at the core of reform efforts that are truly intended to create schools in which adults feel competent in their work and all students develop to their full potential" (p. 21).

Those who have opportunities for growth, development, and promotion often raise their aspirations, value their own skills, engage in improving performance, form political alliances with an improvement orientation, and actively participate in and support reforms. Those without such opportunities lower their aspirations, undervalue their skills, disengage from work improvements, form protective peer groups, and resist passively. Positive attitudes are encouraged by the ability to influence others within the organization. If the individual has very limited power, his or her knowledge and ability will not be respected. Powerlessness leads to petty domination, not leadership, reform, or improved performance.

Powerlessness usually manifests as focusing on means, not the ends, and adherence to standard operating procedures and past practices. How can leaders provide school personnel the development, opportunity, and power needed to encourage ambitious, committed staff members who willingly put in the kind of work that reform efforts require? How can teachers share their knowledge so that it can be synthesized in improved practice?

LEARNING OBJECTIVES

- To acquire an understanding of the complexity of achieving school reform
- To examine the types of organizational structures that will promote staff development and curriculum and instructional improvement
- To analyze the types of leadership styles that will best promote successful school reform and the types of support these styles will need to be successful
- To examine methods by which the knowledge and ability of very different groups of people may be brought together in an ongoing, mutually beneficial way; to determine how groups can share their talents, knowledge, and resources, thus supporting each other in relationships that merge their abilities for the purpose of improving the school
- To distribute power and responsibility in such a way that it encourages mutual respect and willingness to work together to jointly improve schools

GUIDING QUESTIONS

1. How can you get staff members to develop their full potential and encourage their full participation in a school-improvement process? What are the characteristics of a job that provides and supports opportunities for development and advancement?

2. If power means the capacity to mobilize resources, influence others, and "get things done," how can different staff members be given power so they can develop the credibility needed to be respected and ultimately "get school reform done"?

3. What are the sources of order, power, and purpose within the school?

4. What types of efforts will facilitate complex learning, creativity, experimentation, and continuous improvement of the school?

5. How will you know that you are nurturing potential and capacity?

HICKORY RIDGE HIGH SCHOOL

Hickory Ridge High School is a large urban school of approximately 1,800 students, 15% exceptional or special-needs students, 46% white, 40% African American, 12% Hispanic, and 2% Asian, of whom many are recent immigrants. The mean composite score on standardized tests such as the Iowa Test of Basic Skills have improved from the 45th to the 49th percentile, but some students score in the bottom quartile.

The faculty members and school community have sought to meet the needs of the students, but those needs have significantly changed over the past 4 years and the system has been unable to keep pace. During the past year, the Hickory Ridge faculty, staff, parents, and business partners worked toward a variety of reform initiatives but achieved very limited success. The district's reform efforts allowed a core of Hickory teachers to participate in activities. They took technology-based industry tours and attended forums on the implementation of pilot programs to reform the schools. Although Hickory has formulated a new mission statement and vision for the school, the teachers and administrators are in conflict about how best to proceed. The school is generally viewed as unable to meet new reform guidelines, out of date, and in serious conflict.

The makeup of the teaching staff members at Hickory Ridge High School is illustrated in Table 1. There is concern over standardized test scores that, having fallen slightly over the past 3 years, had risen last year.

All rooms at the high school are wired and each has at least 15 computers. The district was seen as a leader in obtaining the needed equipment to make the schools technological centers. The actual use of the computers by both teachers and students, however, was disappointing and major pressure was put on the system to incorporate the computers into the curriculum and daily instruction. Even though the scores and performance of the students on standardized tests were disappointing, the school board and community believed that these changes would result in "better teaching and learning for all kids," and "give their children a head start by providing them with critical thinking and technological skills."

Hickory High has a very supportive parent group who are civic minded, young, technically advanced, and middle class. The turnover in this neighborhood is high because it is considered a stepping-off point to greater affluence. The central administrative staff and you hold the teachers at Hickory High in high regard.

THE PROBLEM

You are the superintendent for Wingfield School District. You were hired 4 years ago to help the school district achieve its newly established vision of becoming a technologically driven, innovative school district. The focus of the reforms was to be school based, beginning at Hickory Ridge High School and spreading to other schools.

The faculty members at the high school are aging and many have been teaching for 20 years or longer. Jim O'Connor, the principal, was a teacher for 8 years at the middle-school level before moving to the assistant-principal position. He served as an assistant principal for 13 years before being promoted last year to his present job of principal at Hickory Ridge High.

Jim O'Connor is not seen as an individual who will advance any further than high school principal. He is the keeper of the history and, although he relates well to children and their parents, he lacks understanding of their needs in the 21st century. No one, however, is more knowledgeable about the community, people, and existing programs and policies within the school district. You called on him to gain perspective on reactions of both internal and external publics to issues being considered within the school district. His staff members see him as knowledgeable but not well respected and unable to understand the school district's vision for Hickory Ridge High School. He has a lot to offer, particularly to younger staff, in

TABLE 1   Makeup of the Teaching Staff Members at Hickory Ridge High School

FACULTY DEMOGRAPHICS	ALL TEACHERS (PERCENTAGE)
TOTAL	100.0
SEX	
Male	35.0
Female	65.0
AGE	
Under 26 years old	21.4
26–30 years old	16.4
31–35 years old	2.1
36–40 years old	4.5
41–45 years old	10.0
46–50 years old	11.3
51–55 years old	20.0
56–60 years old	8.0
61 or more years old	6.3
RACE/ETHNICITY	
Asian or Pacific Islander	0.0
Hispanic, regardless of race	1.3
African American, not of Hispanic origin	20.6
White, not of Hispanic origin	75.6
Native American	2.5
HIGHEST ACADEMIC DEGREE	
High school diploma	0.0
Business/technical school certificate	0.0
Associate degree (2 years or more)	0.0
Bachelor's degree	38.3
Master's degree	56.9
Education specialist or professional diploma	2.4
Doctorate	1.2
Professional degree	1.2

perspective and understanding the community; however, younger staff members see him as having limited power, importance, and as not being able to help them to gain desired promotions.

Over the last 4 years, you have placed 27 new teachers at Hickory, all of whom are identified as having very high potential, although still relatively young. They have all been in the top 10% in their programs of study. They have been well prepared regarding the desired school reforms and are experts in technology. These new high-potential people are highly likely to become administrators themselves someday—they are "fast trackers."

You placed these "fast trackers" at Hickory in hopes that O'Connor and the aging teaching staff would learn from them regarding new, innovative programs. At the same time, you hoped that the fast trackers would learn more about the community, families, and children and the school district's past successes from O'Connor and the more experienced teachers. You hoped that the younger and older staff would share their talents, resources, knowledge, and skill and support each other and the school in the achievement of needed reforms. However, this respect and appreciation of each other's abilities and knowledge never developed.

Two of the top fast trackers, Michael Scott and Kerri Beth, have recently requested to be taken off the site-based planning team for the school. Many of the new teachers have been complaining about O'Connor's management and the attitude of a number of older teachers on the staff, first to O'Connor and then, more delicately, to Sandi Walchek, the associate superintendent O'Connor reports to, and to you. They told Walchek that O'Connor is always looking over their work, second guessing how they teach their classes and what they say to parents, and is endlessly critical.

They are beginning to raise questions about whether Jim and a few of the older teachers can really do their jobs. They see Jim and the older teachers as being out of touch with modern times, too bureaucratic, and too concerned about the parents and the community. They are concerned that the principal and staff will hold back their careers and are not in touch with the power base within the district. The principal measures performance by adherence to routine procedures and community relations, not accomplishments, responsiveness, or reform efforts. Walchek, concerned, has asked O'Connor about this situation without, of course, identifying the people involved.

O'Connor explains that he has a lot of experience and sees the new hires as not understanding the community or kids or appreciating the significant progress made in this school district. He complains that they seem to look down on him and everything the experienced teachers have to say. As a result, they do not understand the culture, the children, or the community and are trying to make too many changes that will not work. This requires that he pay very close attention to their work and that educating children and maintaining the good relations with the community is simply too important to risk. "Anyhow," he says, "they're not as smart as they think. It takes time, experience, and an understanding of the school's heritage and community to develop the skills you need to be a good educator." Although O'Connor does not say so, Walchek can tell that he is also very angry.

You now find yourself under some pressure from the board. You do agree with the direction that the board has established for the schools and you are empathetic with their frustration with what is occurring at Hickory Ridge High School. You have won the trust of the board, staff, and community, and you do not want to lose it. You also realize that the staff and parents at Hickory seem to be beginning to divide themselves in support of either the older or the younger staff. You also know that O'Connor has many friends within the community, including some board members. You are frustrated that this perfect marriage between the younger staff, who are so technologically competent and so knowledgeable about needed reforms, and the older staff and principal, who have so much knowledge about Wingfield children, programs, services, and families, is not working. You do not want to give up on this idea, because you see no other option that has a higher probability of succeeding.

In reflecting on the situation, you believe that perhaps you have not structured the plan properly for success and that you can do something to get these groups to respect one another and work together on reforming the school. You believe that the principal and teachers have the right combination of knowledge, experience, and ability to be successful if they would work together. You are now going back to the drawing board to come up with ideas to make this plan work.

Some of the problems that you see as holding back the reform efforts at Hickory High include lack of trust, confidence, and power; misunderstanding about roles; insufficient communication; lack of respect for each other and the important knowledge each has to share; the principal seen as lacking power with central administration and the superintendent; neither side feels involved or important; the juniors regret the lack of opportunity for powerful mentorship; and the seniors feel disrespected and lack motivation to change what already exists.

YOUR CHALLENGE

You, as superintendent of Wingfield school district, realize that the organizational culture at Hickory Ridge High School is hindering the needed school reform efforts. All parties need to work together to achieve the desired curriculum and instructional improvements. The staff members, from O'Connor to the newest teachers, now seem to feel a sense of helplessness and powerlessness. They are unable to act at a time when they are absolutely essential to needed reform efforts. You realize that you must identify ways to give the principal and teachers a sense of purpose, direction, responsibility, power, respect, optimism, and mission.

You have been given a free hand by the board to insure that all Hickory staff members develop a plan of action and have a common direction, are working together and supporting one another, and have the time and power "to develop needed reforms and then deliver on those plans." The idea is to develop respect for each person's unique talents as an important resource so all parties can work together to create and implement a plan of improvement for the school.

The board chairman has challenged you: "Free up the energy, creativity, and commitment in individual schools, then step back and marvel at the results." You now realize the full meaning in the challenge of this statement. Everything you ask staff members to do appears to be an add-on. They seem incapable of working together. There is a lack of respect for the principal. Energy and focus gets lost; stress and anxiety are running high.

The plan should address the following elements:

1. Helping Jim O'Connor to gain the respect of the new faculty
2. Developing collegiality, honest and open communication, and support among all the faculty members
3. Creating a structure and sense of direction for the development of school improvement and reform
4. Encouraging more design and greater experimentation and risk taking
5. Providing tangible support and empowerment for all members of the staff members
6. Encouraging them to reach out to the extensive research and knowledge pertinent to the desired reforms and to look into promising innovative programs
7. Protecting what is important and good about Hickory High while reforming it to better meet the needs of 21st-century students

You have been told that "it takes a few mistakes before you get it right." You want to get it right this time.

PRODUCT SPECIFICATIONS

You realize you must, in a way, remake Hickory High so it is better prepared to meet the demands for school reform. As one board member warned, with a smile on his face, "You can't bludgeon people into greatness." The initial focus of your plan will be building the needed relationships and exploring structural, process, and cultural changes. You need to give O'Connor greater symbolic power so he will be seen with greater respect. You need to see that teachers work together to share knowledge and expertise. You must create a catalyst for needed reform at Hickory Ridge High School. You will want to help the school staff in their development of a sense of direction and to support the development and implementation of needed improvements.

You are to create conditions whereby purpose, values, information, and relationships are meaningfully connected and aligned around the school system's desire to develop an integrated, technologically supported curriculum. You are to address the conditions that must be created at Hickory High School if the school is to be successfully reformed. You are to create a process at this high school that builds on the capacity of everyone in the school, so as to develop the school's collective intelligence. The plan should create continuous generative learning and staff engagement for the purpose of school reform and improvement. The plan should encourage experimentation and implementation. Your plan should build the school's capacity for participation, engagement, interconnectedness, development, and resilience. You should examine creative ways to distribute power throughout the school district so as to improve respect and each person's opportunity to make a difference. You truly have been given a free hand to solve this very "swampy" problem and to begin developing an effective integrated, technologically supported curriculum.

The process by which the school personnel create needed reforms is an important element in relation to its ultimate success. You will be asked to make an oral presentation to the board on your written plan. The plan should address short-term initiatives (first year) and long-term initiatives (2 to 5 years) and include a chronological sequence of steps to be taken.

(Be sure to refer to the appropriate chapters within this book as a resource.)

INSTRUCTIONAL LEADERSHIP AND STUDENT LEARNING

- - - - -

CHAPTER 6

LEADING LEARNING
IN SCHOOLS

MyEdLeadershipLab™

Visit the **MyEdLeadershipLab**™ site for *Educational Leadership: A Bridge to Improved Practice*, Fifth Edition to enhance your understanding of chapter concepts. You'll have the opportunity to practice your skills through video- and case-based Assignments and Activities as well as Building Leadership Skills units, and to prepare for your certification exam with Practice for Certification quizzes.

LINCOLN ELEMENTARY SCHOOL

Building a Collaborative Team

It is July and Maureen Robinson has been appointed principal at Lincoln Elementary School. The school has had three principals in the last 5 years. Most faculty members have been teaching at the school for more than 15 years; however, seven new teachers out of a total staff of 42 need to be hired. Student achievement levels in all core areas in all grades are either flat or have slightly dropped. During recent years, a large number of families from Somalia, Mexico, and Cambodia have moved into the area. The superintendent has asked Principal Robinson to develop a work plan for her first year.

✳ **What broad areas should Maureen Robinson address in her work plan?**

LEADERSHIP MATTERS

In the previous chapter, we provided an overview of several much-researched as well as more recent theories and models of leadership and management. Those generic leadership and management theories and models are the backdrop for thinking about the unique context of school leadership. This chapter explores the context of schools and what is unique in providing leadership for learning in schools.

Recent research in education has focused on how to improve teaching and learning. In Chapters 3 and 9, we describe some recent school reform efforts, including among other things program reforms, whole school reforms, and greater diversity of teaching strategies. Clearly, in order to improve teaching and learning, successful leadership is a prerequisite. Galvanizing and supporting colleagues (teams) to improve learning for children and youths are crucial ingredients for school reform. But what do we know about successful school leadership? A meta-analysis conducted by Waters, Marzano, and McNulty (2003) found a "substantial relationship between leadership and student achievement. . . . [T]he average effect size between leadership and student achievement is .25" (p. 3). Thus, a quarter of the total school effects on student learning can be attributed to leadership. Another key finding from their analysis is that principals can have a negative impact on student achievement, as well. "When leaders concentrate on the wrong school and/or classroom practices, or miscalculate the magnitude or 'order' of the change they are attempting to implement, they can negatively impact student achievement" (p. 5). Their study concludes that there are two key variables that determine whether leadership will have a positive or a negative impact on learning: (1) the focus of the change and (2) the magnitude of the change.

A review of the literature conducted by Leithwood, Seashore Louis, Anderson, and Wahlstrom (2004), found that:

> [R]esearch also shows that schools that demonstrated effects of successful leadership are considerably greater in schools that are in more difficult circumstances. . . . [T]here are virtually no documented instances of troubled schools being turned around without intervention by a powerful leader. (p. 3)

So, how do these powerful school leaders turn around troubled schools? Are there differences in the skills needed by administrators leading 'troubled' schools compared with schools that have demonstrated success based on multiple indicators? The research literature is beginning to provide some clarity in identifying school leadership models and practices needed by administrators in order to lead successful schools.

Based on their review of the research literature, Waters et al. found that there were certain practices associated with greater student achievement. Figure 6.1 lists school and teacher practices as well as student factors that influence student achievement. A school leader must drill down in each of these areas. Let's take one area from Figure 6.1—"instructional strategies." "Drilling down" refers to the need to understand not only what instructional strategies are being used in all classrooms in the school, but also what the research tells us about the impact of certain instructional strategies. Are there certain instructional strategies that should be used to teach a child whose native language is not English? What do we know about children who are literate in their first language versus those who come to us without being able to read and write fluently in their native language? Or what about a child who enters 1st grade without having attended preschool or kindergarten and has little experience with print literacy? What might it mean for

School	1.	Guaranteed and viable curriculum
	2.	Challenging goals and effective feedback
	3.	Parent and community involvement
	4.	Safe and orderly environment
	5.	Collegiality and professionalism
Teacher	6.	Instructional strategies
	7.	Classroom management
	8.	Classroom curriculum design
Student	9.	Home environment
	10.	Learned intelligence/background knowledge
	11.	Motivation

FIGURE 6.1   School and Teacher Practices and Student Factors Influencing Student Achievement

the learning of a math teacher if she or he knew that in a high school math classroom, the research literature finds a strong positive correlation between the types of problems used by teachers and the achievement scores of their students? What does it look like if teachers use authentic intellectual work in order to raise math achievement scores?

Many school administration books and articles use the metaphor of a principal as an instructional leader. Although it is an interesting metaphor, we really have little understanding of what being an instructional leader means in different types of schools and at different levels. Clearly, a principal of a small elementary school leads instruction in different ways from the principal of a large comprehensive high school. Additionally, a high school principal cannot be an expert in mathematics, chemistry, English, and so on; however, an administrator who is an instructional leader must know what good teaching in mathematics looks like compared to poor teaching, and she or he must know what effective learning for students in any classroom looks like. Let's use a high school math classroom as an example. An administrator who is an instructional leader visits math classrooms to look at student time on task, student–teacher interactions, what "big" mathematical ideas are being taught, what materials were prepared to teach this particular lesson, what skills the teacher wants the students to learn that day, what routines or warm-ups are provided, and how the teacher launches the lesson. Was the purpose and rationale of the learning understood by the students? Was the purpose connected to prior learning? Were the tools and materials available identified? Were expectations set (e.g., learning outcomes, time, and structures)? Was there instruction by whole group, individual, pairs, or small group? At the conclusion of the lesson, did the teacher provide opportunities to make public the learning accomplished by students by sharing what was learned? Did the teacher provide opportunities for students to analyze, share, discuss, extend, clarify, connect, and record thinking strategies? Was a summary of the learning articulated and connected to the lesson's purpose? Can the students articulate the learning/understanding of the mathematical concept being taught? And finally, is meaningful practice in the form of homework assigned to extend the learning? These are some of the key areas and questions that an instructional leader will note when observing a class.

Whatever the teaching background of the principal, these practices are part of what makes good teaching and can be applied to math or any other subject area. If an administrator is to be an instructional leader, then she or he must ensure that all teachers continuously have opportunities to fine-tune their practice. We know from the adult learning research that attending professional development workshops a few times per year, which has been one of the primary mechanisms afforded to teachers to improve their practice, is not necessarily the most effective way of acquiring new knowledge. Learning transfer is a key issue, and no study has found that more than 10% of what is learned in one-session workshops, without any follow-up, is actually transferred into the workplace (Detterman, 1993). According to adult learning theorist Merriam (2001) "the learning process is much more than the systematic acquisition and storage of information. It is also making sense of our lives, transforming not just what we learn but the way we learn, and it is absorbing, imagining, intuiting, and learning formally with others" (p. 96).

> ✻ **What structures and activities should Principal Robinson consider if she wants to develop leadership opportunities for the teachers at Lincoln Elementary School?**

ADULT LEARNING

Being an effective school leader requires a deep understanding of how adults learn. It is important for school administrators to not only recruit and hire teachers, but also to ensure that all teachers continue to have optimal opportunities to learn so they can improve their teaching practices. There is no single theory of adult learning; however, there are various models and sets of practices that will prove helpful as school administrators increase their own understanding of how to lead a successful school. According to Mezirow (1991), central to the process of adult learning is critical reflection. He argues that it is our work as adult educators "to assist adults to learn in a way that enhances their capacity to function as self-directed learners" (p. 137). So, perhaps instead of using "instructional" to describe principal leadership, we should think of "adult educator" as being a more apt metaphor.

Merriam (2001) agrees that two goals of self-directed learning include developing the learner's capacity to be self-directed and deepening the critical reflection done by the learner. If we examine the typical learning opportunities afforded to teachers (workshops, professional development conferences, university coursework, etc.), increasing one's capacity for self-direction and deepening critical reflection are not often the goals. Therefore, designing learning opportunities for teachers is the core role of the school leader. Whether the administrator actually leads the professional development is not the important point. The key issue is to be involved in designing the opportunity. Too often an outside expert is brought into a school or district to present on a particular topic. These people know little about the context in which they are presenting, have not held critical conversations with school leaders in order to contextualize the work for this school, and, after delivering the workshop, do not return for follow-up. Chapter 9 discusses declarative (factual), procedural (practical or strategic), and contextual knowledge. If school leaders do not plan with the consultant on how to address procedural and contextual knowledge issues, then, at best, teachers may learn some declarative knowledge. However, again, we have evidence that, at most, only 10% of what is learned in this type of professional development format is transferred to the classroom (see Chapter 9 for a discussion of learning transfer). This fact alone has major learning and fiscal implications.

The following research-based findings were synthesized from the adult learning literature:

- Critical reflection is essential to adult learning (Mezirow, 1991).
- Learning can be gradual or it can result from sudden, powerful experiences (Clark, 1993).
- Learning is an interdependent relationship built on trust; thus, relationships are of key importance (Taylor, 2000).
- Action learning and collaborative learning are important strategies resulting in sustained changes in organizational culture (Yorks & Marsick, 1999).
- Power dynamics are a crucial part of learning and people seen as authority figures must state their values and "model questioning their own values" (Cranton, 1994, p. 201).
- Contextual factors that influence the ability to learn well enough to implement the desired solution include the availability of appropriate sources (time, money, people from whom to learn); willingness and motivation; and "the emotional capacity to take on new capabilities in the middle of what could be a stressful challenge" (Marsick & Watkins, 2001, p. 30).

✳ **How might Maureen Robinson integrate these findings into her work plan?**

If the school leader were to take these findings from the adult learning literature and apply them to learning opportunities in his or her school, what might teacher professional development opportunities then include? Throughout the history of the United States, from the one-room schoolhouse to many of today's schools in which classroom doors are closed until bells ring and visitors are infrequent, teaching has been, and still too often continues to be, lonely and isolated work. If a key ingredient of adult learning involves collaboration, then clearly school administrators must develop expertise in identifying powerful learning strategies that will allow teachers to engage in collaborative activities. The work of teachers must be made public. In the next section, we list several learning practices that can operationalize the adult learning research findings discussed.

EFFECTIVE SCHOOL LEADERSHIP PRACTICES

> Our work as principals is to improve instruction for every child, in every single classroom in the school.
>
> E. Fink, 2002, p. 5[1]

In the previous section, we briefly examined some of the key findings from the adult learning research literature. Now let us examine the practices that the educational research literature has identified as those of effective school leaders.

- Direct involvement with teacher selection (Maryland State Department of Education, 1978)
- Close monitoring of student progress (Venezky & Winfield, 1979)
- Influence on aspects of instructional strategies (Venezky & Winfield, 1979)
- Encouragement of risk taking (Berman & McLaughlin, 1977)
- Attention to details focusing on connecting routine decisions and actions within the school to a larger strategy of instructional leadership (Bossert, Dwyer, Rowan, & Lee, 1982)
- Focus on student assessment (Purkey & Smith, 1982)
- Possession of an explicit, mutually shared, concrete vision for the school (Cunningham & Gresso, 1993)
- Belief that "relational" trust is key to urban school improvement (Bryk & Schneider, 2002)
- Expertise at diagnosing and analyzing complex problems (Portin, Schneider, DeArmond, & Gundlah, 2003)
- Setting of directions, development of people, and redesign of the organization so that learning conditions are optimal (Leithwood et al., 2004)

The principal must be the lead learner in the school. This means that she or he is modeling what it means to be a good learner: relentlessly asking questions, continuously seeking assistance in strategizing how to solve problems, constantly examining his or her own practices, inviting and receiving feedback on his or her own behavior and decisions, and so forth. Clearly, in order to be a good learner, a school principal must know what she or he believes about education and its many complexities. This is why in Chapter 1 we began with a focus on values and beliefs and the importance of creating your educational leadership platform. We cannot lead others if we do not know what we believe about learning and leading. Our beliefs cannot merely be opinions; instead, they must be based on practice (experience), educational values, research data, and reflection. Effective school

---

[1]Quote taken from interview transcripts conducted by educational sociologist Lea Hubbard (2002) with Elaine Fink, former New York City District Two superintendent and recently retired executive director of the Educational Leadership Development Academy (ELDA) at the University of San Diego.

leadership places adult and student learning at the center of the school. We know a lot about how students learn and what conditions are optimal for that learning. We must pay far more attention to the role that school leaders need to play in helping the adults in the building to learn.

ACCELERATING STUDENT AND ADULT LEARNING

Figure 6.2 illustrates the steps for accelerating student and adult learning in a school. Once the school leader has developed a "voice" and can clearly articulate personal educational beliefs, then it is crucial to hold conferences with teachers, visit classrooms, and engage in meetings with parents. School leaders need to understand and articulate instructional practices not only in regular education settings, but they must also understand good practice for children with special needs and for those whose native language is not English. Expertise at assessing the quality of instruction is crucial and involves diagnosing problems and analyzing solutions (Portin et al., 2003). Some problems may require what Waters et al. (2003) call *first-order change*, whereas others may need second-order changes. First-order change is an extension of the past. It is focused, bounded, incremental, and solution oriented. It is consistent with the prevailing values and norms of the school. "A change becomes second order when it is not obvious how it will make things better for people with similar interests, it requires individual or groups of stakeholders to learn new approaches, or it conflicts with prevailing values and norms" (Waters et al., 2003, p. 7). They maintain that recognizing whether a change is first or second order helps school leaders to select leadership practices and strategies that are appropriate. "Doing so enhances the likelihood of sustainable initiatives and a positive impact on achievement. Failing to do so will just as likely result in the negative impact on achievement" (Waters et al., 2003, p. 8). Another key aspect of learning instruction is adult learning. In order to provide structures to develop and strengthen teaching skills, school leaders must analyze teacher strengths and weaknesses. Finally, developing an accountability system is a crucial component for leading a school. The school leader needs to have timely and accurate data so that instructional and budgetary decisions will support student learning.

DEVELOPING AND SUPPORTING TEACHER LEADERSHIP

What is teacher leadership? Following are five definitions that show how the literature contains varying views of what the term means.

> Teacher leadership refers to a sense of empowerment to lead, a self-knowledge about one's potential for leading. (Dawson Gonzalez, 2004, p. 22)

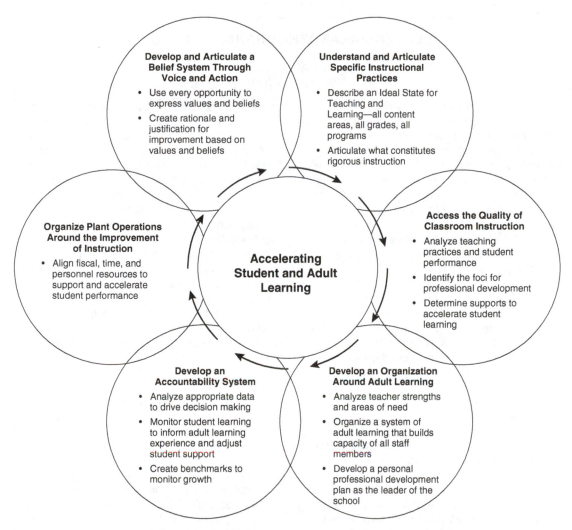

FIGURE 6.2   Accelerating Student and Adult Learning

Source: VanSickle, A., & Beldock, D. (2007). Reprinted with permission from the authors and reprinted from the University of San Diego Educational Leadership Development Academy Handbook. San Diego, CA. Based on a model developed by Elaine Fink.

Teacher leadership facilitates principled action to achieve whole-school success. It applies the distinctive power of teaching to shape meaning for children, youth, and adults. And it contributes to long-term, enhanced quality of community life. (Crowther, Kaagan, Ferguson, & Hann, 2002)

Teacher leadership includes: (a) modeling positive attitudes and enthusiasm; (b) devoting time to doing whatever it takes to make the school work better; (c) enhancing student learning through work with other teachers on

LEADERSHIP AND THE CHANGE PROCESS

MICHAEL FULLAN
University of Toronto

What makes the principal's role so critical in the change process? The answer stems from the conclusion that neither top-down nor bottom-up strategies are effective by themselves. It is only when bottom-up and top-down forces interact and are mediated in purposeful directions that improvement occurs. The principal is the one person ideally placed to play this mediating role.

It has always been said that the principal is key to change, but only recently has research given a detailed understanding of what that role means in practice. We set forth a rationale and framework for the role of the principal in our *What's Worth Fighting For* trilogy (Fullan, 1997; Fullan & Hargreaves, 1992; Hargreaves & Fullan, 1998). I also illustrate the role in practice from the evaluation of the Chicago schools reform (Bender, Sebring, & Bryk, 1998).

We wrote *What's Worth Fighting For* to provide principals and teachers guidelines for action to enable them to take greater control over the change process in a system that is fragmented and overloaded—one that places them in dependent positions. In the first book, *What's Worth Fighting for in the Principalship* (Fullan, 1997), we argued that the starting point for reform is not to hope for or wait for "systemic change" but to look for actions that we ourselves could take. We formed a number of guidelines for action for school principals, such as:

- Avoid "if only" statements, externalizing the blame, and other forms of wishful thinking.
- Practice fearlessness and other forms of risk taking.
- Build a vision in relation to goals as well as change processes.

In the second book, *What's Worth Fighting for in Your School* (Fullan & Hargreaves, 1992), we widened the problem to focus on the culture of the school. We suggested there are at least four cultures in schools—individualized, balkanized, contrived collegiality, and collaborative. Only the last one really makes a difference in school improvement. Since the publication of that book, our analysis has been confirmed precisely in Newman and Wehlage's (1993) careful study of school restructuring in over 800 schools. All schools were engaged in reform, but some were especially successful in increasing student performance.

The three intraschool factors that distinguished the successful schools were (1) the existence of a professional learning community (none other than the collaborative culture), (2) continual review and refinement of instructional practice, and (3) evaluation of student progress. These professional communities constantly examined student work and achievement and revised their teaching accordingly. Newman and Wehlage concluded, as we had, that the role of the principal was to foster and shape collaborative cultures that focus on student achievement using strategies that will accomplish that goal—focused professional development, organization of teaching, use of data, school improvement plans as a tool of developing new school cultures and the like. We said in short that "reculturing" (creating professional learning communities) was the main goal of principals and teachers.

In the third book, *What's Worth Fighting for Out There* (Hargreaves & Fullan, 1998), we extended the analysis even further to say that the context for schools has radically changed and that the "out there" in the form of community, technology, media, government

(continued)

policy, and so on, is now "in here." Therefore, the roles of principals (and teachers) are extended even further. They must in this new environment not only help contend with external forces, but also *form alliances* with many of them. We acknowledged that this was dangerous terrain, but that there were inevitable, indeed sound, reasons for "moving toward the danger." The reasons were inevitable because the outside forces were relentlessly in the school anyway and sound because the job could not be done in the absence of new partnerships with the outside. Our guidelines for principals included:

- Steer clear of false certainty (don't look for the silver bullet, but create your own change models drawing on external ideas).
- Respect those you wish to silence (learn new things from resistance).
- Move toward the danger in forming new alliances.
- Fight for lost causes (be hopeful when it counts).

Our analysis has been corroborated recently by the Chicago schools' reform evaluation. Bender et al. (1998) found that "the quality of the principal's leadership is a critical factor in determining whether a school moves forward to improve learning opportunities for students" (p. 1). More particularly, they found that principals who are most effective (1) focus on student learning, (2) use support and pressure to enable others to act, and (3) attack incoherence through planning that provides continuity. Moreover, effective principals moved forward on two big issues: promoting stronger social ties between school staff and community and creating a viable professional community among the school staff (Bender et al., 1998)

School leadership has never been more critical. It is essential in these complex times because of the need to mediate and integrate bottom-up with top-down forces. There will be tremendous turnover in teachers and principals over the next 5 to 10 years. This will be a difficult time for new leaders, but also an enormously exciting period with a real opportunity to make a difference in the life of students, teachers, and parents.

improving pedagogy; and (d) being recognized, appreciated, and/or valued for such efforts. (LeBlanc & Shelton, 1997, p. 33)

Teacher leadership generally refers to actions by teachers outside their own classrooms which involve an explicit or implicit responsibility to provide professional development to their colleagues, to influence their communities' or districts' policies, or to act as adjunct district staff to support changes in classroom practices among teachers. (Miller, Moon, & Elko, 2000, p. 4)

Teacher leadership is the process by which teachers, individually or collectively, influence their colleagues, principals, and other members of school communities to improve teaching and learning practices with the aim of increased student learning and achievement. (Yorks-Barr & Duke, 2004, pp. 287–288)

Lieberman and Miller (2004) discuss three roles teachers can play that will make a difference: Teachers can serve as: (1) advocates for new forms of accountability and assessment; (2) innovators in the reconstruction of norms of achievement and expectations for students; and (3) stewards for an invigorated profession. They believe that if teachers are taking up these roles, then they will be "critical partners in transforming schooling" (p. 12). Lieberman and Miller maintain that the profession has moved from one of isolation to a profession that involves forming a learning community, and that the teaching act itself has shifted from the act of teaching to the process of learning; thus, teachers can be leaders by assuming the roles listed earlier. For example, if a teacher is a steward 'for an invigorated profession,' then he or she might support colleagues during their candidacy for certification by the National Board of Professional Teaching Standards.

So what can school principals do to nurture and sustain teacher leadership in their schools? Numerous authors (e.g., Murphy, 2005; Prestine, 1991; Sherrill, 1999; Smylie & Brownlee-Conyers, 1992) identify three characteristics found in schools where teacher leadership is promoted. First, it is vital for principals and teachers to have trusting relationships. The relationship between the principal and teacher leaders must be one of respect, trust, and cooperation in order to support and sustain teacher leadership. Second, structures that afford teachers the authority to assume various roles need to be in place. These structures can be formal or informal, but they must be present to allow leadership to be distributed across the school. Third, adults in the school must view power in a way that allows principals to delegate and give authority to others to make decisions. In the next section, we expand on the structures that will facilitate the nurturing of teacher leadership.

STRUCTURES AND PROCESSES THAT PROVIDE OPPORTUNITIES FOR TEACHER COLLABORATION

Organizing a school around adult learning, a key element in leading instruction that is depicted in Figure 6.2, means that certain structures are built into each school. Key structures that operationalize findings from adult learning research include study groups, teacher conferences, school visitations, district and/or instructional conferences, action research, and learning communities and networks.

Study Groups

Study groups can reinforce, clarify, and deepen teacher learning by providing opportunities for teachers to teach each other. They can vary in size, content, and length. Ideally, they would not be too large so that all involved have ample opportunity to discuss and critically reflect on practice. Study groups work best when the participants themselves decide where they need to focus. For example, if teachers believe they need to learn better ways to monitor and assess student learning, then they might decide to invite a colleague whom they believe has strong skills in this area to work with them. How long and how often they meet and over what time period are other factors to consider.

For example, what might a study group of math teachers look like? It might mean that they, as self-directed learners, would decide to visit each other's classes. It might include deciding what kind of feedback they would like to receive after those visits. It could also include what they might jointly read and reflect on. Perhaps it would include what lesson plans they would share and critique. One teacher might ask someone to videotape her lesson, and then she might take the study group through key parts of the tape, soliciting their input on how she taught the particular mathematical concept. Study groups work best when teachers set their own agenda, the schedule they will follow, and the activities they will conduct. The central focus is always on what teachers can do to improve student achievement. They may use resources such as Web sites, videos, professional books, and presenters (experts).

Instructional Walk-Throughs

Walk-throughs are being used in many schools throughout the nation and can take various forms. They usually involve small groups and a facilitator spending time in classrooms looking for evidence of good instructional practice. Often walk-throughs involve using an observation guide that has general components of quality teaching. Participants focus on those identified areas and may record items during the observation. The main reason for conducting walk-throughs is to help improve the teaching skills of the staff. Methods seen as effective can then be shared with other teachers at the school. Often it is the school principal, or others who coach teachers, who conduct the walk-throughs. However, a study group might decide they would like to conduct classroom walk-throughs of the teachers in their group and then meet to discuss what they observed. Walk-throughs could include the same concept being taught in different classrooms so that teachers can observe the impact of different strategies.

Walk-throughs help to keep the school staff focused on instruction. These informal walk-throughs promote meaningful dialogue about instruction and inspire inquiry as teachers and administrators learn about best research-based practices as they are incorporated into practice in the context of individual lessons. The walk-through should be very focused with the overall purpose of improving student achievement as an instructional team. The observer looks at specific activity, student work, teacher plans, lessons, and so on before assembling the information in a way that helps to better portray what students have learned. This provides "bite-sized pieces" that can be more easily discussed and shared. They might focus on instructional modalities, assignments, instructions, questioning, instructional strategies, and so on. The principal's presence is viewed as a sign of support for instructional improvement.

Teacher Conferences

After an administrator, staff developer, or master teacher (peer coach) has observed a classroom, the feedback process then needs to follow. If conducted appropriately, teacher conferencing can be a powerful vehicle for teacher learning. A strong relationship built on trust is key to supervisor–supervisee conferences in order for optimal teacher learning to occur. Instructional leaders need to know what each individual teacher needs in order to improve learning in his or her classroom. Ideally, teacher conferencing would take place both before and after the classroom visit. Teacher conferences should not be sessions in which the supervisor is telling the teacher what to do. Instead, the administrator might begin with any of the following statements: "Tell me about the class I observed"; "Tell me what you have been doing since I last visited your class"; "Tell me where in your lesson you were having difficulty and what you are doing to problem solve how to change that"; "Tell me what you want me to focus on when I visit your class"; "What do you think I am going to see when I visit your class?" Teacher conferencing can be difficult work. Administrators must be in teachers' classrooms on a regular basis, and they need to know what they are looking at. Knowing what is happening in classrooms is the core of the school leaders' work. If administrators are unwilling to visit classes on a regular basis, and if they do not know what aspects of instruction they need to focus on, then they might want to consider a different job.

School Visitations

Visits to other schools by administrators and teachers should be a normal part of professional development. During these visits, educators can observe specific teaching practices, or they may want to examine particular approaches to learning or models being implemented in a school. It is crucial that school visits be focused and that educators have opportunities to discuss what they observed and learned from the visit. During the visit, they need to ask questions and probe for deeper understanding. Needless to say, carefully choosing the school for the site visit is crucial. If a teacher or administrator is to critically and constructively examine a practice, then she must first be sure that the site itself has good practice. Seeing effective practice and then having the opportunity to critically reflect on what was observed, so that learning can then be transferred to the observer's classroom, are key to ensuring that the visit results in teacher or administrator learning.

District and/or School Instructional Conferences

For many years, school districts have been offering in-services. Often, this means teachers either choosing from a list of offerings (e.g., a 2-hour workshop in cooperative learning or working with second language students, etc.) or all teachers (or administrators) being required to attend a workshop that, hopefully, is conducted by a knowledgeable and engaging speaker. If a school district's central office is going to regularly offer professional development conferences, then those conferences or workshops should be highly focused and tied to the district's instructional goals. The content of professional development conferences should always be on improving instruction and tied to specific district or school goals. Instructional conferences should be carefully planned and structured so that teachers are engaged throughout, and they should provide opportunities for teachers to practice what is being taught. Finally, two other vital ingredients are evaluation and follow-up. What evidence exists that what was taught in the instructional conference was learned and that it was appropriately transferred to the classroom?

In order for learning to be deep, teachers need to have multiple opportunities to practice and receive feedback. Study groups, walk-throughs, teacher conferences, school visits, and instructional conferences are five structures that school officials, both principals and teacher leaders, can provide for the adult learners in their building in order to improve practice. In his thoughtful book on professional development, Bredeson (2003) discusses the importance of creating professional learning communities. He maintains that in order for professional development to be effective, it must involve "teachers and principals in the identification and design of learning experiences to meet individual and collective needs" (p. 14). Thus, active involvement of the principal and teacher leaders in professional development is crucial to creating a professional learning community.

Action Research (AR)

AR is inquiry or research in the context of focused efforts to improve student performance. It typically is designed and conducted by teachers and other educators who analyze data to improve their own practice. Glickman, Allen, and Weiss, in an expert opinion on page 85 in Chapter 3, maintain that an action research process that is focused on students can help keep a school on track while informing the decision-making process as to what is working and what needs further attention. AR can be an individual tool, helping classroom teachers reconsider their teaching methods or to adapt in order to solve a problem. It can also be done by teams of colleagues. The team approach is called *collaborative inquiry*.

To begin the process of AR, the teacher first needs a question or problem. Then a plan of action is created. Next, data need to be collected (e.g., student work samples) and analyzed. This is followed by the teacher researcher reflecting on the findings and then sharing the findings. Findings can be shared with colleagues in many ways: through a presentation to colleagues in the school, at a professional conference, through a research paper submitted for publication in an education journal, Internet site, and/or in an online discussion goup.

Learning Communities

The term *learning community* has been used in education for many years. In more recent years, educators have talked about creating *professional communities of learners* or *professional learning communities* (PLCs). Learning communities are when teachers and administrators in a school continuously seek and share learning and then act on what they learn. In learning communities, educators embrace high levels of learning for all students. Educators involved in a PLC create a clear vision of what the school needs to become in order to ensure all students learn. Collectively they decide what each member will do to create such a school, and they use results-oriented goals to guide their progress. Learning communities focus on student learning, not on teaching.

Learning communities are based on research from adult learning (e.g., critical reflection, action learning). Practitioners work together to clarify what each student must learn, regularly monitor each student's learning, provide systematic interventions so that students receive additional support for learning if they are struggling, and extend learning when students have achieved mastery of the learning outcomes. There are many Web sites that support learning communities (See allthingsplc.info/; sedl.org/change/issues/issues61.html).

Networks for School Personnel

For many years, teachers and other educators have been able to participate in various types of networks. For example, the National Writing Project (NWP) works with K–12 teachers from all over the nation to improve writing and learning for all learners and has a network of sites located in colleges and universities. Additionally, professional associations serving teachers in certain content areas offer various types of opportunities (e.g., conferences, workshops) for teachers to collaborate and learn more about their pedagogy, content area, and student learning.

The Internet has brought a new generation of research tools and techniques such as blogs, online access to classroom videos, and free access to print resources. These sites range from chatboards (teachers.net/states/) that include lesson plans and other resources as well, to sites offering blogs, discussion groups, and profiles and videos of schools that have been effective in improving student learning. Many of these sites are not only for teachers but have learning opportunities for all school personnel (see edutopia.org/). Additionally, many of these Web sites and networks offer a place for sharing reports of action research.

SUPPORTING THE CHANGE PROCESS

Earlier, we discussed what Waters et al. (2003) referred to as first-order and second-order change. Some changes are incremental or technical (first order) and others are second-order changes that require what Heifetz (1994) calls *adaptive change.* School leaders need to define problems, and using these two categories can be helpful in determining how one might best respond. Adaptive change is needed when the problem cannot be solved with one's existing knowledge or skills. It also requires people to make a shift in their expectations, attitudes, values, or habits of behavior.

The concerns-based adoption model (CBAM), developed by Hall and Hord (1987), provides tools and assistance for those involved in implementing change in schools. The model includes six dimensions referred to as "stages of concern" detailing the feelings and perceptions of those involved in the change or innovation experience. Additionally, the model has eight "levels of use" describing the various levels that users of an innovation experience as they move from becoming oriented to the innovation and then preparing to

PRINCIPALS AS INSTRUCTIONAL LEADERS: MODELING AND SUPPORTING TEACHING AND LEARNING

PAUL V. BREDESON
University of Wisconsin–Madison

Given the nature of schools and professional work in them, highly successful principals have learned to be selective in their professional work, balancing what others expect them to do (role taking) with their own work priorities and goals as educational leaders (role making). Thus, effective leadership requires balancing many conflicting activities and responsibilities. Through their work, principals create, nurture, and sustain successful and healthy teaching and learning environments for teachers as well as students. The principal's primary role is in modeling and supporting the learning of others, the essence of instructional leadership.

PLAY THE BALL

From the sidelines, a softball coach yells advice to the players on the field. "Play the ball. Don't let the ball play you." In other words, the players need to make the plays, not let the ball determine how they should move or play the game. This advice is as useful on the ball field as it is for principals in schools. Like players facing a number of possibilities to field balls, principals face countless daily events, some predictable, others not. What is important is that principals use their expert knowledge and skills in ways that support the primary teaching and learning goals. On a daily basis, principals must deal with sick children, conflicts among staff, student discipline problems, unexpected visits by parents, telephone calls, piles of paperwork, emergencies, central office meetings, bus and cafeteria duties, and student records. In addition, let us not forget about instruction, curriculum, staff development, and school improvement initiatives. The sheer number of activities can overwhelm even the most experienced principal.

To cope, successful principals keep in mind the big picture, nurturing and supporting a healthy and successful teaching and learning environment, while simultaneously attending to the details of all their administrative responsibilities. Principals influence student-learning outcomes directly and indirectly by what they do, what they believe, and how they use symbols. By viewing their work through the lens of instructional leadership, principals "play the ball," knowing that what they do has the potential to ripple across the school, amplifying its effect on teaching and learning processes and on student and organizational outcomes.

INSTRUCTIONAL LEADERSHIP IN ACTION

For principals, keeping the focus on teaching and learning is more than the application of technical knowledge and expertise. How principals choose to spend their time, what they do substantively and symbolically, and what they believe are steeped in values, intentions, and understandings about teaching, learning, and educational outcomes for children. The fact that principals pay attention to some things in schools while ignoring or de-emphasizing others infuses the continuous stream of actions, substantive and symbolic, with clarity, consensus, and commitment to what's important in teaching and learning. Ordinary routines become expressions of values and purpose.

To illustrate how principals' behaviors, values, and purposes come together, let's examine one common instructional leadership behavior: principals' visits to classrooms. For instructional leaders, classroom visits are more than opportunities to monitor teacher work. They become occasions for principals to clarify the primary mission of the school

(continued)

(teaching and learning), validate this mission for others (students, teachers, and parents), engender excitement and high expectations for teaching and learning, and infuse the daily routines of students, teachers, and support staff with meaning and significance.

PRINCIPALS AS TEACHERS AND LEARNERS

In addition to exercising their influence as instructional leaders on teaching and learning, principals are themselves teachers and learners. "Principals as teachers need not be omniscient paragons of pedagogy. Rather, they are coaches and facilitators who help students, teachers, and other staff understand the mental models and basic assumptions about teaching and learning in particular schools and communities" (Hart & Bredeson, 1996, p. 137).

Principals are also learners. As Schein (1985) reminds us in his discussion of leadership and organizational culture, if you want to know what is important and valued in a school, watch what the principal pays attention to and does, rather than what he or she *says* is important. For example, principals who greet staff at the beginning of a planned in-service and then give their apologies for not staying because they have other work to do send a clear, albeit negative, message regarding the use of time and learning. If learning is important in a school, the principal will model the behaviors of an active learner. Principals who read broadly and remain knowledgeable in their fields, who participate actively in professional development opportunities, and who see their own learning as an important part of their professional work are modeling the beliefs and behaviors they espouse for others in schools.

CHALLENGES FOR INSTRUCTIONAL LEADERS

Many challenges await principals as instructional leaders in the 21st century. Here I describe three in particular. The first centers on clarifying and articulating the values and principles that will guide you as an instructional leader. Understanding and being committed to the values will guide you and your school colleagues as you work together to meet such challenges as inclusive education for children with disabilities, charter school competition, new state and national curriculum standards, public school choice, and bilingual education, to name a few.

A second challenge for principals in the future will be to determine work priorities. As described earlier in this piece, there is no shortage of activity and responsibility for principals. There will always be unexpected and routine tasks that need to be carried out. The question is whether you as leader let the flow of events and activities define you as an instructional leader or whether your values and beliefs about teaching and learning set the tone and substance of your work. Finally, principals as instructional leaders are confronted with the perennial paradox of continuity and change. The certainty of change may be the most predictable factor in your future work, yet the certainty of change brings anxiety and ambiguity.

use it, to later focusing on developing effectiveness in using the innovation. In the final level the user is seeking even more effective alternatives to the original use of the innovation.

Whether you use a framework of technical and adaptive change or a model such as CBAM, the key point is that the school leader needs to develop knowledge about the change process. Fostering the growth of a professional learning community may be a long and challenging process in some schools; however, it has enormous potential to result in greater teacher and student learning.

RECRUITMENT, SELECTION, INDUCTION, SUPPORT, AND EVALUATION

In this section, we primarily focus on teacher selection and recruitment, but the school prinicpal is usually involved in hiring other school personnel such as counselors, librarians, and other administrators, to name a few. Depending on the size of the district, central office personnel usually play a key role in hiring staff such as custodians, cafeteria workers, and so on. However, input is often solicited from site-based personnel.

Staff Planning

A prerequisite to any efforts to recruit and select employees is an assessment of the organization's needs for employees. This includes teachers, counselors, administrators, school nurses, clerical staff, and custodians, among others. Staff planning is a forecast of the number and kinds of employees the school district as a whole will need in each position over a given period of time.

Once the educational program has been determined, it is necessary to prepare enrollment projections. An error in enrollment projections will result in expensive and disruptive overstaffing or understaffing of the school system. Most assignments are based on the number of students expected to enroll in each school. Usually, the district's central office works with each school in helping with enrollment and staffing projections.

For public schools, minimum personnel-to-student ratios are often controversial and established by state boards of education. For example, a school system with 1,610 enrolled 3rd-grade students and a teacher-staffing ratio of 23 students per certified 3rd-grade teacher might require 70 (1,610/23) 3rd-grade teachers. Staff requirements are calculated for all grade levels, all schools, and the school district office. Adjustments are made for special programs and special student needs. Final hiring requirements are determined by comparing the school district's future human resource needs with the numbers of those already employed who will remain with the school district. Retirements, resignations, sabbatical leaves, dismissals, and deaths affect the number of personnel to be replaced. The totals help pinpoint needed new hires, highlight areas of overstaffing for reduction in force (RIF), identify employees for possible intrasystem movement (promotions, transfers, demotions, and so on), identify needs to support an increasingly diverse workforce, and ultimately identify the number and kinds of individuals who must be recruited to satisfy future needs.

RECRUITMENT

The effort to successfully match human resource demands with human resource supply is one of the most important efforts educational leaders make. The process begins with developing ways to attract qualified people to apply for open positions within the school district. Vacancy announcements, advertisements, employment agencies, university visits, professional organizations, employee referrals, job fairs, incentive programs, and other school systems are all potential sources. Perhaps the single most important factor in attracting qualified candidates is the reputation and image of the school district and community. Other factors that influence any recruitment plan are affirmative action and equal employment opportunity, professional negotiations, salary and fringe benefits, school system policy, employment continuity, employee relations, staff development, availability of opportunity, and the work itself. Both equity and excellence must be goals for recruiting and hiring teachers.

There is projected to be a shortage of educational personnel over the next 10 to 15 years. Those presently in teacher preparation programs are far less than needed to fill the projected demand—especially in key subject areas such as math, science, special education, and bilingual education. In fact, the pipeline will fill only slightly more than half of those that will be needed in a few states. This problem is partially caused by the 25% to 50% of new teachers who leave education within the first 5 years. This begs the question, "Are our systems for preparing and developing teachers and principals sufficient to provide the number of high-quality school professionals we will need?" Most states believe the answer is no and have developed emergency licensing procedures and alternative routes to teacher licensing such as the Military Career Transition Program (MCTP), Troops to Teachers (TTT), and career switcher programs that are being funded by the federal government.

Without significant salary increases, many agree that these second-career people in education are essential to fully staffing the schools. Linda Darling-Hammond (2003) states, "Although no state will permit a person to write wills, practice medicine, fix plumbing, or style hair without completing training and passing an examination, these states fill nearly 100,000 vacancies a year with teachers who do not meet basic requirements" (p. 78). She goes on to suggest the problem is compounded by minimal, one-shot professional development activities.

Some districts are trying to turn this situation around with creative staffing and use of time; aggressive recruitment; quality professional development; career ladders; teacher assessment, mentoring, and support; active involvement in internships; teacher retention; reallocation of time (so teachers can work intensively with students and collaboratively with each other); incentives; and competitive salaries.

Recruiters are also working to determine the factors that are causing education to lose many of the best and brightest students. Higher salaries, stock option plans, benefits and bonuses, and other offerings (living allowances, matching 401K and 403B plans, lucrative retirement plans, and so on) in private companies, although a main reason, are not the only reason. Lack of teacher respect is another. Obviously, the quality of the application pool is only as good as those who choose to enter the profession. One idea for increasing the application pool in high-need poverty areas and subjects that have shortages (like math, science, and special education) is to pay bonuses in those positions or even higher salaries in order to induce more applicants to enter the job pool in these areas of greatest need.

School districts are turning to technology for online job vacancies, recruitment materials, applications, electronic evaluation forms, portfolios, interviews, and electronic ordering of transcripts, teaching certificates, and so on. A number of groups have developed educational databases to link school divisions with candidates and include the California State University system (teachcalifornia .org/), the American Association for Employment in Education (aaee.org), and the National Teacher Recruitment Clearinghouse (joeant.com/DIR/info/ get/574/2790). Although recruitment and screening can be through the central office of the district, it is best that selection be decentralized to the school level in which the individual will work. It is important to follow up quickly, particularly with strong candidates who are probably being recruited by other systems.

The National Board of Professional Teaching Standards (NBPTS) certifies that teachers have met standards for what accomplished teachers need to know in order to advance the quality of teaching and learning. Research has suggested that board-certified teachers have a substantial positive impact on teaching and learning (nbpts.org) and better meet the NCLB requirements for highly qualified teachers.

The NCLB legislation stated that by 2006 teachers needed to be "highly qualified" in the subjects they teach. This legislation waives the hiring of teachers on emergency, temporary, or provisional bases. The law defines that "highly qualified" teachers must demonstrate competence by passing a rigorous subject exam or possess an academic major or equivalent coursework or certification or credential in the subject taught. There is some evidence (Jerald & Ingersoll, 2002) that more than 25% of teachers lack training (33% in high-poverty schools) in core academic classes.

These NCLB provisions have caused schools to step up their recruitment. Hard-to-staff schools now require teachers to be "highly qualified" in the content they are to teach. Hard-to-staff schools traditionally are low-income or predominantly minority schools who have low-achieving students. The difference in annual achievement growth for a student taught by an effective teacher rather than an ineffective teacher can be as much as one grade level equivalent (Hanushek, 2002). The impact of an effective teacher is still measurable 2 years later regardless of the effectiveness of the intervening teachers.

There are many important questions a school principal needs to ask regarding the policies and practices the district follows to recruit new teachers. What processes does the district use to recruit teachers? How can a school-site leader influence that process? Does the district or the principal contact university faculty and ask who their best graduates are? Is the district involved with college students studying to be teachers from the time of their admittance to the teacher education program? If the answer is no, then why not? Does it not behoove school district leaders to try and shape who enters the teaching profession? What induction and support does the district have for beginning teachers? Are new teachers assigned mentors? Do local college and university programs partner with the district in supporting new teachers during their induction period?

   ✳ **What factors should principal Maureen Robinson consider when hiring new teachers? What process might she and her colleagues use?**

THE TEACHER SELECTION PROCESS

Earlier in this chapter, we discussed two of the most important jobs of the school administrator: (1) recruiting and selecting teachers and (2) ensuring that all teachers continue to have optimal learning opportunities to improve their teaching practices. Bear in mind that other personnel such as counselors, librarians, and assistant principals also need to have rigorous recruitment, selection, and induction processes. However, in this section we focus on the classroom teacher. Clearly, the work of ensuring that all teachers continue to learn is far easier if teachers begin with the disposition that lifelong learning is a requirement for being an effective educator.

The Interview

The selection process involves matching applicants' qualifications to the selection criteria, job description, specifications, and work unit. The determination to hire is related to technical skills (*can* he or she do the job?) and motivation (*will* he or she do the job?). The selection process may include an interview, an observation of the candidate teaching class, and a candidate's portfolio with samples of evidence such as lesson plans, student work, a teaching video, and so on.

Those involved in the interview process should be trained in its use and familiar with all legal requirements that govern employee selection. Regardless of whether a single individual or a number of staff members jointly perform the tasks of interviewing, the steps remain basically the same, with six typical steps to the structured interview process (Arons, 1999):

1. Introduction and welcoming
2. Obtaining information
3. Providing information
4. Responding to questions
5. Concluding the interview
6. Evaluating the candidate

The *introduction and welcoming* step begins by setting the environment and schedule for the interview. Schedule enough time for the interview, which should be free of disruptions. The interviewer should form a positive relationship with the interviewee while collecting all needed information and retaining control of the interview. Study information on the applicant before the interview, checking appropriate experiences and their sequence; the quality, attitude, style, and tone of the materials; and the strength of supporting documents. Make notes on items to follow up in the interview. Background investigations are very useful, but all legal requirements must be followed. The interview should begin by putting the applicant at ease and setting up ground rules related to time frame, people to be seen, use of note-taking or recording devices, and the time when the interviewee's questions will be answered.

Obtaining information is the heart of the interview, with success resting on the interviewer's skills in questioning. Good interviewing is the process of getting valid and complete information related to the interviewee's ability and motivation to perform the job. Questions should be specific, probing the individual's ability to carry out the responsibilities of the position and assessing the specific characteristics sought. Questions should be open ended, giving the applicant an opportunity to provide a fair amount of information (see next section).

Hiring is the most important activity in administration and most problems can be avoided by hiring the best people up front. It is not always teaching ability that causes serious problems but personal characteristics like intentions, tone of voice, respect, perseverance, honesty, dedication, work ethic, and character that cause the difficulties in education. The interviewer needs to be aware of these important personal characteristics during the screening and hiring process. Interview questions that are particularly good at revealing a person's character place candidates in situations and ask them how they would handle values that are presented in opposition to one another: loyalty to a supervisor versus a staff member; truth to a parent versus silence for a child's welfare; justice versus kindness. Ask if you might call the person who worked next to him or her if no one was included as a reference (Slosson, 1999).

The interviewer should not lead the response with any form of directive or point of view. For example, "We use cooperative education in this school. Do you think this is an effective approach?" is an ineffective question, because it is both a leading and close-ended question. A number of questions are also not in compliance with federal legislation and most state laws (e.g., questions are age; race, ethnicity, or color; gender or sex; country of national origin or birth place; religion; disability; and marital or family status or pregnancy). It is best only to ask questions that are directly related to the job.

Effective listening is important to the interview process. Some common suggestions for improved listening skills include: getting the interview candidate to clarify, elaborate, and reflect (e.g., tell me more, turn a statement into a question, silence); getting the main points and test for understanding (e.g., paraphrase); letting the candidate do the talking; and watching your body language, to name a few. Finally, it is best to make brief notes during the interview to help remember what was said. Then immediately after the interview, record your observations.

In the *providing information* stage, the interviewee needs information about the nature of the position, the community, and the school system itself. Key concerns are typically about salary, benefits, working conditions, policies and procedures, colleagues, reporting relationships, opportunities, staff development, and community support. Brochures, manuals, fact sheets, and promotional materials can provide needed information to the candidate. Information allows the candidate to make better decisions regarding his or her fit within the organization. For this reason, it is very important to set a positive environment and put the best possible face on the organization, without being deceptive or overselling. Always allow time for the interviewee to ask any questions and keep notes on the questions asked. Keep responses to questions brief, always maintaining control of the interview.

Concluding the interview is important to inform the candidate what happens next and give time frames in which decisions will be made and when and how the individual will be notified. Everyone who is interviewed, whether or not he or she receives the job, should receive a letter of appreciation or a telephone call indicating that it obviously was a difficult decision but the position has been filled.

Evaluating the candidate results in recording and rating significant attributes of the candidate that contribute to the effectiveness of final selection. It is best to have an interviewer rating form so that information on all candidates is similarly recorded for easier comparison. Some interviewers find it helpful to construct a matrix on which to compare applicants in terms of their responses to job-related questions. Selecting employees is among the most important decision any administrator makes because an organization can be no better than the people it employs. Recording information helps in making appropriate final decisions and provides a clean audit trail against charges that decisions were based on discrimination, bias, or favoritism.

Interview Questions

Because the interview is a key part of the selection process, the questions asked are particularly important. Here are some sample questions:

- What is your teaching philosophy?
- Describe your classroom management style.
- What experience have you had with (e.g., second language learning, children with special needs, etc.)?
- Give an example of a key idea or important concept in your subject matter and how you developed a lesson to teach it.
- Tell us about a difficult instructional problem you have worked on.
- What experience do you have in working with classroom volunteers, parents in the room, or classroom aides?
- Describe a time when you learned something about teaching or an individual student by listening to a parent.
- How do you assess student learning?
- What techniques would you employ to handle discipline problems that may arise in your classroom?
- Describe some teacher-led organization, support group, or network from which you have benefited.
- How can this school help you to become a better teacher?
- How do you think this interview went?

The interview itself, although very important, is only one part of the selection procedure; it should not be the entire process. Is the prospective teacher asked to teach a lesson or submit a video of a lesson? What criteria does the committee use to evaluate the lesson? Is a portfolio required? What criteria does the committee use to evaluate the portfolio? These are a few of the key issues that must be considered in recruiting and selecting teachers. Teacher selection is one of the most important decisions administrators will make. Identifying well-prepared novice teachers and providing mentoring and support will result in a much greater likelihood that student achievement will significantly increase. Selecting teachers who do not have the disposition for lifelong learning and are ill prepared for teaching will result in a much greater likelihood that student achievement will not improve. An administrator who is an educational leader knows that teacher recruitment and selection are crucial ingredients for an effective school.

> ✳ **How might Maureen Robinson use some of these ideas to talk about the seven new teachers she needs to hire? What questions should prospective teacher candidates for Lincoln Elementary School be asked?**

PEER MENTORING AND COACHING

Peers can be an excellent source for information, knowledge, and skills. Peer Assistance and Review (PAR) is an approach that involves teachers as mentors to evaluate and provide support and development to other teachers. These mentor teachers or coaches are usually released from some to all teaching duties so they can conduct evaluations and provide needed support and development. The mentor reports the progress of participatory teachers relative to meeting standards and making planned improvements. These reports are typically presented to a panel and decisions are made regarding further development. In cases of unsatisfactory performance, the coach and principal makes recommendations about continued employment or possible future plans of assistance.

Coaches typically visit participating teachers' classrooms for an hour or two every 2 weeks. Coaches complete evaluations, assist in planning and modeling lessons, and help in development, often discussing other teachers' teaching practices. This is especially helpful for new teachers and veteran teachers needing more help; they often do not receive this needed support. "Districts that have successfully implemented peer assistance and review, have found it an effective means to systematically improve the quality of teaching, and, in the process, to honor and recognize the best teachers" (Goldstein & Noguera, 2006, p. 36). A concern with this process is that the principal will lose power and authority; however, the benefits of both improved classroom-based support and serious teacher evaluation far outweigh such concerns (Goldstein & Noguera, 2006).

Wiggins and McTighe (2006) discuss teacher isolation and stress the importance of regular opportunities to consider, observe, and analyze best practice and to receive helpful, nonevaluative feedback. An important element in discussions of effective teaching is what some call a "set of learning principles." This can help in providing depersonalized feedback based on the school's instructional goals or principles.

Opportunities for organized feedback and development are paramount to the improvement of teaching and learning—ongoing adjustments of what is not working based on analysis and discussion of best practice. The distributed leadership approach supports the development of grade-level or departmental teams to work together in the process of teacher evaluation and performance improvement.

PERFORMANCE APPRAISAL AND EVALUATION

Performance evaluation is one of the hardest jobs in education and one of the most important. The primary goal of performance appraisal is the professional improvement of employees and thus the instructional process. It has two purposes. Formative evaluation identifies areas for improvement and designs developmental plans. Summative evaluation accumulates records regarding the overall quality and degree of improvement in an employee's performance in order to make and support decisions regarding the individual's continued employment, salary, and promotion potential. In this way, evaluation is a continuous process throughout one's entire career in education. Its use in granting tenure is quite important because once it is granted, the court assumes the teacher is competent.

Planning the Evaluation

Employees typically make needed adjustments if they are made aware of required performance improvements. The absence of such feedback will result in more, longer, and larger errors in their work. In this way, the purpose of the evaluation process is always related to continued improvement of employee performance and/or accountability for implementing needed improvements. The appraisal includes a feedback delivery system on employee progress along with an effective means of communication on performance and development. The system must have integrity if employees are to trust and act on the results (Joint Committee on Standards for Education Evaluation, 1988). Unless skillfully conducted, the appraisal process often results in ill feelings and misunderstandings for both parties and probably does more harm than good.

Following are some of the most compelling reasons to complete the appraisal process:

- Helps the employee assess and improve performance
- Motivates the employee to improve knowledge, skill, and methods
- Makes the employee accountable for performance improvements
- Recognizes and rewards outstanding performance
- Identifies and remediates ineffective performance

- Terminates incompetent employees
- Plans professional development and training

Evaluations provide an opportunity for employees to discuss their professional growth and ways they and the organization might improve curriculum, instruction, and student learning.

There have been a number of efforts to link teacher evaluation, teacher development, teacher pay, and teacher promotion to national and state standards. There is an effort by the National Board for Professional Teaching Standards (NBPTS), Education Testing Service (ETS), and the Interstate New Teacher Assessment and Support Consortium (INTASC) to advance standards of practice and methods of measuring teaching excellence. Many states and districts reward teachers with bonuses and/or salary increases if they obtain National Board Certification.

Some are suggesting that to be considered for the principalship, an individual should first be a National Board–certified teacher, especially to close this option off to people who may never have been in the classroom. Others suggest that leadership requires a different set of characteristics than teaching and administrators should be selected because they have knowledge and skill and have displayed these characteristics in their jobs.

Collecting Performance Data

Although multiple assessment methods may be used to appraise performance, most school systems have a specific form that evaluators complete as they observe the employee's performance on the job. Both evaluator and evaluatee assume responsibility for collecting and exchanging a variety of performance data. The most common techniques are the checklist and rating scales, but essay approaches have gained in popularity. The essay method requires the evaluator to describe in writing how well each employee has performed. The instrument usually spells out evaluation criteria as a cue for the rater who checks, rates, or describes the level of performance.

Supervisors usually complete the instrument, but 360-degree systems, for which supervisor, colleagues, and subordinates all complete performance appraisals on an individual, have proved to improve the quality of information provided (Church & Bracken, 1997; Lepsinger & Yukl, 1995; Manatt, 1998). The researchers suggest that the 360-degree feedback process is more reliable, valid, and credible than any other performance assessment process. Employees achieve an increased self-awareness of their strengths and weaknesses. Other techniques such as portfolios, self-evaluation, cognitive coaching, parent and student evaluation, structured simulations, videotaping, interaction analysis, and action research are also used to provide information.

Student scores on standards-based performance tests are being used by an increasing number of school divisions and states as part of the teacher evaluation and are used to guide feedback, instructional improvement planning, and staff development. Stronge and Tucker (2000) support the use of student achievement information in teacher and administrative evaluation if the following nine practices are followed, in order to reduce bias and increase fairness:

1. Use student learning as only one component of a teacher evaluation
2. Consider the context in which teaching and learning occurs
3. Use measures of students' growth
4. Compare gains from one point in time to another for the same student
5. Recognize gain scores have pitfalls that must be avoided
6. Allow a time frame for patterns of student learning to be documented
7. Use fair and valid measures of student learning
8. Align assessment measures and the curriculum
9. Do not narrow the curriculum and limit teaching to fit a test

Education approaches such as constructivist or authentic learning will require the gathering of more diverse data to get an accurate picture of performance (Darling-Hammond, 1997; Millman & Darling-Hammond, 1990; Wiggins, 1998). Teachers being evaluated might include portfolio artifacts such as samples of student work over time linked to evidence of teaching plans and activities, teacher feedback to students, and analyses of student needs and progress. The focus is on how student learning grows out of specific teaching actions and decisions and emphasizes effective performance assessment employed to measure high-level knowledge and skills (Darling-Hammond, 1998).

USING INFORMATION

In the using-information phase, evaluator and evaluatee jointly diagnose, analyze, and discuss evaluative data and plan and agree on follow-up action. Some suggest that this collaborative process is made easier by using a clinical supervision (Glickman, Gordon, & Ross-Gordon, 2009; Cogan, 1973; Goldhammer, 1969) five-step type of process. The process involves a preobservation conference (to focus the observation); the classroom observation (focus on items selected in the preobservation conference); analysis of the evaluative data collected; postobservation conference; and postconference analysis (evaluation of process and outcome). The evaluator and evaluatee emphasize those specific areas in which they have the greatest interest in order to discuss and develop ideas and activities for improvement. An alternative to clinical supervision is collegial supervision, by which teachers work with one another as colleagues in a more informal process. They can use the clinical supervision process or a less intense informal process. The National Education Association favors the concept of peer review and assistance. This process can also complement peer coaching and mentoring.

If the teacher's performance meets minimum standards, a "development plan" is constructed to build on his or her performance. If performance falls below standards, the teacher is placed on a "plan of assistance" to help him or her improve performance and thus remain employed. Unless an evaluation conference is completed, a performance appraisal has not occurred.

The postobservation conference is the critical step in which the evaluator provides useful information for reflection, discussion, and development. Following are some suggestions for providing useful feedback:

1. Be descriptive rather than judgmental
2. Be specific rather than general
3. Concentrate on things that can be changed
4. Consider your own motives
5. Focus on things that can be reasonably documented
6. Show respect for the other's opinions and use good listening skills
7. Do not overload the person being evaluated with information or developmental efforts
8. Ask open questions
9. Discuss both strengths and areas to focus on for improvement
10. Check to ensure that all parties are clear on what was communicated and there are no discrepancies
11. Set benchmarks for follow-up

The feedback is used to help individuals see how they can continuously improve their performance and better achieve the organization's and their own goals.

Disagreements are expected and are resolved through discussion and mutual problem solving. Performance improvement might require changes in policy, performance expectations (resource availability, or job skills), or it might require increased performance from the employee. The final developmental plan should do the following:

- Protect the individual's pride
- Show how evaluation and developmental plans are credible
- Consider the urgency relative to the area being developed
- Think about feasibility and the impact of the plan
- Consider reasonableness and manageability
- Consider sufficient duration
- Think about costs involved in the plan

All evaluations, performance improvement and developmental plans, supportive documents, and validating data are placed in the employee's personnel file along with comments, recommendations, or rebuttals of all parties. Due process requires the existence of substantiative written documentation and credible judgments, establishment of plans of assistance, and disciplinary action that is consistent and reasonable. A hearing and appeals procedure must exist, and all laws must be followed. Stronge (1997) states:

> When evaluation is treated as less than it deserves (i.e., superficially, with little or no resource allocation, invalid evaluation systems, and flawed implementation designs),

the school, its employees, and the public at large are deprived of opportunities for improvement and the benefits that accountability can afford. All of us, whatever our relationship to the educational enterprise, deserve high-quality evaluation. (p. 18)

STAFF DEVELOPMENT

As discussed earlier in this chapter, there are numerous structures that support the adults in a school to improve their practice. The National Staff Development Council (NSDC) has developed Standards for Staff Development and organized the standards into three strands, including context, process, and content, that focus on the improvement of student learning.

Wiggins and McTighe (2006) recommend using eight principles to discuss items such as selection of instructional strategies, areas of performance appraisal, and focus for staff development.

1. A key goal of learning is fluent and flexible transfer—successfully using one's knowledge and skill on worthy tasks in important realistic situations.
2. Engaged and sustained learning, a prerequisite for understanding, requires that learners see the value of their work and experience a growing sense of efficacy when facing worthy challenges.
3. Success at transfer depends on understanding the big ideas that connect otherwise isolated or inert facts, skills, and experiences, enabling learners to meet and understand new challenges.
4. An understanding is a realization that the learner directly experiences the power of an idea. We cannot give understandings; we need to engineer them so that learners see for themselves how an idea can empower them to make sense of things.
5. Learners require clear priorities and a practical knowledge of the work products involved to meet goals and understand standards of excellence.
6. Learners require regular, timely, and user-friendly feedback to understand goals, produce quality work, and meet high standards.
7. Learners attain understanding only through regular reflection, self-assessment, and self-adjustment as they apply prior learning to new situations and tasks through assessments that demand reflection and transfer.
8. The capacity to deeply understand depends on the capacity to re-examine our thinking because any insight typically requires us to refine our earlier ideas. Being willing and able to rethink requires a safe and supportive environment for questioning assumptions and habits, as well as curriculum designed to foster rethinking.

Thus, staff development is most effective when it is personalized—when it honors learners' interests, curiosity, strengths, contributions, and prior knowledge, making staff members feel that they are an important part of something larger than themselves.

The National Staff Development Council former Executive Director, Dennis Sparks, suggests that 10% of the school budget and 25% of teachers' time be used for professional learning. The council also recommends the creation of teacher teams, sharing responsibility for students, improving student performance, reducing teacher isolation, and providing opportunities to learn from each other.

Employee Assistance and Wellness Programs

All school systems have employees whose health or personal problems adversely affect their performance, productivity, and job satisfaction. Now employers are providing assistance to these employees as an alternative to poor performance appraisals, plans of assistance, and termination, because organizations recognize that helping otherwise good employees is much less expensive and much more motivating than replacing them. Employees who exhibit excessive absenteeism or tardiness, decreased work performance, inconsistent behavior, loss of interest, accidents, depression, physical illness, temper outbursts, or substance abuse might have personal problems that cannot be resolved by disciplinary action and warrant intervention through an employee assistance program (EAP).

EAP is a free, confidential, voluntary program providing a formal structure that helps employees get counseling and clinical services for health and personal problems. It provides a method for disentangling an employee's problems from her or his performance ability. The program typically allows for self-referral, peer referral, or referral by supervisor, but it is the employee who decides whether he or she will participate in an EAP. Directed referrals are often used as a management tool to assist the supervisor and employee in improving unacceptable job performance that could be resulting from personal problems. According to school districts, participants reported substantial increases in functioning in work and nonwork settings, and their supervisors reported sharp increases in employee work performance. Over 90% of participants reported they would recommend the program.

Statistics show a significant decrease in medical care costs and employee absenteeism as a result of wellness programs (Health Insurance Association of America, 1986). The idea of a wellness program is to stimulate health-enhancing behaviors in areas such as smoking, alcohol and drug abuse, nutrition, physical fitness, safety, stress, and environmental sensitivity. Myriad wellness programs stress taking responsibility for a healthy lifestyle, practicing preventive health habits, and educating employees regarding the control of risk factors.

CONCLUSION

This chapter provided a brief overview of the literature on effective school leadership, adult learning, and developing teacher leadership. We believe that two of the most important aspects of effective school leadership are the recruitment and selection of teachers and then providing support for their ongoing learning. We offered seven structures and practices that can help to provide that support: study groups, instructional walk-throughs, teacher conferences, school visitations, instructional conferences, collaborative action research, and professional networks.

These structures allow for building and strengthening the capacity of teachers and other school professionals as well as supporting and nurturing teacher leadership. The research tells us that school leadership matters. Along with teaching, leadership is the most important school-related factor that impacts student learning.

MyEdLeadershipLab™

Go to Topic 4: *Instructional Leadership* in the MyEdLeadershipLab™ site (www.MyEdLeadershipLab.com) for *Educational Leadership: A Bridge to Improved Practice,* Fifth Edition, where you can:

- Find learning outcomes for *Instructional Leadership* along with the national standards that connect to these outcomes.
- Complete Assignments and Activities that can help you more deeply understand the chapter content.
- Apply and practice your understanding of the core skills identified in the chapter with the Building Leadership Skills unit.
- Prepare yourself for professional certification with a Practice for Certification quiz.

PORTFOLIO ARTIFACTS

- Create your own definition of teacher leadership. Revisit your educational leadership platform. How does it address your definition of teacher leadership?
- Interview a school principal who you or your colleagues believe is an outstanding educational leader. Ask him or her how they promote teacher and student learning in their schools.

- With the assistance of a fellow teacher or principal, conduct an instructional walk-through.

- Identify a school that is known for using specific teaching practices or models of learning. Visit that school and observe teaching. Ask questions of those you observe about why they are using those particular teaching techniques or models of teaching.

- How is adult learning encouraged in your school? What other structures could be in place to support teacher learning?

- Ask to serve on a teacher selection committee. Find out how the candidates were recruited. How were candidates selected for interviewing? What was included in the interview process? Who was included? How might the process have been improved?

- Provide ongoing coaching and feedback to an individual or group (informally observe, write up findings, and provide feedback, including one–on–one and in small groups).

- Pair up with someone and interview one another for the position to which you both aspire. Write up the results of your interview and discuss the effectiveness of the interviewee and interviewer.

KEY TERMS

- Action learning
- Action research
- Adult learning
- Clinical supervision
- Collaborative action research
- Collaborative inquiry
- Collaborative learning
- Contextual knowledge
- Critical reflection

- Declarative knowledge
- Differentiated staffing
- Disposition
- Effect size
- Employee assistance program (EAP)
- Instructional conferences
- Learning transfer
- Performance appraisal
- Plan of assistance

- Procedural knowledge
- Professional networks
- School visitations
- Study group
- Teacher conferences
- Teacher networks
- Teacher leadership
- Walk-throughs

SUGGESTED READINGS

Danielson, C. (2006). *Teacher leadership that strengthens professional practice.* Alexandria, VA: Association for Supervision and Curriculum Development.

Farr, S. (2010). *Teaching as leadership: The highly effective teacher's guide to closing the achievement gap.* San Francisco, CA: Jossey-Bass.

Marshall, K. (2009). *Rethinking teacher supervision and evaluation: How to work smart, build collaboration, and close the achievement gap.* San Francisco, CA: Jossey-Bass.

Schlechty, P. C. (2009). *Leading for learning: How to transform schools into learning organizations.* San Francisco, CA: Jossey-Bass.

Schmoker, M. (2011). *Focus: Elevating the essentials to radically improve student learning.* Alexandria, VA: Association for Supervision and Curriculum Development.

CHAPTER 7

TECHNOLOGY AND LEARNING

MyEdLeadershipLab™

Visit the MyEdLeadership**Lab**® site for *Educational Leadership: A Bridge to Improved Practice*, Fifth Edition to enhance your understanding of chapter concepts. You'll have the opportunity to practice your skills through video- and case-based Assignments and Activities as well as Building Leadership Skills units, and to prepare for your certification exam with Practice for Certification quizzes.

LYONS HIGH SCHOOL

Lyons HS: Embracing Technology and Engaging with the World

You have been hired to be the new principal of Lyons High School. Lyons High School is located in a suburban community just outside a major coastal city. Overall, it is a fairly affluent community comprised of many professional families, including a growing population of newly arriving immigrants from India, China, Korea, and Taiwan who have jobs in high-tech fields.

Lyons is a new school still under construction and it will be the second high school in the district. Lyons is scheduled to open in 6 months and you have been charged with identifying the core components (design principles) of the curriculum, and hiring teachers. You are particularly excited because during the 3-day interview process, teachers, parents, district administrators and community members talked about the importance of preparing students for our global society. You were asked questions about your experiences in designing interdisciplinary curricula, experiential learning, personalized learning, the importance of learning other languages, authentic forms of assessment, project-based learning, and the use of mobile learning devices in helping facilitate student learning.

Superintendent Tutu has asked you to develop an outline of how you intend to proceed, what the timeline for your work will be, what resources you need, and how you will involve the various stakeholders in creating the design principles and hiring the new teachers. She would like the outline from you within the next 2 weeks.

✳ **Begin thinking about an outline for the superintendent. How and who will you involve in creating the unique core components (design principles) of the school's curriculum and in hiring teachers? What resources might you need?**

HARNESSING TECHNOLOGY

The increasing importance of technology in the workplace and daily life makes it imperative for students and critical in education today. Teachers and students are now able to exchange ideas and experiences with individuals anywhere on the globe, thus removing classroom walls. Teachers have the capacity to download homework and display student portfolios online. Administrators possess the functionality to offer curriculum tips through bulletin-board functions and deliver training through customized feedback programs. Superintendents have access to school personnel in real time and school performance reports ranging from financial data to graduation statistics and testing data. Members of the board of education have the ability to monitor all schools within their district from their home computers.

Students, teachers, and others can have instant access to student work and create notes or comments or communicate online directly to the originator. People can create networks to participate in discussions or conferences on shared topics and interests. Expert volunteers in various organizations can answer students' questions, comment on their work, and pose questions for students to address.

Communications with parents increasingly occurs electronically, as well. Parents can have access to student assignments and work and be able to leave notes and schedule appointments. Parents can work with their children at home and have computer access to classroom materials 24 hours a day. Teachers can instantly access students' performance records to determine what students are having difficulty learning. They can access a resource repository for advice on how to best reach students who are having trouble and apply specific content, curriculum, and instructional strategies. Students are able to abstract information from different sources and include it in their multimedia reports and presentations.

The computer has become a window to the whole world. Students engage with their counterparts in other cities, states, and nations to complete research and reports, working together online. Students in classrooms at diverse locations talk directly with other students giving joint multimedia reports and other presentations. Constructivist types of learning accelerate as we move beyond the limits of classroom walls.

There are thousands of educational sites on the World Wide Web widely ranging in quality and reliability. Different sites may contain misinformation or harmful information such as pornography, not to mention computer viruses. Martindale, Cates, and Qian (2003) suggest that "this massive collection of online learning materials and activities is largely unfiltered, particularly when compared to the process of print publishing" (p. 47). Organizations such as the International Academy of Digital Arts and Sciences, Homeschool.com, *PC Magazine,* and the

Eisenhower National Clearinghouse for Mathematics and Science Education provide helpful information and publish lists of what they believe to be the best educational Web sites.

Using the appropriate software for instruction is a key element in integrating technology into day-to-day teaching and learning. In addition, within e-learning, there are at least four different categories of learning strategies—individual, assisted, collaborative, and reciprocal. For example, the collaborative model uses a mix of synchronous learning such as face–to–face teaching and collaborative online activities such as virtual classrooms, Web seminars, coaching, conference calls, online meetings, video conferencing, instant messaging, and chats, all of which take place in real time (all participants online simultaneously; see Table 7.1 for key terms and definitions). The reciprocal model uses a form of self-paced asynchronous learning (independent of time and space) among collaborative groups using Web pages, e-mail, simulations, bulletin boards, video streaming, computer-based instructional modules, assessments, recorded events, and so on. The point is that issues surrounding the use and adoption of different learning systems, network services, and technologies are relatively complex (Khan, 2001). Administrators and others are expected to acquire familiarity with the related technologies in order to be able to communicate with the experts and to implement and use these developing technologies in their schools.

Internet cameras are another use of technology that will give parents, community members, and principals' access to what is occurring in the classroom. Sick students will be able to keep up from home. Tests will be taken at diverse locations and scored and reported electronically. Entire classes will be able to video conference (on services such as Skype) with individuals or groups in far-away places.

Another area that holds considerable promise is podcasting, in which users connect their portable audio devices to their computers so that audio feeds can be downloaded to the users' iPod or mp3 players. Users can then listen and learn while they walk, ride the bus, sit in the car, or are otherwise away from direct instruction (e.g., out-of-school suspension) or their computer screen, making education much more portable. Podcast aggregators (those making many podcasts available in one spot) are expanding their reach into book discussions, historic reenactments, poetry slams, and so on. Podcasts are designed to be both entertaining and instructive.

> People who recommend more computers for the schools are like doctors who prescribe more medicine. What medicine? How much medicine? For what reason? The same questions apply to computers.
>
> Tapscott, 1998, p. 135

THE EVIDENCE BASE

With the exponential growth of various forms of technology, school leaders need answers to the question: Does the use of technology improve student learning? The problem inherent in this question is that we do not know what pedagogies

TABLE 7.1   Key Terms and Definitions

Asynchronous communication	Communications not occurring at the same time
Blended learning	Combines face–to–face teaching with elements of distance learning (sometimes called *hybrid learning*)
Blog	Short for Web log; a Web site where an individual can post information for others to access
Chat rooms	A location for person–to–person synchronous interaction by typing messages
Clickers	Remote control devices for responding to posed questions by teachers using student participation systems
Cloud computing	A Web-based server hosting e-mail, school business documents, etc. allowing the central office to cut down on a host of tech-based hardware and utility costs
Database management system (DBMS)	Software that allows the user to edit, sort, retrieve, store, and search through computer databases
Distance education	The delivery of instruction to learners who are separated from their teacher by time and/or location
Mobile learning devices (MLDs)	Smart phones, iPads, iPods, MP3 Players, tablets, PDAs, E-book readers, etc.
Online learning	Course of study or training usually delivered via the Internet
Personal digital assistant (PDA)	A handheld mobile electronic device that allows users to access the Internet, calendars, contact information, e-mail, and some even allow word processing and spreadsheets
Social networking	Web applications (e.g., Facebook, LinkedIn, Skype) that allow individuals to share information in an online community
Synchronous communications	Real time; communication occurring at the same time
Two-way interactive video	A distance education technology in which sending and receiving sites are equipped with cameras, video monitors, and microphones and are linked via some means of transmission (e.g., cable, fiber-optic cable)
Virtual reality	A computer interface simulating an interactive environment that appears to the observer to be another reality; VR uses special hardware and software to project a three-dimensional representation of an environment and responds to the other's motion in that environment
Virtual school	An institution that is not "bricks and mortar"; all student services and courses are conducted through Internet technology
Web 2.0	Term for second-generation Web technologies (e.g., blogs, wikis) that allow for communication and collaboration of people in Web-based communities
Webinar	Short for Web seminar; an interactive synchronous meeting or presentation conducted over the Web
Wiki	Web pages created and maintained by multiple contributors (from the Hawaiian word for *rapid*)

are being used with the technology. Thus, when exploring the evidence base, it is crucial to also know the teaching strategies employed as well as the type of technology used. Overall, there is little empirical research about the impact on student learning of using various types of technology and, too often, the research is not even conducted in PK–12 setting. For example, in 2010, the Department of Education reported that there were ". . . only a small number of rigorous published studies contrasting online and face–to–face learning conditions for K–12 students" (p. xii). The report also cautioned the reader in generalizing to the K–12 population any results from studies in other settings such as in medical training or higher education. Thus, action research, described in Chapter 6, might be a highly effective strategy that collaborative teams in schools can use to identify various types of technologies and pedagogies that can enhance student learning because there is so little evidence, yet we have more and more technology in classrooms.

There are some studies that show that students with access to either computer-assisted instruction, integrated learning systems technology, simulations and software that teach higher-order thinking and use collaborative networked technologies, and design and programming technologies show positive gains on researcher-constructed standardized tests and national tests (Schacter, 1999). According to Lemke and Coughlin (1998), while further research studies are needed, emerging trends indicate that, under the right conditions, technology: accelerates, enriches, and deepens basic skills; strengthens teaching; and motivates and engages students in learning.

There are numerous challenges schools face as they embrace various forms of technology. School leaders must recognize that it is far more important to effectively use technology for learning than it is to learn how to use the technology. Bracewell, Breuleux, Laferriere, Beniot, and Abdous (1998) maintain that the integration of educational technology into the classroom, in conjunction with supportive pedagogy, typically leads to increased student interest and motivation in learning, more student-centered classroom environments, and increased real-life or authentic learning opportunities. Davis (1997) agreed that technology integration led to student-centered classrooms, which increased student self-esteem. Schacter (1995) concludes that technology initiatives have to focus on teaching and learning, not the technology, to be successful: "One of the enduring difficulties about technology and education is that a lot of people think about the technology first and the education later" (p. 11).

Although there is significant agreement on the need to create integrated technological programs in our schools today, research suggests that school use of technology is too often limited to learning games, drill and practice, and/or occasional word processing with almost no integration of technology. Not all the research demonstrates that using technology enhances learning. Some studies show little or no academic improvement (Mathews, 2000). Other researchers believe technology takes funding away from other resources and programs that may be more beneficial to students (Healy, 1999); that an overreliance on technology can rob from children opportunities to express creativity, build human relationships, and experience hands-on learning (Alliance for Childhood, 2000); and that technology often

TECHNOLOGY FOR SCHOOL LEADERS

CHRISTOPHER J. DEVERS
University of San Diego

It is not hard to see the impact technology is having on education. Schools are quick to implement technology (Gray, Thomas, Lewis, & Tice, 2010). Interactive whiteboards, laptops, games, and other technologies are constantly being adopted and integrated into classrooms. However, before technology is purchased and implemented, school administrators should explore the research on the processes by which, and environments in which, technology enhances learning. Specifically, administrators should investigate empirical evidence (research) that first address how students learn (Willingham, 2009; Blakemore & Frith, 2005; Stigler & Hiebert, 2009) and then how technology influences learning (Gardenfors & Johansson, 2005).

Some professionals argue that due to the digital revolution, students actually learn differently than previous generations (Prenksy, 2001). Additionally, students often self-report that they learn differently and can multitask (Dretzin, 2010). However, some evidence suggests that *generations Y/Z* do not learn differently from other generations (Bennett, Maton, & Kervin, 2008) and cannot multitask (Ophir, Nass, & Wagner, 2009; Rubinstein, Meyer, & Evans, 2001; Tugend, 2008; Dretzin, 2010). In fact, some controversial research suggests that because young children are using digital devices at an early age, they use their temporal lobes more and therefore their frontal lobes may be developing to a lesser extent than past generations (Small & Vorgan, 2009). This suggests that young children's use of digital technologies should be very limited, in order to allow the frontal lobe to fully develop. Elementary schools should be cautious when implementing technology in the primary grades, because the effects on children might be harmful to brain development.

Another common misconception in education is that students have different learning styles (Gardner, 2006). Administrators and teachers often think adopting new technology benefits students who have different learning styles. For example, administrators might implement interactive whiteboards in the hope of teaching to different learning styles—visual, verbal, and so on. However, virtually all empirical research on interactive whiteboards suggests that they do not improve learning (Higgins, Beauchamp, & Miller, 2007; Smith, Higgins, Wall, & Miller, 2005; McCrummen, 2010) and that learning styles do not exist (Pashler, McDaniel, Rohrer, & Bjork, 2009; Willingham, 2009; Waterhouse, 2006). Reviewing the evidence is critical before adopting new technologies in order to help ensure that the technology implemented actually improves learning. It is essential to remember that although some theories are interesting, not all interesting theories are supported by empirical evidence—as in the case of learning styles and interactive whiteboards. Empirical research can help administrators make informed decisions, and prevent them from simply relying on unsupported theories or personal ideas.

The study of how self-explanation improves learning (Chi, De Leeuw, Chiu, & Lavancher, 1994) provided a framework for the study of how technology (i.e., cognitive tutors) facilitates self-explanation (Aleven & Koedinger, 2002). This research found that students, who self-explained their procedures with the cognitive tutor, outperformed those who did not explain their steps. This is just one example of how administrators can use empirical evidence to support learning using technology. The idea of using a learning-centered approach helps administrators develop a critical mindset toward learning and technology.

School administrators should critically evaluate new technologies as they emerge and not simply purchase the latest fad (e.g., interactive whiteboards, clickers), but rather first explore the intersection between learning and technology before purchasing new equipment. Therefore, as technology evolves, administrators should be able to effectively and efficiently implement technology that enhances learning.

There are many technologies that improve learning, most of which are free and open for education. Cognitive Tutors (http://www.carnegielearning.com/), from Carnegie Mellon University, is one such technology. The program successfully teaches mathematics at many different levels (middle school to college). Vanderbilt University created a similar program, Teachable Agents (http://www.teachableagents.org/), in which students first learn a subject, and then teach an agent what he or she previously learned. Both of these programs have been proven to be very successful in helping students learn and have been empirically validated (Ritter, Anderson, Koedinger, & Corbett, 2007; Aleven & Koedinger, 2002; Basu, Biswas, & Sengupta, 2011; Biswas, Jeong, Kinnebrew, Sulcer, & Roscoe, 2010; Leelawong & Biswas, 2008). Learning outcomes and fiscal responsibility should be a priority for schools, and technology has the potential to address student learning, while also maintaining a low cost.

What action plan should administrators take when exploring learning and technology? First, connect with local universities and other technology-related research centers. Professors and research centers can point to relevant literature to explore regarding which technologies might be helpful in improving learning in a given situation. Second, invest in free and open software or technologies. Explore sites such as The World is Open (http://worldisopen.com/), Connexions (http://cnx.org/), Wikiversity (http://www.wikiversity.org/), Merlot (http://www.merlot.org/), the Open Content Alliance (http://www.opencontentalliance.org/), edNovo (http://www.ednovo.org), TED (http://www.ted.com/), School of One (http://schoolofone.org/), and the University of the People (http://www.uopeople.org/) for learning and technology resources. Third, be very critical of technology and its influence on learning. Evaluate the literature as a whole, and remember that a single study does not invalidate years of research. Also, be cautious of self-reported results, and rely more heavily on basic research. Last, be prepared to fail. Not everything will work well, and sometimes experimental research does not transfer easily into schools. However, be persistent and create an environment that cultivates the use of empirically validated strategies for improving learning through the use of technology.

sits idle and is underutilized. Others come to very different conclusions. After reviewing the available research, the National Association of School Boards of Education Study Group on e-Learning concluded "e-Learning will improve American education in valuable ways and should be universally implemented as soon as possible" (NASBE, 2001, p. 4).

PERSONALIZED LEARNING

Personalized learning is the tailoring of curriculum, pedagogy, and the learning environment to meet the needs and interests of individual learners, often with extensive use of technology. Personalized learning is not a new concept, but with advancements in technology we now have considerable potential to customize learning for students in ways that were never before possible. According to Yong Zhao (2009), personalized learning is a promising way to prepare citizens for the 21st century and an effective approach to helping students develop the skills and knowledge for the future. With personalized learning, the role of the learner is much more active, the curriculum is customized for different types of learners, and learning is more student centered. As instruction is becoming reusable and shared, learners are being asked to be more responsible for time management and their progress through the instructional system. Technology allows instruction to be continuously up to date and timely assessments provide feedback regarding a student's individual progress. Personalized learning differs from individualized learning.

In our global society, there are several important trends emerging that have implications for education. First, learning is becoming ubiquitous. Students can use the Internet from anywhere and at any time. Rather than look for information in an encyclopedia or a newspaper, learners can simply go online and quickly find the information they seek. Secondly, today's students are part of the mobile generation. They use smart phones, iPads, iPods, and other mobile devices to listen to music, watch movies, play games, and communicate with friends. Another trend involves the many social opportunities technology provides. Students can communicate through social networking sites and we are also seeing that technology is becoming computer free. Web 1.0 required a platform and specific software. Web 2.0 is the second generation for Web technologies and allows learners to communicate and collaborate in Web-based communities; it allows users to do more than simply retrieve information. Another trend is the personalization of learning. We are beginning to see more and more learner-specific assessments and applications ("apps") to deliver personalized learning experiences. Finally, the augmentation of learning is another trend. *Augmented learning* is an on-demand learning technique in which the environment adapts to the student. Instead of focusing on memorizing information, supplemental information is presented to the student based on the current context. The augmented content is tailored to the student's environment by displaying images, video, or even playing audio (music or speech). In computer-based environments, this additional information usually appears in a pop-up window. Additionally, there are more and more ways for students to interact with subject matter such as virtual field trips and virtual worlds, allowing students to create their own avatars, which are graphic representations of themselves.

Schools with the traditional structures as we have known them are outdated. We can no longer organize schools around classes, age cohorts, and classrooms. One teacher standing in front of a room and teaching the entire class at the same time, day after day, does not result in highly motivated students. Schools need to be organized around the needs of learners. At the same time, technology can support and enable personalized learning and encourage student voice. Zhao (2008) maintains that involving students in making educational decisions is an important element of personalized learning.

Online Learning

According to Horn and Staker (2011), "Online learning is sweeping across America. In the year 2000, roughly 45,000 K–12 students took an online course. In 2009, more than 3 million K–12 students did" (p. 1). In their best selling book, *Disrupting Class* (2008), Christensen, Horn, and Johnson make a projection that ". . . by 2019, 50% of all high school courses will be delivered online" (p. 98). Although there is growth in students taking an entire course online, ". . . Most of the growth is occurring in blended learning environments, in which students learn online in an adult-supervised environment at least part of the time" (Horn & Staker, 2011, p. 1).

Blended learning (sometimes called *hybrid learning*) can be defined as an instructional format that combines in person, face–to–face teaching and learning with elements of distance learning. Figure 7.1 depicts six models of blended learning identified by Horn and Staker (2011).

Online learning, or e-learning, appeals to many students due to the flexibility and convenience it offers and it has the potential to dramatically change schools as we currently know them. As education becomes more personalized, online learning can serve as a foundation for personalization. The bottom line is that technology will not completely eliminate the opportunity for face–to–face instruction; however, it provides an important resource to facilitate learning that should be integrated throughout the curriculum because it is already a major component of students' personal lives.

Virtual Schools

There are many definitions of virtual schools, but we will define them here as educational organizations that offer K–12 courses entirely or primarily through Web-based methods. Virtual schools are sometimes called *cyber schools*. Virtual schools exist around the world. In 2001, 14 states had virtual schools (Clark, 2001). Today, it is estimated that there are more than 250 virtual schools serving close to 200,000 students across the country (Wilks, 2011). Virtual schools can be operated by: states, universities, school districts, regional education agencies, charter schools, private companies, or consortia comprised of the mentioned entities.

Most virtual schools use external course providers that are private companies such as Apex Learning or Blackboard as delivery platforms. Most schools developing their own courses use development tools from external vendors, while some have created their own systems. A majority of virtual schools use Web- or Internet-based instruction as their only distance learning method, but offer other courses by methods such as independent study or video conferencing.

Instead of replacing conventional schools, virtual schools appear to be extending teaching resources and expanding curricular offering for students in those schools, and for home.

✳ **What roles will technology play at Lyons High School? How will technology be integrated into the curriculum? What types of technology will be used?**

Model	Example of a Program That Typifies This Model	Other Examples Among Those Profiled
Face–to–face driver	**Leadership Public Schools** allows Hispanic students who are struggling to learn English to sit at a computer in the back of the classroom and catch up with the traditional class at their own pace by using an online textbook that provides Spanish-English translations.	• Big Picture Learning • High Tech High
Rotation	Class periods at **Carpe Diem Collegiate High School** are 55 minutes long. For each course, students spend one period in an online-learning room for concept introduction and one period in a traditional classroom for application and reinforcement. They complete two to three rotations per day.	• Rocketship Education • KIPP LA (Empower Academy) • K12 (@-Day hybrid)
Flex	Each of **AdvancePath Academics'** dropout-recovery academies features a computer lab, where students spend most of their time learning online. But face–to–face, certified teachers also call the students into an offline reading and writing zone or small-group instruction area for flexible, as-needed help.	• San Francisco Flex Academy • Miami-Dade County Public Schools (Prep Academy)
Online lab	Faced with a teacher shortage, Miami-Dade County Public Schools turned to **Florida Virtual School's Virtual Learning Labs** for help. Students complete courses online at their traditional school under adult supervision, but with no face–to–face instruction.	• Metropolitan Nashville Public Schools (Virtual Learning) • Riverside Unified School District (Riverside Virtual School)
Self-blend	Alison Johnson, an 11th-grade student in Detroit, Michigan, self-blends by completing a **Michigan Virtual School** AP Computer Science course in the evenings after she gets home from her traditional high school, which does not offer this course.	• Florida Virtual School • Jesuit Virtual Learning Academy • All-online school that offers a la cart courses that can be taken remotely
Online driver	Students at **Albuquerque Public Schools' eCADEMY** meet with a face–to–face teacher at the beginning of the course. If they maintain at least a C grade, they are free to complete the rest of the course online and remotely, although some choose to use the onsite computer labs.	• EPGY Online High School • Northern Humboldt Union High School (Learning Centers)

FIGURE 7.1   Examples of the Six Models of Blended Learning

Source: Permission granted to reprint by Inno Institute 2011.

THE EVOLVING ROLE OF THE TEACHER

Personalized learning, online learning, virtual schools, blended learning, and other applications of the myriad forms of technology used in schools have significant implications for how teachers teach. Teachers are no longer the experts, standing in front of a class and in some cases lecturing. Nor is whole class instruction the dominant or pervasive teaching approach that is required or favored. We live in a world where students are surrounded by mobile technology. To quote Zhao (2008), we have witnessed the "death of distance" because communication technologies have been a key force in globalization. Thus, a quiet revolution has been taking place in front of our eyes. Because the United States is so large and the availability of technology dramatically differs from school district to school district, it is sometimes hard for the educator to step back and view schools and education from a wide-angle lens. There are hundreds of examples of schools around the nation where some teaching resources are becoming obsolete (e.g., blackboards, overhead projectors), where there is considerable student–student interaction via technology and where students have more control and responsibility for what they are learning and where. Additionally, many of these schools lack traditional educational structures and practices such as classrooms, age cohorts, PA systems, hall passes, bells, and so on. In fact, many of these changes are occurring in the majority of schools in the nation, albeit at vastly different speeds.

Teachers in our contemporary, technology-rich world need to be open-minded, independent professionals who actively collaborate with other educators and experts around the world. They have to be mediators between learners and what they need to know. Twenty-first century teachers are facilitators, designers, coaches, creators, and constructors of learning environments. They monitor student progress and activities electronically, nurture collaborative working practices, and facilitate individualized instruction and pacing. Given the changes taking place in education today and the resulting changes to the roles of teachers need to play, Barnett Berry and the TeacherSolutions 2030 Team (2011) propose a new framework with varying roles for teachers. Those roles include: resident teachers, apprentice teachers, adjunct teachers, virtual teachers, individualized instruction specialist teachers, professional teachers, and master teachers. These various categories of teachers would have differing salaries, knowledge and skill impact, market demands, student learning impact, and teaching activities.

New Competencies for Teachers

Teachers need new skills so that they can take full advantage of the potential of technology to enhance student learning. Knowing how to operate computers and use basic software for e-mail, word processing, and spreadsheets are basic requirements for all teachers. Teachers also need to apply evidence-based teaching principles and use appropriate assessment practices utilizing of technology. Teachers have to be able to search the Internet for resources, create computer-based presentations, and design multimedia documents to support learning. They must be skillful at integrating technology tools into student learning activities across the curriculum, evaluating educational software and keeping up to date with educational technology. While promoting information literacy, teachers need to assist students to make judgments about the quality and validity of new sources and knowledge, especially because the focus is on developing higher levels of cognitive skills rather than only content knowledge. Teachers must continuously upgrade their knowledge and acquire new skills in pedagogy, curriculum development, and the integration of technology into the curriculum.

Staff Development

School administrators must ensure that teachers have ongoing support for the integration for technology. Teachers need coaching on how to develop an appropriate, effective curriculum that enables students to construct meaning, develop new knowledge, and communicate understanding. At the same time, they need practice developing strategies to meaningfully integrated technology into the curriculum. Activities that simply provide skills in using particular software applications have shown little impact on students' classroom learning. Student success depends on teachers using technology to support sophisticated, hands-on multidisciplinary learning projects (project-based learning). These projects must be tightly linked to state and national standards. Therefore, teachers need a system of support at various levels for integrating technology and overcoming their isolation as they struggle with unfamiliar approaches to teaching and tools for learning. They also need real-time technical support in resolving problems related to hardware, software, and computer networks; problems that often interfere with or even derail the learning of both teachers and students (see Dede, 1998; Forcheri & Molfino, 2000; and Papa, 2010).

Technology also offers many advantages regarding the development of professional learning communities (Williams, 2006), whether for professional development, interactions with other professionals, feedback and suggestions, or moral support. When teachers become more comfortable in using technology and trying new instructional practices, students become excited about having increased access and authentic technological experiences in class and are more engaged in learning (Atkinson, Williams, Applegate, & O'Hair, 2006).

Curriculum

Why do we have computer labs? They never had pencil labs.

Larry Rosenstock, CEO High Tech High, June, 2011

Technology cannot be treated as a subject to be taught—it must be used as a tool for learning. Too often, teachers are taught about the technology instead of using the technology to enhance learning experiences and develop rich curricula. Teachers need to develop strategies to integrate technology into the curriculum in all areas and they need training so they can provide appropriate technology-based curriculum materials. If administrators fail to support the appropriate opportunities for teachers developing curriculum, then technology will sit idle and will most likely be used inappropriately by students.

Let's take a detailed look at one school's curriculum design.

✳ **What kinds of teachers do you want at Lyons High School? What types of experiences should they have had? What structures will you put in place to support their ongoing learning?**

HIGH TECH HIGH, SAN DIEGO CALIFORNIA (http://www.hightechhigh.org)

High Tech High (HTH) is an integrated network of 11 schools located in San Diego County. All students complete projects designed by their teachers. Projects are utilized by teachers to demonstrate what students have learned, and to share ideas from other teachers. HTH students and faculty publish their work on Web sites and produce books. In order to hold themselves accountable for the work that they do, they present their projects to a real audience comprised of parents, friends, and community members. These exhibitions are public demonstrations of what students have accomplished and how project-based learning (PBL) facilitates their learning.

All of the HTH schools embody four design principles: personalization, adult world connection, common intellectual mission, and teacher as designer.

HTH DESIGN PRINCIPLES

Personalization
- Each student creates a personal digital portfolio to document the year's learning.
- Networked wireless laptops are available for use.
- Technology is integrated into the academic content.
- Students only play video games created at HTH.

Adult World Connection
- Technology allows students to engage with the world outside the school.
- Students shadow adults in the community.

Common Intellectual Mission
- Student learning is evaluated through performance-based assessments.
- Students are integrated across social class.
- School and community are integrated.

Teacher as Designer
- Teachers work collaboratively and meet together regularly.
- Projects are designed by teachers.
- Through a variety of professional development offerings (e.g., workshops, a speaker series, summer institutes, a journal) HTH educators and others learn about the school's design principles, develop curriculum, and network with colleagues.

Reusable Learning Objectives (RLOs)

An emerging technology that holds a great deal of promise is the concept of reusable learning object databases. In the education industry, creating new courses and curriculum can be extremely costly, especially given the fact that many educators may have already expended time and energy to create the exact same courses. Similar courses are even developed by different departments within the same district. Employing RLOs works to diminish this situation by implementing a state/national/international central repository for all types of courses.

The idea of RLOs stems directly from Web-based sharing of knowledge. If the technology exists for Internet users to instantaneously share photos, videos, music, books, and documents, why can't a system be designed to share courses? Despite such issues as bandwidth restrictions and potential intellectual property rights violations (copyright, trademark, etc.), commercial development companies like CISCO and not-for-profit organizations like the Carnegie Foundation—and even the Department of Defense—rushed to provide methods to share course content, giving rise to the technology behind RLOs. The Department of Defense has embraced the concept of RLOs and made their use a systemwide goal, creating (in conjunction with several civilian agencies) a system of databases collectively known as the Advanced Distributed Learning Network (ADLN).

RLO databases vary in form and presentation, but the most common arrangement is a relational database with keyword search capability. Instructors submit course content to database managers, who in turn break down the content to the smallest level possible. This step ensures course developers the greatest level of access to content. The types of information that can be stored include class presentations, diagrams, syllabi, and tests/evaluations. For-profit systems simply pay their contributors while not-for-profit systems often only offer name recognition and access to other content as their payment for contributions. RLO databases appear to function best when developing courses that are standardized or are taught to a standard. This technology has potential for use in American public schools due to the No Child Left Behind Act. In preparation for state tests, subject matter is related to state standards of learning. Course presentations deemed successful in preparing students for these state standardized tests could be highlighted and made available for curriculum planners and teachers alike. The system provides a Web-supported keyword-accessible database for a plethora of course content. If this task is accomplished, it should serve to limit duplication and speed advancement of this collective knowledge base.

THE ROLES OF ADMINISTRATORS

Administrators have a responsibility to promote and integrate technology into the teaching and learning process. They can serve as role models by demonstrating a commitment to using various types of technology. According to Brockmeier, Sermon, and Hope (2005):

> [A] review of the literature suggests that without a thorough understanding of computer technology's capabilities, principals will not be ready to provide the leadership in technology necessary to restructure schools. Principals who are prepared to act as technology leaders are central to computer technology's integration into teaching and learning and for achieving technology's promise. (p. 4)

Administrators see a major role for technology in maintaining and analyzing data, accessing data and information, completing research, integrating teaching and learning, publishing student work, creating independent learning, communicating to stakeholders, as well as a number of administrative applications.

Administrative Applications of Technology

In addition to instruction, computers and other mobile devices are tremendous resources for expanding the capabilities and efficiencies of educational leaders. Technology empowers educators to make more timely decisions, allowing far greater focus on students and instructional leadership. Different types of data can be connected such as student attendance, discipline records, schedules, assessments, teacher evaluations, budgeting, accounting, purchasing, employee records, and attendance. Administrative systems can interact with one another, sharing data and producing key reports, answering queries, and saving significant time.

Administrators will find certain types of software to be particularly helpful such as word processing, presentation software, spreadsheets, and database management systems. Word processing allows administrators to create memos, letters, forms, and newsletters. Presentation software makes it easy to create materials for meetings, workshops, and conferences. Spreadsheets allow administrators to prepare charts of numerical data, budgets, and so on. Database management systems allow administrators to organize and track student learning, prepare inventories and mailing lists, monitor class cohort progress, and disaggregate data by age, gender, and other variables.

Today's educators face a dizzying assortment of choices for school data management and analysis (DMA). Trying to determine which marketer's and vendor's system best suits the needs of a school or a district is a very challenging task. Some vendors provide a more comprehensive set of management software whereas other companies might focus on only one system. Most systems have a data warehousing component and a data analysis and reporting component. These systems allow for the manipulation and integration of multiple databases that are interconnected. Again, issues such as comprehensiveness, affordability, reliability, support, training, and customizability become important factors to consider. The ability to store data in one place and combine it with data across multiple domains in analysis and reporting, so as to provide comprehensive analytical capabilities, adds greatly to the future effectiveness of the school management software. Schools use data warehousing to analyze longitudinal data, disaggregate data, and follow students over time. These systems can be used to analyze the impact of instruction on student learning. This facilitates data-driven decision making by exploring relationships among data such as student achievement and attendance or expenditure, or teacher professional development and teacher effectiveness.

Instructional management systems are used to look at students' performance over time at the school. They help teachers align lessons to standardized learning objectives, instructional resources, and assessments; they also help measure student performance on learning objectives. Instructional management systems provide teachers with needed information to help align curriculum and instruction to the students' individual needs.

These data warehousing, mining, analysis, and reporting systems support data-driven decision making at any level of education. Various data fields—class, grade, school, teacher, single student—or some combination of fields can be used to report data. Predefined reports can be produced or "on-demand" requests can be made for real-time results to meet accountability requirements and improve instruction. The systems can also support longitudinal analysis as data are collected over time. Students and parents can have improved access to information by having information delivered to computers in classrooms, schools, and homes.

There is much administrative/instructional software to store, access, and query data on students, grading rubrics, staff members, assessments, student performance, discipline, finances, and inventory, among others. Selecting among the various administrative and instructional systems software can be a daunting, even overwhelming task, as is the maintenance and use of these rich databases. These systems force administrators to deal with issues such as security, privacy, liability, engagement, user friendliness, accuracy, affordability, efficiency, accessibility, flexibility, reliability, and many other related issues. Regardless of the complexity, technology offers a rich source for improved teaching, learning, and administration that far outweigh any challenges to 21st-century educators.

Figure 7.2 depicts a continuum leading to a digital school. This model is based on four pillars: leadership, learning, infrastructure, and community. It's crucial for the school leader to be aware of where the school is in relation to each pillar. For example, the school may already have adopted a vision but there may have been minimum professional development in order to implement the vision. Or, the school board might be quite supportive, but few teachers have easy access to computers or other forms of technology.

Technology does have its critics when it comes to depending too much on computers to instruct students, particularly in the lower grades. Harvard Professor Alvin Poussaint and a number of child advocacy groups such as the Alliance for Childhood argue that too much dependence on computers can damage

	Entry	Adoption	Adaptation	Appropriation	Innovation
Leadership	No clear Leader or Power Sponsor	Leadership trying to establish itself	Clear leader, Power Sponsor	Credible, articulate leader	Leaders seen as visionary by peers
	Leadership is delegated	Top-down leadership	Many stakeholders engaged	Shared Leadership	District of school seen as model for effective leadership
	Little or no vision	Recognize vision in other districts	Creating a vision	Clear vision and goals	Demonstrated vision
	No improvement plans	Asking for assistance	Creating a plan	Stakeholders can articulate plan and their role in it	Commitment to excellence
	High aversion to risk	Open to new approaches	Allow new ideas	Encourage innovation	Innovation is part of culture
Learning	Print materials only	Basic C&I – drill and practice	Use of technology for higher-order thinking	Use of digital authoring for teaching and learning	24/7 access to digital content and tools for learning
	No professional development (PD) planning	Some PD	PD aligned to learning goals	Comprehensive PD plan	PD supports and is validated by student learning
	Outdated teaching methods	Exploring new teaching methodologies	Implementing new teaching methodologies	Project-based learning is evident throughout the institution	C&I is model for other districts
	Little or no use of technology	Know that technology can help	Pockets of excellent teaching with technology	Use of technology for learning is pervasive	Technology supports the complete learning environment
	Standardized tests only measure of achievement	Weak connection between assessment and learning	Clear connection between assessment and learning	Integrated authentic assessment	Multiple assessments inform instruction

(continued)

FIGURE 7.2   The Road to the Digital School

Source: Printed with permission from Apple™.

Category	Entry	Adoption	Adaptation	Appropriation	Innovation
Infrastructure	Network unreliable, slow	School has a reliable network	High bandwidth network	High bandwidth out to the classrooms (some wireless)	24/7 access available to teachers and students
	No teachers have computers	Many teachers have their own computers	Teachers have notebooks and productivity tools	Network and web-based teacher tools	Web apps support learning
	Labs and/or limited classroom computers	Some classroom computers	Computers in all classrooms	Mobile carts deployed	All students have a dedicated laptop
	Network limited to administration	Teachers have access to the network	Understand that mobility and wireless are in the future	Realize mobility and wireless are possible now	Pervasive wireless action
	Grading done on papers	Teacher administrative tasks done with computers	Resources dedicated to application and Internet support	Fast, responsive support system in place for break fix	Replacement policy in place for existing systems
Community	Disengaged parent community	Community without vision but receptive to new ideas	Parents engaged and involved in planning	Community understands and supports vision	Community is seen as a model
	Divisive board	Board has low communication	Supportive board	Policymaking board	Board seen as visionary by peers
	Negative press	Positive and negative press	Reactive public relations (PR)	Proactive PR	Comprehensive PR and community outreach
	Special-interest groups wreak havoc	Special-interest groups not controlled	Majority supportive	Strong sponsors in community	Pervasive community support
	New ideas shut down	New ideas tolerated but not embraced	Open to new ideas but unclear on what to do	Clear link between vision and school improvement	Innovation becomes part of larger community culture

FIGURE 7.2   The Road to the Digital School (Continued)

the health and intellectual and social development of our children. Complaints include shrinking attention spans, decreasing motivation and imagination, increased loneliness and isolation, problems with risk taking and negotiating political situations, and possibly eye problems. Teachers can reduce some of these by having students work in pairs and teams when using mobile learning devices. The consensus seems to be that the advantages far outweigh any disadvantages. Some scholars argue that technology can provide a very rich environment for learning, which increases intelligence, nonverbal communication skills, long-term memory, higher-order thinking skills, and self-esteem (Haugland, 1992; Balacheff, 1993; Cradler, McNabb, Freeman, & Burchett, 2002; Papa, 2010).

✳ **What administrative applications might you, as Principal of Lyons High School, use? What types of systems might you incorporate to support administrative and instructional responsibilities?**

Preparing Teachers and Administrators

The future of education will be influenced by instructional technology applications such as broadband Internet access, open-source software, wireless Internet access, and groupware or online collaboration. To meet these technological challenges, we need to make profound changes in the way we prepare prospective administrators and teachers. Future administrators and teachers need to be trained to enter tomorrow's schools prepared to use technology-infused methods. Technology must be integrated into subject area content and methods classes and into college students' field experiences (Moursund & Beilefeldt, 1999). In order to provide a more shared understanding of what teachers and administrators need to know about technology, the International Society of Technology Education (ISTE) created the National Education Technology Standards for Teachers (NETS-T) (see Appendix 7A) and The National Technology Standards for Administrators (NETS-A) in Table 7.2.

TABLE 7.2   NETS for Administrators 2009

1. VISIONARY LEADERSHIP
Educational administrators inspire and lead development and implementation of a shared vision for comprehensive integration of technology to promote excellence and support transformation throughout the organization. Educational administrators:
a. inspire and facilitate among all stakeholders a shared vision of purposeful change that maximizes use of digital-age resources to meet and exceed learning goals, support effective instructional practice, and maximize performance of district and school leaders.
b. engage in an ongoing process to develop, implement, and communicate technology-infused strategic plans aligned with a shared vision.
c. advocate on local, state, and national levels for policies, programs, and funding to support implementation of a technology-infused vision and strategic plan.

(continued)

TABLE 7.2   NETS for Administrators 2009   (Continued)

2. DIGITAL AGE LEARNING CULTURE
Educational administrators create, promote, and sustain a dynamic, digital-age learning culture that provides a rigorous, relevant, and engaging education for all students. Educational administrators:
  a. ensure instructional innovation focused on continuous improvement of digital-age learning.
  b. model and promote the frequent and effective use of technology for learning.
  c. provide learner-centered environments equipped with technology and learning resources to meet the individual, diverse needs of all learners.
  d. ensure effective practice in the study of technology and its infusion across the curriculum.
  e. promote and participate in local, national, and global learning communities that stimulate innovation, creativity, and digital-age collaboration.

3. EXCELLENCE IN PROFESSIONAL PRACTICE
Educational administrators promote an environment of professional learning and innovation that empowers educators to enhance student learning through the infusion of contemporary technologies and digital resources. Educational administrators:
  a. allocate time, resources, and access to ensure ongoing professional growth in technology fluency and integration.
  b. facilitate and participate in learning communities that stimulate, nurture, and support administrators, faculty, and staff members in the study and use of technology.
  c. promote and model effective communication and collaboration among stakeholders using digital-age tools.
  d. stay abreast of educational research and emerging trends regarding effective use of technology and encourage evaluation of new technologies for their potential to improve student learning.

4. SYSTEMIC IMPROVEMENT
Educational administrators provide digital-age leadership and management to continuously improve the organization through the effective use of information and technology resources. Educational administrators:
  a. lead purposeful change to maximize the achievement of learning goals through the appropriate use of technology and media-rich resources.
  b. collaborate to establish metrics, collect and analyze data, interpret results, and share findings to improve staff members' performance and student learning.
  c. recruit and retain highly competent personnel who use technology creatively and proficiently to advance academic and operational goals.
  d. establish and leverage strategic partnerships to support systemic improvement.
  e. establish and maintain a robust infrastructure for technology including integrated, interoperable technology systems to support management, operations, teaching, and learning.

5. DIGITAL CITIZENSHIP
Educational administrators model and facilitate understanding of social, ethical, and legal issues and responsibilities related to an evolving digital culture. Educational administrators:
  a. ensure equitable access to appropriate digital tools and resources to meet the needs of all learners.
  b. promote, model, and establish policies for safe, legal, and ethical use of digital information and technology.
  c. promote and model responsible social interactions related to the use of technology and information.
  d. model and facilitate the development of a shared cultural understanding and involvement in global issues through the use of contemporary communication and collaboration tools.

Source: ISTE. Reproduced by permission.

WILSON ELEMENTARY SCHOOL DISTRICT: FIVE STEPS TO A SUCCESSFUL TECHNOLOGY PROGRAM

JANE M. JULIANO, PHD

Principal, Wilson Charter High School, Phoenix, Arizona

The Wilson Elementary School District in Phoenix, Arizona, is an example of a school district that has successfully implemented the first 5 years of an 8-year technology plan. Currently, all students have their own computers and teachers are able to meet each student's curriculum goals by integrating subject-matter software activities into the classroom curriculum.

STEP ONE: THE VISION

The most important part of the technology plan is the statement of the reason for the technology program and how its success will be measured. For the Wilson district, which has a high-minority, low-socioeconomic status population, the overriding goal for the technology program is to increase student achievement scores. It is also to give students, who otherwise would not have access to computers, the skills necessary to compete in a technological world. Of course, goals must be in line with the budget, and together these factors will set the vision for your plan and guide each aspect of the implementation.

Technology plans and budgets are never static. When you involve key stakeholders, you will obtain the support needed to implement the plan and keep it moving forward. At Wilson, following the superintendent's vision of a computer for every student, all administrators along with school board members, parents, teachers, students, and technology staff were included in the development of the plan. The technology coordinator for the district held monthly meetings with the superintendent, administrators, technology staff, and teachers to keep the plan on track.

STEP TWO: DESIGN THE IMPLEMENTATION

Next, your plan needs to specify what the implementation will look like. Will reaching your technology goals translate into installing a computer lab in your school, distributing a certain number of computers in every classroom, or both? What software will you purchase to meet your goals? The software you choose will determine the hardware to purchase and whether the computers will need to be networked or standalone. A total software curriculum package was purchased at Wilson so teachers are able to customize activities for each student based on his or her instructional needs. This type of implementation meant that all 1,500 computers would be networked and distributed into every classroom. Teachers are able to print reports that evaluate student performance on prescribed activities as well as track the information the district needs to measure the effect of the program on student achievement.

STEP THREE: "WHEELING AND DEALING"

During the next stage of your implementation, you will be making all of the major purchases to get started. The technology team at Wilson learned much during this stage. They quickly realized that hardware and software continually change and that a portion of the budget needs to be reserved for updates and replacements. It also became apparent how dynamic the turnover rate of personnel is in the technology industry. Everything negotiated with a salesperson needs to be specified in your contract so agreements will stand through any changes in company salespeople, CEOs, or ownership. Most school districts require the use of a bidding procedure for major purchases. Typically, a district-wide group with representation from the appropriate units comprises a committee to participate in the process and assess products, services, and vendors.

(continued)

Budget planning and purchasing is ongoing; be creative when you look for funding. At Wilson, two major bond elections 3 years apart have supported the costs of the technology program. Grants have helped finance teacher training activities. Every purchase, big or small, needs to be evaluated in terms of the big picture. For instance, although the network infrastructure at Wilson required a lot of capital up front, it was less expensive to complete the entire project than to install it piece by piece over 4 years' time. Student safety and hardware security also required a large portion of the budget. Customized student desks were built to house each computer. The monitor sits below a glass panel and the CPU and all wires are locked behind side and back doors. Custom shelving units were installed in the classrooms with tubing to house the wires that connect the computer to the network. These design strategies reduce the possibility of damage, theft, or vandalism. They also increase student safety and facilitate integration of computer activities into a teacher's daily curriculum.

STEP FOUR: STAFF DEVELOPMENT

Now, with your vendor contracts in hand and installation imminent, a long-term teacher training plan must be set in motion. At Wilson, with a teaching staff of 100, a full-time teacher trainer became part of the technology team from the beginning of the implementation. Not only do teachers need to learn new ways of teaching, they also need to learn the new software updates, programs, and operating systems, as well as how to implement the new phases of the technology plan such as the addition of the Internet. The teacher trainer at Wilson individualizes training as much as possible so that all teachers feel successful and supported. Throughout the school year, teachers are released from their classrooms for 2-hour blocks of training. In addition, the teacher trainer often works collaboratively in the classroom to model and facilitate the overall management of the classroom technology.

Mentor teachers are trained to assist their colleagues. Annual pay incentives are given to teachers who increase their computer literacy skills by taking community college technology courses.

STEP FIVE: SHOW YOUR SUCCESS

Finally, plan for community access to the computers at your school, and promote what you have accomplished. Evenings at Wilson are busy with adult computer classes. Parents are invited to improve typing skills and learn word processing. Elementary and high school students work on homework projects. International and national visitors tour the two Wilson district campuses on a regular basis. Members of the technology team present the district technology plan at national conferences and submit articles to national publications. Teaching with technology has become part of the district's culture, and so it can become yours, if you plan with the future in mind before you take the first step.

CONCLUSION

Technology has the potential to improve teaching and learning, but it depends on the teachers' purposes in using the technology, and under which contexts and in which ways they use it. The changes resulting from the implementation and use of technology are ongoing and immense and the shift from teacher as expert to teacher as facilitator of learning is well underway. There are many schools around the world that have embraced the principles outlined in this chapter and much can be learned from their efforts. School leaders need to ensure a system of support for teachers and students as well as simply provide help for teachers to cope with these rapid changes.

MyEdLeadershipLab™

Go to Topic 5: *Curriculum Planning, Assessment, and Accountability* in the **MyEdLeadershipLab**™ site (www.MyEdLeadershipLab.com) for *Educational Leadership: A Bridge to Improved Practice,* Fifth Edition, where you can:

- Find learning outcomes for *Curriculum Planning, Assessment, and Accountability* along with the national standards that connect to these outcomes.
- Complete Assignments and Activities that can help you more deeply understand the chapter content.
- Apply and practice your understanding of the core skills identified in the chapter with the Building Leadership Skills unit.
- Prepare yourself for professional certification with a Practice for Certification quiz.

PORTFOLIO ARTIFACTS

- Visit the following Web site: http://www.sandiego.edu/soles/centers/cepal/recent_studies/ecd_project/index.php and read the suggested school district policy for student misuse of electronic communication devices. Compare and contrast it with your school district's policy.

- Use a new software program in your current work setting.

- Explore these Web sites detailing the research on using technology to facilitate student learning: Cognitive Tutors http://www.carnegielearning.com and Teachable Agents http://www.teachableagents.org/.

- Integrate a current technology that you have never used before into your current work setting.

- Examine Figure 7.2, The Road to the Digital School, and identify where you believe your school is along each continuum.

- Visit the Web sites of the High Tech High system of schools http://www.hightechhigh.org/ and the School of One http://schoolofone.org/. In what ways are technology tools used in these schools?

- Visit a school in your district or state that is engaged in some of the practices described in this chapter. What implications does this visit have for your leadership platform?

- Explore the Web site of the Science Leadership Academy in Philadelphia http://www.scienceleadership.org/. In what ways is technology integrated in their work with PBL?

- Schools continue to experiment with various types of teaching roles: co-teachers, master teachers, peer coaches, apprentice teachers, specialist teachers, and so on. Discuss these roles with a fellow teacher.

- What new tools and environments do teachers need to use and create for teaching in the 21st century? Discuss this with your classmates. What implications does this have for your leadership platform?

KEY TERMS

- Asynchronous learning
- Augmented learning
- Avatar
- Blended learning
- Blogs
- Cloud computing
- Distance learning
- Discussion board

- Handheld devices
- Mobile learning devices
- Net Generation
- Online learning
- Podcasting
- Social networking
- Synchronous learning
- Smart phones

- Social networking
- Virtual schools
- Virtual world
- Web 2.0
- Webinar
- Webpage
- WiFi
- Wiki

SUGGESTED READINGS

Christensen, C., Horn, M., & Johnson, C. (2008). *Disrupting class: How disruptive innovation will change the way the world learns.* New York, NY: McGraw-Hill.

McLeod, S., & Lehmann, C. (2011). *What school leaders need to know about digital technologies and social media.* San Francisco, CA: Jossey-Bass.

November, A. (2009). *Empowering students with technology* (2nd ed.). Arlington Heights, IL: Skylight.

Papa, R. P. (2010). *Technology leadership for school improvement.* Newbury Park, CA: Sage.

Zhao, Y. (2009). *Catching up or leading the way: American education in the age of globalization.* Alexandria, VA: Association for Supervision and Curriculum Development.

APPENDIX 7A

ISTE's National Education Technology Standards for Teachers (NETS-T)

1. Facilitate and Inspire Student Learning and Creativity

Teachers use their knowledge of subject matter, teaching and learning, and technology to facilitate experiences that advance student learning, creativity, and innovation in both face–to–face and virtual environments. Teachers:

a. promote, support, and model creative and innovative thinking and inventiveness.

b. engage students in exploring real-world issues and solving authentic problems using digital tools and resources.

c. promote student reflection using collaborative tools to reveal and clarify students' conceptual understanding and thinking, planning, and creative processes.

d. model collaborative knowledge construction by engaging in learning with students, colleagues, and others in face–to–face and virtual environments.

2. Design and Develop Digital-Age Learning Experiences and Assessments

Teachers design, develop, and evaluate authentic learning experiences and assessment, incorporating contemporary tools and resources to maximize content learning in context and to develop the knowledge, skills, and attitudes identified in the NETS•S. Teachers:

a. design or adapt relevant learning experiences that incorporate digital tools and resources to promote student learning and creativity.

b. develop technology-enriched learning environments that enable all students to pursue their individual curiosities and become active participants in setting their own educational goals, managing their own learning, and assessing their own progress.

c. customize and personalize learning activities to address students' diverse learning styles, working strategies, and abilities using digital tools and resources.

d. provide students with multiple and varied formative and summative assessments aligned with content and technology standards and use resulting data to inform learning and teaching.

3. Model Digital-Age Work and Learning

Teachers exhibit knowledge, skills, and work processes representative of an innovative professional in a global and digital society. Teachers:

a. demonstrate fluency in technology systems and the transfer of current knowledge to new technologies and situations.

b. collaborate with students, peers, parents, and community members using digital tools and resources to support student success and innovation.

c. communicate relevant information and ideas effectively to students, parents, and peers using a variety of digital-age media and formats.

d. model and facilitate effective use of current and emerging digital tools to locate, analyze, evaluate, and use information resources to support research and learning.

4. Promote and Model Digital Citizenship and Responsibility

Teachers understand local and global societal issues and responsibilities in an evolving digital culture and exhibit legal and ethical behavior in their professional practices. Teachers:

a. advocate, model, and teach safe, legal, and ethical use of digital information and technology, including respect for copyright, intellectual property, and the appropriate documentation of sources.

b. address the diverse needs of all learners by using learner-centered strategies providing equitable access to appropriate digital tools and resources.

c. promote and model digital etiquette and responsible social interactions related to the use of technology and information.

d. develop and model cultural understanding and global awareness by engaging with colleagues and students of other cultures using digital-age communication and collaboration tools.

5. Engage in Professional Growth and Leadership

Teachers continuously improve their professional practice, model lifelong learning, and exhibit leadership in their school and professional community by promoting and demonstrating the effective use of digital tools and resources. Teachers:

a. participate in local and global learning communities to explore creative applications of technology to improve student learning.

b. exhibit leadership by demonstrating a vision of technology infusion, participating in shared decision making and community building, and developing the leadership and technology skills of others.

c. evaluate and reflect on current research and professional practice on a regular basis to make effective use of existing and emerging digital tools and resources in support of student learning.

d. contribute to the effectiveness, vitality, and self-renewal of the teaching profession and of their school and community.

Source: ISTE. Reproduced by permission.

CHAPTER 8

DIVERSITY AND LANGUAGE LEARNING

MyEdLeadershipLab™

Visit the MyEdLeadershipLab™ site for *Educational Leadership: A Bridge to Improved Practice*, Fifth Edition to enhance your understanding of chapter concepts. You'll have the opportunity to practice your skills through video- and case-based Assignments and Activities as well as Building Leadership Skills units, and to prepare for your certification exam with Practice for Certification quizzes.

CHAVEZ HIGH SCHOOL

Cultures Clash in New Bedford

The trouble didn't start in September. The brief but fierce brawls only announced it. Minutes after school let out at New Bedford's Chavez High on September 29, hundreds of students poured into the street. The melee was on. Between 20 and 30 teenagers went at each other with shoes, sticks, belts, rocks, and canes.

Combatants were from virtually every ethnic group in attendance at the high school. "But," Assistant Principal Henry Barros suggested, "the two predominant groups were African American and Somali." It lasted about 10 minutes, by the estimate of Brent O'Brien, Chavez's principal. Police and staff intervened, and a New Bedford police helicopter ordered the crowd to disperse.

A second street fight broke out the following afternoon at the edge of Memorial Park,

a few blocks away. Police cars and the vehicles of private citizens were pelted, and one motorcycle officer was struck with a rock. Tensions have receded in the last 2 weeks, but everyone involved has seen these lulls before. No one's offering a guarantee that this one is permanent.

For the Somalis, the brawls were simply the latest eruption of an ongoing series of smaller conflicts that could be titled "Somalis Versus Everybody Else." In the past, many Somali children in the New Bedford neighborhood of Mesa Grande have found themselves at odds with students of various ethnic backgrounds, particularly Indochinese and Latino.

The causes for conflict are many, subtle, and complex. The Somalis' experience provides a window into exactly what difficulties can arise as a cultural group is introduced into U.S. society.

It began among the children with name calling, taunts, and bullying. In discussing these issues with Somali community members and students, Principal O'Brien learned that it started in 1993 when Somalis began arriving in New Bedford. Thousands of miles away, their African homeland was being consumed in violent clan warfare, anarchy, and mass starvation after the collapse of the government. Somali refugees arrived in New Bedford in significant numbers with little or no advance notice. Such is often the case with refugee groups who are literally airlifted out of countries in turmoil and deposited in the United States perhaps a mere 24 hours later.

Somali students say that practically from the beginning, other students have made fun of their cultural dress, with remarks such as "It's not Halloween." They are picked on, they say, and attacked when they pass through Memorial Park on their way to and from school.

For the most part, the Somali refugees who have come to New Bedford have settled in Mesa Grande, an area that is often called a "Little UN" in which more than 25 different languages are spoken.

Last spring, according to school district officials, Chavez High School, which draws much of its population from Mesa Grande, was 29.7% Indochinese, 27.3% Hispanic, 26.3% African American, 13.3% Anglo, 1.5% other Asian groups, and 1.9% other. Included in the African-American population are 270 Somali students.

According to Omar Jama, president of the East African Youth Center, Somali children tend to keep to themselves at school. Somalis are relatively new to the United States and find the culture very different. In school, Somali children form a distinct group. Most are Muslim. Women and girls wear veils and scarves that cover their hair. Mr. Jama argues that these are only superficial differences, and the divide goes much deeper than appearance.

In Somalia, few women work outside their homes or drive cars. Men generally do not take direction from women. Islamic law forbids alcohol, drugs, and premarital sex; violations incur severe penalties. Somalis do not touch members of the opposite sex who are not related to them. They follow certain dietary restrictions; for example, they eat no pork. As Muslims, they pray several times a day. And, English is new language for them.

These cultural and linguistic differences have led other students to consider Somali students standoffish, and many take offense. Somali parents complain to school administrators that students deliberately poke and touch Somali girls to provoke reaction. Boys of other ethnic groups try to speak to them. "That's just not possible," comments Mr. Jama.

For school officials, police, and outside groups, issues are magnified because of communication difficulties presented by language and customs. Mr. Jama comments that Somali parents of all clans are anguished and alarmed at the tensions their children are experiencing: "Somalis come from a country ruined by civil war. We are looking for peace."

Assistant Principal Barros believes that the public is not accustomed to distinguishing between immigrants and refugees. He maintains that how the Somalis arrive in the United States plays a role in how they are received.

Last year, Somali parents took their complaints to Pinto Middle School, a feeder to Chavez. The Somalis expected the school to decree an end to the taunting and name calling. The school did not do as they expected. Meetings were convened and attended by members of the Somali community, school staff, New Bedford police, parents of other ethnic groups, and various interested parties. "Steps were taken," says Mr. Jama, "but they were not deep enough. The Somali parents came away very disappointed in school officials."

The Somali parents also believe the police have failed them. "The perception is that the police are only doing things against the Somali kids," says Sergeant David Melholf of the New Bedford juvenile services team. "The kids are telling just one side of the story to their parents."

Various groups such as the Urban League of African Students at New Bedford College have offered their services to Chavez and to the Somali community since last month's disturbances. Hardly anyone believes the troubles are over for good. "They are only over," says Mr. Jama, "until the next incident, which could be next week or next year."

✻ **If you were Principal O'Brien, how would you go about decreasing the likelihood that these incidents will recur? In what ways might parents, family members, and community groups be involved in dealing with these issues at Chavez High? Is there basic content knowledge in areas of cultural diversity that all involved should have? If so, what is it?**

DIVERSITY IN SCHOOLS

School leaders are charged with the responsibility to create a school climate that is sensitive to diverse cultures (Dukes, 2006). Principals are responsible for ensuring that all aspects of the school are culturally sensitive and accepting. In order to be successful at responding to diversity, administrators need to value diversity—promoting instructional practices that recognize diversity, building connections between schools and diverse communities, and so on (Gardiner & Enomoto, 2006). School leaders must be self-reflective and aware of their own cultural biases and differences. Leaders will want to construct an inclusive leadership team to develop a diversity plan of action. Walker (2006) suggests a four-component plan that involves students, school staff, parents, the community, and universities that prepare teachers, school counselors, and administrators.

The four components of the plan include: (1) recognizing and honoring diversity; (2) acknowledging the implications of diversity and challenging sameness; (3) extending the knowledge level at the school and in the community; and (4) soliciting the commitment of cultural programming in the preparation of teachers, counselors, and administrators. Walker (2006) states that:

> [A] culturally proficient school [is] where the culture of the school promotes inclusiveness and institutionalizes processes for learning about differences, promoting differences, and appropriately responding to differences. It is a place where educators and students are valued and community members are involved in facilitating cultural understanding. (p. 58)

School leaders are also responsible for ensuring that teachers employ strategies within the classroom to stimulate a culturally sensitive environment and promote learning for all students. These might include classroom discussions of cultural diversity, one–on–one conversations with diverse students, and use of multicultural literature.

One common theme throughout the research on integrating cultural diversity into the classroom is literature. Wan (2006) states:

> Literature is the essence of communication. Through it, we share our opinions, values, experiences, and what makes us who we are. We share the most personal aspects of our culture and the ways in which we identify with a particular ethnicity, geographical region, religion, or other culture groups . . . [and] the study of literature allows us to see that people of different cultures are more similar than different. (p. 142)

School leaders and teachers can utilize and encourage the reading, in classrooms, of literature from all over the world to open students' eyes to the differences in themselves and each other.

Chang (2006) stresses the importance of looking into "the collection of the set of possible solutions from many different cultures or societies to recurrent problems that are common to the human condition and that no one culture has managed to solve completely" (p. 371). Students from various cultures investigate how their particular culture would solve a problem and present that to the class. This classroom experience becomes a tool to introduce various ideas, opinions, and traditions from all the cultures represented in one classroom. Students and teachers develop an appreciation for one another's unique responses to the same problems, creating a sense of similarity within the differences. Despite the challenges of creating a culturally competent environment, there are many practices that are quite effective. "Initiatives must be taken by both teachers and administrators to implement and maintain cultural activities and strategies that are embedded in existing classroom and school routine" (Dukes, 2006, p. 44).

Diversity is the norm in all schools. Staff and student populations are diverse, whether a school is located in North Dakota or along the border between the United States and Mexico, whether it consists predominantly of one racial or ethnic group or of a variety of cultural groups. Diversity includes differences in age, gender, sexual orientation, political beliefs, socioeconomic status, religion, physical and mental ability, language, and ethnicity. Although some schools have greater diversity than others, all schools must acknowledge and act on the diversity found in their populations, the community itself, the state, the nation, and on our planet. Staff and students need to (a) be aware of diversity, (b) have knowledge and understanding about diversity, and (c) on the basis of that knowledge take action, sometimes called *praxis*.

Many educators, when talking about diverse schools, assume that urban schools are the most heterogeneous. The words *diversity, urban,* and *minority student*, however, are not synonymous. For example, an inner-city school with a student population of all Mexican American students who are from a low socioeconomic background may have less diversity than a typical suburban school.

Socioeconomic Status and Social Class

Socioeconomic status (SES) refers to stratification that can be measured by factors such as economic status, family background, and job prestige. A broader term is *social class,* which involves large categories of people of similar SES who have in common such attributes as cultural identification, lifestyle, and attitudes.

SES is strongly correlated with academic success. When we talk about correlation, we are not addressing causation. Instead, researchers have found that children coming from low socioeconomic backgrounds are *more likely* to do poorly in school than children coming from high socioeconomic backgrounds. This does not mean that all children who are poor will do less well in school because they are poor. Families that are financially stable or affluent have greater access to resources, whereas families struggling to survive are more concerned with paying rent than buying a computer. This correlation has been found to be true in nearly every nation in the world and certainly is not a surprise to anyone. Generally, the greater the socioeconomic resources available to children, the better will be the children's educational attainment (Luster & McAdoo, 1994).

Inequities in social class intersect with other areas of difference in U.S. society (see Table 8.1). According to Parker and Shapiro (1993), "Social class plays a strong role in the struggle by people of color to achieve equal educational opportunity and vertical equity in school resources" (p. 42).

U.S. Population Demographics

The 2010 Census questionnaire lists 15 racial categories, as well as places to write in specific races not listed on the form. The 2010 Census continues the option first introduced in the 2000 Census for respondents to choose more than one race. Only about 2% of Americans identified with more than one race in the 2000 Census, but the percentage was much higher for children and young adults in 2010. Only about 2% of Americans identified with more than one race in the 2000 Census, but the percentage was much higher for children and young adults in 2010 (see Table 8.2).

As Table 8.3 depicts, it is estimated that by the middle of the 21st century just over half of the U.S. population will fall into the category of white (this

TABLE 8.1   Children Living in Poverty in 2009

ETHNIC/RACIAL GROUP	PERCENTAGE OF CHILDREN
Non-Hispanic White	12%
African American	36%
Native American	35%
Asian and Pacific Islander	13%
Hispanic or Latino	20%

Source: Data from the Annie E. Casey Foundation.

TABLE 8.2   Percent Distribution of U.S. Population by Race and Hispanic Origin

	1990	2005	2010	2015	2030
White	75.7	81.3	80.5	79.7	77.6
Black	11.8	13.2	13.5	13.7	14.4
American Indian	0.7	0.9	0.9	0.9	1.0
Asian	2.8	4.6	5.1	5.6	7.0
Hispanic	9.0	12.6	13.8	15.1	18.9
White, not Hispanic	—	69.6	68.0	66.1	60.5
Black, not Hispanic	—	12.4	12.6	12.7	13.1
American Indian, not Hispanic	—	0.8	0.8	0.8	0.8
Asian, not Hispanic	—	4.4	4.8	5.3	6.6

Source: Data from the Bureau of the Census: http://www.census.gov/.

TABLE 8.3   Distribution of U.S. Population by Race/Ethnicity, 2010 and 2050

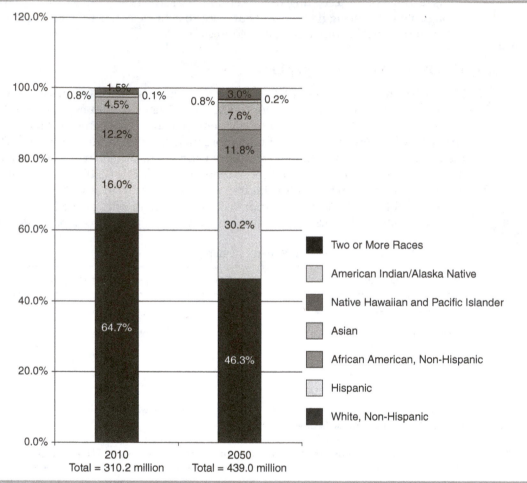

Source: U.S. Census Bureau, 2008, Projected Population by Single Year of Age, Sex, Race, and Hispanic Origin for the United States: July 1, 2000 to July 1, 2050. Retrieved from http://www.census.gov/population/www/projections/downloadablefiles.html.

category includes persons not of Hispanic origin). An increase among nonwhite populations is projected for the next 50 years, with dramatic increases in the number of Hispanics.

The terminology used to describe people is constantly changing. We often hear of four ethnic or racial groups in the United States: whites, Native Americans, African Americans, and Hispanics. In 1960, Americans were offered two categories to describe themselves: white and nonwhite. By 1990, there were six major categories including "Other." In the 2010 census, there were two questions about race and ethnicity. Is this person of Hispanic, Latino, or Spanish Origin? And what is this person's race? This question about race listed 15 racial categories, as well as places to write in specific races not listed on the form. The 2010 census continued the option first introduced in the 2000 census for respondents to choose more than one race. Only about 2% of Americans identified with more than one race in the 2010 census, but the percentage was much higher for children and young adults, and according to the U.S. Census Bureau, will increase in the future.

CULTURAL IDENTITY

In Chapter 5, we discuss organizational culture, which differs in many respects from national or ethnic group culture. Countless authors have defined the word *culture* in a variety of ways. Anthropologists Levinson and Holland (1996) maintain that emphasis should be "placed on culture as a continual process of creating meaning in social and material contexts, replacing a conceptualization of culture as a static, unchanging body of knowledge 'transmitted' between generations" (p. 13).

Anthropologist Rosaldo (1989) argues that culture is open ended, dynamic, and permeable. In regard to a cultural group he was investigating, he writes, "Immigrants and socially mobile individuals appeared culturally invisible because they were no longer what they once were and not yet what they could become" (p. 209).

Rosaldo discusses the concept of *borderlands*, liminal zones where cross-cultural encounters take place, often for the first time. Not only are schools that are located along national borders such as those near the U.S.–Mexico border in California, Arizona, New Mexico, and Texas dealing with the concept of *borderlands* as defined by Rosaldo, but also nearly all schools can be considered borderlands. Children representing nearly every ethnic group on this planet can be found in U.S. public school classrooms.

Bullivant (1989) believes that in the borderlands, groups' cultural programs evolve historically as their members adapt to changes in the social environment. A growing number of classrooms typify borderlands where children and adults from diverse backgrounds influence each other. In these borderlands, students forsake some aspects of their native cultures if the cultures conflict with the values and behaviors that produce social acceptance and success in school. It is important for educators to remember that schools are often the first places in which children internalize their ethnicity as a category for describing themselves.

If we accept the definition of culture as "a continuous process of creating meaning in social and material contexts," then each element composing cultural identity (see Box 8.1) has the potential to change considerably over time.

⁎ **How might issues of cultural identity be addressed at Chavez High School?**

BOX 8.1

ELEMENTS OF CULTURAL IDENTITY

LANGUAGE
  Dominant language (English) versus native language
  Nonverbal communication: kinesics and proxemics
  Linguistic style

GENDER ROLES
  Male and female relationships and roles
  Views of sexuality
  Religious/spiritual beliefs and practices
  Religious beliefs
  Religious holiday observances

FAMILY AND KINSHIP PATTERNS
  How are people related?
  Close versus distant relations; extended families
  Familial expectations and duties

**BEHAVIORAL NORMS/MORAL/
SOCIAL PRACTICES**
  Rules and norms of the culture
  Appropriate versus inappropriate activities and behaviors
  Dress

  Diet; food and eating-related issues
  Personal hygiene

ADULT–CHILD RELATIONSHIPS
  Acceptable/unacceptable behavior between adults and children

**LEARNING STYLES/EDUCATIONAL BELIEFS/
VIEWS OF INTELLIGENCE**
  Preferred learning modality (auditory, visual, kinesthetic)
  Cooperative versus competitive approaches to learning
  Value of education/schooling
  Country of origin education system
  Ways of knowing

CULTURAL TRADITIONS
  Mores and customs
  Holidays

**VIEW OF THE INDIVIDUAL
AND LIFE VIEWS**
  "Rugged individualism" versus collectivism
  Historical awareness of the culture

What, then, does the borderlands concept mean for schools and school administrators? One implication is that because new "cultures" are constantly being created, educators must discard the notion that they need to *understand* children's cultures (or countries). Because (1) the culture or country a child came from 2 years ago is not necessarily the same today, and (2) the child himself or herself is not necessarily the same person he or she was 2 years ago because of entering a new culture, the notion of *understanding* or *knowing* other cultures is as complex as the notion of understanding one's own culture. Thus, although Box 8.1 discusses various aspects of cultural identity, the notion that together these factors comprise cultural identity is far too simplistic. Cultural identity, too, is constantly in a state of flux, especially in the borderlands.

Gender roles differ substantially from culture to culture. We can see within the United States how the roles of males and females, as well as people's views about sexuality, are in a constant state of change. Acceptable gender roles in one culture might not be acceptable in another. Why a girl from a particular ethnic group does not speak in class might have little to do with language proficiency. The explanation for her hesitation or reluctance to raise her hand in class might be because the female role in her culture always allows boys to speak first.

In recent years, a subtle change with major implications is occurring in the area of religion in the United States, where the majority of citizens are Christian. Several religious populations are increasing significantly. For example, the number of people in the United States who call themselves Muslims range anywhere from 2 to 7 million depending on the source. Most educators know little about the Muslim faith and its beliefs. What are the implications for schools with Muslim students who are called to pray five times each day? What might be some implications of the tragic events of September 11, 2001, with regard to students' understanding, or lack of understanding, of the Muslim faith?

Another key element of cultural identity involves behavioral, moral, and social practices. Cultures differentiate themselves by dress, diet, mores, and norms. What are the implications for school policies when students, such as Sikhs, wear turbans, although the school policy states that no hats can be worn? What does it mean to a teacher or fellow students when deodorant is not typically used in a particular culture, and the group believes a student "smells"?

Family and kinship patterns differ within many cultures as well. In some cultures, the extended family plays a major role in raising a child. This family may include a grandparent, cousin, aunt, uncle, older sibling, or a nonblood relative. These kinship patterns can have considerable implications for family involvement in schools.

Learning styles and beliefs about how people learn, as well as beliefs about what constitutes intelligence, differ widely from culture to culture within the United States. There is some research that supports that cultural groups differ in their preferred learning style (Ramirez & Casteñeda, 1974; Stodolsky & Lesser, 1971). Additionally, children come to U.S. schools from many different educational systems. Helping families understand the U.S. educational system's structure is crucial to obtaining their participation in their children's learning process.

Although all children deal with issues of identity, immigrant children often feel torn between worlds. One Mexican-American high school student said she felt "like a jalapeño in a candy jar" (Cordeiro, Reagan, & Martinez, 1994, p. 105). One of the challenges for educators is to know how to respond, within the school environment, to the marginalization of ethnic groups in the mainstream culture.

Cultural Transitions

People experience stages as they encounter new cultures. One helpful frame for exploring these stages is Adler's five-stage model of culture shock (see Table 8.4). The stages include (1) initial contact with the culture, (2) disintegration of the familiar, (3) reintegration of new cues about the culture, (4) new identity formation with this new culture, and (5) biculturalism. People's perceptions, emotional ranges, and behaviors change depending on which stage they are in. These stages are not unidirectional; an event may trigger a person's returning to an earlier stage.

TABLE 8.4 The Five Stages of Culture Shock

STAGE	PERCEPTION	EMOTIONAL RANGE	BEHAVIOR	INTERPRETATION
Contact	Differences are intriguing. Perceptions are screened and selected.	Excitement Stimulation Euphoria Playfulness Discovery	Curiosity Interest Self-assurance Impressionistic Depression Withdrawal	The individual is insulated by his or her own culture. Differences as well as similarities provide rationalization for continuing of status, role, and identity.
Disintegration	Differences have impact, and are contrasted. Cultural reality cannot be screened out.	Confusion Disorientation Loss Apathy Isolation Loneliness Inadequacy	Depression Withdrawal	Cultural differences begin to intrude. Growing awareness of being different leads to loss of self-esteem. Individual experiences loss of cultural support ties and misreads new cultural cues.
Reintegration	Differences are rejected.	Anger Rage Nervousness Anxiety Frustration	Rebellion Suspicion Rejection Hostility Exclusiveness Opinionatedness	Rejection of second culture causes preoccupation with likes and dislikes; differences are projected. Negative behavior, however, is a form of self-assertion and growing self-esteem.
Autonomy	Differences and similarities are legitimized.	Relaxation Warmth Empathy	Self-assurance Self-control Independent Comfortableness Confidence	The individual is socially and linguistically capable of negotiating most new and different situations; he or she is assured of ability to survive new experiences.
Independence	Differences and similarities are valued and significant.	Trust Humor Love Full range of previous emotions	Expression Creativity Actualization	Social, psychological, and cultural differences are accepted and enjoyed. The individual is capable of exercising choice and responsibility and is able to create meaning for situations.

Source: Adapted from Atkinson, D. R., Morten, G., & Sue, D. W. (1993). *Counseling American minorities* (4th ed.). New York, NY: McGraw Hill.

Adler's framework can be applied by educators to students in U.S. schools who come from other cultures. A student's ability to reach the stages of autonomy and independence in the United States is related to many factors. The culture of the school (see Chapter 4) and the school's relationship with the student's family are key factors in minimizing the negative behaviors that might result from culture shock.

✳ **If most people experience stages of cultural transition as they move from culture to culture or from place to place, what implications do these stages have for students, staff, and families at Chavez High School?**

Sexual Identity

Lesbian, gay, and bisexual youth must also cope with the prejudice, discrimination, and violence in society and, in some cases, in their own families, schools, and communities.

Just the Facts Coalition, 2008, p. 3

Many educators are uncomfortable dealing with issues of student and faculty sexual identity. Whatever your beliefs and experiences are, it is absolutely crucial that you have good information about sexual identity, because schools are increasingly involved in controversies surrounding this topic. For example, in 2004 a California suburban school district experienced a controversy involving gay and straight students that became highly volatile. This controversy captured the attention of the national media and continued months later and involved a series of lawsuits (Soto, 2004).

The controversy involved a student (Harper) who wore a T-shirt that read on the front: "Be ashamed, our school has embraced what God has condemned" and on the back read "Homosexuality is shameful." The shirt was worn on the day following the high school campus's observance of "A Day of Silence." Organized nationally by the Gay, Lesbian, and Straight Education Network, based in New York, it encourages college and high school students to take a vow of silence in opposition to antigay harassment. A teacher told the student that the school's dress code prohibited slogans of "hate behavior" and sent the student to the administration office. Fearing that violence might erupt on the campus, the administrators told the student to remain in the office for the remainder of the day. There are disagreements as to whether the student was suspended and chose to stay in the principal's office instead, or whether in fact he was actually suspended. This case, *Harper v. Poway School District*, was heard at the appellate court level and the decision was appealed. The Supreme Court heard it in 2008. The Supreme Court vacated the 9th Circuit's previous opinion as moot because Mr. Harper had graduated. This is one small example of a controversy that administrators will deal with increasingly in our schools.

In the Suggested Readings for this chapter, we include a reference guide about sexual orientation created by the American Psychological Association that may be helpful to you as an administrator; as with all issues of diversity, it is vital that school administrators are well informed. A school administrator has an obligation to protect all students from antigay harassment just as he or she must ensure protection of students from other forms of harassment (see Chapter 11 for more information about school safety and bullying). In a 1999 Supreme Court decision (*Davis v. Monroe County Board of Education, 526 US 629*), the Court explained that "school administrators will continue to enjoy the flexibility they require" in responding to sexual harassment as long as they are not deliberately indifferent or the response is not "clearly unreasonable in light of the known circumstances." At the same time, the Office of Civil Rights requires school districts to "take steps reasonably calculated to end any harassment, eliminate a hostile environment if one has been created, and prevent harassment from occurring again."

Cyberbullying (harassing online) and sexting (sending, receiving, or forwarding sexually suggestive nude or nearly nude photos through a cell phone) are becoming increasingly common among teenagers. Many educators and parents do not even know when a child has been a victim or been involved with sexting or cyberbullying. Gay, lesbian, bisexual, and transgender students are among the most likely to be targeted. Educators must take great care in creating a school culture where harassing behaviors are not tolerated.

It is also important to remember that educators too have various sexual identities. For school administrators, attracting and maintaining qualified teachers, regardless of gender and sexual orientation, is critically important. Administrators need to create safe environments not only for students, but also for educators.

Sexual identity is a key facet of cultural identity. It is a complex and multifaceted issue. Additionally, various ethnic groups have a wide range of views on sexuality. For example, in some Middle Eastern and African cultures it is typical for males to walk down the street with their fingers entwined. This cannot be interpreted to mean these men are gay; it is a cultural tradition to do this. As people prepare to become school administrators and as they practice administration, becoming knowledgeable about, and comfortable with, discussing issues of all forms of cultural identity is imperative.

Student Behavior and Security

Research and experience suggest that much violence in schools is motivated by teasing, being left out, threats, stealing, prejudice, harassment, intimidation, aggression, slurs, taunts, derogatory remarks, and being hit or kicked by one or more other students. Research suggests that as many as 4.8 million U.S. students are victimized and bullied by other students. Bullying does seem to occur more often based on a student's race or ethnicity, religion, disability, gender, or sexual orientation. Bullies enjoy harassing certain types of children—provocative and passive—gaining satisfaction from the pain of their victims. This bullying is unacknowledged, underreported, and too often ignored.

Harris, Petrie, and Willoughby (2002) believe:

> Bullying is part of the daily life of the students in this study. Nearly three out of four students observe some type of bullying at their school. Although most of the bullying is confined to teasing and name calling, such treatment is still hurtful and cruel, and one in four bullied students feels anger or sadness. Victims are most likely to tell their mother or a friend; they rarely tell a teacher. However, telling is likely to not change anything; it might even make things worse for the victim. In general, students do not feel administrators or teachers support a stop to bullying. Who students tell about being bullied, what happens when they tell, and their perceptions of teacher and administrator support are critical, given that one of the main components in intervention programs is encouraging students to tell someone in authority. (p. 11)

All schools should have policies that prohibit the expression of hate and/or violence against others. (An excellent resource for school administrators on hate crime prevention can be downloaded at justice.gov/crs/pubs/prevyouhatecrim .pdf.)

PREJUDICE AND DISCRIMINATION

Prejudice is a negative or narrow attitude or belief toward an entire group of people. It is related to the use of stereotypes—generalizations about people. Triandis (1971) differentiates between stereotypes and sociotypes. Sociotypes are accurate characterizations about social and cultural groups, and stereotypes are inaccurate and possibly dangerous beliefs about a group. Aboud (1988) argues, "The less that is known about a group, the easier it is to assign to it negative attributes" (p. 21). Thus, one possible cause for prejudice against a certain cultural group might be lack of contact and firsthand experience with that particular group.

One of the first psychologists to focus on the study of personality was Gordon Allport. Allport (1979) believed that children begin categorizing and stereotyping certain kinds of differences among people at a very young age. Later, in adolescence and adulthood, they learn to modify their categories by incorporating exceptions into their stereotypes. Depending on a person's environment and experiences, however, some stereotypes may be reinforced instead of disregarded.

According to Allport, prejudices are rigid and exaggerated preferences. All people hold prejudices. Allport maintained that if a prejudice is not acted on, then it does "no great harm. It merely stultifies the mind that possesses it. But prejudice expressed leads to discrimination" (p. 127). Allport developed a continuum of social relationships among human groups that ranges from friendly to hostile. He believed that "we define the degrees of hostile relationships that are readily distinguishable, starting with predilection, the mildest and most normal form of group-exclusion, through active prejudice and discrimination, to scapegoating itself" (p. 127). This process could be viewed as a continuum of relationships, with cooperation at one end and scapegoating at the other extreme.

Cooperation
Respect
Tolerance
Predilection
Prejudice
Discrimination
Scapegoating

Allport referred to scapegoating as "full-fledged aggression," in which "the victim is abused verbally or physically." If, as Allport stated, "No child is born prejudiced. His prejudices are always acquired" (p. 307), the focus for educators should not be on discerning *how* children acquire prejudices but, instead, on helping them to question *why* they hold these prejudices.

Discrimination occurs when people act on their beliefs. When teachers develop grading criteria that are as fair as possible and then decide that one student's paper is better than another's, they are discriminating. Discrimination is not only acceptable; it is also, in fact, necessary. Problem discrimination arises when people's beliefs and actions are not based on evidence. For example, if a teacher has certain criteria for grading and arbitrarily changes the criteria or uses inappropriate criteria, then any resulting discrimination is harmful. When we discuss the problems of societal and educational discrimination, we should concentrate on inappropriate kinds of discrimination.

Allport (1979) identified 10 sociocultural conditions that foster prejudice:

1. Heterogeneity in the population
2. Ease of vertical mobility
3. Rapid social change with attendant anomie
4. Ignorance and barriers to communication
5. The relative density of minority group populations
6. The existence of realistic rivalries and conflict
7. Exploitation sustaining important interests in the community
8. Sanctions given to aggressive scapegoating
9. Legend and tradition that sustain hostility
10. "Unfavorable attitudes toward both assimilation and cultural pluralism" (p. 233)

Allport had a profound influence on the field of psychology and social psychology and many of the concepts and ideas he discussed are foundational to researchers and educators today. His framework can be useful to school administrators when trying to understand racial and ethnic dynamics in the school and community.

   ✳ **Which of Allport's sociocultural conditions may have contributed to the bias incidents at Chavez High School?**

DISCRIMINATION IN SCHOOLS

It is rare in schools to find purposeful discrimination against students based on Allport's categories. For example, law prohibits barring an African-American child from a public school on the basis of skin color. However, as Nieto (2000) argues, "Racism and discrimination are manifest in numerous practices and policies . . . for example, many studies have found that rigid tracking is most evident in poor communities with large numbers of African American, Latino and American Indian students" (p. 38). Nieto has identified nine educational structures in which prejudice and discrimination affect student learning:

1. Tracking
2. Standardized testing
3. Curriculum
4. Pedagogy
5. The physical structure of the school
6. Disciplinary policies
7. The limited role of students
8. The limited role of teachers
9. The limited role of parents and families

Bullock and Stewart (1978, 1979) identified what they call "second-generation discrimination," which includes practices that deny minority students access to education and limit integration of schools. Academic grouping and disciplining students in a discriminatory manner are examples of second-generation discrimination. Meier and Stewart (1991) found that minority students are overrepresented among those who are expelled, disciplined, or drop out. Their research argues that Hispanics and African-American students are denied access to high-quality education. In an in-depth study of Hispanic students in 142 school districts, Meier and Stewart (1991) found that second-generation discrimination exists because Hispanic populations lack the political power to prevent certain conditions that would preclude discrimination. According to their research, "School districts with greater Hispanic representation on the school board and among teaching faculty experience significantly less second-generation discrimination against Hispanic students" (p. xvii).

Educational leaders need to ask critical questions about the educational structures in schools. If a secondary school, for example, has a high dropout rate, educators must ask a variety of questions. A school administrator might ask: Who is dropping out? Are there differences in ethnicity, social class, or gender of the students who drop out? What reasons do these students report for dropping out? Are there program structures (e.g., bilingual programs, special education classes) that these students were a part of? For example, Meier and Stewart found that "Hispanic high school graduation rates are negatively associated with corporal punishment and bilingual classes, and positively associated with gifted classes.

Hispanic dropout rates are positively associated with suspensions and negatively associated with gifted class enrollments" (p. 177).

Additionally they noted, "The pattern that Hispanics receive more corporal punishment, more suspensions, and more expulsions when blacks receive less, and vice versa, implies that administrators compensate for disciplining one group by lessening discipline of the other group" (p. 154).

> ✳ **What types of records could Chavez High School staff keep to ensure they are not guilty of various forms of second-generation discrimination?**

COMPETING PERSPECTIVES: THEORIES, MODELS, AND APPROACHES TO RACE, CLASS, AND GENDER

Educational institutions can approach issues of cultural diversity in a number of ways. Theories, models, and approaches to learning about diversity are categorized into six areas. None of these approaches is independent of the others; each category overlaps and draws on other theoretical areas. The approaches are cultural deficiency, cultural difference, human relations, single-group studies, multicultural education, and social justice education.

Cultural Deficiency Approach

Historically, U.S. educators have viewed students from backgrounds other than the dominant culture in two ways: the deficit perspective and the cultural difference perspective. Some educators believe that students from other cultures come to U.S. schools with deficiencies. They might argue, for example, that students are *deprived* because they have minimal proficiency in the English language, or they might believe that because students are from low socioeconomic backgrounds or single-parent families, they are *disadvantaged*. Identification of students as deprived or disadvantaged implies that they have deficiencies that must be remediated. Similarly, in the 1990s the term *at-risk* became a popular label.

Educational researchers such as Harry (1992) and Trueba (1989) have argued that language-biased educators have incorrectly placed language-minority students in classes for the learning disabled or mentally retarded. Because language-biased educators think such students have "language deficiencies" (i.e., they are not highly proficient in English), they put them in remedial classes.

Another deficiency perception that many educators hold is that children from low socioeconomic backgrounds lack appropriate role models for their development. In a 1992 article in the *New York Times National*, Gross stated, "A mother is sometimes present in these homes, but she is often a drug addict or a teenager who comes and goes. . . . Scarred by years of abuse and neglect, many of these children are angry and disruptive" (pp. 1 & 166). Some minority groups (e.g., African-American males) are blamed for abandoning their families, thus causing these families to be *deprived* or *deficient*. A more enlightened way to frame these issues is to focus on access to resources and support systems instead of focusing on lack of morals or family psychological instability. The deficit perspective has been severely criticized in recent years.

Cultural Difference Approach

According to Sleeter and Grant (1993), "The main idea behind Teaching the Culturally Different Approach . . . is to ensure as much cultural compatibility as possible" (p. 44). The focus is on building bridges between the two cultures because there is a *cultural mismatch*. An example might be a child who has minimal proficiency in English. The programmatic response might be to include partial- or full-day English as a second language (ESL) classes or sheltered English classes. Providing a sign language interpreter in a regular classroom for a child who is deaf might be a programmatic response for his or her cultural difference.

As we look at ethnic minority groups, according to the cultural difference approach, some minority students fail because they do not adapt themselves to the dominant cultural style of the school or as Trueba states (1988), the schools have not provided appropriate "activity settings" to accommodate the minority student. Although this approach is important because it offsets the racist *cultural deprivation* or *genetic inferiority* approach, it ignores the historical and social factors responsible for the reproduction of "cultural differences" in schools.

Ogbu (1992) was one of the first researchers to criticize the cultural difference approach. He argued that there has been a lack of critical analysis among educators and that this absence of critique has allowed educators to attempt to approach school conflicts over cultural styles through remediation programs.

Human Relations Approach

Sometimes called *intergroup education,* the major goal of a *human relations* approach is to help *all* students develop more positive attitudes toward people who are members of different racial, cultural, and gender groups. This approach seeks to improve the relationships that students have with one another. Another objective of a human relations approach is to help students become better communicators. Group processes and group facilitation, which are part of *cooperative learning,* are methods of achieving these goals.

A human relations approach is supported by theories and concepts developed by research that started in the 1940s. Researchers were originally interested in studying the nature of racial prejudice. Myrdal (1944) and others such as Deutsch (1963) discovered that interaction across racial lines tended to increase racial tolerance. Several explanations were given for the finding that contact reduces prejudice.

Cognitive dissonance theory argued that dissonance occurs when an individual's behavior or experience clashes with the views he or she holds. In other words, individuals want to align their attitudes with their experiences, so they try to bring their behaviors and attitudes together. Another explanation is found in the theory of *interpersonal attraction*. This theory holds that people are attracted to others whose beliefs and values they share. Hewstone and Brown (1986) contend that contact with persons and the opportunity to learn about them will eventually "neutralize the negative relationship that formerly existed" (p. 5). Another possible explanation for increases in racial tolerance when racial lines are crossed is based on the notion that contact can have an educational benefit. Interaction with others can provide more knowledge and can identify false thinking. Thus, it is argued that contact might reduce prejudice because it expands an individual's knowledge and experiences.

In his seminal book *The Nature of Prejudice,* Allport (1958) formulated a hypothesis that attitudes change most often if contact occurs between individuals of equal status. Allport made a crucial point—contact does not automatically reduce prejudice. He believed that contact across racial lines of individuals with similar educational or occupational status would have more positive effects on people's attitudes than would contact among individuals of different status. More recent work in anthropology by Levinson (1996), who studied students in a Mexican *secundaria,* found that students in their first and second years from the

> *pueblitos* [villages close to the city] . . . forge ties with one another across and within *grupos escolares* [heterogeneous cohorts who pass through the 4 years of middle school together]. The shared position that appears to bring them together is that of "country" or "village" dweller in relation to the school's predominantly urban culture." (p. 227)

The work of other researchers, such as Nieto (2009), Gazda, Blazer, Childers, Nealey, Phelps, & Ealters (2005), and Purkey and Novak (1984) has also contributed to our understanding of human relations. Johnson and Johnson advocate *cooperative learning,* which they believe will improve intergroup relations. Purkey and Novak have written about *invitational education.* They argue that educators and schools must be intentionally inviting.

Single-Group Studies Approach

Another approach to addressing cultural diversity in education is what Sleeter and Grant (1993) call *single-group studies.* The curriculum is the main focus of this approach. A single-group focus might be a course (Asian literature), program (women's studies), or an entire school with a particular focus on one group (Afrocentric schools; single-gender schools). According to Sleeter and Grant, the goal in these programs is to "reduce social stratification and raise the status of the group" (p. 123). The approach of Afrocentric schools was instituted in response to a curriculum that has traditionally emphasized the contributions of white middle-class males.

Two classic books are part of the first wave of critical studies of schooling: *Schooling in Capitalist America: Educational Reform and the Contradictions of Economic Life* by Bowles and Gintis (1976) and Bourdieu and Passeron's (1977) *Reproduction: In Education, Society, and Culture.* Their authors argue that schools are not passive sites where culture is simply transmitted. To the contrary, schools actually perpetuate, or *reproduce,* the inequalities that exist in society. Instead of equalizing people, schools reproduce the inequities that separate them. Educators began to ask: What does schooling mean to children who are not members of the dominant societal group (white, middle class)?

Multicultural Education Approach

The term *multicultural education* is most often used inappropriately. Many educators who approach cultural diversity through a *cultural difference, human relations,* or *single-group* approach describe their efforts as multicultural education. Banks (2007; 1994) states that multicultural education is "at least three things: an idea or concept, an educational reform movement, and a process" (p. 3).

Davidman and Davidman (2000) have identified six interrelated goals for multicultural education:

1. Educational equity
2. Empowerment of students and their parents
3. Cultural pluralism in society
4. Intercultural/interethnic/intergroup understanding and harmony in the classroom, school, and community
5. An expanded knowledge of various cultural and ethnic groups
6. The development of students, parents, and practitioners whose thoughts and actions are guided by an informed and inquisitive multicultural perspective

Equity involves not only access to learning opportunities and physical and financial conditions within the school and district, but also "educational outcomes for both individuals and groups" (Davidman & Davidman, 2000, p. 4). *Empowerment* requires members of the school community to take active roles, whether at the local or national level. The empowerment of students and parents is key to a multicultural education approach. *Cultural pluralism* indicates an acceptance of cultural diversity as a valuable and worthwhile facet of society. Teachers who accept cultural pluralism constantly ask themselves how to help students respect and appreciate cultural diversity in the classroom, school, and society.

Social Justice Education Approach

Borrowing heavily from each of the previous approaches, the social justice education approach "deals more directly with oppression, social structural inequality based on race, social class, gender and disability" (Davidman & Davidman, p. 153).

In one of the most informative books on cultural diversity in education, *Affirming Diversity: The Sociopolitical Context of Multicultural Education*, Nieto & Boyd, 2011) states:

> Multicultural education is a process of comprehensive school reform and basic education for all students. It challenges and rejects racism and other forms of discrimination in schools and society and accepts and affirms pluralism (ethnic, racial, linguistic, religious, economic, and gender, among others) that students, their communities, and teachers represent. Multicultural education permeates the curriculum and instructional strategies used in schools, as well as the interactions among teachers and students and parents, and the very way the schools conceptualize the nature of teaching and learning. Because it uses critical pedagogy as its underlying philosophy and focuses on knowledge, reflection, and action (praxis) as the basis for social change, multicultural education furthers the democratic principles of social justice. (p. 318)

According to Nieto (2000), multicultural education has seven basic characteristics: (1) antiracist education, (2) basic education, (3) important for all students, (4) pervasive, (5) for social justice, (6) a process, and (7) critical pedagogy.

Let us examine the concepts of social justice and critical pedagogy in more detail. Figure 8.1 is a model developed by Banks (1999) describing the levels of integration of ethnic content that can be used in curriculum reform.

At the *contributions* level, educators might celebrate Cinco de Mayo or Martin Luther King Day. The focus is on the particular contribution that a group of people (Hispanics or African Americans) or a person made toward a movement, cause, or cultural group. Most U.S. schools have a variety of activities that could fall within this approach. As Banks (2007) states, at the contributions level "students do not attain a global view of the role of ethnic and cultural groups in U.S. society" (p. 218).

Banks (1999) calls the next level the *ethnic additive* approach. In this approach concepts, themes, and various perspectives are added to the curriculum, but the curriculum is not restructured. Adding another perspective, however, does not necessarily enhance the curriculum. For example, if the class is studying a unit titled "Columbus's Discovery of the New World" and the teacher includes a discussion of how people indigenous to the West Indies might have responded to Columbus, an alternative perspective is not necessarily being presented. The title of the unit itself implies that it took a European to *discover* people who already had a long-standing culture. Thus, such an approach still presents only a Eurocentric perspective.

✳ **Use New Bedford's Chavez High School to discuss alternative ways in which the lesson on Columbus might have been given a greater multicultural emphasis.**

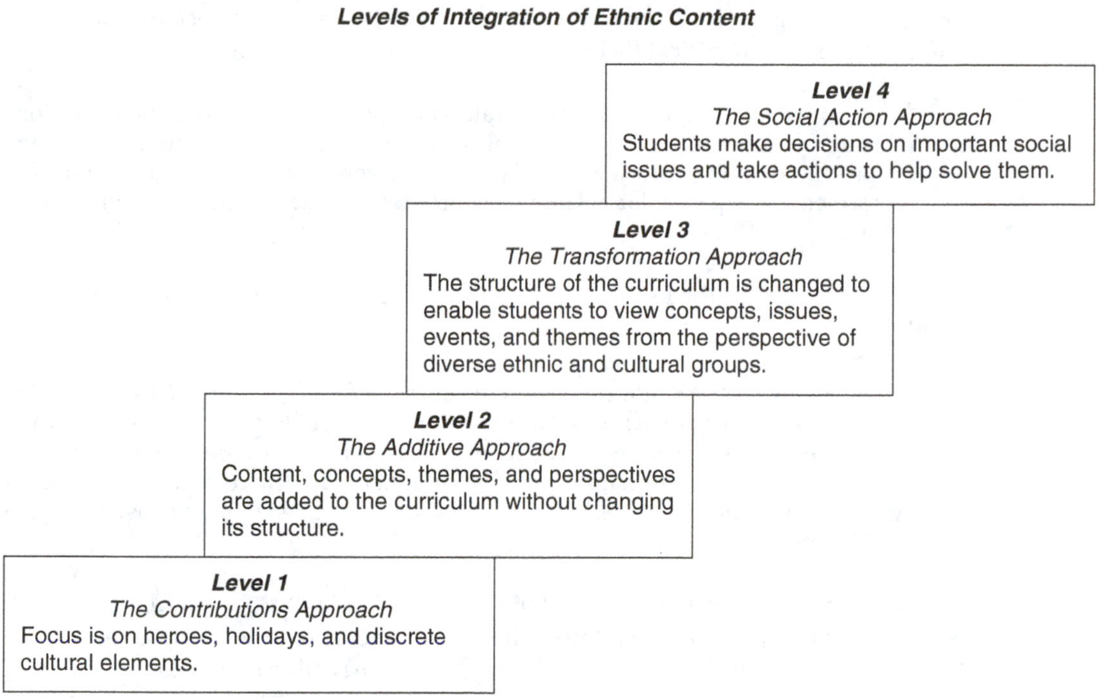

Levels of Integration of Ethnic Content

Level 4
The Social Action Approach
Students make decisions on important social issues and take actions to help solve them.

Level 3
The Transformation Approach
The structure of the curriculum is changed to enable students to view concepts, issues, events, and themes from the perspective of diverse ethnic and cultural groups.

Level 2
The Additive Approach
Content, concepts, themes, and perspectives are added to the curriculum without changing its structure.

Level 1
The Contributions Approach
Focus is on heroes, holidays, and discrete cultural elements.

FIGURE 8.1   Banks's Approaches to Multicultural Curriculum Reform

Source: Banks, J. A. (2002). *An introduction to multicultural education* (3rd ed.). Boston, MA: Allyn and Bacon, p. 30. Reprinted with permission.

At the *transformation* level, a restructuring of the curriculum occurs. Students are provided with ideas, issues, themes, and challenges from a variety of perspectives. Study of the U.S. Civil War, for example, places emphasis on how our many cultures formed the overall U.S. culture at that time. A complex weaving of diverse cultural elements (e.g., from language, music, art) originated from the wide variety of racial, ethnic, cultural, and religious groups. This level is transformational because it transcends the dominant perspective and gives voice to the many cultural elements present in our society.

Banks's fourth level, *social action,* incorporates the three earlier levels, but the concept of social justice is the main criterion of this level. Encouraging social action and developing decision-making skills in students is a key goal. Gordon (1985) includes emancipatory pedagogy. She believes that "categories such as 'critical emancipatory or liberatory pedagogy,' may work as descriptors that not only expand the narrow frames of reference, but also move them from pejorative to self-reflection, critique, and social action" (p. 29).

Some of the research and theory that informs this approach can be found in the works of Luna-Delgado (2005), Romo (2005), Giroux (1992), Apple (1986),

Freire (1985), Ogbu (1992), and Anyon (1980). The terms *critical teaching* and *critical pedagogy* come from critical theory. According to Giroux (1992):

> Critical pedagogy refers to a deliberate attempt to construct specific conditions through which educators and students can think critically about how knowledge is produced and transformed in relation to the construction of social experiences informed by a particular relationship between the self, others, and the larger world. (pp. 98–99)

Brazilian educator Freire (1985) maintains that critical pedagogy promotes greater understanding of this approach.

> A pedagogy will be that much more critical and radical, the more investigative and less certain of "certainties" it is. The more "unquiet" a pedagogy, the more critical it will become. Pedagogy preoccupied with the uncertainties rooted in the issues we have discussed is, by its nature, a pedagogy that requires investigation. This pedagogy is thus much more pedagogy of question than a pedagogy of answer. (Cited in Macedo, 1994, p. 102)

An interesting term used by (2005), Luna-Delgado (2005), and Macedo (2007) is *border pedagogy*. Romo (2005) uses this term to refer to "the study of and practice of inclusive education for all children, particularly [those] in a context of great contrast: language, culture, resources, family backgrounds and political tensions" (p. 2). These authors maintain that critical pedagogy is central to border pedagogy and that "political tensions" are a key aspect of border pedagogy since their work grew from the political conflicts found along the U.S.–Mexican border.

✳ **What are the implications of these approaches for Chavez High School? Would one approach or combinations of several approaches better match Chavez's context?**

Language Diversity in U.S. Schools: Program Options

Although a few earlier examples of bilingual programs in U.S. history can be identified, bilingual education is a relatively recent phenomenon. In 1968, Congress passed the Bilingual Education Act (later, Title VII of the Elementary and Secondary Education Act, ESEA). The Bilingual Education Act states that, "no person shall be subjected to discrimination on the basis of race, color, or national origin." School districts are required to take affirmative steps to provide children with the language skills they need to participate in school. The Bilingual Education Act and the landmark U.S. Supreme Court decision *Lau v. Nichols* (1974) provided a legal basis for equitable treatment of limited-English-proficient children in U.S. schools. It placed non–native English-speaking children at the forefront of an often hotly debated topic.

Bilingual refers to proficiency in at least two languages, and *biculturalism* is participation in two cultures. Bilingual education usually refers to an educational approach involving the use of two languages of instruction at some point in the student's schooling. For decades educators and policymakers have wrestled with questions related to bilingual education: What are the best ways to teach children whose native language is not English? How can the achievement of students with limited proficiency in English be enhanced? There is no debate over the issue that proficiency in English is essential to school and workplace success. Instead, the debate deals with the most appropriate ways for students to learn English as a second language and what roles, if any, the first language should play.

School districts offer several types of programs to language-minority students in the United States (Box 8.2). These include ESL, sheltered English,

---

BOX 8.2

PROGRAM OPTIONS FOR NON–NATIVE ENGLISH-SPEAKING STUDENTS

ENGLISH AS A SECOND LANGUAGE
ESL is a systematic, comprehensive approach to teaching English to students whose native language is not English. It is usually an important component of a bilingual program, but it can also exist by itself.

OPTIONS
- Full/partial day
- Pullout
- Sheltered English
- English for special purposes (ESP)

SHELTERED ENGLISH
In what are sometimes called *transition* or *bridge* classes, students cover the same content offered in classes in which native English proficiency is assumed. The language component of these classes is adapted to suit the English proficiency levels of the language-minority students.

TRANSITIONAL BILINGUAL EDUCATION (TBE)
The Bilingual Education Act of 1968 defined transitional bilingual education as "structured English language instruction, and to the extent necessary to allow a child to achieve

competence in the English language, instruction in the child's native language." Ideally, access to a comprehensible curriculum is assured by providing basic instruction in the child's native language until the student attains English competency and comprehension in speaking, writing, and reading. The goal of these programs is for students to learn English as quickly as possible so they can exit the programs.

TWO-WAY BILINGUAL EDUCATION
Two-way bilingual programs offer a means of encouraging bilingualism in both language minority and language majority students.

MAINTENANCE BILINGUAL EDUCATION
The goal in maintenance bilingual programs is to provide students with instruction that helps the development of the native language.

SUBMERSION OR IMMERSION
Sometimes called the "sink or swim" approach, submersion (immersion) places students in a totally English-speaking environment with no use of their native language. It is not a form of bilingual education.

transitional bilingual education, two-way bilingual education, maintenance bilingual education, and structured immersion. It is important for educational leaders to determine which of these approaches is most appropriate for the children in their schools or districts. Language proficiency, the number of students whose native language is not English, the ages of children, and whether they are able to speak and read their native language proficiently are but a few of the factors that need to be examined. Most bilingual educators favor maintenance programs; the majority of existing programs, however, are transitional.

ENGLISH LANGUAGE LEARNERS IN U.S. PUBLIC SCHOOLS

Many languages other than English have always been spoken in U.S. public schools, and this increasingly continues to be the situation. English language learners (ELLs), also known in some states as ELs (English learners), can be defined as those students who have not developed listening, speaking, reading, and writing proficiencies in English sufficient for participation in the regular school program. Examining the growth in ELLs during the last decade, from 1993 to 1994 ELL students made up approximately 5% of the total school population in the nation. In 1999–2000, the percentage grew to nearly 7%. Although the percentage increases are not the same in all regions, states in the Midwest, South, and West have all shown an increase in the ELL student population, both in total and as a percentage of the total school population. There are approximately 1.6 million EL students in California's public schools alone and California serves one third of all EL students in the nation.

Because linguistic diversity will always be a part of U.S. public education, school administrators must be knowledgeable about the optimal types of programs needed for ELs. Currently, Spanish, Chinese, Vietnamese, Hmong, Cantonese, Filipino, and Cambodian are the most prevalent languages spoken by immigrant children and youths in schools. It is estimated that 85% of all ELs in the United States are Spanish speaking. In 2010, the fastest-growing foreign languages spoken in U.S. homes are Chinese, Vietnamese, Russian, Arabic, and French Creole.

English Only, English Plus, and Programs for Nonstandard English Speakers

In recent years, some states and organizations have called for English to be the *only* language used in state documents, in business transactions, and in schools. Other groups have pointed out the importance of being multilingual. The latter group takes a view that some call *English Plus*: People should not only speak English, but they also should have fluency in another language. The U.S. federal government does not specify an official language; however, all official documents in the U.S. are written in English, though some are also published in other languages.

As of 2011, 26 states have voted to make English the official language of that state. Although these state and national debates may be important, they have not yet had a direct impact on schools.

One debate that garnered considerable attention in 1997 was the controversy surrounding a decision by the Oakland (California) School Board to offer African-American speakers of Ebonics, or Black English, special instruction. Additionally, during the debate, other school districts such as that in Los Angeles were found to already be offering "Ebonics" programs. Once the issues were dissected, several common factors could be identified regardless of the voices in the debate: (1) African-American students were lagging behind other ethnic groups in academic achievement, (2) something had to be done to address this lack of achievement, and (3) everyone involved (parents, teachers, students, and community members) agreed that all students must be able to speak standard English. Most linguists agree that a student who develops awareness of her or his own variety of English will make a better learner of standard English.

In volatile situations such as these, the challenges for school leaders include examining the complexity of the issues, identifying needs, identifying options, and working collaboratively to choose the best option(s).

Promoting the Academic Success of Linguistically Diverse Learners

In exploring why some students who are non–native English speakers do better academically than other students, a study of ELLs in 257 elementary schools in California (Williams et al., 2007) found that some schools have far better results than others. The study used the Academic Performance Index (API), which is the cornerstone of California's Public Schools Accountability Act of 1999. It measures the academic performance and growth of schools on several academic measures, and each California school receives a score between 200 and 1,000. For elementary schools, students' results on the California Standards Test in the core academic subjects of math and English language arts are a major portion of the index. Using these scores to identify how well schools were doing with English language learners, the study attempted to examine some large differences in school scores. Some California elementary schools serving similar proportions of low-income Spanish-speaking EL students differed by over 250 points on California's new EL Academic-Performance Index score. What practices can help explain this API gap?

The researchers found that the EL–API gap among schools with similar populations could likely be narrowed if schools focused on improving schoolwide practices in four domains: (1) using assessment data to improve student achievement and instruction; (2) ensuring availability of instructional resources; (3) implementing a coherent standards-based curriculum and instructional program; and (4) prioritizing student achievement, using measurable and monitored objectives. The full report can be downloaded at edsource.org.

Specially Designed Academic Instruction in English (SDAIE)

When effective bilingual programs are not available for English language learners, an alternative is for classroom teachers to use an approach called *specially designed academic instruction in English (SDAIE)*. SDAIE, or *Sheltered English*, allows students to move forward with academic courses such as biology or mathematics and at the same time learn English through the contextual clues provided by the course. The pedagogy of SDAIE is based on linguistic theories developed by researchers such as Steven Krashen and Jim Cummins. At the heart of contextual interaction theory, which they developed, are two major components that impact the SDAIE classroom: a "supportive affective environment" and "comprehensible second language input." Teacher training in SDAIE methodology revolves around the idea that successful lesson design and course development hinge on the teacher's ability to provide these two key elements.

SDAIE is an important aspect of some structured English immersion programs. It is a method of teaching students in English so that they gain skills in both the subject matter and in using English. SDAIE requires that ELLs possess some degree of fluency in English as well as their native language. The SDAIE approach incorporates many different types of instructional strategies, including comprehension checking, choral reading, brainstorming, or using graphic organizers, writing prompts, learning logs, journals, and idea starters. SDAIE strategies involve teachers using modified speech such as speaking at a slower rate, avoiding idiomatic speech, clearly enunciating, or using cognates. Teachers also use contextual clues. For example, teachers might use gestures and facial expressions, props and manipulatives, word banks, and audiovisual materials. In SDAIE, lessons are designed so that the fluency level of the student is reflected. There is evidence of scaffolding and a strong emphasis on vocabulary building. The curriculum is not watered down; instead, there is a rigorous core curriculum. Key topics are organized around main themes, and topics are appropriate for the grade level. During formative assessment of learning, the teacher employs strategies such as confirmation checks, clarification requests, expansions, repetitions, and a variety of question types. Summative assessment strategies might include review of main topics and vocabulary, mastery assessment using a variety of modalities, and written assessment that would be appropriate for intermediate or early advanced ELLs.

Clearly, the SDAIE teaching strategies discussed here are often employed for native English-speaking students. However, explicit training in the many types of teaching strategies used in SDAIE methodology means that teachers consciously and purposefully employ strategies and techniques that are effective for not only learning English, but also the subject material.

English Learners, the Achievement Gap and Literacy

Research (Cummins, 2009) has shown that any discussion of improving education for disadvantaged children has to include addressing the problems of literacy. When we choose to frame the universe of discourse about underachievement primarily in terms of children's deficits in some area of psychological or linguistic functioning, we expel culture, language, identity, intellect, and imagination from our image of the child. A much broader perspective requires the linking of literacy engagement to the development of reading comprehension. The construct of *literacy engagement* incorporates notions of *time on task* (reading extensively), *affect* (enthusiasm and enjoyment of literacy), *depth of cognitive processing* (strategies to deepen comprehension), and *active pursuit of literacy activities* (amount and diversity of literacy practices in and out of school). The Organization for Economic and Cooperative Development (OECD) showed that "the level of a student's reading engagement is a better predictor of literacy performance than his or her socioeconomic background, indicating that cultivating a student's interest in reading can help overcome home disadvantages" (p. 8).

Literacy engagement will be enhanced when (a) students' prior knowledge is activated; (b) their ability to understand and use academic language is supported through specific instructional strategies; (c) their identities are defined; and (d) the student's knowledge of and control over language is extended across the curriculum. ELL teachers and other school personnel often focus on what the ELL student lacks rather than on the intelligence, imagination, and linguistic talents that the student brings to the classroom and school. However, by following simple changes to the social structure and practices of the classroom and school, students are often able to express intelligence, feelings, and identity in ways that lead to improved achievement. Cummins (2009) has developed an audit system to allow schools to begin to look at their language and literacy policies. In addressing these issues, Cummins states that educators might want to think in terms of the following questions: *Where are we now—what are our current realities? Where would we like to be—what is our vision for the future? How do we get there—what is our action plan?* Table 8.5 might help administrators and teachers to begin to audit or access existing practices and to begin to think through improved approaches.

Overall, the research literature (Cummins, 2009; Hand & Anderson, 2009) has found four critical components of reading instruction for ELLs: speech, comprehension, word recognition, and vocabulary. Most ELLs lag behind native speakers in the oral language skills that are necessary for reading success. Secondly, ELLs, like other students, need to be taught comprehension strategies for making sense of the texts they need to be able to read. The research has shown that explicit instruction in word recognition or phonics can help ELLs, within 2 to 3 years, to acquire skills equivalent to native speakers. Finally, ELLs begin with many fewer words than native speakers of English, and the gap grows during schooling unless a strong focus is placed on acquiring new vocabulary.

In a recent report on early grade literacy, Deitrick (2011) summarized the research about ELLs.

TABLE 8.5   Pedagogies of Choice: Collaborative Auditing of School Organization and Instructional Practice

A. OVERALL SCHOOL IDENTITY—*To what extent does the school become a site of empowerment for students and communities? To what extent do school leaders do the following?*

- Promote respect for and high expectations in relation to students' cultural, linguistic, and intellectual resources and actively seek to use these resources in the instructional program
- Establish strong parental and community participation as a priority
- Establish a climate where student voice is heard and students share in the ownership of the school as a learning organization
- Establish a collaborative ethos among school staff members, and work to support teachers in developing the knowledge base to teach diverse learners effectively
- Recruit staff with the cultural/linguistic expertise and sensitivity to connect with students and communities
- Initiate a language policy process within the school that articulates belief systems about language and literacy development and directions for attaining articulated goals

B. PROMOTION OF MULTILITERACIES—*To what extent does the school encourage and provide opportunities for students to interpret and create multimodal and multilingual texts in the school, home and community?*

To what extent are students engaged in social networks organized around the comprehension, creation, and critical discussion of multiple forms of texts?	Medium: Electronic, print based, live (e.g., drama)
	Modality: Aural, oral, sign, visual, written (either multimodal or unimodal)
	Language: Multilingual, unilingual
	Variety: Standard variety, group-specific variety
	Genre: Expository text, fiction, poetry, music, etc.

C. STUDENT LEARNING—*To what extent are students developing the cognitive, linguistic, and affective dispositions for critical literacy engagement?*

1. *With respect to cognitive processing, do students systematically:*	Relate their pre-existing knowledge to academic content?
	Integrate facts with conceptual structures? Actively control, self-regulate, and develop metacognitive awareness of the learning process?
2. *With respect to the processing of language, do students systematically:*	Focus on meaning, ranging from comprehensible input to critical literacy?
	Focus on language, including attention to language forms and genres and the intersections between language and power?
	Focus on use, including using language to generate new knowledge, create literature and art, and act on social realities?
3. *With respect to affect, do students consistently:*	Experience affirmation of identity in the process of creating multimodal and multilingual texts?

D. INSTRUCTION—*To what extent do teachers enable forms of learning that promote student empowerment and literacy engagement?*

To what extent do teachers:

Scaffold access to textual meanings?

Scaffold production of identity texts?

Encourage student participation in literate communities of practice?

Make explicit the linguistic structure of academic content?

Demystify linguistic and social codes of language use?

Orchestrate classroom interactions that construct linguistic and cultural diversity as a resource for learning?

Implement assessment strategies (e.g., portfolio assessment) that encourage and capture the full range of students' creative work?

Engage parents and community members in partnerships related to literacy?

Source: Cummins, J. (2009). Transformative multiliteracies pedagogy: School-based strategies for closing the achievement gap. *Multiple Voices for Ethnically Diverse Exceptional Learners, 11*(2), 38–56.

- The number of English learners in schools in the United States increased by nearly 300% between 1979 and 2006. Latino youth comprise the largest percentage of English learners, with Spanish being the most frequently spoken language at home (Billings, 2009).
- All young children are capable of learning two languages. Becoming bilingual has long-term cognitive, academic, social, cultural, and economic benefits (AECF, 2010, p. 33).
- ELL students need systematic support for the continued development of their home language. Loss of the home language has potential negative long-term consequences for the ELL student's academic, social, and emotional development, as well as for the family dynamics (AECF, 2010, p. 33).
- Teachers and programs can adopt effective strategies to support home language development even when the teachers are monolingual English speakers. Dual-language programs are effective approaches to improving academic achievement for ELL students, while also providing benefits to native English speakers (AECF, 2010, p. 33).
- Students experience either success or failure in their English literacy acquisition depending on what occurs in their homes and classrooms. If teachers make linguistically informed decisions about curriculum and instruction, students can learn to read and write in English in the context of linguistically diverse classrooms (Barnitz, 1997; Perry, Soltero-Gonzalez, 2009).
- In order to increase the chances of all learners' successful acquisition of language and literacy, classroom strategies for teaching students from

all language backgrounds must involve the orchestration of the learners' total language and the activation of their prior knowledge as they compose and comprehend authentic texts supported by natural classroom discourse (Barnitz, 1997; see also Markose, 2008).

■ "While there are universal similarities across all languages, variations across basic linguistic systems exist in phonology, morphology, syntax, lexicon, text structure, oral discourse, and orthographies. Cultural variation of oral discourse needs to be considered in literacy instruction, as does variation in text structures found across languages" (Barnitz, 1997, p. 265).

■ Native languages and dialects play an important role in learning English. Respecting and appreciating diverse language is a necessary first step in successful literacy instruction (Barnitz, 1997; see also Soltero-Gonzalez, 2009).

■ ELL students benefit from literature-based instruction because it provides authentic, natural, uninterrupted texts with contextual support from illustrations (Barnitz, 1997; see also Lynch).

■ "Family literacy programs are defined as those that involve the three separate, but highly connected constituencies of family, school, and community; family literacy services are defined as those provided to participants on a voluntary basis that are of sufficient intensity in terms of hours, and of sufficient duration, to make sustainable changes in a family (such as eliminating or reducing welfare dependency) and that integrate all of the following activities: interactive literacy activities between parents and their children, equipping parents to partner with their children in learning; parent literacy training that leads to economic self-sufficiency; and appropriate instruction for children of parents receiving parent literacy services" (Crawford, 2006, p. 262).

One important issue to remember from the literature on early grade literacy for ELLs (and any struggling reader) is that family literacy programs can play a key role in helping young children more quickly acquire reading fluency in English. The elementary school principal, in particular, needs to play a major role in improving literacy initiatives in his or her school. Principals need to ensure that all elementary teachers have strong literacy training. Additionally, the principal must ensure that teachers have numerous opportunities for high-quality professional development in language arts and reading. Finally, it is vital that the elementary school principal have a deep understanding of how native English-speaking students and ELLs acquire language skills and also he or she must be familiar with the evidence base of the many family literacy programs available. Crucial to the success of ELLs is a strong partnership with families and schools around language learning.

A Word About Language Programs in the United States

As a nation, the United States has a tentative history with regard to the importance of students learning other languages. Because English is so widely spoken and is used in commerce worldwide, many Americans do not see the importance of offering other languages, especially in elementary schools. In recent years, there has been a resurgence in language learning, due to the globalization of our planet as well as a variety of other reasons. Today, Mandarin, English, Spanish, Arabic, Russian and Portuguese are the most widely spoken languages in the world. And, as distances become shorter, the value of speaking other languages is beginning to become recognized, appreciated, and valued in the United States.

In the late 1950s in response to the Russians beating the United States into space by launching the first space shuttle, the federal government started investing in foreign language programs in elementary schools (FLES). Until that time, secondary schools had typically offered languages such as Latin, Greek, and French, while elementary schools had rarely offered any language other than English. Over time, the federal government decreased the financial support available for FLES programs and by the early 1970s most had disappeared. Today most long-standing foreign language programs in elementary programs are the result of local initiatives. However, given the enormous changes taking place due to globalization, there is a resurgence at all levels of education of the importance for students to learn a second or even third language. Today, secondary schools throughout the nation routinely offer Spanish, French, Japanese, Russian, Mandarin, Portuguese, and/or Arabic, to name a few. Foreign language programs in elementary schools are also on the rise with Spanish, French, Mandarin, Russian, Arabic, and other languages beginning to flourish in a growing number of school districts; often because parents are requesting that their children learn a second language.

CREATING A MULTICULTURAL LEADERSHIP FRAMEWORK

We have discussed the enormous diversity in society and how that diversity is transforming America's school. In spite of the diversity of languages, racial and ethnic groups, socioeconomic status, sexual identity, cultural traditions, and so on, ethnocentricity continues to be prevalent. Bordas (2007) defines ethnocentricity as ". . . seeing the world from one cultural orientation and believing it to be the universal standard—or even superior" (p. 8). Bordas maintains that a multicultural leadership orientation ". . . incorporates many cultural perspectives, appreciates differences, values the unique contributions of diverse groups, and promotes learning from many orientations" (p. 8). Table 8.6 illustrates two different organizational paradigms: hierarchical and egalitarian. The paradigm of schools is in the process of moving from one in which the dominant cultural perspective has been hierarchical and is transitioning to one that is egalitarian and includes the traditions and diversity of numerous cultures and groups. Because this transition can be slow, stressful, and unsettling for some, it requires that school leaders guide the way for this shift.

TABLE 8.6   Two Organization Paradigms

HIERARCHICAL PLURALISM	EGALITARIAN PLURALISM
▪ History is seen from the dominate cultural perspective—and believed to be "the truth" or "reality."	▪ History and tradition reflect the experiences and backgrounds of diverse cultures that comprise the whole.
▪ Everyone must conform to dominant cultural values and perspectives. There is only one world view. Ethnocentric.	▪ The values, perspectives, and worldviews of all subgroups are respected and integrated. Multicultural.
▪ Diverse people must *conform* to dominant-culture behavior, dress, norms, thinking, and communication patterns. Homogenous and homogenized.	▪ Diversity is infused at all levels of the culture, organization, and society—"differences add value." Heterogeneous.
▪ Operating rules, structures, and systems are in alignment with dominant cultural values and orientation. Business as usual.	▪ Operating rules, structures, and symptoms are dynamic, flexible, and responsive to people's needs.
▪ Intelligence is measured by reading comprehension, critical thinking, and problem solving—I.Q. standardization. Rational.	▪ Intelligence and ability are assessed by a variety of measures (emotional, kinetic, and spiritual.) Emotional, spiritual, and cultural I.Q.
▪ Primary learning is through information reading and scientific method use of experts. Analysis.	▪ Different styles of learning and processing information are all validated: "we can all learn from one another."
▪ Tokenism—one can speak for the many.	▪ *Bienvenidos*, inclusiveness is a cherished trait—welcome to the table.
▪ Traditional thinking is sequential and linear. Action- and task-oriented thinking.	▪ Multidimensional thinking—there are many paths to the same goal.
▪ The long-term end is to retain and expand power and to control resources and people.	▪ The long-term end is to include equitable representation at all levels of the organization and society. Share resources.
▪ Few at the top, generally White males. Privilege, advantage, and entitlement. Inner circle. Clubby.	▪ Many share power and responsibility. Competency, education, and hard work are the avenues to success. Empowerment.
▪ Collaboration as a decision-making and team-building tool. Competition based.	▪ Collaboration as a tool for advancing authentic representation; all voices are heard.
▪ Scope: pervasive, institutionalized, covert discrimination, normative, dominance unrecognized.	▪ Scope: interactive, fluid, change-oriented, synergistic, adaptive, encouraging diverse approaches.
▪ Cultural patriarchy and dominance.	▪ Multicultural: circular shared leadership.

Source: Bordas, J. (2007). *Salsa, soul and spirit: Leadership for a muliticultural age.* San Francisco, CA: Berrett-Koehler Publishers.

CONCLUSION

A number of social and cultural factors affect children's learning. Ethnicity, social class, gender, sexual identity, disability, family, home environment, and language are some of the many factors that must be better understood by educators. Thoughtful consideration of these factors will assist educational leaders in analyzing issues so that prudent decisions regarding educational programming can be made. In recent years, there have been many high-profile, shocking incidents of harassment and bullying of gay youth, some of whom have committed suicide. It is imperative that school leaders create safe environments where harassing behaviors are not tolerated. There is great diversity in our schools, among students as well as adults in the building. Creating a supportive learning environment that fosters a culture of inclusion is vital to the academic success of all students.

The United States is a nation of immigrants and waves of refugees and immigrants continue to enter our doorstep with these immigrant children sitting in the nation's clasrooms. The acquisition of English is vital for student success in schools. In recent years, there has been a growing research base of strategies to help ELL students as well as struggling readers. School leaders need a strong experiential background in reading, language arts, and second language acquisition so they can support teachers working with ELL students. Because we live in a society that is a kaleidoscope of diversity, crafting a multicultural leadership paradigm will allow students, families, and school staff to better work together to form what Starratt (Chapter 1) calls the *moral enterprise of learning*.

MyEdLeadershipLab™

Go to Topic 5: *Curriculum Planning, Assessment, and Accountability* in the MyEdLeadershipLab™ site (www.MyEdLeadershipLab.com) for *Educational Leadership: A Bridge to Improved Practice*, Fifth Edition, where you can:

- Find learning outcomes for *Curriculum Planning, Assessment, and Accountability* along with the national standards that connect to these outcomes.
- Complete Assignments and Activities that can help you more deeply understand the chapter content.
- Apply and practice your understanding of the core skills identified in the chapter with the Building Leadership Skills unit.
- Prepare yourself for professional certification with a Practice for Certification quiz.

PORTFOLIO ARTIFACTS

- Revisit your educational leadership platform. What does your platform say about your beliefs regarding issues of educational equity? How does it address issues related to multicultural education and language learning?

- Travel to a community or country different from your own. Reflect on the similarities and differences.

- Examine a curriculum. Is that curriculum reflective of the issues of diversity discussed in this chapter?

- Spend time with people who are different from you in regard to race, socioeconomic status, ethnicity, ability/disability (e.g., switch jobs for a day with someone in a school serving a population different from yours). Reflect on the experience.

- Spend a period of time riding along with a police officer in a community that is different from the one in which you live. Many police departments have special programs for citizens. Reflect on the experience.

  Explore what foreign languages are offered in elementary and secondary schools in your region or state. Have there been any changes in the last 10 years?

- Search the Web for the National Association of Multicultural Education (http://www.nameorg.org). Do you think an administrator would find this site helpful? If yes, why? If no, why not?

KEY TERMS

- Adequate yearly progress
- Afrocentric schools
- Assimilation
- Bilingual education
- Border pedagogy
- Critical teaching (pedagogy)
- Cultural deficit theory
- Cultural difference theory
- Cultural diversity
- Cultural identity/ethnic identity
- Cultural pluralism
- Cultural relativism
- Culture shock
- Cyberbullying
- Desegregation

- Discrimination
- Ebonics
- English as a second language (ESL)
- English learner (EL) or English language learners (ELLs)
- Equal access
- Ethnocentricity
- FLES
- Lesbian, gay, bisexual, transgender, questioning (LGBTQ)
- *Harper v. Poway*
- Inclusion (inclusive)
- Integration
- Intergroup education
- Language minority student
- Language proficiency

- *Lau v. Nichols*
- Learning style
- Limited English proficiency (LEP)
- Mainstreaming
- Prejudice
- Race
- Racism
- Second-generation discrimination
- Segregation
- Sexual identity
- Sheltered English
- Socioeconomic groups
- Sociotypes
- Specially designed academic instruction in English (SDAIE)
- Stereotypes

SUGGESTED READINGS

Biegel, S. (2010). *The right to be: Sexual orientation and gender identity in America's public schools.* Minneapolis, MN: University of Minnesota Press.

DomNwachukwu, C. S. (2010). *An introduction to multicultural education: From theory to practice.* Lanham, MD: Rowman & Littlefield Publishers, Inc.

Goldenberg, C., & Coleman, R. (2010). *Promoting academic achievement among English learners: A guide to the research.* Thousand Oaks, CA: Corwin Press.

Just the Facts Coalition. (2008). *Just the facts about sexual orientation and youth: A primer for principals, educators, and school personnel.* Washington, DC: American Psychological Association. Retrieved from http://www.apa.org/pi/lgbt/resources/just-the-facts.aspx.

Nieto, S., & Bode, P. (2011). *Affirming diversity: The sociopolitical context of multicultural education.* Boston, MA: Allyn & Bacon.

Payne, R. K. (2005) *A framework for understanding poverty* (4th ed.). Highlands, TX: Aha! Process.

Williams, T., Hakuta, K., Haertel, E., et al. (2007). *Similar English learner students, different results: Why do some schools do better? A follow-up analysis based on a large-scale survey of California elementary schools serving low-income and EL students.* Mountain View, CA: EdSource.

MEDIA RECOMMENDATION

Cohen, R. (2004). *Going to School (Ir a La Escuela).* Venice, CA: Richard Cohen films. A documentary about inclusion, diversity, and empowering students with disabilities. http://www.richardcohenfilms.com.

CHAPTER 9

CURRICULUM DEVELOPMENT AND ASSESSMENT

MyEdLeadershipLab™

Visit the MyEdLeadershipLab™ site for *Educational Leadership: A Bridge to Improved Practice*, Fifth Edition to enhance your understanding of chapter concepts. You'll have the opportunity to practice your skills through video- and case-based Assignments and Activities as well as Building Leadership Skills units, and to prepare for your certification exam with Practice for Certification quizzes.

LOGAN ELEMENTARY SCHOOL

Program Improvement

A parent approached Principal Robert Carmo of Logan Elementary School regarding the 2nd-grade health curriculum. This parent believed the curriculum taught by the school psychologist was inappropriate for 2nd-grade students; he indicated that several other parents shared his views. The principal listened to the parents' complaints and wrote down the specific concerns.

Although in his third year as principal of Logan, Carmo was not familiar with the details of this 2nd-grade health curriculum. Following the meeting with the parent, Principal Carmo asked the opinions of the three 2nd-grade teachers. All three agreed that the curriculum was of value and well received by the students. In speaking with the school psychologist, Principal Carmo discovered that the psychologist's predecessor had introduced the curriculum. The incumbent was in her first year at Logan and her first position in an educational setting. The psychologist stated that she, like the parent, had similar reservations concerning the curriculum. Because of her lack of experience, however, she had not brought forward the concerns.

Principal Carmo immediately asked the assistant superintendent for curriculum and instruction when the school board had approved this particular curriculum. The assistant superintendent could not recall any such approval during her 4-year tenure; eventually, it was discovered that the curriculum had never been presented to, or approved by, the school board.

Board policy stated that the decision to retain or reject curriculum materials would be based on specific criteria, including whether the material represented life in true proportions, whether circumstances were dealt with realistically, and whether the materials had literary or social value. Policy required that factual material be included in all instructional material collections.

✳ **How do you assess the "value and worth" of a curriculum? This school district's board policy had guidelines for choosing this curriculum. Does your school district have board policy in this area? What does it say? How does it compare with the policy in Principal Carmo's district?**

CONCEPTIONS OF ACADEMIC ACHIEVEMENT

According to Cole (1990) there are currently two major conceptions of academic achievement. The first, called *basic skills and facts*, grew out of the 1950s and 1960s when behavioral psychology dominated the way educators viewed learning. The second conception of achievement involves the notions of higher-order thinking skills, problem solving, and advanced knowledge. These achievement skills could be regarded as a progression as described by Bloom and Krathwohl (1984): knowledge, comprehension, application, analysis, synthesis, and evaluation.

As Cole (1990) maintains, "Conceptions of educational achievement change with the times, are influenced by many factors, and take different forms for different people" (p. 2). Cole finds the two conceptions of academic achievement inadequate in helping us to think about learning, concluding that educators need to formulate an alternative conception that integrates divergent views of achievement, carries clear instructional implications, and focuses on long-term educational goals. Choices are related to what is valued, what is teachable, how it is organized, how much time should be devoted, who should be involved, what best communicates intentions, and what goals are served, to name a few of the elements of these alternatives (Costa, 1997).

Theories of Intelligence

In recent years, two theories of intelligence have proved particularly useful to educators: Robert Sternberg's triarchic theory and Howard Gardner's multiple intelligence (MI) theory.

Sternberg (1996b) maintains that intelligence, defined by its underlying components, can be altered through instruction. Sternberg's triarchic theory of intelligence comprises three parts—synthetic, analytic, and practical—each of which is related to creativity.

The *synthetic* part of intelligence generates ideas and redefines problems. "Synthetic" relates to a person's internal thinking and consists of three processes. The first process is used in planning, monitoring, and evaluating the performance of a task. The second governs behavior in the performance of the task itself;

Sternberg maintains that a person can become more or less intelligent by learning what to acknowledge and what to ignore. The final internal component of intelligence controls the previous knowledge a person brings to a new situation. According to Sternberg, it is this previously acquired knowledge a person brings to the new situation that is more important than the mental speed or memory skills a person uses.

The *analytic* part of intelligence recognizes ideas, structures, and themes; allocates resources; and evaluates the quality of ideas. It addresses the basics of problem solving. The *practical* part of intelligence makes ideas work. It promotes and refines ideas based on how the learner critiques the information he or she gets from others.

A key aspect of Sternberg's theory is that intelligence depends heavily on how people learn to cope with the world around them. Sternberg (1996b) believes that "academic intelligence of the kind measured by IQ tests matters, but really it doesn't matter that much" (p. 22). Sternberg (1996a) argues that his concept of successful intelligence is of paramount importance because it is the type of intelligence that is used to achieve important goals and is needed in the 21st century.

In his 1983 seminal book on intelligence, *Frames of Mind,* Gardner groups people's broad range of abilities into seven categories of intelligence: linguistic, logical–mathematical, spatial, bodily–kinesthetic, musical, interpersonal, and intrapersonal. In recent years, Gardner added an eighth intelligence: a naturalist intelligence, which allows people to recognize and discriminate among living things (Checkley, 1997).

Gardner's theory is called *multiple intelligence (MI)* theory. He maintains that each person possesses all eight intelligences to varying degrees. Those intelligences include: musical, kinesthetic, logical, spatial, linguistic, interpersonal, and naturalistic. Within each category are multiple ways to be intelligent. Each of these intelligences interacts with other intelligences, and the context of learning is crucial. Gardner disavows the notion that knowledge and ability in one area (e.g., musical intelligence) is less important than knowledge in another area (e.g., logical–mathematical).

Acceptance of the idea that (1) intelligence comprises multiple forms and that (2) it can be altered through instruction challenges the traditional school curriculum, which emphasizes linguistic and logical–mathematical forms of intelligence. One need only examine the allocation of time in schools to see which disciplines are most valued. Little learning time is devoted to spatial, bodily–kinesthetic, musical, interpersonal, and intrapersonal intelligences, compared with the amount devoted to the areas of linguistic and logical–mathematical intelligences. It is a rare U.S. elementary school that does not begin the school day with reading or language arts. If, as Armstrong (1994) suggests, teaching activities, materials, and instructional strategies were to incorporate all of the intelligences, then students with "less intelligence" in one area than another would not be left out of the learning loop or made to believe they are "dumb." Confusion sometimes exists between mismatches in styles of teaching and learning being mistakenly described as poor teaching and/or lack of student ability (teachability grouping).

Even though Gardner's work has been criticized for not having a research base supporting it, this theory is helpful in reminding educators that intelligence is a complex, fluid concept. The traditional school curriculum includes the notion that intelligence can be measured by an instrument. This reification of intelligence through IQ tests has had a detrimental effect on thousands of schoolchildren throughout the last century. If there are numerous forms of intelligence, and if there is only one definition, a more useful goal should be to determine how people best learn certain types of knowledge.

Both Sternberg's and Gardner's theories of intelligence have important implications for teaching and learning. If people possess varying degrees of intelligence in different areas and if intelligence can be altered through instruction, then a school's curriculum can influence the degree of student learning significantly.

Types of Knowledge

What does it mean for a person to learn something? Are some ways to learn superior to others? Is a person's learning style defined by what he or she is learning? Researchers (Leithwood, Begley, & Cousins, 1994; Sternberg & Caruso, 1985; Sternberg & Frensch, 1993) suggest that there are various types of knowledge: declarative knowledge, practical and procedural or strategic knowledge, and contextual knowledge. Declarative knowledge is factual; it is knowledge about something. Sternberg and Caruso (1985) define practical knowledge as "procedural knowledge that is useful in one's everyday life" (p. 134). Leithwood and colleagues (1994) add the descriptor "strategic." They maintain that practical knowledge is "concerned with *how* to solve problems rather than knowledge *about* problem solving" (p. 192), which they term *declarative knowledge*. Contextual knowledge is knowledge that depends on context.

Learning Transfer

Transfer has been defined as "the degree to which a behavior will be repeated in a new situation" (Detterman, 1993, p. 4). Educators are often perplexed when they have a student who learned something in the recent past but is unable to transfer that learning to a similar situation. For example, in Spanish class, a student might have spent considerable time learning the past tense form of a verb and might demonstrate that knowledge on a written and oral test. Yet the student is often unable to remember the correct verb form when required to use it in a conversation. Are there mechanisms that will increase the likelihood that learning in one situation will be transferred to another situation?

According to Sternberg and Frensch (1993), the degree of transfer from one situation to another depends on four mechanisms. First, there must be *encoding specificity*. The degree of transfer depends on the original encoding of the knowledge. Retrieval of the knowledge depends on how the learner has encoded it. If students are not taught (in the classroom) how to apply information, then the likelihood of their being able to transfer information to a situation is reduced. For example, most educators are well versed in adolescent development but may be unable to transfer such knowledge to raising their own children.

A second mechanism that influences transfer is *organization*—how information is originally organized in a person's memory. Sternberg and Frensch (1993) believe "that organization of information from old situations can either facilitate or impede transfer to new situations" (p. 26). When we learn something in a particular way (e.g., memorizing verbs by conjugation), we must reorganize the information to apply it.

A third mechanism involves *discrimination,* in which information is retrieved depending on whether it was tagged or stored as relevant to a new situation in which it might be applied. Discrimination occurs frequently, of which tagging is the key process. What makes a learner tag one piece of information and not another? Reinforcement and review of information might make it more likely that the learner will tag certain knowledge.

Sternberg and Frensch (1993) label the fourth mechanism for transfer the *mental set.* Whether a person "sees a useful way of doing something depends in part upon the mental set with which he or she approaches the task" (p. 26). In most schools, academic subjects are taught in isolation. Subjects such as algebra are infrequently made relevant to real-world use. Yet educators expect students to transfer the knowledge of the algebraic formula to practical applications. Many students study algebra for 2 years in high school with little perceived relevance other than that it is usually required for college entrance.

One day while sailing, a person tried to explain to one of the authors how to plot a course and stated, "This is just basic algebra." This statement enabled the author to transfer what had been learned in algebra class to an actual situation. If the learner has an appropriate mental set, transfer is more likely to occur.

Each of these mechanisms has implications for teaching and learning. Current research on teaching and learning calls for approaches that recognize students' transfer of learning and that make sense of what they learn.

✳ **What criteria should be used to evaluate Logan's 2nd-grade health curriculum and how it is being taught?**

CONSTRUCTIVISM

By the mid-1980s, the educational community was beginning to talk about a "constructivist" way of learning. Constructivist literature calls for a marked departure from behaviorist theory, which continues to drive much educational practice today. Different theories of learning such as behavioral, cognitive, and constructivist approaches have both advantages and disadvantages, but each has much to offer educators in improving student learning.

Behaviorist learning theory includes measurable behavioral objectives (e.g., by the end of this unit the student will have . . .) and sequenced curricula. In language texts before the mid-1980s, for instance, students were taught language structure sequentially—the present tense followed by the past tense. Many language teachers believed a natural progression existed that was the best way for people to learn. Conditionals such as "can" and "may," for example, were not often presented until midway through a course or toward the latter part of a text, if at all. Requesting something—May I go to the restroom? May I borrow a pen?—are language statements that beginners require. A behavioral approach to language learning, however, with its tight control on presentation of grammar and vocabulary, precludes a beginner's ability to make such requests.

Behaviorist approaches segment knowledge and skills into small pieces, with an overall idea that if each of these small pieces can be mastered, they will, taken together, result in acquisition of complex language skills. It pays little attention to conceptions and misconceptions that students might hold about the knowledge or skills being introduced. We now understand that, like thinking, learning a language is more than the sum of its parts. It is possible to know all grammar tenses and possess a large vocabulary and still be unable to speak a language.

According to Woolfolk (2001), "Cognitive theories of learning deal with thinking, remembering, and problem solving" (p. 2). The focus with cognitive theory is on how learners process information. Teaching techniques such as strategies to improve memorization, graphic organizers, or note-taking skills are examples of cognitive theory in action.

Constructivism, by contrast, is based on the belief that students learn best when they acquire knowledge through exploration and active learning. Individuals construct knowledge rather than receive it. According to Airasian and Walsh (1997), constructivism is a theory about how people learn: "Constructivism is based on the fundamental assumption that people create knowledge from the interaction between their existing knowledge or beliefs and the new ideas or situations they encounter" (p. 445).

Constructivist theory posits that students learn by actively constructing knowledge, comparing new information to previously learned information, thinking about and working through discrepancies, and ultimately reaching new understandings. Constructivist views have strongly influenced the movement toward national standards. Constructivism reminds us that ordering of information takes place in the minds of individuals, so when we as teachers impose our order on students, we rob them of the opportunity to create knowledge and understand themselves.

Building a Culture of Learning

Throughout the 1970s, numerous studies explored variables that showed high correlations with increased academic achievement (Bossert, Dwyer, Rowan, & Lee, 1982; Brookover & Lezotte, 1979; Lezotte, Edmonds, & Ratner, 1974; Rutter, Maughan,

Mortimore, Ouston, & Smith, 1979; Spartz, Valdes, McCormick, Meyers, & Geppert, 1977). These factors include:

- A safe and orderly environment
- An academic focus on basic skills
- Close monitoring of instruction by testing and supervision
- Strong instructional leadership from the principal
- High expectations and clear goals for students

The 1970s research findings, however, oversimplified the notion of effectiveness, and little attention was paid to the contexts in which these studies were conducted. What might be a successful practice in one context does not necessarily transfer to another. Programs often do not travel well to other locations regardless of how meticulously they were originally crafted.

In more recent studies that longitudinally examine academic achievement, other factors related to achievement present a more comprehensive picture (Cunningham & Gresso, 1993; Duke, 1987; Lipsitz, 1984; Reyes & Scribner, 1999; Wimpelberg, Teddlie, & Stringfield, 1989). These researchers discuss the broad-based conditions necessary for successful schools. Themes include leadership and management, changing school culture, and implementing challenging curricula and instruction. According to a study by Binkowski (1995), higher-performing schools include the following themes: participative leadership and management, communication and collaboration between central office and school staff regarding district and school goals, parental involvement, and staff development tied to curriculum and instruction.

In a provocative study of a school using site-based management, Beck and Murphy (1996) identified four imperatives for successful schools:

1. A consistent and powerful focus on learning
2. Strong, facilitative leadership
3. A commitment to nurturing a sense of internal and external community
4. Resources aimed at building the capacity of people within the community to lead, learn, and teach. (p. ix)

Beck and Murphy (1996) observed that staff members were highly motivated to increase learning in schools that have site-based management. "We found a school where promoting learning was a clear priority and, for some teachers and the principal, a consuming passion" (p. 43). They noted that more attention was paid to student learning than to adult education. Additionally, they discovered that certain instructional strategies worked well in a particular school. These strategies matched students' interests and needs.

Beck and Murphy (1996) noted that the principal and a number of teachers exercised leadership. Additionally, parents contributed to children's success "by actively and enthusiastically supporting the work of educators" (p. 79). Finally, they found that site-based management provided more opportunities for parents to take leadership roles.

Beck and Murphy's third imperative for successful schools refers to the role of the community. Site-based management of schools creates opportunities for collaboration with organizations and agencies in the community. This comprehensive focus on children was a crucial factor in academic success.

Beck and Murphy's fourth imperative deals with capacity building. They found that site autonomy "encouraged a sense of agency on the part of teachers and parents" (Beck & Murphy, 1996, p. 114). Site-based management allows teachers greater freedom to control their professional lives. Autonomy and a degree of budgetary control allow teachers to more quickly make decisions regarding curriculum, program innovations, and professional development.

A strong focus on learning, sufficient resources, strong facilitative leadership, and human capital from the school, district, and community are essential conditions for learning. Once these optimal learning conditions exist in a school, then attention must be given to the most appropriate teaching and learning approaches for the various types of knowledge that are part of the curriculum.

* **What conditions must exist at Logan Elementary School to ensure that an effective health curriculum is being taught?**

TEACHING AND LEARNING APPROACHES

A multitude of teaching and learning approaches can be used to optimize learning, and it is important to keep in mind Wiggins's (1990) idea of the futility of trying to teach everything of importance. He maintains, "Students cannot possibly learn everything of value by the time they leave school, but we can instill in them the desire to ask questions throughout their lives" (p. 44).

A number of different constructs can be used to analyze and determine what and how students should learn. Glatthorn (1994) believes that "some knowledge and skills seem to have high importance for all students, and they are the essential learning that all students need to master" (p. 27). They include major concepts, principles, ideas, and skills of a subject. Glatthorn also maintains that the structure of learning should be analyzed: "Understanding the principles of genetics is learning of high structure; it must be explicitly planned, taught, and tested. But developing scientific curiosity seems to be learning of low structure" (p. 27). He argues that teachers should nurture students' developing curiosity when possible, rather than simply spout facts that are taught "and then forgotten" (p. 27). Content raises questions and provides answers as it moves the learner from a basic grasp to a sophisticated and systematic view.

In this section, we briefly describe learning and teaching models embedded in a constructivist approach to learning and in multiple intelligence and triarchic intelligence theories.

Apprenticeship Learning

Much has been written about apprenticeship, one of the oldest models for learning. Researchers have recently revisited the potential of this model. As Gardner (1991) states, "Apprenticeships may well be the means of instruction that builds most effectively on the ways in which most young people learn" (p. 124). He posits that "the best chance for an education leading to understanding lies in the melding of certain features of apprenticeships with certain aspects of schools and other institutions" (p. 125).

Why are a growing number of educators and researchers (Gardner, 1991; Lave & Wenger, 1993; Moffett, 1994) advocating apprenticeship learning? One major reason might be that in addition to situating learning in context, apprenticeships provide interaction, which is a key part of psychologist Lev Vygotsky's (1978) *zone of proximal development*. This "zone" is the space between what a student can do when working alone compared with what he or she can do when working with an experienced adult or peer. Learning and mastery occur through active joint participation. This zone represents the gap between the individual learner's problem-solving ability and the total capacity demonstrated by those with whom the learner interacts.

According to Moffett (1994), natural learning methods such as witnessing, attuning, imitating, helping, collaborating, interacting, experimenting, transmitting, and investigating are all combined into the educational practice of apprenticing. Apprenticeships, however, are not the only learning formats that involve interaction in the zone of proximal development.

Cooperative Learning

Over the last 20 years, professionals in education have become increasingly familiar with the practice of cooperative learning. Students are arranged in groups of heterogeneous ability levels in which they work together to accomplish shared goals. Cooperative learning can be used in any class level and subject area.

A substantial body of research documents the effectiveness of cooperative learning strategies (Slavin, 1990; Stevens & Slavin, 1995). Children learn by piggybacking on the ideas of others through collaboration; they serve as instructional agents for one another. Work is carefully structured; students work in cooperative groups and thereby obtain a sense of positive interdependence.

Cooperative learning fosters problem solving and works best if there are five or fewer in a team. It promotes cooperative interpersonal behavior, mutual encouragement, and individual responsibility and accountability. Cooperative learning has been found to improve student achievement, intergroup relations, and self-esteem (Slavin, 1996) and is a sturdy platform for problem-based learning.

Project-Based Learning or Problem-Based Learning

"Doing projects" is an important tradition in American education and the roots of project-based learning (PBL) lie in this tradition. In recent years, PBL has gained momentum because of two important developments. First, there has been a revolution in our understanding of how people learn. Research in neuroscience and psychology has extended cognitive and behavioral models of learning—which support traditional direct instruction—to show that knowledge, thinking, doing, and the contexts for learning are inextricably tied. We now know that learning is partly a social activity and that it takes place within a context that includes culture, community, and experiences.

An important forerunner to project-based learning was problem-based learning. Problem-based learning, also referred to as PBL, is widely used in medical education, and in recent years it has found a place in a variety of disciplines, including engineering, law, architecture, social work, and educational administration (Boud & Feletti, 1998; Bridges & Hallinger, 1995; Clarke, 1998; Taylor, Cordeiro, & Chrispeels, 2008).

Problem-based learning begins with a practical problem that the student is likely to encounter in the real world. Problems are selected to illuminate core concepts in the curriculum. Subject matter is organized around the problem rather than around a discipline, and students have considerable responsibility and autonomy for directing their learning. Most learning is done in dyads or small teams (cooperative learning groups). Students must demonstrate their learning through a product or performance. Clearly, the role of the instructor in PBL differs considerably from that of the teacher as expert. In PBL, the teacher challenges, facilitates, and questions. In small groups, students work on PBL projects that are situated in a learning context and have multiple opportunities to work within the zone of proximal development.

Students are required to struggle with complicated real-world issues within the classroom setting. Problems should provide just enough information to guide investigation and student-directed inquiry. Students grapple with open-ended problems and are expected to propose solutions. They gain experience in self-direction, reasoning, problem solving, and collaboration. Teachers become facilitators, helping students understand their own thinking and guiding them as they search for new information. Students interact with others and acquire information before deciding how to deal with the problem.

According to the Buck Institute for Education (bie.org) which promotes project-based learning, research shows that learners not only respond by feeding back information, but also actively use what they know to explore, negotiate, interpret, and create. In doing this, the process shifts from emphasizing the process of teaching to emphasizing the learning process. In addition, the research coming from cognitive science has revealed more about the nature of how problems are solved. As educators apply the findings from cognitive research, teachers have learned how to effectively scaffold content and activities to amplify and extend the learning opportunities for students.

At the same time that we are learning from cognitive science, the growth of technology has afforded learners around the world access to information they never had before. As Friedman (2006) states, "The first and most important ability you can develop . . . is the ability to 'learn how to learn'—to constantly absorb, and teach yourself, new ways of doing old things or new ways of doing new things"

(p. 302). It is clear that children need both knowledge and skills to succeed. This need is driven not only by workforce demands for high-performance employees who collaborate and communicate, but also by the need to help all children learn their new roles as global citizens.

There is no one accepted definition of PBL; however, according to the Buck Institute, PBL is a standards-focused, systematic teaching method that engages students in learning knowledge and skills through an extended inquiry process structured around complex, authentic questions and carefully designed products and tasks (Buck Institute for Education, 2009). This definition encompasses a spectrum ranging from short-term projects that may only last a few days, to semester or yearlong projects. Projects might be based on a single subject in one classroom to interdisciplinary projects involving community partners.

Apprenticeship learning, cooperative learning, and project-based or problem-based learning are three approaches embedded in constructivist philosophy. It is important that the school administrators understand the various approaches to learning and how to implement them in the curriculum. Other approaches related to constructivism are thematic, authentic, and differentiated instruction.

Thematic Instruction.   In a thematic instruction approach, various related disciplines are brought to bear on a theme, issue, problem, topic, or experience. It is best when the themes or problems emerge from the student's world. Teachers and students are engaged in a learning partnership to examine a specific area in-depth and from multiple perspectives. Teachers in separate disciplines are united to team-teach around a selected set of issues. Information is viewed in a holistic manner. This orientation shows how different subject areas relate, thus affirming their relevance.

Authentic Instruction.   Students learn best from actual experiences rather than from simulations. Authentic instruction requires that the teacher work with students in choosing a topic on which to focus and obtaining needed information. Information gathering might include contacting expert practitioners, students from another culture, and authors, as well as collecting data from researchers, foundations, governments, and others. Technology is often used in obtaining, organizing, manipulating, and displaying information. The teacher serves as a coach, providing structure and actively supporting students. Some educators refer to certain types of problem-based learning as a form of authentic instruction.

Differentiated Instruction.   The approach called *differentiated instruction* is based on a diagnosis of student readiness, interest, and learning profile. All students are engaged in a continual progression of challenging work. Use of time, space, and groupings is flexible.

Research indicates the importance of meeting varying learning needs, even though in practice the process has proved difficult. This type of study allows students to pursue topics of interest in a direction or depth that might not be suitable or likely to be pursued by the class as a whole. Students ready for independence from teacher direction will be released from persistent supervision, and those requiring assistance are provided greater structure. Differentiated instruction involves such strategies as curriculum compacting, independent study, interest centers or interest groups, tiered assignments, flexible grouping, mentorships and apprenticeships, learning contracts, and anchoring activities. Other types of curricular and instructional approaches include brain-based, discovery, interdisciplinary, and whole language.

✳ **What instructional model(s) might work best for health education at Logan Elementary? Explain why.**

CURRICULUM DESIGN AND EDUCATIONAL PROGRAMMING

According to Glatthorn (1997), "principals can best discharge their leadership role if they develop a deep and broad knowledge base with respect to curriculum" (p. 3). What is it that school administrators need to know about curriculum?

Functions of Curriculum

Textbooks on curriculum development traditionally discuss four curriculum levels: state, district, school, and classroom. For example, one role at the classroom level is to develop units of study. Those units of study emanate from one of the school functions—developing a program of studies. This program is, in turn, embedded in a district function—identifying a common program of studies. At the state level, administrators develop frameworks embodying broad goals and general standards. Thus, there is a connection and an alignment among the functions at the various levels.

A fifth curriculum level should be added to Glatthorn's four levels: the emerging roles played by national professional organizations, national and international research groups, and the U.S. Department of Education in Washington, DC. These groups can be described not only as influencing local curriculum, but also as being major players in the creation of frameworks and in the development of national tests and standards.

THE STANDARDS MOVEMENT

In recent years, a variety of national and state agencies and professional organizations have been involved in the development of curriculum standards or frameworks. Almost all states have standards of learning in English, language arts, history/social studies, mathematics, science, and writing. Many of these frameworks have influenced the development of local school curricula. Certainly, an administrator should carefully consider the standards developed by these organizations when setting curriculum at the local level.

Standards are norms for quality control. They tell us what students should know and be able to do. According to Ravitch (1995), there are three types of standards: content standards, performance standards, and opportunity-to-learn (OTL) standards. Content standards are the descriptions of the knowledge and skills desired for students to learn. Performance standards refer to the level of proficiency, or degree of mastery, at which the knowledge or skill is to be displayed. OTL standards have to do with the availability of resources. The premise of OTL standards is that schools, districts, and states must provide the necessary programs, staff, and other resources to meet the basic needs of students.

PRINCIPAL AS CURRICULUM LEADER

ALLAN A. GLATTHORN
University of East Carolina

When I told a friend that the title of one of my books was *Principal as Curriculum Leader,* she responded, "That's an oxymoron if I ever heard one." Her reaction is understandable: Most principals do not believe that they have any role in setting curriculum. However, I believe that they do have a key part to play in this essential component of schooling.

Curriculum development and implementation are nested processes: The state, the school system, the school, and the classroom all have legitimate roles to play in learning enhancement. The state should identify curriculum standards for each subject; the school district should use those standards in developing coordinated curricula for grades K–12, with appropriate benchmarks. The school should develop its own program of studies, within district guidelines. The classroom teacher should operationalize the district curriculum guides in several ways: develop long-term plans, write units of study, enrich the district curriculum, and adapt it so that it responds to individual student needs.

School-level leadership functions with respect to curriculum, as follows:

1. Influencing district curriculum guides
2. Developing the school's program of studies
3. Developing a learning-centered schedule
4. Determining the nature and extent of curriculum integration
5. Aligning the curriculum
6. Monitoring the curriculum
7. Helping teachers make long-term plans
8. Helping teachers develop curriculum units
9. Helping teachers provide enrichment and remediation
10. Evaluating the curriculum

This list does not mean that the principal must do all the work. Instead, I encourage principals to play an active role but to use a team-leadership approach that recognizes the strengths and needs of classroom teachers.

While educators need to strengthen curricula at all levels, I believe that the most important challenge is to develop curriculum competence at the school and classroom levels. In responding to this challenge, principals are the key agents in curriculum reform.

Currently, national curriculum standards documents are available in the following areas: arts (dance, music, theatre, visual arts), civics, economics, English/language arts, foreign languages, geography, health, history, mathematics, physical education, science, social studies, and technology. Each document is organized differently but many include the knowledge, skills, and dispositions that students need to have in order to achieve. Some of these standards documents, such as those for technology, have student, teacher, and administrator standards.

As discussed in Chapter 2, there are currently 42 states that have adopted the Common Core State Standards; however, those standards are only in mathematics and language arts. There is considerable national debate and discussion about whether having common standards for all states will improve academic achievement. Some politicians, practitioners, and scholars maintain that the standards were developed and adopted by states too quickly. They argue that the standards do not pay sufficient attention to the need for an interdisciplinary curriculum and that they disregard the role that schools play in preparing students for citizenship. Advocates for the Common Core State Standards assert that common standards not only bring coherence, but are more rigorous than most states' current standards. Global education advocate Zhao (2009) states:

> Theoretically national curriculum standards for each subject can be useful, but unless we can develop sound standards for all subjects and knowledge we think our students should have, unless we can develop and implement valid and reliable assessment for all standards, unless we can enable our students to choose from a wide range of offerings, and unless we can attach equal value to a broad range of knowledge and skills, national standards will do more harm than good. (p. 202)

✳ **What is the role of the principal and teachers at Logan Elementary School regarding the health curriculum, and how might standards help in this effort?**

CURRICULAR AND INSTRUCTIONAL CHANGE

Whether curriculum is based on national, state, or locally developed standards, the process of change is key to understanding curriculum implementation and program innovation. Fullan (1993a) argues, "It is probably closer to the truth to say that the main problem in public education is not resistance to change, but the presence of too many innovations mandated or adopted uncritically and superficially on an *ad hoc* fragmented basis" (p. 23). The successful development and implementation of programs thrives on abundant opportunity for dialogue that encourages educators to critique the curriculum. This dialogue will more than likely involve conflict. If we think of conflict in terms of "conflict with civility," then it is not only healthy, but a necessary ingredient in curriculum and program development.

Several researchers have discussed the stages of change in schools (Cordeiro, 1998; Fullan, 1991; Kilmann, 1989). A model for program development including four approaches to change, and the stages inherent in each, is particularly appropriate to this discussion.

As Figure 9.1 shows, there are four overarching types of approach to change: a top-down approach ("This district will use computer technology in all courses"); a model adoption approach ("We are considering adopting the Accelerated Schools model"); a change agent approach ("Several teachers have piloted the Success for All curriculum and are recommending that it be used by the school"); and a catalytic events approach ("After this terrible racial incident, we must consider a multicultural approach to our curriculum").

Whatever the approach, all innovations pass through a series of stages. Change proceeds along a continuum. Initiation might involve conceptualization, awareness, and commitment. Implementation might include development, experimentation, adaptation, and refinement. Finally, institutionalization might involve refocusing, continuation, routinization, or possibly consolidation.

Modification of a curriculum and educational program begins in a specific proposal to modify what already exists. Curriculum change focuses on what will be taught, and instructional change focuses on the way the curriculum will be taught. The proposal grows from the staff's knowledge of the goals, standards, and research as well as of the students and community. Participants can become knowledgeable by reading, visiting other schools, experimenting, discussing, and

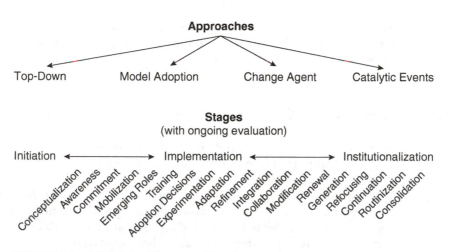

FIGURE 9.1   **A Model of Program Development**

consulting. The formal proposal includes a rationale for change and an analysis of the change's potential impact on resources.

The proposal should be presented to all concerned, including faculty and parents, for final review before it is submitted through the school system's review process. Those involved might choose to join one of the networks to help develop the curriculum and provide needed support (see Chapter 3). The final step after approval is determining how the curriculum will be organized and delivered.

✳ **What steps should Logan Elementary School staff members take to develop and refine the existing health curriculum?**

Developing Curriculum and Programs

According to Eisner (1995), all schools teach three curricula: explicit, implicit, and null. The explicit curriculum is the actual curriculum the school uses to teach pupils. The explicit curriculum usually takes the form of curriculum guides, but all too often it consists of textbooks. The implicit curriculum is not a formal part of the curriculum, yet it is taught in school. For example, the importance of punctuality and respect for others is part of many schools' implicit curriculum. Eisner (1995) maintains that "the implicit curriculum of a school is what it teaches because of the kind of school it is" (p. 97). Eisner's thesis is that "what schools do not teach is just as important as what they do teach" (p. 97).

Eisner defines the null curriculum in two dimensions. First, educators need to look at the subjects or content areas that may or may not be present in the curriculum. Teachers might ask such questions as: Why do we teach pre-algebra? Why do we have five tracks for English classes? Why are no advanced placement courses offered? Why do so few female students enroll in advanced math classes? What should students be expected to know as part of U.S. literature?

The second dimension involves the intellectual processes that the school emphasizes or neglects. Eisner (1995) maintains that "not all thinking is mediated by word or number, nor is all thinking rule-abiding" (p. 98). Critical questions educators might ask include: What forms of knowing (i.e., visual, metaphoric) are absent or marginal? In what ways do we cultivate students' imaginations?

Asking questions such as these is not only helpful in curriculum development and implementation, but also in evaluating curriculum and programs. Clearly, many factors affect curriculum development.

Designing, Managing, and Mapping the Curriculum

A variety of policies and factors are associated with effective programs. Whether a curriculum is based on a national, state, or local framework, the goal of curriculum development is to create a coherent educational program. Regardless of the design of the curriculum, important issues to consider are curriculum *congruity, integration, sequence,* and *student access.* Administrators must foster a school environment that continuously raises questions related to these four areas. Following are some of these questions:

Curriculum Congruity

- How consistent is the curriculum across grade levels and schools?
- What criteria are used to determine whether a student has achieved mastery of a concept?
- What enables the student to understand the interpretation of knowledge and how it is used to examine authentic problems?

Curriculum Integration

- Is the curriculum socially relevant?
- Which is more important—breadth or depth of subject matter?
- Should additional time be given to a specific subject?
- Is the program balanced between essential knowledge and special interests?
- What requirements and standards should be established?

Curriculum Sequence

- Should certain topics precede other topics?
- Should a topic be taught chronologically?
- Should a topic be taught from a developmental viewpoint?
- Should a topic be taught inductively or deductively?

Student Access

- What program options are available to students?
- How are students assigned to classes and teachers?
- How do policies regarding promotion, required courses, and the like affect students?
- How is the program of studies responsive to the special needs of the students served?
- What information is provided to students and families about course and program options?
- How are students grouped or tracked into courses?
- What are the enrollments by gender and race or ethnicity in courses?

When a teacher has identified the culminating task or performance and has considered how to assess it, then it is important to work backward to determine what is needed to teach so that students can actually accomplish the culminating task. This is called *backward mapping.* The teacher has to determine what foundational knowledge, deeper understandings, and performance skills students will actually need in order to complete the culminating task.

SEEING THE CURRICULUM WHOLE: THE FUNCTION OF A REAL EDUCATIONAL LEADER

LAUREL N. TANNER
Temple University

The school administrator's task, of course, involves the entire curriculum. Nowhere is the task more beautifully set forth than in Lawrence Cremin's *The Genius of American Education* (1965): "Someone must look at the curriculum whole and raise insistent questions of priority and relationship" (p. 58). No individual, he writes, can or ought to have the sole responsibility for this concern, but it certainly must be the main business of anybody who sees himself or herself a principal, superintendent, or director of curriculum.

Specialists do not look at how the parts must relate to the whole. Principals must have a larger vision and see the entire curriculum. Because we lack such a vision, schools are wrestling with some intractable problems that might have been avoided. In the famous curriculum reform movement of the 1960s, priority was given to science, mathematics, and modern foreign languages because these subjects were deemed essential for our national defense. Daniel Tanner and I found, as a result of the reforms that were instituted, that the schools were left with problems stemming from misguided curriculum priorities, curriculum imbalance, and failure to articulate the curriculum with the nature of the learner (Tanner & Tanner, 1995).

Two of our most difficult problems—discipline and dropping out—are due in no small way to the failure to look at the curriculum whole. For example, some school districts that reduced their offerings in the studio and industrial arts experienced an increased dropout rate (Tanner, 1997). The loss to individual students was tremendous. Unable to develop in the one area in which they excelled, they decided to leave school.

The literature is filled with references to the "strong" educational leader. The principal's strength derives from professional knowledge and experience in working out problems by using theoretical principles. It is in no sense an arbitrary thing. Three constructs provide strength for a principal to see the curriculum as an entirety.

THE SCHOOL'S PHILOSOPHY

First, the curriculum and how it is taught must be governed by a statement of philosophy and goals—a theory of what the school hopes to achieve. Tyler (1949) suggests that a school have 7 to 15 broad educational goals. Without a goals statement, a school is susceptible to whatever schemes are fashionable at a given time and the whims of individual faculty members.

Hoy and Tarter (2007) provide an interesting example of a high school principal who denied a member of the English faculty's request to offer an elective in Latin American literature. The department chair had already turned down the request because it was inconsistent with the thrust of the program. The school had a statement of philosophy and goals and tried to make decisions that were consistent with it.

As Cremin (1965) warned, "To refuse to look at curricula in their entirety is to relegate to intraschool policies a series of decisions that ought to call into play the most fundamental philosophical principles" (p. 58). The strong educational leader derives his or her strength from a statement of philosophy and goals developed collaboratively with the faculty. No philosophy, however, should be a barricade against change. "Any person who is open-minded and sensitive to new perceptions, and who has concentration and responsibility in connecting them has, in so far, a philosophic disposition," observed Dewey (1910, p. 380).

(continued)

WHAT A WHOLE CURRICULUM LOOKS LIKE

The second source of strength is knowledge of what the entire curriculum looks like. Such a comprehensive vision is a difficult thing for any one person, because there are so many knowledge categories. It is little wonder that administrators regard the curriculum as specialized and compartmentalized knowledge over and beyond their domain of expertise. But there is a manageable way of looking at the macrocurriculum, in terms of five inclusive functions (Tanner & Tanner, 1995):

1. General education or the common understandings and competencies necessary for responsible citizenship in a free society
2. Specialized education that enables the learner to become a productive earner as well as a lifelong learner
3. Enrichment education—avocational instruction that enriches the life of every individual
4. Exploratory education that stimulates the individual to extend his or her reach into untried realms
5. Special-interest education that provides for intensive learning experiences beyond one's vocational and avocational pursuits

Like the fingers of a hand, these five functions are interdependent. Equipped with a comprehensive view of the curriculum, the administrator can help faculty develop a shared vision and put it into practice as an ongoing operation.

A good leader asks what Cremin (1965) called "insistent questions of priority and relationship" (p. 58). The point is that a good school is always involved in curriculum development and better teaching methods. Interestingly, even top-scoring countries, with which the United States is told to compare itself, are dissatisfied with their practices in teaching science and mathematics and "are investing large sums to change" (Atkin & Black, 1997, p. 28). There is a big difference between the reform movement of the 1960s and the present one: Teachers are involved in working out the curriculum at the classroom level.

PUTTING THE VISION INTO PRACTICE

The third strength is the way the administrator orchestrates the vision of a whole curriculum. How does he or she bring the specializations into relationship? The best answer is an approach pioneered by Tyler (1949). It concerns what happens—or should happen—immediately after a school has firmed up its goals statement. The faculty has already answered Tyler's question, "What educational purposes should the school seek to attain?" (p. v). Tyler shows the way a high school English department might use these broad goals to open up the question, How do we in the English department not just teach literature but also help achieve our school's seven or nine or twelve educational goals? Every teacher has a responsibility to deal with the school's goals—academic, social, personal, and vocational. Attention to the goals is key. The strong leader uses the goals not just to test and screen curriculum proposals but to bring the specializations together.

We have provided a few of the questions that address issues of curriculum congruity, integration, sequencing, and access. These questions and a variety of critical factors must be investigated in the design and development of curriculum and programs. Critical factors include nature and scale of the program, community expectations, resources needed, stakeholders involved, the utilization of time, community and school demographics, incentives for teachers, timeline implementation, program monitoring, and desired learning outcomes. Once a curriculum is developed or a program or model adapted to a school, the work of program improvement has just begun. And it is an ongoing process.

＊ **What are some of the questions that need to be asked regarding Logan Elementary's health curriculum?**

PROGRAM IMPROVEMENT AND EVALUATION

The notion of evaluation is integral to the change process. Too often it is an afterthought and is tacked on to a completed or near-completed program. Genuine program improvement requires that evaluation be built into the curriculum from the beginning. Program improvement may be conducted by those involved in the program itself or by an outside organization such as an accrediting agency. Regardless of the approach used, evaluation is an ongoing part of the improvement process of the school.

CRESST, the UCLA Center for Research on Evaluation, Standards, and Student Testing (cresst.org), proposes six steps for guiding evaluation (see Table 9.1). Two of the six steps include the involvement of key constituencies. Guba and Lincoln (1989), in their book *Fourth Generation Evaluation,* maintain that "the claims, concerns and issues of stakeholders [should] serve as organizational foci (the basis for determining what information is needed)" (p. 50). Therefore, an initial step in any approach to evaluation involves identification of stakeholders.

Fenwick English (Frase, English, & Poston, 1995) developed a curriculum auditing process that is widely used by school districts and is part of an auditing approach sponsored by the American Association of School Administrators. A key concept in curriculum auditing is the alignment of goals and objectives, curriculum content, and testing. The audit determines the degree to which the written, taught, and tested curricula are aligned. The audit provides information for curriculum and instructional planning by validating what currently exists within a school district. The results of an audit are used to improve the quality of the curriculum and instruction and to ultimately improve the quality of learning.

＊ **How might the health curriculum at Logan Elementary School be evaluated?**

UTILIZING TIME

Perhaps the two most important jobs of a school administrator are recruiting and hiring faculty and deciding how time in a school year will be allocated. The length of the school year, day, and class session, as well as their organization, have significant impact on teacher–student and student–student relationships. In recent years, there has been renewed interest in various types of scheduling. Additionally, the notion of looping—teachers moving with students over a 2- or 3-year period—is growing in popularity.

TABLE 9.1   Principles of Sensible Evaluation

STEP	SENSIBLE ACTIONS
Focus the evaluation	Involve significant constituencies Include improvement and accountability concerns Look at long- and short-term targets of change Look at relationships between processes and outcomes based on your theories of action Look for unanticipated side effects
Identify tracking strategies	Use strategies well aligned with school goals Use multiple indicators Build in checks for validity of inferences Build measures on existing information
Manage instrument development and data collection	Consider accountability mandates Match instruments with specific evaluation questions
Score and summarize data	When appropriate, use scoring sessions for staff development Assure valid inferences by choosing appropriate scores
Analyze and interpret information	Involve key constituencies Examine progress over time Consider and refine your theories of action Be alert to unanticipated side effects Corroborate findings by using multiple indicators
Act on findings and continue program monitoring	Use the principles guiding focusing activities to monitor actions based on your findings

Source: Center for Research on Evaluation Standards and Student Testing. (1997). *Sensible evaluation.* Los Angeles, CA: Author. Reprinted with permission.

Year-Round Education

Year-round education (YRE) is not a new idea in the United States or in other nations. The literature on year-round education in the United States first appeared with some degree of regularity in the 1970s. Most of the discussion, unfortunately, focused on the importance of utilizing the school building, rather than on efficiency and effectiveness as has been done more recently. YRE is slowly and steadily increasing and by 2008 nearly 2.5 million schools were on year-round calendars. It is estimated that "by 2012 more than 5 million pupils—about 10 percent of all children enrolled in American public schools—could be going to school year-round" (Johnson, 2010).

YRE involves a reorganization of the school calendar into instructional blocks, with vacations (or special intersessions) distributed throughout the calendar year, rather than concentrated in the summer. Learning opportunities need to be continuous throughout the year. School districts can operate on single-track or multitrack schedules. The most common year-round schedule is the single-track, 45–15 day plan. Students attend school for 45 days, followed by 15 days with no school. This pattern is repeated four times. According to the research literature, the several advantages to year-round education include:

- Increased attendance of teachers and students
- Lower student dropout rates, greater flexibility in instruction, greater retention of learning
- Greater flexibility in teacher planning, student assessment, and curriculum development
- Additional opportunities for remedial and accelerated classes during the intersessions (Ballinger, 1988; Doyle & Finn, 1985; Gee, 1997).

Block Scheduling

Canady and Rettig (1995) estimated that more than 50% of U.S. high schools use some form of block scheduling (flexible modular scheduling). There are numerous formats for block scheduling. Two widely used models include the 4/4 semester plan and the alternative day or A/B schedule. In a 4/4 semester block schedule, each semester students attend four classes a day, completing the course during this time. In the alternative day, or A/B schedule, a course meets every other day for the entire school year. Figure 9.2 depicts a typical A/B block schedule.

A powerful variation of block scheduling is the Copernican Plan (Carroll, 1994). In this scheduling model, class periods are longer so that teachers have fewer students each semester. Students have two 85- to 90-minute classes each day, lunch, and either one or two electives. Classes meet for 90 days and then another class is scheduled. In the Copernican Plan, credit is awarded for mastering course objectives, and students graduate at the end of the semester in which they complete the required number of credits.

There are many reasons secondary schools are experimenting with allocating time differently from seven- or eight-period schedules. Criticisms of these schedules are numerous: Time is lost passing in hallways, hallway time increases discipline problems, students are overwhelmed by having seven or eight teachers each day, teachers are overwhelmed with having 120 to 150 students per day, an impersonal assemblyline atmosphere is created, far too many subjects might be assigned homework for the same evening, and so on.

Monday	Tuesday (even)	Wednesday (odd)	Thursday (even)	Friday (odd)
Period 1 7:27–8:14 **Period 2** 8:20–9:07	**Block 1** 7:27–9:06 Period 1	**Block 2** 7:27–9:06 Period 2	**Block 1** 7:25–9:04 Period 1	**Block 2** 7:25–9:04 Period 2
Period 3 9:13–10:07 **Period 4** 10:13–10:53	**Block 3** 9:13–10:53 Period 3	**Block 4** 9:13–10:53 Period 4	**Block 3** 9:13–10:53 Period 3	**Block 4** 9:13–10:53 Period 4
Lunch Period—A 11:00–11:30 5 **Class Period—B** 11:00–11:49	**Block 3** 11:00–11:30 5 Class Period—B 11:00–11:49	**Block 3** 11:00–11:30 5 Class Period—B 11:00–11:49	**Block 3** 11:00–11:30 5 Class Period—B 11:00–11:49	**Block 3** 11:00–11:30 5 Class Period—B 11:00–11:49

12-Minute Overlap

Monday	Tuesday	Wednesday	Thursday	Friday
Class Period—A 11:37–12:26 5 **Lunch Period—B** 11:56–12:26	Class Period—A 11:37–12:26 5 Lunch Period—B 11:56–12:26	Class Period—A 11:37–12:26 5 Lunch Period—B 11:56–12:26	Class Period—A 11:37–12:26 5 Lunch Period—B 11:56–12:26	Class Period—A 11:37–12:26 5 Lunch Period—B 11:56–12:26
Period 6 12:33–1:20 **Period 7** 1:26–2:12	**Block 4** 12:33–2:12 Period 6	**Block 4** 12:33–2:12 Period 7	**Block 4** 12:33–2:12 Period 6	**Block 4** 12:33–2:12 Period 7
After School	**After School**	**After School**	**After School**	**After School**

FIGURE 9.2   Example of a Block Schedule

In a study of 820 high schools, Glickman (1998) found that activity-learning methods, which are more likely to be found in schools with longer class periods, led to higher achievement. Additionally, fewer class changes resulted in fewer discipline problems and a less stressful school setting. The research data describe several advantages to block scheduling:

- Reduction in disciplinary referrals and suspensions (Carroll, 1994; Einedar & Bishop, 1997; Glickman, 1998; Meadows, 1995; Reid, 1995)
- Positive effects on school climate (Carroll, 1994; Glickman, 1998; Reid, 1995)
- Lower dropout rates (Carroll, 1994; Hottenstein & Malatesta, 1993; Reid, 1995)
- Improved student attendance (Cameron, 1995; King, Clements, Enns, Lockerbie, & Warren, 1975; Schoenstein, 1995)

- Improved student attitudes (Carroll, 1994; Einedar & Bishop, 1997; Hottenstein & Malatesta, 1993; Meadows, 1995; Seinost, 2009)
- Improved teacher attitudes (Carroll, 1994)

Varying the structure of the school day and the school year can provide numerous academic benefits. In a study that focused on block scheduling and its effect on math instruction, Kramer (1997) noted that transitioning to block schedules can lead to achievement gain given sufficient staff development, planning time, and curriculum modification. It is evident that when transitioning to a block schedule, the major role of the school administrator is to provide faculty with adequate support.

Looping

Perhaps one of the most important strategies for affording students more contact time with the same teacher, and additional opportunities for group learning, can be met through the concept of looping. *Looping,* or multiyear interactions between cohorts of students and a single teacher, is common practice in many countries. In Spain, for example, students in kindergarten and grades 1 and 2 have the same teacher for all 3 years. Beginning in grade 3, the student cohort has a different teacher for the next 3 years (grades 3–5). Finally, this student cohort has another new teacher for grades 6, 7, and 8. Similarly, in Mexico, the heterogeneous grouping of students into cohorts facilitates students' passage through the curriculum. These *groupos escolares* remain together for 3 years. A growing body of research supports the notion that long-term relationships with teachers and multiyear relationships with peers can increase student learning (Cordeiro, 1990; Liu, 1997; Baran, 2011).

Time on Task

According to Stallings (1980), efficient allocation of time spent on a task can increase student achievement. The research literature has identified three levels of time: allocated time, engaged time, and academic learning time. *Allocated time* is the amount of time that is actually assigned for a class. *Engaged time* is the amount of allocated time in which the student is actively engaged in the learning activity. *Academic learning time* is a refinement of engaged time and reflects the quality of the learning (e.g., high, moderate, or low degree of success; appropriateness of the instructional materials).

Research indicates that the allocation of time, including models that examine the school year, day, multiple years, and time in the classroom, is an important approach that enhances learning opportunities (Cangelosi, 2007).

ASSESSING STUDENT PROGRESS

Considerable discussion and debate centers around the best ways to assess student progress. Some of the most common forms of student assessment include standardized achievement testing (norm-referenced tests), criterion-referenced testing, and performance or alternative assessment.

Standardized tests, which are designed to compare the performance of students to the performance of a normative group, inspire much debate (Kean, 1986; Neill, 1997). The National Forum on Assessment, which included a group of 80 education and civil rights organizations, concluded that multiple-choice testing (e.g., true or false, selecting one item among several) should be only a small part of any assessment program (Marzano & Kendall, 1997; Popham, 2010). Students in the United States regularly take standardized tests. In addition, U.S. students are compared with students in other countries through tests such as PISA (Program for International Student Assessment) taken by 15-year-old students every 3 years in reading, math, and science, and the TIMSS (Trends in International Mathematics and Science Study) assessment of educational progress test taken by 4th- and 8th-grade students every 3 years. The main standardized test taken by U.S. students for state comparison is NAEP (National Assessment of Education Progress). NAEP assessments are conducted periodically in mathematics, reading, science, writing, the arts, civics, economics, geography, and U.S. history. NAEP results are based on representative samples of students at grades 4, 8, and 12 for the main assessments, or samples of students at ages 9, 13, or 17 years for long-term trend assessment.

Criterion-referenced tests are meant to ascertain a learner's status with respect to a learning task. They are used to see if a student has mastered specific material. Most tests and quizzes written by steachers are criterion-referenced tests.

Performance assessment is a relatively new method that provides more appropriate indicators of student learning than do multiple-choice tests. Performance assessments are sometimes called *alternative assessments* and can assume many forms. Herman, Aschbacher, and Winters (1992) define alternative assessments as measures with common characteristics. Such assessments (a) ask students to perform, create, or produce; (b) tap higher-level thinking and problem-solving skills; (c) use tasks that represent meaningful instructional activities; (d) involve scoring; and (e) require new instructional and assessment roles for teachers.

Some educators maintain that assessments must be authentic. Wiggins and McTighe (2011) define authenticity as the extent to which a test, performance, or product in an assessment bears a relationship to a real-world referent.

Portfolios and Exhibitions

A portfolio is a collection of individual students' work that results from participation in a developmental process. Decisions related to what is collected depend on the purpose of the portfolio—assessment, culmination, display, or future study, to name a few. Through reflection, students can become increasingly aware of themselves as learners. Portfolios tend to focus attention on what students are learning, how well they are learning it, how well they demonstrate learning, and how well they reflect on this work.

Except in arts education, portfolios and other types of performance assessments are a relatively recent phenomenon. Some teachers specify what goes into a portfolio, whereas others allow the student to select what will be included. This work should exhibit to the student, teacher, and others the student's progress and achievement in a particular area. A portfolio should show the various stages through which a project has passed. For example, a portfolio could contain a series of drafts of a paper. Or it might contain video clips from different time periods showing how a dance performance has improved as the student practiced.

An exhibition is an authentic assessment activity by which students demonstrate or perform what they have learned. An exhibition might be a project, an essay, an oral or written report or performance, a portfolio, or piece of artwork. Effective exhibitions define essential learning and focus the curriculum, teacher, and students. Exhibitions involve real audiences viewing student work and give students and teachers frequent opportunities to gauge strengths and weaknesses and reflect on what is working (and not working) in the classroom. The result is that assessment and evaluation become learning opportunities that provide students and teachers with dynamic measures of progress toward their goals.

ASSESSING STUDENT PERFORMANCE

GRANT WIGGINS
President and Director for the Center on Learning Assessment
and School Structure (CLASS)

Assessment should be educative, not merely a quick audit of performance as is now too often the case. Students and teachers need useful and timely feedback, not arcane item analysis provided in the summer when school is out. Educative assessment thus requires an approach and schedule very different from what is typically found in classroom, district, and state testing.

Assessment should be educative in two senses: It should teach students (and teachers) what kinds of performance tasks and standards are most valued. It should reflect situations in the wider world—real problems, real situations, real audiences, and real purposes. Assessment should also provide timely, ongoing, user-friendly feedback to make possible the slow but steady mastery of such tasks (as opposed to one-shot testing and ranking).

The use of such feedback—the student's ability to self-adjust—should become increasingly central to what and how we assess. As is true of Little League, Nintendo games, karate, or cooking, the assessment system should provide ongoing feedback using standards and measures of progress over time. It should also provide opportunities to use the feedback as part of what we assess—the assessment of self-adjustment.

Four maxims about reform follow from this idea of educative assessment:

1. *Assessment must be grounded in authentic tasks if it is to inform and improve performance.* To improve and not just audit student performance, we need assessment based on what adults actually do in the world. Although tests and quizzes have a place in rounding out the performance picture, they must be made secondary to more "authentic" tasks.

An assessment is authentic if it:
a. replicates or simulates the ways in which a person's knowledge and abilities are "tested" in real-world situations;

(continued)

b. requires the student to use knowledge and skills wisely and effectively to solve complex, multistep problems (where the solution involves more than just following a set routine or procedure or "plugging in" knowledge);

c. asks the student to "do" the subject—to *do* science or history, not just recite or replicate through demonstration what was taught or is already known;

d. replicates the *contexts* in which adults are "tested" in the workplace, in civic, and in personal life. By "context," we mean the situations, purposes, audiences, constraints, and the "messiness and murkiness" so common to life's challenges—but so typically absent from neat-and-clean school tests;

e. tests the student's ability to use a repertoire of knowledge and skill to solve complex, multifaceted performance challenges. By contrast, most test items are "plug-in" questions—similar to the sideline drills in athletics (as opposed to the actual game, which requires integrated use of all the drills). While there is, of course, a place for drill tests, *performance is always more than the sum of the drills;* and

f. allows for *appropriate* opportunities to rehearse, practice, consult resources, get feedback on and refine performances and products.

Only by ensuring that the assessment system *models* genuine performance challenges, requirements, and feedback will student performance and teacher instruction be improved over time. This model makes teaching more appropriately like coaching athletic, artistic, and intellectual performances.

2. *Assessment must do more than audit performance. It must be designed to*

improve performance. This principle exposes the weakness of one-shot typical tests. Students, teachers, and administrators need timely, ongoing, user-friendly feedback about the key performance challenges of learning and adult performance. As in athletics and the arts, students need clear, worthy, and recurring tasks that can be slowly mastered over time.

By contrast, all current testing typically "audits" student performance once. Tests use a small number of relatively simplistic indirect "items" that can be easily and quickly scored. A more direct assessment of performance would look at whether students can use knowledge in real-world ways and judge whether they can improve over time on known tasks and standards.

Consider an analogy with athletics. Imagine if a basketball season consisted of one game, played on the last day of the year, in which the players did not know the plays they would be asked to make. Imagine further that they would not know if their shots went in the basket until weeks later. Imagine further that if instead of playing the game of basketball, teams of measurement experts each year invented an arcane series of drills to test with—valid to measurement experts, but unconnected to basketball playing in the minds of players and coaches. Finally, imagine a scoring system fully understandable only to the assessors and not the players and coaches. Who would improve at the game under these conditions? Yet state testing consistently provides feedback that cannot easily be deciphered or used on tasks that do not mirror real performance, where the test is unknown until test day, and where the feedback comes at the end of the school year, when it cannot be used to improve the performance of the student or the cohort.

3. *Assessment must be credible and open if genuine reform is to occur.* Accountability occurs only when adults not only are *responsive* to results but also feel *responsible* for them. Genuine accountability thus requires credible assessment tasks. As in athletics and the arts, where teachers typically work overtime to enable students to meet high standards, that sense of responsibility is attributable to the fact that (1) the standards and tasks are credible and worthy and (2) the assessment system (and the results generated) are open and defensible as a system. No coach complains that the "test" of the game or recital is somehow unfair or unknown; there are many opportunities to improve performance over time. A system of assessment must meet the test of local credibility if we are to get beyond local excuses for poor performance.

Assessment must not rely solely on secret test items and performance standards and one-shot tests. Although simplistic test items (kept secure until test day) are relatively inexpensive to use and easy to measure, implementing them as standard policy is counterproductive to student, teacher, and school improvement. How can anyone improve his or her performance if what specifically is going to be tested is kept secret?

4. *An effective assessment plan must build local high-quality assessment capacity.* An assessment system should be deliberately designed to improve the quality of local tests, standards, grading, and reporting.

Consider another analogy. The district's or state's goal should not be that of a narrow-minded doctor who merely forces patients to have an annual physical exam based on a handful of simple tests. Rather, the physician's goal should be to promote daily healthfulness.

As things now stand, however, the state "doctor" seems interested only in seeing whether schools "pass the physical."

The unintended but powerful effect of the current system causes the school "patient" to fixate on the simple tasks of the physical exam rather than on attaining daily standards of health and fitness. As a result, few teachers understand how to test for genuine intellectual "health" and "fitness." Fewer still see that their own testing need not mimic the *form* of state testing. Teachers do not need to "teach to the (simplistic) test" for their students to do well on it. Teachers become (wrongly) convinced that the only way to get good test results is to teach to and practice the checkup, ignoring the fact that a multiple-choice test is based on a reverse logic: If you are "healthy" and meet high standards day in and day out, your health will show on the checkup.

The goal of improving local intellectual "fitness" thus requires a system that models good assessment practice as it audits local fitness, so that local assessment improves. Tests teach teachers and students what we value, regardless of an intent merely to measure. The district (and the state) should provide models of "health" (good performance) and "physical fitness standards" (exemplary tests) in its assessment system. And incentives should be provided to ensure higher-quality local assessment, grounded in clear policies about design and use.

Note: A thorough discussion of these points can be found in Wiggins, G. (1998). *Educative assessment: Designing assessment to inform and improve student performance.* San Francisco, CA: Jossey-Bass.

Reporting Student Progress

Of the many formats used for reporting student progress, letter grades (A, B, C, D, F) are the most common. Numbers (percent correct), symbols (S = Satisfactory, N = Needs Improvement, U = Unsatisfactory), or descriptors (Emerging, Developing, Maturing) are sometimes used at the elementary level.

Another format is a dual-marking system. The student gets two marks in a subject—one for the student's level of achievement and the other perhaps the student's achievement in relation to personal ability (student improvement).

Pass–Fail, or Pass–No Pass, is another option for reporting student progress. One advantage to this option is that students will be more likely to explore new areas of knowledge if they know they will not receive a poor grade. A disadvantage, some educators argue, is that students will do the minimum to receive a "pass," rather than being motivated to do better by receiving a letter grade.

Some schools report success with narrative reports. A letter grade may or may not be included. This narrative is a description of the student's progress in a particular subject area and may be developed from a listing of characteristics related to the student's progress. Computer programs are often used to print out selected comments.

Presenting Student Outcomes to the Community

Who are stakeholders in the assessment process? Parents, students, teachers, administrators, state officials, and community members—all of whom are stakeholders—have potentially differing expectations of program and student assessment.

Administrators must also ask what kinds of information each stakeholder needs and how that information will be used. The answers to these questions will help administrators communicate more effectively and efficiently with each stakeholder.

Stiggins (1994) and Stiggins and Chappuis (2011) provide a helpful way to evaluate the users and uses of assessment results (Table 9.2). Stiggins lists the various stakeholders, the key questions that need to be answered, and the information needed to answer those questions. Staff members should be informed first and oriented to the results of testing programs. Then the community should be informed through the appropriate means. Special meetings should be held to discuss and explain test results.

There has been a national trend to move toward high-stakes student assessment, attaching real consequences to low performance. Students who do not perform well on assessment tests are required to go to summer school, are retained, or are awarded less-than-standard high school diplomas. Research has not provided evidence that such consequences improve student performance. As a result, a number of districts are looking at smaller class sizes, enriched and more rigorous curriculum, focused attention on areas of weakness, and enrichment programs. Some states want to hold principals and teachers accountable by tying their evaluations and salaries to assessments of student progress.

Some argue against high-stakes assessment, suggesting that it works best when it is a central part of teaching, influencing the way we think about curriculum, teaching, and learning. Assessment is to "educate and improve" performance, not merely to audit it. Assessment establishes clear linkage between state and district standards and local testing and grading of students' work. Wiggins and McTighe

TABLE 9.2   USERS AND USES OF ASSESSMENT RESULTS

USERS	KEY QUESTION(S) TO BE ANSWERED	INFORMATION NEEDED
CLASSROOM LEVEL		
Student	Am I meeting the teacher's standards? What help do I need to succeed? Are the results worth my investment of energy?	Continuous information about individualized student attainment of specific instructional requirements
Teacher	Which students need what help? Who among my students should work together? What grade should appear in the report card? Did my teaching strategies work? How do I become a better teacher?	Continuous information about individual student attainment of specific program requirements Continuous assessment of group performance
Parent	Is my child succeeding in school? What does my child need to succeed? Is my child's teacher(s) doing the job? Is this district doing the job?	Continuous feedback on individual students' mastery of required material
INSTRUCTIONAL SUPPORT LEVEL		
Principal/vice principal	Is instruction in particular areas producing results? Is this teacher effective? What kinds of professional development will help? How shall we spend building resources to be effective?	Periodic assessment of group achievement
Lead teacher (mentor, support teacher, deptartment chair)	What does this teacher need to do the job?	Periodic assessment of group achievement
Counselor/ psychologist	Who needs (can have access to) special support services such as remedial programs? What student should be assigned to which teachers to optimize results?	Periodic assessment of individual achievement
Curriculum director	Is our program of instruction effective?	Periodic assessment of group achievement

(continued)

USERS	KEY QUESTION(S) TO BE ANSWERED	INFORMATION NEEDED
POLICY LEVEL		
Superintendent	Are programs producing student learning?	Periodic assessment of group achievement of district curriculum
	Is the building principal producing results?	
	Which programs need/deserve more resources?	
School board	Are students in the district learning?	Periodic assessment of group achievement
	Is the superintendent producing results?	
State department of education	Are programs across the state producing results?	Periodic assessment of group achievement of state curriculum
Citizen/legislator (state or national)	Are students in our schools achieving in ways that will allow them to be effective citizens?	Periodic assessment of group achievement of valued achievement targets

Source: Stiggins, R. J. (1994). *Student-centered classroom assessment.* Columbus, OH: Merrill. A teacher's handbook distributed by the Assessment Training Institute, 50 SW Second Ave., Suite 300, Portland, OR 97204.

(1998; 2011) tell us that assessment is central to instruction; that authentic tasks anchor assessment, which anchors teaching; and that performance improvement is locally achieved.

A partial list of Wiggins and McTighe's (2011) strategies for the future includes:

- Turn tests into prompts and prompts into performance tasks;
- Change typical contextual constraints or limits on resources available during a test;
- Redefine passing to ensure that a grade is standard based;
- Get colleagues to "own" the problem of quality;
- Go for scoring consistency;
- Establish a set of R & D task forces;
- Make self-assessment and self-adjustment more central to the job; and
- Provide opportunities, incentives, and criteria that allow each teacher to engage in more careful research into what constitutes effective practice. (pp. 327–329)

School districts devise plans for conducting assessments to provide all stakeholders understandable and accurate information about student achievement.

CONCLUSION

The curriculum provides a statement of what knowledge, skills, and moral principles students will be expected to acquire during their time in school. Program development and delivery "is a decision-making process—constantly balancing the emerging and ever-changing needs of students, society, and the content to be taught. As research adds to the knowledge base, as political systems change, as trends in society change, as technology advances, as we learn more about learning, and as we gain greater insight into the functioning of the human brain, so too must the curriculum change" (Costa, 1997, p. 49).

It is important to realize that one's perspective will determine how the results of program and student assessment will be perceived. Spring (1998) states:

> A newspaper headline reads "Lower Test Scores in City Schools." A religious-right group might give a spin that "lower scores exemplify the lack of instruction in traditional moral values." Another group might spin an interpretation that "lower scores are the result of low academic standards." Or another interested party might respond, "Poor-quality instruction is causing test scores to decline." A spokesperson for a teacher union might put the following spin on the story: "Low teacher salaries make it impossible to keep good teachers, causing test scores to fall." And a union spokesperson might say "inadequate school funding causes a decline in test scores." A spokesperson for a group representing a cultural minority might provide the following spin: "Culturally biased curriculum causes low test scores. This means that it is very important that the school division take control by characterizing the causes for the scores and actions to be taken in the future regarding curricular and instructional changes. Otherwise they become the fuel for future ideological battles and limited improvement in student performance. (p. 24)

MyEdLeadershipLab™

Go to Topic 5: *Curriculum Planning, Assessment, and Accountability* in the MyEdLeadershipLab™ site (www.MyEdLeadershipLab.com) for *Educational Leadership: A Bridge to Improved Practice*, Fifth Edition, where you can:

- Find learning outcomes for *Curriculum Planning, Assessment, and Accountability* along with the national standards that connect to these outcomes.
- Complete Assignments and Activities that can help you more deeply understand the chapter content.
- Apply and practice your understanding of the core skills identified in the chapter with the Building Leadership Skills unit.
- Prepare yourself for professional certification with a Practice for Certification quiz.

PORTFOLIO ARTIFACTS

- What does your educational leadership platform say about teaching and learning? Developing curriculum? The allocation of time in schools? Developing assessments?

- Analyze and critique a variety of different secondary school schedules. What are the strengths and weakness of each? What are the implications for teachers in each of these schedules?

- Explore who is involved in scheduling classes in a school. Meet with the people involved and investigate what decision rules they use in creating the schedule.

- Participate on a curriculum development or auditing team at the state or local level.

- Examine the state and national test data available for your school. What trends do you see over time?

- Disaggregate testing data for a particular subject (e.g., mathematics) for a school. Disaggregate the data by grade level, gender, native language, and so forth.

- Implement a curriculum change at your school that has an impact on children from more than one classroom.

- Select a teaching approach that you know little about (e.g., PBL, cooperative learning), visit Web sites and learn about the approach, then visit and observe in a school using that approach.

- Visit the Edutopia (http://www.edutopia.org) Web site and watch several of the videos on assessment. What implications might what you have heard have for your platform?

KEY TERMS

- Adequate yearly progress (AYP)
- Apprenticeship learning
- Authentic instruction
- Backward instructional design; backward mapping
- Constructivism
- Cooperative learning
- Curriculum alignment
- Curriculum audit
- Curriculum maps

- Differentiated instruction
- Hidden curriculum
- Learning transfer
- Looping
- Multiple intelligence theory
- National standards
- NAEP
- Opportunity to Learn (OTL) standards
- Performance assessment

- PISA
- Portfolios
- Problem-based learning (PBL)/project-based learning (PBL)
- Thematic instruction
- TIMMS
- Triarchic theory
- Zone of proximal development

SUGGESTED READINGS

Chappuis, S. J., Stiggins, R. J., Arter, J. A., & Chappuis, J. (2009). *Assessment for learning: An action guide for school leaders* (2nd ed.). Boston, MA: Allyn and Bacon.

Friedman, T. L. (2006). *The world is flat* (expanded edition). New York, NY: Farrar, Straus & Giroux.

Glatthorn, A. (2008). *The principal as curriculum leader: Shaping what is taught and tested.* Thousand Oaks, CA: Corwin Press.

Popham, W. J. (2010). *Everything school leaders need to know about assessment.* Thousand Oaks, CA: Corwin Press.

Schmoker, M (2011). *Focus: Elevating the essentials to radically improve student learning.* Alexandria, VA: Association for Supervision and Curriculum Development.

Wiggins, G., & McTighe, J. (2011). *The understanding by design guide to creating high-quality unit.* Alexandria, VA: Association for Supervision and Curriculum Development.

Zhao, Y. (2009). *Catching up or leading the way. American education in the age of globalization.* Alexandria, VA: Association for Supervision and Curriculum Development.

A JALAPEÑO IN A CANDY JAR: ADDRESSING DIVERSITY

PAULA A. CORDEIRO
University of San Diego

One of the greatest challenges facing schools today is the diversity of the children at our doorsteps. The demographics of the United States are shifting in important ways. American families are rapidly becoming more diverse—the definition of what is meant by "family" is being reconceptualized. Increasing numbers of single-parent families, more families with stepchildren, more fathers raising children alone, more children raised by parents of the same sex, and more mothers in the labor force are all factors. The cumulative effect of a significant influx of immigrants in the last 30 years promises to be both profound and interesting. Many of our recent immigrants represent cultural groups that have never immigrated to the United States before in significant numbers. These immigrants fall into three categories: refugees, legal immigrants, and undocumented immigrants. In absolute numbers, this migration is among the largest in U.S. history.

Most teachers and administrators have not been trained to deal with the unique needs these children bring to schoolhouse doors. The structure of local governments in many cities and towns do not lend themselves easily to linking services that might be available to other community members and schoolchildren. Additionally, racism rises to the surface as jobs are lost and financial constraints on local governments increase.

LEARNING OBJECTIVES

- To collaboratively develop a plan incorporating knowledge from the research on diversity in education
- To develop specific strategies for the implementation programming that is inclusive
- To examine personal beliefs and assumptions about language and cultural issues

GUIDING QUESTIONS

1. Reflect on the ways in which your ethnic and racial background, gender, religion, ability or disability, and sexuality affect your beliefs. Share with your team some of your basic beliefs. How have they changed over time? Why?

2. What should a school administrator know about issues related to diversity? Do you know these things? If so, how did you learn them? If not, how might you learn them?

3. What should a teacher know about cultural diversity? If a teacher has had little training in this area, what are the best ways for him or her to learn more?

4. What roles, if any, should parents, families, school boards, and community members play in working with schools? In the case of Seaview School District, and Silvermine Middle School in particular (see the following section), how might they be actively involved in multicultural educational programming?

5. How might Banks's (1999) (see Chapter 8) "Approaches to Multicultural Curriculum Model" be applied to this situation?

6. Chapters 6, 8, 9, 10, and 11 discuss legal and ethical considerations, learning, learning transfer, student services, diversity, bullying, and staff development. What implications do these readings have for the development of your team's plan?

SEAVIEW SCHOOL DISTRICT

Seaview School District is adjacent to a large city in the northeastern part of the United States. Seaview has approximately 2,970 students. Until the mid-1990s, the demographics of the district were relatively stable. Seaview had been a predominantly white, middle-class community. However, since that time the African-American and Hispanic (Puerto Rican and Mexican-American) populations have steadily increased. Additionally, two local organizations have sponsored Laotian and Vietnamese immigrants. One of these groups also has plans in the near future to sponsor Hmong immigrants.

SILVERMINE MIDDLE SCHOOL

Silvermine Middle School has approximately 520 students and 30 certified staff members. Currently, there are no bilingual programs, but as the Spanish-speaking population increases steadily, the assistant superintendent has begun discussing the need to consider some type of bilingual (Spanish/English) program. The district employs two full-time ESL teachers and six aides. One ESL teacher covers the middle and high schools, and the other teacher works in three elementary schools that have the highest proportions of non–native English-speaking students. Each of the aides works in a different elementary school "tutoring" students and helping those elementary teachers who have non–native English-speaking children in their classes.

All Silvermine staff members (certified and noncertified) are White. Twenty-seven percent of the students are currently receiving free or reduced-priced meals; this percentage has doubled in the last 10 years.

Silvermine offers the typical content areas found in a middle school. The staff members and students are especially pleased with their technology education program. The school has a strong library information center as well as a computer lab. It does not offer any language classes except English and ESL.

THE PROBLEM

You are the new principal of Silvermine Middle School. One day last fall after your first 2 weeks on the job, a serious racial incident occurred on school grounds. The incident involved students from your school and from another middle school in a nearby city. Several students had black eyes and were badly bruised from having been hit with baseball bats. These students required medical attention. After a complete investigation, which included community groups, 11 students from the two schools were suspended. Two parents claimed that their children were unfairly punished. They argued that there was a lack of evidence to prove that their children were involved and that suspension was too severe a punishment.

During the investigation you discovered that numerous racial, ethnic, and religious incidents have occurred over the last 5 years. Additionally, you have heard that there has been a history of occurrences of bullying. A series of minor incidents have taken place throughout your first year. After exploring the curriculum and talking with your assistant principal and staff members during the school year, you have seen little evidence that issues of diversity are being addressed. Additionally, you have found that more than half your staff and your assistant principal do not feel that these incidents were bias-related incidents. They believe them to be "typical problems encountered by adolescents."

Several African-American and Spanish-speaking families have complained to you and the central office staff members, both formally and informally, that some teachers at Silvermine are treating their children unfairly. In your observations this year, you have seen some evidence of such discrimination as well. Also, at the last school board meeting, several African-American parents called these issues to the attention of the board. The school board promised to investigate and report back to the parents.

More than 60% of the teachers have been at Silvermine for more than 17 years. You believe that many of these staff members are dissatisfied with the "different" kinds of children the district has now, as compared with 15 years ago. Although most staff members have had little experience working with children from non–native English-speaking backgrounds or with children representing racial and ethnic groups other than White, several faculty members do have teaching experiences with LEP students and students from culturally diverse backgrounds. Mrs. Sasse recently told you a story of a Hispanic student who confided in her that at Silvermine she felt "like a jalapeño in a candy jar." She felt the jar was filled with beautiful jelly beans and she was this odd-looking jalapeño amongst the brightly colored beans.

As a result of the information collected during the investigation of the fight as well as through exploring the curriculum, you are keenly aware that Silvermine Middle School cannot continue to be reactive in its approach to dealing with racial, cultural, and religious incidents. Meanwhile, the superintendent has sent a memo to all administrators in the district (see the following memorandum).

Memorandum

June 2

To: All Principals, Assistant Principals, and Instructional Leaders
From: Valerie Blandy, Superintendent
Re: Cultural Diversity in Seaview

As you may be aware, the population of Seaview school district is rapidly changing. Additionally, we are seeing an increase in serious confrontations among students. There is increasing evidence of the inability of all of us to understand the nature of the new, diverse population of students in our schools.

These changes make it imperative that schools at all levels begin addressing issues of cultural diversity. Diversity is not solely a racial issue. Our focus is to ensure we are inclusive of all groups that experience prejudice and discrimination in our society. The purpose is to reduce discrimination against them and to provide equal educational opportunities for all. To meet this goal, the district will:

- Nurture lifelong respect and compassion in students for themselves and other human beings regardless of race, ethnic origin, gender, social class, disability, religion, and sexual orientation.
- Remain steadfast in guaranteeing equal opportunity for high-quality education for all students, and not unlawfully discriminate.
- Endeavor to secure equal opportunities for all students.

Inclusiveness is a major concern, and we encourage all schools to begin to address this issue through curriculum and staff development. By beginning the process now, we can eliminate problems at a later date.

Each school is to develop a 3-year plan to address these issues starting in the following school year. I will be contacting each school in the next few weeks to set up a meeting in which you will present an outline of your plan.

YOUR CHALLENGE

Today is June 3, and the superintendent has scheduled a meeting with you at 10 A.M. on June 29. You have been working with a team of staff members on the plan requested by the superintendent. She has asked you to present a draft outline of the written plan at that meeting. She and the assistant superintendent would like to familiarize themselves with what your team is proposing for your school so that they can marshal district resources.

Seaview School District

SCHOOL	GRADE	ENROLLMENT	SCHOOL	GRADE	ENROLLMENT
Unity Elementary	K–5	380	Seaview Middle School	6–8	468
Hope Elementary	K–5	438	Silvermine Middle School	6–8	522
Praxis Elementary	K–5	291	Seaview High School	9–12	870

Silvermine Middle School

TOTAL CERTIFIED STAFF MEMBERS	25	TOTAL NONCERTIFIED STAFF MEMBERS	14
Regular classroom teachers	20	Instructional	4
Special-program teachers	2	Noninstructional	10
Administration	2		
Pupil personnel services	1	Average class size	26

Silvermine Middle School

	SCHOOL ENROLLMENT		
		PERCENTAGES	
	NUMBERS	NOW	IN 3 YEARS (APPROX.)
Total	522		
Race/ethnicity			
Asian American	34	7	10
African American	62	11	15
Hispanic	60	12	20
Native American	5	1	1
White	361	69	51

PRODUCT SPECIFICATIONS

Prepare an action plan that reflects your solution to the superintendent's request for Silvermine Middle School. Your plan should include the following sections:

1. *A definition of the problem* as you view it at Silvermine. If your team identifies more than one problem, please prioritize what you choose to address.
2. *A 3-year draft plan* for addressing the important components of the problem. The plan should include sample activities, the sequence in which you intend to proceed with them, and a rationale for the selection and sequence.
3. Your *strategy* for gaining the support of faculty members, staff members, students, and families. It should include how you will overcome the potential obstacles you will face in implementing the plan.

(Please refer to appropriate chapters in this book as a resource.)

Four Silvermine Middle School Staff Members

Joi Spencer has been teaching social studies at Silvermine for 17 years, and she currently serves as a team leader. Before working at Silvermine, Kathy taught for 5 years at an International American School in Spain. Kathy usually spends her summer vacations in Spanish-speaking countries (Mexico, Spain, Guatemala). She has a keen interest in Latino cultures and is well respected by many of the Spanish-speaking families.

Scott Newkirk is in his 8th year of teaching English. Before coming to Silvermine, he taught in New York City for 10 years. Scott has spoken with the principal several times about his concerns with the LEP students. He believes that he cannot adequately meet their language needs because the ESL teacher has to cover both the middle school and high school, and many students have only one class of ESL each day.

Helen Sasse has been teaching ESL at Silvermine and Seaview High School for the last 4 years. Before that time she taught English three-quarter time and ESL one-quarter time at Silvermine. Helen has a master's degree in teaching English as a second language (TESOL). Last summer she attended her third special weeklong workshop, which focused on LEP students from specific language backgrounds.

Lonnie Rowell is a guidance counselor who has been at Silvermine for 11 years. Lonnie has been particularly adept in working with students involved in some of the racial and ethnic incidents in the last few years. He is married to a woman who is African American and has strong ties with the black community.

PART III

OPERATIONAL SUPPORT FOR EFFECTIVE TEACHING AND LEARNING

CHAPTER 10

STUDENT SUPPORT SERVICES

MyEdLeadershipLab™

Visit the MyEdLeadershipLab™ site for *Educational Leadership: A Bridge to Improved Practice*, Fifth Edition to enhance your understanding of chapter concepts. You'll have the opportunity to practice your skills through video- and case-based Assignments and Activities as well as Building Leadership Skills units, and to prepare for your certification exam with Practice for Certification quizzes.

OAK GROVE MIDDLE SCHOOL

Special Education

Oak Grove Middle School currently houses 1,134 students in grades 6 through 8. Oak Grove's staff is comprised of 3 administrators, 38 classroom teachers, 3 guidance counselors, 2 gifted and 2 special education resource teachers, and 1 computer teacher, in addition to other staff members. The teachers in the school feel pushed to the limit with issues such as large class loads, discipline problems, attendance issues, student apathy, an increase in the special education population, inclusion, and accountability. The teachers are being asked to do more and more, when in reality, the teachers have extended all their resources and are having great difficulty dealing with existing responsibilities. The general feeling is that they have been "pushed over the edge."

You, as principal of this school, are very proud of the individualized education plan (IEP) process and inclusion model used in this school. Your assistant principal (AP) typically chairs these IEP meetings, but you are sitting in because the AP is absent and you feel it to be a good opportunity to get a firsthand sense of how the process is working. The first student to be discussed at today's IEP meeting is Natasha, who has a recent history of behavior problems. Natasha was found eligible for special education services in the 4th grade under the category of learning disabled (LD) while attending Calcutta Elementary School. She was referred for a re-evaluation in the 6th grade, and her category was changed from LD to emotional disturbance (ED). This change in category was made because of escalated incidents of verbal and physical aggression. During the 6th grade, Natasha was suspended seven times for a total of 12 days of absences.

Natasha's suspensions were for spitting in the teacher's face, hitting and kicking other students, running out of the classroom without permission, and disrupting class.

Natasha, a black female, receives instruction in a special education resource class for reading/language arts. Instruction for science, math, health, and social studies are provided in an inclusion classroom. She also receives speech/language therapy twice a week for 30 minutes. Natasha is performing well below grade level and is receiving failing grades. She is experiencing difficulty following directions and acquiring basic skills. She frequently refuses to attempt class assignments even though her class work is at her current achievement level. Her distractibility, impulsiveness, and short attention span have adversely affected her academic achievement. Natasha has been diagnosed with attention-deficit/hyperactivity disorder (ADHD), bipolar disorder, and oppositional defiant disorder. Natasha is currently taking the following medications: Zoloft, Wellbutrin, and Prozac.

The IEP meeting involving the annual review of Natasha's educational program is barely under way when Natasha's mother starts yelling at you. She calls her daughter's classroom teacher and the rest of the staff in the school, including you, uncompassionate. She is very unhappy with the planned IEP modification to place her daughter at Behavior Horizon, which serves students who are unable to maintain appropriate behavior, and with the way her daughter is being treated by the regular classroom teacher within her inclusion class. She cannot be calmed down and gets up and says she is going to the superintendent's office to report you, the student's regular classroom teacher, and others for totally neglecting her special education student's welfare. The mother is very aware of the laws related to special education and said she is also going to contact her lawyer because the first IEP was never implemented and her daughter never received the services spelled out in the IEP, which she had consented to.

After the mother leaves, you discuss this case with all those involved. The classroom teacher immediately becomes very defensive and states that the expectations in this school are ridiculous and that inclusion puts the responsibilities over the top. The special education resource teacher feels that the environment in the classrooms does not support good instruction for the diverse populations and behaviors within the classroom and that most teachers seem to be struggling with inclusion and basically ignoring student IEPs and her efforts on their behalf.

The school psychologist questions the lack of active participation and planning for IEP meetings, the development of behavior improvement plans (BIP), the resistance that her suggestions meet regarding the needs of specific students, and the refusal to adhere to the IEP team's recommendations; the school counselor concurs. It is further discussed that the school often uses a somewhat standard IEP and BIP that are completed prior to the meetings. The staff believes this is efficient and that because everyone involved is very pressed for time, the IEP meetings are best kept short. They also mention that parents do not understand the pressure that teachers are under and that the meetings are not cordial and have become a real chore. The classroom teacher says she is tired of so-called experts telling her what to do all the time.

You sense a decline in the school culture from increases in discipline problems, parent and teacher complaints, and, of course, the fall in scores on state standardized tests. You believe this is caused by the increase in special education students but that it would work its way out. Obviously, the situation is not getting better. You are now quite concerned about this parent's meeting with the superintendent.

✳ **How will you determine if students and teachers in Oak Grove Middle School are struggling with inclusion? How might this be relevant to Natasha's case?**

PUPIL PERSONNEL–STUDENT SERVICE TEAM

Pupil personnel services (sometimes called *student support services* in secondary schools) are an essential component of an effective, modern school system. It is readily acknowledged that children's emotional, social, physical, and mental conditions and their out-of-school experiences are powerful influences on their in-school performances (Center for the Future of Children, 1992; Children's Defense Fund, 2011). Most all now agree that schools should address the root causes of youth disability and special needs. This service typically requires collecting student information, assessing student needs, and planning and developing comprehensive programs to ensure that students are receiving needed services. When exceptionality that is environmentally caused lowers a student's chance of success, the student is described as "at risk." Organic causes of exceptionality are described as handicapping conditions or disabilities.

The pupil personnel services team consists of professionals who specialize in fostering the healthy educational, social, emotional, intellectual, and career development of all students. Specialists serve as counselors and other guides who provide psychological services, special education, and remedial instruction. They are concerned with child accounting and school safety, school health, speech and hearing therapy, appraisal, testing and diagnostics, and school–court liaison. They also function as social workers and visiting teachers. Figure 10.1 lists the essential services that are part of pupil personnel.

Teachers (although parents and students can request services) typically arrange to consult with a specialist to discuss needs for intervention and then make arrangements to discuss the referral with parents and to complete referral forms. This referral often results in a child being screened by the child study team, followed by a decision regarding formal evaluation. Once a child has been determined to be eligible for special education services, an IEP is written to outline the specific pupil personnel services a student will begin receiving. Public Law 94-142, the Education for All Handicapped Children Act of 1975, and now called the Individuals with Disabilities Education Improvement Act (IDEA), ensures the rights of children with disabilities to a free, appropriate public education, an IEP, special education services, due process procedures, and the least restrictive learning environment.

The 1997 amendments to IDEA have specifically addressed the issue of discipline for students with disabilities. In the case of a child with disabilities whose behavior impedes his or her learning or that of others, the IEP team shall consider strategies and supports to address that behavior. A behavioral intervention plan (BIP) detailing the interventions and supports must be included as part of the IEP for such students. The 2004 reauthorization aligned this act with the high expectations of NCLB and improved on the way that students are identified and classified.

✳ **Whom might you call on to assist in determining if appropriate programs and services were in place to meet the needs of all students, including Natasha? Describe how they might help.**

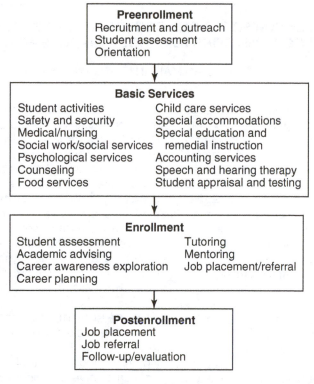

Three Stages of Enrollment

Preenrollment—the period when a student is preparing to enroll in a school
Enrollment—the period when a student is enrolled
Postenrollment—the period when a student has left the program, whether he
or she has advanced to the next level or withdrawn

FIGURE 10.1   Essential Services to Facilitate Student Success

Source: Maddy-Berstein, C., & Cunanan, E. S. (1995). Improving student services in secondary schools. *Office of Student Services Briefs, 7*(2), 3–6. Adapted with permission.

COUNSELING, GUIDANCE, AND PSYCHOLOGICAL SERVICES

The major role of counseling and psychological services is to facilitate wise choices and to promote positive adjustment, mental health, learning abilities, and development. Students' personal, social, educational, and career needs are the focus of the work of guidance counselors and school psychologists. These professionals assist in orientation, provide information, analyze and interpret results, increase possibilities and create new ones, help with decisions and commitments, remove obstacles, and identify emotional problems and learning disabilities, including reading problems. However, their role in addressing severe abnormalities should be very limited. Such conditions should be referred to an external professional who is an expert in the identification and treatment of such abnormal development.

HOW PRINCIPALS EMPOWER SCHOOL COUNSELORS TO BECOME LEADERS AND CONTRIBUTORS TO SCHOOL IMPROVEMENT

IAN MARTIN
The University of San Diego

As a Research Fellow within the Center for School Counseling Outcome Research and Evaluation (CSCORE) at the University of Massachusetts, Amherst, I had the great fortune of seeing dynamic school counseling leadership and practice across the country. Here I focus on several factors important to school leaders wishing to empower school counselors to reach their full potential as leaders and contributors to school improvement within their schools.

IS SCHOOL COUNSELING BEST A POSITION OR A PROGRAM?

A crucial place to start a discussion about maximizing the contribution of school counselors is the distinction between positions and programs. Based on my experience, when school counseling is viewed as a position, leaders typically want to see a person who works well with students and who can respond effectively when crises arise. This position perspective is also linked to the common perceptions of school counselors as "quasi-administrators" and/or "master schedulers." While there is merit to putting out fires and making sure that students fulfill their graduation requirements, school leaders should ask themselves, "Is there a better way?"

Research and scholarship over the last 40 years in the field clearly supports the conceptualization of school counseling practice as primarily programmatic. This research played a major role in the American School Counselor Association (ASCA) creating the National Model (ASCA, 2003). The National Model maintains that programs should have their own curriculum and offer a mixture of preventative–developmental and intervention services in a range of modalities (whole-classroom instruction, consultation, group counseling, and individual counseling). Because

many schools, school districts, and state departments of education adopted and/or adapted the National Model as their model for organizing and delivering school counseling programs (Martin, Carey, & DeCoster, 2009), it can be considered fundamental to the practice of modern school counseling in the United States. Furthermore and most important, research indicates that students benefit academically, socially, and have more positive outlooks on the future when exposed to such programs (Lapan, Gysbers, & Sun 1997; Lapan, Gysbers, & Petroski, 2001; Sink & Stroh, 2003; Sink, Akos, Turnbull, & Mvududu, 2008).

WHY ARE SCHOOL COUNSELING PROGRAMS IMPORTANT TO SCHOOL LEADERS?

In addition to the positive research supporting the establishment of school counseling programs, there are some very pragmatic reasons school leaders would want to consider encouraging their school counselors to pursue a program approach to their work. Because school counseling programs are context specific and allow school counselors to adapt their programs to the needs of individual schools, school counseling programs are well suited to support other school-related initiatives. Here are some examples of educational initiatives that can be operationalized within a school counseling program:

- *Positive Behavior Interventions and Supports (PBIS)*—A common model for improving schoolwide student behavior and conduct. Within PBIS, schools actively create and reinforce positive behaviors that contribute to effective learning environments and promote school safety (for a good example, see Sherrod, Getch, & Ziomek-Daigle, 2009).

- *Antibullying Programs*—Many schools purchase and implement curricular materials designed to prevent and/reduce bullying behaviors.
- *Response to Intervention (RTI)*—A common approach for determining a student's eligibility and need for special education services involves closely tracking several cycles of interventions that include basic classroom accommodations to more targeted academic and behavioral interventions.
- *Dropout Prevention Programs*—Many schools are working to create structures that better support students at risk of dropping out. Research on dropout prevention highlights the importance of counseling (Edmondson & White, 1998).

These initiatives just scratch the surface of the types of activities school counselors and programs could help to support. Unfortunately, many school leaders do not initially recognize that school counselors and school counseling programs could take an active leadership role in organizing and delivering crucial school initiatives. In my experience, most school leaders simply have not seen the possibilities. For example, as a former elementary school counselor, I worked closely with my school's special education team. After adopting an RTI approach, it became clear that we needed a more systematic pre-referral process for special education eligibility. Based on this need, we redesigned the process into the school counseling program so that I could work with teachers, parents, and students to track interventions and contribute data to be used within our team meetings. After the first year, we were able to reduce the number of students identified as needing special education services by 50%.

Similar scenarios are relatively rare because few principals have had formal exposure to effective organization and management strategies for school counseling programs (Dollarhide, 2003). Based upon national research of state school counseling models and

programs, many states delegate educational decision making to local school districts and/or individual schools (Martin et al., 2009). This arrangement results in many principals being directly responsible for establishing the nature and organization of school counseling within their schools and requires that work be done to inform and aid principals in understanding the conditions, organization, and expectations that could lead to positive school counseling outcomes directly linked core school goals. Therefore, here are some Web resources that may help school leaders to become more informed about effective school counseling practices:

- umass.edu/schoolcounseling/
- schoolcounselor.org/
- missouricareereducation.org/index. php?view=content_area&section=admin (The Missouri Department of Elementary and Secondary Education has a long history of school counseling leadership and has designed webinars specifically for school administrators.)

WHY SHOULD SCHOOL COUNSELORS BE INCLUDED IN SCHOOL LEADERSHIP?

In today's schools, there is a tremendous amount of school-generated data. School counselors have unrestricted access to most formal and informal school data. This unique position has prompted leaders in the field to identify the effective use of data as a major component of school counselor leadership (Stone & Dahir, 2007) and have developed resources that promote the use of evidence within the decision-making process (Dimmit, Carey, & Hatch, 2007). In addition to data use, Borders and Shoffner (2003) identified school counselors' training in human relations, problem solving, change processes, human and career development, group work, learning theories, and program evaluation as particularly advantageous leadership qualities (p. 52–53). In addition to these qualities and training trends, Janson, Stone, and Clark (2009) recommend the use of a "distributed leadership"

(*continued*)

perspective to better understand and differenti-ate school counselor leadership from principal leadership. Distributed leadership involves leaders engaging in a process of continu-ous learning and improvement that enhances the entire organization's leadership capacity (Elmore, 2000; Halverson, 2003; O'Day, 2004). Within this perspective, there is recognition that school counselors must collaborate and build a sense of shared responsibility amongst several leaders to move school goals forward.

For example, as a school counselor, I worked closely with my principal. We devel-oped a relationship and grew to understand our individual strengths and weaknesses. He invited me to share my perspective on situations both informally and formally and over time, he

learned about school counseling and I learned about his vision for the school. Ultimately, our re-lationship evolved into a place where all school counseling program activities were intentionally tied to recognized school needs and/or goals.

Finally, this section outlined some of the ways school counselors and school counseling programs can aid school leaders in school im-provement. Though it also stressed that school leaders need to see the potential value of school counseling beyond the stigma of the position and invite school counselors to do more than just put out fires. Establishing relationships with school counselors and encouraging them to design pro-grams directly linked to important school goals may help school counselors to better access their unique set of skills and realize their full potential.

School counselors and psychologists work with students individually and in groups, consulting parents, teachers, and a diverse group of community service providers. They make recommendations regarding curriculum, instruction, and classroom management to meet the needs of the child. They suggest ways parents can work with the school to help their children. They also provide various edu-cation programs for parents, children, teachers, and administrators. School psy-chologists and counselors often assist in compiling significant information, which becomes part of the student's cumulative school record.

Certification for counselors and psychologists is required in all states, al-though the requirements vary. The school counselor's professional organization is the American School Counselors Association (ASCA), which is a division of the American Counseling Association. The National Association of School Psycholo-gists (NASP) is the professional organization for school psychologists.

The main function of school psychologists is to provide testing and con-sultation for special education students. Because the training in school psychol-ogy tends to be in testing, human development, and system change, school psychologists are usually not licensed by the state to do counseling or psycho-therapy. They are experts in identifying learning disabilities, developmental disorders, physical impairments, or other special needs including the gifted.

The school psychologist works with a team to design a program of services. It blends the best methods of teaching and the most conducive learning environ-ment for the child into a remedial plan to be implemented within the classroom. They share and interpret results at parent conferences and with child-study teams before writing final reports. They follow up on the progress of students and work with others to make needed adjustments for the student.

School counselors provide a diverse array of services to help students, including advising in academic, social, emotional, and behavioral matters. They address a wide array of issues such as course selection, vocational placement, college selection, parental divorce, dating, loneliness, study habits, controlling aggressiveness, violence, depression, bullying, and many other developmental issues.

✳ **What role do counselors have in helping students like Natasha with their problems, even going back to earlier grades?**

SPECIAL EDUCATION AND INDIVIDUALS WITH DISABILITIES EDUCATION IMPROVEMENT ACT (IDEA)

The 1975 passage of P. L. 94-142, now called IDEA, stressed the placement of services in the least restrictive environment. IDEA defines *special education* as specially designed services and instruction to meet the unique needs of students with disabilities. Turnbull, Turnbull, Shank, and Leal (1995, p. 53) outline five principles for educators in implementing the law.

PRINCIPLE	COMMAND TO EDUCATORS
Zero rejects (nondiscriminatory evaluation)	Enroll the student.
	Determine if the student has a disability and, if so, whether the student needs special education and related services.
Appropriate education	Provide beneficial special education and related services.
Least restrictive environment	Include the student with children who do not have disabilities.
Due procedural process	Check to determine if schools and parents are complying with IDEA.
Parent participation	Collaborate with parents.

To remove barriers presented by a disability, students who will require some modification or accommodations in the environment or the instructional methodology will have a document called a 504 plan. Students who have a disability requiring special education services will have an IEP. The 1997 IDEA lists the following as disabilities that must be addressed by an IEP:

Autism, deaf-blindness, deafness, hearing impairment, mental retardation, multiple disabilities, orthopedic impairment, other health impairment, serious emotional disturbance, specific learning disability, speech or language impairment, traumatic brain injury, and visual impairment.

In addition, the following conditions are to be covered under section 504:

> Attention deficit disorder—ADD (also attention-deficit hyperactivity disorder—ADHD); chronic medical conditions (such as cancer, Tourette's syndrome, asthma, or epilepsy); communicable diseases; some temporary medical conditions; physical impairment; and disorders of emotion or behavior. To qualify, there must be a demonstrated and substantial limitation of a major life activity.

Almost 90% of students identified with disabilities typically are categorized as specifically learning disabled, speech or language impaired, mentally retarded, or emotionally disturbed. If you knowingly do not provide needed accommodations, it can be viewed as discrimination and the school system and you can be liable for legal action.

When evidence of an exceptionality appears, the psychologist conducts a complete diagnosis of the student to pinpoint strengths and weaknesses and to plan a comprehensive IEP. The diagnosis and classification of children is based on a comprehensive set of assessments in the areas of behavior, achievement, and functioning profiles as measured through interviews, examining records, observation, a battery of psychoeducational assessment instruments, and IQ scores. The functional assessment identifies the abilities, accomplishments, conditions, potential, and full range of challenging behaviors. The results are used by the IEP team to develop complementary strategies that provide the greatest potential for success. Federal law requires that the team include the student's parents or guardian, student's regular education teacher(s), school representative (assistant principal), special education teacher(s), an individual to interpret evaluation results (school psychologist), and other individuals with knowledge and special expertise.

The 2004 reauthorization of IDEA aligned this act with NCLB so that the education of students with disabilities is held to the same high standards as for other students. It also attempted to ease the number of lawsuits filed by requiring states to offer mediation to parents and school districts. In addition, this reauthorization law, now called the Individuals with Disabilities Education Improvement Act, spearheaded some significant changes, including the way students are classified for special education.

Overrepresentation and underrepresentation of children from minority groups and diverse backgrounds has been a dilemma for many years (National Research Council, 2002a). The concern is warranted because misplacement into special education often stigmatizes students, denies them a high-quality education, limits their future opportunities, and takes valuable resources away from truly disabled students (Garcia, 2006).

The reauthorization attempts to put a system in place to decrease the number of children incorrectly referred for special educational services. Determination of disability was previously based on significant discrepancy between ability and achievement. The revised version of IDEA includes new requirements for identifying children with special learning disabilities by incorporating early intervening services. Response to intervention (RTI), as authorized in IDEA, is a multi-tiered process requiring regular education teachers to identify students who warrant an evaluation to determine their eligibility for the special education classification (Zirkel, 2007).

Advocates of RTI support requiring educational specialists to monitor the student's response to regular instruction and to try multiple strategies to promote learning for an individual student instead of simply labeling the student with a disability. Students have the opportunity to participate in the regular education setting, receiving the necessary accommodations, and possibly experience success without the disabilities label.

> Rather than devoting extensive resources to finding out whether students have 'Disabilities,' we should devote those resources to assessing students' exact instructional needs. . . . [S]chools will meet to provide this instruction through collaboration between General and a special education personnel to ensure that all students continue to have full access to the general curriculum. (Harry & Klingner, 2007, p. 18)

After determining the student's educational program, placement, and need for related services, the team then determines long- and short-term objectives and specific support plans for students in general education placements. These plans meet the individual student's needs while maintaining the integrity of lessons for classmates without disabilities (Giangreco, Cloninger, & Iverson, 1993). The students' progress is re-evaluated periodically, and specialists work with the classroom teacher to obtain maximum success.

IEPs are legal documents that must be signed and therefore can create legal issues as well as instructional ones. It is very important to include all the student's teachers in the planning process for all accommodations and modifications. The principal and/or his or her designee should attend these meetings and be prepared to discuss the resources the school is able to commit. Once it is in the IEP, the district must provide for it. The disorder itself cannot be the sole reason for placement and special education students must be placed with students of the same chronological age and developmental ability. Accommodations should be consistent and not applied selectively. Important decisions related to students' tests include alternative assessment, extended time, providing a test reader, involvement in high-stakes testing, and so on. All decisions should be made to meet the spirit and the letter of the law (Armenta & Beckers, 2006).

Students might need a variety of related services. The *school-community worker, visiting teacher,* or *school social worker* provides a link between the school, home, and community, rendering interpretation, support, assistance, coordination, advocacy, and investigation services. He or she also assists in the proper enforcement of all laws pertaining to juveniles. *Speech, hearing,* and *learning specialists* address problems such as sensory loss, speech and language delays, academic achievement delays, writing difficulties, and other communication disorders. These experts provide remediation and compensation and should be certified specialists in their respective fields.

The *special education teacher* helps identify basic disabilities and develops instruction, lesson plans, materials, and tests. He or she also tests approaches to determine if they are successful and transfers the procedures and materials to the classroom teacher. The specialist's main function is to adapt curriculum materials such as assignments, worksheets, reading books, and tests for individual students. Sometimes the special education teacher works as a co-teacher, jointly planning and team-teaching lessons with the regular classroom teacher. Other times, the special education teacher may work with small groups or individual special-needs children within the regular classroom to provide tutorial or remedial assistance.

The special education teacher may also pull students out of regular classrooms for intensive individualized and small-group instruction. Children with severe disabilities are sometimes placed with a special education teacher in a self-contained classroom and also are included in the mainstream. Special education staff members provide consultation and training for regular classroom teachers in alternative assessment, instruction, and discipline strategies. These teachers receive specialized training and licensing to work with the special-needs population of students. Some of the additional services from which special education students can benefit are audiology, medical and health services, occupational therapy, physical therapy, recreation, transportation, and assistive technology services (for more information, see cec.sped.org).

Administrators must advocate the rights of all children to receive needed services and to promote inclusive school practice. An enormous responsibility for a school administrator is to establish and maintain a learning environment that meets the needs of a diverse student body. Administration and leaders will be under continuous pressure to ensure that applicable regulations regarding students with disabilities are observed and that all students achieve success in their schools.

A number of new issues are occurring regarding special education students. One such decision is whether and how to include a special education student in state testing and to ensure that such policies are not seen as a way to maneuver students out of state testing so as to raise schoolwide scores. In addition, there is a continuous need to train administrators and teachers so they are prepared to provide leadership for special education programs.

Inclusion

Inclusion requires the elimination of two separate systems—general education and special education—and the development of unified general education that includes all students. This includes subjects, school-based programs, curriculum, clubs, sports, extracurricular activities, and transportation.

Inclusive classrooms place students with exceptionalities in general classrooms, and special education resource teachers work with general classroom teachers in team-teaching modes. Children in inclusive classrooms can take advantage of cooperative learning, curriculum adaptations, classroom aides, environmental accommodations, cooperation between regular and special education teachers, proactive behavior plans, and peer tutoring. Requirements for

educating students with disabilities in the least restrictive environment are specified in the IDEA amendments of 1997 as follows:

> To the maximum extent appropriate, children with disabilities, including children in
> public or private institutions or other care facilities, are educated with children who
> are not disabled. Special classes, separate schools, or other removal of children with
> disabilities from the regular educational environment occurs only when the nature or
> severity of the disability of a child is such that education in regular classes with the use
> of supplementary aids and services cannot be achieved satisfactorily. [(sec. 612.(a)(5)]

The research suggests that the setting itself is less important than the quality of
the program and the transformation within the school to support what is going
on in the setting. Effective best practice teaching strategies and an individualized
approach are the critical ingredients in special education (Zigmond, 2003). The
NCLB Act of 2001 emphasized the addition of effective instructional strategies,
where teachers will need to implement best practices to meet the needs of their
increasingly diverse student population.

The Individuals with Disabilities Education Improvement Act (IDEIA) of
2004 requires that students with disabilities have access to the general education
curriculum in the least restrictive environment. As a result, teachers are realiz-
ing that they are part of a collaborative support team comprised of specialists
(e.g., special educators, reading specialists) and service personnel (e.g., speech
and language pathologists, occupational and physical therapists, psychologists,
paraprofessionals), all of whom are involved in diagnosing and responding to
student needs. These resources are available to provide assistance to the whole
class as well as specific individuals with special needs.

General education classes are the placement of first choice for all learners,
including disabled learners, and all special services and supplemental supports
are brought into the classroom, as opposed to removing students from general
education classrooms to receive services. The number of students with disabilities spending 80% or more of their time in general education classes went from
25% in 1985 to 47.4% in 1999. That percentage has continued to increase in the
2000s to greater than 50%. However, disparities exist among schools, districts,
and states. For instance, these percentages range from a low of 18% in Hawaii to a
high of 82% in Vermont (U.S. Department of Education, 2003).

The administrator plays a key role in the success of efforts at inclusion. Villa
and Thousand (2005) have delineated five essential actions administrators must
take to facilitate inclusive practices:

1. Building consensus for a vision of inclusive schooling
2. Developing educators' skills and confidence to be inclusive educators
   through ongoing professional development
3. Creating incentives (time, training, responding to concerns) and recognition
4. Reorganizing and expanding human and other teaching resources
5. Planning for and taking actions to help the community see and get excited
   about a new vision

Administrators must model acceptance of all students and celebrate the diversity within the schools. They must continually encourage all staff members to support and become part of these programs and to collaborate on how best to support students and their families. The key to success is instructional responsiveness to individual learning needs.

Generally, the following characteristics can be found in inclusive schools:

- Programs and procedures are planned to meet the needs of all students rather than a one-size-fits-all approach.
- Classrooms are differentiated and use a wide range of curricular materials and instructional strategies.
- Curricular materials are accessible to all and not retrofitted after the fact.
- Peer learning and cross-age tutoring support classroom learning.
- Instructional technology is infused into the curriculum.
- Collaboration between and among school personnel brings greater expertise to instruction and allows for professional development.
- Accommodations and modifications in testing are used to measure what students know and can do.
- Superintendents and principals assume responsibility for the planning, implementation, and outcomes of the education of all their students (Lipsky & Gartner, 2003).

The bottom line is that curriculum and instruction, leadership practices, and school structure might need to change to meet the needs of students of all abilities, handicapping conditions, and disabilities (Bartlett, Weisenstein, & Etscheidt, 2002; Hall, 2007).

According to Villa and Thousand (2003), the degree of administrative support and vision was the most powerful predictor of general educators' attitudes toward inclusion. They stress the importance of meeting the needs of a diverse student population by using:

> initiatives and organizational best practices to accomplish this aim, including supportive parallel and complementary co-teaching, peer mediated instruction, transdisciplinary teaming, block scheduling, multi-age student grouping and looping, schoolwide positive behavior support and discipline approaches, detracking, and school-within-a-school family configurations of students and teachers. These initiatives facilitate the inclusion and development of students with disabilities within general education. (p. 20)

They also stress approaches such as parallel teaching, supportive teaching (support personnel provide needed assistance), complementary teaching, coteaching, alternative teaching, model interactive teaching, and station teaching. Other important best practice elements include cooperative learning, constructivist learning approaches, differentiated instruction, partner learning, authentic learning, demonstrations, whole language approaches, phonics instruction, thematic/interdisciplinary approaches, curriculum overlapping, authentic assessment, and

LEADERSHIP FOR SPECIAL SERVICES

JUDY MANTLE
National University

School leaders have the responsibility of improving the performance and learning outcomes for all students. When the needs of students depart significantly from others perceived to be in the "mainstream," various opinions frequently arise about the types of services that should be provided and in what context. In times of fiscal restraint, tensions can easily arise from among interdisciplinary team members about what constitutes an "appropriate education program." Even the best of school leaders can be challenged by circumstances posed by various students and sometimes from among their family members. In spite of these challenges, school leaders must ensure that all students are given the resources and supports needed so that these individuals can fully access their educational environments and reach their maximum potential.

Contemporary educational leaders who oversee special services can greatly enhance their effectiveness if they embrace the following principles and practices:

1. *Stay updated on the laws* as well as district policies that apply to school-aged special-needs populations and their families and become clear about everyone's role and responsibilities in providing these services. It is important to learn about contact persons and other resources available to you should you need advice or technical assistance in this area.

2. *Select highly qualified competent teachers and support personnel* who possess suitable dispositions for working with special-needs populations. Continue to develop them and reward them for their performance as appropriate. This is especially important because of the frequent stress factors resulting in high

turnover rates among those who serve these populations.

3. *Explore research-based models of inclusive practice* and service delivery and engage others in the creative process of brainstorming with you about new possibilities for your school or district. Gather baseline data and monitor results over time to determine whether better results are gleaned from student outcomes data as a result of shifts in service delivery practices.

4. Stay apprised of instructional trends, innovations, and cutting-edge practices that *can benefit all learners,* and especially those who manifest special needs. For example, knowledge of universal design for learning (UDL) principles, differentiated instruction, and coteaching practices provide great promise for improving learning outcomes for all and may prove to greatly assist in closing the achievement gap between general and special education students.

5. *Institute a model of collaborative engagement* that will impress upon everyone the importance of effective teamwork at all levels. Because key decision making is typically made within the context of interdisciplinary teams, one's proficiency in team dynamics is vital for communicating findings from assessments, determining instructional needs, and designing needed services within and across program areas. Team members must learn and value the knowledge, skills, and expertise that each has to offer when crafting programs and support services for students with special needs. School leaders need to model and clearly communicate their expectations for team

(continued)

members, set the tone for interacting in a respectful manner, and provide feedback when necessary. The capacity of an interdisciplinary team can be better realized within the context of a healthy and constructive interactive teaming environment compared to one that is fraught with undesirable dynamics and plagued by various levels of dysfunction.

School leaders can significantly impact others by setting intentions and taking action that will affect the lives of those who require special support to achieve their education goals. Becoming as independent as possible and experiencing a high quality of life are important goals for persons with disabilities and/or special needs and for their families. Future educational leaders who are truly committed to serving all learners have the potential to greatly inspire these individuals and their families. They are the gatekeepers for many resources that might possibly unleash the potential of these challenged individuals. The decisions and actions of the special services leader also set an example and give a strong message to those who teach these students. Effective leadership in the special service area can lead to powerful outcomes and can truly make a positive difference in the lives of many.

technology support (imsglobal.org/accessibility). These approaches require scheduling time for planning teams to work and teach each other and to collaborate with parents.

One of the concerns regarding NCLB is that it might cause administrators to move low-performing students from a special education category to a regular category. Most schools and districts are fearful that the special education cell will cause them to not make AYP. This may result in the shuffling of such students to a place where they will have the least effect. On the other side, if special education students were opted out of NCLB it would needlessly drive many low-performing students into special education. What is needed is an appropriate measure of improvement for disabled students (Watsa, 2006).

✳ **What evidence will be needed to support the decision to remove Natasha from Oak Grove Middle School and send her to Behavior Horizon? How might this case influence the service delivery model and the use of proactive strategies for students?**

SCHOOL HEALTH SERVICES

The school nurse performs a number of services, including screening for hearing and visual problems, head lice, tuberculosis, and heart defects; checking teeth and throat; teaching units on human development and personal hygiene; providing emergency first aid; consulting about health problems with teachers and students; and assisting in homebound instruction and in referring children to physicians and social workers. School administrators are expected to determine whether the health services provided within the school meet the needs of students (Zepeda & Langenbach, 1999). That means periodically assessing the current state of health delivery in the school by reviewing with the school nurse the numbers of students and teachers served, types of services being offered, and services needed.

Educators know that children need to be healthy and feel safe in order to learn, particularly at the elementary level (actionforhealthykids.org; ashaweb.org; nationalguidelines.org). The 2004 Child Nutrition Reauthorization Act requires every school district receiving federal funds to have wellness policies in place that address the physical health, mental health, and safety of students and staff. One way to ensure that comprehensive health needs are being met is to designate a school health team to oversee health and safety within the school. The Centers for Disease Control and Prevention developed a School Health Index to help elementary schools assess their school health activities cdc.gov/healthyyouth/shi). Marx, Wooley, and Donica (2006) state:

> Because elementary schools reach more young people than any other social institution (other than families), they are well positioned to lay the foundation for students' success in school and in life. The need for a coordinate approach to health and learning is greater now than ever before. In fulfilling their primary responsibilities to foster an environment conducive to learning, principals cannot afford to neglect the health and safety of their students and staff. (p. 14)

STUDENT DISCIPLINE

Most schools have codes of student conduct that are to be enforced by the teachers, administrators, and pupil personnel workers. Administrators are responsible for reinforcing teacher disciplinary actions and taking responsibility for the more difficult or unusual behavior problems. Traditional methods (Kimbrough & Burket, 1990, p. 277) for correcting student behavior include (1) reprimands, (2) detention, (3) enforced duties, (4) suspension from school, (5) in-school suspension, and (6) expulsion from school. The disciplinarian must be consistent, strict, deliberate, fair, just, and compassionate and perceived as such. Youth, and particularly inner-city youth, want the security and predictability that accompany clear codes of conduct and consistent, clear, and firm discipline. Inner-city youth seek the concern and security conveyed by strong discipline as long as they perceive the discipline as swift, certain, and fair (McLaughlin, Irby, & Longman, 1994).

In order of teachers' perceived frequency of occurrence, school problems over the past decade include:

- Physical conflict among students
- Conflict and abuse involving teachers and other staff
- Student use of alcohol
- Student use of illegal drugs
- Vandalism of school property
- Robbery and theft
- Student possession and occasional use of weapons

Teachers suggest that the nature of each of these school problems is more serious than in the past (Shen, 1997). All of these problems are much more serious in secondary schools than in elementary schools.

The 1989 U.S. Supreme Court decision in *Honig v. Doe* found that students with disabilities cannot be unilaterally suspended or expelled for more than 10 days without due process. This triggered many new procedures. Functional behavior assessment (FBA) is a systematic process for identifying the causes of problem behaviors and developing an effective plan to reduce the severity or eliminate the behaviors. The purpose of an FBA is to collect information to explain the relationship among associated environmental factors and the problem behavior. The problem behavior can then be addressed through the IEP process and behavior intervention plan (BIP).

The FBA addresses the relationships among precipitating conditions, the behavior, its consequences, and the function of the behavior. The precipitating conditions identify specific triggers related to the behavior such as setting, time, cause, provocation, persons present, and so on. The specific behavior describes the pattern of behavior that the student has demonstrated, including a specific description of the student's actions. The consequences describe the responses or events, both situational and personal, that typically follow the behavior. The function of the behavior allows professionals to hypothesize about the purpose the behavior serves such as avoidance, gaining attention, anger, frustration, vengeance, control, intimidation, anxiety relief, and so on. Assessment techniques (e.g., observation, rating, interview, taping) and related information (e.g., academic, social/peer, family) are also provided (Fad, Patton, & Polloway, 2000).

Section 612(a)(1) of the IDEA amendment of 1997 and the 1999 IDEA final regulations state that free, appropriate public education (FAPE) shall be available to all children with disabilities, ages 3–21, and restricts suspensions to 10 school days and interim alternative education settings (IAES) to 10 days except in cases involving weapons or illegal drugs. Weapons or drug violations warrant suspension for not more than 45 days. The expulsion and discipline provision requires a hearing to determine whether there is a manifestation (disability causes behavior). The manifestation hearing must be held in cases of (a) weapons, (b) drugs, (c) dangerous behavior, or (d) any discipline for more than 10 days. If the school has not already conducted an FBA and implemented a BIP before disciplining the student, the IEP team must do so. If the school, however, has conducted a functional behavioral assessment and developed a behavioral intervention plan, the IEP team must review and modify the plan, "as necessary, to address the behavior."

The purpose of the BIP is to provide appropriate responses, including strategies for improving the student's behavior, in order to complement the IEP. Appropriate practice suggests that BIPs include the following components: specific goals, proposed interventions, person(s) responsible, methods, evaluation criterion, and the timelines to be followed. Table 10.1 provides a list of possible intervention strategies for improving student behavior.

TABLE 10.1   Intervention Strategies for Improving Student Behavior

A. RESTRUCTURING PRECIPITATING CONDITIONS (ANTECEDENTS)
1. Remove distracting materials.
2. Provide quiet, separate seating area.
3. Modify academic requirements.
4. Use visual cues/signal/advance organizers.
5. Provide written or visual schedule.
6. Use proximity cues.
7. Provide choices related to assignments.
8. Use gestures, physical cues.
9. Minimize transition time.
10. Other: _____

B. INSTRUCTIONAL TECHNIQUES
1. Teach class rules and establish expectations/set limits.
2. Model desirable behavior.
3. Use strategic placement.
4. Role-play.
5. Coach through use of corrective feedback.
6. Provide literature-based lessons.
7. Monitor and provide written feedback.
8. Develop student–teacher contract.
9. Develop student–parent contract.
10. Teach self-monitoring.
11. Show and discuss videotapes.
12. Use team-building activities.
13. Provide social skills games.
14. Organize group discussions.
15. Other: _____

C. CONSEQUENCES FOR POSITIVE BEHAVIORS
1. Use frequent, consistent, specific verbal praise.
2. Provide positive social reinforcement.
3. Establish point system.
4. Establish in-class or in-school reward system.
5. Establish home-school reward system.
6. Establish token economy.
7. Provide consumable reinforcement.
8. Provide tangible reinforcement.
9. Refer to other adults for praise.
10. Use privileges/responsibilities.
11. Use private praise.
12. Other: _____

D. CONSEQUENCES TO REDUCE MISBEHAVIOR
1. Use nonverbal signals.
2. Provide verbal reminder/reprimand.

(continued)

3. Set up system of planned ignoring.
4. Use a structured warning system.
5. Assign essays/writing assignments.
6. Use cost response procedures.
7. Provide time to cool off at desk or other area.
8. Implement loss of privileges.
9. Arrange student–teacher conference.
10. Implement previously agreed-on behavior contract.
11. Refer to counselor or mentor.
12. Telephone parent(s).
13. Use lunch detention.
14. Use after-school detention.
15. Implement in-school suspension for _____ periods/days.
16. Contact parent and send student home for remainder of day.
17. Set up in-school suspension up to 10 school days without committee meeting.
18. Suspend up to 3 consecutive days without committee meeting.
19. Place in alternative educational placement up to 10 school days without committee meeting.
20. Other: _____

E. EVALUATION METHODS
1. Behavior monitoring forms (e.g., contracts, point sheets).
2. Grades on assignments recorded in grade book.
3. Anecdotal records.
4. Attendance records.
5. Tally sheets or handheld counter of the frequency of target behavior(s).
6. Tape recordings (audio or video).
7. Progress reports/interim notices.
8. Portfolios/work samples.
9. Student self-assessments or ratings.
10. Teacher/parent rating scales.
11. IEP review forms.
12. Parent feedback forms.
13. Time totals on stopwatches.
14. Graphing behavioral performance.
15. Other: _____

Source: Fad, K., Patton, J., & Polloway, E. (2000). *Behavior intervention planning.* Austin, TX: Pro-ED.

According to Johns (1998), success lies in administrators establishing total staff commitment to the process. Plans should treat students with respect, place responsibility on students, encourage appropriate choices, and teach social skills. School personnel need in-depth training, the opportunity to practice behavioral management, and technical support in these applications. Students must know what is expected of them in all school settings. Staff members must recognize students who follow the rules and must establish logical consequences for those who do not. Ultimately, parents and community agencies will need to be involved to get students the right kind of help.

Horner, Sugai, and Horner (2000) suggest, "Too often efforts to remove or contain the small number of the most disruptive students simply results in identification of an ever-increasing number of these students" (p. 22). They found that functional behavior assessment and implementation plans resulted in problem behaviors being reduced. They also suggest that zero tolerance and get-tough punishment and exclusion policies without proactive approaches to improvement "is associated with increases in aggression, vandalism, truancy, and dropouts" (p. 22). They conclude that "administrators, in particular, need to define schoolwide discipline as a major goal within their school, build disciplinary systems to complement traditional reactive systems and establish assessment and intervention programs" (p. 22) (pbis.org; ed.gov/offices/osers/osep/earlywrn.html).

✳ **If Natasha were to stay at Oak Grove Middle School, what might be some proactive strategies to give her and the teacher greater support? What is Natasha's impact on school safety and security and how might discipline policies help in this case?**

Positive Behavioral Interventions and Supports (PBIS)

PBIS is a systems-based discipline method for improving student behavior, which was developed at the University of Oregon and is gaining wide support and usage (pbis.org). There are approximately 10,000 schools nationwide implementing PBIS. States like Illinois and Maryland have implemented statewide systems providing support networks for statewide technical assistance focused on applying the science of PBIS at a schoolwide level.

PBIS offers a schoolwide approach to improving student behavior. The system is based on three simple principals: be respectful, be responsible, be resourceful. The system claims many possible improvements, including:

- Reduced office referral rates of up to 50% per year
- Improved attendance and school engagement
- Improved academic achievement
- Reduced dropout rates
- Reduced delinquency in later years
- Improved school atmosphere
- Reduced referrals to special education

PBIS is a proactive system based on principals of applied behavior analysis, the use of systems of reinforcement designed to draw attention to pro-social student behavior, and reduce the focus on student misbehavior. It uses student and school-level data to make decisions about behavioral and academic practices within the school. The system also attempts to increase parental support and community involvement.

The system matches the level of interventions to the presenting problems following a three-tiered PBIS prevention model. Eighty percent of the students within a school fall in the primary prevention category, which provides a schoolwide system for all students, staff members, and settings. Fifteen percent of the students will require secondary prevention in specialized group systems for students at risk. The remaining 5% will be placed in specialized individual systems for students with at risk behaviors.

PBIS is comprised of seven key features including: *Expectations Defined* (three to five positive schoolwide behavioral expectations are defined); *Behavioral Expectations Taught* (these expectations are taught to all children in the school); *System for Rewarding Behavioral Expectations* (rewards are provided for meeting the behavioral expectations); *System for Responding to Behavioral Violations* (a consistently implemented continuum of consequences for problem behavior is in place); *Monitoring and Evaluation* (behavior patterns are monitored and the information is used for ongoing decision making); *Management* (an administrator actively supports and is involved in the PBIS effort, and a comprehensive schoolwide behavior support team is formed); and *District-Level Support* (the school district provides support to the school in the form of functional policies, staff training, and data collection opportunities) (Bradshaw, Reinke, Brown, Bevans, & Leaf, 2008).

STUDENT APPRAISAL, TESTING, AND DIAGNOSTICS

Testing and diagnostic programs are often organized schoolwide or systemwide for administering standardized tests. Tests are used to diagnose difficulties, identify aptitudes and discrepancies, appraise achievement, group students, identify needs, assess competencies, and create accountability. They are also used to inform the public (see Chapter 1). A major part of most testing and diagnostic programs is achievement testing. A common approach is a standardized norm-referenced test. Other types include criterion-referenced, objective-referenced, domain-referenced, intelligence, minimum competency, and performance assessment tests.

A major concern in testing and appraisal as a result of NCLB is "How are our students, teachers, and administrators doing and are things improving in our schools?" High-stakes testing is being used to determine if students are promoted and will graduate (28 states by 2010) and to provide a "school report card" for the teachers and administrators. The data collected is used to both facilitate instruction (a diagnostic tool) and to make comparisons and hold administrators, teachers, and students accountable (communicating with parents and community). Testing is used to compare schools and districts, plan curriculum, assess effectiveness, stimulate reform, and provide recognition.

According to an Education Sector report entitled "Margins of Error: The Education Testing Industry in the No Child Left behind Era," by Thomas Toch, nine companies control nearly 100% of expenditures from states for tests and testing services. However, the surge in testing has created immense challenges for both the industry that writes, scores, and reports the vast majority of the new statewide tests and the state agencies and school districts charged with carrying out NCLB's requirements (Toch, 2006). According to Toch, there are not enough experts in the field to deal with these new testing responsibilities. Toch states that the surge in state testing under NCLB has created a severe shortage of those experts (p. 9).

Many state testing offices and some districts suffer from heavy turnover and shortages of skilled staff as a result of underfunding and hiring freezes introduced during the 1990s (Toch, 2006). Toch also maintains that a survey of state testing directors revealed that over half the states have problems recruiting and retaining the testing staff they need to respond to NCLB adequately.

As a result, scoring errors, reporting delays, and lack of state oversight of testing contractors are some of the many problems that exist because of NCLB (see Chapter 1). States report the following problems: 52% find it difficult recruiting and retaining qualified staff for testing-related positions, 35% have experienced a significant error by a contractor in scoring a state test since 2000, and 20% did not receive test results from a contractor in a timely fashion. Toch relates how scoring errors have sent thousands of students to summer school when they had in fact passed their tests and how administrators have lost their jobs for low scores on tests that, had they been scored correctly, would have shown improvements in student achievement. In fact, so many errors have been discovered that testing companies are even giving students college scholarships to atone for the fact that scoring errors deprived them of their high school diplomas.

These problems aside, data-driven decision making is a major theme in educational leadership today. The major data used is the state student performance test, which reports the percentage of students in the school who answered questions correctly and met state standards. The focus is placed on maintaining progress in areas of success and giving additional attention to the weak content or skills areas (did not meet state standard or average yearly progress).

The analysis identifies problem areas that stand out by comparing scores to standards, to previous years' performances, to resources available and time devoted, to supporting materials and textbooks, to other schools and leaders, and to curriculum and instructional strategies to help target areas needing attention. The analysis should focus on causes of poor performance such as alignment issues, changes from year to year, problems with special education or at-risk students, literacy problems, differences among teachers or schools, as well as ineffective use of time, resources, and/or supporting materials and so on.

Figure 10.2 provides an illustration of the type of data that might be used to track performance in an elementary school. This data can be used to track the performance and progress of the student, teacher, program, school, and district. The data is most helpful when it is in a sequence and format that disaggregates the data in such a way that problems, trends, comparisons, and so on can easily be made.

Whether tests really measure what students need to be able to do to succeed in the 21st century is a growing concern. Many believe that performance assessment and demonstrations are better suited to measure the skills and abilities that students will need to be successful in a world that is undergoing significant

Key Performance Indicators—For Each Content Area (Language Arts/English, Mathematics, Science, History/Social Science)

- Number/percentage of students passing each of the standard of learning (SOL) tests (grades 3 and 5)
- Number/percentage of students failing each of the SOL tests (grades 3 and 5)
- Number/percentage of students requiring remediation for each of the SOL areas
- Number/percentage of students successfully completing remediation for each SOL area
- Number/percentage of 4th-grade students scoring above the 50th percentile on the Stanford 9 achievement tests
- Number/percentage of the 4th-grade students scoring in the first quartile on the Stanford 9 achievement tests
- Number/percentage of students meeting or exceeding expectations of SOL objectives in grades K–3 (score of 3 or 4 on a 1–4 scale)
- Number/percentage of students in grades 3–5 with satisfactory report card grades
- Number/percentage of students reading on grade level
- Number/percentage of students promoted to the next grade

Demographic Indicators

- Number/percentage of minority students passing each of the SOL tests (grades 3 and 5)
- Number/percentage of mobility (transfer) students passing each of the SOL tests (grades 3 and 5)
- Number/percentage of special education students participating in SOL tests
- Number/percentage of students (by disability category) participating in SOL tests

Community Indicators

- Number/percentage of parents in PTA
- Number/percentage of parents satisfied with quality of education students are receiving at school

School Characteristics Indicators

- Number/percentage of teachers with advanced degrees
- Number/percentage of students attending school on a daily basis—missing 10 or fewer days per year
- Number/percentage of students receiving free or reduced-price lunches
- Number of student referrals for discipline

Use this space to list other school data you want to track yearly.

- Percentage of teachers meeting state licensure requirements
- Percentage of staff involved in professional development activity

---

FIGURE 10.2   Core Data Elements to Track Yearly Elementary Schools

Source: Core Data Elements to Track Yearly, copyright 2000 by Successline, Inc. Reproduced by permission of Deborah Wahlstrom.

transformation (see Chapter 6). Given the debate, testing and research experts must determine the role of testing within their school districts. Perhaps the single best resource for gaining greater understanding of these and other related complex concerns is the American Educational Research Association (AERA). (For more information, see aera.net.)

It is clear that test scores and how to improve them will occupy significantly more time in the school leader's future. This will include choosing assessments, determining how to interpret them, providing incentives and sanctions to encourage improvement, and developing programs that will allow students to be successful on assessments. The curriculum, the standards, and the assessment must all flow together. The general purpose of all final reports is to summarize, organize, and interpret test results so that a meaningful picture of the school or the individual emerges. For more information, see nces.ed.gov/nationsreportcard.

✳ **What sources of data will be used in an inquiry-oriented data-driven approach when working toward the success of Natasha and other such students at Oak Grove Middle School?**

EXTRACURRICULAR ACTIVITIES

Athletics tends to be the most prominent of all extracurricular activities. Through athletics, students set personal goals, learn to be responsible, develop self-discipline, learn to work with others, adjust to the many personalities and situations that arise, develop lifelong physical fitness habits, and learn dedication, sacrifice, and patience. Studies suggest that participation in sports contributes to better academic performance, serves to keep many students in school, and inspires greater involvement and leadership (Holland & Andre, 1991; Reith, 1989).

The press magnifies athletics and it is quite important to operate an honest, well-organized, and safe program. Schools typically must follow the athletic rules and regulations that are established for the region and state. Student athletes should put academics first and should model exemplary behavior. An athletic director typically reports to the principal and is responsible for the entire athletic program. The coaches and assistant coaches report to the athletic director. The athletic trainer also reports to the athletic director and is responsible for medical coverage for all athletics. In addition, good managers are critical to running an efficient program. Coaches, along with the athletic director, are responsible for schedules, uniforms, player eligibility, tryouts, parental contacts, coaching, team travel, safety, discipline, recognition, and many other aspects of athletic programs.

Sports are not the only extracurricular activities within schools. Many different honorary, service, class-related, and special interest clubs exist, as well as various types of field trips and community service projects. The primary purpose of all of these programs is to meet the needs and interests of as many students as possible, providing unique learning experiences while developing a positive school climate, school spirit, and fellowship, which add to the overall morale of the school. Gerber (1996) found that the amount of participation in extracurricular activities also was positively related to academic achievement. Students involved in these kinds of extracurricular activities find opportunities to shine and are less likely to become disengaged from school. A Gallup survey showed that participation in extracurricular activity is positively correlated with high school and post–high school academic achievement as well as occupational status after graduation.

DEVELOPING PROGRAMS OF SCHOOL, FAMILY, AND COMMUNITY PARTNERSHIPS: ADMINISTRATORS MAKE A DIFFERENCE

JOYCE L. EPSTEIN

Director, Center on School, Family, and Community Partnerships, Johns Hopkins University

Over and over again we learn that principals, district administrators, and state education policy leaders make the difference between successful and unsuccessful schools. Administrators have different leadership styles, but all effective leaders focus on important goals, encourage hard work, inspire excellence, and recognize the efforts and contributions of others. Only with outstanding support will all teachers, students, parents, community members, and others remain committed to improving schools, classrooms, and children's learning. This support is especially necessary for developing comprehensive programs of school, family, and community partnerships.

What is a comprehensive program of partnerships? First, such programs are *theory driven*. The theory of "overlapping spheres of influence" recognizes that students learn and grow at home, at school, and in their communities. Students are at the center of this model, because they are the main actors in their education. Second, comprehensive programs of partnership are *research based*. From the results of many studies in elementary, middle, and high schools, I developed a framework of six major types of involvement:

Type 1—Parenting: Assist families with parenting skills, family support, understanding child and adolescent development, and setting home conditions to support learning at each age and grade level. Assist schools in understanding families' backgrounds, cultures, and goals for children.

Type 2—Communicating: Communicate with families about school programs and student progress in varied, clear, and productive ways. Create two-way communication channels (school to home and home to school) so that families can easily communicate with teachers, administrators, counselors, and other families.

Type 3—Volunteering: Improve recruitment, training, activities, and schedules to involve families as volunteers and as audiences at the school or in other locations. Enable educators to work with regular and occasional volunteers who assist and support students and the school.

Type 4—Learning at Home: Involve families with their children in academic learning activities at home, such as homework, goal setting, and other curriculum-related activities and decisions. Encourage teachers to design homework that enables students to share and discuss interesting work and ideas with family members.

Type 5—Decision Making: Include families as participants in school decisions, governance, and advocacy activities through school councils or improvement teams, committees, PTA/PTO, and other parent organizations. Assist family and teacher representatives to obtain information from, and give information to, those they represent.

Type 6—Collaborating With Community: Coordinate resources and services for families, students, and the school with community businesses, agencies, cultural and civic organizations, colleges or universities, and other community groups. Enable students, staff, and families to contribute their service to the community.

There are hundreds of practices for the six types from which elementary, middle, and high schools may choose. Each type of involvement has explicit challenges that must be met in order to turn an ordinary program into an excellent one. Each type of involvement leads to different results for students, families, teachers, schools, and communities.

From many studies, we have learned that schools make progress in home/school/community connections if plans are written and if an action team for school, family, and community partnerships charts progress. The team of teachers, parents, administrators, and others completes an inventory of present practices, constructs a 3-year vision, and writes annual 1-year action plans that address school goals with good practices from the six types of involvement.

Many studies indicate the following results of good programs of partnership:

- Families are important for children's learning, healthy development, and school success from preschool through high school.
- State, district, and school policy statements about partnerships are not enough. Schools need assistance, support, recognition, and ongoing guidance to develop, improve, and maintain successful programs of school, family, and community partnerships.
- All communities have resources to promote students' social and intellectual development and to assist schools and families. Community resources must be organized, mobilized, and incorporated in comprehensive programs of partnership.
- Students are more positive about school and learning and do better in school if their families and communities are involved in their education in productive ways. Specific results (e.g., improvements in attendance, behavior, homework completion, reading, writing, math, or other achievement) are linked to goal-oriented and subject-specific activities for family and community involvement.
- When elementary, middle, and high schools develop excellent programs of partnership, families become involved, including those who would not become involved on their own or who are typically "hard to reach."

For administrators to organize and improve their leadership on school, family, and community partnerships requires understanding, action, and persistence, as well as knowing the framework of the six types of involvement, the challenges that must be met to reach all families, and the connections of involvement to specific goals and results.

Guidelines for action are available from the National Network of Partnership Schools at the Center on School, Family, and Community Partnerships at Johns Hopkins University. Members receive handbooks, newsletters, training workshops, assistance by phone, e-mail, and Web site, and opportunities for research and sharing best practices. There are no fees for these services, but members must invest in their own staff, identify budgets, implement annual plans, develop comprehensive programs, and share progress with the center.

Developing excellent home, school, and community partnerships is an ongoing process that takes time, organization, and effort. Progress is accelerated if efforts in school, family, and community partnerships are targeted in annual professional evaluations of teachers, principals, and superintendents.

No longer a separate topic off to the side of "real" reform efforts, school, family, and community partnerships now are seen as a central component of whole-school change and school improvement. Information for families and their involvement and input are needed for students to succeed with bilingual programs, challenging curricula, innovative instruction, and new tests and assessments. In sum, good programs of partnerships help improve schools, strengthen families, energize communities, and increase student success.

Note: This work is supported by grants from the U.S. Department of Education and the DeWitt Wallace's Digest Fund. The ideas are the author's and do not necessarily represent the policies of either funding source. For information on the National Network of Partnership Schools or lists of related publications, contact the Center on School, Family, and Community Partnerships, Johns Hopkins University/CRESPAR, e-mail: sfc@csos .jhu.edu; Web site: http://www.csos.jhu.edu/p2000.

In many schools, the student cooperative association (SCA) has a responsibility to oversee and to disseminate information about school activities. The faculty sponsor and the treasurer of each organization participate in the management of finances according to the policy of the state board of education, school board, and superintendent. Itemized day-by-day receipts and expenditures are recorded with the school bookkeeper. Extracurricular activities also receive support from student services, parent–teacher associations, and a number of community sponsors.

Usually, one person is designated in each school to coordinate extracurricular activity. Sometimes students must meet specific criteria to be allowed to participate in an extracurricular activity. Written and well-understood rules and regulations for the governance of these activities are important. Issues sometimes develop around adult interference, broken rules, over competitiveness, overemphasis, interference with academics, irrelevance, financial problems, faculty supervision, equitable treatment, transportation, and prejudice.

Extracurricular activities are becoming even more important, because safe spaces for children are shrinking as those for adults are expanding, such as restaurants, health clubs, tennis clubs, spas, golf courses, sports and entertainment complexes, and resorts. Many argue that technology as well as television is further privatizing lives and making needed human interactions even less available to children who desperately need them.

✳ **Should students like Natasha participate in extracurricular activities? Why or why not? What policies and supporting activities should exist regarding student participation in extracurricular activities? How would you respond to Natasha's mother's right to challenge the appropriateness of educational services being planned for her daughter?**

CONNECTING SCHOOLS AND COMMUNITY ORGANIZATIONS

In education, partnerships are either school linked or school based. These school partnerships range in complexity from a collaboration with one person, organization, or agency to multilayered alliances. Research supports the observation that the partnering service model is not only useful but in today's economic and social climate also quickly becoming recognized as mandatory (Sheldon & Simon, 2008; Cordeiro & Loup, 1996; Gardner, 1993; Jehl & Kirst, 1992).

Figure 10.3 depicts the numerous human service agencies and community organizations that constitute what some researchers call "cultural capital" or "sociocultural capital" (Bourdieu & Passeron, 1977, p. 90; Coleman, 1993; Cordeiro, Reagan, & Martinez, 1994). At the center is the child, encompassed first by family, then by the school and school district.

A variety of other entities influence the child's school and family life either directly or indirectly. These include religious organizations, higher-education institutions, nonprofits such as museums and local arts organizations, government

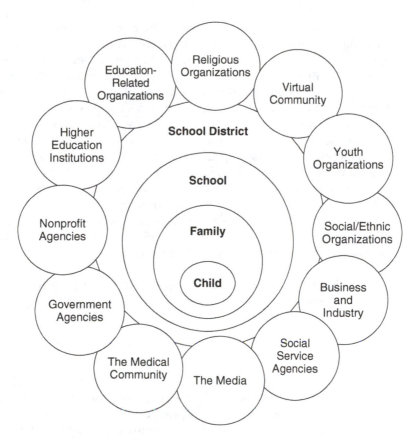

FIGURE 10.3   Educational Partners

agencies, the medical community, the media, social service agencies, business and industry, social and ethnic organizations, youth organizations such as the YM/YWCA or Boys and Girls Clubs, parks and recreation department programs, education-related organizations, and the rapidly growing outside world—the virtual community. Each of these agencies or organizations is part of a network of services available to all children. One fairly new role that schools and school districts need to play is the coordination of these many entities not only with the school, but also with the family.

Cordeiro and Monroe-Kolek (1996) identified five key factors among these organizations and schools that are preconditions for successful partnerships: leadership, trust, stability, readiness, and a common agenda. These factors interact to form a foundation on which partnerships can be constructed. Without this basic framework, it is doubtful that solid school–community partnerships will improve children's lives.

Research has identified four conditions that support collaboration if these preconditions exist. Communication is crucial to any partnership. The form of communication does not appear to be the key factor but rather the fact that regular and sustained communication occurs. The notion that both partners are benefiting in some way so that there appears to be reciprocity is another element in maintaining successful partnerships (Cordeiro & Monroe-Kolek, 1996; Epstein & Associates, 2009). Aligning and pooling of resources is another factor. Johnson and Galvan (1996) argue that the interests and transaction costs associated with such efforts suggest that certain partnerships might in fact increase the actual costs for both organizations involved. Thus, it is imperative that partners not duplicate services but instead fill in the gaps in service provision. The final crucial element these authors identify to maintaining and sustaining a partnership is the notion of knowing the community. One way to address this issue is McKnight and Kretzman's (1993) concept of asset mapping. Especially in urban and low-SES communities, there is a tendency to look at what is *not* present to support the growth and development of children. McKnight and Kretzman argue that poor neighborhoods have a multitude of assets, such as schools, ethnic and religious organizations, institutions of higher education, churches, and libraries, to name but a few.

✳ **What types of community partnerships might be important to Natasha's success?**

CONCLUSION

Pupil personnel services help schools confront difficult issues that keep students from achieving academic success. All the professionals within a school are encouraged to contribute their unique knowledge and skills to the goal of achieving competent, well-educated, and well-adjusted students, and, ultimately, self-sufficient adults.

With the support of public policy, more and more special-needs students are receiving assistance and being accommodated in regular classes. The inclusion of a pupil personnel plan to complement classroom activity has proven absolutely essential to student success. The focus of pupil personnel services is to help remediate developmental issues within a student's life and to enable the student to reach his or her full potential. When pupil personnel services are well organized and integrated into the culture of the school and community, they make a substantive contribution to student achievement by better preparing students to participate in academic work and by improving their lives. Professionals who provide these services have a formidable responsibility to adhere to the highest professional and ethical standards. Changes within a variety of disciplines, judicial decisions, legislation, societal changes, child development research, technological and other advancements, and many other forces will continue to have enormous impact on pupil personnel practices. Keeping up with the trends and issues in the decades ahead will be an exciting, challenging, sometimes frustrating—but always rewarding—endeavor.

MyEdLeadershipLab™

Go to Topic 8: *Community Relations* in the MyEdLeadershipLab™ site (www.MyEdLeadershipLab .com) for *Educational Leadership: A Bridge to Improved Practice*, Fifth Edition, where you can:

- Find learning outcomes for *Community Relations* along with the national standards that connect to these outcomes.
- Complete Assignments and Activities that can help you more deeply understand the chapter content.
- Apply and practice your understanding of the core skills identified in the chapter with the Building Leadership Skills unit.
- Prepare yourself for professional certification with a Practice for Certification quiz.

PORTFOLIO ARTIFACTS

- Prepare a BIP or FBP for a chronically disciplined student.

- Discuss a discipline referral with a teacher, hold a conference with the persons involved, and assign an appropriate disciplinary action.

- Develop strategies for creating inclusive learning communities that promote equity and learning for all students.

- Explore the following Web site: http://pbis.org.
  Do RTI or PBIS have any implications for your educational leadership platform?

- Explore the resources for special needs students at the Iris Center Web site: http:// iris.peabody.vanderbilt.edu/index.html.

- Identify a variety of curriculum accommodations and teaching techniques that respond to a wide range of individual differences.

- Examine a district's policy on antiharassment/antibullying. What strategies, if any, does the district promote?

- Conduct or oversee a child-study team and oversee an individualized educational plan (IEP) causality meeting.

- Visit a home with a school social worker and write a report on your experience.

- Participate in a group counseling session with a school counselor and keep a reflective journal of your experiences.

- Work with a school psychologist in administering and interpreting tests.

- Interview a person working in a community agency who partners with a school. How does this person's perspective influence your views on schools and their communities?

- Serve as a faculty sponsor for an extracurricular activity.

KEY TERMS

- Antibullying programs
- Behavior intervention plan (BIP)
- Data disaggregation
- Data-driven decision making
- Dropout prevention programs
- The Education for All Handicapped Children Act
- Extracurricular activity

- Functional behavior assessment (FBA)
- Individualized education plan (IEP)
- Individuals with Disabilities Education Act (IDEA)
- In-school suspension
- Learning disability (LD)
- Mainstreaming and inclusion
- Norm-referenced test

- Positive behavior supports (PBS)
- Response to intervention (RTI)
- School counselor
- School psychologist
- Universal design for learning (UDL)
- 504 plan

SUGGESTED READINGS

Dimmitt, C., Carey, J. C., & Hatch, T. (2007). *Evidence-based school counseling: Making a difference with data-driven practice.* Thousand Oaks, CA: Corwin Press.

Epstein, J. & Associates. (2009). *School, family and community partnerships: Your handbook for action.* Thousand Oaks, CA: Corwin Press.

Hall, S. (2007). *Implementing response to intervention: A principal's guide.* Thousand Oaks, CA: Corwin Press.

McLaughlin, M. J. (2008). *What every principal needs to know about special education.* Thousand Oaks, CA: Corwin Press.

Sherrod, M., Getch, Y. Q., & Ziomek-Daigle, J. (2009). The impact of positive behavior support to decrease discipline referrals with elementary students. *Professional School Counseling, 12*(6), 421–427

CHAPTER 11

LAW AND POLICY

MyEdLeadershipLab™

Visit the MyEdLeadershipLab™ site for *Educational Leadership: A Bridge to Improved Practice*, Fifth Edition to enhance your understanding of chapter concepts. You'll have the opportunity to practice your skills through video- and case-based Assignments and Activities as well as Building Leadership Skills units, and to prepare for your certification exam with Practice for Certification quizzes.

EMPIRE I.S.D.

Not Following School Board Policy

It was 7:45 a.m. and Principal Julia Holladay was sitting at her desk contemplating her next step. Yesterday, high school teacher Angel Chavarin had chosen not to follow school district policy on field trips. The policy required that parents give written permission prior to their children going on a field trip. Chavarin knew what the policy was, but in his own mind the circumstance was different and justified deviation from the policy. Clearly it wasn't. He had chosen not to get prior permission, and the car he was driving with the four students had been involved in an accident around 4 p.m. No permission slips constituted a clear violation.

Principal Holladay knew that Chavarin was a fine educator. She had worked with him for nearly 12 years. Before she became principal, Holladay had been a teacher in the school. Holladay and Chavarin had spent hours discussing education and how to improve

schools for youths. In fact, Chavarin was one of the top teachers in the building. Two years before, he had received the district's "Outstanding Teacher" award. He just hadn't thought about the possible implications of his field trip decision.

The previous afternoon Principal Holladay and her assistant principal had tried to find out as much as possible about the situation. One of the students was still in the hospital and was scheduled to be released the next day. Chavarin and the three other students had suffered minor injuries and were released from the hospital that same night. Holladay called the superintendent to inform her of what had occurred. Because the superintendent was out of town, Holladay left a message at her hotel.

Last night, after arriving home around midnight from a work-related dinner, Holladay had found a long message on her answering machine from Daryl Turner, the board president. Outraged by what had happened, he demanded that Chavarin be fired, tenured or not. "This is gross negligence," he clamored. There was also a message from her superintendent asking her to call her first thing in the morning. The superintendent had spoken to Daryl Turner and was very concerned about the situation.

✳ **If you were principal Holladay, what would you do next? Obtain a copy of your state's policy regarding the dismissal or suspension of teachers. What does it say?**

LEGAL RESPONSIBILITY

Every week, federal and state courts hand down decisions that have the potential to affect every school in the nation. It is therefore important for educational leaders to learn about current legal issues and their potential impact on schools. School districts are involved in a number of major litigation areas, and knowledge of several key concepts in school law is essential. It is also important for administrators to understand compliance with policies, procedures, and risk management.

Learning about Schools and Legal Issues

One way to begin to acquire a basic understanding of the legal system and the laws and statutes that pertain to schools is to take a basic course in school law. Although such a course provides a foundation, keeping up to date must become an ongoing part of professional development. School leaders should have an understanding of, and appreciation for, the legal rights of teachers and students. Educators need a basic understanding of the federal Constitution and Bill of Rights as well as their state constitutions and statutes. Common law is a general, overarching statewide or nationwide precedent that derives from earlier legal controversies. It prescribes social conduct enforced by courts by the doctrine of the supremacy of law.

One of the functions of school boards is to adopt policies in accordance with state legislation. Thus, educational leaders must understand school district policies. There are a variety of professional organizations that are helpful. The National Association of Secondary School Principals (NASSP) has a "Principal's Online School Law Guide" (NASSP.org/knowledge-center/principals-online-school-law-guide). Educational newspapers and journals have special sections pertaining to legal issues (see *Kappan*, Phi Delta Kappa's monthly magazine with its special section "Courtside" or Pi Lambda Theta's magazine *Educational Horizons* with a special section "Legal Talk"). Other resources include Web sites and publications that serve as guides to federal and state cases. The official newspaper of the U.S. government, available online, is the *Federal Register* (gpoaccess.gov/fr). It is the vehicle through which all federal agencies publish their regulations and legal notices.

A graduate-level university course in school law and professional reading on a regular basis will help administrators stay current on school legal issues. For interpretations of court decisions, which can sometimes be difficult to follow, a telephone call to the school district's lawyer (most districts have legal counsel) might be appropriate.

THE U.S. LEGAL SYSTEM

Federal Role in Education

Education is not specifically discussed in the U.S. Constitution. Box 11.1 lists those amendments that are particularly relevant to typical school legal issues. The 10th Amendment states, "The powers not delegated to the United States by the Constitution, nor prohibited by it to the States, are reserved to the States respectively, or to the people." This does not mean that the federal government has little influence on schools—in fact, the amendments to the Constitution, U.S. Supreme Court decisions, and congressional acts have considerable influence on both public and private educational institutions.

Federal Courts

The three levels of federal court are shown in Box 11.2. Each state has at least one federal district court; some have several, depending on population density. Appeals from federal district courts can go to the next level, the U.S. appeals courts, and even on rare occasions to the U.S. Supreme Court.

The procedures and functions of intermediate and the highest appellate courts differ from those of trial courts. These courts do not conduct trials, nor do

---

BOX 11.1

SELECTED AMENDMENTS OF THE U.S. CONSTITUTION

AMENDMENT I (1791)
Congress shall make no law respecting an establishment of religion, or prohibiting the free exercise thereof; or abridging the freedom of speech, or of the press; or the right of the people peaceably to assemble, and to petition the Government for a redress of grievances.

AMENDMENT IV (1791)
The right of the people to be secure in their persons, houses, papers, and effects, against unreasonable searches and seizures, shall not be violated, and no Warrants shall issue, but upon probable cause, supported by Oath or affirmation, and particularly describing the place to be searched, and the persons or things to be seized.

AMENDMENT IX (1791)
The enumeration in the Constitution of certain rights, shall not be construed to deny or disparage others retained by the people.

AMENDMENT X (1791)
The powers not delegated to the United States by the Constitution, nor prohibited by it to the States, are reserved to the States respectively, or to the people.

AMENDMENT XIV (1868)
Section 1. All persons born or naturalized in the United States, and subject to the jurisdiction thereof, are citizens of the United States and of the State wherein they reside. No State shall make or enforce any law which shall abridge the privileges or immunities of citizens of the United States; nor shall any State deprive any person of life, liberty, or property, without due process of law; nor deny to any person within its jurisdiction the equal protection of the laws.

BOX 11.2

THE FEDERAL COURT SYSTEM*

U.S. SUPREME COURT
(highest court of the country)

U.S. CIRCUIT COURTS OF APPEALS (APPELLATE COURTS)
(13 intermediate appeal courts)

U.S. DISTRICT COURTS (TRIAL COURTS)
(89 district courts)

*For more information, see http://www.uscourts.gov.

---

they hear any new evidence or conduct fact finding. Their function is to review records of lower courts to determine whether any errors of law have occurred. Errors of law might include procedural mistakes, misinterpretations of the Constitution or statutes, and incorrect instructions to juries, to name a few.

There are 13 circuit courts of appeal (see Table 11.1). One, the Federal Circuit Court of Appeals, has jurisdiction to hear special claims such as those related to

TABLE 11.1   Jurisdictions of the Federal Circuit Courts of Appeal

CIRCUIT	JURISDICTION
1st	Maine, Massachusetts, New Hampshire, Puerto Rico, Rhode Island
2nd	Connecticut, New York, Vermont
3rd	Delaware, New Jersey, Pennsylvania, Virgin Islands
4th	Maryland, North Carolina, South Carolina, Virginia, West Virginia
5th	Louisiana, Mississippi, Texas
6th	Kentucky, Ohio, Michigan, Tennessee
7th	Illinois, Indiana, Wisconsin
8th	Arkansas, Iowa, Minnesota, Missouri, Nebraska, North Dakota, South Dakota
9th	Alaska, Arizona, California, Guam, Hawaii, Idaho, Montana, Nevada, Northern Mariana Islands, Oregon, Washington
10th	Colorado, Kansas, New Mexico, Oklahoma, Utah, Wyoming
11th	Alabama, Florida, Georgia
DC	Washington, DC
Federal	Three specialized courts, Washington, DC

taxes, patents and copyrights, customs, and international trade. The remaining 12 are those to which an education-related case would be appealed.

Decisions rendered in a federal appellate court are binding only in the states that fall within that circuit's jurisdiction. For example, the 1st Circuit Court of Appeals includes Maine, Massachusetts, New Hampshire, Puerto Rico, and Rhode Island. A decision rendered in the 1st Circuit Court of Appeals pertains to these states and territory only; however, the decisions rendered by individual courts of appeals often *influence* the decisions of other courts dealing with similar issues.

The U.S. Supreme Court is the court of highest appeal on questions of federal law. The Supreme Court has heard numerous education cases dealing with particular provisions of the U.S. Constitution. In particular, the 14th Amendment's *equal protection clause* (e.g., *Plessy v. Ferguson* and *Brown v. Board of Education*); the 14th Amendment's *due process clause* (e.g., *Meyer v. Nebraska*); and the 1st Amendment's *establishment clause* (e.g., *Board of Education v. Allen*) are cited more often than other amendments in school law cases.

In addition to federal courts, the federal government enacts legislation (federal statutes) directly affecting educational institutions. Statutes are regularly updated, supplemented, and revised by successive legislatures (see the *Federal Register*). Courts determine the validity and meaning of these legislative acts. These acts are binding for all citizens as long as they satisfy constitutional requirements. Civil rights legislation such as the Individuals with Disabilities Education Act (IDEA), Section 504 of the Rehabilitation Act of 1973, and Title VII of the Civil Rights Act of 1964 are examples of federal statutes.

One example of federal legislation that affected nearly all school districts in the country was Goals 2000. This legislation was introduced by President George Bush Sr. in 1989 and later passed by Congress and signed by President Bill Clinton in 1994. Consisting of eight goals, it appropriates federal money each year for states that adopt voluntary standards. These standards must meet federal guidelines for student achievement. It is not required that a state applies for the funding, but, if it does, it would then make subgrants to local education agencies (LEAs may include school districts, regional service centers, and others). This legislation also established two other acts: The Gun-Free Schools Act and the Safe Schools Act. (For more details about federal involvement in education, see Chapter 2.)

The Department of Education's (DOE) role is to implement the administration's policies regarding education. The chief executive officer of the DOE is the secretary of education. The Department of Education maintains a home page at ed.gov/.

The operationalizing of the administration's policies can be seen in the federal education budget. (Chapter 12 provides an example of how federal monies are distributed to certain program areas for use in local school districts.) The federal government can penalize or sanction local education agencies that do not adhere to federal policies. Additionally, guidelines and policies from federal agencies,

UNDERSTANDING COURT DECISIONS

PERRY A. ZIRKEL
Lehigh University
KATHLEEN A. SULLIVAN
Lehigh University

Published court opinions form an important body of law that fills in the gaps and resolves the interactions between other sources of law, such as the Constitution and legislation, in relation to specific factual situations. Not all court decisions result in published opinions. Generally, the proportion of published opinions is higher in federal than in state courts and in appellate than in trial courts.

Citations provide identifying information for published court decisions. This sample citation illustrates the key elements: *Yankton School District v. Schramm,* 93 F.3d 1369 (8th Cir. 1996). The first element, the name of the case, is customarily underlined or italicized and contains the names of at least one party on each side of the case. Inasmuch as many of the published opinions, including this one, are at the appellate level, the order of the names does not necessarily convey who was the plaintiff, or suing party. Instead, at the appellate level, the first of the two names (here "Yankton") is the appellant, or the party who lost at the level below and, as a result, has brought the appeal.

The second element consists of numbers and an abbreviation that tell where to find the case. The central piece of information, here "F.3d," signifies the reporter, or set of volumes for a particular group of courts. The *Federal Reporter,* originally abbreviated as "F." and now in its third series, contains published decisions of the intermediate appellate courts in the federal system. The number in front of the abbreviation, here "93," is the volume in that series, and the number after the abbreviation, here "1369," is the page in that volume where the court's opinion starts.

The final element, which is in parentheses, contains the year in which the decision was issued and, if not indicated by the reporter abbreviation, an abbreviation for the court that issued

the decision. Because only Supreme Court decisions appear in the alternative *Supreme Court Reporter* as "U.S." and "S. Ct.," no additional notation beyond citation to the reporter is necessary to identify the court. As in the sample citation, the United States circuit courts of appeal, the level below the Supreme Court, is identified by circuit number. An opinion rendered by the highest state court will contain only the state's abbreviation in parentheses, and opinions from lower levels will contain further abbreviations for the name of the court.

The court opinion also has identifiable elements that help the reader understand the import of the decision. The first part, which follows the name of the judge who authored the opinion, typically contains the facts that were distilled from the evidence in the case. The facts include who did what to whom, giving rise to the specific controversy. At the appellate level, this section also includes the disposition of the case in the lower court(s).

The central element of the opinion, which might take several readings to accurately identify, is the issue of the case. Usually a single question answerable by yes or no, the issue poses the relevant facts in a sufficiently generalizable form. In the *Schramm* case, for example, the issue may be stated as follows: "Whether instructional accommodations fulfill the 'special education' criterion for eligibility under the Individuals with Disabilities Education Act (IDEA)."

The court's answer to this question, along with the basis, or legal source, and rationale for the decision provide the final part of the court's opinion. The court's answer is called the *rule* or *holding* in the case. In *Schramm,* the 8th Circuit Court of Appeals answered the question affirmatively, based on the definition of "special education" in IDEA. The rationale was that the plain meaning of the words in the definition, such as "specially designed instruction" to meet individual needs, conveyed a congressional intent to include instructional accommodations for otherwise qualified students. Usually the court presents its rationale through a logical discussion and application of the law to the facts of the case.

Opinions also often contain statements made by the court that are not necessary for the holding, such as a comment on how the decision might change if the facts were different. These comments, known as *dicta,* should not be confused with the holding. Only those statements or observations essential to the judge's decision form the holding in the case and may be relied on for guidance.

Usually a court's decision applies both to the immediate parties and to future cases that have the same circumstances. These past cases and their effect on future cases are called *precedents.* Precedent is binding on courts at the same or higher level within a jurisdiction. Because our legal system contains both federal and state branches, each with different boundaries of authority, not all decisions are binding on all other courts. Decisions from outside jurisdictions, although not binding, might be persuasive to other courts.

Judicial opinions offer insight into the probable outcome of similar cases and establish boundaries to guide future conduct. Deciphering the elements of not only the citation but, more important, the opinion, enables school leaders to locate and use court decisions. Because they cannot afford to leave such matters entirely to lawyers, school leaders can benefit by knowing how to find and understand court decisions to answer as well as ask key questions.

such as the Equal Employment Opportunities Commission (EEOC), are often cited in employment discrimination claims.

✳ **What federal laws are relevant to addressing issues related to Chavarin, the injured students, and the field trip? What are the relevant laws in your state?**

The State's Legal Role in Education

Although state court systems vary, most state courts have three levels: trial courts, intermediate appellate courts, and the state supreme court (see Box 11.3).

The majority of education-related cases are heard at the state level because education is a function of the state, rather than the federal government. A state supreme court case can be appealed to a federal court only if it involves a question of federal law. Appellate courts, whether at the federal or state level, do not review an entire case. Instead, they take appeals only on questions that the lawyers properly "preserve" for appeal. The narrowness of the appeals process explains why some school law cases are litigated several times before all the important issues are finally settled. Examining one state education case will be illustrative.

Sheff v. O'Neill was filed in 1989 on behalf of 17 schoolchildren in Hartford, Connecticut. Milo Sheff was a 4th-grade African-American student (16 other white and Hispanic children living in the city of Hartford and the suburbs were also plaintiffs). William A. O'Neill, the defendant, was then governor of Connecticut. The plaintiffs argued that it was up to the state to alleviate the educational deprivation associated with living in a racially and socioeconomically isolated urban area

BOX 11.3
STATE COURT SYSTEMS

STATE SUPREME COURT
(highest state court)

STATE APPELLATE COURTS
(intermediate appellate courts)

TRIAL COURTS
(district, circuit, or county courts)

such as Hartford. The case was originally filed in the lowest court in the state—the superior court. This district court ruled against the plaintiffs, Milo Sheff and the other children. The superior court ruled that because the state did not create the segregation that now held sway, it need not take measures to dismantle it.

The case was appealed by the plaintiffs to the state appellate court. The appeal was granted and in 1995 the case went to the Connecticut State Supreme Court. In 1996, this court ruled in favor of the plaintiffs. It declared that the state constitution's education and equal protection clauses require the legislature to ensure that students in the Hartford public schools are provided with integrated and equal educational opportunities. Although this case is not binding outside Connecticut, it has the potential to influence similar claims in other states.

State Legislatures, Administrative Agencies, and Local Boards of Control

States have the power to enact statutes within the limitations of state and federal constitutions. Valente & Valente (2004), in their text on school law titled *Law in the Schools,* maintains that within the realm of education,

> legislative power includes authority to (1) create, alter, and abolish school districts; (2) alter the structure and powers of school boards; (3) remove incumbent school board members and abolish offices; (4) prescribe the school calendar and curriculum; (5) determine the sources and procedures for raising school revenue and school spending; (6) fix the appointment, term, and qualifications of teachers; (7) require local schools to admit children of nontaxpayers; and (8) revoke charters of public schools for noncompliance with state regulations. (p. 17)

For example, a Connecticut statute (Sec. 46b-56) regarding the rights of noncustodial parents reads:

> Sec. 46b-56. (Formerly Sec. 46-42). Superior court orders re custody and care of minor children in actions for dissolution of marriage, legal separation, and annulment. Access

RACIAL ISOLATION IN SCHOOLS

FRANK KEMERER
University of San Diego

At first glance, American public schools appear to be racially diverse. Data from the National Center for Education Statistics show that public school enrollment is over 50% White, about 15% Black, and over 20% Latino.[1] But, as educators know, schools rarely reflect this degree of diversity. In fact, data from the Civil Rights Project/Proyecto Decrechos Civiles at the University of California, Los Angeles show that the average White student attends a school that is nearly 80% White, whereas the average Black or Latino student attends a school that is less than a third White.[2] Viewed another way, only 1% of White students attend schools that are 90% to 100% of color, but nearly 40% of both Black and Latino students do. Because race and class overlap, Black and Latino students are three times as likely as White students to attend high-poverty schools. And these schools are likely to be among the lowest performing. The same pattern of racial clustering is evident in charter and private schools.[3]

It is apparent that the U.S. Supreme Court's 1954 seminal ruling in *Brown v. Board of Education* has not eradicated racial segregation in schooling.[4] When the decision was handed down, many commentators were unsure exactly what the extent of the ruling was. Some believed it was targeted only at de jure segregation, that is, segregation maintained by law, and did not address de facto segregation (segregation resulting from such factors as housing preference). Others believed its intent was to end racial segregation regardless of cause. The source of the ambiguity was Chief Justice Earl Warren's statement in the opinion that "Segregation of white and colored children in public schools has a detrimental effect upon the colored children. The impact is greater when it has the sanction of law."[5] In other words, segregation of children by race in schools for whatever reason is harmful.

Later, the high court clarified that it was addressing only de jure segregation (*Milliken v. Bradley,* 1974).[6] Thus, while racial integration progressed rapidly in the South after the enactment of the 1964 Civil Rights Act and the aggressive use of federal desegregation court orders, substantial racial segregation remained in the North. Still, educators in many school districts without a history of de jure segregation took strides to reduce or eliminate racial clustering. The assumption was that they had authority to do so, based on what Chief Justice Warren Burger had written in a 1971 unanimous Supreme Court decision (*Swann v. Charlotte-Mecklenburg Board of Education*):

> School authorities are traditionally charged with broad power to formulate and implement educational policy and might well conclude, for example, that in order to prepare students to live in a pluralistic society each school should have a prescribed ratio of Negro to white students reflecting the proportion for the district as a whole. To do this as an educational policy is within the broad discretionary power of school authorities.[7]

Both the federal government and the federal courts have pulled back in recent years from aggressively pursuing school racial integration, but many school leaders have continued efforts to reduce racial isolation in response to research studies showing the positive academic and socialization benefits of racial integration. In 2007, the U.S. Supreme Court confronted this approach. The case involved the Jefferson County School District in metropolitan Louisville, Kentucky, and the Seattle School District in Washington state. The Jefferson County

(continued)

district had continued to use race in assigning students to school to achieve racial balance after a desegregation court order had ended. The Seattle school district had never been under a desegregation court order but used race as a tie-breaker to further diversity if any of its 10 high schools was oversubscribed under the district's school choice plan. The purpose was to reduce racial clustering in the high schools resulting from segregated housing.

The U.S. Supreme Court declared the use of race in both districts unconstitutional (*Parents Involved in Community Schools v. Seattle School District No. 1, 2007*).[8] However, only four justices ruled that any use of race in student assignment is prohibited. A fifth justice, Anthony Kennedy, agreed that, absent a court order, assigning students to schools based on their race is invalid. However, he did approve a more nuanced use of race. Specifically, he suggested that race could be considered in choosing sites for new schools, drawing attendance zones, allocating resources for special programs, and targeted recruiting of both students and teachers. The other four justices on the Court voted to uphold the explicit use of race in student assignment as practiced in the two school districts. With the Court split four to four, Justice Kennedy's view prevails.

So what should a school leader who is faced with growing racial imbalance in a school or district do? The first task is to examine what state law and district policy require. For example, the Connecticut Supreme Court ruled in 1996 that the state constitution requires action to end racial and ethnic isolation in public schools regardless of cause (*Sheff v. O'Neill*).[9] The California Supreme Court ruled the same 20 years before (*Crawford v. the Board of Education of the City of Los Angeles*), but a later change to that state's constitution from voter approval of Proposition 209 in 1996 prohibits preferential treatment or discrimination based on race, sex, color, ethnicity, or national origin.[10] If there is a requirement to address racial isolation in states like these or if school leaders in other states desire to do so for pedagogical reasons, how should this be done in light of the U.S. Supreme Court's 2007 *Parents Involved* decision?

In addition to employing Justice Kennedy's suggestions, proxies for race such as family income can be used to assign or recruit students to schools. Although not as effective as using race, they are more likely to be legally permissible and they add other dimensions to diversity. For example, requiring every school in a district to have, say, 20% of its students from low-income families increases diversity by class and, to some extent, by race as well. What can be done, of course, will be influenced by community attitudes. Even relatively routine decisions such as where to construct new schools can generate considerable controversy unless efforts are undertaken firsthand to build community support.

Simply taking efforts to achieve race and class diversity in student populations is no guarantee that positive outcomes will occur. Self-sorting by students, coupled with academic tracking and course selection, may result only in the appearance of diversity. The challenge for leaders is to design academic and extracurricular programs that ensure student and parent buy-in. Only in this way will the positive outcomes of integration have a chance to occur.

1. National Center for Education Statistics. http://nces.ed.gov/programs/coe/2006.section1/table.asp?tableID=436

2. Orfield, G., & Lee, C. (2006). *Racial transformation and the changing nature of segregation.* http://civilrightsproject.ucla.edu/research/deseg/deseg06.php

3. Frankenberg, E., & Lee, C. (2003). *Charter schools and race: A lost opportunity for integrated education.* Harvard University. http://www.civilrightsproject.ucla.edu/research/deseg/CharterSchools.php; Reardon, S., & Yun, J. (2002). *Private school racial enrollments and segregation.* Harvard University. http://www.civilrightsproject.ucla.edu/

4. *Brown v. Board of Education,* 347 U.S. 483 (1954). p. 494.

5. *Brown v. Board of Education,* 347 U.S. 483 (1954).

6. *Milliken v. Bradley,* 418 U.S. 717 (1974).

7. *Swann v. Charlotte-Mecklenburg Board of Education,* 402 U.S. 1 (1971), p. 16.

8. *Parents Involved in Community Schools v. Seattle School District No. 1,* 127 S.Ct. 2738 (2007).

9. *Sheff v. O'Neill,* 211 Conn. 627 A.2d.518 (1996).

10. *Crawford v. the Board of Education of the City of Los Angeles,* 551 P.2d 28 (Cal. 1976).

to records of minor children by noncustodial parent. (a) In any controversy before the superior court as to the custody or care of minor children, and at any time after the return day of any complaint under section 46b-45, the court may at any time make or modify any proper order regarding the education and support of the children and of care, custody, and visitation if it has jurisdiction under the provisions of chapter 815o. Subject to the provisions of section 46b-56a, the court may assign the custody of any child to the parents jointly, to either parent, or to a third party, according to its best judgment upon the facts of the case and subject to such conditions and limitations as it deems equitable. The court may also make any order granting the right of visitation of any child to a third party including but not limited to grandparents.

Some statutes are designated as education statutes. For example, Sec. 10-221 of the Connecticut statutes pertains to rule prescription by boards of education:

Sec. 10-221. Boards of education to prescribe rules. (a) Boards of education shall prescribe rules for the management, studies, classification, and discipline of the public schools, and, subject to the control of the state board of education, the textbooks to be used; shall make rules for the control, within their respective jurisdictions, of school library media centers and approve the selection of books and other educational media therefore, and shall approve plans for public school buildings and superintend any high or graded schools in the manner specified in this title.

All states have a *state superintendent of instruction* or *state commissioner of education*. This person is the chief state school officer and serves as the chief executive of the state department of education. (For more information, see CCSSO.org.) State education departments typically comprise a variety of divisions, such as teaching and learning, educational programs, vocational–technical schools, finance and administration, and so forth. The size of the department often depends on the state's population as well as whether there are regional or county departments of education. For example, Texas has regional service centers with appointed directors, whereas California has county service centers that fall under the aegis of the county board of education, an elected board and, in most cases an elected superintendent. The roles of these service centers vary but often include providing direct services to school districts such as special education services, adult education programming, family service coordination, and cooperative purchasing programs, to name but a few. (See Chapter 10.)

Administrative agencies include not only the state department of education but also other state and regional agencies that might have jurisdiction over all or some schools in a given state. In some states, boards of education are called *school committees* and in others they are called *school boards*. States cannot implement the general supervision of schools, so it is delegated to local boards of education. (Hawaii is an exception because it is composed of a single school district.) Because local school boards have the authority to enforce federal and state policies, their actions must be within federal and state constitutions and statutes. (See Chapter 4.)

The statutes of each state contain provisions that concern certain aspects of teachers' and administrators' behavior. Statutes dealing with a variety of topics can be found in the state's education statutes, including information regarding teacher and administrator certification; discipline; dismissal; the denial, revocation or suspension of certification; and contract termination, for example. The school administrator must be familiar with the statutes in the state's education code and refer to them when needed.

✳ **What specifically does your state's education code say regarding the tenure, nonrenewal, or dismissal of teachers? What implications, if any, does this have for Angel Chavarin?**

School Districts and Litigation

According to a study conducted by Underwood and Noffke (1990), the number one cause for school district litigation was employee-related issues. Table 11.2

TABLE 11.2   Issues That Land Schools in Court

ISSUES	PERCENTAGE OF TOTAL CASES INITIATED	PERCENTAGE OF TIMES DISTRICT PREVAILED
EMPLOYEE ISSUES (TOTAL)	42.6	81.4
Dismissal/nonrenewal	14.2	93.3
Contract negotiations/implementation	11.6	75.0
Discipline	10.5	88.8
Other	1.6	33.3
Hiring	1.0	100.0
DISTRICTWIDE ISSUES (TOTAL)	37.4	67.5
Negligence	22.6	63.1
District property	4.7	60.0
Desegregation	3.2	66.7
Curriculum	2.6	0.0
Finance	2.1	50.0
Other	2.1	90.0
STUDENT ISSUES (TOTAL)	20.0	65.4
Special education	8.9	50.0
Discipline practices	6.8	87.5
Discrimination	2.1	33.3
Grades and promotion	1.0	100.0
Constitutional issues	0.5	100.0
Other	0.5	33.3

Source: Underwood, J. & Noffke, J. (1990). School law news: You're winning. *The Executive Educator,* *12*(3), 18–20. Reprinted with permission.

displays the percentage of total cases initiated in three categories: employee issues, districtwide issues, and student issues.

In all categories, negligence is the primary reason for litigation. However, as Underwood and Noffke (1990) point out, "It's most likely to be settled by the parties, rather than being litigated in court" (p. 20). The authors identify the second-highest litigation area as employment-related issues. Under the category of student issues, special education ranked highest. According to the authors, litigation in this area is on the upswing.

LEGAL ISSUES AND SCHOOLS

Common law, statutes, and constitutional law touch on such issues as tenure, contracts, student rights, civil rights, collective bargaining, finance, property, desegregation, intergovernmental relations, instructional programming, and teacher rights. These and other issues are governed to some extent by law. A few important issues that educational administrators might face are due process, freedom of expression, student discipline, records, and tort liability.

Due Process

According to the 14th Amendment, a person cannot be deprived arbitrarily of "life, liberty, or property, without due process of law." Before the state can deprive citizens of these rights, due process must be afforded. According to Data Research Inc. (1991), an organization that publishes law texts, "There are many variations, and the courts do not always agree on what constitutes due process of law" (p. 92).

Of the two types of due process, substantive and procedural, substantive due process deals with the entire process of being fair. According to Strahan and Turner (1987), substantive due process includes the necessity for a rule not to be unduly vague and that discipline should be based on written rules. Further, decisions should be supported with evidence, the identity of a witness should be revealed, an impartial hearing must be afforded each person, and if the accused so requests, a public or private hearing should be offered. Procedural due process involves providing notice and fair hearing so that an impartial and just settlement of a conflict between parties can be reached; thus, procedural due process is an established system.

Notice refers to making the rules orderly and ensuring that each party involved is aware of them and how they should be followed, as well as possible penalties for their violation. Inherent in this notion is that people have a right to know the standards by which they are to be judged. It would be unreasonable and unfair to hold people accountable for meeting expectations if they are ignorant of those expectations. For example, if a school system has a teacher-evaluation system and the procedures and standards involved in that system are not explained to teachers, then it would be unfair and unreasonable to expect teachers to be evaluated using that system. Similarly, if there is a student discipline code, including the procedures and penalties for certain behaviors, and the code is not explained to a student, it is unreasonable to punish the student for not following it. Standards must be known in advance, and they should be clear so that a person knows that what he or she has done counts as meeting, or not meeting, the standards.

Fair hearing includes several aspects: a written statement of the charges and the type of evidence that should be given to the individual, explanation of procedural right, adequate time to prepare a defense, and an opportunity for a formal hearing. According to McCarthy, Cambron-McCabe, and Thomas (1987), in cases where a teacher is terminated, the following procedural elements must be afforded:

- Notification of charges
- Opportunity for a hearing
- Adequate time to prepare a rebuttal to the charges
- Access to evidence and names of witnesses
- Hearing before an impartial tribunal
- Representation by legal counsel
- Opportunity to present evidence and witnesses
- Decision based on evidence and findings of the hearing
- Transcript or record of the hearing
- Opportunity to appeal an adverse decision (pp. 381–382)

✳ **What implications do these procedural elements have for Principal Holladay's decisions?**

Freedom of Speech and Expression

The First Amendment covers written, oral, and symbolic forms of expression, including:

- Academic freedom (e.g., *Keyishian v. Board of Regents of New York,* 1967)
- Censorship (e.g., *Planned Parenthood v. Clark County School District,* 1991)
- Community service programs (e.g., *Steirer v. Bethlehem Area School District,* 1993)
- Defamatory expression, which includes slander (oral) and libel (written) (e.g., *Scott v. New-Herald,* 1986)
- Symbolic expression (e.g., in *Tinker v. Des Moines Independent School District,* 1969, the Supreme Court ruled that a rule prohibiting students from wearing black arm bands in school as a protest against the Vietnam War was invalid)
- Hate speech (e.g., *Doe v. University of Michigan,* 1989)
- Obscene, vulgar, or inflammatory expression (e.g., *Miller v. California,* 1973; *Fenton v. Stear,* 1976)
- Freedom of the press (e.g., *Hazelwood School District v. Kuhlmeier,* 1988)

- Distribution of religious materials (e.g., *Walz ex rel. Walz v. Egg Harbor Township Board of Education,* 2003)
- Dress and hair codes (e.g., *Karr v. Schmidt,* 1972)

Numerous controversies over freedom of speech erupted starting in the 1960s. Many educators argue that schools should not tolerate student speech and expression that is inconsistent with the school's basic educational mission. Given a compelling purpose, speech can be regulated; but no one can be prohibited from speaking simply because her or his ideas differ from those of the administration or staff.

Discipline and Students With Disabilities

As previously noted in Table 11.2, Underwood and Noffke rank special education highest in litigation areas related to students, They maintain that litigation in special education is on the upswing. Discussing the disciplining of regular and special education students, legal expert Perry Zirkel (1996) recommends that policies and practices be "in accord with federal constitutional requirements and any procedural safeguards under state law" (p. 21).

Substantive and procedural due process must clearly be kept in the forefront as regards disciplining students. Essex (2006) states, "It has long been held that children with disabilities may not be punished for conduct that is a manifestation of their disability. . . . In situations where certain types of discipline are warranted, an effort must be made to ensure that the punishment does not materially and substantially interrupt the child's education" (p. 97). Exercise caution and work with the district's legal counsel to protect your schools and district from legal costs and liability awards.

School district personnel make many common mistakes when dealing with children having special needs and their families. Often these mistakes result in litigation that could have been avoided if due process had been followed. First, parents must be informed and their consent obtained. They need to be notified of all due process procedures and be given lists of all procedural safeguards upon the initial referral for evaluation. Additionally, parents should once again be informed at each IEP meeting about due process procedures and procedural safeguards. Another common mistake involves improper or insufficient evaluations. Evaluations must be administered by knowledgeable and trained personnel and must be in accordance with any instructions provided by test producers. Also, students should be assessed in all areas of suspected disability, including, if appropriate, health, vision, social and emotional status, hearing, academic performance, general intelligence, and motor abilities. The findings from these evaluations need to be translated into a single coherent view of the child. The document should be easily understood, detailed, and should have realistic and concrete recommendations.

Another common mistake made by school personnel is to deny an independent educational evaluation. If the parent disagrees with the district's evaluation *and* the district's evaluation is not appropriate, the parent, at public expense, has the right to an independent evaluation. Another error often made is an insufficient or incomplete IEP. This may include not including measurable objectives; omitting current levels of performance based on recent data; failing to summarize discussions at IEP meetings such as areas of concern, agreement, disagreement, and the length of the meeting, among others; and failing to get partial consent when parents disagree or refuse to sign the document. Another common mistake is to deny services based on cost considerations. Districts are required to provide free appropriate public education (FAPE) without regard to the funds they receive. Costs can only be considered when the choice is between two equally appropriate educational programs.

Another common mistake is conducting a deficient IEP meeting. It is crucial that the mandatory people be present. In some states such as California, this includes at least one regular education teacher if the student has regular education classes (see California Education Code 56341). Other issues that signify a deficient IEP meeting are the need to video- or tape-record, not having an attorney present, and attempting to exclude persons. There also may be a need to have note takers, sign language interpreters, English language interpreters, and so on. Another common mistake is to give in to parent demands. Educators are the experts, and because they are trained to conduct IEPs, they should provide guidance for parents. FAPE is a student right that parents cannot waive. Another common error is to deny access to student records or to not protect confidentiality. It is crucial that school personnel are knowledgeable about what their state education code asserts on this topic. In many states, teachers must be informed of who commits suspendable or expellable offenses. Finally, a common mistake that leads to litigation is procrastination. Neglect and indifference are often reasons for litigation. It is imperative that school personnel follow through on mediated agreements and due process decisions. It is easy to become busy and allow deadlines to pass and services to be ignored.

The Confidentiality of Student Records

The Family Educational Rights and Privacy Act (FERPA, Public Law 93-380), enacted by the U.S. Congress in 1974, established a student's right to privacy. Also included in this act is the requirement that schools adopt and publicize the procedures for accessing and obtaining school records as well as explaining how information can be removed. FERPA stipulates that a parent's written consent is required for a third party to obtain access to a student's record. An amendment to this act, the Buckley amendment, threatens the withdrawal of federal funds if parents are prevented from seeing their children's complete records.

Administrators should formulate guidelines regarding student records that include developing procedures for allowing access to the files, keeping a log of all people who have obtained access to the records, allowing parents and students to submit outside materials to the record, and developing procedures to obtain informed consent from students and parents before data in the student's

TABLE 11.3   Family Educational Rights and Privacy Act

The Family Educational Rights and Privacy Act (FERPA) (20 U.S.C. § 1232g; 34 CFR Part 99) is a Federal law that protects the privacy of student education records. The law applies to all schools that receive funds under an applicable program of the U.S. Department of Education.

FERPA gives parents certain rights with respect to their children's education records. These rights transfer to the student when he or she reaches the age of 18 or attends a school beyond the high school level. Students to whom the rights have transferred are "eligible students."

■ Parents or eligible students have the right to inspect and review the student's education records maintained by the school. Schools are not required to provide copies of records unless, for reasons such as great distance, it is impossible for parents or eligible students to review the records. Schools may charge a fee for copies.

■ Parents or eligible students have the right to request that a school correct records which they believe to be inaccurate or misleading. If the school decides not to amend the record, the parent or eligible student then has the right to a formal hearing. After the hearing, if the school still decides not to amend the record, the parent or eligible student has the right to place a statement with the record setting forth his or her view about the contested information.

■ Generally, schools must have written permission from the parent or eligible student in order to release any information from a student's education record. However, FERPA allows schools to disclose those records, without consent, to the following parties or under the following conditions (34 CFR § 99.31):
  ■ School officials with legitimate educational interest;
  ■ Other schools to which a student is transferring;
  ■ Specified officials for audit or evaluation purposes;
  ■ Appropriate parties in connection with financial aid to a student;
  ■ Organizations conducting certain studies for or on behalf of the school;
  ■ Accrediting organizations;
  ■ To comply with a judicial order or lawfully issued subpoena;
  ■ Appropriate officials in cases of health and safety emergencies; and
  ■ State and local authorities, within a juvenile justice system, pursuant to specific State law.

Schools may disclose, without consent, "directory" information such as a student's name, address, telephone number, date and place of birth, honors and awards, and dates of attendance. However, schools must tell parents and eligible students about directory information and allow parents and eligible students a reasonable amount of time to request that the school not disclose directory information about them. Schools must notify parents and eligible students annually of their rights under FERPA. The actual means of notification (special letter, inclusion in a PTA bulletin, student handbook, or newspaper article) is left to the discretion of each school.

Source: U.S. Department of Education. Retrieved from http://www2.ed.gov/policy/gen/guid/fpco/ferpa/index.html

record can be released to a third party. Table 11.3 is from the Web site of the federal government (ed.gov) and details who has access to student records. Clearly, the issue of the privacy of records is an important one, and the development of clear guidelines is not only an important legal issue but an ethical one, as well.

Securing Student Records and Student Attendance

Schools may also provide some directory information without consent. Schools must notify parents and eligible students annually of their rights under FERPA; however, parents do not have the right to inspect counselor, psychologist, and teacher records unless these are part of the student's cumulative records.

Many associated activities, such as compulsory attendance, class scheduling, follow-up services, school reports, student eligibility, and dropout prevention depend on accurate student data. To focus on one example, attendance records can be used to ensure that the child's right to receive a free public education up to a certain age is being enforced. School attendance and other student rights are usually covered in the students' rights, responsibilities, and disciplinary rules pamphlets each family receives, which must comply with school system policy and procedures. Good attendance habits should be established early so problems related to academics, deportment, drop-out rates, and later employment do not develop. Irregular attendance, frequent tardiness, and low achievement are strong predictors that a child might drop out of high school and have later social and economic problems (Achilles & Smith, 1994; Kaplan, Peck, & Kaplan, 1997). The attendance clerk provides monitoring and communication and triggers intervention strategies involving attendance problems.

Many students with discipline and attendance problems receive no interventions (Schwartz, 1995). For those who do, the most frequent interventions by school personnel are counseling, remedial education, peer tutoring and mentoring, adult–student mentoring, training, special placement, student advising, safe and disciplined school programs, family partnership, and comprehensive support systems. These programs have proven successful for early intervention for attendance problems, discipline problems, and delinquency prevention.

Torts

A tort is a civil (not a criminal) wrong, not including contracts, for which a remedy in damages can be sought. According to Valente (2004) tort liability is created by federal and state law. Actions alleging failure of schools to protect students against sexual harassment and violence are being brought against schools under federal law. According to state tort law, "A person who causes injury to another through violation of some legal duty is liable to pay compensatory money damages to the injured party" (p. 442). Claims are usually covered by a district's group insurance; minimizing the potential for tort litigation, however, should be a prominent concern of educational leaders.

A basic concept of tort law is *fault*. Torts may be intentional, or may result from negligence or carelessness. According to Taylor (1996), three factors must be met for a party to be "liable for negligence: (1) there must be a duty on the part of the defendant toward the victim either to act or to refrain from acting

TEACHER AND STUDENT FREEDOM OF EXPRESSION

FRANK KEMERER
University of San Diego

In the late 1960s, the U.S. Supreme Court began handing down several key decisions that have helped define the parameters of public school teacher and student expression rights under the 1st Amendment. Because the Bill of Rights applies only to the public sector, the extent of expression rights in private schools depends primarily on the policies of the schools.

With regard to teachers, the U.S. Supreme Court ruled in 1968 that teachers cannot be fired for speaking out on school-related matters of public concern unless it can be shown that in doing so they undermined their effectiveness or disrupted the school (*Pickering v. Board of Education*).[i] The justices overturned the dismissal of a teacher for writing an editorial in a local newspaper criticizing the school board for its handling of a bond election. Nearly a decade later, the Court qualified the decision by ruling that marginally effective teachers cannot insulate themselves from a negative employment decision simply by speaking out on a public issue involving the school. If there are job-related reasons unrelated to protected expression, then the negative employment action can go forward.[ii] The key lesson for school leaders is to have sufficient documentation of job-related deficiencies to overcome the allegation of retaliation for the exercise of free speech (the same would be true for other rights such as the right to freedom from race, gender, age, and disability discrimination). In 1983, the high court ruled that, unlike teacher comments on matters of public concern, comments about on-the-job personal concerns (e.g., extra duty assignments) are not constitutionally protected under the 1st Amendment.[iii]

Teacher freedom of expression generally does not encompass the classroom. There are no U.S. Supreme Court decisions defining academic freedom rights for public school teachers, and very few federal and state courts rulings have done so. Thus, academic freedom is much more an asserted professional prerogative than a legal right. The classroom largely remains under the control of the school. One of the few exceptions is a ruling of the U.S. Court of Appeals for the 5th Circuit, whose jurisdiction encompasses Texas, Louisiana, and Mississippi. That court decided in 1980 that a high school teacher has a right to lead classroom discussion on controversial issues as long as doing so does not overbalance the teacher's effectiveness.[iv] It is important to note, however, while a state cannot restrict federal rights, nothing precludes its expanding them. Thus, school leaders must look to state law, school board policies, and collective bargaining contracts to determine the extent to which teachers have a "right to teach" and can speak out about personal job-related matters at school.

The idea that public school students are to be seen and not heard ended in 1969 when the U.S. Supreme Court ruled in the famous *Tinker v. Des Moines Independent School District* that students cannot be suspended from school for wearing black armbands symbolizing their opposition to the war in Vietnam.[v] In writing for the seven justices in the majority, Justice Abe Fortas clearly endorsed the view that the school is a marketplace of ideas: "In our system, state-operated schools may not be enclaves of totalitarianism. School officials do not possess absolute authority over their students. . . . In our system, students may not be regarded as closed-circuit recipients of only that which the State chooses to communicate."[vi] Under *Tinker*, student expression loses its protection only if it materially disrupts the school environment

(continued)

or substantially interferes with the rights of others.

Several points are worth noting about this ruling. First, the Court pointed out that a student's freedom of expression encompasses both the classroom and areas outside it. Later, the Court backed away from the classroom assertion. Second, the decision applies only to secondary school students. The majority did not address the expression rights of elementary school students, and few courts have done so. Third, because a student is not on the school's payroll, the Court's ruling against protection of teacher comments on internal school matters of personal concern does not apply to students.

More recently, the Supreme Court has cut back a bit on student expression rights. In 1986, the justices ruled that student speech that is lewd, profane, or indecent is not entitled to any constitutional protection.[vii] Four years later, in *Hazelwood School District v. Kuhlmeier* the Court ruled that school authorities have the right to control the content of student expression in school-sponsored channels of communication such as the student newspaper, theatrical productions, and other venues supervised by faculty members that are intended "to impart particular knowledge or skills to student participants and audiences." With the latter statement, the Court appears to have encompassed the classroom. The school can exert content control over these areas as long as it has a "legitimate pedagogical concern" and has not converted the channel of communication into an open forum.[viii]

Once again, it is important to note some caveats. First, if a school-controlled channel of communication is operated as an open forum for student expression, then viewpoint discrimination is not possible. For example, a social studies teacher who holds a general discussion on the causes of warfare would have a hard time justifying restricting a student's assertion that religion is the main culprit. Second, a number of states have enacted laws giving students freedom of expression in official school publications regardless of whether they are financed by the school. In effect, the state has converted these channels of communication

into open forums for student free expression, and the *Kuhlmeier* ruling does not apply. Third, the *Kuhlmeier* ruling has relevance to the school's computer and e-mail system. Most schools assert content control over these channels of communication through what are called "Acceptable Use Policies" that must be signed by parents and by teachers. Whereas a school can impose sanctions on both teachers and students for misuse of these electronic means of communication, its control over what students and teachers communicate on their own computers outside of school is limited to situations where demonstrable safety issues arise or, in the case of teachers, where job effectiveness has been significantly compromised.

The most recent decision from the U.S. Supreme Court on student freedom of expression involved a high school student's display of a banner bearing the odd message "Bong Hits 4 Jesus" at a school-related off-campus activity. Five justices ruled in *Morse v. Frederick* that the message was not constitutionally protected, because it could be construed to promote or endorse the use of drugs.[ix] However, two of the five justices clearly indicated that they would not approve any other restrictions on student expression. In effect, then, the U.S. Supreme Court continues to recognize the core principle of *Tinker* that for older students, the school is a marketplace of ideas where free speech reigns.

i.   *Pickering v. Board of Education,* 391 U.S. 563 (1969)

ii. *Mt. Healthy City School District Board of Education v. Doyle,* 429 U.S. 274 (1977)

iii. *Connick v. Myers,* 461 U.S. 138 (1983)

iv. *Kingsville Independent School District v. Cooper,* 611 F.2d 1109 (5th Cir. 1980)

v.   *Tinker v. Des Moines Independent Community School District,* 393 U.S. 503 (1969)

vi. *Tinker v. Des Moines Independent Community School District,* 393 U.S. 503 (1969) p. 511

vii. *Bethel School District No. 403 v. Fraser,* 478 U.S. 675 (1986)

viii.*Hazelwood School District v. Kuhlmeier,* 484 U.S. 260 (1988)

ix. *Morse v. Frederick,* 127 S.Ct. 2618 (2007)

in a particular way, (2) this duty must be breached through failure to exercise a reasonable standard of care, and (3) there must be injury caused by this breach" (p. 66).

All school employees are required to carry out their duties in a reasonable manner so that no damage or injury is incurred. Typical tort liability settings include laboratories, shops, playgrounds, field trips, spaces for physical education, and classrooms.

With regard to negligence:

- School employees have a duty to protect students in their care (*in loco parentis*, a legal concept meaning "in place of the parent").
- School employees must act with a reasonable standard of care.
- Once a cause of injury is established, the school leader must ask if the employee failed to act with a reasonable standard of care.
- There must be evidence that damage to the plaintiff was the result of the injury.

✳ **What implications does the discussion about torts in this chapter have for the students involved in the accident and their parents?**

MONITORING COMPLIANCE WITH POLICIES AND PROCEDURES

How can the school administrator ensure that the policies of the school district are followed and that teachers and students understand them? What systems can be put in place to monitor compliance? As schools continue developing partnerships and collaborations with individuals and community organizations, complying with state and district policies is crucial to risk management. According to Shoop and Dunklee (1992), "Risk management is a coordinated, effective pre-event and post-event response to a school district's liability exposure, developed through planning, organizing, leading, and monitoring a district's activities and assets" (p. 307).

Risk management is a concept that started in the insurance industry, and the business manager of a school district should be keenly aware of its importance. It includes areas such as safety, security, transportation, and health. Given the growth of litigation against school districts and the simultaneous decentralization of management from the district to the site level, risk management is a concept with which all administrators should have familiarity. A key way of operationalizing the myriad issues involved in risk management is the development of clear and succinct policies and procedures, which are then explicated to students and teachers in school handbooks.

Another important concept is the *legal audit*. In the case of school districts, this refers to a *professional* review of the legal affairs of the district, carried out on a periodic basis and reported to the school board. Shoop and Dunklee (1992) cite two advantages of a legal audit:

1. The likelihood is increased that significant, but preventable, legal problems will come to the attention of district administrators and the board of education.
2. The flow of information to district administrators and the board of education is increased, with the assurance that the parties are receiving accurate facts on which to base preventive action.

Part of the legal audit involves examining the policies the school board has developed and the procedures for informing school district personnel and students of those policies. School-based administrators should be aware that the central office arranges for legal audits to be conducted and that these reports might have implications for the daily operations of their schools.

Figure 11.1 exemplifies a school district policy regarding the acceptable use of electronic information systems. The school district in Plainville, Connecticut, has community relations, business, instruction, personnel, and student policies that appear not only in student handbooks, but also on the district's website. The policy in Figure 11.1 is for students. Note that a policy on "acceptable use" was originally approved in 1997, revised in 2002, again in 2003 and again in 2005. One of the first things an administrator new to a district needs to do is become familiar with district policies and where to find them.

To ensure that students are familiar with district policies that pertain to them, it is typical for the student handbook to include all such policies. Usually, there is a signature sheet in the student handbook that must be signed by the student and his or her parent acknowledging that they have indeed read the policies.

It then becomes imperative that the school site administrator develop mechanisms to monitor that all such forms are returned and filed. This is part of what is referred to as *preventive law*. Shoop and Dunklee (1992) define it as "a branch of law that endeavors to minimize the risk of litigation or to secure, with more certainty, legal rights and duties" (p. 308).

※ **How might the school district ensure that problems like the one caused by Chavarin's negligence do not occur in the future?**

SCHOOL SAFETY AND SECURITY

In today's world of public education, we are all too familiar with the presence of daily violence. Every person in the United States can remember instances of school violence such as at Columbine High School. Research also shows that violent crime is on the increase across the nation—Philadelphia, Miami, Boston, Indianapolis, Charlotte, Washington (DC), Wilmington, Oakland, St. Louis, to name a few—and this is particularly true among youths. The effect has been greatest on the nation's poorest neighborhoods. Murder, assault, robbery, and weapons arrest increased

STUDENTS DETAILS	
Section	(5000) Students
Policy Name	Acceptable Use Policy (AUP)
Policy Number	5131.8
Date Approved	04/14/1997
Date Revised	01/14/2002
Date Revised	10/14/2003
Date Revised	06/13/2005
Date Revised	
Policy	Plainville Community Schools provides electronic information systems for improving teaching, learning, and managing. These systems shall be used by members of the school community in accordance with policy and procedures established by the school district and laws enacted by state and federal governments. The following acceptable use policy (AUP) applies to supervised and independent use of all forms of technology. It does not attempt to articulate all access scenarios and user behaviors. For the purposes of this AUP, the definition of information systems is any configuration of hardware and software, which provides users access to information stored electronically. The configuration can be a single unit or multiple units networked together. Networks include computer hardware, operating system software, application software, and stored text and data files, regardless of source and content. Users shall be defined as any person who utilizes these information networks. Users include all students, district employees and members of the Board of Education. It may also include other persons outside of these groups who, in the course of using district facilities, require access to the systems. The Plainville Board of Education expects all users of its technologies and electronic information systems to demonstrate responsible, courteous behaviors. Responsible behavior includes abiding by the law and the terms of the AUP with regard to privacy, confidentiality, security, and intellectual property. *(continued)*

FIGURE 11.1   Board of Education Policy Detail View

Computers, computer files, the e-mail system, software furnished to users and other pieces of the school's information network are school district property. Students should not consider any of their use of computers to be private, including all electronic communications. Use of passwords to gain access to the school's information systems does not imply privacy in that use. There should be no expectation of privacy in aspects of computer use. The school district has the right but is not required to monitor any and all aspects of its information systems, including all materials students create, store, send or receive.

The Superintendent of Schools or his/her designee will be responsible for implementing this policy, establishing procedures and guidelines, and supervising access privileges. Such guidelines shall be used to enforce the measures to block or filter Internet access and to preserve the students' and staff's rights to examine and use information to meet the educational goals and objectives of the Plainville Community School District.

Violations of this policy may result in revocation of access to and privileges relating to use of the information systems and networks. Encouraging, allowing, or ignoring student use of the computer resources in a manner contrary to this policy is strictly prohibited. Violations of this policy by students may result in disciplinary action, up to and including suspension and/or expulsion. Violations may also result in civil and criminal liability. Students will be responsible for any losses, costs or damages incurred by the school district as a result of unauthorized use or intentional destruction of its information network or pieces.

Legal Reference:
    17 U.S.C. § 101 et. seq., The Copyright Act
    20 U.S.C. §1232g Family Education Rights and Privacy Act (FERPA)
    20 U.S.C. §1400 et. seq., Individuals with Disabilities Education Act
    C.G.S. §10-15b Access to student records
    C.G.S. §53a-182b through §53a-183, Harassment
    C.G.S. §53a-251 et. seq., Computer Crime

FIGURE 11.1 Board of Education Policy Detail View (Continued)

5% for White juveniles between 2004 and 2005 and by 20% for Black juveniles. During the 2009–10 school year, the rate of violent incidents per 1,000 students was higher in middle schools (40 incidents) than in primary schools or high schools (21 incidents each) (Institute of Education Sciences [IES], 2010). Of course, this is an example of the extremes; however, less violent examples occur on a daily basis. Aggressive behavior, roughhousing, bullying, cyberbullying, threats, harassment, terrorizing, and physical violence take place in a majority of children's lives beginning in elementary school. On many occasions, different schools have had riots and multiple episodes of gang activity. Police officers, resource officers, and undercover officers have been assigned to high schools in order to deter violence. Examples of incidents that occur regularly nationwide include alcohol possession, arson, battery against school personnel, sexual offenses, drug violence, fights, and possession of firearms and violent weapons. Research shows that by high school three out of four children will have felt bullied or threatened in school or on the way to school. If a child is scared or severely depressed by the way they are treated in school, that child will not learn or progress with his or her study. Given these concerns, our schools are still considered relatively safe (IES, 2010).

The belief today is that cyberbullying is the fastest growing and most prevalent form of youth violence today. Instant messaging, online profiles, Facebook, and similar social networking sites allow children to unwittingly reveal too much information about themselves. This opens up possibilities for cyberstalking, sexual harassment, identity theft, and other types of hacking violations. Principals must take a hard look at technology safety issues. Other problems include online insults, read by large populations, about a person's physical appearance, friends, family, clothing, sexuality, and so on. Many states and networking sites are cracking down on cyberbullying.

Homemade bombs, anthrax scares, concealed weapons, and other "new crimes for new times" now present school administrators with the formidable task of developing security and crisis preparedness guidelines at both building and district levels. Along with the "traditional" security threats, recent shifts in school violence are driving administrators in even the safest of schools and communities to realize that "it could happen here." And staff members, students, parents, politicians, lawyers, and the media want to know what you, as a school administrator, have done to prevent incidents from happening.

Dealing with misbehavior is often focused on some form of negative discipline—verbally challenging behaviors, placing in an undesirable classroom status, more work, referrals to the office, detention, suspension, and/or expulsion. This tends to create a downward spiral of lower morale, less academic emphasis, a harsher school culture, and more referrals. Many discipline problems can be dealt with in a more proactive way by analyzing a problem area and developing a more positive corrective strategy. For example, many problems tend to start in school hallways and meeting spaces. By displaying positive messages and sweeping these areas with adults who address students respectfully and see that they get to where they need to be, discipline problems are decreased dramatically. To be successful, discipline has to be more than a policy of forced compliance or removal.

School safety is the responsibility of everyone—administrators, staff, students, parents, and the community. Trump (2002) states:

> The safety of your students and staff members might very well depend upon your ability to evaluate, plan, and implement a comprehensive school safety program. As many school administrators struggle to learn about drug trafficking trends, gang identification, stranger danger, and the prevention of aggressive and violent behavior, even newer challenges have arrived at the schoolhouse doorway. (p. 11)

Most states require all schools in the state to conduct a building-level school safety audit. Each school should conduct a complete safety audit every 3 years. This is an internal inventory of existing practices, policies, and procedures as they relate to school safety. This proactive process helps to ensure that students maximize their learning potential within a safe and secure environment. For best results and credibility, assessments should be performed by individuals with expertise in professional school security in cooperation with other key school staff and community members. A comprehensive safety audit provides a useful basis for faculty and staff in-service, as well as for generating recommendations and modifications for current policies, practices, and procedures related to the health, safety, and well-being of students, faculty members, and staff members. The assessment helps to identify and evaluate student safety concerns occurring on school property or at school-sponsored events. The audit should provide guidelines for improving school security and safety (Flanary, 1997).

The following ten domains provide examples of what might be assessed annually for school safety:

- Development and enforcement of policies
- Procedures for data collection
- Development of intervention and prevention plans
- Personnel security
- Level of staff development (education and training)
- Opportunities for student involvement
- Level of parent and community involvement and linkages
- Role of law enforcement
- Standards for safety, security personnel, and police staffing
- Safety and security of buildings and grounds
- Development of emergency response plans (crisis preparedness)

Most school districts are required by law to have school safety audit guidelines. A helpful Web site is: schoolsecurity.org.

The challenge is creating the delicate balance between protecting individual rights and ensuring general welfare (wiredsafety.org; isafe.org).

McCarthy and Webb (2000) discuss this delicate balance:

Some limitations on student behavior are necessary to prevent violence in public schools, but students' rights must be protected in imposing such restrictions. Student handbooks should clearly describe the rationale for any conduct regulations and the consequences for noncompliance. Disciplinary rules should be discussed with the students, their justification should be debated, and rules should be eliminated if they lack a sound educational or safety rationale. Any constraints imposed on students' freedom must be necessary to protect the general welfare and advance the school's educational mission. Students should feel safe, but they should not view schools as prisons where they have lost all personal liberties.

Moreover, school authorities' emphasis should be on the prevention of antisocial and illegal behavior rather than on punitive action. Schools need to make every effort to encourage students to engage in civil conduct and healthful living and to use mediation to resolve conflicts. Student assemblies and group and individual counseling sessions can assist students in learning to treat others with respect and to expect such treatment in return. Various programs, some of which include simulations and role-playing exercises, are available to help students acquire mediation skills so they can resolve conflicts without resorting to violence and can empathize with individuals who are the victims of disrespectful or harassing behavior. (p. 43)

Another aspect of school security is to lock doors, install video cameras and metal detectors, and assign police to patrol the school. These signal a fear of violence, however, and certainly do not make students feel safe. Today's children need to be respected and helped to feel secure within their schools. Students need to have a clearly defined forum in which they can express their concerns. That requires an active counseling staff, teachers who care about students, and administrators who are welcoming and have an open door to students and their parents. Educators should invite and welcome both written and verbal expression of student concerns and feedback and be prepared to address those concerns. Most of all, everyone within the school should take harassment of any form very seriously and help put procedures in place to prevent disrespectful behavior.

Critical Incidents

Principals must be prepared to handle *critical incidents* that typically occur with little or no advance warning. Difficult issues such as racial disharmony, sexual misconduct, religious freedom, educational equity, drugs, anti-American sentiment, and violence have found their way into schools across the United States. Principals can misjudge the nature, direction, and scale of the conflict resulting in the underestimation or exaggeration of conditions. How the principal deals with critical incidents is another crucial determinant of his or her effectiveness and that of the school.

Principals also need an instinct to recognize potential "time bombs." Many principals who lose their jobs have experienced a critical incident that turned the

LEGAL AND ETHICAL DIMENSIONS OF EDUCATIONAL LEADERSHIP

MARTHA MCCARTHY
Indiana University

An important purpose of public education in our nation is to instill core values for citizenship—values that form the foundation of a democratic society, such as love of liberty, justice, democracy, equality, fairness, and freedom of thought (Etzioni, 1993; McCarthy, Bull, Quantz, & Sorenson, 1993). A related function of public schools is to teach how our legal system and ethical codes protect these values. Many school administrators, however, currently are hesitant to engage teachers and students in reflecting on legal and ethical concerns. Legal discussions are sometimes avoided because school leaders are uneasy about their own knowledge of the law and consequently fear that such discussions will identify legal problems or make schools more vulnerable to legal challenges. Ethical deliberations may be avoided because they frequently surface value conflicts. Public schools have been faulted by some conservative citizen groups for encouraging students to clarify their values (Cohen, 1990).

Educators should not fear the law, apologize for exploring ethical concerns, or try to eliminate value-oriented material from the public school curriculum (an impossible feat). On the contrary, school leaders have an obligation to encourage their staff members and students to examine their values and the fundamental values undergirding the Constitution and laws in our nation.

All actions of school leaders have legal and ethical dimensions, yet many school administrators hold the erroneous impression that law and ethics simply set boundaries for their behavior (Bull & McCarthy, 1995). Indeed, the law is often viewed as a bothersome, external constraint—a prescriptive limitation—imposed on administrators' discretion and creativity. And some view ethical considerations as more concrete and settled—a precise list of "correct" behaviors—than they are.

Prospective school leaders should be encouraged to embrace a broader view of law and ethics. The law provides the basic framework for all interactions in an ordered society, and it specifies mechanisms for conflict resolution. The law emanates from experience, is constantly evolving, is designed to facilitate individual and collective activities, and reflects political and social changes over time. Thus, understanding the law is not simply a mechanical process of locating rules and regulations that govern our behavior. When educators do not understand the law, they often have unfounded fears of legal sanctions and they focus solely on the legal directives rather than on the process of developing, interpreting, and applying the law. Increased awareness of fundamental legal principles and the tensions between individual and collective interests leads to greater respect for the responsibilities that accompany legal rights.

Ethical deliberations also are more complex than school leaders often perceive them to be. Ethics is a social process of justifying human actions and exploring the validity of reasons for actions. By examining school situations through the lens of ethical behaviors (e.g., what is considered "just" and why), individuals can acquire a deeper understanding of their own values and biases as well as those of society. One's ethical code is more than a list of virtuous behaviors; it involves an examination of the concept of "virtue" and other concepts (e.g., "good," "moral"). To gain an understanding and appreciation of ethics, one must explore various ethical perspectives on a range of issues.

Although there are similarities between law and ethics, the commonalties should not be overstated. Some actions may be considered ethical but violate the law and vice versa. Individuals continue to be willing to suffer legal consequences for breaking laws they consider morally wrong (civil disobedience). Also, practices that some view as unethical, such as misleading a colleague regarding a professional matter, have no legal ramifications. This is why many professional organizations have developed codes of ethics in an effort to regulate behavior for which legal sanctions are not available.

If school leaders are to develop a deep understanding of law and ethics and translate such knowledge into action, these topics must be approached differently in educational leadership preparation programs. The notion is no longer widely supported that school administrators should be taught to deal with school situations as objective problems to be solved in a scientifically rational manner. Many now believe that preparation programs should guide school leaders in exploring complex, messy school situations that have no concrete answers and in understanding that personal beliefs influence what they do on the job (Beck & Murphy, 1997).

Yet most preparation programs still do not encourage future school leaders to think critically about the legal and ethical aspects of their roles or to challenge their own values and world views. Preparation programs should expose future school leaders to scholarship in law and ethics and provide them ample opportunities to practice legal and ethical discourse and engage in intense personal reflection and critique (McCarthy et al., 1993; Starratt, 1994). Moreover, if school leaders become comfortable with legal and ethical deliberations during their preparation programs, their comfort level should carry over into their professional roles.

Whereas law has been a part of the educational leadership curriculum for several decades (although often too technically focused), only recently has ethics received systematic attention in some programs (Beck & Murphy, 1997). Both law and ethics lend themselves to problem-based instruction and the exploration of legal and ethical implications of real and simulated school situations. By identifying and exploring dilemmas and considering alternative perspectives in formulating responses, school personnel can ask penetrating questions and make thoughtful decisions.

---

tide against them. Thomas and Davis offer an example of a critical incident in their Phi Delta Kappa publication titled *Legal and Ethical Bases for Educational Leadership* (1998). As the principal of a high school, you are confronted with a number of challenges related to an incident from the previous day. The headline of the morning newspaper, in an article about your school, reads "Teacher Steps on Flag." The superintendent has already left an e-mail directing you to immediately suspend the teacher involved without pay. Parents of a boy sent out of class in the incident and a policeman, there to serve a warrant on the teacher, are waiting to see you. This critical incident has a number of red flag characteristics that could embroil the principal and the entire school system in destructive conflict and embarrassment. Red flag issues are those that (1) endanger the health, safety, and security of students and/or employees; (2) escalate in intensity; (3) fall under close media or community scrutiny; (4) interfere with the normal operation of the school; and (5) jeopardize the positive public image of the school district. Violence, racial discrimination, sexual misconduct, and other such issues are automatic red flags needing immediate attention.

The previous day, a student in Mr. Calisch's class showed up wearing a swastika—a Nazi symbol—on a necklace. The teacher requested that the young man put the necklace in his pocket. The student admittedly refused and the teacher asked the student to go to the assistant principal's office for further discussion. The student and others in the class asked for an explanation. Mr. Calisch explained that he was Jewish and several of his relatives had been killed in concentration camps during World War II. In trying to help the students to understand, Mr. Calisch took out his handkerchief and asked: "What is this made of?" "Cloth," responded the class. He dropped the handkerchief to the floor and stepped on it. "Does it bother you that I stepped on this piece of cloth?" "No," was the unanimous answer.

Then Mr. Calisch took down the American flag. "What is this made of?" he asked. "Cloth," responded the class. He then proceeded to drop the flag on the floor and stepped on it. The class was offended. The responses were quick and direct:

> "You can't step on the flag, it is a symbol for our country."
> "The flag is sacred, it is a symbol of democracy and all the values held by our nation."
> "It's wrong to desecrate the flag; you could go to jail for stepping on it."

At this point, all class members, except one, agreed that the Nazi symbol held sufficient symbolism to offend the teacher. The boy wearing the necklace disagreed and left the room. The rest of the class period went on as usual.

How the principal handles this situation has the potential to affect not only his future career and his relations with a number of key individuals, but also students' and teachers' respect for the beliefs of others, the reputation of the school, and the level of conflict related to this issue that will develop in the community. The potential dangers make this an example of a critical incident.

The principal's first duty is to educate the students, manage the school, and make decisions that do not disrupt the educational process. Although the superintendent ordered suspension without pay, the principal is also governed by the rights of the teacher and due process and the principal will be responsible, not the superintendent. The principal must balance individual student rights with his obligation to provide an education without disruption, including overt disruption, potential disruption, disruption caused by symbols of immoral or illegal acts contrary to prevailing community values, and nexus disruption. The decisions the principal makes regarding this critical incident have tremendous implications for many people. This can become a smooth positive learning experience, or it can become a catalyst for volatile and cataclysmic events with the principal in the middle.

The examples are endless. A health teacher tells middle school students that they "are going to experiment with sex and that her own child had it at the age of 15." A high school girl complains that she wants the derogatory and sexually explicit graffiti about her removed from the boys' bathroom. A teacher falsifies a student's individualized education plan; a teacher assaults a child; a teacher propositions a child for sex; a student says he is going to kill teachers and students; drugs are being sold in school; there are increasingly violent racial tensions.

When reasonable norms of behavior are breached, there is a demand for quick action and control and the development of appropriate sanctions. This is even more pressing when the health, safety, and security of students and/or employees are endangered. The best approach is to develop a plan for the crisis during a noncrisis period, and to build good relations with those whom you might need in a crisis—teachers, students, parents, lawyers, police, media, ministers, and social services. As the flow of events escalates, the key is to maintain control and not to panic. This is much easier if you are already prepared for the possibility of such events. Take charge and communicate, communicate, communicate! Then rebuild, recover, and heal.

COLLECTIVE BARGAINING

Collective bargaining is the process of negotiating an agreement between an employer and an employee organization, usually for a specific term, defining the conditions of employment, the rights of employees and their organization, and the procedures to be followed in settling disputes. States have legislated regulations in areas such as unfair practices, administration of labor law, determination of bargaining units, impasse procedures, and prohibiting teacher strikes in order to create a more orderly negotiation process. In addition, school boards have tightened up on the scope of negotiations with teachers. As a result, many see a decrease in the power of professional associations in the collective bargaining process. However, this condition varies by state, school district, and decade.

If there is a persistent contract disagreement between the employee organization and the employer and an agreement has not been worked out approximately 90 days before the due date for the budget, a district is automatically at impasse. In the *meet-and-confer process*, the bargaining unit is advisory in capacity and the school board, which has legal responsibility for the contract, writes the contract with the teachers' input. However, teachers' input might have minimal impact because it can be ignored.

A significantly greater number of items reach impasse under a meet-and-confer agreement than in situations in which an appeals process exists. An appeals procedure permits the employee organization, the employer, or both to seek assistance in resolving impasses through mediation, fact finding, arbitration, or other forms of assistance from a third party. *Mediation* is voluntary and advisory in order to come up with a nonbinding compromise solution. In *fact-finding* situations, a neutral panel gathers data, studies the impasse, publishes a report of the facts and issues involved, and makes a recommendation for settlement. Fact finding is not binding, but it has significant power in that the results are generally published and known by all parties and may carry considerable political weight.

Arbitration is a process whereby the disputing parties at impasse submit their differences to a third party, sometimes from the American Arbitration Association, for a decision. The decision can be advisory and voluntary or compulsory and binding as agreed on by both parties.

Final steps such as sanctions and strikes must follow the laws that govern the collective-bargaining process. Court-ordered injunctions can be obtained to keep individuals or groups from committing acts that the court determines to be illegal or harmful. When strikes are legal, it is important for the district to have a strike plan. The most important part of this plan is a communication component to provide information, notification, and quick response to news media, parents, staff, safety and security officials, and others in the community. The plan will also identify specific spokespersons and a decision-making center.

Let's examine how one state resolves impasses over negotiating mandatory bargaining topics. In 1975, California enacted the Educational Employment Relations Act (EERA). Many states have acts similar to EERA. This acts regulates when bargaining is mandatory, when consulting is mandatory, and when an issue falls under the prerogative of management. For example, mandatory bargaining is required when there are issues about topics such as wages, employment conditions, benefits, class size, layoffs of probationary certificated employees, etc. Representatives of certificated employees have the right to consult with management on issues such as the determination of curriculum and the selection of textbooks. It is the prerogative of management to decide issues when matters are not specifically enumerated by the act. However, each state has an "Education Code" and it's important that school district management is familiar with what is exempted in the code.

California has a Public Employment Relations Board (PERB) that administers the EERA. Appointed by the governor, its five members as well as the paid staff members decide appropriate bargaining units, establish lists of mediators, determine what is within the scope of negotiations and of meeting and conferring, among other duties.

With respect to teachers, there are five states that prohibit bargaining (South Carolina, North Carolina, Georgia, Texas, Virginia) while in 11 other states, bargaining is permitted but not mandatory as it is in California. Tennessee is unusual in that state law makes teachers the only public employees who can collectively bargain. States vary considerably in the topics that can be addressed through collective bargaining but often they include: wages, fringe benefits, teacher workload, duties, evaluation, and development assignments; the school calendar; curriculum content and quality; grievance procedures; a no-strike provision; and reduction in force. An obvious problem that develops is determining what is negotiable and what falls under the policy responsibilities of the school board. A written agreement regarding all the issues is essential because it serves to formalize the basic rights governing the parties to the agreement and prevents controversies later.

EMPLOYEE RECORDS AND REPORTS

A school district's human resource department is responsible for collecting, maintaining, analyzing, and reporting large amounts of employee information. It begins with job analysis, recruitment, affirmative action, and application information and covers all information through exit interviews, unemployment insurance claims, and retirement. Technology has made the collection, storage, and transmittal of information more efficient and thereby the quality of decision making has improved. Information is more likely to be credible if it is maintained in a single automated personnel file. All updates are made to this single integrated file.

A number of laws address the importance of protecting employee privacy rights, which must be considered in record keeping and reporting. Effective record keeping is essential to the smooth operation of the school system. Accurate information is required to successfully respond to every aspect of the organization, from educational planning to prevention or defending against litigation.

CONCLUSION

It is critically important that educational leaders keep abreast of school law issues. Administrators need a comprehensive knowledge of both education and law to make prudent judgments. Consulting professional publications and, when appropriate, contacting the district's legal counsel are important preventive measures for protecting your school from litigation. Follow these guidelines:

- Schools may regulate speech only when it is necessary to achieve a compelling purpose and when regulations are no more extensive than necessary.
- Schools cannot prohibit speech simply because the ideas expressed differ from those of the administration or staff.
- The prohibition of speech can occur only when it disrupts the school's educational purpose or if it invades the rights of others.
- Students must be given an opportunity for a hearing before exclusion from school for disciplinary purposes.
- Students with disabilities, as well as limited-English-proficient students, must be afforded an education from which they may reasonably be expected to benefit.
- State statutes establish the only acceptable bases for termination or nonrenewal of contract of a teacher after that teacher has passed a probationary period.
- It is imperative that all school personnel act reasonably with regard to the rights of others.

In the *International Handbook of Educational Leadership and Administration*, Shorten (1996) reminds readers, "Prudent administrators will establish operational mechanisms which enable the changes in the law to be brought to their notice as soon as it is possible to do so, and have in place an adequate communication system to enable that information to be disseminated to those who need to know it" (p. 83). This is sound advice, and the prospective educational administrator must be keenly aware of the importance of this type of communication system.

MyEdLeadershipLab™

Go to Topic 12: *Legal Issues* in the MyEdLeadershipLab™ site (www.MyEdLeadershipLab .com) for *Educational Leadership: A Bridge to Improved Practice*, Fifth Edition, where you can:

- Find learning outcomes for *Legal Issues* along with the national standards that connect to these outcomes.
- Complete Assignments and Activities that can help you more deeply understand the chapter content.
- Apply and practice your understanding of the core skills identified in the chapter with the Building Leadership Skills unit.
- Prepare yourself for professional certification with a Practice for Certification quiz.

PORTFOLIO ARTIFACTS

- Explore the following Web site for the Plainville Public Schools in Connecticut (http://www.plainvilleschools.org/boepolicies2/) Notice how the manual is organized. Note the types of sections and policies found in the manual. How does this compare with your school district?

- Some states produce one (or several) document(s) referred to as the education code. Does your state have such a code book? If so, review a copy. Examine one topic, such as teacher evaluation and dismissal. What is the essence of the code? How many times has it been revised?

- Interview a school principal and ask questions related to legal issues in schools. The ISLLC standards (see Chapter 1) can be used to create your questions. See Standards 3, 5, and 6 in particular.

- Talk with your school district's HR offfice. Find out what the total value is of your salary and benefits combined.

- Spend a day observing cases in family and domestic relations court or follow an educational case through the courts.

- Review the policy manual of a school district.

- Visit the Web site of the National Association of Secondary School Principals: http://www.nassp.org/tabid/3632/default.aspx and explore the online school law guide. There is a tutorial and legal modules that you may find most helpful.

- Review the salary schedule and fringe benefit plan for a school system with that of another organization.

KEY TERMS

- Acceptable use policy
- Arbitration
- Circuit court
- Collective bargaining
- de facto segregation
- Defendant
- de jure segregation
- Desegregation
- Differentiated staffing
- Due process
- Equal protection clause

- Family Educational Rights and Privacy Act (FERPA, 1974)
- FAPE (free appropriate public education)
- IDEA (Individuals with Disabilities Education Act)
- IEP (individualized educational program)
- *in loco parentis*
- Libel

- Line and staff
- Meet and confer process
- Merit pay (pay for performance)
- Single salary schedule
- Negotiation
- Negligence
- Plaintiff (complainant)
- School safety audit
- Slander
- Statute
- Tort

SUGGESTED READINGS

Dunklee, D. R., & Shoop, R. J. (2006). *The principal's quick-reference guide to school law: Reducing liability, litigation, and other potential legal tangles* (2nd ed.). Thousand Oaks, CA: Corwin Press.

Essex, H. L. (2011). *School law and the public school: A practical guide for educational leaders* (5th ed.). Boston, MA: Allyn and Bacon.

Hannaway, J., & Rotherham, A. J. (2006). *Collective bargaining in education: Negotiating change in today's schools.* Cambridge, MA: Harvard Education Pub Group.

Kemerer, F., Sansom, P., & Kemerer, J. (2009). *California school law* (2nd ed.). Palo Alto, CA: Stanford University Press.

Walsh, J., Kemerer, F., & Maniotis, L. (2010). *The educator's guide to Texas school law.* (7th ed.). Austin, TX: University of Texas.

COURT CASES

Bethel School District No. 403 v. Fraser, 478 U.S. 675 (1986).

Board of Education v. Allen, 392 U.S. 236, 88 S. Ct. 1923, 20 L. Ed 1060 (1968).

Brown v. Board of Education of Topeka, 347 U.S. 483, 74 S. Ct. 686, 98 L. Ed. 873 (1954).

Connick v. Myers, 461 U.S. 138 (1983).

Doe v. University of Michigan, 721 F. Supp. 852 (1989).

Fenton v. Stear, 423 F. Supp. 767 (W.D. Pa) (1976).

Hazelwood School District v. Kuhlmeier, 484 U.S. 260 (1988).

Karr v. Schmidt, 460 F.2d 609 (5th Cir.) (1972).

Keyishian v. Board of Regents of New York, 385 U.S. 589 (1967).

Kingsville Independent School District v. Cooper, 611 F.2d 1109 (5th Cir.) (1980).

Meyer v. Nebraska, 262 U.S. 390, 43 S. Ct. 625, 67 L. Ed. 1042 (1923).

Miller v. California, 413 U.S. 15 (1973).

Milliken v. Bradley, 418 U.S. 717 (1974).

Morse v. Frederick, 127 S. Ct. 2618 (2007).

Mt. Healthy City School District Board of Education v. Doyle, 429 U.S. 274 (1977).

Parents Involved in Community Schools v. Seattle School District No. 1, 127 S. Ct. 2738 (2007).

Pickering v. Board of Education, 391 U.S. 563 (1969).

Planned Parenthood v. Clark County School District, 941 F. 2d 871 (9th Cir.) (1991).

Plessy v. Ferguson, 163 U.S. 537, 16 S. Ct. 1138, 41 L. Ed. 256 (1896).

Scott v. News-Herald, 496 N.E.2d 699 (Ohio) (1986).

Sheff v. O'Neill, 211 Conn. 627 A. 2d. 518 (1996).

Steirer v. Bethlehem Area School District, 987 F.2d. 989 (3rd Cir.) (1993).

Swann v. Charlotte-Mecklenburg Board of Education, 402 U.S. 1 (1971).

Tinker v. Des Moines Independent Community School District, 393 U.S. 503 (1969).

Walz ex rel. Walz v. Egg Harbor Township Board of Education, 342 F.3d 271 (3rd Cir.) (2003).

CHAPTER 12

RESOURCE ALLOCATION AND MANAGEMENT

MyEdLeadershipLab™

Visit the MyEdLeadershipLab™ site for *Educational Leadership: A Bridge to Improved Practice,* Fifth Edition to enhance your understanding of chapter concepts. You'll have the opportunity to practice your skills through video- and case-based Assignments and Activities as well as Building Leadership Skills units, and to prepare for your certification exam with Practice for Certification quizzes.

BAYVIEW VALLEY SCHOOL DISTRICT

Identifying Funding Sources for Hartley High

Bayview Valley School District is located adjacent to a large city in the West. It is comprised of seven elementary schools, two middle schools, and a high school with nearly 2,500 students. Hartley High School (HHS), like many of its counterparts throughout the nation, is experiencing problems with an aging facility.

HHS, originally built in 1930, nearly doubled its size in 1980 by means of an addition. Although the facility has been well maintained, it needs retrofitting. Referring to the science and computer labs, the faculty members have often told Principal Kate Sheridan that, although safety requirements have been met, the facilities are in a "deplorable condition." The faculty members say they are "completely embarrassed" about the lack of equipment,

particularly when visitors pass through the rooms. A typical high school class has 30 students, but the computer lab has only 10 computers. In science labs, students have to share microscopes and other equipment.

Principal Sheridan has discussed these concerns with the central office; however, they have informed her that in the foreseeable future no additional money will be available. Sheridan has requested that the school-site council include discussion of these issues on the next agenda. The school-site council is comprised of five teachers, one student, the principal, two parents, and two community members. Because Bayview Valley School District has decentralized authority in recent years, HHS has considerable influence in budget planning and expenditures.

✳ **If you were formulating next year's budget, what approach might you use to help real-locate funds within the existing budget? How can money be identified so that additional resources will be available to students in the science and computer laboratories?**

FINANCING SCHOOLS

To address fiscal issues in operating a school and to speak knowledgeably with school community members, administrators need to have a basic understanding of school finance.

Taxes

Tax revenues are used to finance many public services, including social service agencies, police departments, fire departments, transportation systems, and schools. Public schools are primarily funded through the revenues generated from property, consumption, and state income taxes. Each of these taxes has advantages and disadvantages when evaluated on such criteria as equity, yield, tax base, economic impact, and compliance.

The *equity* of a tax refers to fairness. One of the basic assumptions since the inception of American taxation has been progressivity, based on the belief that an equitable tax is one that takes a higher percentage from those whose net worth increases the most, because they are gaining the most from society and that such taxes do not take away from the basic necessities of life but only from luxuries. Former Secretary of Labor Robert Reich (1997), expressing concerns about recent policies that have lowered the taxes of the wealthiest income earners, stated, "I find this trend deeply disturbing. We have the most unequal distribution of income of any industrialized nation" (p. 32). This trend of lowering taxes for the wealthiest Americans occurred as part of the Tax Reform Act of 1986 and became an issue again at the turn of the century.

Yield refers to the revenue produced by a tax. Questions regarding yield look at which tax yields the most revenue at the lowest tax rate and whether income from a tax increases as the economy improves and decreases as the economy slows down.

The *tax base* refers to the particular category of income and assets to which a tax rate can be applied. Typical tax base classifications include income, wealth, property value, and consumption.

Economic impact is another factor used to evaluate taxation systems. Key questions to ask are whether the tax is a disincentive to the U.S. business owner or worker or whether the tax produces negative impacts on the economy.

The *administration of taxes* can be highly cumbersome. The question to ask is how to generate maximum revenue while keeping tax administration costs to a minimum.

Finally, *compliance* involves ensuring that taxes are actually paid. One example is the automatic nature of withholding of income taxes. Some contract workers pay income taxes on a quarterly or yearly basis and the taxes are not deducted from the paycheck; thus, compliance becomes an important issue.

In recent years, the federal government has moved more toward a proportional or flat tax, which reduces the taxes on the wealthy and increases the taxes on the middle class as a percentage of income.

As states examine their school finance legislation, there is a trend toward reducing the reliance on property taxes and increasing the amount of revenue from other types of taxes (e.g., consumption taxes such as the revenues generated from state lotteries). Property taxes and some other types of taxes are often regressive—that is, they ask middle-class taxpayers to pay a higher percentage of their wages in taxes than higher-income groups. Knowledge of taxation for education and its effect on citizens is important because taxes provide much of the revenue stream for public education.

FEDERAL INVOLVEMENT IN FINANCING SCHOOLS

Although education is a state rather than a federal responsibility, the federal government plays a role in financing specific education programs supported by the government. The federal government's role as a source of revenue has changed little since 1970. The percentage of a local school budget contributed by the federal government is usually less than 10%. This figure varies according to the type of school.

For example, large urban school districts are more likely to have federally financed initiatives such as bilingual programs, magnet schools, migrant programs, Head Start, and school-to-work programs. Thus, the percentage of their budget contributed by the federal government is larger than that in districts not offering these programs.

Table 12.1 depicts a budget outlay for a variety of programs supported by the U.S. government. Aid is usually distributed to school districts as block grants, categorical aid, or as general aid. These monies are usually sent to the state office of education, which distributes funds to local education agencies.

STATE INVOLVEMENT IN FINANCING SCHOOLS

Most states have complex systems of funding; however, one particularly important concept is what is called the *foundation program*. The foundation program refers to the established minimum of financial support that a district receives for each enrolled student. School districts are reimbursed by the state on an average daily membership (ADM) or average daily attendance (ADA) basis. The amount, sometimes called a *per-pupil allotment*, might be affected by several factors, including the amount of local fiscal effort, the number of special, vocational, and bilingual education students, and the number of students from families below the poverty level. Figure 12.1 depicts the total revenues per pupil for fiscal years 1990 to 2002.

TABLE 12.1   Where Do Federal School Dollars Go?

A breakdown of average per-pupil spending by category in nine selected districts in 1967, 1991, and 1996.

PROGRAM AREA	1967	1991	1996
Regular education	80.1%	58.5%	56.8%
Special education	3.6%	17.8%	19.0%
Food services	1.9%	3.3%	4.8%
Compensatory education	5.0%	4.2%	3.5%
Pupil support (attendance and counseling)	2.1%	3.5%	3.2%
Transportation (regular education)	3.6%	3.9%	3.1%
Vocational education	1.4%	2.8%	2.7%
Bilingual education	0.3%	1.9%	2.5%
Desegregation	0.0%	1.9%	1.5%
Regular health and psychological services	1.4%	1.0%	1.1%
After school athletics	0.4%	0.7%	0.6%
"At-risk" youth education, alternative education	0.1%	0.6%	0.6%
Security and violence prevention	0.1%	0.5%	0.6%
Total	100.0%	100.0%	100.0%

*Programs listed in order of 1996 share of total per pupil spending.
Source: Economic Policy Institute, 1996.

In addition to the foundation concept, other approaches to financing public schools include a flat-grant model, power-equalizing plan, guaranteed tax base plan, and a weighted-student model. Several states use more than one method for financing schools.

With a *flat-grant model*, state aid to local school districts is based on a fixed amount. This amount is then multiplied by the number of students in the district. Many people argue that this approach to funding schools is unequal because it is more expensive to educate some children than others. For example, a child requiring special education services or bilingual education would cost a school district more to educate than a child not needing these services.

A *power-equalizing model* pays a percentage of local school expenditures in an inverse ratio to the school district's wealth. The wealthier the district, the less matching state monies it receives. The goal is equalization between wealthier school districts and those of less wealth. Because those living in wealthy districts can pay a much lower percent of their income and yet raise considerably more

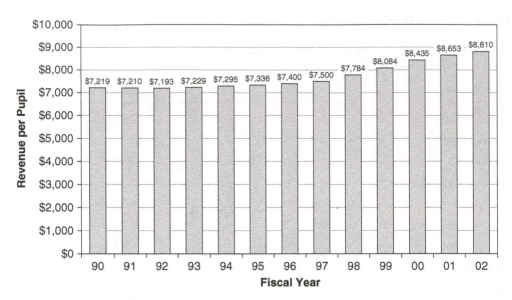

FIGURE 12.1   Inflation-Adjusted Total Revenues per Pupil for Public Elementary and Secondary Education in the United States: Fiscal Years 1990–2002

Source: U.S. Department of Education, National Center for Educational Statistics, Common Core of Data (CCD), "National Public Education Financial Survey, Fiscal Years 1990–2002."

money for the education of every child in average daily membership, the state tries to make adjustments for these inequities.

In a *weighted-student model* of financing public education, students are weighted in proportion to their special needs. For example, students requiring bilingual education, special-needs classes, or vocational classes would be allotted additional money according to the costs of those services. One of the problems with this model is the complexity involved in assigning weights. For example, some children receive not only special education services but also bilingual program services. Calculating weights for special programs can become highly complex.

The school financial issue that has received the greatest sustained court attention is the alleged inequities in financing public education. The issue is inequality of educational opportunity caused by educational funding that is "a function of district property wealth; whether or not a disputed financial scheme provides each child with at least a basic or adequate education; the importance of local control; and the extent, if any, of courts' involvement in providing remediation" (LaMorte, 1999, pp. 351–352).

A related issue is providing choices of educational services at public expense. LaMorte (1999) goes on to say:

Unfortunately for discussion purposes, the notion of choice does not describe a single, well-defined plan but is an umbrella term for a host of programs. . . . Its proponents argue that bringing a concept—consumer choice—to education will break the alleged monopolistic stranglehold of the educational bureaucracy by introducing the necessary ingredient of a measure of needed competition, with all the positive connotations that term implies, to the public schools. (p. 374)

Charter schools are a form of choice that encourages innovative educational ideas. Charter schools, which are public schools that have many of the characteristics of independent schools, are also financed through taxes. Typically, certain per-pupil allotment is given by the district or state directly to the charter school for each child enrolled, rather than to a district central office. If a student chooses to leave a school, she or he takes the funding away from that school (for more information, see nationalcharterschools.org).

Let us examine the sources of funding for schools in one state, using California as an example (see Figure 12.2). Approximately 13% of the K–12 education budget for a California school district is from federal government funds. These monies are allotted through categorical or block grants. About 55% of the funding comes from the state's budget. These monies come from business, corporate, and personal income taxes as well as sales taxes and other special taxes. Local property taxes comprise about 22% of the funding. This varies depending on the state's overall budget for a given year. There are other local revenues as well. Comprising approximately 8% of the funding, these sources might include: fees on commercial or residential construction; contributions from parents, businesses, and foundations; special elections for parcel taxes; interest on investments by local school districts; and cafeteria sales, and interest on investments by local school districts,

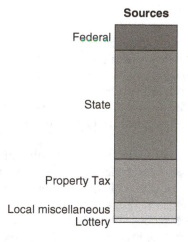

Sources

Federal
State
Property Tax
Local miscellaneous
Lottery

- Funds from the federal government are about 13% of the K–12 education budget.
- About 55% of the total comes from the state's budget: business, corporate and personal income taxes, sales taxes, and some special taxes.
- Local property taxes are about 22%, an amount that is determined within the state's budget.
- Miscellaneous local revenues, about 8% of the total, include such items as fees on commercial or residential construction; special elections for parcel taxes; contributions from parents, businesses, and foundations; cafeteria sales; and interest on investments by local school districts.
- The smallest amount at the bottom is the California Lottery, which provides 1.5% of the total, or about $125 per student annually.

These percentages represent the average contribution that each funding source has contributed during the past 10 years.

FIGURE 12.2   The Sources of Funding for Schools

Source: Retrieved from http://www.ed-data.k12.ca.us/Pages/Home.aspx.

TABLE 12.2   Sources of Revenue for California Schools

	1994–1995	1998–1999	2003–2004	2009–2010
Federal aid	8.3%	9.6%	13%	9.2%
State aid	53.2%	54.0%	53%	60.2%
Property tax	29.1%	28.0%	27%	21.4%
Local miscellaneous	7.2%	7.0%	6%	7.6%
Lottery	2.2%	2.4%	1%	1.6%

among others. Finally, approximately 1% of the funding for schools comes from the California Lottery (about $125 per student annually). As Figure 12.2 shows, these sources of funding vary slightly from year to year. Table 12.2 describes the sources of revenue for one state (California) and with the exception of the category of "lottery," it would be similar to most other states.

LOCAL INVOLVEMENT IN FINANCING SCHOOLS

State governments have granted school districts the power to tax individuals and companies. The main revenue source for public schools is the local property tax. The property tax is a function of three variables: the tax base, the assessment practice, and the tax rate. The tax base includes all taxable property in the district except that owned by the federal government, public hospitals, state parks, churches, and nonprofit entities, which are not taxable.

States vary as to how they assess property. Usually a percentage rate, established by the taxing authority, is applied to the property's market value. The market value is the amount the owner would receive on selling the property. Depending on the state, the tax rate is expressed in a variety of ways: per thousand dollars of assessed valuation, dollars per hundred dollars of assessed valuation, and mills. According to Sharp (1994), "The school district's tax rate is multiplied by the assessed value of the tax base of the community to yield the amount of money the school will receive" (p. 2).

Let's look at an example for a single home. If the market value of a home is $120,000 and the taxing authority's assessment practice is 80%, the assessed value of the home would be $120,000 × 0.80, or $96,000. This is the amount on which the homeowner would be taxed. If the rate were $2.00 per $100.00 of assessed value, the property tax on this house would be $96,000 × 0.02, or $1,920. Keep in mind, however, that the homeowner's overall tax rate includes other taxes in addition to school taxes (e.g., water district, hospital district).

This is a simplified version of the tax process. Often, homeowners and businesses are eligible for certain types of exemptions. Additionally, when a community is trying to lure businesses into town, it often offers tax abatements (a lesser amount of taxes in the first few years).

Here is a typical formula for a school district's income:

General purpose (Revenue limit × ADA)
+ Special purpose (categorical aid)
+ Miscellaneous local and other (i.e., sale of assets, investment income)
+ Lottery

= Total District Income

VOUCHERS

In the mid-1950s, economist Milton Friedman proposed that every family be given a voucher of equal worth for each child attending public schools. Under his plan, a family could choose any school meeting the basic requirements set by the government. Parents could add their own resources to the voucher, and schools could set their own tuition level and admission requirements.

Throughout the last 40 years, various versions of a voucher system have been debated at local, state, and national levels. Vouchers have been tied to the concept of school choice, with a voucher program being proposed as one form of schooling that should be made available to children and families.

School choice has become a major policy issue affecting schools throughout the nation. At present, only one state (Indiana) has a voucher system. Several cities across the nation are utilizing voucher systems (e.g., Milwaukee, Chicago, Cleveland) with limited measures of success. In 1998, the Wisconsin Supreme Court upheld the use of vouchers, and the U.S. Supreme Court declined to review the case. The city of Milwaukee, Wisconsin started a voucher program in 1990 and now has nearly 15,000 students using vouchers. Former Florida Governor Jeb Bush proposed a voucher plan in 2000 providing up to $4,000 for each student attending a failing school (based on the school's test scores) that could be used to attend public, private, or religious schools; however, it was struck down by a Florida state court. In 2004, Washington, DC launched a voucher program providing support for tuition, transportation, and school fees. The program was ended by the Obama administration in 2009, and was revived again in 2011. Arizona passed a law in 2011 allowing students with disabilities to sign up for "empowerment scholarships." These "scholarships" can be used to pay for tuition, online courses, tutoring, college classes, or classes at home. The families could also choose to save the money and use it toward full-time college enrollment after high school graduation (Shah, 2011, p. 4).

In 2011, Indiana's legislature approved the formation of one of the most ambitious voucher programs in the nation. Indiana's law allows students from middle-income backgrounds to receive vouchers. Children from lower socioeconomic backgrounds receive larger amounts of aid, but this is the first time a state's middle-income students can use vouchers to pay for private school tuition. More and more states are proposing voucher legislation or have small voucher programs.

In addition, school vouchers (or *education vouchers,* as they are sometimes called), are used in a growing number of countries throughout the world. For example, the Netherlands began using vouchers early in the last century and Chile has had vouchers since the 1980s. In addition, other nations such as Ireland and Sweden have voucher systems. The school choice movement includes ideas such as vouchers, magnet schools, home schools, and charter schools. These movements have the potential to change the allocation of revenues and have implications for revenue generation for schools.

NONTRADITIONAL REVENUE SOURCES

To expand services, many school districts have begun to look at a variety of nontraditional sources of revenue. Meno (1984) identified three categories for nontraditional funding sources: donor, enterprise, and cooperative. According to the research of Garnos and King (1994), superintendents and principals believe that nontraditional revenues are viable ways to enhance public school budgets. As the charter school movement expands nationwide, these sources will become more commonly used. Additionally, much can be learned from independent schools (both private and religious) about alternative sources of revenue generation; in order to exist, these institutions have had to utilize a variety of funding strategies. School administrators must be skilled in fostering partnerships, securing donors, and establishing enterprises.

School Foundations

A school foundation is similar to a university's development office. A foundation has a tax-free status; thus, donors can benefit from their gifts. Foundations allow community members to raise funds through gifts from individuals and corporations. Funds can be used to pay for field trips, special projects, scholarships, and awards.

Thayer and Short (1994) maintain that the principal must be a key player in forming a foundation. They recommend the following steps in creating a foundation:

- Organize a team to study the feasibility of such a move.
- Obtain 501(c)(3) status and authorization to transact business, subject to all applicable state and federal laws.
- Inform stakeholders why a foundation is needed and of the history behind the process.
- Set specific, reasonable goals.

REVENUE SOURCES FOR INDEPENDENT SCHOOLS

Independent schools include both religious and private schools located in the United States and overseas. Independent schools are primarily funded through tuition and gifts. Alumni are among the largest sources of gifts for independent schools. One difference between independent private schools and religious schools is that for the latter, religious institutions sometimes support a portion of the school budget.

Much can be learned from independent schools, not only regarding their fundraising strategies, but also in how they market their programs.

✳ **What implications do funding mechanisms have for the plans of the school-site council of Hartley High?**

OBTAINING FUNDING FOR EDUCATIONAL PROGRAMS

HARVEY B. POLANSKY, PHD
Former Superintendent of Schools, Southington, Connecticut

Funding has become an intricate part of district and school management. Strategies in the development, procurement, and public approval of school funds vary greatly but have one common strand: accountability. Accountability is less a process of bookkeeping and more one of intense taxpayer scrutiny of what value the public receives for its educational dollars. With much more emphasis on state and local government transparency in recent years comes even greater scrutiny and criticism of school funding. Administrators will be forced to defend funding strategies and seek alternative and creative means to obtain funds. They will have to manage the funds with greater competency and preparation. Many of us started our educational journey in the spend-free 1980s. Since then, a quasi–tax revolt has diminished educational dollars.

WHERE DO SCHOOL FUNDS COME FROM?
Nationally, over 80% of all school funds come from local and state funding, entitlements, and tax revenue. Tax revenues have decreased, placing both tax revenues and entitlements in jeopardy. School districts seek other means to develop strategies in obtaining funds for worthwhile programs. No longer can administrators expect the municipality to cover all expenses. Creative strategies to find school funding include the following five.

Development of Educational Enterprise Zones. Schools can no longer sit back and expect tax dollars to cover the costs of innovative programs. In many cases, school must put up an "open for business" sign. Fees for extended-day programs, day-care programs, and enrichment programs often come from consumers. Principals must learn how to market and create fiscal systems of accountability to manage these programs. School will be open from 6 a.m. to 6 p.m., and the fees earned can be used for staff, materials, and building initiatives. Governance teams and building improvement teams must be coordinated.

(continued)

Preschool Programs. Schools will have to compete with private day-care providers. Are preschool programs educationally sound, providing the students fewer transitions? Can they be an economic cash cow? Effective preschool programs will enhance feeder programs, engage parents at early ages, and offer community outreach to a population that is politically strong. Funds can be used for schoolwide initiatives. In addition, research suggests that the experience of children in the first 4 years has a strong influence on their future development.

Resource Sharing. School districts tend to view their existence in isolated management camps. Regional service centers attempt to develop resource sharing but are often in the market themselves. School districts should learn to share business and support side functions, such as transportation, substitute teachers, food service, custodial service, bidding services, and innovative technological and curricular programs across district lines. Sharing will diminish personnel costs and enhance district funding. Cooperative arrangements with museums, corporations, and businesses will also bring needed services to schools. Most corporate giving has ceased or is part of a competitive grant program.

Grant Writing. School administrators must turn to the Internet and find grants. Entitlements are drying up and competitive categorical grants are becoming increasingly available. Dream a little. Put your thoughts on paper, go online, and find out what grants are available. The National School Boards Association (http://www.nsba.org) and the U.S. Department of Education (http://www.sdoe.org) have Web sites and periodicals listing available grant programs. Local organizations might also list grant opportunities. Some administrators are hesitant to submit a grant proposal. Remember, the worst that could happen is that they reject it. You will still be learning a great innovative approach to finding alternate funding.

Distance Learning. While some teacher unions oppose the concept of distance learning, satellite, interdistrict distance learning programs can decrease costs (thereby allowing administrators to use funds elsewhere) and offer opportunities to charge for programs. Latin 4, French 6, and esoteric math and science courses can be taught via interactive distance learning programs. Equipment is expensive but does tend to attract grant funding. Universities also offer programs that can reduce costs and provide much-needed studio facilities.

We can no longer rely on traditional funding sources. It is the entrepreneurial administrators who will find funds that best meet the needs of their schools and programs.

GRANT WRITING

Given the increase in the need for schools and school districts to obtain funding from nontraditional sources, skills in understanding grant writing are now requisite for school administrators. Ruskin and Achilles (1995) summarize the grant-writing process as follows:

1. Identify a philanthropist or foundation interested in your type of project.
2. Develop a comprehensive and individualized plan to interest this person.
3. Design a short-term strategy and a long-range plan for support.
4. Make personal contact with the funder.

5. Devise a plan to enlist support of other key people.
6. Send a letter of inquiry and interest.
7. Submit the required proposal.
8. Establish ongoing dialogue with the funder.
9. Steward the funder through various phases of your project to ensure that the funder becomes a stakeholder. (p. 30)

Not only do school administrators have to understand the process of applying for grants, but they also need to understand what information is typically found in any grant. Ruskin and Achilles (1995) provide eleven suggestions for grant writers to use when supporting their case in a grant proposal:

1. Provide a clear picture of your school site—demographics, curriculum, special programs, best features, and the problem.
2. Clearly present the needs you are attempting to meet, with supporting data about the impact of needs on the quality of education provided to students.
3. Articulate the plan you are proposing to meet these needs, including how the plan was developed. Provide a comprehensive picture of the reasons this plan is the best means to address the educational needs. Support your ideas with other successful models, and provide a timetable for implementation.
4. Outline direct and indirect educational benefits derived through successful implementation of your plan. Emphasize the impact of your project on the quality of education and its implications for the individual student.
5. List funder costs for your plan. Depending on what the funder is seeking, you may need to convince the funder that you have given careful attention to costs and that you can complete the project within your budget.
6. Provide an evaluation design for your plan as part of your implementation timeline. Tie it to measurable objectives.
7. Provide a convincing argument about the professional and personal qualifications of the proposed project director.
8. Delineate future funding needs and a strategy to secure needed resources.
9. Develop a plan to continue the project after initial funding is completed. How will you institutionalize the grant?
10. Provide appropriate support information in appendixes.
11. Develop a calendar with your agenda for grant follow-up. Specify important targeted grant deadlines and appointments on this calendar to ensure ongoing contact with the funder. Details of stewardship activities could be added here. Make it easy for the grant manager to take one glimpse at the calendar and anticipate any significant deadlines. (pp. 53–54)

BUDGETING, ACCOUNTING, AND FACILITY MANAGEMENT

The receipt of the budget provides that moment of truth when the administration learns the type of educational program that the community can afford or is willing to support. Budgeting ensures that required resources will be available at the right time and in the right amount to accomplish the educational plan. It is a financial plan that needs to be interpreted to the school board and community so that it can be approved.

The Budgeting Process

The budgeting process involves planning, formulating, presenting, administering, and evaluating. Many states follow a calendar that determines when certain stages of a school district's budget must be met. Often the process begins in September, and the budget is adopted the following June or July.

Planning. The academic program should drive the budget; therefore, in the planning stage of the budget process, factors such as needs, program goals and objectives, alternatives for achieving goals, and selecting cost-effective alternatives must be considered.

Formulating. To formulate the budget, it is crucial to have input from the many constituencies of the school. Schools can no longer jealously guard the budget, keeping secret how and why money is spent. Teachers are being asked to assume a greater role in the budget process in many school districts, especially in schools that are site managed. Creating and detailing the budget should involve input and discussion from faculty, staff, and other groups who are part of the school's community.

Box 12.1 displays a checklist for developing a school budget. It includes the process, the organizing of the budget document, and the types of data needed to compile the budget.

Presenting. A crucial part to presenting a school budget is the development of a rationale. In most school districts, principals meet with superintendents and other central office personnel involved with the budgeting process to discuss their budget. The final school district budget is presented to the school board and, in the case of dependent school districts, to the city council or board of county supervisors. It is crucial that an administrator be able to articulate a strong rationale for budget priorities.

Administering. One way to administer the budget is to allocate money to each program or department and allow staff to spend as they wish as long as they stay within the assigned amount. The responsibilities related to purchasing and accounting, however, are very important. Often, it can take several months between the time an item is ordered and the time the bills actually arrive (encumbrances). The money that will be used is encumbered until the bill is actually paid. Thus, although the money is technically available, it should not be used. A multitude of computer programs are available to help school administrators manage the school budget and ensure that encumbered monies are not used and that the budget is not overexpended.

Evaluating. The school budget is usually organized into categories such as programs (early childhood, bilingual, language arts), functions (instructional,

BOX 12.1

SCHOOL BUDGET DEVELOPMENT CHECKLIST

PROCESS: PROCEDURES FOR CONDUCTING HEARINGS

_____	Roles of board and superintendent clearly defined
_____	Board finance policies updated regularly
_____	Financial data accurate and timely
_____	Staff adequately in budget request
_____	Public hearing held with citizen participation
_____	Budget document (or summary) widely distributed
_____	Process complies with legal requirements
_____	Community/political support generated for budget
_____	Contingency strategy (budget options) exists
_____	Efficient accounting/financial reporting system used

FORMAT: PREPARING THE DOCUMENT

_____	Cover, title page, appearance attractive
_____	Table of contents or index; number pages
_____	Board members and officers' names included
_____	Organizational chart and school administrators listed
_____	Budget message or transmittal letter included
_____	Graphics/artwork, charts, figures, tables
_____	Clarity of style; avoidance of technical jargon
_____	Manageable size and shape of document
_____	Glossary of key terms
_____	Concise executive summary (budget in brief)

CONTENTS: DATA COMPILATION

_____	Feasibility of bottom-line requests
_____	School system goals and objectives
_____	Budget guidelines or priorities
_____	Object budget summary (e.g., salaries, supplies)
_____	Site budget summary (e.g., individual campuses)
_____	Budget history (expenditures for previous 5 years)
_____	Unit cost analysis (per-pupil expenditures)
_____	Estimated revenue summary (all sources)
_____	Explanation of tax rate impact
_____	Explanation of major cost factors (contracts, inflation)
_____	Budget coding system explained (account charts)
_____	Performance measures included (test data)
_____	Pupil enrollment projections by grade
_____	Staffing history and projections
_____	Long-range plans (5 years) for district
_____	Major decisions justified (layoffs, closings)
_____	District or state comparisons
_____	Capital budget summarized (improvement projects)
_____	Budget detail (line-item expenditure data)

Source: Hartley, H. (1990). Boardroom bottom line. _American School Board Journal, 177_(2), 31. Reproduced with permission.

transportation, facilities management), and objects (supplies, salaries, staff development, travel). These areas can be evaluated separately or in combination. Questions such as the following need to be asked: How well did the budget serve the goals it was meant to accomplish? How will we determine whether the goals and objectives were achieved? Were the goods and services purchased actually used? Should the program be expanded? Should the program be eliminated? As programs are evaluated, school administrators should ask if the approach used was the most effective as well as most efficient way to accomplish the goals.

TYPES OF BUDGETING

The following four types of budgets are not mutually exclusive; each can provide useful and needed information. One might become more important depending on organizational needs and situations. If the computer system used is sophisticated enough for financial records and the data are properly organized, the computer program can prepare cost and budget information in a number of different formats.

Line-Item Budgeting

Line-item budgeting is the most widely used budgeting approach in school system budgeting. An *object budget* is a listing of the objects of expense, such as salaries, supplies, equipment, services, insurance, travel, professional improvements, postage, maintenance, utilities, fringe benefits, rents, debt reduction, and so forth. A *function classification* lists estimates of expenditures in terms of the purposes for which they are made—administration, instruction, health service, pupil transportation, food service, operation, fixed charges, summer school, adult education, and so on. Today's general line-item budget has evolved from a combination of these two organizational categories.

The wide variety of classification systems used to account for school expenditures and revenues complicate the process, along with the consequent difficulties involved in securing expenditure and revenues. Additionally, the difficulty involved in securing comparable data concerning the financial operation of the school systems impelled the U.S. Office of Education to issue a handbook, *Financial Accounting for Local and State School Systems*, which is periodically updated. The handbook provides recommendations regarding expenditure and revenue accounts to be used in budgeting and accounting. For the most part, state requirements and local school budgets have followed the basic recommendations made by the U.S. Office of Education.

Budget estimates are typically made from one year to the next by adding a percentage increment of the previous year's budget. The typical procedure is to record expenditures for a given budget classification for 1 or 2 years prior, enter the request for the future year, and note the additional amounts requested. Then the budget director, superintendent, and school board arrive at a final figure by taking a fixed percentage cut (or addition) in the school's requests. This is the basis of stability in the appropriations process and provides an excellent mechanism for control.

Planning, Programming, Budgeting System (PPBS)

Typically, the line-item budget deals primarily with the functions and objects of expense but not with the programs. A program-budgeting system provides a method of determining the costs of programs. Sometimes called *PPBS* and at other times called *PPBES*, with the *E* referring to evaluation, this approach to budgeting requires that the budget be organized around program goals and the processes to accomplish these goals. Although it originated in the 1940s, PPBS did not gain momentum until the 1960s.

According to Ubben and Hughes (1997), PPBS involves five steps:

1. Establish the general goals to be achieved.
2. Identify the specific objectives that define this goal.
3. Develop the program and processes that it is believed will achieve the objectives and goals.
4. Establish the formative and summative evaluation practices.
5. Implement a review and recycle procedure that indicates whether or not, or the degree to which, the program and processes resulted in the achievement of the objectives and the goals, and, if not, to help determine other procedures, processes, and programs. (p. 308)

Program budgets are not increased incrementally, but require leadership to decide how much to spend on achieving program goals and objectives. The administrator might select a more favorable alternative for one program and a less favorable one for another based on cost-and-benefit analysis. Candoli, Hack, Ray, and Stollar (1984) maintain that PPBES is a cyclical process that constantly requires feedback. The two-way arrows in Figure 12.3 depict the recursive nature of this budgeting approach. One disadvantage of PPBES is that it is far more time-consuming than other budgeting approaches and might not provide as efficient fiscal control; it is, however, excellent for planning purposes.

Zero-Based Budgeting

Zero-based budgeting requires administrators to justify all expenditures on an annual basis. Thus, starting with a zero amount, current and new expenditures must be fully justified so that monies can be allocated for them. Zero-based budgeting also requires yearly evaluations so that priorities based on program evaluation data can be set.

According to Bliss (1994), zero-based budgeting involves five steps:

1. Identify decision units (defined as any programs that consume resources).
2. Analyze decision packages (documents that describe a decision's objectives, activities, resources, and costs).
3. Rank decision packages.
4. Allocate funds.
5. Prepare official budgets.

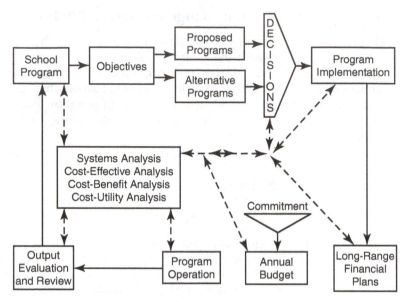

FIGURE 12.3   Illustration of Way in Which Planning, Programming, Budgeting, Evaluation System (PPBES) Might Work

One of the key benefits is that functions or programs can be ranked as to desirability and marginal activities can be identified. Administrators can reassess their operations from the ground up and justify every dollar spent in terms of current goals. However, the major focus is typically on those program increments that are just above or below the projected funding level. The heart of zero-based budgeting is, therefore, the ranking process. This ranking procedure establishes priorities among the decision packages. One disadvantage to zero-based budgeting is its time intensiveness. A major advantage is the elimination of expenditures that were valid in the past but are no longer relevant.

Incremental Budgeting

The most common budgeting in schools is incremental budgeting, which involves adding to or subtracting from the current year's budget. Budget development for the current year begins with the previous year's budget. An assumption is made that the upcoming year's budget will be similar to the current year's budget. Last year's programs are regarded as a base and allowed to grow by some fixed percent; whatever resources are left over are then assigned to new or improved programs. Incremental budgeting does not include formal evaluation of needs and programs. Often, programs that do not necessarily fulfill existing needs continue to be allocated monies, while more effective, newer programs might go underfunded. These are serious problems for a nation calling for greater accountability.

Items such as special programs and facility renovations are handled separately. Additionally, money coming from federal sources is usually addressed separately.

Trends in Budgeting and Management

In recent years, various types of organizations have been calling for performance-based budgeting, results-based budgeting, or mission-based budgeting and management. Results-based budgeting is based on the premise that managers should seek to obtain control over human and financial resources by developing budget systems that fund outcomes rather than inputs. Advocates of results-based budgeting maintain that it is a vehicle for moving beyond short-term increments to a long-term view of strategies to address priorities. A results-based budgeting system defines the mission and the outcomes, but it does not directly link dollars spent to the quality of the outcomes.

Performance-based budgeting requires strategic planning regarding the organization's mission, goals, and objectives and a process that requires quantifiable data that provides meaningful information about program outcomes (Willoughby & Melkers, 1998). Performance-based budgeting may also require that an organization assess its progress toward specified target goals.

Gaining considerable popularity in universities and colleges, and to a lesser degree in schools, is mission-based management and mission-based budgeting. Mission-based management refers to introducing a new reporting system that tracks revenues and expenses and measures faculty activities and contributions on a mission-specific basis. It also involves the implementation of a new management and decision-making structure and processes that are enabled by these new reporting systems. A key issue in mission-based management is allocating resources based on a better understanding of the distribution of faculty effort.

Poston (2010) advocates for performance-based (curriculum-driven) budgeting. Sometimes this is called *result-based* or *data-driven budgeting*. The key "... is to tie measured performance, or achievement of established outcomes or objectives, into the decision-making process" (p. 9). With performance-based, curriculum-driven budgeting funding is based on the value received from the program and the level. Thus, there is a direct link between the resources invested and the results of the program or initiative.

Whatever approach to budgeting is used, identifying concrete district and school goals is crucial. For example, if one districtwide goal is to improve student achievement in mathematics, then this may result in a request to add a part-time or full-time math instructor at a particular school. Recent years have seen an increase in the use of metrics to measure student and school performance; thus, there will continue to be greater focus on quantifying teacher and administrator performance in relation to student achievement data.

❋ **What budgeting approach(es) might help the school-site council at Hartley High School in reallocating funds for the science and computer labs? In what way?**

ACTIVITY FUNDS

Typical student activity funds include accounts for student organizations (e.g., sports clubs, student council), profit earnings (e.g., concessions and school pictures), special-purpose accounts (e.g., field trips, hospitality), and others. Monitoring accounts is essential to a well-managed school.

The Association for School Business Officials (ASBO) has recommended 12 guidelines for managing student activity accounts (Box 12.2). Additionally, most school districts have policies regarding activity funds as well as soliciting funds (Figure 12.4).

BOX 12.2

ASBO GUIDELINES FOR MANAGING STUDENT ACTIVITY ACCOUNTS

1. All money received should be acknowledged by issuing prenumbered receipts or prenumbered tickets to the person from whom the money is received.
2. Deposits should be made daily, if possible. Cash should never be left in the school over the weekend or holidays.
3. Receipts should be issued to the person making the deposit. Deposit slips should be retained by both the depositor and the school accountant or bookkeeper.
4. Purchase orders or requisitions should be initiated by the person in charge of the activity fund.
5. Payments should be made by check, prepared and mailed from the business office to the payee.
6. The principal should designate two or more persons in addition to himself or herself who will be authorized to sign checks. Two of the three authorized signatures should also be required for all withdrawals.
7. No payment should be made unless supported by a written purchase order and by a signed invoice certifying receipt of merchandise and accuracy of prices.
8. Student activity funds should not be used for any purchase that represents a loan or accommodation to any school district employee or other nonstudent. Emergency loans may be made to students for lunches, carfare, and the like upon written permission of the principal. Individuals may not make purchases through the student body in order to take advantage of better prices.
9. Student bodies may enter contracts for the purchase of supplies, equipment, and services from an approved vendor provided the term of the contract is within the tenure of the students of the school (usually 3 years).
10. The student body should operate on a budget reflecting past experience and future plans; like the school and school district budget, the student budget should serve as a guide for the year's financing activities.
11. Student activity books and financial procedures should be subjected to periodic internal and external audits. An annual examination by outside, independent accountants is also recommended.
12. Regular reports (monthly and annual) should be prepared and submitted to the principal, business office, or any others responsible for the supervision of student activity funds.

MILFORD SCHOOL DISTRICT
Milford, Delaware 19963
POLICY
5104

STUDENT ACTIVITY FUNDS

This policy governs all student organizations under the jurisdiction of the Board of Education and serves as recommended guidelines and procedures for all affiliated organizations.

(1) STUDENT ORGANIZATION: Shall be defined as any student group under the direct supervision of a building principal or other designated member of the district staff.

(2) AFFILIATED ORGANIZATION: Shall be defined as any parent, booster, or other group whose purpose is supportive of a student organization.

GENERAL GUIDELINES

1. Any monies raised by fund-raising activities shall be for the benefit of the students, student organizations, and/or the school.
2. Activities or expenditures that require the raising of funds shall be appropriate to the needs of the school, organization, and students who will benefit.
3. All fund-raising will be scheduled and regulated by the principal.
4. All accounts shall require multiple signatory parties. For the high school, one of the signatories must be a student representative.
5. No organization shall permit the Treasurer of the organization to be a district employee.
6. No product, materials, or publications will be sold or distributed by anyone to students during school hours without prior approval of the building principal.
7. Any fund-raising activities, which could be construed as gambling (such as raffles and lotteries), must also adhere to existing legal requirements and may not be advertised in school nor involve students.
8. Any uniform purchase must have prior approval of the District's administration.
9. Any equipment, uniforms, etc., purchased and/or donated to the school becomes district and/or school property and must adhere to the requirements of the Delaware Division of Purchasing.
10. The hiring of personnel and providing of stipends to staff (direct employees) is prohibited.
11. Any fund-raising that benefits organizations other than student or affiliated groups is not permitted, unless by special permission of the Board of Education.
12. The giving of awards or other incentives to students may affect the athletic eligibility of students and will not be given without the approval of the principal and district administration.
13. All student and affiliate organizations are to develop annual budgets, plan, and request approval for fund-raising activities early in the school year so they can be properly scheduled.
14. The person disbursing the funds for any organization shall be different from the person serving as the bookkeeper.
15. The bookkeeper shall not be a signatory authority for checks issued to themselves.

(continued)

FIGURE 12.4   Board of Education Policy: Student Activity Funds

Source: Retrieved from http://www.milfordschooldistrict.org/district/board/policies.jsp.

SPECIFIC PROCEDURES

1. The funds of school and student organizations shall be placed in internal accounts, which are regulated by the building principal and comply with district guidelines.
2. Affiliated organizations must register with the building principal prior to any solicitation for funds using the school name.
3. The principal or his designee is to orient the sponsors of student organizations to these guidelines on an annual basis.
4. All fundraising requests must be submitted and approved in advance as specified by Board Policy #5103.
5. All fundraising requests must identify specific budgeted items for which the funds will be used.
6. Solicitation by adults on behalf of students is permitted.
7. Any student solicitation of relatives and other adults familiar to students is permitted, but other door-to-door solicitation is prohibited.
8. Only high school student organizations are permitted to solicit businesses.
9. The utilization of an automated checkbook is encouraged.
10. Specific check request/authorization forms previously approved by multiple persons shall be utilized prior to disbursement of a check.
11. Receipts and other pertinent financial data shall be secured and safeguarded.
12. Specific procedures to maintain a permanent record of all bank accounts shall be established and followed.
13. A ledger of account shall be established, kept up to date at all times, and shall be designed to follow standard bookkeeping practices.
14. Receipts for all monies received by the organization shall be issued. All receipts are to be posted to the respective account on a timely basis and deposited in the appropriate bank account on the day received, or in the case of a holiday, weekend, or evening activity, the next business day.
15. No monies shall be kept overnight by an employee and/or sponsor.
16. Disbursement (payments) shall be made by checks only.
17. Detailed meeting minutes with special emphasis for notations regarding authorizations to expend funds shall be recorded.
18. The pre-signing of disbursement items (checks) is prohibited and inappropriate.
19. The organization shall provide the school's administration with an up-to-date list (name, address, and telephone number) of office holders.
20. At the end of each month, the account ledger for each organization is to be totaled and balanced, the bank statement must be reconciled, and a Treasury Report is to be issued to the President and Secretary of the organization as well as to the principal.
21. At least annually, the district shall conduct an internal review/audit of all student activity accounts.
22. The account balance of the graduating class must be exhausted at the time of graduation. Any account balance of the graduating class that has not been expended or designated as a donation to other school classes or organizations shall be considered a donation to the Milford High School. Such donation shall be expended for the benefit of the Milford High School as determined by the school administration.

ADOPTED: 8/25/03; 2/28/05

FIGURE 12.4   Board of Education Policy: Student Activity Funds (Continued)

FISCAL ACCOUNTING

Fiscal stewardship is of the utmost importance and is a responsibility that no administrator should take lightly. The funds an administrator allocates each day are public funds, and there is an inherent expectation that they will be accounted for properly.

Once the budget for the school district has been approved, it is the responsibility of the administration to ensure that the money that has been appropriated is expended properly. Fiscal accountability is maintained through the district's accounting system and its reporting, auditing, and inventory procedure.

Administrators must maintain accurate records of all money spent and received during the fiscal cycle and provide an accurate accounting at the end of the budget year. Administrators must be knowledgeable and skilled in maintaining accounts for revenues and expenditures as well as for inventories of materials and equipment. The accounting system must adequately control requisitions, purchase orders, contracts, payments, claims, payrolls, and other actions influencing the assets of the organization. The expectation is that all records will be accurate and provide assurance to the board that its financial policies are being observed.

The typical accounting system is described as a double-entry system. For example, the most common entry would be to increase (purchase) an asset and to decrease capital (money) or to increase a liability (debt to creditors). Transactions are entered into the accounts as debits and credits. A debit typically increases an asset or decreases a capital or liability account. The debits and credits in all the school system's accounts must be equal, and all assets, resources, and liabilities must be accounted for in the financial records. The books in which financial records are maintained are called *journals* and *ledgers*. The journal provides a historic record of all transactions, and the ledger provides all transactions made to a given account.

Each school system has its own procedures for maintaining fiscal accountability, but the administrator or his or her designee is expected to code expenditures properly and follow accounting system procedures to accurately maintain ledger accounts and a cash receipt and payment journal. One of the most important decisions an administrator makes is selecting financial officers and bookkeepers to help maintain the financial records. Nonetheless, the administrator is ultimately responsible and should understand basic accounting procedures.

THE AUDIT

Checking for accuracy in accounting is called *auditing*. Internal and external audits should be conducted regularly, and reports should be prepared. Most states require that a certified public accountant conduct an external audit on an annual or biannual basis. It is in the best interests of the school that audits be conducted regularly to maintain credibility and accountability. An administrator should ensure that an audit has been completed before taking responsibility for a budget.

✳ **What accountability procedures need to be addressed at Hartley High?**

ACQUIRING, ALLOCATING, AND ACCOUNTING FOR RESOURCES

RICHARD A. KING
University of Northern Colorado

Acquisition of adequate resources to attain performance goals challenges educational leaders at all levels. Finding funds for desired programs entails several aspects of school finance: (1) gathering resources, which is often called a *revenue* dimension; (2) directing appropriate resources to educational programs, which forms an *allocation* dimension; and (3) ensuring that resource use makes a difference in program outcomes, which entails both a *management* function (to be sure resources are directed where intended) and an *accountability* dimension (to relate allocations to school performance measures).

BALANCING UNIFORMITY AND LOCAL CONTROL

Many state courts concluded that wealth-based spending inequities violate state constitutions' equal-protection provisions or articles mandating "uniform" or "thorough and efficient" educational systems. Other courts upheld finance policies, finding that revenue variations do not deny equal protection, because they are a consequence of legitimate state interests in maintaining local control over schooling. State legislatures responded to judicial and political pressures to equalize resources, and in the 1990s the average state share rose to 48%—exceeding the local contribution of 45%—with the remainder financed by federal revenue.

Partnerships with businesses, educational foundations, and sales of advertising space on facilities and buses have promised new resources. These funds, however, account for but a small portion of total revenue, and, like property taxation, they raise questions about resulting inequities when opportunities to generate new resources differ greatly from community to community.

Leaders will be increasingly pressed to secure more revenue to expand programs, obtain essential instructional materials and technologies, finance necessary professional development, and be competitive with private schools and charter schools. Educational leaders will address such questions as: Will our school community be satisfied with the level of resources provided through traditional channels, or will we aggressively seek additional resources to meet parental demands and student needs despite resulting inequities among schools?

DECIDING PRIORITIES WHEN ALLOCATING RESOURCES

Planning and budgeting frameworks help school personnel determine goals and objectives, the most cost-effective mix of human and material resources to reach goals, the funds necessary to deliver programs, and evaluation of outcomes in relation to resources as new budget cycles begin. These budget development processes raise questions about priorities. The difficulty of reaching consensus about priorities among stakeholders makes the allocation dimension highly political. For this reason, it is tempting to adopt an incremental approach and thus ease tensions by increasing all prior budgets by a given percentage. However, as new instructional approaches and technologies emerge, as program demands shift along with a school's demography, and as the productivity of traditional programs is challenged, discussions about resource priorities are inevitable.

In the context of school-based decision making, budget decisions will increasingly be made at building levels. Allocations among existing and proposed programs will challenge educational leaders to address many questions, including: Will we incrementally raise all current program budgets, or will we examine which instructional approaches and consequent resource allocations best enable school personnel to meet changing student needs and improve student performance?

ACCOUNTING FOR THE USE OF FINANCIAL RESOURCES

Budget management and accounting functions within central offices and schools are concerned primarily with ensuring the lawful use of public money within designated funds. This dimension of school finance has been expanded in recent years to embrace a broader accountability function: relating resource decisions to improvements in program outcomes.

Relationships between human and financial inputs and resulting outcomes define a traditional view of school productivity and efficiency. Another perspective on efficiency calls for maximizing the satisfaction of consumers—parents, students, employers, and legislators—at the same or perhaps at an even lower investment of society's resources.

An emerging policy direction is to induce school improvement and greater efficiency through performance-based school finance. This entrepreneurial restructuring of schools aligns resources, as well as potential sanctions, with state standards and assessments. By rewarding those schools or districts whose students' performance meets desired standards or whose performance improves toward such targets, this approach is intended to stimulate school leaders and teachers to redesign curriculum and instruction in ways that achieve educational reform goals. There are concerns, however, that "high-stakes" accountability brings unintended consequences.

To the degree that program and financial accountability relates future school resources to performance, educational leaders will address questions such as: Will budget management be primarily concerned with proper accounting for revenue and expenditures within designated funds, or will we also lead schools in ways that help all personnel to maximize the results of programs financed by those resources—and ultimately strengthen public accountability and support for public education?

WAGE AND SALARY CONSIDERATIONS

Approximately 80% of school district budgets come from the salary and benefits of personnel. Job classification systems group jobs into classes or grades that represent different pay levels, ranging from minimum to maximum for a particular grade of jobs. The compensation system determines the way salary payments are allocated between and within levels. The ultimate objective is to establish proper compensation for positions as well as for individuals holding the positions. The plan should attract, retain, and motivate qualified and competent employees; remain consistent with pay plans in other industries; and meet the acceptance of the taxpayers. The compensation system takes the form of wages, salaries, and benefits.

There is considerable debate over the amount of money paid to educators compared with the salaries of those in comparable positions in business, industry, and commerce. The Educational Research Service (ERS), a nonprofit organization, conducts salary surveys that cover the pay of all classifications of public school employees including teachers, bus drivers, clerical workers, principals and many others. Conducted every 10 years, the 2003–2004 found that classroom teachers' salaries had lost ground from the 1993–1994 survey. In real dollars, the average teacher salary fell 1.87% during this period (Jacobson, 2004). Trends in administrator salaries are dependent on the region of the nation, size of the school, and size of the district. Overall, elementary principals salaries are lower than middle school principals whose salaries are lower than high school principals. It is important to remember that there is a relationship between salary and a district's enrollment, per-pupil spending, and location.

CEOs and middle-level managers earn more than do their counterparts in education. The same inequities exist for teachers who receive significantly lower salaries than comparable college graduates in other fields. A major responsibility of human resources management professionals in a school district is to work with superintendents and school boards to ensure that salaries and benefits are competitive and attract qualified individuals to the profession.

The problem with these compensation plans is that they do not consider performance. The most-competent and the least-competent teachers in the school system will be paid the same throughout their professional careers as long as they have the same preparation and number of years of experience. Performance pay plans factor in merit to the automatic step increases found in most single-salary schedule pay plans. Performance pay plans include merit pay, differentiated staffing, performance contracting, and/or incentive pay.

Merit pay is paying an educator, at least in part, according to the quality of his or her work. Merit adjusts salaries to recognize different levels of job performance. It is based on the belief that individuals should be rewarded in proportion to their contributions and, more pragmatically, that sustaining productivity requires a close link between performance and rewards. The performance evaluation system is the key to a successful merit pay plan. If employees trust the performance appraisal plan, they often will be able to support merit pay.

In its simplest form, performance increments—ratings from unsatisfactory to exceptional—are added to the single-salary schedules. More complex approaches include point or unit systems and salary performance formulas. The arguments against merit pay include the creation of jealousy, envy, distrust, and conflict; breakdown of collegiality, cooperative spirit, and teamwork; too much discretionary power in the hands of the evaluator; failure because of weak performance appraisal systems and insufficiently qualified evaluators; and inequitable pay for the same job. However, in many other organizations a merit pay system has been effective. Recently, the governor of Virginia invited 57 districts with struggling schools to apply for $3 million in state funding for merit pay (Education Week, 2011). If lackluster performance continues, many school districts will be experimenting with various forms of merit pay for educators.

Differentiated staffing, or career ladders, create different roles that permit educators to assume responsibilities, initiative, authority, and pay commensurate with their interests, talents, abilities, and performance. In general, differentiated staffing plans require as many promotion channels and layers as possible to provide for advancement in responsibility and pay. For example, positional advancements and pay incentives now do not reinforce teaching as a career; they reinforce educational administration. All promotion channels in teaching lead away from the classroom. At the same time, all teachers are treated as interchangeable parts, regardless of talent, work ethics, or performance because there are no structural provisions for differences among them.

Possible promotion channels within teaching might include associate teacher, staff teacher, senior teacher, and master teacher. Master teachers, as instructional leaders, might work on curriculum, instruction, testing, performance appraisal, and student support, spending only 40% of their time in the classroom. Master teachers would be paid comparably to assistant principals. In 1998, Massachusetts created a master teacher corps for high-performing teachers certified by the National Board of Professional Teaching Standards. Former head of the National Council for Accreditation of Teacher Education Arthur Wise (2001) stated:

> In a differentiated staffing structure, with corresponding levels of compensation, qualified teachers would supervise those without proper qualifications. . . . A staffing structure could include board-certified teachers, fully licensed teachers, beginning interns, teacher candidates and those with little or no preparation. Individuals would have distinct titles and different pay scales. This structure would provide a career ladder for highly qualified teachers by encouraging them to stay in teaching and it would give school districts a way to fulfill staffing needs with integrity. (p. 37)

Benefits

Fringe benefits provide assistance and protection to all employees and are not contingent on performance. They have risen in cost to represent approximately 35% of total compensation paid to employees. Under the provisions of law, school districts as employers are required to provide benefits related to social security, retirement insurance, health insurance, unemployment compensation, long-term care, and worker's compensation. These six, along with a minimum paid vacation, are often considered core benefits in a flexible-benefit, sometimes called a *cafeteria* program.

Other possible fringe benefits include leaves of absence, safety and security, duty-free lunch periods, periodic health screening, dental insurance, savings incentive plans, legal services, wellness and health consultants, travel awards, tuition assistance, paid holidays, recreation programs, and extended core coverage, among others. Fringe benefits are an important part of all compensation programs and influence recruitment, hiring, and employee motivation.

✳ **How might teachers at Bayview Valley be rewarded for outstanding student performance?**

MANAGING SCHOOL SUPPLIES AND EQUIPMENT

Managing school supplies includes purchasing, storing, distributing, and accounting. Computer programs can be particularly helpful in managing supplies and equipment. Table 12.3 describes the process of purchasing and control and enumerates those responsible for the process.

MAINTAINING SCHOOL BUILDINGS AND GROUNDS

Creating a meaningful and appropriate learning environment for students is a challenge for educators. It demands not only an excellent curriculum but also designing and maintaining the school building and grounds. Bullock and Foster-Harrison (1997) describe 12 requisite factors of the school environment: furniture, color, aesthetics, carpet, building and grounds maintenance, decorating detail, comfort, space and design, lighting, classroom elements (e.g., ceiling fans, sinks), instructional items (e.g., areas for displaying student work), and professional items (e.g., access to a telephone).

✳ **How will you include needed improvements for the building and grounds in your proposal?**

TABLE 12.3   The Supply Process and Its Control

PROCESS OF PURCHASING AND CONTROL	STAFF MEMBER OR DEPARTMENT INVOLVED
1. Develop standard list of supplies and equipment	1. By users in cooperation with business manager
2. Stock catalogs refined from standard list; includes all possible supplies normally handled with necessary ordering data	2. Business office
3. Annual supply and equipment request (detailed statement of requirements for year)	3. Entire staff, including teachers and custodians
4. Budget document (listing, in general, supplies and equipment authorized and money available)	4. Supply and equipment budget developed by business office, approved by superintendent and board of education
5. Requisition and approval	5. Initiated by individual approved by designated administrative officer
6. Purchase order	6. Designated purchasing office
7. Note of receipt in good order	7. Receiving clerk
8. Spot-checks made on weight, quality, and quantity; notations made	8. Business office
9. Material placed in supply or equipment accounting ledger	9. Supply clerk
10. Bill paid by accounting office	10. Sent to accounting office by purchasing officer
11. Distribution records material sent to accountable individual buildings, based on annual requests and periodic requisitions	11. Principal of school
12. Building distribution personnel records for each teacher who gets basic supplies at beginning of year and periodically as requested	12. Principal administers, may be coordinated with central office computer
13. User accountability: user signs for supplies	13. Users (teacher, custodians, etc.) and equipment in room at beginning of year; list provided by supply clerk
14. User "use" chart: materials checked off as used; form provided by supply, appraisal may be computerized	14. User (teacher, custodian, etc.)
15. Spot-checks and inspections	15. Business office and principal
16. Yearly inventory of all areas of supply storage	16. Business office (supply)
17. Use charts, reports, summaries	17. Business office (supply)

CONCLUSION

School administrators must have at least a basic understanding of how schools are financed. There are various sources for school revenues, and some sources have a more important role than others in revenue generation. As the new century goes forward, issues in generating revenue and allocating resources for schools will continue to dominate the discussion at both the state and national levels.

In addition to the acquisition of resources, budgeting, accounting, and maintenance are vital to a well-managed school. Planning, management, and control each play their own distinctive part in the complete budgeting and accounting process. One does not operate at the expense of the other; rather, they all coexist as multiple purposes of fiscal stewardship.

MyEdLeadershipLab™

Go to Topic 10: *Finance/Resource Allocation* in the MyEdLeadershipLab™ site (www .MyEdLeadershipLab.com) for *Educational Leadership: A Bridge to Improved Practice*, Fifth Edition, where you can:

- Find learning outcomes for *Finance/Resource Allocation* along with the national standards that connect to these outcomes.
- Complete Assignments and Activities that can help you more deeply understand the chapter content.
- Apply and practice your understanding of the core skills identified in the chapter with the Building Leadership Skills unit.
- Prepare yourself for professional certification with a Practice for Certification quiz.

PORTFOLIO ARTIFACTS

- Compare and contrast the school budgets of two comparable schools within the same district and between two different districts.

- Collaborate with colleagues in your school or in your internship site school in writing a small grant. When you have completed the project, describe in writing what you learned.

- Investigate a school that has a foundation. Interview some of the people on the foundation's committee. How did the foundation first begin? How does it currently operate? Describe in writing what you learned about school foundations from your interviews.

- Examine a safety plan for a school. What is included in the plan? Who is involved in implementing it?

- Work with the bookkeeper to make entries in a school's accounting records or follow a purchase order through the system.

- Attend a school board meeting at which the budget is discussed.

- Explore the following Web sites to learn more about charter schools http://www .charterschoolcenter.org/; U.S. independent schools (http://www.nais.org); and independent schools abroad (http://www.aaie.org and http://www.academyish.org).

KEY TERMS

- Average daily attendance (ADA)
- Charter schools
- Flat-grant model
- Independent schools
- Mission-based budgeting
- Parcel tax

- Per-pupil allotment
- Power-equalizing model
- Planning, programming, budgeting system (PPBS)
- Planning, programming, budgeting, and evaluation system (PPBES)

- School foundation
- School vouchers/ education vouchers
- Wages and benefis
- Weighted-student model

SUGGESTED READINGS

Brimley, V. R., Verstegen, D. A., & Garfield, R. R. (2011). *Financing education in a climate of change* (11th ed.). Upper Saddle River, NJ: Prentice Hall.

Burke Smith, N., & Works, E. G. (2006). *The complete book of grant writing: Learn to write grants like a professional.* Naperville, IL: Sourcebooks, Inc.

Lubienski, C. A., & Weitzel, P. C. (Eds.). (2010). *The charter school experiment: Expectations, evidence and implications.* Cambridge, MA: Harvard Education Press.

McMormick, D., Ferguson, D., & Bauer, D. (2000). *Creating foundations for American schools.* Sudbury, MA: Jones & Bartlett Learning.

Poston, W. K. (2010). *School budgeting for hard times.* Thousand Oaks, CA: Corwin Press.

APPENDICES

Appendices A and B are two resources for better understanding project-based learning. We recommend that students read both expert inquiries prior to beginning work on any of the PBL projects in this text.

PROBLEM-BASED LEARNING

This textbook contains four problem-based learning (PBL) projects. It is recommended that only one project be used in a typical 3-credit university course. The instructor and students might decide to use the same PBL project with more than one group, or different groups could complete different projects at the same time. Project selection might depend on the interests of students and the level of school (elementary, middle, or high school, or school district) in which they would like to focus their learning. The table in this Appendix lists the main features of each project.

Problem-based learning (PBL) is an instructional approach that uses typical problems of practice as the context for an in-depth investigation of core content. According to Bridges and Hallinger (1995), PBL has five elements:

1. The starting point for learning is a problem.
2. The problem is one that students are apt to face as future professionals.
3. The knowledge that students are expected to acquire during their professional training is organized around problems rather than disciplines.
4. Students, individually and collectively, assume a major responsibility for their own instruction and learning.
5. Most of the learning occurs within the context of small groups rather than lectures. (p. 6)

A key part of PBL involves the nature of the problems used in a project. Leithwood, Begley, and Cousins (1994) categorize problems that confront educational leaders into two types: high ground and swampy. They discuss the characteristics of preparation programs for developing expert school leaders and urge programs to focus on "swampy" problems. High-ground problems are those "of a more technical nature, where a well-rehearsed procedure for solving [is] available" (p. 53). Swampy problems are complex, at least to the person who has to solve them. The authors explain that problems are swampy when "one only vaguely understands the present situation, has no clear way of knowing what solutions would be superior, and lacks procedures for addressing the obstacles or constraints in the situation" (p. 43). Given the vast array of constituents and needs that face school administrators, it is crucial that the preparation of future educational leaders focus on solving swampy, ill-structured problems.

MAIN FEATURES OF PBL PROJECTS

PROJECT NAME	GRADE LEVEL	RELATED CHAPTERS	RELATED TOPICS AND CONCEPTS
Marveling at the Results	High School	1, 2, 3, 4, 5, 6, 7, 9	School improvement Change School reform Leadership theory Values Professional learning communities
A Jalapeño in a Candy Jar	Middle school	3, 5, 6, 8, 9, 10, 11	Cultural diversity Change Staff development Curriculum Learning theory Equity, student rights Central office and board roles
Safe Havens	K–8	1, 3, 4, 5, 10, 11	Service integration Partnerships Grant writing Site-based management Transformational leadership Facilities management and allocation Change
Personalizing Learning Through Technology Integration	High school	2, 3, 4, 5, 7, 8, 10, 11, 12	Technology Staff development Change curriculum Program evaluation Instruction

At the same time, educational administration students need to have conversations with experts to probe how effective practitioners solve identical or similar problems. Working with real audiences for the culminating activity of the PBL project, as well as people who are used to developing solutions to problems, affords students opportunities to learn how experts engage in problem solving and reflection. The goal of such reflection is for the learner to examine swampy problems by analyzing, exploring, gathering data, and critiquing.

Leithwood (1995), for example, discusses the high level of reflection that was an integral part of the problem-solving practice of reputationally effective superintendents he studied. Similarly, Schön (1983) advocates "reflection-in-action through which practitioners sometimes make new sense of uncertain, unique, or conflicted situations of practice" (p. 39). Schön maintains that if instructors encourage reflection, students will not assume "that existing professional knowledge fits every case nor that every problem has a right answer" (p. 39). Reflective thinking is crucial to helping educational leaders improve their problem-solving expertise.

In the real world of schools, problems are not solved independently. The complexity of the problems addressed by school leaders requires collaboration. Collaboration requires learning to listen to others, collectively reviewing outcomes, and responding to and partaking of relevant discussion. Vygotsky's (1978) concept of the "zone of proximal development" may be particularly relevant to PBL. This zone is the gap between a person's individual capacity for problem solving and the capacity of the group or peer with whom the learner is working. The group processes of discussing and critically reflecting afford the individual learner opportunities to internalize the group's problem-solving capacities. Ultimately, the ability to show good judgment, take control of situations, and communicate effectively will determine the success of solutions to problems, pinpoint perceptions, rank options, and resolve the issue at hand. The leader's future effectiveness depends on how well he or she handles problems, whether they are high ground or swampy (see Table 3.1, Chapter 3, pages 91–92).

Because learning group-processing skills is essential to problem-based learning, peer and instructor feedback are integral components of projects. Students are usually asked to reflect on their role in the group with peers, and instructors provide feedback to students about those roles. Part of a discussion might include exploring why certain decisions have been made and how other factors might be involved. Thus, opportunities for what Argyris (1982) calls *double-loop learning* can be built into the feedback and assessment process.

PROBLEM-BASED LEARNING IN EDUCATIONAL LEADERSHIP

ED BRIDGES
Stanford University

PHILIP HALLINGER
Vanderbilt University

Problem-based learning (PBL) provides a context in which participants can develop various leadership skills, acquire the knowledge needed to deal with problems of leadership, and experience what it means and feels like to be a leader. PBL develops leaders who solve problems through thoughtful deliberation with people who have a stake in the outcome and, in the end, are committed to implementing the group's decision.

When people first encounter PBL, they often initially feel "lost at sea." The sea can become rough as the group struggles with defining the problem and agreeing on what should be done about it. If a lot of wheel spinning occurs and deep divisions develop within the group, the experience can be less than satisfying, result in a shoddy product, and thwart learning. Over the years we have learned that these undesirable consequences can be minimized or avoided by using particular methods and techniques. In this brief commentary, we share some of what we have learned with you.

GROUP SIZE

Through experimenting with various group sizes, we have discovered that groups of six or seven members are ideal and are large enough to permit members to occupy and learn different roles (e.g., leader, facilitator, recorder, group member). Moreover, groups of this size afford opportunities for everyone to participate and contribute ideas. Three-person groups are especially troublesome because there is an inherent tendency in these groups for two people to form an alliance against the third. As groups increase in size beyond seven, they constrain the amount of "airtime" each member can have. The potential for problems to develop that interfere with group functioning increases unless an extremely skilled facilitator guides the discussion.

METHOD FOR CONDUCTING EFFECTIVE MEETINGS

The vast majority of people have worked in groups; some have undoubtedly wasted time and accomplished little, and others have worked much more efficiently and effectively. When groups go awry, people tend to attribute their difficulties to personality clashes. While these clashes might account in part for troubles in the group, more often discord is due primarily to a lack of methods for conducting effective meetings.

In our search for ways to assist groups in functioning more effectively, we have introduced them to the interaction method (Doyle & Straus, 1993). Groups that use this method initially find it too constraining; the discomfort gradually disappears, however, as group members begin to internalize the method and acquire the skills and tools. Occasionally, after trying it once or twice, groups abandon the method on the grounds that they function well together and do not need such a method. Typically, these groups run into difficulty and revert to the interaction method with a greater appreciation of the contribution it makes to effective group functioning.

CRITERIA FOR PROBLEM FRAMING AND ANALYSIS

Learning in PBL, as the term implies, begins with a problematic situation. Some problems are fairly well structured, and others are ill-structured, messy, complex, and multifaceted. Identifying and stating the problem concisely poses a challenge for most people. The vast majority of PBL groups rush to solve the problem without fully understanding it. Yet, as Dewey (1910) and others have taught us, "A problem well-stated is a problem half solved" (p. 221). Unless the problem is well-defined, problem solvers may follow a path that fails to remedy the existing situation while creating additional difficulties in the process because they fail to consider an adequate range of alternative courses of action.

To facilitate the problem-framing phase of the problem-solving process, we have found it beneficial to provide PBL groups with two criteria for evaluating the adequacy of a problem statement. The first criterion underscores the importance of stating the problem without embedding a solution in it. Groups commonly incorporate a solution into their statement of the problem, thus shutting off consideration of solution alternatives. A brief example might help to clarify this point.

In a Desert Survival exercise we use in our leadership program, groups either bypass the problem-framing stage or frame the problem as "Should we stay at the crash site, or should we leave and walk to safety?" Either of these formulations of the problem contains a solution to the "real" problem: "How can we survive?" The choice the group makes, to stay or leave, has profound consequences on its chances of survival. Groups that identify the "real" problem are much more likely to make the right choice of whether to stay or leave.

In addition to the solution-free criteria for judging the adequacy of a problem statement, we encourage PBL participants to look for facts in the problem scenario that support their definition of the problem. By testing their definition of the problem against the facts

(*continued*)

contained in the description of the problem, participants have a basis for evaluating their particular definition of the problem.

USE OF RESOURCES

With many PBL projects, the instructor supplies a list of resources that might have relevance to the problem; in some instances, the instructor also includes a copy of the suggested readings. Group members often decide to assign each person a different set of readings. At the next meeting of the group, members take turns providing brief synopses of what they have read. Having completed their reading "assignments," they turn to attacking the problem. By following this procedure, group members are apt to focus simply on the knowledge without regard to its application and might compromise their own in-depth knowledge of the content.

Because knowledge and application are of equal importance in PBL, we encourage group members to postpone reading the pertinent resources until they agree on a formulation of the problem. As individuals proceed to read the material, they ask themselves a question such as, "How does what I read apply to the problem we are facing?" When reporting back to the group, members discuss how what they have read may apply to their problem. If two members read the same material, they can share their perspectives on the same issue. We have learned that group members are much more likely to use the knowledge in solving the problem if they study the resources after, not before, they have framed it.

FACILITATING GROUPS

The Institute for Development of Educational Activities, Inc. (I/D/E/A) has been involved in a number of projects that require the development of effective facilitator skills. The following discussion of group facilitation is based on the I/D/E/A projects.

The success of the group in solving problems is interrelated with the facilitator's ability to help the group work as a productive team (Cunningham & Gresso, 1993). The facilitator works with the group to establish a climate of mutual understanding, trust, and commitment to work together as a team to develop the best possible solution to the problem at hand. Facilitation requires a sensitivity to, and appreciation of, the diverse talents on the team and the skill to value each person's unique contribution to the group. The ability to model positive reinforcement of members but also to stick to a reasonable plan of action is essential for a successful group leader. The facilitator must be nonthreatening, supportive, and positive.

Group members clarify their thinking by expressing their perspectives and attaining consensus relative to the solution to the problem. One of the key decisions a facilitator makes is when to keep quiet and when to intervene in the group.

The major role of the facilitator is to:

- Build the capacities and stature of group members.
- Nurture diverse values and perspectives among group members.
- Create ownership among group members.
- Nurture creative thoughts of others.
- Ask questions that help members rethink positions.
- Ensure that team members identify resources, outside information, and ideas needed to address the problem.
- Use effective, solid, time-tested group processes to maximize the efficacy of the group and its individual members.
- Demonstrate effective listening, processing, and communication skills.
- Encourage goal-directed behavior and foster a patient and encouraging environment.

Depending on the approach used for the division of duties for team members playing various roles, the facilitator's tasks might include working with team members to develop schedules, agendas, and assignments in regard to solving the problem. The facilitator should begin by establishing mutual understanding of why the group exists and setting forth what will happen. Members should be encouraged to be open, take risks, share expertise, stay focused, and suspend judgment until the problem has been solved.

To be successful, group members need to be able to solve problems together and make effective decisions to which they are all committed. Cunningham and Gresso (1993) state, "The role of the group facilitator is to provide support by serving as a catalyst during the consideration, discussion, and resolution phase of team deliberation" (p. 23). The facilitator should help the group to be aware of the needs of the individual members and assist the group to focus on its purpose. "The facilitator models appropriate forms of participation and assists the individual to be as effective as possible. The main function of the facilitator is to continuously encourage and support human development, resulting in individual, team, and organizational improvement" (p. 243).

UNDERSTANDING GROUP PROCESS

CHERYL GETZ
University of San Diego

Unlike traditional learning, problem-based learning (PBL) is an instructional approach that affords participants opportunities to examine real-life problems, while at the same time gaining knowledge about group process, group dynamics, and leadership in groups. My comments herein are drawn from emerging perspectives of "experiential learning groups" (Gillette & McCollom, 1995), which are heavily influenced by previous work in experiential group instruction at the National Training Institute (NTL) (http://www.ntl.org/) that focuses primarily on interpersonal skills in relation to the group, and by scholars and consultants working at the A. K. Rice Institute (http://www.akriceinstitute.org/), whose focus is on the study of social systems and group relations. Both offer valuable perspectives about groups and how they function.

Typically, candidates in educational administration programs bring with them a wealth of knowledge, skills, and experiences, with which all members can apply to their own learning. However, those attempting to complete PBL projects often lose sight of the process, due to a variety of factors such as time constraints, a strong desire to focus primarily on outcomes, and differences of opinion or

personalities present in the group. Given this scenario, the valuable learning that can occur by examining the *process* of getting to the final product is often lost.

At this juncture, one might ask, "what can we learn from the *process* of working on a PBL project?" To answer this question, I begin with a typical example that I will use throughout to demonstrate the powerful learning that can transpire by reflecting on the group process. A group of six administrative candidates are assigned Project 2: "A Jalapeño in a Candy Jar" (p. 431). The group consists of three men and three women. The task of the group is to prepare an action plan to address issues in multicultural education.

In the initial phase of the PBL group, members are encouraged to identify formal roles for members of the group. Generally, the group designates roles such as facilitator, recorder, and timekeeper, recognizing that this will contribute to the overall effectiveness of the group. In this phase of a group's life, members are seeking safety and a certain level of comfort with each other. The identification of specific roles helps members feel more secure about the process, as they work together to accomplish the task at hand.

Using the example described earlier, one of the males asks to be the facilitator and suggests that one of the women be the recorder. She agrees, and one of the other women volunteers to be the timekeeper. There is no discussion about the reason for the assignments, and the group spends the next couple of meetings discussing the PBL project and trying to outline a plan of action. The first two meetings of the group seem to go very well, but as the group enters the next phase of the life of the group, differences of opinion arise, and the group cannot seem to agree on a direction. Five members of the group agree on a direction to take, but one of the women strongly opposes the direction the group is taking. She thinks discussions about cultural differences are divisive, and she proposes an alternate plan to the direction the group had been taking. After the meeting, the other five members blame the sixth member; after all, she is the one who "just doesn't understand the value of multicultural education." The sixth member now becomes the scapegoat for everything that goes wrong in the group, because other members project (on her) their own hidden fears and doubts about multicultural education but are unable, unaware of, or not willing to confront their hidden anxieties. Members of the group quite naturally bring expectations with them, and each member of the group will act in accordance with the expectations and the valences that they bring. It is in this phase that these expectations begin to influence the *life of the group*.

The *life of the group* can be defined in two ways; first as the beginning and end of the group, which is bounded in time (the beginning and end of each group meeting and the entire time allotted for completion of the project) and space (where the meetings are located); and the second, is ways in which the group recreates the social systems that are present in our everyday lives.

Consider again our example. During the next meeting, the facilitator (speaking on behalf of the five members who are aligned against the sixth member) confronts the sixth member. He tells her that the group has decided to stay with their original plan, because the majority of the members agree, and it seems impossible to reach any consensus. With tears in her eyes, she angrily responds, "Sure, this is how the group has been going all along; you decided you would be the facilitator, and I would be the recorder, so I'll just be quiet and take notes." The comment frustrates the group; some members think the facilitator was too harsh, and they feel empathy for her. Others are secretly glad that she remains quiet for the remainder of the meeting. A new alignment emerges, informal roles shift, but the group continues to work.

Careful observation of any group reveals the numerous roles that members take up or are drawn into by the group, often without their conscious awareness. For example, the formal roles that were designated by the group, and informal roles that surfaced and may change at any time. As previously mentioned, in PBL groups, designated roles such as facilitator, recorder, and timekeeper serve important functions and keep the group on task. However, informal roles also emerge, such as silent observer, dissenter, scapegoat, and so forth that often threaten group members and prevent the group from completing the assigned task. What happens then? Members try to patch things up, further conflict is avoided, people take sides, judgments are made that further diminish the possibility of some members ability to contribute to the groups work, and usually two or three members take on the major responsibilities of task completion.

What *could* happen, if members discussed in advance the possibility (and probability) of the various roles emerging? Recognizing that during the life of any group members will take on a variety of roles, and without making judgments members can give and receive feedback on the roles they find themselves and others taking up during the life of the group. As the group's life unfolds over time, the results will be discussions that provide all members with critical feedback

(continued)

as each grapples with what it means to be a leader. Some questions that might surface include how the formal roles were determined or negotiated. Whose voice is heard more often and why? Whose values are received positively or negatively by the group and why? How are individual and group biases and prejudices played out in the group? How do societal expectations of individuals and the roles they bring influence the group?

This observation of self and others and the difficult discussions that follow often creates an onerous task, one that can illuminate differences, and instigate conflict. Yet, much can be learned about exercising leadership by examining the group and the role each member experiences during the time the group is together. The individual and group observation includes reflecting on one's own attitudes, behavior, and roles in relation to the various attitudes, behaviors, and roles present in members that together form the *life of the group*. Groups operating at this level are more likely to uncover the root causes of the conflict by examining their own role in undermining the group's process.

When exploring the dynamics of any group, understanding and discussing the concept of boundaries (physical, task, time, and role) can serve as a starting point. Some boundaries are less permeable than others, for example, the *physical* boundary (membership and location) and the *task* of the assigned PBL group are generally quite impermeable because neither is likely to be altered in any way. The *task* of the group has several levels worth considering, such as the task of completing a final product, the task of each member (usually assigned by the group) in between meetings, and the various tasks of the group during designated meetings. However neither is completely impermeable, for example, intrusions on the physical boundary often affect the group. For instance, if the group wants to meet at a coffee shop or a member wants to bring a pet or child to a meeting. The boundaries should be renegotiated to ensure that this does not negatively affect the group.

In contrast to the physical and task boundaries, boundaries such as *time* and *role* are much more permeable and are likely to change over the life of the group. When working in a PBL group, setting time limits on the group's work contributes to the group's effectiveness. Time limits can be set for each group meeting for a discussion about a specific topic during a group meeting, as well as for the completion of the final product. While time boundaries should be closely monitored to ensure that the group stays on task, groups that are able to make adjustments to the agreed-upon time boundaries, as a result of a changing task, are likely to benefit from their ability to accept this flexibility.

The most complex boundary is that of *role*. The various roles that members participate in during the life of the group can change frequently or not at all, depending on the group and its members. Some roles may be familiar roles that members are accustomed to outside of the group; other roles that members find being placed on them by the group, are less familiar. Back to our example: Suppose at the very first meeting, the male member who offered to be the facilitator and suggested that one of the women be the recorder asked himself why he made that suggestion, and then shared his perspective with the group. This might open a dialogue about all of the roles that needed to be assigned, and the tendency for each member to take on specific roles. Perhaps the woman who agreed to be the recorder would then speak to her frustration of agreeing to this role because she was often the note taker in previous settings, and this restricted her ability to bring her ideas forward. Both might still agree to take on these roles, but the individual and group awareness has been elevated.

When conflicts arise, such as when the woman could not agree with the plan, the group can benefit from looking at her dissention, from a *group* perspective versus an individual or *interpersonal* one. Group members typically respond to each other on an interpersonal level, that is, they attribute conflicts within the group to *individual* personalities, behaviors, or attitudes. However, groups are much more complex! A more effective, parallel reflective process includes a dialogue that considers the interpersonal aspects of group members and an awareness of the group as a social system. The group might ask: What is she representing for us? Who are the constituents in our schools that she represents? Individuals at various points throughout the group's life might also ask themselves the same question: What am I representing for the group? If the group can move away from making judgments on an interpersonal level, members will be more apt to see that dissention offers the group powerful learning. An individual may embody a strong sentiment in the entire group, as well as in other social systems, such as the school communities that each member is associated with.

As a leader, one can imagine the difficulties that might arise when attempting to adopt a new policy or advance a strategic plan when the leader does not notice or pays little attention to the dynamics present in the groups she or he will be leading. The value of the PBL process is the opportunity for participants to gain awareness of group dynamics, including an awareness of self and others. Like high-performing teams, group members who understand themselves and each other and work together in the service of learning, are more likely to produce work that represents the integration of ideas from all members, and a culmination of the groups ideas are likely to be reflected in the final product.

References
Gillette, J., & McCollom, M. (Eds.). (1995). *Groups in context: A new perspective in group dynamics.* New York, NY: University Press of America.

PERSONALIZING LEARNING THROUGH TECHNOLOGY INTEGRATION: A PLAN FOR SHERIDAN HIGH SCHOOL

PAULA A. CORDEIRO

University of San Diego
(adapted from a PBL project created by Dr. Barbara Campbell,
retired assistant superintendent, Wolcott Public School, CT)

Microchip technology's power to store, manage, and transmit large amounts of information rapidly has transformed all aspects of living and working in our society. Information mediated by microchips is the commodity of the future. In the past, the mission of education was to equip students with competencies that would serve as their stock in trade (e.g., in agriculture, industry) to live a productive, high-quality life. Schools currently are information-based institutions charged with the same mission, so one would expect them to be aggressive adopters and users of technology.

They have not, however, been successful in adopting and integrating technology. The reasons frequently cited are:

- Insufficient hardware
- Inappropriate and or insufficient software
- Lack or inadequacy of technical support
- Lack or inadequacy of teacher training and staff development
- Lack of administrative support
- Mismatch between the technology and educational need
- Lack or inadequacy of initial and continuing funding

If schools are to be successful in preparing productive, informed citizens for a global society, they will have to overcome the problems they have had with integrating technology into the teaching and learning process. Administrators, who are responsible for curriculum and program development, must meet this challenge.

LEARNING OBJECTIVES

- Define the opportunities and challenges associated with technology integration.
- Collaboratively design a plan for adopting and implementing technology in a school that incorporates prior learning, field experiences, and best-practice models gleaned from available resources.
- Using various types of technology, prepare the plan and present it to central office team that includes the superintendent, assistant superintendent for curriculum and instruction, the district's technology specialist, and several directors including the director of special education.

GUIDING QUESTIONS

1. Whom will you involve in developing the plan? In implementing it? What role will you play?
2. Which technology is "right" for your building's initial experience? What kinds of implementation challenges are associated with the technology?
3. What potential leverage points do you have for developing and implementing the plan?
4. What elements constitute an exemplary building technology plan?
5. Based on what you have learned about change, staff development, curriculum/instruction, and school reform, how will you address the issues that have caused previous attempts at integrating technology to fail?

THE PROBLEM

As the new principal of Sheridan High School, you have spent most of the year gathering information about the school's culture. Even though many of the problems are characteristic of comprehensive high schools in the area, you are beginning to feel frustrated and overwhelmed by the way in which each issue compounds another.

Sheridan is the only high school in the Mountjoy district of 2,800 students. Its enrollment of 730 students is beginning to increase as larger classes make their way through the system. The district seems to be a buffer zone. It is surrounded by affluent suburban districts on one side, and a large urban district on the other. From your conversations with other district principals, you sense a tension between the achievement levels of the suburban schools and having to deal with more at-risk students from the inner city whose parents have moved into Mountjoy. Data show that your minority, free or reduced lunch, and special-education numbers are increasing annually.

The faculty members (55 certified) are veteran staff members who, for the most part, view themselves as content experts. The head of the social studies department summed up their beliefs: "We cover our content in the limited time we have. That stuff (e.g., learner-centered methodologies, alternative assessments, technology, any of the literacies) is for the elementary and middle school teachers, anyway!" They note that the only ongoing "fad" has been the district's commitment to technology. However, since the initiative started at the elementary level, they believe that money and commitment will run out before the technology gets to them.

Feedback from students is conflicting. You are disturbed by the "listlessness" you feel as you walk down the halls during passing times and that you observe in class. Many students respond to your questions regarding issues affecting them with "I don't know" or a shrug. On the other hand, a few students have come to you with complaints about boring classes, the lack of any types of technology including too few computers, and the absence of student input into decision making.

You suspect that student experiences in the lower grades might be a significant contributing factor to negative student behavior and attitudes. Your conversations with other principals lead you to believe that the expectations of incoming freshmen have been dramatically changed by the success of the district's technology initiative at the elementary and middle-school levels. By the time students leave the elementary schools, they are accustomed to generating their assignments using word processing, graphics, and charts in fully networked environments. Their experiences at the middle school build on this expertise. Students are used to working with a team of teachers in long blocks of time. They are accustomed to being in charge of their learning. Confronted with the technology wasteland of Sheridan and lecture-style teaching delivered in 42-minute segments, students seem to respond with behaviors that rapidly degenerate into apathy or disciplinary issues.

The school's crumbling physical infrastructure compounds all these problems. It is poorly designed and poorly equipped for implementing more effective programs. Electrical wiring is inadequate. You suspect that any facilities monies in the district have been consumed in attempting to respond to ever-increasing enrollments at the elementary and middle levels.

There is no area with computers that can accommodate a class of more than 18, and the average class size is 23. The few computer areas in English, business, and science education are considered exclusively for the use of those respective departments. The computers themselves are a hodge-podge of various types of PCs and Macs. Some on run Windows while others do not. Of the mini-networks in the building (office, technology education, and business), none connects with the others. The building is not wireless and there are few connections to the Internet (e.g., the computer lab, library, and main offices). The school only has few digital cameras, one Sympodium, one document camera, and two iPads.

Sheridan's parents seem to be divided into two camps. One group wants to perpetuate the status quo; the other argues strongly in favor of raising levels of academic performance and expanding the program of studies. The president of Sheridan's Parent Group, Karen Strong, belongs to the former. She has not found her participation in the newly formed district parent council (whose membership consists of the presidents of all of the school parent councils) worthwhile. She has told you that the group is comprised of parents who think that Mountjoy schools are private technology academies. Her recommendation to drop out of the group was overturned by high school parents interested in academics and increased use of technology.

At your last meeting with Superintendent Garcia, you learned that monies will be available during the next budget year to begin the process of making Sheridan High School a technology-rich environment. She has asked you to develop the first part of a 3-year plan for the project and informed you that she will send you a memo outlining details.

PRODUCT SPECIFICATIONS

1. Develop Sheridan's technology-based plan. The plan must include:
   a. A brief description of how the plan was developed (e.g., who was involved, when they met, how they organized their task, what the principal's role was)
   b. A list of the technology(ies) chosen for initial adoption and implementation with a brief rationale for the selection
   c. An outline of the adoption and implementation stages and strategies, with a brief rationale for each major stage and strategy
   d. A description of how you will monitor the progress and success of the plan
2. Using a presentation program (e.g., Prezi), prepare the plan.
3. Prepare for and participate in a review of the plan by the administrative council.
   Note: The council will read your plan in advance. During the review, you must be prepared to answer questions about it.
   Plan Due: _____

Memorandum

April 15

To: Deborah Carroll

From: Esmeralda Garcia, Superintendent

Re: Technology initiative

At our last meeting, I reviewed our district's technology initiative with you and asked you to begin developing a technology plan for your building. We will review your plan at the September administrative council meeting the following year. Final adoption is scheduled for the October meeting. To assist you with plan development, I am providing these conditions and guidelines:

- Consider the district's goals for technology—improved teaching, learning, and leading with technology.
- Our corporate partners and the Board of Education have been willing to provide generous funding for well-thought-out plans. Therefore:
  - The network infrastructure will be provided for your building.
  - Funding to cover plan development costs (e.g., summer work by staff, consultant fees, visitations, training, materials) is readily available.
  - Cost should not be a primary decision-making criterion when selecting technology(ies).
- Think long range but develop the plan *only* for Sheridan's first year of adoption and implementation. You should list "next steps" for years 2 and 3.
- Technology coordinators and principals from other buildings stand ready to assist you at any point in your plan development.
- Please send a copy of your plan to me by September 15, so that we can duplicate and distribute it before the meeting.

SELECTED READINGS FROM THE PRINCIPAL'S JOURNAL

May 1

I toured my building today. Reality hit me in the face. What an ugly monster of a place! Ceiling tiles stained, floor tiles mismatched, walls painted in awful institution colors. . . . And those awful chairs with arms placed in rows.

According to Frank, the head custodian, Sheridan has antiquated heating and intercom systems and problems with asbestos and electricity. He also informed me that he does not have enough staff to manage a building of its size.

My assistant Elaine interrupted the tour because the computer network had crashed while she was running schedules. The level of anger was incredible. I learned from Fred and Carol [assistant principals] that the network spends most of its time crashed. When I asked what we do about a crashed network, I unleashed the office staff's frustration. The contracted service responds on its time schedule, not on the basis of our needs.

May 24

When I got back to the building, I ran into Kelly, our library media specialist. As we chatted, I gathered some valuable information. Although her budget is not adequate, it seems that she has been working with Fred, Nancy, and Pat to move away from textbooks to resource-based learning. Kelly implied that I might see some kind of proposal from the group. I assured her I look forward to reviewing it. She asked whether I thought funding would be available to automate Sheridan's library media center in the near future. It seems the other buildings have online circulation and catalog systems, CD-ROM reference materials, and telecommunications!

May 28

Here are my initial impressions about the department leaders:

Fred Gollner (English): Articulate, seems to know the latest buzzwords. Peers tease him about being the "bleeding edge" of education; wants more computers for writing.

Nancy Heisey (Science): Believes her staff is doing some interesting things. Hinted at issues related to the district policy that every course must have an approved textbook. Seems to know how to help her colleagues to compromise. Listens in a group more than she speaks. Has jury-rigged computers that others don't want; used to form a small computer-based learning lab.

Hank Keller (Social Studies): Has he read or thought about anything since the early 1980s?! Seems attached to the expression "If it ain't broke, don't fix it." Complains about all the work he has to do as department head, but has been in the position 10 years.

Terry Rankin (Health and Physical Education): Apparently he has been used to excusing himself regularly from these meetings, because his area isn't an "academic" subject. Body language during the meeting ranged from apathy to hostility.

Carl Groff (Mathematics): Behaves like Hank's yes man. Informed me that the high school has enough technology and that his math teachers are experts. How does he explain our low test scores in math? Hedges on responding whenever I bring up NCTM standards.

Jose Gomez (Foreign Language): Seems to know his stuff! Desperately needs and wants additional staff members and some computer setup so that kids can interact with native language speakers. Great sense of humor.

Sally Ball (Combined Arts): What a powerhouse! Two years ago she single-handedly persuaded the BOE to fund Arts Propel and graphics computers for kids to use and then proceeded to have kids earn all kinds of awards. She seems to value Fred's input.

George Crandall (Career Technical Education): When asked what changes he'd like to see, he replied that all students should take keyboarding. He informed me that he will not entertain major revisions of the home economics or automotive programs, because they meet the needs of Sheridan's nonacademic kids.

Pat Green (Special Services): Seems ostracized by the group—sat alone, no one greeted her. Several times she was addressed indirectly by the phrase "your kids" or "Green's kids." She seems pleasant and knowledgeable. I wonder whether she is shunned because of the district's strong focus on inclusion.

May 29

Although I had met many of the staff members earlier, this was the first time I had them together. I've formed some initial hypotheses: (1) New staff members are regarded as outsiders; (2) most of the staff members do not link what they do instructionally with student performance; (3) many staff members believe that only some students can achieve at high levels; (4) staff members identify strongly with their respective departments. It is amazing that some of these people don't know the names of recent hires in other departments! This is a staff of 55 teachers, not 200.

My initial categories: the movers and shakers (a smattering of teachers across departments, Kelly, and Pat); the middle majority; and the "guys," as they call themselves, a group made up of Hank, Carl, George, and Terry. They took their lunches to the AV area to watch a baseball game.

June 3

I suppose I shouldn't be disappointed with the list the faculty brainstormed, but I am. Vision is absent but need is apparent. Imagine four or five intercom interruptions to class, and having only one copier that serves administrative and instructional needs in a school this size! Another big issue is that the teachers feel that many of the meetings they are contractually obligated to attend are meaningless.

I think I made some allies when I promised no intercom announcements during class time and rotation of events like pep rallies.

I also asked them to form a committee to make recommendations for their copying and intercom needs. Dead silence was followed by a maelstrom of complaints regarding the absence of any kind of technology in sufficient numbers and condition. Finally, Kelly offered to provide me with an inventory of most of the AV equipment. Apparently, no one has updated computer and software inventories.

Then Mary, the teacher association president, sarcastically noted that many of the meetings are contractual. I see some room to use time more effectively, but wasn't ready to make my ideas public. So I proposed that the teachers who volunteered to serve on the copier/intercom committee hold their first meeting during the faculty meeting, which contractually must be scheduled at the end of the school day (whose crazy idea is that?!). That went over well, and the meeting ended.

Harry (science) and Kelly, who had volunteered to co-chair the committee, came up to ask whether I would consider letting a secretary meet with the committee, because office staff members also use the technologies. I agreed—much to their surprise.

June 5

I'm in trouble with Dr. Garcia. (One of the staff members must be an informant.) By the time I arrived at school this morning, I had a note to call the superintendent after 9:00. When I did, I was told very firmly that I was to hold teachers to their required meetings. After I explained my rationale and plan (use the time flexibly for staff development, small study groups, etc.), she seemed to accept the idea "because you need to build a relationship with the staff" but warned me about the importance of "holding their feet to the fire." Hmmm . . . this is a potential area of conflict.

June 10

Harry and Kelly met with me today on the copier recommendations. I agreed to budget for their copier and telephone requests. Their report also raised some important issues regarding other technologies. The AV inventory is ancient and inadequate for our needs. There is only an outdated building inventory of computers and software because of intense department territoriality.

June 12

How depressing! Seven of the last eight observations have shown me that teachers lecture and students sit; worksheets, questions at the end of the chapter. No student engagement, no ties to their lives or current events.

I think I'll mix my observations from now on. I balance this last bunch with some of the really gifted educators I have on staff—veteran and new. I have to find a way to get the traditional teachers to see some of their techniques.

The topic of discussion was the state mastery test scores (low, low, low!). I had asked the chairs to analyze the results to see what we could do to improve our students' performance. I don't think I was prepared for their responses.

> Sheridan kids are all good kids.
> Some Sheridan kids can learn because they are motivated.
> We can help the motivated ones. (A group they think comprises approximately 20% of the student body. Like improving their scores will significantly impact our results!!)
> Their teachers work hard but will try even harder. (Doing what??)
> It's the middle school's fault for coddling kids rather than teaching them.

Only Fred and Nancy had even discussed the test results with their departments. Nothing I said or did could move most of the group toward linking instruction and curriculum and student achievement.

June 13

I finished my initial meetings with students and student groups. I am deeply troubled by what I heard and observed. Apathy and anger co-exist. Students feel outside the decision-making process. The present clubs and athletic programs do not seem of interest to many. On the other hand, a small group of students expressed interest in building "school spirit." This group wants to restructure everything from the extracurricular program to the number of computers available during the day.

I reviewed my findings with both vice principals. They were a bit defensive, citing little time to deal with the issues because of the increasing amount of time they have to spend on discipline.

I am surprised how many teachers have, in casual conversation, wanted to know whether Sheridan will ever be able to have the kinds of technology-rich environments other schools in the district have. It seems they have heard from students about what other buildings have, but many have never been to the buildings themselves!!

REFERENCES AND BIBLIOGRAPHY

Aboud, F. (1998). *Children and prejudice.* New York, NY: B. Blackwell.

Achilles, C. M., & Smith, P. (1994, 1999). Stimulating the academic performance of pupils. In L. W. Hughes (Ed.), *The principal as leader.* New York, NY: Merrill.

Adams, J. E., & Kirst, M. W. (1999). New demands and concepts for educational accountability: Striving for results in an era of excellence. In J. Murphy & K. Seashore Louis (Eds.), *Handbook of research on educational administration.* San Francisco, CA: Jossey-Bass.

Agosto, D. (2002). Bounded rationality and satisfying in young people's Web-based decision making. *Journal of the American Society for International Science and Technology, 53*(1), 16–27.

Airasian, P., & Walsh, M. (1997). Constructivist cautions. *Phi Delta Kappan, 78*(6), 444–449.

Aleven, V., & Koedinger, K. R. (2002). An effective metacognitive strategy: Learning by doing and explaining with a computer-based Cognitive Tutor. *Cognitive Science, 26*(2), 147–179.

Alexander, L. (1986). Chairman's summary. In National Governor's Association, *Time for Results.* Washington, DC: National Governor's Association.

Alliance for Childhood. (2000). *Fool's gold: A critical look at computers in childhood.* College Park, MD. Retrieved from http://drupal6.allianceforchildhood.org/fools_gold

Allison, G. (1971). *Essence of decision making: Exploring the Cuban missile crisis.* Boston, MA: Little, Brown.

Allport, G. (1958). *The nature of prejudice.* Cambridge, MA: Addison-Wesley.

Allport, G. (1979). *ABC's of scapegoating.* New York, NY: Anti-Defamation League of B'nai B'rith.

American Association of School Administrators. (1981). *Statement of ethics.* Arlington, VA: Author.

American Association of School Administrators. (1991). *America 2000: Where school leaders stand* (Report No. ISBN-0-8762-172-3). Arlington, VA: AASA (ERIC ED 344 325).

American Association of School Administrators. (1993). *1994 Platform and resolutions.* Arlington, VA: Author.

American Association of School Administrators. (2007). "State of the Superintendency." Retrieved from http://www.aasa.org/content.aspx?id=330

American School Counselor Association. (2003). *The ASCA national model: A framework for school counseling programs.* Alexandria, VA: Author.

Anderson, G. (1991). Cognitive politics in principals and teachers: Ideological control in an elementary school. In J. Blase (Ed.), *The politics of life in schools: Power, conflict, and cooperation* (pp. 120–145). Newbury Park, CA: Sage.

Anderson, L., & Shirley, R. (1995). High school principals and school reform: Lesson learned from a statewide study of project re: Learning. *Educational Administration Quarterly, 31*(3), 405–423.

Anderson, R. S., & Reiter, D. (1995). The indispensable counselor. *The School Counselor, 42,* 268–276.

Anyon, J. (1980, Winter). Social class and the hidden curriculum of work. *Journal of Education, 162,* 67–92.

Apple, M. (1986). *Teachers and texts: A political economy of class and gender relations in education.* New York, NY: Routledge.

Argyris, C. (1982). *Reasoning, learning, and action.* San Francisco, CA: Jossey-Bass.

Argyris, C. (1993). *The individual and the organization: Some problems of mutual adjustment.* New York, NY: Irvington.

Argyris, C., & Schön, D. (1974). *Theory in practice: Increasing professional effectiveness.* San Francisco, CA: Jossey-Bass.

Argyris, C., & Schön, D. (1978). *Organizational learning: A theory of action perspective.* Reading, MA: Addison-Wesley.

Arias, B. (1986, November). The context of education for Hispanic students: An overview. *American Journal of Education,* 26–57.

Armenta, T., & Beckers, G. (2006, May). The IEP: How to meet its demands and avoid its pitfalls. *Principal Leadership, 6*(9), 22–26.

Armstrong, T. (1994). *Multiple intelligences in the classroom.* Alexandria, VA: Association for Supervision and Curriculum Development.

Arons, E. L. (1999). *Successful interviewing techniques.* Mimeographed sheet, p. 18. Rockville, MD: Montgomery County Public Schools.

Associated Press. (April 27, 2011) *Virginia Governor Rolls out Teacher Merit-Pay Plan.* Education Week. p. 2.

Atkin, J. M., & Black, P. (1997). Policy perils of international comparisons. *Phi Delta Kappan, 79*(1), 22–28.

Atkinson, L., Williams, L., Applegate, P., & O'Hair, M. (2006). "High achieving schools." Norman, OK: K20 Center for Education and Community Renewal (www.k20center.org).

Atkinson, L., Williams, L., Applegate, D., & O'Hair, M. (2006, November). Paper presented at the 2006 UCEA Annual Conference, San Antonio, TX.

Avery, R., & Campion, G. (1982). The employment interview: A summary and review of recent research. *Personal Psychology, 35*(2), 281–322.

Bacharach, S. B., & Mundell, B. (Eds.). (1995). *Images of schools: Structures and roles in organizational behavior.* Thousand Oaks, CA: Corwin Press.

Baker, E. T., Wang, M. C., & Walberg, H. J. (1995). The effects of inclusion on learning. *Educational Leadership, 52*(4), 33–35.

Ball, S. (1987). *The micropolitics of the school: Toward a theory of school organization.* New York, NY: Methuen.

Balacheff, N. (1993). Advanced Educational Technologies: Knowledge Revisited. In T. Liao (Ed.). *Advanced Educational Technology: Research Issues and Future Potential,* 1-20. New York: Springer-Science.

Ballinger, C. (1988). Rethinking the school calendar. *Educational Leadership, 35*(5), 57–61.

Banks, J. A. (1993). The canon debate, knowledge, construction, and multi-cultural education. *Educational Researcher, 22*(5), 4–14.

Banks, J. A. (1999). *An introduction to multicultural education.* Boston, MA: Allyn & Bacon.

Banks, J., & Banks, C. (Eds.). (1994). *Multicultural education: Issues and perspectives.* Boston, MA: Allyn & Bacon.

Banks, J. (2007). (4th ed.). An Introduction to Multicultural Education. Boston, MA: Allyn & Bacon.

Barker, J. A. (1992). *Paradigms: The business of discovering the future.* New York, NY: HarperCollins.

Barnett, B. G. (1991). The educational platform: Articulating moral dilemmas and choices for future educational leaders. In B. G. Barnett, F. O. McQuarrie, & C. G. Norris (Eds.), *The moral imperatives of leadership: A focus on human decency.* Memphis, TN: National Network for Innovative Principal Preparation.

Barnitz, J. (1997). Emerging awareness of linguistic diversity for literacy instruction. Reading Teacher, 51(3), 264.

Bartholomew, S., Melendez-Delaney, G., Awilda, O., & White, S. (2005). Untapped resources: Assistant principals as instructional leaders. *Principal Leadership 5*(9), 22–26.

Bartlett, D., & Steele, J. (1994). *America: Who really pays the taxes.* New York, NY: Simon & Schuster.

Bartlett, L., Weisenstein, S., & Etscheidt, S. (2002). *Successful inclusion for educational leaders.* Upper Saddle River, NJ: Merrill Prentice Hall.

Bass, B. (1998). *Transformational leadership: Industrial, military, and education impact.* Mahwah, NJ: Erlbaum.

Basu, S., Biswas, G., & Sengupta, P. (2011). Scaffolding to support learning of ecology in simulation environments. In S. Bull & G. Biswas (Eds.), *Proceedings of The 15th International Conference on Artificial Intelligence in Education.* Auckland, New Zealand.

Beck, L. (1994). *Reclaiming educational administration as a caring profession.* New York, NY: Teachers College Press.

Beck, L., & Murphy, J. (1996). *The four imperatives of a successful school.* Thousand Oaks, CA: Corwin Press.

Beck, L., & Murphy, J. (1997). *Ethics in educational leadership programs: Emerging models.* Columbia, MO: University Council for Educational Administration.

Begley, P. (1996). Cognitive perspectives on values in administration: A quest for coherence and relevance. *Educational Administration Quarterly, 32*(3), 403–426.

Bell, C. (1997). Passionate leadership. In K. Shelton (Ed.), *A new paradigm of leadership* (pp. 195–198). Provo, UT: Executive Excellence.

Bell, T. H. (1993). Reflections: One decade after a nation at risk. *Phi Delta Kappan, 74*(8), 592–598.

Bellah, R., Madsen, R., Sullivan, W., Swindler, A., & Tipton, S. (1985). *Habits of the heart.* Berkeley, CA: University of California Press.

Bemak, F., Chung, R. C., & Siroskey-Sabdo, L. (2005). Empowerment groups for academic success: An innovative approach to prevent high school failure for at-risk, urban African-Americans. *Professional School Counseling 8*(5), 377–389.

Bender, W., Sebring, P., & Bryk, A. (1998). *School leadership and the bottom line in Chicago.* University of Chicago, Consortium on School Research.

Benham, M. (1997). The story of an African-American teacher–scholar: A woman's narrative. *Qualitative Studies in Education, 10*(1), 63–83.

Benham, M., & Cooper, J. (1998). *Let my spirit soar! Narratives of diverse women in school leadership.* Newbury Park, CA: Corwin Press.

Bennett, C. I. (1998). *Comprehensive multicultural education: Theory and practice.* Boston, MA: Allyn & Bacon.

Bennett, S., Maton, K., & Kervin, L. (2008). The 'digital natives' debate: A critical review of the evidence. *British Journal of Educational Technology, 39*(5), 775–786.

Bennis, W. G. (1983). *The chief.* New York, NY: Morrow.

Bennis, W., & Nanus, B. (1985). *Leaders: The strategies for taking charge.* New York, NY: Harper & Row.

Berlew, T., & Hall, F. (1988). Pygmalion effect of first time bosses. *Harvard Business Review, 62*(3), 150–168.

Berman, P., & McLaughlin, M. (1977). *Federal programs supporting educational change, Vol. VIII: Implementing and sustaining innovations.* Santa Monica, CA: Rand.

Bernard, C. I. (1938). *The functions of the executive.* Cambridge, MA: Harvard Press.

Bernhardt, V. (1998). *Data analysis for comprehensive school improvement.* Larchmont, NY: Eye on Education.

Bernstein, B. (1964). Elaborated and restricted codes: Their social origins and some consequences. *American Anthropologist, 66,* 55–69.

Berry, B. & The Teacher Solutions 2030 Team. (2011). Teaching 2030: What We Must Do for Our Students and Our Public Schools—Now and in the Future. New York: Teachers College Press.

Biddle, B., & Saha, L. (2006, March). How principals use research. *Educational Leadership, 63*(6), 72–77.

Billings, E. (2009). El alfabetismo y las familias latinas: A Critical Perspective on the Literacy Values and Practices of Latino Families With Young Children. Journal of Latinos & Education, 8(4), 252–269.

Binkowski, K. (1995). *Factors contributing to school improvement in high performing elementary schools.* Unpublished doctoral dissertation. University of Connecticut.

Birdwhistell, R. (1970). *Kinesics and context.* Philadelphia, PA: University of Pennsylvania.

Biswas, G., Jeong, H., Kinnebrew, J., Sulcer, B., & Roscoe, R. (2010). Measuring self-regulated learning skills through social interactions in a teachable agent environment. *Research and Practice in Technology-Enhanced Learning, 5*(2), 123–152.

Blackmore, J. (2009). Re/Positioning Women in Educational Leadership. In H.C. Sobehart (Ed.). Women Leading education Across the Continents. (73–00).

Blake, R. R., & McCanse, A. A. (1991). *Leadership dilemmas—Grid solutions.* (Formerly *The managerial grid* by Robert R. Blake and Jane S. Mouton.) Houston, TX: Gulf Publishing.

Blake, R. R., & Mouton, J. S. (1964). *The managerial grid.* Houston, TX: Gulf Publishing.

Blake, R. R., & Mouton, J. S. (1978). *The new managerial grid.* Houston, TX: Gulf Publishing.

Blakemore, S.-J., & Frith, U. (2005). *The learning brain: Lessons for education.* Malden, MA: Wiley-Blackwell.

Blanchard, K. H., & Peale, N. V. (1988). *The power of ethical management.* New York, NY: William Morrow.

Blase, J., & Blase, J. (1998). *Handbook of instructional leadership: How really good principals promote teaching and learning.* Thousand Oaks, CA: Corwin Press.

Blase, J., & Blase, J. (2003). *Breaking the silence: Overcoming the problem of principal mistreatment of teachers.* Thousand Oaks, CA: Corwin Press.

Blase, J. G. (1990). Some negative effects of principals' control-oriented and protective behaviors. *American Educational Research Journal 27*(4), 727–753.

Blase, J. G. (1993). The micropolitics of effective school-based leadership: Teachers' perspectives. *Educational Administration Quarterly, 29*(2), 142–163.

Bliss, W. (1994). Managing budgets. *NAASP Bulletin, 78*(566), 327–344.

Bloom, B. (1956). *Taxonomy of educational objectives: A classification of educational goals. Handbook I: Cognitive domain.* New York, NY: David McKay.

Bloom, B. (1971). Mastery learning. In J. Block (Ed.). *Masterly learning: Theory and Practice,* New York, NY: Holt, Rinehart & Winston.

Bloom, B., & Krathwohl, D. R. (1984). *Taxonomy of educational objectives.* Boston, MA: Addison-Wesley.

Bloom, L., & Munro, P. (1995). Conflicts of selves: Nonunitary subjectivity in women administrators' life history narratives. In J. Hatch & R. Wisniewski (Eds.), *Life history and narrative* (pp. 99–112). Washington, DC: Falmer Press.

Blount, J. (1993). One postmodern perspective on educational leadership: And ain't I a leader? In S. Maxcy (Ed.), *Postmodern school leadership* (pp. 47–62). Westport, CT: Praeger.

Blumberg, A., & Greenfield, W. (1980). *The effective principal: Perspectives on school leadership.* Boston, MA: Allyn & Bacon.

Bolman, L. G., & Deal, T. E. (1991, 2003). *Reframing organizations: Artistry, choice, leadership.* San Francisco, CA: Jossey-Bass.

Bolman, L. G., & Deal, T. E. (1995). *Leading with soul: An uncommon journey of spirit.* San Francisco, CA: Jossey-Bass.

Bonk, C. J. (2009). *The world is open: How web technology is revolutionizing education.* San Francisco, CA: Jossey-Bass.

Bordas, J. (2007). *Salsa, soul and spirit: Leadership for a multicultural age.* San Francisco, CA: Berrett-Koehler Publishers.

Borders, L. D., & Shoffner, M. F. (2003). School counselors: Leadership opportunities and challenges in the schools. In J. D. West, C. J. Osborn, & D. L. Bubenzer (Eds.), *Leaders and legacies: Contributions to the profession of counseling* (pp. 51–64). New York, NY: Brunner-Routledge.

Borman, G., Hewes, G., Overman, T., & Brown, S. (2003, Summer). Comprehensive school reform and achievement: A meta-analysis. *Review of Educational Research 73*(2), 125–230.

Bossert, S., Dwyer, D., Rowan, B., & Lee, G. (1982). The instructional management role of the principal. *Educational Administration Quarterly, 18*(3), 34–64.

Boud, D., & Feletti, G. (1998). *The challenge of problem-based learning.* New York, NY: St. Martin's Press.

Bourdieu, P., & Passeron, J. (1977). *Reproduction: In education, society, and culture.* Newbury Park, CA: Sage.

Bowles, S., & Gintis, H. (1976). *Schooling in capitalist America.* New York, NY: Basic Books.

Bracewell, R., Breuleux, A., Laferriere, T., Beniot, J., & Abdous, M. (1998). *The emerging contribution of online resources and tools to classroom learning and teaching.* Montreal: Universite Laval. Retrieved from http://www.tact.fse.ulaval.ca/ang/html/review98.html

Bracey, G. W. (2003, January). Investing in preschool. *American School Board Journal, 190*(1), 32–35.

Bracey, G. W. (2003, October). The condition of public education. *Phi Delta Kappan, 85*(2), 148–164.

Bradshaw, C., Reinke, W., Brown, L., Bevans, K., & Leaf, P. (2008). Implementation of school-wide positive behavioral interventions and supports (PBIS) in elementary schools: Observations from a randomized trial. *Education and Treatment of Children, 31*(1), 1–26.

Brandt, R. (1992, February). On rethinking leadership: A conversation with Tom Sergiovanni. *Educational Leadership, 49*(5), 46–49.

Brandt, R. (1992, September). On building learning communities: A conversation with Hank Levin. *Educational Leadership, 50*(1), 19–23.

Bredeson, P. V. (2003). *Designs for learning: A new architecture for professional development in schools.* Thousand Oaks, CA: Corwin Press.

Brewer, D. (1993). Principals and student outcomes: Evidence from U.S. high schools. *Economics of Education Review, 12*(4), 281–292.

Bridges, E. M. (1986). *The incompetent teacher.* Philadelphia, PA: Falmer.

Bridges, E., & Hallinger, P. (1995). *Implementing problem-based learning in leadership development.* University of Oregon, ERIC Clearinghouse on Educational Management.

Brockmeier, L., Sermon, J., & Hope, W. (2005) Principals' relationship with computer technology. *NASSP Bulletin, 89*(643), 45–64.

Brookover, W., & Lezotte, L. (1979). *Changes in school characteristics in coincidence with changes in student achievement.* East Lansing, MI: Michigan State University.

Brown, B., & McLenighan, H. (2005). Only the extraordinary for next generation's leaders. *The School Administrator, 62*(6), 44–45.

Brown, F. (1995). Privatization of public education: Theories and concepts. *Education and Urban Society, 2*(2), 116.

Brown, K., & Anfara, V. (2002) From the Desk of the Middle School Principal: Leadership Responsive to the Needs of Young Adolescents. Blue Ridge Summit, PA: R & L Education.

Brown, R. (1983). Some Impractical Suggestions for Renewal. The Quarterly, Vol. 5, No. 3, 1–5.

Brown-Ferrigno, T. (2003). Becoming a principal: Role conception, initial socialization, role-identity transformation, purposeful engagement. *Educational Administration Quarterly, 39*(4), 468–503.

Bryk, A., Bender Sebring, P., Allensworth, E., Luppescu, S. & Easton, J. (2010). Organizing Schools for Improvement: Lessons from Chicago. Chicago: University of Chicago Press.

Bryk, A., & Schneider, B. L. (2002). *Trust in schools.* Newbury Park, CA: Sage.

Buck Institute for Education. (1999). *Project based learning handbook.* Novato, CA: Author.

Bull, B. L., & McCarthy, M. M. (1995, November). Reflections on the knowledge base in law and ethics for educational leaders. *Educational Administration Quarterly, 31*(4), 613–631.

Bullivant, B. M. (1989). Culture: Its nature and meaning for educators. In J. Banks & C. A. McGee Banks (Eds.), *Multicultural education: Issues and perspectives* (pp. 27–45). Boston, MA: Allyn & Bacon.

Bullock, A., & Foster-Harrison, E. (1997, November-December). Making the best decisions: Designing for excellence! *Schools in the Middle, 7*(2), 37–39, 60–61.

Bullock, C. S., & Stewart, J. (1978). *Compliant processing as a strategy for combating second generation discrimination.* Paper presented at the annual meeting of the Southern Political Science Association, Atlanta, GA.

Bullock, C. S., & Stewart, J. (1979). Incidence and correlates of second-generation discrimination. In M. L. Palley & M. B. Preston (Eds.), *Race, sex, and policy problems* (pp. 115–129). Lexington, MA: Lexington Books.

Burns, J. M. (1978). *Leadership.* New York, NY: Harper and Row.

Bynham, W. C. (1971, December). The assessment center as an aid in management development. *Training and Development Journal, 25*(12), 10–22.

Callahan, R. E. (1962). *Education and the cult of efficiency.* Chicago, IL: University of Chicago Press.

Cameron, T. (1995, October). Block scheduling one year later, or, what's your schedule done for you lately? *Oklahoma Association of Secondary School Principals Newsletter.*

Campbell, C. A., & Dahir, C. A. (1997). *Sharing the vision: The national standards for school counseling programs.* Alexandria, VA: American School Counselor Association.

Campbell, R. (1987). *A history of thought and practical educational administration.* New York, NY: Teachers College Press.

Campbell, R. F., Cunningham, L. L., Nystrand, R. O., & Usdan, M. D. (1980). *The organization and control of American schools.* Columbus, OH: Merrill.

Canady, R. L., & Rettig, M. (1995). *Block scheduling: A catalyst for change in high schools.* Princeton, NJ: Eye on Education.

Candoli, I. C., Hack, W. G., Ray, J., & Stollar, D. H. (1984). *School business administration: A planning approach.* Boston, MA: Allyn & Bacon.

Cantano, N., & Stronge, J. (2006, September). What are principals expected to do? Congruence between principal evaluation and performance standards. *NASSP Bulletin, 90*(3), 221–237.

Carlson, R. (1989). *Restructuring schools: International memorandum.* Washington, DC: District of Columbia Public Schools.

Carlson, R. (1996). *Reframing and reforms.* White Plains, NY: Longman.

Carnegie Forum on Education and Economy. (1986). *A nation prepared: Teachers for the twenty-first century.* New York, NY: Report of the Task Force on Teaching as a Profession.

Carr, N. (2003). Leadership: The toughest job in America. *American School Board Journal, 14*, 20.

Carr, N. (2008). Is Google making us stupid? *The Atlantic.* Retrieved from http://www.theatlantic.com/magazine/archive/2008/07/is-google-making-us-stupid/6868/

Carroll, J. M. (1994). The Copernican plan evaluated: The evolution of a revolution. *Phi Delta Kappan, 76*(2), 105–113.

Carson, C. C., Hiwelskamp, R. M., & Woodall, T. D. (1992, April). *Perspectives on education in America.* Albuquerque, NM: Sandia National Laboratories.

Carspecken, P., & Cordeiro, P. (1995). Being, doing, and becoming: Textual interpretation of social identity and a case study. *Qualitative Inquiry, 1*(1), 87–109.

Carter, G. R., & Cunningham. W. G. (1997). *The American school superintendent: Leading in an age of pressure.* San Francisco, CA: Jossey-Bass.

Castetter, W. B. (1996). *The human resource function in educational administration.* Englewood Cliffs, NJ: Prentice Hall.

Center for Educational Leadership. (2007). *Leadership as learning: Closing the achievement gap by improving instruction through content-focused leadership.* Seattle, WA: University of Washington.

Cetron, M., & Cetron, K. (2004, January). A forecast for our schools. *Educational Leadership, 61*(4), 22–29.

Chang, J. (2006). A transcultural wisdom bank in the classroom: Making cultural diversity a key resource in teaching and learning. *Journal of Studies in International Education, 10*(4), 369–377.

Chapman, J., Sackney, L., & Aspin, D. (1999). Internationalization in educational administration: Policy and practice, theory and research. In J. Murphy & K. Seashore Louis (Eds.), *Handbook of research on educational administration* (pp. 73–98). San Francisco, CA: Jossey-Bass.

Chappuis, S. J., Stiggins, R. J., Arter, J. A., & Chappuis, J. (2009). *Assessment for learning: An action guide for school leaders* (2nd ed.). Boston, MA: Allyn and Bacon.

Charles, F. (2006). *Technology in education: What the research says.* Cisco Systems, Inc. Cheryl Lemke, CEO, Metiri.

Checkley, K. (1997). The first seven . . . and the eighth: A conversation with Howard Gardner. *Educational Leadership, 55*(1), 8–13.

Chi, M. T. H., De Leeuw, N., Chiu, M.-H., & Lavancher, C. (1994). Eliciting self-explanations improves understanding. *Cognitive Science, 18*(3), 439–477.

Children's Defense Fund. (1991). *The state of America's children.* Washington, DC: Children's Defense Fund.

Childress, S., Elmore, R., & Grossman, A. (2006, November). How to manage urban school districts. *Harvard Business Review, 85,* 55–68.

Chrisman, V. (2005, February). How schools sustain success. *Educational Leadership, 62*(5), 16–20.

Christensen, C., Horn, M. B., & Johnson, C. W. (2008). Disrupting Class: How Disruptive Innovation Will Change the Way the World Learns. New York: McGraw-Hill.

Church, A., & Bracken, D. (1997, June). Advancing the state of the art of 360-degree feedback. *Organizational Management, 22*(2), 149–162.

Cibulka, J. G. (1997). Two eras of urban schooling: The decline of the old order and the emergence of new organizational form. *Education and Urban Society, 29*(3), 317–341.

Clark, K. E., & Clark, M. B. (1996). *Choosing to lead.* Greensboro, NC: Center for Creative Leadership.

Clark, T. (2001). Virtual Schools: A Study of Virtual Schools in the United States. San Francisco: Distance Learning Resource Network (DLRN) WestEd.

Clarke, G. H. (1998). *Real questions, real answers.* Alexandria, VA: Association for Supervision and Curriculum Development.

Clemmer, E. F. (1991). *The school policy handbook: Primer for administrators and school board members.* Boston, MA: Allyn & Bacon.

Cogan, M. (1973). *Clinical supervision.* New York, NY: Houghton Mifflin.

Cohen, D. K., & March, J. G. (1974). *Leadership and ambiguity: The American college president.* New York, NY: McGraw-Hill.

Cohen, D. K., & Spillane, J. P. (1992). Policy and practice: The relations between governance and instruction. In G. Grant (Ed.), *Review of research in education.* Washington, DC: American Educational Research Association.

Cohen, J. J. (Ed.). (1990). *The fundamentalist phenomenon.* Grand Rapids, MI: William B. Eerdmans.

Cohen, J. M., & March, J. G. (1977, September). Almost random careers: The Wisconsin superintendency, 1940–1972. *Administrative Science Quarterly, 22,* 79–92.

Cole, N. S. (1990). Conceptions of educational achievement. *Educational Researcher, 19*(3), 2–7.

Coleman, J. (1993, March). *Family involvement in education.* Paper prepared for The Milken Family Foundation, National Education Conference, Los Angeles, CA.

Coleman, J. S., & Hoffler, T. (1987). *Public and private high schools: The impact of communities.* New York, NY: Basic Books. Guidance and Counseling. New York, NY: College Entrance Examination Board.

Collins, G. C., & Porras, G. I. (1994). *Build to last: Successful habits of visionary companies.* New York, NY: HarperCollins.

Collins, J. (2001). *Good to great: Why some companies make the leap . . . and others don't.* New York, NY: HarperCollins.

Comer, J. P., Joyner, E. T., & Haynes, N. M. (1996). Lessons learned. In J. P. Comer, N. Haynes, E. Joyner, & M. Ben-Avie (Eds.), *Rallying the whole village.* New York, NY: Teachers College Press.

Commission of Skills of the American Workforce. (2006). *Tough choices, tough times.* Washington, DC: National Center on Education and the Economy.

Commission on Standards for the Superintendency. (1993). *Professional standards for the superintendency.* Arlington, VA: American Association of School Administrators.

Congressional Quarterly Inc. (2007). *No child left behind.* Retrieved from http://web.lexis-nexis.com.proxy.lib.odu.edu

Constas, M. A. (1998, March). The changing nature of educational research and a critique of postmodernism. *Educational Researcher, 27*(2), 26–32.

Cooper, B., Fusarelli, L., & Carella, V. (1999). *Career crisis in the superintendency.* Arlington, VA: American Association of School Administrators.

Cooper, B., Fusarelli, L., & Randall, E. (2004). *Better policies, better schools.* Boston, MA: Allyn & Bacon.

Cooper, J., & Heck, R. (1995). Using narrative in the study of school administration. *Qualitative Studies in Education, 8*(2), 195–210.

Copland, M. A. (2001, March). The myth of the super-principal. *Phi Delta Kappan, 82*(7), 528–533.

Cordeiro, P. (1990). *Growing away from the barrio: An ethnography of high achieving, at-risk, Hispanic youths at two high schools.* Dissertation Abstracts International. University of Houston, Houston, TX.

Cordeiro, P. (1998). The principal's role in curricular leadership and program development. In L. W. Hughes (Ed.), *The principal as leader.* New York, NY: Merrill.

Cordeiro, P., & Loup, K. (1996). Partnering changes the roles of school leaders: Implications for educational leadership preparation programs. In P. Cordeiro (Ed.), *Border crossings: Educational partnerships and school leadership.* San Francisco, CA: Jossey-Bass.

Cordeiro, P., & Monroe-Kolek, M. (1996). Connecting school communities through the development of educational partnerships. In P. Cordeiro (Ed.), *Border crossings: Educational partnerships and school leadership.* San Francisco, CA: Jossey-Bass.

Cordeiro, P., Reagan, T., & Martinez, L. (1994). *Multiculturalism and TQE: Addressing cultural diversity in schools.* Newbury Park, CA: Corwin Press.

Corey, M., & Corey, G. (1987). *Groups: Process and practice.* Pacific Grove, CA: Brooks/Cole.

Costa, A. L. (1997). Curriculum: A decision-making process. In A. L. Costa & R. M. Liebmarin (Eds.), *Envisioning process as content.* Thousand Oaks, CA: Corwin Press.

Covey, S. R. (1989). *The 7 habits of highly effective people.* New York, NY: Simon & Schuster.

Covey, S. R., Merrill, A. R., & Merrill, R. R. (1994). *First things first.* New York, NY: Simon & Schuster.

Cradler, J., McHabb, M., Freeman, M., & Burchett, R. (2002). How does technology influence student learning? *Learning and Leading with Technology, 29*(8), 46–49.

Craig, R. (1994). Ethical frameworks to guide action. In L. Hughes (Ed.), *The principal as leader.* New York, NY: Merrill.

Craig, R. (1999). Ethical frameworks to guide action. In L. Hughes (Ed.), *The principal as leader* (2nd ed.). Upper Saddle River, NJ: Prentice Hall.

Cranton, P. (1994). *Understanding and promoting transformative learning: A guide for educators of adults.* San Francisco, CA: Jossey-Bass.

Crawford, P., & Zygouris-Coe, V. (2006). All in the Family: Connecting Home and School with Family Literacy. *Early Childhood Education Journal, 33*(4), 261–267.

Cremin, L. (1965). *The genius of American education.* New York, NY: Vintage.

Crow, G., Mathews, L., & McCleary, L. (2002). Leadership. In P. Chance & E. Chance (Eds.), *Introduction to educational leadership and organizational behavior.* Larchmont, NY: Eye on Education.

Crowther, F., Kaagan, S., Ferguson, M., & Hann, L. (2002). *Developing teacher leaders: How teacher leadership enhances school success.* Newbury Park, CA: Corwin Press.

Cuban, L. (1976). *The urban school superintendency: A century and a half of change.* Bloomington, IN: Phi Delta Kappa Education Foundation.

Cuban, L. (1988). *The managerial imperatives and the practice of leadership in schools.* Albany, NY: State University of New York Press.

Cuban, L. (1989). *The urban school superintendency: A century and a half of change.* Bloomington, IN: Phi Delta Kappa Education Foundation.

Cubberly, E. (1909). *Changing conceptions of education.* Boston, MA: Houghton Mifflin.

Culbertson, J. A. (1981). A century's quest for a knowledge base. In N. J. Boyan (Ed.), *Handbook of research on educational administration.* New York, NY: Longman.

Cummins, J. (2009). Transformative multiliteracies pedagogy: School-based strategies for closing the achievement. *The Multiple Voices for Ethnically Diverse Exceptional Learners, 11*(2) 38–56.

Cunningham, L., & Hentges, G. T. (1982). *The American school superintendent.* Arlington, VA: American Association of School Administrators.

Cunningham, P., Hall, D., & Defee, M. (1998, May). Nonability-grouped, multilevel instruction: Eight years later. *Reading Teacher, 51*(8), 652–664.

Cunningham, W. (2007a). *A handbook for educational leadership interns: A rite of passage.* Boston, MA: Allyn & Bacon.

Cunningham, W. G. (1982). *Systematic planning for educational change.* Palo Alto, CA: Mayfield.

Cunningham, W. G. (1991). *Empowerment: Vitalizing personal energy.* Atlanta, GA: Humanics.

Cunningham, W. G., & Gresso, D. W. (1993). *Cultural leadership: The culture of excellence in education.* Boston, MA: Allyn & Bacon.

Cunningham, W. G., & Sperry, J. (2001a, February). Where's the beef in administrator pay? *The School Administrator, 58*(2), 32–38.

Cunningham, W. G., & Sperry, J. (2001b, April). The underpaid educator. *American School Board Journal, 188*(4), 38–44.

Dantley, M. (2005). African American spirituality and Cornel West's notions of prophetic pragmatists. *Educational Administrative Quarterly, 41*(4), 651–674.

Danzberger, J. P. (1998). School boards—Partners in policy. In R. Spillane & P. Regnier (Eds.), *The superintendent of the future.* Gaithersburg, MD: Aspen.

Daresh, J. (2002). *Building leaders for the future: The Socorro Independent School District assistant principal's academy.* Paper presented at the annual meeting of the National Council of Professors of Educational Administration, Houston, TX, August 7–19.

Darling-Hammond, L. (1997). *The right to learn.* San Francisco, CA: Jossey-Bass.

Darling-Hammond, L. (February, 1998). Standards for assessing teaching effectiveness are key. *Phi Delta Kappan, 79*(6), 471–472.

Darling-Hammond, L. (2003). Enhancing teaching. In W. Owings & L. Kaplan (Eds.), *Best practices, best thinking.* Thousand Oaks, CA: Corwin Press.

Darling-Hammond, L., & Falk, B. (1997). Using standards and assessments to support student learning. *Phi Delta Kappan, 79*(3), 190–202.

Data Research, Inc. (1991). *U.S. Supreme Court education cases.* Rosemount, MN: Data Research.

Datnow, A. (2005, February). The sustainability of comprehensive school reform models in changing district and state contexts. *Educational Administration Quarterly, 41*(1), 121–153.

David, J. L. (1989, May). Synthesis of research on school-based management. *Educational Leadership, 46*(8), 45–53.

Davis, L., Johnson-Reid, M., Saunders, J., Williams, J., & Williams, T. (2005). Academic self-efficacy among African American youths: Implications for school social work practice. *Children & Schools, 27,* 5–14.

Davis, S. (1997, November) How mastering technology can transform math class. *Educational Journal,* 49–51.

Davis, S., Darling-Hammond, L., LaPointe, M., & Meyerson, D. (2005). *School leadership study: Developing successful principals (Review of Research).* Stanford, CA: Stanford University, Stanford Educational Leadership Institute.

Dawson Gonzales, L. (2004). *Sustaining teacher leadership: Beyond the boundaries of an enabling school culture.* Lanham, MD: University Press of America.

Deal, T. E., & Kennedy, A. A. (1982). *Corporate cultures.* Reading, MA: Addison-Wesley.

Deal, T. E., & Peterson, K. E. (1990, September). *The principals' role in shaping school culture.* Washington, DC: Office of Education Research and Improvement.

Dede, C. (1998). Learning with Technology. The 1998 Yearbook. Alexandria, VA: Association for Supervision and Curriculum Development.

DeFranco, J., & Golden, N. (2003). *Educational Leadership Improvement Tool.* Eugene, OR: Center for Educational Policy Research/University of Oregon.

Deitrick,L. (2011). Literacy literature review report for the United Way San Diego. San Diego, CA: Caster Family Research Center, University of San Diego.

Delbecq, A. L., Van De Ven, A. H., & Gustafsan, P. H. (1975). *Group techniques for program planning.* Dallas, TX: Scott Foresman.

Deluca, J. (1999). *Political savvy.* Berwyn, PA: EBG Publications.

Deming, W. E. (1986). *Out of crisis.* Cambridge, MA: MIT Center for Advanced Engineering Studies.

Deming, W. E. (1991). Foundations for management of quality in the western world. In *An introduction to total quality for schools.* Arlington, VA: American Association of School Administrators.

Deming, W. E. (1993). *The new economics for industry, government and education.* Cambridge, MA: MIT Center for Advanced Engineering Studies.

Deming, W. E. (1997). Quality leaders. In K. Shelton (Ed.), *A new paradigm of leadership* (pp. 121–126). Provo, UT: Executive Excellence.

DePree, M. (1989). *Leadership is an art.* New York, NY: Dell.

Detert, J., Kopel, M., Mauriel, J., & Jenni, R. (2000, March). Quality management in U.S. high schools: Evidence from the field. *Journal of School Leadership, 10*(2), 158–187.

Detterman, D. (1993). The case for the prosecution: Transfer as an epiphenomenon. In D. Detterman & R. Sternberg (Eds.), *Transfer on trial: Intelligence cognition and instruction.* Norwood, NJ: Ablex.

Deutsch, M. (1963). The disadvantaged child and the learning process. In A. H. Paslow (Ed.), *Education in depressed areas* (pp. 163–180). New York, NY: Teachers College Press.

Dewey, J. (1910). *How we think.* Boston, MA: DC Heath.

Dewey, J. (1938). *Logic: The theory of inquiry.* New York, NY: Holt, Rinehart & Winston.

Diangreco, M. F., Cloninger, C. J., & Iverson, V. S. (1993). *Choosing options and accommodations for children.* Baltimore, MD: Brookes.

Diaz, C. (1992). *Multicultural education for the twenty-first century.* Washington, DC: National Education Association.

Digest of Education Statistics. (1995). Washington, DC: National Center for Education Statistics.

Dimmitt, C., Carey, J. C., & Hatch, T. (2007). *Evidence-based school counseling: Making a difference with data-driven practice.* Thousand Oaks, CA: Corwin Press.

DiPaola, M. F., & Stronge, J. H. (2001, February). Credible evaluation: Not yet state-of-the art. *The School Administrator, 58*(2), 18–21.

DiPaola, M., & Tschannen-Moran, M. (2003, March). The principalship at a crossroads: A study of the conditions and concerns of principals. *NASSP Bulletin, 87*(634), 43–63.

Doggett, L., & Wat, A. (2010). Why preK for all? *Phi Delta Kappan, 92*(3), 7–13.

Dolan, L. J. (1992). *Models for integrating human services into the school.* (Report no. 30). Baltimore, MD: Center for Research on Effective Schooling. (ERIC Document Reproduction Service No. ED 347 244.)

Dollarhide, C. T. (2003). School counselors as program leaders: Applying leadership contexts to school counseling. *Professional School Counseling, 6*(5), 304–308.

Domenech, D. (2005, November). Situation governance: A continuum of board types. *The School Administrator, 62*(10), 6–14.

Donmoyer, R. (1999). The continuing quest for a knowledge base. In J. Murphy & K. Seashore Louis (Eds.), *Handbook of research in educational administration* (2nd ed.). San Francisco, CA: Jossey-Bass.

Donmoyer, R. (2007). Foreword. In C. Bellamy, C. Fulmer, M. Murphy, & R. Muth (Eds.), *Principal accomplishments: How school leaders succeed* (pp. ix–xi). New York, NY: Teachers College Press.

Donoghue, E., & Kraft, C. (2009). *Managing chronic health needs in child care and schools.* Elk Grove Village, IL: American Academy of Pediatrics.

Doyle, D., & Finn, C. (1985). Now is the time for year-round schools. *Principal, 65,* 29–31.

Doyle, M., & Straus, D. (1993). *How to make meetings work* (3rd ed.). New York, NY: The Berkley Publishing Group.

Drake, T. L., & Roe, W. H. (1999). *The principalship.* Upper Saddle River, NJ: Merrill.

Dretzin, R. (2010). Digital nation. Frontline. Retrieved from http://www.pbs.org/wgbh/pages/frontline/digitalnation/view/

Drucker, P. F. (1954). *The practice of management.* New York, NY: Harper & Row.

Drucker, P. F. (1974). *Management: Tasks, responsibilities, and practices.* New York, NY: Harper & Row.

Drucker, P. F. (1980). *Managing in turbulent times.* New York, NY: Harper & Row.

Drucker, P. F. (1992). *Managing for the future: The 1990's and beyond.* New York, NY: Truman Tally Books.

Drucker, P. F. (1993). *Managing for the future: The 1990's and beyond.* New York, NY: Penguin Books.

Drucker, P. F. (1998). *Managing the nonprofit organization.* New York, NY: Diane Publishing.

Drucker, P. F. (2002). *The effective executive.* New York, NY: Harper Collins.

Drucker, P. F. (2006) Managing the Nonprofit Organization. New York: Harper Paperbacks.

Dryfoos, J. (1994). *Full-service schools: A revolution in health and social services for children, youth, and families.* San Francisco, CA: Jossey-Bass.

DuFour, R., & Eaker, R. (1998). *Professional learning communities at work: Best practices for enhancing student achievement.* Bloomington, IN: National Education Service.

Duhaney, D., & Zemel, P. (2000). Technology and the education process: Transforming classroom activities. *International Journal of Instructional Media, 27*(3), 27–32.

Duke, D. (1987). *School leadership and instructional improvement.* New York, NY: Random House.

Duke, D. (1998, April). The normative context of organizational leadership. *Educational Administration Quarterly, 34*(2), 165–195.

Duke, D., & Grogan, M. (1997). The moral and ethical dimensions of leadership. In L. Beck & J. Murphy (Eds.), *Ethics in educational leadership programs.* Columbia, MO: UCEA.

Dukes, K. (2006). Fostering cultural competence through school-based routines. *Multicultural Education, 14*(1), 42–48.

Duncan, A. (2009). A video address of Secretary of Education Arne Duncan at the Wallace Foundation's National Conference. http://www.wallacefoundation.org

Eberts, R., & Stone, J. (1988). Student achievement in public schools: Do principals make a difference? *Economics of Education Review, 7*(3), 291–299.

E.C.I.S. (1998). *The directory of the European council of international schools.* Petersfield, UK: European Council of International Schools.

Edger, M. (2006). Administration of schools. *College Student Journal, 40*(4), 846–851.

Edmonds, R. (1979). Effective schools for the urban poor. *Educational Leadership, 37*(1), 15–24.

Edmondson, J. H., & White, J. (1998). A tutorial and counseling program: Helping students at risk of dropping out of school. *Professional School Counseling, 1*(4), 43–51.

Education Trust. (2006). *Education watch.* Washington, DC: Author.

Education Week. (1999, January 11). *Quality counts: Education Week/Pew Charitable Trusts report on education in the 50 states.* Bethesda, MD: Author.

Education Week. (2006). *The information edge: Using data to accelerate achievement.* Bethesda, MD: Author. Retrieved from http://www.edweek.org/ew/toc/2006/05/04/index.html

Education Week. (2006). *The curriculum in instructional improvement.* Bethesda, MD: Author. Retrieved from http://www.edweek.org/ew/collections/focus-on-curriculum-and-assessment/index.html

Educational Research Services. (1998). *Is there a shortage of qualified candidates for openings in the principalship? An exploratory study.* Arlington, VA: Author.

Einedar, D., & Bishop, H. (1997). Block scheduling the high school: The effects on achievement behavior, and student-teacher relationships. *NASSP Bulletin, 51*(589), 45–54.

Eisner, E. (1995, Spring). Preparing teachers for schools of the 21st century. *Peabody Journal of Education, 70*(3), 99–111.

Eisner, M. (1997). Creative leadership. In K. Shelton (Ed.), *A new paradigm of leadership* (pp. 105–108). Provo, UT: Executive Excellence.

Elmore, R. (2000). *Building a new structure for school leadership.* New York, NY: The Albert Shanker Institute.

Elmore, R. (2005, Winter). Accountable leadership. *The Educational Forum, 69*(2), 134–142. Retrieved from http://www.eric.ed.gov/PDFS/EJ683739.pdf

Elmore, R. (2006, November 11). *Educational leadership and practice: Some new directions.* Mitstifer Lecture at the 2006 annual UCEA Meeting, San Antonio, TX.

Elmore, R. F., Peterson, P. L., & McCarthy, S. J. (1996). *Restructuring in the classroom: Teaching, learning, and school organization.* San Francisco, CA: Jossey-Bass.

English, F. (2006, August). The unintended consequences of a standardized knowledge base in advancing educational leadership preparation. *Educational Administration Quarterly, 42*(3), 461–472.

English, F. (2008). *Anatomy of professional practice.* Lanham, MD: Rowman and Littlefield Education.

English, F. W. (1993, Spring). A post-structural view of the grand narratives in educational administration. *Organization theory dialogues.* Bloomington, IN: Organizational Theory SIG (AERA) Indiana University.

English, F. W. (1995). Toward a reconsideration of biography and other forms of life writings as a focus for teaching educational administration. *Educational Administration Quarterly, 31*(2), 203–233.

English, F. W., & Steffy, B. E. (1997, February). Using films to teach leadership in educational administration. *Educational Administration Quarterly, 33*(1), 107–115.

Epstein, J. & Associates. (2009). *School, family and community partnerships: Your handbook for action.* Thousand Oaks, CA: Corwin Press.

Epstein, J. L. (1992). School and family partnerships. In M. Alkin (Ed.), *Encyclopedia of educational research.* New York, NY: Macmillan.

Epstein, J. L. (2001). *School, family, and community partnerships: Preparing educators and improving schools.* Boulder, CO: Westview Press.

Epstein, J. L., Coates, L., Salinas, K. C., Sanders, M. G., & Simon, B. S. (2002). *School, family, and community partnerships: Your handbook for action.* Thousand Oaks, CA: Corwin Press.

Epstein, J. L., & Jansorn, N. (2004, January-February). Developing successful partnership programs. *Principal, 83*(3), 10–15.

Etzioni, A. (1967, December). Mixed scanning: Their approach to decision-making. *Public Administration Review, 27,* 385–392.

Etzioni, A. (1986). Mixed scanning revisited. *Public Administration Review, 46,* 8–14.

Etzioni, A. (1993). *The spirit of community.* New York, NY: Crown.

Evers, C. W., & Lakomski, G. (1996). *Exploring educational administration.* New York, NY: Pergamon Press.

Fad, K., Patton, J., & Polloway, E. (2000). *Behavioral intervention planning.* Austin, TX: PRO-ED.

Fairman, M., Holmes, M., Hardage, J., & Lucas, C. (1979). *Manual for the organizational health instrument.* Fayetteville, AR: Organizational Health: Diagnostic and Development.

Fashola, O. S., & Slavin, R. E. (1998, January). Schoolwide reform models: What works? *Phi Delta Kappan, 79,* 370–379.

Fayol, H. (1949). Administrator industrielle et generale. In C. Starrs (Ed.), *General and industrial management.* London, England: Sir Issac Pitman and Sons.

Federal Communications Commission. (2007). *Children's Internet Protection Act.* Retrieved from http://www.fcc.gov/cgb/consumerfacts/cipa.html

Ferrero, D. (2006, May). Having it all. *Educational Leadership, 63*(8), 8–14.

Fiedler, F. (1967). *A theory of leadership effectiveness.* New York, NY: McGraw-Hill.

Fiedler, F., & Cherners, M. (1974). *Leadership and effective management.* Glenview, IL: Scott Foresman.

Fiedler, F., & Cherners, M. (1984). *Improving leadership effectiveness: The leader match concept.* New York, NY: Wiley.

Fiedler, F., & Garcia, J. (1987). *New approaches to effective leadership: Cognitive resources and organizational performances.* New York, NY: Wiley.

Fink, D., & Brayman, C. (2006, February). School leadership succession and the challenges of change. *Educational Administration Quarterly, 42*(1), 62–89.

Fink, E. (2002). Interview tape transcript conducted by L. Hubbard. San Diego, CA: University of San Diego, ELDA archives.

Firestone, W. A., & Gonzalez, R. A. (2007). Culture and processes affecting data use in school districts. In P. Moss (Ed.), *The 106th yearbook of the National Society for the Study of Education: Evidence and decision making* (pp. 132–153). Malden, MA: Blackwell Publishing.

Fisher, C., Duyer, D., & Yocam, K. (Eds.). (1996). *Education and technology.* San Francisco, CA: Jossey-Bass.

Flanary, R. A. (1997). Making your school a safe place for learning. *Schools in the Middle, 7*(20), 43–47.

Fleishman, E., & Hunt, J. (1973). *Current developments in the study of leadership.* Carbondale, IL: Southern Illinois University Press.

Follett, M. P. (1924). *Creative experience.* London, England: Longmans Green.

Follett, M. P. (1942). *Dynamic administration.* New York, NY: Harper.

Forsheri, P., & Molfino, M. T. (2000). ICT as a Tool for Learning to Learn. In D. Watson & T. Downes (Eds.). Communications and networking in education: learning in a networked society. Boston, MA: Kluwer Academic Publishing.

Foster, W. (1986). *Paradigms and promises: New approaches to educational administration.* Buffalo, NY: Prometheus Books.

Foster, W. (2004, April). The decline of the local: A challenge to educational leadership. *Educational Administration Quarterly, 40*(2), 176–191.

Frank, J. (1970). *Law and the modern man.* Gloucester, MA: Peter Smith. (Original work published 1930.)

Frankl, V. (1984). *Man's search for meaning.* New York, NY: Simon & Schuster. (Original work published 1949.)

Franklin, C., & Allen, P. (1997, July). School social workers are a critical part of the link. *Social Work in Education, 19*(2), 131–135.

Frase, L., English, F., & Poston, W. (1995). *The curriculum management audit: Improving school quality.* Arlington, VA: AASA.

Freeman, E. (2010). The shifting geography of urban education. *Education and Urban Society, 42*(6), 672–693.

Freire, P. (1973). *Pedagogy of the oppressed.* New York, NY: Seabury Press.

Freire, P. (1985). *The politics of education.* South Hadley, MA: Bergin and Garvey.

Friedman, T. L. (2006). *The world is flat: A brief history of the twenty-first century.* New York, NY: Farrar, Straus, and Giroux.

Fuhrman, S. H. (1994). Legislature and education policy. In R. F. Elmore & S. H. Fuhrman (Eds.), *The governance of curriculum*. Alexandria, VA: Association for Supervision and Curriculum Development.

Fullan, M. (1991). *The new meaning of educational change*. New York, NY: Teachers College Press.

Fullan, M. (1993). *Change forces*. Bristol, PA: Falmer Press.

Fullan, M. (1997). *What's worth fighting for in the principalship*. New York, NY: Teachers College Press.

Fullan, M. (2003). *Change forces: With a vengeance*. New York, NY: Routledge Falmer.

Fullan, M., & Hargreaves, A. (1992). *What's worth fighting for in your school*. New York, NY: Teachers College Press.

Fuller, E., Young, M., Barnett, B., Hirsch, E., & Byrd, A. (2007). Examining school leadership behavior. Paper presented at the 2007 UCEA annual conference, Alexandria, VA.

Furman, G. (2002). *School as community: From promise to practice*. New York, NY: State University of NY Press.

Furman, G., & Gruenewald, D. (2004, February). Expanding the landscape of social justice: A critical ecological analysis. *Educational Administration Quarterly, 40*(1), 49–78.

Garcia, V. (2006, Winter). High school students' perspectives on the 2001 No Child Left Behind Act's definition of a highly qualified teacher. *Harvard Educational Review, 76*(4), 698–724.

Gardenfors, P., & Johansson, P. (Eds.). (2005). *Cognition, education, and communication technology*. Mahwah, NJ: Lawrence Erlbaum Associates.

Gardiner, M., & Enomoto, E. (2006). Urban school principals and their roles as multicultural leaders. *Urban Education, 41*(6), 560–584.

Gardner, H. (1983). *Frames of mind: The theory of multiple intelligences*. New York, NY: Basic Books.

Gardner, H. (1991). *The unschooled mind: How children think and how schools should teach*. New York, NY: Basic Books.

Gardner, H. (1993). *Multiple intelligences: The theory in practice*. New York, NY: Basic Books.

Gardner, H. (2006). *Multiple intelligences: New horizons*. New York, NY: Basic Books.

Gardner, H., & Boix-Mansilla, V. (1994, February 7). Teaching for understanding—Within and across the disciplines. *Educational Leadership, 51*(5), 14–18.

Gardner, S. (1993). Key issues in developing school-linked, integrated services. *Education and Urban Society, 25*(2), 141–152.

Garnos, M. L., & King, R. A. (1994). Non-traditional sources of revenue: South Dakota's experience. *NASSP Bulletin, 78*(566), 27–38.

Gazda, G. M., Blazer, F. J., Childers, W. C., Nealy, A., Phelps, R. E., & Ealters, R. P. (2005). (7th Ed.). Human Relations Development: A Manual for Educators. Boston, MA: Allyn & Bacon.

Gee, W. (1997). The Copernican plan and year-round education: Two ideas that work together. *Phi Delta Kappan, 78*(10), 793–796.

Gerber, S. B. (1996, Fall). Extracurricular activities and academic achievements. *Journal of Research and Development in Education, 30*(1), 42–50.

Gerke, W. (2004). More than a disciplinarian. *Principal Leadership, 5*(3), 39–41.

Gerzon, M. (2006). Leading through conflict. *The School Administrator, 63*(10), 28–31.

Giangreco, M. F., Cloninger, C. J., & Iverson, V. S. (1993). *Choosing options and accommodations for children*. Baltimore, MD: Brookes.

Gill, B., Timpane, M., Rose, K., & Brewer, D. (2001). *Rhetoric versus reality: What we know and need to know about vouchers and charter schools* (MR-1118-EDU). Santa Monica, CA: RAND.

Gillette, J., & McCollom, M. (1995). *Groups in context: A new perspective on group dynamics*. New York, NY: University Press of America.

Gilligan, C. (1982, 1993). *In a different voice*. Cambridge, MA: Harvard University Press.

Ginsberg, B., Lowi, T., & Weir, M. (1995). *We the people*. New York, NY: Norton and Co.

Giroux, H. (1992). *Border crossings: Cultural workers and the politics of education*. New York, NY: Routledge.

Glass, T. E. (1992). *The study of the American school superintendency*. Arlington, VA: The American Association of School Administrators.

Glass, T. E. (2000, Fall/Winter). The politics of school board education. *The School Community Journal, 10*(2), 83–97.

Glass, T. E., Bjork, L., & Brunner, C. (2000). *The study of the American school superintendency 2000: The superintendency in the new millennium*. Arlington, VA: American Association of School Administrators.

Glatthorn, A. A. (1994). *Developing a quality curriculum*. Alexandria, VA: Association for Supervision and Curriculum Development.

Glatthorn, A. A. (1997). *The principal as curriculum leader: Shaping what is taught and tested*. Thousand Oaks, CA: Corwin Press.

Glickman, C. D. (1998). *Revolutionizing American schools*. San Francisco, CA: Jossey-Bass.

Glickman, C. D., Gordon, S. P., & Ross-Gordon, J. M. (2009). (8th Ed.) SuperVision and Instructional Leadership: A Developmental Approach. Upper Saddle River, NJ: Prentice-Hall.

Goerty, M. E., Floden, R. E., & O'Day, J. (1996, October). *Systematic reform*. Washington, DC: U.S. Office of Educational Research and Improvement.

Goldhammer, R. (1969). *Clinical supervision*. New York, NY: Holt, Rinehart & Winston.

Goldstein, J., Halverson, R., & Murphy, J. (2007). *Distributed leadership and power: Responses and new direction*. Paper presented at the 2007 UCEA annual conference, Alexandria, VA.

Goldstein, J., & Noguera, P. (2006, March). A thoughtful approach to teacher evaluation. *Educational Leadership, 63*(6), 31–37.

Good, T., Biddle, B., & Brophy, J. (1975). *Teachers make a difference*. New York, NY: Holt, Rinehart & Winston.

Goodlad, J. I. (1991). *Teachers for our nation's schools.* San Francisco, CA: Jossey-Bass.

Goodlad, J. I. (1994). *Educational renewal: Better teachers, better schools.* San Francisco, CA: Jossey-Bass.

Goodlad, J. I., & Lovitt, T. C. (Eds.). (1993). *Integrating general and special education.* New York, NY: Macmillan.

Goodwin, R. (2004). The changing principalship: A summary of the finds of the 2003 NCPEA Morphet Award Dissertation. *NCPEA Educational Leadership Review, 5*(1), 16–19.

Goodwin, R., Cunningham, M., & Childress, R. (2003, March). The changing role of the secondary school principal. *NASSP Bulletin, 87,* 26–42

Gordon, B. M. (1985). Toward emancipation in citizenship education: The case of African-American cultural knowledge. *Theory and Research in Social Education, 12,* 1–23.

Gould, S. J. (1981). *The mismeasure of man.* New York, NY: Norton.

Gould, S. J. (1995, November). The geometer of race. *Discover, 109,* 64–69.

Grant, C. A. (Ed.). (1992). *Research and multicultural education: From the margins to the mainstream.* London: Falmer Press.

Grant Foundation Commission on Work, Family, and Citizenship. (1988). *Citizenship through service.* Washington, DC: Grant Commission.

Gray, L., Thomas, N., Lewis, L., & Tice, P. (2010). *Educational technology in U.S. public schools: Fall 2008. Educational technology.* Washington, DC: National Center for Education Statistics.

Greenfield, T. B. (1978, Spring). Reflections on organizational theory and the truth of irreconcilable realities. *Educational Administration Quarterly, 14*(2), 1–23.

Greenfield, T. B. (1979). Ideas versus data: How can the data speak for themselves? In G. L. Immegart & W. L. Boyd (Eds.), *Problem-finding in educational administration.* New York, NY: Lexington Books.

Greenfield, T. B. (1980). The man who comes back through the door in the wall: Discovering truth, discovering self, discovering organizations. *Educational Administration Quarterly, 16*(3), 26–59.

Greenfield, T. B. (1985). Theories of educational organization: A critical perspective. In T. Husen & T. B. Greenfield (Eds.), *International encyclopedia of education.* Oxford, England: Pergamon Press.

Greenfield, T. B. (1988). The decline and fall of science in educational administration. In D. E. Griffiths, R. T. Stout, & P. B. Forsyth (Eds.), *Leaders for American schools.* Berkeley, CA: McCutchan.

Greenfield, T., & Ribbins, P. (Eds.). (1993). *Greenfield on educational administrations: Towards a humane science.* London, England: Routledge.

Greenfield, W. D. (1982). *A synopsis of research on school principals.* Washington, DC: National Institute for Education.

Greenfield, W. D. (1990). Five standards of good practice for the ethical administrator. *NASSP Bulletin, 74*(528), 32–37.

Greenfield, W. D. (1993). Articulating values and ethics in administrative preparation. In C. A. Capper (Ed.), *Educational administration in a pluralistic society.* Albany, NY: State University of New York Press.

Greenfield, W. D. (1995, February). Toward a theory of school administration: The centrality of leadership. *Educational Administration Quarterly, 31*(1), 61–85.

Greenhow, C., Robelia, B., & Hughes, J. (2009). Learning, teaching, and scholarship in a digital age. *Educational Researcher, 38*(4), 246–259.

Greenleaf, R. K. (1977). *Servant leadership: A journey into the nature of legitimate power and greatness.* New York, NY: Paulist Press.

Greenleaf, R. K. (1996). *On becoming a servant leader.* San Francisco, CA: Jossey-Bass.

Greifer, L. (2007, February). Technology standards. *Education Week, 26,* 45.

Griffiths, D. E. (1959). *Administrative theory.* New York, NY: Appleton-Century-Crofts.

Griffiths, D. E. (1979). Intellectual turmoil in educational administration. *Educational Administration Quarterly, 13*(3), 43, 65.

Griffiths, D. E., Stout, R. T., & Forsyth, P. E. (Eds). (1988). *Leaders for America's schools: The report and papers on the national commission on excellence in educational administration.* Berkeley, CA: McCutchan.

Grogan, M. (2000, February). Laying the groundwork for a reconception of the superintendency from feminist postmodern perspectives. *Education Administration Quarterly, 36*(1), 117–142.

Grogan, M. (2002). Guest editors' introduction: Leadership for social justice. *Journal of School Leadership, 12,* 112–115.

Grogan-Kaylor, A. (2004). The effect of corporal punishment on antisocial behavior in children. *Social Work Research, 28,* 154–163.

Gronn, P. (1984a). I have a solution. . . .: Administrative power in a school meeting. *Educational Administration Quarterly, 20*(2), 65–92.

Gronn, P. (2002). Distributed leadership as a unit of analysis. *Leadership Quarterly, 13,* 423–451.

Gronn, P. (2003). Leadership: Who needs it? *School Leadership and Management, 23*(3), 267–290.

Gronn, P., & Ribbins, P. (1996). Leaders in context: Postpositivist approaches to understanding educational leadership. *Educational Administration Quarterly, 32*(3), 452–473.

Grosso De León, A. (2006, Fall). The school leadership crisis: Have school principals been left behind? *Carnegie Reporter, 4*(1), 1–9.

Guarino, C., Sanlibarney, L., & Daley, G. (2006, Summer). Teacher recruitment and retention: A review of the recent empirical literature. *Review of Educational Research, 76*(2), 173–208.

Guba, E., & Lincoln, Y. (1989). *Fourth generation evaluation.* Thousand Oaks, CA: Sage.

Guba, E., & Lincoln, Y. (1994). Competing paradigms in qualitative research. In N. K. Denzin & Y. S. Lincoln (Eds.), *Handbook of qualitative research.* Thousand Oaks, CA: Sage.

Guskey, T. (2005, September). A historical perspective on closing the achievement gap. *NASSP Bulletin, 89*(644), 76–89.

Hall, G. E., & Hord, S. M. (1987). *Change in schools: Facilitating the process.* Albany, NY: State University of New York Press.

Hall, S. (2007). *Implementing response to intervention: A principal's guide.* Thousand Oaks, CA: Corwin Press.

Hallinan, M. (1979). Structural effects of children's friendships and cliques. *Social Psychology Quarterly, 42,* 54–77.

Hallinger, P. (2005). Instructional leadership and the school principal: A passing fancy that refuses to fade away. *Journal of Leadership and Policy in Schools, 4*(3), 221–239.

Hallinger, P., & Heck, R. (1998). Exploring the principal's contribution to school effectiveness: An assessment of methodological progress. Paper presented at the AERA, New York.

Hallinger, P., & Heck, R. (2000). *Exploring the principal's contribution to school effectiveness, 1980–1995.* Washington, DC: Institute of Educational Leadership.

Hallinger, P., & Murphy, J. (1987). Instructional leadership in the school context. In W. Greenfield (Ed.), *Instructional leadership: Concepts, issues, and controversies* (pp. 79–207). Boston, MA: Allyn & Bacon.

Hallinger, P., Bickman, L., & Davis, S. (1989). *What makes a difference? School context, principal leadership and student achievement.* Paper presented at the annual meeting of the American Educational Research Association, San Francisco, CA.

Halpin, A. W. (1956). *The leader behavior of school superintendents.* Columbus, OH: Ohio State University College of Education.

Halpin, A. W. (1966). *Theory and research in administration.* New York, NY: Macmillan.

Halverson, R. (2003). Systems of practice: How leaders use artifacts to create professional community in schools. *Educational Policy Analysis Archives, 11*(37), 1–35.

Hanson, E. M. (1979; 1991; 1996; 2003). *Educational administration and organizational behavior.* Boston, MA: Allyn & Bacon.

Hanushek, E. (2002). *The importance of school quality.* Stanford, CA: Hoover Press.

Hardage, J. G. (1978). *Development of an instrument to measure the task-centered and the internal state components of organizational health.* Unpublished doctoral dissertation. Fayetteville, AR: University of Arkansas.

Hargreaves, A., & Fullan, M. (1998). *What's worth fighting for out there?* New York, NY: Teachers College Press.

Hargreaves, A., & Goodson, I. (2006). Educational change over time? The sustainability and nonsustainability of three decades of secondary school change and continuity. *Educational Administration Quarterly, 42*(1), 3–41.

Harris, B., & Monk, B. J. (1992). *Personnel administration in education.* Boston, MA: Allyn & Bacon.

Harris, S., Petrie, G., & Willoughby, W. (2002, March). *NASSP Bulletin, 86*(630), 3–14.

Harry, B. (1992). *Cultural diversity, families, and the special education system.* New York, NY: Teachers College Press.

Harry, B., & Klingner, J. (2007). Discarding the deficit model. *Educational Leadership, 64*(5), 16–21.

Hart, A. (1993, August). Reflection: An instructional strategy in educational administration. *Educational Administration Quarterly, 29*(3), 39–63.

Hart, A. W. (1994). Creating teacher leadership roles. *Educational Administration Quarterly, 30*(4), 472–497.

Hart, A. W., & Bredeson, P. V. (1996). *The principalship: A theory of professional learning and practice.* New York, NY: McGraw-Hill.

Hartley, H. (1990). Boardroom bottom line. *American School Board Journal, 177*(2), 29–31.

Hattie, J. A. C. (2009). *Visible learning: A synthesis of over 800 meta-analyses relating to student achievement.* New York, NY: Routledge.

Haugland, S. (1992). The effect of computer software on preschool children's developmental gains. *Journal of Computing in Childhood Education, 3*(1), 15–30.

Health Insurance Association of America. (1986). *Wellness at the worksite: A manual.* Washington, DC: Author.

Healy, J. M. (1999, April). The mad dash to compute. *The School Administrator,* 6–10.

Heck, R., & Hallinger, P. (1999). Next generation methods for the study of leadership and school improvement. In J. Murphy & K. Seashore Louis (Eds.), *Handbook of research on educational administration* (pp. 141–162). San Francisco, CA: Jossey-Bass.

Heifetz, R. A. (1994). *Leadership without easy answers.* Cambridge, MA: Harvard University Press.

Heifetz, R. A., Linsky, M., & Grashow, A. (2009). *The Practice of Adaptive Leadership: Tools and Tactics for Changing Your Organization and the World.* Cambridge, MA: Harvard Business Press.

Heller, M. F., & Firestone, W. A. (1995). Who's in charge here? Sources of leadership for change in eight schools. *Elementary School Journal, 96*(1), 65–86.

Hemphill, J. K., & Coons, A. (1950). *Leadership behavior description.* Columbus, OH: Personnel Research Board, Ohio State University.

Henderson, A., & Mapp, K. (2002). *A new wave of evidence: The impact of school, family and community connections on student achievement.* Austin, TX: Southwest Education Development Laboratory.

Henderson, C., Buehler, W., Stein, W., Dalton, J., Robinson, T., & Anfara, V. (2005, September). Organizational health and student achievement in Tennessee middle level schools. *NASSP Bulletin, 89*(644), 54–75.

Henkin, A., & Dee, J. (2001, January). The power of trust: Teams and collective action in self-managed schools. *The Journal of School Leadership, 11*(1), 48–62.

Herman, J. J., & Herman, J. L. (1993). *School-based management: Current thinking and practice.* Springfield, IL: Charles C. Thomas.

Herman, J., Aschbacher, P., & Winters, L. (1992). *A practical guide to alternative assessment.* Alexandria, VA: Association for Supervision and Curriculum Development.

Herman, R., Aladjem, D., McMahon, P., Masem, E., Mulligan, I., O'Malley, A., . . . Woodruff, D. (1999). *An educator's guide to schoolwide reform.* Washington, DC: American Institutes for Research. Retrieved from http://www.eric.ed.gov/PDFS/ED460429.pdf

Hersey, P., & Blanchard, K. H. (1977; 1982) *Management of organizational behavior: Utilizing human resources.* Englewood Cliffs, NJ: Prentice Hall.

Hersey, P., & Blanchard, K. H. (1993). *Management of organizational behavior: Utilizing human resources* (6th ed.). Upper Saddle River, NJ: Prentice Hall.

Hersey, P., Blanchard, K., & Johnson, D. (1996). *Management of organizational behavior: Utilizing human resources* (7th ed.). Upper Saddle River, NJ: Prentice Hall.

Hess, F., & Meeks, O. (2010). Unbundling schools. *Phi Delta Kappan, V92*(3), 39–45.

Hewstone, M., & Brown, R. (Eds.). (1986). *Contact and conflict in intergroup encounters.* New York, NY: Basil Blackwell.

Higgins, S., Beauchamp, G., & Miller, D. (2007). Reviewing the literature on interactive whiteboards. *Learning, Media and Technology, 32*(3), 213–225.

Hill, M. S., & Raglan, J. C. (1995). *Women as educational leaders.* Thousand Oaks, CA: Corwin Press.

Hill, R. B. (1991). *The strengths of black families.* New York, NY: Emerson Hall.

Hirsch, E. D. (1996). *The schools we need: And why we don't have them.* New York, NY: Doubleday.

Hodgkinson, C. (1991). *Educational leadership: The moral art.* Albany, NY: State University of New York Press.

Hodgkinson, E. (1982). *Toward a philosophy of administration.* Oxford, MA: Blackwell.

Hodgkinson, H. L. (1993). Keynote address by Harold Hodgkinson. In S. Elarn (Ed.), *The state of the nation's public schools.* Bloomington, IN: Phi Delta Kappa.

Hodgkinson, H., & Montenegro, X. (1999). *The U.S. school superintendent: The invisible CEO.* Washington, DC: Institute for Educational Leadership.

Hofstede, G. (1991). *Cultures and organizations: Software of the mind.* London, England: McGraw-Hill.

Hofstede, G. J. & Minkov, M. 3rd Ed. (2010). *Cultures and Organizations: Software of the Mind.* New York: McGraw-Hill.

Hole, S., & McEntee, G. (1999). Reflection is at the heart of practice. *Educational Leadership Journal, 56*(8), 34–47.

Holland, A., & Andre, T. (1991). Is the extracurriculum an extra curriculum? *American Secondary Education Journal, 19*(2), 1–12.

Honig, M. (2003, August). Building policy from practice. *Educational Administration Quarterly, 39*(3), 305–338.

Hooper-Brian, K., & Lawson, H. A. (1994, October). *Serving children, youth, and families through interprofessional collaboration and service integration: A framework for action.* Philadelphia, PA: National Forum for the Danforth Foundation and the Institute for Educational Renewal at Miami University.

Horn, M. B., & Staker, H. C. (2011). The rise of k-12 blended learning. Innosight Institute, Inc. (www.innosightinstitute.org).

Horner, R., Sugai, G., & Horner, H. (2000, February). A school-wide approach to student discipline. *The School Administrator, 57*(2), 20–23.

Horvat, E., Weininger, E., & Lareau, A. (2003, Summer). From social ties to social capital: Class differences in the relations between schools and parent networks. *American Educational Research Journal, 40*(2), 391–351.

Hossell, C.H. (2005). Magnet Schools: No longer famous but still intact. Education Next. 5(2), 44–49.

Hottenstein, D., & Malatesta, C. (1993). Putting a school in gear with intensive scheduling. *High School Magazine, 2*, 23–29.

House, N. G. (2005, January). Reclaiming children left behind. *The School Administrator, 62*(1), 10.

House, R. (1971). A path-goal theory of leadership effectiveness. *Administration Science Quarterly, 16*, 321–339.

House, R., & Boetz, M. (1990). Leadership: Some empirical generalizations and new research directions. In B. Staw (Ed.), *Research in organizational behavior* (p. 219). Greenwich, CT: JAI Press.

Houston, P. D. (2000, December). A stake through the heart of high-stakes tests. *The School Administrator, 57*(11), 58.

Houston, P. D. (2006). Nearly famous. *The School Administrator, 63*(8), 52–53.

Hoy, W. K. (1994, May). Foundations of educational administration: Traditional and emerging perspectives. *Educational Administration Quarterly, 30*(2), 178–198.

Hoy, W. K., & Miskel, C. G. (1991; 1995; 2008). *Educational administration: Theory, research and practice.* New York, NY: McGraw-Hill.

Hoy, W. K., Tarter, C. J., & Hoy, A. (2006, Fall). Academic optimism for schools: A force for student achievement. *American Educational Research Journal, 43*(3), 425–446.

Hoyle, J. R., English, F. W., & Steffy, B. E. (1990). *Skills for successful school leaders* (2nd ed.). Arlington, VA: American Association of School Administrators.

HT Media Ltd. (2007). Senator Salazar releases results of Colorado statewide survey regarding no child left behind law. Retrieved from http://web.lexisnexis.com.proxy.lib.odu.edu

Hubbard, L. (2002). Transcript of interview with Elaine Fink, June 26, 2002. Educational Leadership Development Academy, University of San Diego.

Huerta, L., & Gonzalez, E. (2006). Cyber charter schools: Can accountability keep pace with innovation? *Phi Delta Kappan, 88*(1), 23–30.

Hughes, L. W., & Achilles, C. M. (1971). The supervisor as change agent. *Educational Leadership, 28*(8), 840–848.

Hymes, D. L., Chafin, A. E., & Gonder, P. (1991). *The changing face of testing and assessment.* Arlington, VA: American Association of School Administrators.

Iannoccone, L. (1978). *Public participation in local school districts.* Lexington, MA: Lexington Books.

IBM. (1992, June 22). *EduQuest: The journey begins.* Armonk, NY: IBM Educational Systems.

Industry Report 2000. (2000, October). The tech emergence. *Training, 37*, 10, 87–95.

Institute of Education Sciences. (2010). Crime, violence, discipline and safety in U.S. public schools. Washington, DC: U.S. Department of Education.

International Society for Technology in Education. (2000). *National education technology standards for students: Connecting curriculum and technology.* Eugene, OR: ISTE.

Ivey, G. (2002). Supporting literacy in the later years: It takes extended reading time and more to get a 12-year-old to enjoy reading. *Middle Matter, 1–2,* 6. Retrieved from http://www.edreadysearch.org/content/821/preview-naesp524_supportingliteracy inthelaterye.pdf

Jacobson, L. (July 15, 2004). Teacher Salary Gains Tempered By Health-Benefit Costs, Says AFT 23(42), page web only. Retrieved 12/3/11 http://www.educationweek.org

Janis, I. L., & Mann L. (1977). *Decision making: The psychological analysis of conflict, choice, and commitment.* New York, NY: Free Press.

Janson, C., Stone, C., & Clark, M. (2009). Stretching leadership: A distributed perspective for school counselor leaders. *Professional School Counseling, 13*(2), 98–106. doi:106.10.5330/PSC.n.2010-13.98

Jehl, J., & Kirst, M. (1992). Getting ready to provide school-linked services: What schools must do. In *The future of children* (2nd ed., pp. 95–106). Los Altos, CA: Center for the Future of Children.

Jerald, C., & Ingersoll, R. (2002). *All talk, no action: Putting an end to out-of-field teaching.* Washington, DC: The Education Trust.

Johns, B. H. (1998). Translating the new discipline requirements of the 1997 Individuals with Disabilities Education Act into practice. In L. M. Bullock & R. A. Gable (Eds.), *Implementing the 1997 IDEA: New challenges.* Reston, VA: Council for Exceptional Children.

Johnson, B., & Galvan, P. (1996). Conceptualizing school partnerships and inter-organizational relationships: A consideration of the public choice and organizational economics frameworks. In P. Cordeiro (Ed.), *Border crossings: Educational partnerships and school leadership.* San Francisco, CA: Jossey-Bass.

Johnson, D. W., & Johnson, R. (1975). *Learning together and alone.* Englewood Cliffs, NJ: Prentice Hall.

Johnson, S. M. (1990). *Teachers at work: Achieving success in our schools.* New York, NY: Basic Books.

Johnston, E. W. G. (1988). *Organizational health instrument: Technical manual.* Fayetteville, AR: Organizational Health Diagnostic and Development Corporation.

Joint Committee on Standards for Educational Evaluation. (1988). *The personnel evaluation standards: How to assess systems for evaluating educators.* Newbury Park, CA: Sage.

Jones, B. (2002). Recommendations for implementing internet projects. *Journal of Educational Technology Systems, 30*(3), 271–291.

Joyce, B., Weil, M., & Showers, B. (1992). *Models of teaching.* Boston, MA: Allyn & Bacon.

Kagan, S. L. (1991). *United we stand: Collaboration for children.* New York, NY: Teachers College Press.

Kanter, R. M. (1983). *The change masters.* New York, NY: Simon & Schuster.

Kaplan, D. S., Peck, B. M., & Kaplan, H. B. (1997, August). Decomposing the academic failure-dropout relationship: A longitudinal analysis. *Journal of Educational Research, 90*(6), 331–343.

Kaplan, L., & Owings, W. (1999, November). Assistant principals: The case for shared instructional leadership. *NASSP Bulletin, 83*(610), 80–94.

Kean, T. H. (1986, November). Who will teach? *Phi Delta Kappan, 18,* 205–208.

Keesor, C. (2005). Administrative visibility and its effect on classroom behavior. *NASSP Bulletin, 89*(693), 64–73.

Keith, N. (1996). A critical perspective on teacher participation in urban schools. *Educational Administration Quarterly, 32*(1), 45–79.

Keller, B. K. (1995). Accelerated schools: Hands-on learning in a unified community. *Educational Leadership, 52*(5), 10–13.

Kelley, C. (1999, October). Leveraging human and fiscal resources for school improvement. *Educational Administration Quarterly, 35*(4), 642–657.

Khan, B. (Ed.). (2001; 2004). *Web-based training.* Englewood Cliffs, NJ: Education Technology Publications.

Kilmann, R. (1989, October). A completely integrated program for creating and maintaining organizational success. *Organizational Dynamics,* 5–19.

Kimball, D. (2005). The cornerstone relationship between CEO and board president. *The School Administrator, 62*(1), 6–8.

Kimbrough, R. B., & Burket, C. W. (1990). *The principalship: Concepts and practices.* Englewood Cliffs, NJ: Prentice Hall.

King, A., Clements, J., Enns, J., Lockerbie, J., & Warren, W. (1975). *Semestering the secondary school.* Toronto, Canada: Ontario Institute for Studies in Education.

Kirby, D., & Lovick, S. (1987). School-based health clinics. *Educational Horizons, 5*(3), 139–143.

Kirby, S. N., Berends, M. & Naftel, S. (1999). Supply and Demand of Minority Teachers in Texas: Problems and Prospects. Educational Evaluation and Policy Analysis, 21, 47–66.

Kirsch, I., Braun, H., Yamamoto, K., & Sun, A. (January 2007) America's Perfect Storm: Three Forces

Changing our Nation's Future. Princeton, NJ: Educational Testing Service.

Kirst, M. (1994). A changing context means school board reform. *Phi Delta Kappan, 75*(5), 378–381.

Knapp, M., & Associates. (1995). *Teaching in high poverty classrooms.* New York, NY: Teachers College Press.

Knapp, M. S. (1995). How shall we study comprehensive, collaborative services for children and families? *Educational Researcher, 24*(4), 5–16.

Knickerbocker, J., & Rycik, J. (2006). Reexamining literature study in the middle grades: A critical response framework. *American Secondary Education, 34*(3), 43–56.

Kochan, F. K., Spencer, W., & Matthews, J. (2000). Gender-based perceptions of the challenges, changes, and essential skills of principalship. *Journal of School Leadership, 10*(4), 290–310.

Kotlowitz, A. (1991). *There are no children here: The story of two boys growing up in the other America.* New York, NY: Anchor Books.

Kottkamp, R. B. (1982). The administrative platform in administrator preparation. *Planning and Change, 13,* 82–92.

Kouzes, J., & Posner, B. (1993). *Credibility: How leaders gain and lose it, why people demand it.* San Francisco, CA: Jossey-Bass.

Kowalski, T., & Reitzug, U. (1993). *Contemporary school administration: An introduction.* New York, NY: Longman.

Kozol, J. (November, 2010). No half steps, no equivocation. *Educational Leadership, 68*(3), 28–30.

Kramer, S. L. (1997). What we know about block scheduling and its effects on math instruction, part II. *NASSP Bulletin, 81*(587), 69–82.

Kuiper, E., Volman, M., & Terwel, J. (2005, Fall). The Web as an information resource in K-12 education. *Review of Educational Research, 75*(3), 285–328.

LaMorte, M. W. (1999). *School law.* Boston, MA: Allyn & Bacon.

Land, D. (2002, Summer). Local school boards under review: Their role and effectiveness in relation to students' academic achievement. *Review of Educational Research, 72*(2), 229–278.

Lankford, M., Loeb, S., & Wyckoff, G. (2002). Teacher sorting and the plight of urban schools: A descriptive analysis. *Educational Evaluation and Policy Analysis, 24*(1), 37–62.

Lapan, R. T., Gysbers, N. C., & Petroski, G. F. (2001). Helping seventh graders be safe and successful in school: A statewide study of the impact of comprehensive guidance and counseling programs. *Journal of Counseling and Development, 79,* 320–330.

Lapan, R. T., Gysbers, N. C., & Sun, Y. (1997). The impact of more fully implemented guidance programs on the school experiences of high school students: A statewide evaluation study. *Journal of Counseling & Development, 75,* 292–302.

LaPointe, M., & Davis, S. (2006, September-October). Effective schools require effective principals. *Leadership, 36*(1), 16–38.

Larson, R., & Rader, T. (2006, May). Working together. *American School Board Journal, 193*(5), 32–33.

Lashway, L. (2006). The landscape of school leadership. In S. Smith & P. Piele (Eds.), *School leadership* (pp. 18–49). Thousand Oaks, CA: Corwin Press.

Lave, J., & Wenger, E. (1993). *Situated learning: Legitimate peripheral participation.* New York, NY: Cambridge University Press.

Lawler, E. E. (1986). *High involvement management.* San Francisco, CA: Jossey-Bass.

Lawler, E. E. (1992). *The ultimate advantage.* San Francisco, CA: Jossey-Bass.

Lawrence, T. E. (2011). The Seven Pillars of Wisdom (The Complete 1922 Text). Radford, VA: Wider Publications.

LeBlanc, P., & Shelton, M. (1997). Teacher leadership: The needs of teachers. *Action in Teacher Education, 19*(3), 32–48.

Leelawong, K., & Biswas, G. (2008). Designing learning by teaching agents: The Betty's Brain system. *International Journal of Artificial Intelligence in Education, 18*(3), 181–208.

Leithwood, K. (Ed.). (1995). *Effective school district leadership.* Albany, NY: State University of New York Press.

Leithwood, K. (1999). *Changing leadership for changing times.* Bristol, PA: Taylor & Francis.

Leithwood, K., Aitben, R., & Jantzi, D. (2001). *Making schools smarter: A system of monitoring school and district progress.* Thousand Oaks, CA: Corwin Press.

Leithwood, K., Begley, P., & Cousins, B. (1994). *Developing expert leadership for future schools.* Bristol, PA: Falmer.

Leithwood. K., Day, C., Sammons, P., Hopkins, D., & Harris, A. (2006, March 30). *Successful school leadership: What it is and how it influences student learning.* Toronto, Canada: Report to the Department for Education and Skills.

Leithwood, K., & Duke, D. (1994). A century's quest to understand school leadership. In J. Murphy & K. Seashore Louis (Eds.), *Handbook for research on educational administration.* San Francisco, CA: Jossey-Bass.

Leithwood, K., & Jantzi, D. (2005). A review of transformational school leadership research 1996–2005. *Leadership and Policy in Schools, 4*(5), 177–199.

Leithwood, K., & Jantzi, D. (2006). *Linking leadership to student learning: The contributions of leader efficacy.* Toronto, Canada: Ontario Institute of Studies in Education.

Leithwood, K., & Riehl, C. (2005). What do we know about educational leadership? In W. A. Firestone & C. Riehl (Eds.). A New Agenda for Research in Educational Leadership. New York: Teachers College Press.

Leithwood, K., Seashore Louis, K., Anderson, S., & Wahlstrom, K. (2004). *How leadership influences student learning.* Bloomington, MN: Center for Applied Research and Educational Improvement, University of Minnesota.

Leithwood, K. A. (1992, February). The move toward transformational leadership. *Educational Leadership, 49*(5), 8–12.

Leithwood, K. A. (1994). Leadership for school restructuring. *Educational Administration Quarterly, 30*(4), 498–518.

Leithwood, K. A., Steinback, R. S., & Raun, T. (1993). Superintendent's group problem-solving process. *Educational Administration Quarterly, 29*(3), 364–391.

Lemke, C., & Coughlin, E. C. (1998). *Technology in American schools: Seven dimensions for gauging progress. A policymaker's guide.* The Milken Exchange on Educational Technology. Retrieved from http://www.mff.org/publications/publications.taf?page=158

Lepsinger, R., & Yukl, G. (1995, December). How to get the most out of 360-degree feedback. *Training, 32*(12), 45–50.

Levin, K., Lippitt, R., & White, R. (1939). Patterns of aggressive behavior in experimentally created social climates. *Journal of Social Psychology, 10*(3), 43–195.

Levine, A. (2000, May). The private sector's market mentality. *The School Administrator, 57*(5), 6–12.

Levine, A. (2005). *Educating school leaders.* New York, NY: The Education School Project.

Levinson, B. (1996). Social difference and schooled identity at a Mexican *secundaria.* In B. Levinson, D. Foley, & D. Holland (Eds.), *The cultural production of .the educated person* (p. 370). Albany, NY: State University of New York Press.

Levinson, B., & Holland, D. (1996). The cultural production of the educated person: An introduction. In B. Levinson, D. Foley, & D. Holland (Eds.), *The cultural production of the educated person* (p. 370). Albany, NY: State University of New York Press.

Levy, E. H. (1948). An introduction to legal reasoning. *University of Chicago Law Review, 15,* 501–574.

Lewin, K. (1951). *Field theory in social science.* New York, NY: Harper & Row.

Lezotte, L. (1988a). Base school improvement on what we know about effective schools. *American School Board Journal, 176*(8), 18–20.

Lezotte, L. (1988b). Strategic assumptions of the effective school process. *Monographs on effective schools.* New York, NY: New York State Council of Educational Administration.

Lezotte, L. (1994). The nexus of instructional leadership and effective schools. *The School Administrator, 51*(6), 20–23.

Lezotte, L., Edmonds, R., & Ratner, G. (1974). *A final report: Remedy for school failure to equitably deliver basic school skills.* East Lansing, MI: Michigan State University Press.

Lieberman, A. (1991). *Early lessons in restructuring schools.* New York, NY: Teachers College, Columbia University.

Lieberman, A., & Miller, L. (2004). Teacher leadership. San Francisco, CA: Jossey-Bass.

Likert, R. (1967). *The human organization: Its management and value.* New York, NY: McGraw-Hill.

Lindblom, C. E. (1980). *The policy making process.* Englewood Cliffs, NJ: Prentice Hall.

Lindblom, C. E. (1995). *The intelligence of democracy.* New York, NY: Free Press.

Lindle, G., & Mawhinney, H. (2003, February). Introduction: School leadership and the politics of education. *Education Administration Quarterly, 39*(1), 3–9.

Lipman-Blumen, J. (1996). *The connective edge: Leading in an interdependent world.* San Francisco, CA: Jossey-Bass.

Lipsitz, J. (1984). *Successful schools for young adolescents.* New Brunswick, NJ: Transaction Books.

Lipsky, D., & Gartner, A. (2003). *Inclusion: A service, not a place—A whole school approach.* Port Chester, NY: National Professional Resources.

Little, J. W. (1986, September). The effective principal. *American Education, 72,* 3.

Liu, J. Q. (1997). The emotional bond between teachers & students. *Phi Delta Kappan, 79*(2), 156–157.

Lomotey, K. (1989). *African American principals: School leadership and success.* Westport, CT: Greenwood Press.

Loveless, T., & Jasin, C. (1998). Starting from scratch: Political and organizational challenges facing charter schools. *Educational Administration Quarterly, 34*(1), 9–30.

Lubienski, C. (2003, Summer). Innovation in education markets: Theory and evidence on the impact of competition and choice in charter schools. *American Education Research Journal, 40*(2), 395–443.

Lucas, C. J. (1978). *Development of an instrument to measure form dimensions of organizational health: Innovation, autonomy, adaptation, and problem-solving adequacy.* Unpublished doctoral dissertation, Fayetteville, AR: University of Arkansas.

Luna-Delgado, M. (2005). *Border pedagogy.* Paper presented at the 5th Annual Border Pedagogy Conference, University of San Diego, CA.

Lunenburg, F., & Ornstein, A. (1991). *Educational administration: Concepts and practices.* Belmont, CA: Wadsworth.

Luster, R., & McAdoo, H. P. (1994). Factors related to the achievement and adjustment of young African American children. *Child Development, 65,* 1080–1094.

Lynch, J. (2009). Print Literacy Engagement of Parents from Low-Income Backgrounds: Implications for Adult and Family Literacy Programs. Journal of Adolescent & Adult Literacy, 52(6), 509–521.

Macedo, D. (1994; 2005). *Literacies of power: What Americans are not allowed to know.* Boulder, CO: Westview Press.

Macedo, D. (2007). *Critical pedagogy in a corporate world.* Keynote speech, 7th Annual Border Pedagogy Conference, University of San Diego, CA.

Manatt, R. (1998, Spring), Teacher and administration performance: Benefits of 360-degree feedback. *Journal of Research and Information (ERS Spectrum), 16*(2), 18–23.

March, J. G., & Simon, H. A. (1959). *Organizations.* New York, NY: Wiley.

Markose, S., & Hellsten, M. (2009). Explaining success and failure in mainstream schooling through the lens of cultural continuities and discontinuities: two case studies. Language & Education: An International Journal, 23(1), 59–77.

Marks, H., & Printy, S. (2003, August), Principal leadership and school performance: An integration of transformational and instructional leadership. Educational Administration Quarterly, 39(3), 370–397.

Marshall, C., & Anderson, G. (1995). Rethinking the public and private spheres: Feminist and cultural studies perspectives on the politics of education. In J. D. Scribner & D. H. Layton (Eds.), The study of educational politics: The 1994 commemorative yearbook of the politics of education association (1969–1994) (pp. 169–182). Washington, DC: Falmer.

Marsick, V. J., & Watkins, K. (1999). Facilitating learning organizations: Making learning count. Aldershot, England: Grower Publishers.

Martin, I., Carey, J., & DeCoster, K. (2009). A national study of the current status of state school counseling models. Professional School Counseling, 12, 378–386.

Martin, J. R. (1993). The school home: Rethinking schools for changing families. Educational Leadership, 52(1), 25–31.

Martindale, T., Cates, W., & Qian, Y. (2003, November-December). Education web sites: A classification system for educators and learners. Education Technology, 43(6), 47–57.

Marx, E., Wooley, S., & Donica, B. (2006, February). A coordinated approach to health and learning. Principal 85(3), 12–15.

Maryland State Department of Education. (1978). The role of the elementary principal in program improvement. Baltimore, MD: Author.

Marzano, R., & Kendall, J. (1997). Curriculum frameworks. NASSP Bulletin, 81(590), 26–41.

Marzano, R. J., Waters, T., & McNulty, B. A. (2010). Schools that work. Alexandria, VA: Association for Supervisions and Curriculum Development.

Mathews, J. (2000, May 2). High-tech heretics: Group of skeptical educators questions the usefulness of computers in the classroom. The Washington Post, p. A11.

Matthews, J. (1994, January 19). Analysis of seven frameworks of educational leadership. Charlottesville, VA: National Policy Board for Educational Administration, 1–16.

McCarthy, B. (1997). About learning. Barrington, IL: Excel.

McCarthy, M., Cambron-McCabe, N., & Thomas, S. (1987). Public school law. Boston, MA: Allyn & Bacon.

McCarthy, M., Bull, B., Quantz, R., & Sorenson, G. (1993). Legal and ethical dimensions of schooling: Taxonomy and overview. New York, NY: McGraw-Hill.

McCarthy, M. M., & Webb, L. D. (2000, March). Legal principles in preventing and responding to school violence. NASSP Bulletin, 84(614), 33–45.

McChesney, J., & Hertling, E. (2000, April). The path to comprehensive school reform. Educational Leadership, 57(7), 10–15.

McCrummen, S. (2010). Some educators question if whiteboards, other high-tech tools raise achievement. The Washington Post. Washington, DC. Retrieved from http://www.washingtonpost.com/wp-dyn/content/article/2010/06/10/AR2010061005522.html

McDermott, K. (2000, Spring). Barriers to large-scale success models in urban reform. Education and Policy Analysis, 22(1), 85–89.

McGregor, D. (1960). The human side of enterprise. New York, NY: McGraw-Hill.

McKnight, J. L., & Kretzman, J. P. (1993). Mapping community capacity. Michigan State University Community and Economic Development Program Community News, 1–4.

McLaughlin, M. W., Irby, M. A., & Longman, J. (1994). Urban sanctuaries. San Francisco, CA: Jossey-Bass.

Mead, M. http://www.interculturalstudies.org/faq.html Institute for Intercultural Studies. Retrieved 12/1/11

Meadows, M. E. (1995). A preliminary program review of the four-period day as implemented in four high schools. Doctoral dissertation. College Park, MD: University of Maryland.

Meier, K., & Stewart, J. (1991). The politics of Hispanic education: Un paso Pa'lante y Dos Pa'tras. Albany, NY: State University of New York Press.

Meno, L. R. (1984). Sources of alternative revenue. In L. D. Webb & V. D. Mueller (Eds.), Fifth annual 1. Cambridge, England: Ballinger.

Merriam, S. B. (2001). The new update on adult learning theory. San Francisco, CA: Jossey-Bass.

Mertz, N. (1997a). Knowing and doing: Exploring the ethical life of educational leaders. In L. Beck & J. Murphy (Eds.), Ethics in educational leadership programs. Columbia, MO: UCEA.

Mertz, N. T. (1997b). Voices from the field: Principal perceptions. Presented at the 1997 Annual Conference of the University Council of Educational Administration, Orlando, FL.

Metcalf, H., & Urwick, L. (Eds.). (1941). Dynamic administration and the collected papers of Mary Parker Follett. New York, NY: Harper.

Meyer, H. H., Kay, E. E., & French, R. P. (1965, February). Split roles in performance appraisals. Harvard Business Review, 48(2), 196–241.

Mezirow, J. (1991). Transformative dimensions of adult learning. San Francisco, CA: Jossey-Bass.

Miles, M., & Louis, K. (1990, May). Mustering the will and skill for change. Educational Leadership, 47(8), 57–61.

Miller, B., Moon, J., & Elko, S. (2000). Teacher leadership in mathematics and science. New York, NY: Heinemann.

Miller, E. (1995, November-December). Shared decision making by itself doesn't make for better decisions. Harvard Education Letter, XI(6), 1–4.

Millman, J., & Darling-Hammond, L. (Eds.). (1990). *The new handbook of teacher evaluations: Assessing elementary and secondary school teachers.* Newbury Park, CA: Sage.

Mills, L. (2005). Organizing for technology support. *The School Administrator, 62*(4), 8–10.

Mintzberg, H. (1987, July-August). Crafting strategy. *Harvard Business Review, 65*(4), 66–75.

Mintzberg, H. (1989). *Mintzberg on management.* New York, NY: Free Press.

Moffett, J. (1994). *The universal schoolhouse: Spiritual awakening through education.* San Francisco, CA: Jossey-Bass.

Monroe, T. (2004). "Boundaries and Authority." In James McGregor Burns, George R. Goethals, and Georgia J. Sorenson (Eds.). Encyclopedia of Leadership. Thousand Oaks, CA: Sage, 112–117.

Morris, C. (1992, December). Pressure groups and the politics of education. *Updating School Board Policies, 23*(9), 1–5.

Mountford, M. (2004). Motives and power of school board members: Implications for school board superintendent relationships. *Educational Administration Quarterly, 40*(5), 704–741.

Moursund, D., & Bielefeldt, T. (1999). *Will new teachers be prepared to teach in a digital age?* Research report by International Society for Technology in Education. New York, NY: Milken Exchange on Educational Technology.

Muir, M. (2007). Research summary: Technology and learning. Retrieved from http://www.nmsa.org/Research/ResearchSummaries/Technologyand-StudentLearning/tabid/275/Default.aspx

Murphy, J. (1991). *Restructuring schools: Capturing and assessing the phenomena.* New York, NY: Teachers College Press.

Murphy, J. (1993). What's in? What's out? American education in the nineties. In S. Elam (Ed.), *The state of the nation's public schools* (pp. 55–56). Bloomington, IN: Phi Delta Kappan.

Murphy, J. (1999). New consumerism: Evolving market dynamics in the institutional dimension/schooling. In J. Murphy & K. Seashore Louis (Eds.), *Handbook of Research on Educational Administration* (pp. 405–420). San Francisco, CA: Jossey-Bass.

Murphy, J. (2005). *Connecting teacher leadership and school improvement.* Thousand Oaks, CA: Corwin Press.

Murphy, J. (2009). Closing achievement gaps: Lessons from the last 15 years. *Phi Delta Kappan, 91*(3), 8–12.

Murphy, J. (Ed.). (1993). *Preparing tomorrow's school leaders: Alternative designs.* University Park, PA: ULCA, Inc.

Murphy, J., & Beck, L. (1995). *School based management as school reform: Taking stock.* Newbury Park, CA: Corwin Press.

Murphy, J., & Hallinger, P. (Eds.). (1993). *Restructuring schooling: Learning from ongoing efforts.* Newbury Park, CA: Corwin Press.

Myrdal, G. (1944). *An American dilemma: The negro problem and modern democracy.* New York, NY: Harper & Brothers.

Nance, J. (2003, October). Public school administration and technology policy making. *Education Administration Quarterly, 39*(4), 434–467.

Nanus, B. (1992). *Visionary leadership.* San Francisco, CA: Jossey-Bass.

Nathan, J. (1996). *Charter schools.* San Francisco, CA: Jossey-Bass.

National Alliance for Public Charter schools (2011) retrieved, 11/28/11 http://dashboard.publiccharters.org/dashboard/schools/page/overview/year/2011.

National Archives and Records Administration (2007a). Congressional bills: Main page. Retrieved from http://www.gpoaccess.gov/bills/index.html

National Assessment Governing Board. (2004). *2004 12th grade achievement in America.* Washington, DC: NAGB/NAEP.

National Association of Secondary School Principals. (1996). *Breaking ranks: Changing an American institution.* Reston, VA: Author.

National Association of Secondary School Principals. (1998). *Assessment handbook.* Reston, VA: Author.

National Association of Secondary School Principals. (2003). *Measuring leadership: A guide to assessment for development of school executives.* Reston, VA: Author.

National Association of State Boards of Education. (1992). *Winners all: A call for inclusive schools.* Alexandria, VA: Author.

National Center for Education Statistics (NCES). (2003). Internet access in DS/public schools and classroom: 1994–2002. Retrieved from http://nces.ed.gov/pubs2001/200107.pdf

National Commission for Excellence in Teacher Education. (1985). *A call for change in teacher education.* Washington, DC: American Association of Colleges for Teacher Education.

National Commission on Children. (1991). *Beyond rhetoric: A new American agenda for children and families.* Washington, DC: U.S. Government Printing Office.

National Commission on Excellence in Education. (1983). *A nation at risk: The imperative of school reform.* Washington, DC: U.S. Office of Education.

National Commission on Teaching and America's Future. (1996). *What matters most: Teaching and America's future.* New York, NY: Author.

National Commission on the Role of the School and the Community in Improving Adolescent Health. (1990). *Code blue: Uniting for healthier youth.* Alexandria, VA: National Association of State Boards of Education and the American Medical Association.

National Education Goals Panel. (1991). *The national education goals report: Building a nation of learners.* Washington, DC: Author.

National Governors Association. (1986). *Time for results.* Washington, DC: Author.

National Governors Association. (2005). *American's high schools: The frontline in the battle for our economic future.* Washington, DC: Author.

National Research Council. (2002a). *Minority students in special and gifted education.* Washington, DC: National Academics Press.

National Research Council. (2002b). *Scientific research in education.* Washington, DC: National Academy Press.

National School Board Association. (1997). *Urban dynamics: Lessons learned from urban boards and superintendents.* Alexandria, VA: Author.

National School Board Association. (2006, February). Tough choices or tough times. *American School Board Journal, 193*(3), 6–8.

National Science Board. (1983). *Educating Americans for the twenty-first century.* Washington, DC: National Science Foundation.

National Teacher Training Institute (NITI). (2004, October). *Gains and gaps in education technology: An NEA survey educational technologies in U.S. schools.* Retrieved from http://www.eric.ed.gov/PDFS/ED495805.pdf

National Teacher Training Institute. (2007). On writing tests, computers slowly making mark. *Education Week, 26*(23), 10.

Negroponte, N. (1995). *Being digital.* New York, NY: Alfred A. Knopf.

Neil, R., Stoner, E., Bay, S., & Furstenberg, F. (2001). *Connecting entrance and departure: The transition to ninth grade and high school dropout.* Paper presented at Harvard Civil Right Project Conference. Retrieved from http://www.civilrightsproject.ucla.edu/

Neill, D. M. (1997, September). Transforming student assessment. *Phi Delta Kappan, 79*(1), 34–40.

Neill, M. (2003, February) High stakes, high risk: The dangerous consequences of high-stakes testing. *American School Board Journal, 190*(2), 18–21.

Neukrug, E. (2003). *The world of the counselor.* Pacific Grove, CA: Brooks/Cole.

Newmann, F. M., & Wehlage, G. (1993, April). Five standards of authentic instruction. *Educational Leadership, 50*(5), 8–12.

Nieto, S. (2000). *Affirming diversity: The sociopolitical context of multicultural education.* New York, NY: Longman.

Noddings, N. (1992). *The challenge to care in schools: An alternative approach to education.* New York, NY: Teachers College Press.

Norris, C. J. (1994). Cultivating creative cultures. In L. W. Hughes (Ed.), *The principal as leader* (p. 341). New York, NY: Macmillan.

Norris, J. H. (1994, Spring). What leaders need to know about school culture. *Journal of Staff Development, 15*(2), 10–26.

North Central Regional Educational Laboratory (NCREL). (1994). *Designing learning and technology for educational reform.* Elmhurst, IL: NCREL.

Northhouse, P. G. (1997). *Leadership: Theory and practice.* Thousand Oaks, CA: Sage.

Northwest Regional Educational Laboratory. (2000). *Catalog of school reform models* (2nd ed.). Portland, OR: Author. Retrieved from http://education northwest.org/news/1336

O'Callaghan, W., Jr., & Irish, C. (2006). The right place, the right time. *The School Administrator, 63*(2), 18–24.

OECD. (2011). Education at a Glance 2011: OECD Indicators. Paris, France: Organisation for Economic Co-operation and Development.

O'Day, J. (2004). Complexity, accountability, and school improvement. In S. H. Fuhrman & R. Elmore (Eds.), *Redesigning accountability systems for education* (pp. 15–46). New York, NY: Teachers College Press.

O'Donnell, R., & White, G. (2005, December). Within the accountability era: Principals' instructional leadership behaviors and student achievement. *NASSP Bulletin, 89*(645), 56–71.

O'Neil, G. (2000, April). Fads and fireflies: The difficulties of sustaining change: An interview with Larry Cubarn. *Educational Leadership, 57*(7), 6–9.

O'Neil, J. (2000, Summer). Integrating curriculum and technology. *Educational Leadership, 9*(4), 14–19.

O'Neil, R. (1995). On lasting school reform: A conversation with Ted Sizer. *Educational Leadership, 52*(5), 4–9.

Odden, A. R., & Wohlestetter, P. (1994). Making school-based management work. *Educational Leadership, 51*(6), 32–36.

Ogawa, R. (1991). Enchantment, disenchantment, and accommodating: How a faculty made sense of the succession of its principal. *Educational Administration Quarterly, 27*(1), 30–60.

Ogawa, R., & Bossert, S. (1995). Leadership as an organization property. *Educational Administration Quarterly, 31,* 224–243.

Ogbu, J. (1992). Understanding cultural diversity and learning. *Educational Researcher, 21*(8), 5–14.

Ophir, E., Nass, C., & Wagner, A. D. (2009). Cognitive control in media multitaskers. *Proceedings of the National Academy of Sciences of the United States of America, 106*(37), 15583–15587.

Oppenheimer, T. (1997, July). The computer delusion. *Atlantic Monthly.* Retrieved from http://www.theatlantic.com/past/docs/issues/97jul/computer.htm

Orfield, G., & Lee, C. (2006). Racial Transformation and the Changing Nature of Segregation. The Civil Rights Project, Harvard University.

Organisation for Economic Cooperation and Development. (2004). *Messages from PISA 2000.* Paris, France: Author meeting of the American Educational Research Association, San Francisco, CA.

Orr, M. (2006). *Innovative leadership preparation and effective leadership practices: Making a difference in school improvement.* Stanford, CA: Stanford Educational Leadership Institute.

Ouchi, W. (1981). *Theory Z.* Reading, MA: Addison-Wesley.

Ovando, M. (2004). Prospective school leaders' educational platform: A reflection prior to action tool. *NCPEA Educational Leadership Review, 5*(1), 33–40.

Owens, R. G. (1995). *Organizational behavior in education* (5th ed.). Boston, MA: Allyn & Bacon.

Owings, W., Kaplan, L., & Nunnery, J. (2005, January). Principal quality, ISLLC standards, and student achievement: A Virginia study. *Journal of School Leadership, 15*, 99–119.

Palmer, P. J. (1998). *The courage to teach: Exploring the inter-landscape of a teacher's life.* San Francisco, CA: Jossey-Bass.

Papa, R. P. (2010). *Technology leadership for school improvement.* Newbury Park, CA: Sage.

Papert, S. (1980). Teaching children thinking. In R. Taylor (Ed.), *The computer in school: Tutor, tool, tutee* (pp. 161–176). New York, NY: Teachers College Press.

Parker, L., & Shapiro, J. (1993). The context of educational administration and social class. In C. Capper (Ed.), *Educational administration in a pluralistic society.* Albany, NY: State University of New York Press.

Parsad, G., & Jones, B. (2005). Internet access in U.S. public schools and classrooms. Washington, DC: ERIC (#ED484400).

Pashler, H., McDaniel, M., Rohrer, D., & Bjork, R. (2009). Learning styles: Concepts and evidence. *Psychological Science, 9*(3), 105–119.

Payne, R. (1995). *A framework for understanding poverty.* Highlands, TX: RFT Publishing.

Payne, R. (2005). *A framework for understanding poverty.* Highlands, TX: Aha Process, Inc.

Payzant, T. W. (1992). New beginnings in San Diego: Developing a strategy for interagency collaboration. *Phi Delta Kappan, 74*(2), 139–146.

Payzant, T. W. (1994). Commentary on the district and school roles in curriculum reform: A superintendent's perspective. In R. F. Elmore & S. H. Fuhrman (Eds.), *The governance of curriculum* (p. 224). Alexandria, VA: Association for Supervision and Curriculum Development.

Pedersen, P. (1994). *A handbook for developing multicultural awareness.* Alexandria, VA: American Counseling Association.

Perkins, D., & Blythe, T. (1994, February). Putting understanding up front. *Educational Leadership, 51*(1), 4–7.

Perman, P., & McLaughlin, M. W. (1978, May). *Federal programs supporting educational change, volume VII: Implementing and sustaining innovation.* R-1589/8-HEW. Washington, DC: Department of Health, Education, and Welfare.

Perot, R. (1997). Caring leaders. In K. Shelton (Ed.), *A new paradigm of leadership* (pp. 237–240). Provo, UT: Executive Excellence.

Perry, N., Kay, S., & Brown, A. (2008). Continuity and change in home literacy practices of Hispanic families with preschool children. Early Child Development & Care, 178(1), 99–113.

Peters, T. (1987). *Thriving on chaos: Handbook for management revolution.* New York, NY: Knopf.

Peters, T. (1994). *The pursuit of wow!* New York, NY: Vintage Books.

Peters, T. (1997). *The circle of innovation.* New York, NY: Knopf.

Peters, T. J., & Austin, N. (1985). *A passion for excellence: The leadership difference.* New York, NY: Random House.

Peters, T. J., & Waterman, R. H. (1982). *In search of excellence: Lessons from America's best-run companies.* New York, NY: Harper & Row.

Peterson, G., & Dlugosh, L. (2007). *Insulted into reform: The influence of No Child Left Behind on the professional life of the district superintendent.* Paper presented at the annual meeting of UCEA. Washington, DC: November 17, 2007.

Peterson, K. (1978). The principal's tasks. *Administrators Notebook, 26*, 1–4

Phinney, J. (1993). A three-stage model of ethnic identity development in adolescence. In M. Bernal & G. Knight (Eds.), *Ethnic identity* (p. 280). Albany, NY: State University of New York Press.

Pollard-Durodola, S. (2003, November,). Wesley Elementary: A beacon of hope for at-risk students. *Education and Urban Society, 36*(1), 94–117.

Ponder, G., & Stranham, D. (2005). *Deep change.* Washington, DC: IAP.

Popham, W. J. (1997). The standards movement and the emperor's new clothes. *NASSP Bulletin, 81*(590), 21–25.

Popham, W. J. (2003, February). Trouble with testing. *American School Board*, 14–17.

Popham, W. J. (2010). *Everything school leaders need to know about assessment.* Thousand Oaks, CA: Corwin Press.

Porter, A., McMaken, J., Hwang, J., & Yang, R. (2011) Common Core Standards; The New US Intended Curriculum. Educational Researcher, 40(7) 103–116.

Portin, B. S. (1997, November 1). *Complexity and capacity: A survey of principal role change in Washington state.* Paper presented at UCEA annual meeting, Orlando, FL.

Portin, B., Schneider, P., DeArmond, M., & Gundlah, L. (2003). *Making sense of leading schools.* Center on Reinventing Public Education, University of Washington.

Postman, N. (1995). *The end of education: Redefining the value of school.* New York, NY: Knopf.

Poston, W. K. (2010). *School budgeting for hard times.* Thousand Oaks, CA: Corwin Press.

Pounder, D. (1999, August). Teacher teams: Exploring job characteristics and work-related outcomes of work group enhancement. *Educational Administration Quarterly, 35*(3), 317–348.

Pounder, D., & Crow, G. (2005). Sustaining the pipeline of school administrators. *Educational Leadership, 62*(8), 56–60.

Pounder, D., & Merrill, R. (2001). Job desirability of the high school principalship: A job choice theory perspective. *Education Administration Quarterly, 37*(1), 27–57.

Pounder, D., Ogawa, R., & Adams, E. (1995). Leadership as an organization-wide phenomena: Its impact on school performance. *Educational Administration Quarterly, 31*(4), 564–588.

Pounder, D., Reitzug, V., & Young, M. (2002). Preparing school leaders for school improvement, social justice, and community. In J. Murphy (Ed.), *The educational leadership challenge: Redefining leadership for the 21st century*. One hundred-first yearbook of the National Society for the Study of Education. Chicago, IL: National Society for the Study of Education.

Prenksy, M. (2001). Digital natives, digital immigrants. *On the Horizon, 9,* 5, 1–6.

President's Committee of Advisors on Science and Technology. (1997, March). *Report to the president on the use of technology to strengthen K–2 education in the United States.* Washington, DC: Panel on Educational Technology.

Prestine, N. (1991). Political system theory as an explanatory paradigm for teacher education reform. *American Education Research Journal, 23*(2), 237–274.

Prestine, N. A. (1995). A constructivist view of the knowledge base in educational administration. In R. Donmoyer, M. Imber, & J. Scheurich (Eds.), *The knowledge base in educational administration* (p. 326). Albany, NY: State University of New York Press.

Price, W. (2001, February). Policy governance revisited (school boards vs. superintendents). *The School Administrator 58*(2), 46–50.

Public Education Network. (2007). No Child Left Behind: Everything you wanted to know about NCLB: The one-stop resource for community and parent leaders. Retrieved from http://www.publiceducation.org/nclb_main/index.asp

Purkey, S., & Smith, M. S. (1982, December). Too soon to cheer? Synthesis of research on effective schools. *Educational Leadership, 82*(3), 64–69.

Purkey, W. W., & Novak, J. M. (1984). *Inviting school success* (2nd ed.). Belmont, CA: Wadsworth.

Putman, R. D. (1996, Winter). The strange disappearance of civic America. *The American Prospect, 24,* 34–48.

Quigley, M. (1997). Leader as learner. In K. Shelton (Ed.), *A new paradigm of leadership* (pp. 93–96). Provo, UT: Executive Excellence.

Quin, T. (2002) *Succession planning.* Reston, VA: The National Association of Secondary School Principals.

Raferty, J. R. (1992). *Land of fair promise.* Palo Alto, CA: Stanford University Press.

Ragan, S., & Reid, J. (2009) Invest in early childhood education. *Phi Delta Kappan, 90*(8), 571–584.

Ramirez, A., & Carpenter, D. (2009). The matter of dropouts. *Phi Delta Kappan, 90*(9), 656–670.

Ramirez, M., & Casteñeda, A. (1974). *Cultural democracy, bicognitive development and education.* New York, NY: Academic Press.

Ravitch, D. (1995). *National standards in American education.* Washington, DC: Brookings Institution Press.

Ravitch, D. (March, 2010). Why public schools need democratic governance. *Phi Delta Kappan, 91*(6), 23–27.

Razik, T. A., & Swanson, A. D. (1995). *Fundamental concepts of educational leadership and management.* Englewood Cliffs, NJ: Prentice Hall.

Reagan, B. R. (1981, July). *Teacher shortages in Texas.* Presentation at the AASA Summer Instructional Leadership Conference, Washington, DC.

Rebore, R. W. (1998). *Personnel administration in education: A management approach.* Boston, MA: Allyn & Bacon.

Rebore, R. W. (2001). *The ethics of educational leadership.* Upper Saddle River, NJ: Merrill Prentice Hall.

Reeves, D. B. (2000, December). Caught in the middle: State accountability requirements, teacher independence, and local school board policy. *American School Board Journal, 87*(12), 25–27.

Reeves, D. B. (2003). High Performance in High Poverty Schools: 90/90/90 and Beyond. Center for Performance Assessment. www.makingstandardswork.com

Reeves, D. (2007). *Assessing educational leaders: Evaluating performance for improved individual and organizational results.* San Francisco, CA: Sage.

Regan, H. (1990). Not for women only: School administration as a feminist activity. *Teachers College Record, 91*(4), 565, 577.

Reich, R. (1997). *Keynote speech: Employment in the twenty-first century conference.* Pittsburgh, PA: University of Pittsburgh and Carnegie Mellon University.

Reid, W. M. (1995). *Restructuring secondary school with extended time blocks and intensive courses: The experiences of school administrators in British Columbia.* Dissertation Abstracts. Spokane, WA: Gonzaga University.

Reith, K. M. (1989, Winter). Minority athletes: Study breaks stereotypes. *National Coach, 25*(2), 36.

Revenaugh, M. (2006, January). K–8 virtual schools: A glimpse into the future. *Educational Leadership, 63*(4), 60–64.

Reyes, P., & Scribner, J. D. (1999). Creating learning communities for high performing Hispanic students: A conceptual framework. In P. Reyes, J. D. Scribner, & A. P. Scribner (Eds.), *Lessons from high performing Hispanic schools: Critical issues in educational leadership series.* New York, NY: Teachers College Press.

Rhodes, L. A. (1997, January). *Connecting leadership and learning.* A position paper for the American Association of School Administrators. Arlington, VA: American Association of School Administrators.

Richards, A. (2000). Panel call for fresh look at duties facing principals. *Education Week.* Retrieved from http://www.edweek.org/ew/articles/2000/11/01/09iel.h20.html

Richardson, J. (2009). "Quality education is our moon shot": An interview with Secretary of Education Arne Duncan. *Phi Delta Kappan, 91*(1), 24–30.

Richardson, M. D. (1988, June). *The administrative assessment center.* Presented at the Kentucky Association of School Superintendent Annual Conference. Louisville, KY. ED 301–930.

Richardson, W. (2006). *Blogs, wikis, podcasts, and other powerful web tools for classrooms.* Thousand Oaks, CA: Corwin Press.

Ritter, S., Anderson, J. R., Koedinger, K. R., & Corbett, A. (2007). Cognitive tutor: Applied research in mathematics education. *Psychonomic Bulletin & Review, 14*(2), 249–255.

Rivero, V. (2006, June). Teaching with technology: The secrets of their success. *T.H.E. Journal, 33*(11), 44–47.

Robbins, H., & Finley, M. (1995). *Why teams don't work: What went wrong and how to make it right.* Princeton, NJ: Pacesetter Books.

Robinson, V. (1996). Problem-based methodology and administrative practice. *Educational Administration Quarterly, 32*(3), 427–451.

Roethlisberger, F., & Dixon, W. (1939). *Management and the worker.* Cambridge, MA: Harvard University Press.

Rogers, E. M. (1995). *Diffusion of innovations.* New York, NY: Free Press.

Romo, J. J. (2005). *Lives of teachers on the border.* Paper presented at the 5th Annual Border Pedagogy Conference, University of San Diego, CA.

Rosaldo, R. (1989). *Culture and truth: The remaking of social analysis.* Boston, MA: Beacon Press.

Rost, J. C. (1993). Leadership for the Twenty-First Century. Westport, CT: Praeger Publishing.

Rotherham, A., & Mead, S. (2003, June). Teacher quality: Beyond No Child Left Behind. A response to Kaplan and Owings. *NASSP Bulletin, 87*(635), 165–176.

Rubinstein, J. S., Meyer, D. E., & Evans, J. E. (2001). Executive control of cognitive processes in task switching. *Journal of Experimental Psychology: Human Perception and Performance, 27*(4), 763–779.

Ruskin, K. B., & Achilles, C. M. (1995). *Grantwriting, fundraising and partnerships: Strategies that work!* Thousand Oaks, CA: Corwin Press.

Rutter, M., Maughan, B., Mortimore, P., Ouston, J., & Smith, A. (1979). *Fifteen thousand hours: Secondary schools and their effects on children.* Cambridge, MA: Harvard University Press.

Sagor, R., & Barnett, B. G. (1994). *The TQE principal: A transformational leader.* Thousand Oaks, CA: Corwin Press.

Salend, S., Duhaney, L., & Montgomery, W. (2002). A comprehensive approach to identifying and addressing issues of disproportionate representation. *Remedial and Special Education, 23*(5), 289–299.

Salmonowicz, M. (2009). Meeting the challenge of school turnaround: Lessons from the intersection of research and practice. *Phi Delta Kappan, 91*(3), 19–24.

Sanders, K. P., & Theimann, F. C. (1990). Student costing: An essential tool in site-based budgeting and teacher empowerment. *NASSP Bulletin, 74*(523), 95–102.

Sarason, S. B. (1996). *Barometers of change: Individual educational social transformation.* San Francisco, CA: Jossey-Bass.

Sashkin, M., & Walberg, H. (1993). *Educational leadership and school culture.* Berkeley, CA: McCutchan.

Sayers-Kirsch, S. (1985). Understanding behavioral style. *NREL Behavioral Matrix.* Portland, OR: Northwest Regional Education Laboratory.

Schacter, J. (1995). *The impact of educational technology on student achievement.* The Milken Exchange on Educational Technology. Retrieved from http://www.mff.org/publications/publications.taf?page=161

Schacter, J. (1999). *The impact of educational technology on student achievement: What the most current research has to say.* Santa Monica, CA: Milken Exchange on Educational Technology.

Scharmer, C. O. (2009). Theory U: Leading from the Future as It Emerges. San Francisco, CA: Berrett-Koehler Publishers.

Schein, E. (1985; 1991). *Organizational culture and leadership.* San Francisco, CA: Jossey-Bass.

Schewick, J., & Skrla, L. (2003). *Leadership for equity and excellence.* Thousand Oaks, CA: Corwin Press.

Schewick, J. J., & Young, M. D. (1997, May). Coloring epistemologies: Are our research epistemologies racially biased? *Educational Researcher, 26*(4), 4–16.

Schlechty, P. C. (1990). *Schools for the twenty-first century.* San Francisco, CA: Jossey-Bass.

Schmidt, W. (April 2010). Are national standards the right move? *Educational Leadership, 67*(7), 24–25.

Schmitt, N., Noe, R., Meritt, R., Fitzgerald, M., & Jorgensen, C. (1983). *Criterion-related and content validity of the NASSP assessment center.* Reston, VA: National Association of Secondary School Principals.

Schmoker, M. (1996). *Results: The key to continuous school improvement.* Alexandria, VA: Association for Supervision and Curriculum Development.

Schoenstein, R. (1995). The new school on the block. *Executive Educator, 17*(8), 18–21.

Schön, D. (1983). *The reflective practitioner: How professionals think in action.* New York, NY: Basic Books.

School Health Resource Services, Office of School Health. (1995). *School-based health centers: Recommended services.* Denver, CO: University of Colorado Health Sciences Center Resource Packet Series. [Available by writing: 4200 E. 9th Ave./Box C287, Denver, CO 80262 or calling (303) 270-5990.]

School Health Resource Services, Office of School Health. (1995). *School-based clinics that work.* Denver, CO: University of Colorado Health Sciences Center Resource Packet Series.

School Health Resource Services, Office of School Health. (1995). *State initiative to support school-based health centers.* Denver, CO: University of Colorado Health Sciences Center Resource Packet Series.

Schwartz, W. (1995). *School dropouts: New information about an old problem.* Washington, DC: Office of Educational Research and Development. EDO-OD-96-5.

Scott, W. R. (1992). *Organizations.* Englewood Cliffs, NJ: Prentice Hall.

Scribner, J., Sawyer, R., & Watson, S. (2007). Teacher teams and distributed leadership: A study of group discourse and collaboration. *Educational Administration Quarterly, 43*(1), 67–100.

Scribner, J. P., Aleman, E., & Maxcy, B. (2003, February). Emergence of the politics of education field: Making sense of the messy center. *Education Administration Quarterly, 39*(1), 10–40.

Sears, S. J., & Coy, D. R. (1991). The scope of practice of the secondary school counselor. Washington, DC: ERIC Clearinghouse on Counseling and Personnel Services. ED 328830.

Senge, P., Cambron-McCabe, N., Lucas, T., Smith, B., Button, J., & Kleiner, A. (2000). *Schools that learn.* New York, NY: Doubleday Dell Publishing Group.

Senge, P. M. (1990). *The fifth discipline: The art and practice of learning organization.* New York, NY: Doubleday Currency.

Senge, P., Scharmer, C. O., Jaworski, J., & Flowers, B. S. (2005). Presence: An Exploration of Profound Change in People, Organizations, and Society. NEW YORK: Crown Business.

Sergiovanni, T. J. (1992a). *Moral leadership: Getting to the heart of school reform.* San Francisco, CA: Jossey-Bass.

Sergiovanni, T. J. (1992b, February). Why we should seek substitutes for leadership. *Educational Leadership, 49*(5), 41–45.

Sergiovanni, T. J. (1994, May). Organizations or communities? Changing the metaphor changes the theory. *Educational Administration Quarterly, 30*(2), 214–226.

Sergiovanni, T. J. (2001). *The principalship: A reflective practice perspective.* Boston, MA: Allyn & Bacon.

Sergiovanni, T. J., & Starratt, R. J. (1998; 2001). *Supervision: Human perspectives.* New York, NY: McGraw-Hill.

Shah, N. (April 20, 2011). Arizona creates vouchers for special ed. students. *Education Week,* p. 4.

Shakeshaft, C. (1995). A cup half full: A gender critique of the knowledge base in educational administration. In R. Donmoyer, M. Imber, & J. Scheurich (Eds.), *The knowledge base in educational administration* (p. 323). Albany, NY: State University of New York Press.

Shapiro, J. P., & Stefkovich, J. (1997). Preparing ethical leaders for equitable schools. In L. Beck & J. Murphy (Eds.), *Ethics in educational leadership programs.* Columbia, MO: UCEA.

Shapiro, J. P., & Stefkovich, J. (2010). (3rd. Ed.) Ethical Leadership and Decision Making in Education: Applying Theoretical Perspectives to Complex Dilemmas. New York: Routledge.

Sharp, W. (1994). Seven things a principal should know about school finance. *NASSP Bulletin, 78*(566), 1–5.

Sheldon, S. (2003). Linking school-family-community partnerships in urban elementary schools to student achievement on state tests. *Urban Review, 35*(2), 149–165.

Shen, J. (1997, October). The evolution of violence in schools. *Educational Leadership, 55*(2), 18–22.

Shen, J., Cooley, V., & Wegenke, G. (2004). Perspectives on factors influencing application for the principalship: a comparative study of teachers, principals and superintendents. International Journal of Leadership in Education, 7(1), 57–70.

Shen, J., & Crawford, C. (2003, March). Introduction to the special issue: Characteristics of the secondary principalship. *NASSP Bulletin, 87*(634), 2–8.

Sherrill, J. (1999). Preparing teachers for leadership roles. *Theory Into Practice, 38,* 56–67.

Sherrod, M., Getch, Y. Q., & Ziomek-Daigle, J. (2009). The impact of positive behavior support to decrease discipline referrals with elementary students. *Professional School Counseling, 12*(6), 421–427. Retrieved from http://www.thefreelibrary.com/The+impact+of+positive+behavior+support+to+decrease+discipline...-a0206850820

Shoop, R. J., & Dunklee, D. J. (1992). *School law for the principal.* Boston, MA: Allyn & Bacon.

Shoop, R. J., & Sparkman, W. (1983). *Kansas school law.* Dubuque, IA: Bowers.

Short, P. M., & Green, J. T. (1997). *Leadership in empowered schools.* Upper Saddle River, NJ: Prentice Hall.

Shorten, A. R. (1996). Law and the courts. In K. Leithwood, J. Chapman, D. Corson, P. Hallinger, & A. Hart (Eds.), *The international handbook of educational leadership and administration.* Boston, MA: Kluwer Academic.

Shreeve, J. (1994). Terms of estrangement. *Discover, 108,* 57–63.

Simmons, R. (1994). The horse before the cart: Assessing for understanding. *Educational Leadership 51*(5), 22–23.

Simon, H. (1960). *The new science of management decision.* New York, NY: Harper & Row.

Simon, H. A. (1947; 1976). *Administrative behavior* (4th ed.). New York, NY: Macmillan.

Singh, J. V., Tucker, D. J., & House, R. J. (1986). Organizational legitimacy and the liability of newness. *Administrative Science Quarterly, 31,* 171–193.

Sink, C. A., & Stroh, H. R. (2003). Raising achievement test scores of early elementary school students through comprehensive guidance and counseling programs. *Professional School Counseling, 6*(5), 350–365.

Sirotnik, K., & Oakes, J. (Eds.). (1986). *Critical perspectives on the organization and improvement of schooling.* Boston, MA: Kluwer-Nijhoff.

Sizer, T. R. (1996). *Horace's hope: What works for the American high school.* Boston, MA: Houghton Mifflin.

Slater, R. O. (1994). Symbolic educational leadership and democracy in America. *Educational Administrative Quarterly, 30*(1), 97–101.

Slavin, R. (1990). *Cooperative learning: Theory, research, and practice.* Englewood Cliffs, NJ: Prentice Hall.

Slavin, R. (1996). Cooperative learning in middle and secondary schools. *Clearinghouse, 69*(4), 200–204.

Slavin, R. E., & Fashola, O. S. (1998). *Show me the evidence!* Thousand Oaks, CA: Corwin Press.

Slavin, R. E., Madden, N. A., Dolan, L. J., & Waskik, B. A. (1996). *Every child. Every school: Success for all.* Thousand Oaks, CA: Corwin Press.

Sleeter, C., & Grant, C. (1993). *Making choices for multicultural education: Five approaches to race, class and gender.* New York, NY: Merrill.

Slosson, J. (1999, October). Hiring the right people. *The High School Magazine, 7*(2), 20–32.

Smith, H. J., Higgins, S., Wall, K., & Miller, J. (2005). Interactive whiteboards: Boon or bandwagon? A critical review of the literature. *Journal of Computer Assisted Learning, 21*(2), 91–101.

Smith, W. F., & Andrews, R. L. (1989). *Instructional leadership: How principals make a difference.* Alexandria, VA: Association for Supervision and Curriculum Development.

Smylie, M., & Brownlee-Conyers, T. (1992). Teacher leaders and their principals. *Educational Leadership, 28*(2), 150–184.

Smylie, M., & Hart, A. (1999). School leadership for teacher learning and change: A human and social capital development perspective. In J. Murphy & K. Seashore Louis (Eds.), *Handbook for research on educational administration* (pp. 421–443). San Francisco, CA: Jossey-Bass.

Solomon, B., & Preis, S. (2006). *School board relationships, roles, and effectiveness: A case study.* Paper presented at the VCEA Annual Convention, San Antonio, TX.

Soltero-Gonzalez, L. (2009). Preschool Latino Immigrant Children: Using the Home Language as a Resource for Literacy Learning. Theory Into Practice, 48(4), 283–289.

Solomon, R. P. (1992). *Black resistance in high school.* Albany, NY: State University of New York Press.

Soto, O. R. (2004, August 22). Officials had feared violence at high school. *San Diego Union Tribune*, B3.

Sousa, D. (2005). *How the brain learns to read.* Thousand Oaks, CA: Corwin Press.

Sparks, D. (1997, September). A new vision of staff development. *Principal, 77*(1), 20–22.

Spartz, J., Valdes, A., McCormick, W., Meyers, J., & Geppert, W. (1977). *Delaware educational accountability system case studies: Elementary schools grade 1–4.* Dover, DE: Delaware Department of Public Instruction.

Spillane, J. (2006). *Distributed leadership.* San Francisco, CA: Jossey-Bass.

Spillane, J., Halverson, R., & Diamond, G. (2001). Investigating school leadership practices: A distributed perspective. *Educational Research, 30*(3), 23–28.

Spillane, J., Sherer J., & Coldreu, A. (2005) Distributed leadership: Leadership practice and the situation. In W. Hoy & C. G. Miskel (Eds.). *Educational leadership and reform.* Greenwich, CT: InformationAge.

Spring, J. (1998). *Conflict of interests: The politics of American education.* Boston, MA: McGraw-Hill.

SREB. (2010). *The three essentials: Improving schools requires district vision, district and state support, and principal leadership.* New York, NY: The Wallace Foundation.

Sredl, H. G., & Rothwell, W. J. (1987). *Professional training roles and competencies—Volume I.* New York, NY: Random House.

Stallings, J. (1980). Allocated academic learning time revisited, or beyond time on task. *Educational Researcher, 9*, 11–16.

Starratt, R. J. (1991). Building an ethical school: A theory for practice in educational leadership. *Educational Administration Quarterly, 27*(2), 185–202.

Starratt, R. J. (1994). *Building an ethical school: A practical response to the moral crisis in schools.* London: Falmer Press.

Starratt, R. J. (1996). *Transforming educational administration: Meaning, community and excellence.* New York, NY: McGraw-Hill.

State News Service. (2007). No Child Left Behind Act: Five years of results for America's children. Retrieved from http://georgewbush-whitehouse.archives.gov/news/releases/2007/01/20070108-6.html

Stedman, L. (1987). It's time we change the effective schools formula. *Phi Delta Kappan, 69*(3), 215–224.

Steinberg, E. D. (1995, January 6). Margaret Wheatley on leadership for change. *School Administration, 52*(1), 16–20.

Sternberg, R. (1996a). IQ counts, but what really counts is successful intelligence. *NASSP Bulletin, 80*(583), 18–23.

Sternberg, R. (1996b). *Successful intelligence.* New York, NY: Simon & Schuster.

Sternberg, R., & Caruso, O. (1985). Practical modes of knowing. In E. Eisner (Ed.), *Learning and teaching the ways of knowing* (NSSE Yearbook) (pp. 133–158). Chicago, IL: University of Chicago Press.

Sternberg, R., & Frensch, P. (1993). Mechanism of transfer. In D. Detterman & R. Sternberg (Eds.), *Transfer on trial: Intelligence, cognition, and instruction.* Norwood, NJ: Ablex.

Stevens, R., & Slavin, R. E. (1995). Effects of a cooperative learning approach in reading and writing on academically handicapped and nonhandicapped students. *Elementary School Journal, 95*(3), 241–262.

Stiggins, R. (1994). *Student-centered classroom assessment.* Portland, OR: Assessment Training Institute.

Stigler, J. W., & Hiebert, J. (2009). *The teaching gap: Best ideas from the world's teachers for improving.* New York, NY: Free Press.

Stodolsky, S., & Lesser, G. (1971). Learning patterns in the disadvantaged. In *Challenging the myths: The schools, the blacks, and the poor.* Reprint Series #5. Cambridge, MA: Harvard Educational Review.

Stogdill, R. (1974). *Handbook of leadership.* New York, NY: Free Press.

Stogdill, R. (1981). Traits of leadership: A follow-up to 1970. In B. Bass (Ed.), *Handbook of leadership.* New York, NY: Free Press.

Stone, C., & Dahir, C. (2007). *School counselor accountability: A measure of student success* (2nd ed.). Columbus, OH: Merrill Prentice Hall.

Strahan, R. D., & Turner, L. C. (1987). *The courts and the schools.* New York, NY: Longman.

Strike, K., Haller, E., & Solitus, J. (1988). *The ethics of school administration.* New York, NY: Teachers College Press.

Stronge, J. H. (1997). Improving schools through teacher evaluation. In J. H. Stronge (Ed.), *Evaluating teaching* (p. 253). Thousand Oaks, CA: Corwin Press.

Stronge, J. H., & Tucker, P. (2000). *Teacher evaluation and student achievement.* Washington, DC: National Education Association.

Stronge, J. H., & Tucker, P. D. (2001). *Student achievement and teacher evaluation.* Manuscript submitted for publication.

Suters, E. (1997). Inspirational leadership. In K. Shelton (Ed.), *A new paradigm of leadership* (pp. 199–264). Provo, UT: Executive Excellence.

Swap, P. (1993). *Developing home-school partnerships: From concepts to practice.* New York, NY: Teachers College Press.

Synder, J., & Ebmeier, H. (1992). Empirical linkages among principal behaviors and intermediate outcomes: Implications for principal evaluation. *Peabody Journal of Education, 68*(1), 75–107.

Takaki, R. (1993). *A different mirror: A history of multicultural America.* Boston, MA: Little, Brown.

Tannenbaum, R., & Schmidt, W. H. (1958). How to choose a leadership pattern. *Harvard Educational Review, 57,* 92–106.

Tanner, D., & Tanner, L. N. (1995). *Curriculum development: Theory into practice.* Englewood Cliffs, NJ: Prentice Hall.

Tanner, L. N. (1997). *Dewey's laboratory school: Lessons for today.* New York, NY: Teachers College Press.

Tapscott, D. (1998). *Growing up digital: The rise of the net generation.* New York, NY: McGraw-Hill.

Task Force on Teaching as a Profession. (1986). *A nation prepared: Teachers for the twenty-first century.* New York, NY: Carnegie Forum on Education and the Economy.

Taylor, B. B. (1996). *Education and the law: A dictionary.* Santa Barbara, CA: ABC-CLIO.

Taylor, D., Cordeiro, P., & Chrispeels, J. (2009). Pedagogy. In M. Young, G. Crow, J. Murphy, & R. Ogawa (Eds.), *The international handbook of research on the education of school leaders.* Hillsdale, NJ: Lawrence Erlbaum.

Taylor, E. W. (2000). Analyzing research on transformative learning theory. In J. Mezirow & Associates (Eds.), *Learning as a transformation: Critical perspectives on a theory in progress.* San Francisco, CA: Jossey-Bass.

Taylor, F. W. (1947). *Scientific management.* New York, NY: Harper.

Texas Department of State Health Services. (2011). School-based health centers role of DSHS. Retrieved from http://www.dshs.state.tx.us/schoolhealth/healctrrole.shtm#3

Thayer, Y., & Short, T. (1994). New sources of funding for the twenty-first-century school. *NASSP Bulletin 78*(566), 6–15.

Thomas, D., & Davis, G. (1998). *Legal and ethical bases for educational leadership.* Bloomington, IN: Phi Delta Kappa International, Inc. Fastback.

Thomas, R. (2004, May–June). Aligning schools to state standards. *Principal, 83*(5), 12–38.

Thorndike, E. (1910). A scale for merit in English writing by young people. *Journal of Educational Psychology, 2,* 361–368.

Thurston, P., Clift, R., & Schacht, M. (1993, November). Preparing leaders for change oriented schools. *Phi Delta Kappan, 75*(3), 259–265.

Tice, L. (1997). Limitless leadership. In K. Shelton (Ed.), *A new paradigm of leadership* (pp. 79–82). Provo, UT: Executive Excellence.

Toch, T. (2006). *Margins of error: The education testing industry in the No Child Left Behind era.* Washington, DC: Education Sector.

Toch, T. (2009). Seeding success in charter schools. *Phi Delta Kappan, 91*(4), 36–42.

Togneri, W., & Anderson, S.E. (2003). *Beyond islands of excellence: What districts can do to improve instruction and achievement in all schools—A leadership brief.* Baltimore, MD: Association for Supervision and Curriculum Development and the Learning First Alliance.

Triandis, H. (1971). *Attitude and attitude change.* New York, NY: Wiley.

Trueba, H. T. (1988; 1989). *Raising silent voices: Educating the linguistic minorities for the twenty-first century.* Rowley, MA: Newbury House.

Trump, K. (2002, May). Be prepared, not scared. *Principal, 81*(5), 10–12.

Tucker, M. (1990, April). Restructuring: What is it? *Education Leadership, 47*(7), 9.

Tugend, A. (2008). Multitasking can make you lose . . . um . . . focus. *The New York Times.* New York, NY. Retrieved from http://www.nytimes.com/2008/10/25/business/yourmoney/25shortcuts.html?pagewanted=all

Turnbull, A. P., Turnbull, H. R., Shank, M., & Leal, D. (1995). *Exceptional lives.* Englewood Cliffs, NJ: Prentice Hall.

Turnbull, A., Turnbull, R., & Wehmeyer, M. L. (2007). *Exceptional lives: Special education in today's schools.* Columbus, OH: Pearson.

Tyack, D. (1992, Spring). Health and social services in public schools: Historic perspective. *The Future of Children, 2*(1), 19–31.

Tyler, R. W. (1949). *Basic principles of curriculum and instruction.* Chicago, IL: University of Chicago Press.

Ubben, G. C., & Hughes, L. W. (1997). *The principal: Creative leadership for effective schools* (3rd ed.). Boston, MA: Allyn & Bacon.

Ubben, G., Hughes, L., & Norris, C. (2001). *The principal: Creative leadership for effective schools* (4th ed.). Boston, MA: Allyn & Bacon.

Underwood, J., & Noffke, J. (1990). Litigation threat has chilling effect. *The Executive Educator, 12*(3), 18–20.

Urwick, L. F. (1937). Organization as a technical problem. In L. Gulick & L. F. Urwick (Eds.), *Papers on the science of administration* (pp. 47–88). New York, NY: Institute of Public Administration, Columbia University.

U.S. Department of Education. (2003). *Twenty-third annual report to congress on the implementation of the Individual with Disabilities Education Act.* Washington, DC: Author.

U.S. Department of Education. (2007). Carl D. Perkins Career and Technical Education Act. Retrieved from http://www.ed.gov/policy/sectech/leg/perkins/index.html

U.S. Department of Education, Office of Planning, Evaluation, and Policy Development. (2010). *Evaluation of evidence-based practices in online learning: A meta-analysis and review of online learning studies.* Washington, DC: Author.

Valente, W. D. (1997). *Law in the schools* (4th ed.). New York, NY: Merrill.

Valente, W. D., & Valente, C. M. (2004). (6th Ed.) Law in the Schools. Englewood Cliffs, NJ: Prentice Hall.

Van Horn, G., Burrello, L., & DeClune, L. (1992). An instructional leadership framework: The principal's leadership role in special education. *Special education leadership review.* Albuquerque, NM: Council of Administration of Special Education.

Van Voorhis, F. (2001). Interactive science homework: An experiment in home and school connection. *NASSP Bulletin, 85*(675), 20–32.

Varenne, H. (1978). Culture as rhetoric: Patterning in the verbal interpretation of interaction in an American high school. *American Ethnologist, 5*(4), 635–650.

Venezky, R. L., & Winfield, L. F. (1979). Schools that succeed beyond expectations in teaching: Studies in Education Technical Report No. 1. Delaware University (ED1777484).

Villa, R., & Thousand, J. (2003, October). Making inclusive education work. *Educational Leadership, 60*(10), 19–24.

Villa, R., & Thousand, J. (2005). *Creating an inclusive school.* Alexandria, VA: Association for Supervision and Curriculum Development.

Vroom, V. H., & Jago, A. G. (1988). *The new leadership: Managing participation in organization.* Englewood Cliffs, NJ: Prentice Hall.

Vroom, V. H., & Yetton, P. W. (1973). *Leadership and decision-making.* Pittsburgh: University of Pittsburgh Press.

Vygotsky, L. (1978). *Mind in society.* Cambridge, MA: Harvard University Press.

Walberg, H. J., & Lane, J. E. (1989). *Organizing for learning: Toward the twenty-first century.* Reston, VA: National Association of Secondary School Principals.

Walker, J. (2006). Principals and counselors working for social justice: A complimentary leadership team. *Guidance and Counseling, 21*(2), 56–63.

Wan, G. (2006). Teaching diversity and tolerance in the classroom: A thematic storybook approach. *Education, 127*(1), 140–154.

Wang, M. C., Haertel, G. D., & Walberg, J. H. (1977). *What do we know? Widely implemented school improvement programs.* Philadelphia, PA: Temple University Center for Research in Human Development and Education.

Wang, M. C., Haertel, G. D., & Walberg, H. J. (1993). Toward a knowledge base for school learning. *Review of Educational Research, 63*(3), 249–294.

Waterhouse, L. (2006). Multiple intelligences, the Mozart effect, and emotional intelligence: A critical review. *Educational Psychologist, 41*(4), 207–225.

Waters, T., & Marzano, R. (2006). School district leadership that works: The effect of superintendent leadership on student achievement (a working paper). Retrieved from http://www.mcrel.org

Waters, T., Marzano, R. J., & McNulty, B. (2003). *Balanced leadership: What 30 years of research tells us about the effect of leadership on student achievement.* Denver, CO: McREL.

Weber, M. (1947). *The theory of social and economic organization* (trans. by A. M. Henderson; introduction by T. Parsons). New York, NY: Free Press.

Weiss, C. H. (1995, Winter). The four "I's" of school reform: How interests, ideology, information, and institution affect teachers and principals. *Harvard Education Review, 65*(6), 571–592.

Wenglinsky, H. (1998). *Does it compute? The relationship between educational technology and student achievement in mathematics.* Princeton, NJ: Educational Testing Service. Retrieved from http://www.ets.org/Media/Research/pdf/PICTECHNOLOG.pdf

Wenglinsky, H. (2005). *Using technology wisely: The keys to success in schools.* New York, NY: Teachers College Press.

Wenglinsky, H. (2006, December-January). Technology and achievement. *Educational Leadership, 63*(4), 29–32.

West, C. (1992). The new cultural politics of difference. In S. Seidman (Ed.), *The postmodern turn: New perspectives on social theory.* Cambridge, England: Cambridge University Press.

Wheatley, M. (1992). *Leadership and the new science.* San Francisco, CA: Berrett-Koehler.

Whitehurst, G. (2003, April). *The institute of education sciences: New wine in new bottles.* Invited address to the annual meeting of the American Educational Research Association, Chicago, IL.

Wiggins, G. (1990). *The case of authentic assessment.* ERIC ED 328 611.

Wiggins, G. (1998). *Educative assessment.* San Francisco, CA: Jossey-Bass.

Wiggins, G., & McTighe, J. (2006). Examining the teaching life. *Educational Leadership, 63*(6), 26–29.

Wiggins, G., & McTighe, J. (2011). *The understanding by design guide to creating high-quality unit.* Alexandria, VA: Association for Supervision and Curriculum Development.

Wikipedia. (2007). Adam Walsh Child Protection and Safety Act. Retrieved from http://en.wikipedia.org/wiki/Adam_Walsh_Child_Protection_and_Safety_Act

Wilks, J. (2011, February 1). Let our virtual schools flourish. Editorial, *Albany Democrat.* http://www.democraterald.com/news/opinion/editorial/article_ec61b042-2d82-11e0-9261-001cc4c03286.html

Williams, B. (2003). *Closing the achievement gap: A vision for changing beliefs and practices.* Alexandria, VA: Association for Supervision and Curriculum Development.

Williams, L. (2006). *The relationship of technology integration and high school collaboration through the development of a professional learning community.* Norman, OK: University of Oklahoma.

Williams, T., Hakuta, K., Haertel, E., Perry, M., Oregon, I., Kirst, M., & Brazil, N. (2007). *Similar English learner students, different results: Why do some schools do better? A follow-up analysis based on a large-scale survey of California elementary schools serving low-income and EL students.* Mountain View, CA: Ed Source.

Willingham, D. (2009). *Why don't students like school: A cognitive scientist answers questions about how the mind works and what it means for the classroom.* San Francisco, CA: Jossey-Bass.

Willoughby, K., & Melkers, J. (1998). *The state of the states: Performance budgeting requirements in 47 out of the 50 states.* Boston, MA: The Pioneer Institute for Public Policy Research.

Willower, D., & Forsyth, P. (1999). A brief history of scholarship on educational administration. In J. Murphy & K. Seashore Louis, *Educational Administration* (pp. 1–23). San Francisco, CA: Jossey-Bass.

Willower, D. G. (1979). Some issues in research on school organization. In G. I. Immegart & W. Boyd (Eds.), *Currents in administrative research: Problem finding in education* (p. 310). Lexington, MA: Heath.

Willower, D. J. (1996). Explaining and improving educational administration. In C. W. Evers & G. Lakomski (Eds.), *Exploring educational administration.* New York, NY: Pergamon.

Wimpelberg, R., Teddlie, C., & Stringfield, S. (1989). Sensitivity to context: The past and future of effective schools research. *Educational Administration Quarterly, 25*(1), 82–107.

Wise, A. E. (2001, January). Differentiated staffing. *The School Administrator, 58*(1), 34–38.

Wise, B. (2005). Improving adolescent literacy: Middle schools are at the core of helping students learn to read. *Middle Matters, 14*(1), 1–3.

Wolcott, H. (1973). *The man in the principal's office: An ethnography.* New York, NY: Holt, Rinehart & Winston.

Wollons, R. (1992). (Ed.). *Children at risk in America: History, concepts, and public policy.* Albany, NY: State University of New York Press.

Wong, K., & Nicotera, K. (2007). *Successful schools and educational accountability.* Boston, MA: Allyn & Bacon.

Woolfolk, A. (2001, Fall). Leading for learning: An educational psychologist's perspective. *UCEA Review, XLIII*(3), 1–4.

Young, M. D., & Brooks, J. S. (2008). Supporting Graduate Students of Color in Educational Administration Preparation Programs: Faculty Perspectives on Best Practices, Possibilities, and Problems. *Educational Administration Quarterly, 44*(3), 391–423.

Yorks, L., & Marsick, V. (1999). Transformative learning in organizations. In J. Mezirow & Associates (Eds.), *Learning as transformation: Critical perspectives on a theory in process.* San Francisco, CA: Jossey-Bass.

Yorks-Barr, J., & Duke, K. (2004). What do we know about teacher leadership? *Review of Educational Research, 74*(3), 255–316.

Young, M., Petersen, G., & Short, P. (2002). The complexity of substantive reform: A call for interdependence among key stakeholders. *Education Administration Quarterly, 38*(2), 137–175.

Yukl, G. A. (1989). *Leadership in organizations.* Englewood Cliffs, NJ: Prentice Hall.

Yukl, G. (2002). *Leadership in organizations.* Upper Saddle River, NJ: Prentice Hall.

Zepeda, S., & Langenbach, M. (1999). *Special programs in regular schools.* Boston, MA: Allyn & Bacon.

Zhao, Y. (2009). *Catching up or leading the way. American education in the age of globalization.* Alexandria, VA: Association for Supervision and Curriculum Development.

Zhao, Y. (2009). Catching Up or Leading the Way: American Education in the Age of Globalization. Alexandria, VA: Association for Supervision & Curriculum Development.

Zigler, E., Kagan, S., & Klugman, E. (1983). *Children, families, and government.* Cambridge, England: Cambridge University Press.

Zigmond, N. (2003, September). Where should students with disabilities receive special education services? *The Journal of Special Education, 37*(3), 193–199.

Zirkel, P. (1996). Discipline and the law. *The Executive Educator, 18*(7), 21–23.

Zirkel, P. (2007). The pluses and perils of RTI. *The School Administrator, 64*(4), 53–54.

NAME INDEX